Mobil
Travel Guide®

SOUTHWEST

ACKNOWLEDGMENTS

We gratefully acknowledge the help of our representatives for their efficient and perceptive inspections of the lodging and dining establishments listed, the establishments' proprietors for their cooperation in showing their facilities and providing information about them, and the many users of previous editions who have taken the time to share their experiences. Mobil Travel Guide is also grateful to all the talented writers who contributed entries to this book.

Front and back cover images: ©iStockPhoto.com

All maps: created by Mapping Specialists

ISBN: 9-780841-60867-2   Manufactured in Canada

10 9 8 7 6 5 4 3 2 1

TABLE OF CONTENTS

3

★★★★★ SOUTHWEST

WRITTEN IN THE STARS

Because time is precious and the travel industry is ever-changing, having accurate, reliable travel information at your fingertips has never been more important. With this in mind, Mobil Travel Guide has provided invaluable insight to travelers through its Star Rating system for more than 50 years.

The Mobil Corporation (known as Exxon Mobil Corporation since a 1999 merger) began producing the Mobil Travel Guide books in 1958 following the introduction of the U.S.-interstate highway system in 1956. The first edition covered only five Southwestern states. Since then, our books have become the premier travel guides in North America, covering all 50 states and Canada, and beginning in 2008, international destinations such as Hong Kong and Beijing.

Today, the concept of a "five-star" experience is one that permeates the collective conciousness, but few people realize it's one that originated with Mobil. We created our star rating system to give travelers an easy-to-recognize quality scale for choosing where to stay, dine and spa. Based on an objective process, we make recommendations to our readers that we believe will enhance the quality and value of their travel experiences. Our trusted Mobil One- to Five-Star rating system is the oldest and most respected lodging and restaurant inspection and rating program in North America. Most hoteliers, restaurateurs and industry observers favorably regard the rigor of our inspection program and understand the prestige and benefits that come with receiving a Mobil Star rating.

The Mobil Travel Guide process of rating each establishment includes unannounced inspections, incognito evaluations and a review of unsolicted comments from the general public. We inspect more than 500 attributes at each property we visit, from cleanliness to the condition of the rooms and public spaces, to employee attitude and courtesy. It's a system that rewards those properties that strive for and achieve excellence each year. And the very best properties raise the bar for those that wish to compete with them.

Only facilities that meet Mobil Travel Guide's standards earn the privilege of being listed in the guide. Properties are continuously updated, and deteriorating, poorly managed establishments are removed. We wouldn't recommend that you visit a hotel, restaurant or spa that we wouldn't want to visit ourselves.

★★★★★The Mobil Five-Star Award indicates that a property is one of the very best in the country and consistently provides gracious and courteous service, superlative quality in its facility and a unique ambience. The lodgings and restaurants at the Mobil Five-Star level consistently continue their commitment to excellence, doing so with grace and perseverance.

★★★★The Mobil Four-Star Award honors properties for outstanding achievement in overall facility and for providing very strong service levels in all areas. These award winners provide a distinctive experience for the ever-demanding and sophisticated consumer.

★★★The Mobil Three-Star Award recognizes an excellent property that provides full services and amenities. This category ranges from exceptional hotels with limited services to elegant restaurants with a less formal atmosphere.

★★The Mobil Two-Star property is a clean and comfortable establishment that has expanded amenities or a distinctive environment. These properties are an excellent place to stay or dine.

★The Mobil One-Star property is limited in its amenities and services but provides a value experience while meeting travelers' expectations. The properties should be clean, comfortable and convenient.

We do not charge establishments for inclusion in our guides. We have no relationship with any of the businesses and attractions we list and act only as a consumer advocate. We do the investigative legwork so that you won't have to.

Restaurants and hotels—particularly small chains and stand-alone establishments—change management or even go out of business with surprising quickness. Although we make every effort to continuously update information, we recommend that you call ahead to make sure the place you've selected is still open.

STAR RATINGS

MOBIL RATED HOTELS

Whether you're looking for the ultimate in luxury or the best bang for your travel buck, we have a hotel recommendation for you. To help you pinpoint properties that meet your needs, Mobil Travel Guide classifies each lodging by type according to the following characteristics.

★★★★★The Mobil Five-Star hotel provides consistently superlative service in an exceptionally distinctive luxury environment. Attention to detail is evident throughout the hotel, resort or inn, from bed linens to staff uniforms.

★★★★The Mobil Four-Star hotel provides a luxury experience with expanded amenities in a distinctive environment. Services may include automatic turndown service, 24-hour room service and valet parking.

★★★The Mobil Three-Star hotel is well appointed, with a full-service restaurant and expanded amenities, such as a fitness center, golf course, tennis courts, 24-hour room service and optional turndown service.

★★The Mobil Two-Star hotel is considered a clean, comfortable and reliable establishment that has expanded amenities, such as a full-service restaurant.

★The Mobil One-Star lodging is a limited-service hotel, motel or inn that is considered a clean, comfortable and reliable establishment.

For every property, we also provide pricing information. The pricing categories break down as follows:

$ = Up to $150

$$ = $151-$250

$$$ = $251-$350

$$$$ = $351 and up

All prices quoted are accurate at the time of publication; however, prices cannot be guaranteed.

★
★★
★★
★

MOBIL RATED RESTAURANTS

Every restaurant in this book has been visited by Mobil Travel Guide's team of experts and comes highly recommended as an outstanding dining experience.

★★★★★The Mobil Five-Star restaurant offers one of few flawless dining experiences in the country. These establishments consistently provide their guests with exceptional food, superlative service, elegant décor and exquisite presentations of each detail surrounding a meal.

★★★★The Mobil Four-Star restaurant provides professional service, distinctive presentations and wonderful food.

★★★The Mobil Three-Star restaurant has good food, warm and skillful service and enjoyable décor.

★★The Mobil Two-Star restaurant serves fresh food in a clean setting with efficient service. Value is considered in this category, as is family friendliness.

★The Mobil One-Star restaurant provides a distinctive experience through culinary specialty, local flair or individual atmosphere.

Because menu prices can fluctuate, we list a pricing category rather than specific prices. The pricing categories are defined as follows, per diner, and assume that you order an appetizer or dessert, an entrée and one drink:

$ = $15 and under

$$ = $16-$35

$$$ = $36-$85

$$$$ = $86 and up

MOBIL RATED SPAS

Mobil Travel Guide's spa ratings are based on objective evaluations of hundreds of attributes. About half of these criteria assess basic expectations, such as staff courtesy, the technical proficiency and skill of the employees and whether the facility is clean and maintained properly. Several standards address issues that impact a guest's physical comfort and convenience, as well as the staff's ability to impart a sense of personalized service. Additional criteria measure the spa's ability to create a completely calming ambience.

★★★★★The Mobil Five-Star spa provides consistently superlative service in an exceptionally distinctive luxury environment with extensive amenities. The staff at a Mobil Five-Star spa provides extraordinary service beyond the traditional spa experience, allowing guests to achieve the highest level of relaxation and pampering. These spas offer an extensive array of treatments, often incorporating international themes and products. Attention to detail is evident throughout the spa, from arrival to departure.

★★★★The Mobil Four-Star spa provides a luxurious experience with expanded amenities in an elegant and serene environment. Throughout the spa facility, guests experience personalized service. Amenities might include, but are not limited to, single-sex relaxation rooms where guests wait for their treatments, plunge pools and whirlpools in both men's and women's locker rooms, and an array of treatments, including a selection of massages, body therapies, facials and a variety of salon services.

★★★The Mobil Three-Star spa is physically well appointed and has a full complement of staff.

INTRODUCTION

If you've been a reader of Mobil Travel Guides, you may have noticed a new look and style in our guidebooks. Since 1958, Mobil Travel Guide has assisted travelers in making smart decisions about where to stay and dine. Fifty-one years later, our mission has not changed: We are committed to our rigorous inspections of hotels, restaurants and, now, spas, to help you cut through all the clutter, and make easy and informed decisions on where you should spend your time and budget. Our team of anonymous inspectors are constantly on the road, sleeping in hotels, eating in restaurants and making spa appointments, evaluating hundreds of standards to determine a property's star rating.

As you read these pages, we hope you get a flavor of the places included in the guides and that you will feel even more inspired to visit and take it all in. We hope you'll experience what it's like to stay in a guest room in the hotels we've rated, taste the food in a restaurant or feel the excitement at an outdoor music venue. We understand the importance of finding the best value when you travel, and making the most of your time. That's why for more than 50 years, Mobil Travel Guide has been the most trusted name in travel.

If any aspect of your accommodation, dining, spa or sightseeing experience motivates you to comment, please contact us at Mobil Travel Guide, 200 W. Madison St., Suite 3950, Chicago, IL 60606, or send an email to info@mobiltravelguide.com Happy travels.

ARIZONA

HIKE THE GRAND CANYON. RELAX AT A SPA. HIT THE LINKS. THIS RAPIDLY GROWING STATE— its population has more than tripled since 1940—offers all of this and much more.

Arizona is known for its hot summers, mild winters and desert landscape. But the northern mountains, cool forests, spectacular canyons and lakes offer a variety of vacation activities, including fishing, white-water rafting, hiking and camping. The northern, central part of the state is on a plateau at higher altitudes than the desert in the southern region of the state and has a cooler climate.

There are also meadows filled with wildflowers, ghost and mining towns, dude ranches and intriguing ancient American Indian villages. The state has 23 reservations and one of the largest Native American populations in the United States. More than half of that population is Navajo. Visitors can scoop up craft specialties including basketry, pottery, weaving, jewelry and kachina dolls.

Arizona has scores of water parks, interesting museums, zoos and wildlife exhibits. And who says it doesn't snow in Arizona? There are several places for downhill skiing, including the Arizona Snowball in northern Arizona, Mt. Lemmon Ski Valley near Tucson and Sunrise Ski Resort in the east.

Of course, there is also plenty of what people have come to expect here. There are more than 300 golf courses across the state, making it home to several stops on the PGA Tour, most notably the Phoenix Open. You'll also find some of the best SPAS in the country. Enjoy.

Information: www.arizonaguide.com

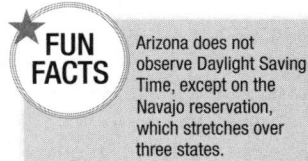

★ FUN FACTS

Arizona does not observe Daylight Saving Time, except on the Navajo reservation, which stretches over three states.

The state is home to 22 tribal nations.

AJO

Once a copper-mining hub, Ajo is located about 40 miles from the Mexico border. It's a prime spot to stop while visiting nearby Organ Pipe Cactus National Monument.
Information: Ajo Chamber of Commerce, 400 Taladro St., Ajo, 520-387-7742, 520-387-3641; www.ajochamber.com

WHAT TO SEE AND DO
ORGAN PIPE CACTUS NATIONAL MONUMENT
10 Organ Pipe Drive, Ajo, 520-387-6849; www.nps.gov/orpi
This 516-square-mile Sonoran desert area on the Mexican border is Arizona's largest national monument. The organ pipe cactus grows as high as 20 feet and has 30 or more arms, which resemble organ pipes. The plant blooms in May and June, and the blossoms are white with pink or lavender flowers. During February and March, depending on rainfall, parts of the area may be covered with Mexican gold poppy, magenta owl clover, blue lupine and bright orange mallow. Many desert plants thrive here, including mesquite, saguaro, several species of cholla, barrel cacti, paloverde

BEYOND THE GRAND CANYON

This loop drive, a side trip for visitors to the South Rim of Grand Canyon National Park, combines scenic beauty with archeological, historical, geologic and scientific sites. It can be done in one full day or divided into a day and a half with an overnight stop in Flagstaff.

From Grand Canyon Village, head south on Highway 64/Highway 180, turning southeast on Highway 180 at Valle for a drive through the San Francisco Mountains. Those interested in the history of the area, including prehistoric peoples and more recent Native Americans, will want to stop at the **Museum of Northern Arizona** *(3101 N. Fort Valley Road, Flagstaff)*. Continue along Highway 180 to the turnoff to **Lowell Observatory** *(1400 W. Mars Hill Road, Flagstaff)*, which has been the site of many important astronomical discoveries since its founding in 1894. Guided tours of the facilities are offered, and there's a public observatory.

You are now on the north edge of Flagstaff. From the city, go east on Interstate 40 (I-40), and take the turnoff to Walnut Canyon National Monument to see dozens of small cliff dwellings built by the Sinagua people some 700 years ago. The monument can be explored via two trails. One is a fairly easy walk along a mesa top; the other is a bit more strenuous but provides a much closer look at the cliff dwellings as it drops about 185 feet into Walnut Canyon.

Leaving the monument, head back toward Flagstaff on I-40 and go north on Highway 89 to the Sunset Crater Volcano/Wupatki national monuments loop road, where there is an extinct volcano, fields of lava rock and ruins of prehistoric stone pueblos. Wupatki National Monument's main attraction is Wupatki Pueblo, a 100-room dwelling built in the 12th century by the Sinagua. This handsome apartment house was constructed of red sandstone slabs, blocks of pale beige limestone and chunks of brown basalt and cemented together with clay. Nearby, Sunset Crater Volcano National Monument offers an intimate look at a dormant volcano, with its rugged landscape of jet-black basalt, twisted into myriad shapes. Sunset Crater's primary eruption was in the winter of 1065.

After rejoining U.S. 89, continue north into the Navajo Reservation and the community of Cameron, with the historic but still operating Cameron Trading Post, which sells museum-quality items as well as more affordable rugs, baskets, jewelry and other American Indian crafts. From Cameron, head west on Highway 64 back into the national park. *Approximately 215 miles.*

trees, creosote bush and ocotillo. You can take two scenic drives, both self-guided: the 53-mile Puerto Blanco and the 21-mile Ajo Mountain drives. There is a 208-site campground near headquarters May-mid-January, 30-day limit; mid-January-April, 14-day limit.

SPECIALTY LODGING
GUEST HOUSE INN
700 Guest House Road, Ajo, 520-387-6133; www.guesthouseinn.biz
Four rooms. Complimentary full breakfast. $

BISBEE

Located in the foothills of the Mule Mountains of southeastern Arizona, Bisbee was a tough mining town known as "Queen of the Copper Camps." Today, it's rich in architecture and culture with many art galleries, period hotels and bed and breakfasts.
Information: Greater Bisbee Chamber of Commerce, 1 Main St., Bisbee, 520-432-5421; www.bisbeearizona.com

WHAT TO SEE AND DO
BISBEE MINING AND HISTORICAL MUSEUM
5 Copper Queen Plaza, Bisbee, 520-432-7071; www.bisbeemuseum.org
Housed in the 1897 office building of the Copper Queen Consolidated Mining Company, this museum depicts early development of this urban center through displays on mining, historical photographs and more. Daily 10 a.m.-4 p.m.

QUEEN MINE
478 Dart St., Bisbee, 520-432-2071, 866-432-2071; www.queenminetour.com
This one-hour guided tour on a mine train takes you 1,800 feet into a mine tunnel. Daily 9-10:30 a.m., noon, 2-3:30 p.m.

HOTELS
CALUMET AND ARIZONA GUEST HOUSE
608 Powell St., Bisbee, 520-432-4815; www.calumetaz.com
Six rooms. Complimentary full breakfast. Pets accepted. **$**

★★COPPER QUEEN HOTEL
11 Howell Ave., Bisbee, 520-432-2216; www.copperqueen.com
48 rooms. Wireless Internet access. Restaurant, bar. Pool. **$**

BULLHEAD CITY

Bullhead City was established in 1945 as a construction camp for Davis Dam, a reclamation facility located three miles to the north. The name is derived from its proximity to Bull's Head Rock, now largely concealed by the waters of Lake Mohave. Bullhead City is across the Colorado River from Laughlin, Nevada, and its casinos.
Information: Chamber of Commerce, 2355 Trane Road, Bullhead City, 928-763-9400; www.bullheadcity.com

WHAT TO SEE AND DO
DAVIS DAM AND POWER PLANT
Bullhead City, 928-754-3626; www.usbr.gov
This dam has a surface area of 28,500 acres and reaches 67 miles upstream to Hoover Dam.

HOTELS
★BEST WESTERN BULLHEAD CITY INN
1126 Highway 95, Bullhead City, 928-754-3000, 800-780-7234; www.bestwestern.com
88 rooms. High-speed Internet access. Complimentary continental breakfast. Pets accepted; fee. Pool. Spa. **$**

★★LAKE MOHAVE RESORT
2690 E. Katherine Spur Road, Bullhead City, 928-754-3245; www.sevencrown.com
51 rooms. Restaurant, bar. Pets accepted. **$**

RESTAURANT
★EL ENCANTO
125 Long Ave., Bullhead City, 928-754-5100
Mexican menu. Breakfast, lunch, dinner. Bar. Children's menu. Outdoor seating. **$**

WHAT TO SEE AND DO
CANYON TOURS
Highway 191 and RR 7, Chinle, 928-674-5841, 800-679-2473
Personnel from Thunderbird Lodge conduct jeep tours into the canyons; half-day (daily) and full-day (April-October, daily) trips.

HOTELS
★★BEST WESTERN CANYON DE CHELLY INN
100 Main St., Chinle, 928-674-5874, 800-327-0354; www.bestwestern.com
104 rooms. High-speed Internet access. Restaurant. Pool. Spa. **$**

CANYON DE CHELLY NATIONAL MONUMENT
The smooth red sandstone walls of the canyon extend straight up as much as 1,000 feet from the nearly flat sand bottom. When William of Normandy defeated the English at the Battle of Hastings in 1066, the Pueblo had already built apartment houses in these walls. Many ruins are still here.

The Navajo came long after the original tenants had abandoned these structures. In 1864, Kit Carson's men drove nearly all the Navajo out of the area, marching them on foot 300 miles to the Bosque Redondo in eastern New Mexico. Since 1868, Navajo have returned to farming, cultivating the orchards and grazing their sheep in the canyon. In 1931, Canyon de Chelly and its tributaries, Canyon del Muerto and Monument Canyon, were designated a national monument.

There are more than 60 major ruins—some dating from circa A.D. 300—in these canyons. White House, Antelope House and Mummy Cave are among the most picturesque. Most ruins are inaccessible but can be seen from either the canyon bottom or from the road along the top of the precipitous walls. Two spectacular, 16-mile rim drives can be made by car in any season. Lookout points—sometimes a short distance from the road—are clearly marked. The only self-guided trail (2½ miles round-trip) leads to the canyon floor and White House ruin from White House Overlook. Other hikes can be made only with a National Park Service permit and an authorized Navajo guide. Only four-wheel drive vehicles are allowed in the canyons—and each vehicle must be accompanied by an authorized Navajo guide and requires a National Park Service permit obtainable from a ranger at the visitor center.
Information: Canyon de Chelly Headquarters, Highway 191, Window Rock, 928-674-5500; www.nps.gov/cach

13

ARIZONA

★
★★
★★
★

★★THUNDERBIRD LODGE
Highway 191 and Route 7, Chinle, 928-674-5841, 800-679-2473; www.tbirdlodge.com
73 rooms. Restaurant. Pets accepted. **$**

CAREFREE
The immense Tonto National Forest stretches to the north and east. In the center of town is the largest and most accurate sundial in the Western Hemisphere.
Information: Carefree/Cave Creek Chamber of Commerce, 100 Easy St.,
480-488-3381; www.carefree.org

SPECIAL EVENTS
CAREFREE FINE ART AND WINE FESTIVALS
15648 N. Eagles Nest Drive, Fountain Hills, 480-837-5637; www.thunderbirdartists.com
At each of these pleasant outdoor festivals, more than 150 booths feature the work of nationally recognized artists. You'll find a wide range of mediums from paintings and pottery to sculptures and stained glass, in all price ranges. In the wine pavilion, host to Arizona's largest wine-tasting event, visitors can sample vintages from around the world. These popular festivals draw more than 180,000 art lovers each year. Late October, early November, mid-January, early March: Friday-Sunday 10 a.m.-5 p.m.

FIESTA DAYS
28th Street and New River Road, Memorial Arena, Carefree, 480-488-3381
This three-day event features a rodeo, family entertainment and a parade. Usually the second weekend in April.

HOTEL
THE BOULDERS RESORT & GOLDEN DOOR SPA
34631 N. Tom Darlington Drive, Carefree, 480-488-9009, 866-397-6520;
www.theboulders.com
Located in the foothills of the Sonoran Desert just north of Scottsdale, the Boulders Resort and Golden Door Spa blends perfectly with the surrounding rock outcroppings, ancient boulders and saguaro cactus plants. The adobe casitas are distinguished by overstuffed leather chairs, exposed beams and Mexican tiles, while one-, two- and three-bedroom Pueblo Villas are ideal for families. The resort boasts a first-rate tennis facility and an 18-hole championship golf course. There's also rock climbing, hiking and tours of Native American cave dwellings and ruins. Guided night hikes using night vision equipment are especially fun. Note that the resort is scheduled to undergo renovations in 2009, but will continue to accommodate guests throughout the year. 215 rooms. Pets accepted, some restrictions; fee. High-speed Internet access. Five restaurants, three bars. Children's activity center. Fitness center. Spa. Three outdoor pools, whirlpool. Golf, 36 holes. Tennis. Business center. **$$$$**

SPA
★★★GOLDEN DOOR SPA AT THE BOULDERS
34631 N. Tom Darlington Drive, Carefree, 480-595-3500, 800-553-1717;
www.theboulders.com
This branch of the original California spa is the jewel in the crown of the Boulders Resort. Many treatments are a nod to the region's Native American history. Ancient

Ayurvedic principles are revived in the mystical treatments of *bindi* balancing, where crushed herbs exfoliate and light oils moisturize your skin, and *shirodhara*, which begins with massaging warm oil into your scalp and concludes with a mini facial massage and a heated hand and foot treatment. The 33,000-square-foot spa also includes a meditation labyrinth inspired by Hopi medicine wheels and a movement studio, which offers yoga, tai chi, Pilates, kickboxing and more. **$$**

RESTAURANT
★★★THE LATILLA
34631 N. Tom Darlington Drive, Carefree, 480-488-9009, 866-397-6520;
www.theboulders.com
The cuisine at this glass-enclosed restaurant in the Boulders Resort and Spa focuses on fresh, organic produce, free-range meats and poultry and responsibly caught seafood from clean waters. Most of the wines are also organic. The rustic, cozy dining room is decorated with Ocotillo branches (called *latillas*, which means "little sticks" in Spanish). The outdoor patio, warmed by a blazing fire, is an ideal spot to have a drink before or after dinner. California menu. Dinner. Bar. Business casual attire. Reservations recommended. Valet parking. Outdoor seating. **$$$**

CASA GRANDE
Named for the Hohokam ruins 20 miles northeast of town, Casa Grande is situated in an agricultural and industrial area.
Information: Chamber of Commerce, 575 N. Marshall St.,
520-836-2125, 800-916-1515; www.casagrandechamber.org

WHAT TO SEE AND DO
CASA GRANDE VALLEY HISTORICAL SOCIETY AND MUSEUM
110 W. Florence Blvd., Casa Grande, 520-836-2223; www.cgvhs.org
Exhibits trace the growth of the Casa Grande Valley from prehistoric times to the present, with an emphasis on farming, ranching, mining and domestic life. September-May, Monday-Saturday 1-5 p.m.; closed summer.

PICACHO PEAK STATE PARK
15520 Picacho Peak Road, Picacho, 520-466-3183;
azstateparks.com/parks/pipe/index.html
This 3,400-acre park includes a sheer-sided peak rising 1,500 feet above the desert floor that was a landmark for early travelers. The only Civil War battle in Arizona was fought near here. Colorful spring wildflowers; desert nature study. Hiking, picnicking. Daily 8 a.m.-10 p.m.

SPECIAL EVENT
O'ODHAM TASH-CASA GRANDE'S INDIAN DAYS
108 W. Second St., Casa Grande, 520-836-4723
Rodeo, parades, ceremonial dances, arts and crafts, barbecue and more. Reservations recommended. Mid-February.

CASA GRANDE RUINS NATIONAL MONUMENT

The four-story Casa Grande was built during the 14th century. It was constructed of caliche-bearing soil (a crust of calcium carbonate on stony soil) and is covered by a large protective roof, making it the only structure of its type and size in southern Arizona. After being occupied for some 100 years, Casa Grande was abandoned. Father Kino, a Jesuit missionary and explorer, sighted and named it Big House in 1694. Museum with archaeological exhibits; self-guided tours.
Information: 1100 Ruins Drive, Coolidge, 520-723-3172; www.nps.gov/cagr

CHANDLER

Chandler is one of the major suburbs of Phoenix. A growing number of high-technology companies have facilities here, including Intel, Motorola and Microchip Technologies.

Information: Chandler Chamber of Commerce, 25 S. Arizona Place, 480-963-4571, 800-963-4571; www.chandleraz.org

WHAT TO SEE AND DO

CASA PALOMA

7131 W. Ray Road, Chandler, 480-777-2272; www.shopcasapaloma.com

It's worth stopping at this upscale strip mall with 35 shops. After shopping, pamper yourself at Rolf's Salon and Spa or dine at one of seven restaurants. Daily.

CHANDLER CENTER FOR THE ARTS

250 N. Arizona Ave., Chandler, 480-782-2680; www.chandlercenter.org

This 64,000-square-foot performance center is known for its superb acoustics. The London City Opera, Jay Leno, Anne Murray, Rita Moreno, Bob Newhart and the Phoenix Boys Choir are among the performers who have helped the center earn its reputation for staging shows that bring audiences to their feet. The main auditorium seats 1,550 but can be subdivided into three separate halls holding 1,000, 350 and 250 people, respectively.

WILD HORSE PASS CASINO

5550 W. Wild Horse Pass, Chandler, 800-946-4452; www.wingilariver.com

With nearly 170,000 square feet of gaming action, this casino offers lots of options. The card room is decked out with 19 poker tables, while the bingo hall has 1,200 seats. There's also a 24-hour live keno section and more than 500 slot machines.

SPECIAL EVENTS

CHANDLER JAZZ FESTIVAL

Chandler, 480-782-2735; www.chandleraz.gov

More than 20 bands perform mostly swing music. The two-day event attracts about 6,000 jazz lovers. Late April.

CHANDLER OSTRICH FESTIVAL

Tumbleweed Park, 2250 S. McQueen Road, Chandler, 480-963-4571;
www.ostrichfestival.com

Features ostrich racing, food, entertainment, arts and crafts, carnival with rides and other amusements such as a petting zoo and pony rides. Early March.

HOTELS
★★★CROWNE PLAZA SAN MARCOS GOLF RESORT

1 San Marcos Place, Chandler, 480-812-0900, 800-528-8071;
www.sanmarcosresort.com

Built in 1912, this was the first golf course in Arizona. Located just a few miles from companies like Motorola and Intel, it's a great choice for business travelers. Families can enjoy tennis and horseback riding. Guest rooms include eye pillows, ear plugs, lavender spray and sleep CDs. 295 rooms. High-speed Internet access. Restaurant, bar. Pets accepted. Pool. Golf. Tennis. Business center. $

★FAIRFIELD INN

7425 W. Chandler Blvd., Chandler, 480-940-0099, 800-228-2800; www.marriott.com
66 rooms. Complimentary continental breakfast. Pool. $

★★RADISSON HOTEL PHOENIX-CHANDLER

7475 W. Chandler Blvd., Chandler, 480-961-4444, 888-201-1718;
www.radisson.com/chandleraz

159 rooms. High-speed Internet access. Restaurant, bar. Airport transportation available. Pets accepted. Pool. Business center. Fitness center. $

★★★SHERATON WILD HORSE PASS RESORT & SPA

5594 W. Wild Horse Pass Blvd., Chandler, 602-225-0100, 800-325-3535;
www.wildhorsepassresort.com

This unique resort on Gila River tribal land blends the décor and traditions of the area with the convenience and services of a modern hotel. Each detail of the interior has been included for its significance to Native American traditions, from the design of the title to the petroglyph-engraved furniture. The destination resort also features two 18-hole golf courses, a 17,500-square-foot spa, equestrian center for riding lessons and trail rides, jogging paths and tennis courts. A two-mile replica of the Gila River runs through the property and offers boat rides to the Wild Horse Pass Casino or the Whirlwind Golf Club. 500 rooms. High-speed Internet access. Three restaurants, three bars. Spa. Airport transportation available. Pets accepted. Golf. Tennis. Pool. $$$

RESTAURANTS
★★C-FU GOURMET

2051 W. Warner Road, Chandler, 480-899-3888; www.cfugourmet.com
Chinese, dim sum, sushi menu. Lunch, dinner. Bar. Casual attire. Reservations recommended. $$

★EL SOL BAKERY

760 N. Arizona Ave., Chandler, 480-786-0811; www.elsolbakery.com
Mexican menu. Breakfast, lunch, dinner. Closed Sunday. Casual attire. $

★★★★★KAI

5594 W. Wild Horse Pass Blvd., Chandler, 602-385-5726; www.whpdining.com
Lodged in the Sheraton Wild Horse Pass, this sophisticated eatery showcases locally grown produce and a surprisingly rich Arizona-made olive oil in recipes that merge contemporary tastes and time-honored Native American techniques. (Kai means "seed" in Pima.) The results include lobster tail, corn and avocado atop fry bread, and rack of lamb sauced with a mole made from American Indian seeds. Southwestern menu. Dinner. Closed Sunday-Monday. Bar. Business casual attire. Outdoor seating. **$$$**

★SOUL IN THE HOLE

601 N. Arizona Ave., Chandler, 480-963-7787
American menu. Lunch, dinner. Closed Monday. Casual attire. **$**

SPA
★★★★AJI SPA

Sheraton Wild Horse Pass, 5594 W. Wild Horse Pass Blvd., Chandler, 602-225-0100;
www.wildhorsepassresort.com
This resort spa will transport you a million miles away. Traditional Native American healing therapies are the backbone of Aji Spa, such as the Ho'dai Massage, which uses hot rocks to soothe muscles. You'll get a dose of culture along with your comfort, too—meditation sessions, medicinal massages and a one-of-a-kind healing treatment that combines massage and ancient Pima techniques are among the treatments that honor Native American traditions.

COTTONWOOD

This town is in the beautiful Verde Valley, an area offering many opportunities for exploration.
Information: Chamber of Commerce, 1010 S. Main St., Cottonwood, 928-634-7593;
www.cottonwoodchamberaz.org.

WHAT TO SEE AND DO
DEAD HORSE RANCH STATE PARK

675 Dead Horse Ranch Road, Cottonwood, 928-634-5283;
www.azparks.gov/Parks/parkhtml/deadhorse.html
This 423-acre park offers fishing, nature trails, hiking, picnicking, camping. Visitor center. Daily from 8 a.m.

SPECIAL EVENT
VERDE VALLEY FAIR

Fairgrounds, 800 E. Cherry St., Cottonwood, 928-634-3290;
www.verdevalleyfair.com
This annual fair features live music, arts and crafts, racing and swimming swine, novelty shows, food and contests. First weekend in May.

HOTEL
★★BEST WESTERN COTTONWOOD INN
993 S. Main St., Cottonwood, 928-634-5575, 800-350-0025; www.bestwestern.com
77 rooms. Wireless Internet access. Complimentary continental breakfast. Pool. Business center. **$**

FLAGSTAFF
In 1876 the Boston Party, a group of pioneers, made camp in a mountain valley on the Fourth of July. They stripped a pine tree of its branches and hung a flag at its top. Afterward, the tree was used as a marker for travelers who referred to the place as the spring by the flag staff. In 1882, Flagstaff became a railroad town when the Atlantic and Pacific Railroad (now the Santa Fe) was built.

Today, Flagstaff, home of Northern Arizona University, is an educational and cultural center. Tourism is the main industry—the city is a good place to see the Navajo country, Oak Creek Canyon, the Grand Canyon and Humphreys Peak (12,670 feet), the tallest mountain in Arizona. Tall pine forests fill the surrounding area.
Information: Chamber of Commerce, 101 W. Route 66, 928-774-4505;
www.flagstaff.az.gov

WHAT TO SEE AND DO
ARIZONA HISTORICAL SOCIETY PIONEER MUSEUM
2340 N. Fort Valley Road, Flagstaff, 928-774-6272; www.arizonahistoricalsociety.org
This museum highlights the history of Flagstaff and northern Arizona. There are changing exhibits throughout the year. Monday-Saturday.

ARIZONA SNOWBOWL SKI & SUMMER RESORT
6355 Highway 180, Flagstaff, 928-779-1951; www.arizonasnowbowl.com
The 50-acre resort has two triple, two double chairlifts; patrol, school, rentals; restaurants, bars, lounge; lodges. Thirty-two trails, longest run more than two miles;

SUNSET CRATER VOLCANO NATIONAL MONUMENT
Between the growing seasons of 1064 and 1065, violent volcanic eruptions built a large cone-shaped mountain of cinders and ash called a cinder cone volcano. Around the base of the cinder cone, lava flowed from cracks, creating the Bonito Lava Flow on the west side of the cone and the Kana'a Lava Flow on the east side. The approximate date of the initial eruption was determined by examining tree rings of timber found in the remains of American Indian pueblos at Wupatki National Monument.

This cinder cone, now called Sunset Crater, stands about 1,000 feet above the surrounding terrain. Mineral deposits around the rim stained the cinders, giving the summit a perpetual sunset hue.

Park rangers are on duty all year. Do not attempt to drive off the roads; the cinders are soft and the surrounding landscape is very fragile. The U.S. Forest Service maintains a campground (May-mid-September) opposite the visitor center. Guided tours and naturalist activities are offered during the summer. Visitor center daily. A 20-mile paved road leads to Wupatki National Monument.
Information: 7133 N. US 89, Flagstaff, 928-526-0502; www.nps.gov/sucr

WUPATKI NATIONAL MONUMENT

The nearly 2,600 archeological sites of the Sinagua and Anasazi cultures were occupied between A.D. 1100 and 1250. The largest of them, Wupatki Pueblo, was three stories high, with about 100 rooms. The eruption of nearby Sunset Crater spread volcanic ash over an 800-square-mile area and for a time, made this an active farming center.

The half-mile ruins trail is self-guided. Books are available at its starting point. The visitor center and main ruin are open daily. Wupatki National Monument and Sunset Crater Volcano National Monument are located on a 35-mile paved loop off of Highway 89. The nearest camping is at Bonito Campground (May-October; 520-526-0866).

Information: 6400 N. Highway 89, Flagstaff, 928-679-2365; www.nps.gov/wupa

vertical drop 2,300 feet. Mid-December-mid-April, daily. Skyride (Memorial Day-Labor Day) takes riders to 11,500 feet.

COCONINO NATIONAL FOREST

1824 S. Thompson St., Flagstaff, 928-527-3600; www.fs.fed.us/r3/coconino

This national forest surrounds the city of Flagstaff and the community of Sedona. Outstanding scenic areas include Humphreys Peak—Arizona's highest point—as well as parts of the Mogollon Rim and the Verde River Valley, the red rock country of Sedona; Oak Creek Canyon (where Zane Grey wrote *Call of the Canyon*) and the San Francisco Peaks. Includes extinct volcanoes and high country lakes. Fishing, hunting, winter sports, camping.

LOWELL OBSERVATORY

1400 Mars Hill Road, Flagstaff, 928-774-3358; www.lowell.edu

The dwarf planet Pluto was discovered from this observatory in 1930. Guided tours, slide presentations, telescope viewing. Telescope domes are unheated so appropriate clothing is advised. Daytime hours: November-February, daily noon-5 p.m.; March-October, daily 9 a.m.-5 p.m. Evening hours: September-May, Wednesday, Friday, Saturday 5:30-9:30 p.m.; June-August, Monday-Saturday 5:30-10:00 p.m.

MORMON LAKE SKI CENTER

5075 N. Highway 89, Flagstaff, 928-354-2240;
www.fs.fed.us/r3/coconino/recreation/mormon_lake/moromon-winter.shtml

This terrain includes snowy meadows, huge stands of pine, oak and aspen, old logging roads and turn-of-the-century railroad grades. Plus, more than 20 miles of marked, groomed trails. School, rentals, ski shop. Guided tours (including moonlight tours on full moon weekends). Restaurant, bar, motel, cabins. Daily 8 a.m.-5 p.m.

MUSEUM OF NORTHERN ARIZONA

3101 N. Fort Valley Road, Flagstaff, 928-774-5213; www.musnaz.org

Exhibits on the archaeology, geology, biology, paleontology and fine arts of the Colorado Plateau. Daily 8 a.m.-5 p.m.

OAK CREEK CANYON

Slide Rock State Park, 6871 N. Highway 89A, Sedona, 928-282-3034;
www.fs.fed.us/r3/coconino/

This spectacular gorge may look familiar to you—it's a favorite location for Western movies. The northern end of the road starts with a lookout point atop the walls and descends nearly 2,000 feet to the stream bed. The creek has excellent trout fishing. At the southern mouth of the canyon is Sedona.

RIORDAN MANSION STATE HISTORIC PARK

409 Riordan Road, Flagstaff, 928-779-4395; azstateparks.com/parks/rima/index.html

This six-acre park features an Arts and Crafts-style mansion built in 1904 by Michael and Timothy Riordan, two brothers who played a significant role in the development of Flagstaff and northern Arizona. Original artifacts, handcrafted furniture, mementos. Picnic area. Guided tours (reservations recommended). Admission: adults $6, children $2.50, children under 7 free. May-October, daily 8:30 a.m.-5 p.m.; November-April, daily 10:30 a.m.-5 p.m.

WALNUT CANYON NATIONAL MONUMENT

Walnut Canyon Road, Flagstaff, 928-526-3367; www.nps.gov/waca

A spectacular, rugged 400-foot-deep canyon with 300 small cliff dwellings dating back to around A.D. 1100. The dwellings are well preserved because they are under protective ledges in the canyon's limestone walls. There are two self-guided trails and an educational museum in the visitor center. Picnic grounds. Daily.

SPECIAL EVENTS

COCONINO COUNTY FAIR

Flagstaff, 928-774-5139; www.coconino.az.gov/parks.aspx

This annual fair in Coconino County features livestock auctions, contests, entertainment, fine arts and food. Labor Day weekend.

HOPI ARTISTS' EXHIBITION

Museum of Northern Arizona, 3101 N. Fort Valley Road, Flagstaff, 928-774-5213;
www.musnaz.org

Exhibition and sale of Hopi artwork. Late June-early July.

NAVAJO ARTISTS' EXHIBITION

Museum of Northern Arizona, 3101 N. Fort Valley Road, Flagstaff, 928-774-5213;
www.musnaz.org

Last weekend in July-first weekend in August.

WINTERFEST

Flagstaff, 928-774-4505; www.flagstaffchamber.com

Features theater performances, sled dog and other races, games, entertainment and more. February.

★
★
★
★
★

HOTELS

★★EMBASSY SUITES

706 S. Milton Road, Flagstaff, 928-774-4333, 800-774-4333; www.embassysuites.com
119 rooms, all suites. Complimentary full breakfast. Wireless Internet access. Bar. Pool. Business center. fitness center. **$**

★FAIRFIELD INN

2005 S. Milton Road, Flagstaff, 928-773-1300, 800-574-6395; www.fairfieldinn.com
131 rooms. Complimentary continental breakfast. Wireless Internet access. Pool. Spa. Fitness center. **$**

★HAMPTON INN

2400 S. Beulah Blvd., Flagstaff, 928-913-0900, 800-426-7866; www.hampton.com
126 rooms. Complimentary continental breakfast. Wireless Internet access. Airport transportation available. Pool. Fitness center. **$**

★★★INN AT 410 BED & BREAKFAST

410 N. Leroux St., Flagstaff, 928-774-0088, 800-774-2008; www.inn410.com
Known as the place with the personal touch, this charming 1894 Craftsman home offers fresh-baked cookies in the evenings. Each room has its own individual theme and is decorated with charming antiques. 10 rooms. Children over five permitted. Complimentary full breakfast. Wireless Internet access. Airport transportation available. **$$**

★★★LITTLE AMERICA HOTEL

2515 E. Butler Ave., Flagstaff, 928-779-7900, 800-865-1401;
www.littleamerica.com/flagstaff
Located on 500 acres of beautiful pine forest, this hotel has its own private hiking trails. The outdoor pool offers views of the mountains. The spacious guest rooms include floor-to-ceiling windows and flatscreen TVs. Complimentary hors d'oeuvres are served nightly. 247 rooms. High-speed Internet access. Restaurant, bar. Children's activity center. Airport transportation available. Business center. **$**

RESTAURANTS

★KACHINA DOWNTOWN

522 E. Route 66, Flagstaff, 928-779-1944, 877-397-2743; www.kachinarestaurant.com
Mexican menu. Lunch, dinner. Bar. Children's menu. Reservations recommended. **$$**

★★MAMMA LUISA

2710 N. Steves Blvd., Flagstaff, 928-526-6809
Italian menu. Dinner. Children's menu. Casual attire. Reservations recommended. **$$**

FOUNTAIN HILLS

An affluent community not far from Scottsdale in the Valley of the Sun, Fountain Hills offers distinct beauty and lots of opportunities for outdoor recreation.
Information: Chamber of Commerce, 16837 Palisades Blvd., Fountain Hills,
480-837-1654; www.fountainhillschamber.com

WHAT TO SEE AND DO
FORT MCDOWELL CASINO
Fort McDowell Road and Beeline Highway, Fountain Hills, 800-843-3678;
www.fortmcdowellcasino.com

This casino boasts the state's largest card room, a 1,400-seat bingo hall with jackpots as high as $50,000, a keno lounge with million-dollar payouts and 475 slot machines that keep the decibel level high night and day. Spend some of your winnings in one of four restaurants or at the lounge, which offers live entertainment daily. Only those 21 and older can come and play. Daily.

HOTELS
★★★COPPERWYND RESORT AND CLUB
13225 N. Eagle Ridge Drive, Fountain Hills, 480-333-1900, 877-707-7760;
www.copperwynd.com

This elegant full-service resort, located on a mountain ridge overlooking Scottsdale, provides views of the Sonoran Desert and the surrounding mountain ranges. The spacious European-inspired guest rooms feature gas fireplaces, private balconies, granite counters and Italian linens. Play tennis on one of the nine courts, or golf at one of the nearby courses. 42 rooms. Wireless Internet access. Two restaurants, three bars. Fitness center. Spa. Pool. Tennis. $$$

★★★INN AT EAGLE MOUNTAIN
9800 N. Summer Hill Blvd., Fountain Hills, 480-816-3000, 800-992-8083;
www.innateaglemountain.com

This small boutique hotel is located on the 18th fairway with views of Red Mountain, overlooking Scottsdale and Arizona. The suites have kiva fireplaces, sitting areas and whirlpool tubs. Six of them have a theme, ranging from the Frank Lloyd Wright inspired décor in the Prairie suite to the cowboy items in the Wild West suite. 42 rooms, all mini suites. Restaurant, bar. Pool. $$

GLENDALE
Located just west of Phoenix in the beautiful and scenic Valley of the Sun, Glendale shares all of the urban advantages of the area. Luke Air Force Base is located here.
Information: Chamber of Commerce, 7105 N. 59th Ave.,
623-937-4754, 800-437-8669; www.glendaleaz.com

WHAT TO SEE AND DO
ARIZONA'S ANTIQUE CAPITAL
Glendale, 623-930-4500, 877-800-2601; www.visitglendale.com

This shopping area in downtown Glendale includes antique stores, specialty shops and a candy factory. Most stores open Monday-Saturday.

BO'S FUNKY STUFF
5605 W. Glendale Ave., Glendale, 623-842-0220

This offbeat emporium proves the old adage that one man's junk is another man's treasure. Two rooms are crammed with old advertising signs, housewares and '50s furniture. Prices range from under a dollar to several thousand. September-May, Monday-Saturday noon-5 p.m.; June-August, Saturday 11 a.m.-6 p.m.

CERRETA CANDY COMPANY

5345 W. Glendale Ave., Glendale, 623-930-9000; www.cerreta.com

It doesn't get any sweeter than this old-fashioned factory, where the Cerreta family has been cooking up mouthwatering confections for more than 30 years. Guided tours are offered at 10 a.m. and 1 p.m. Monday through Friday, but the kitchens are visible to customers, so you can get a flavor for how things are made anytime. Monday-Saturday 8 a.m.-6 p.m.

GLENDALE ARENA

9400 W. Maryland Ave., Glendale, 623-772-3200; www.glendalearenaaz.com

Glendale Arena is home to the Phoenix Coyotes NHL ice hockey team. It also hosts concerts, family shows and more.

HOTELS
★HAMPTON INN

8408 W. Paradise Lane, Peoria, 623-486-9918, 800-445-8667; www.hamptoninn.com

112 rooms. Complimentary continental breakfast. High-speed Internet access. Fitness center. Pool. $

★LA QUINTA PHOENIX INN AND SUITES PEORIA

16321 N. 83rd Ave., Peoria, 623-487-1900, 800-642-4271; www.laquinta.com

108 rooms. Complimentary continental breakfast. High-speed Internet access. Pool. Pets accepted.

GRAND CANYON NATIONAL PARK

Look out over the great expanse of the Grand Canyon and the awe-inspiring vistas reveal a spectacular desert landscape. Rocks in this great chasm change colors from sunrise to sunset and hide an ecosystem of wildlife. It's no wonder millions of visitors pay a visit to this world wonder every year.

Visitors come here to hike the trails, travel down by mule, camp at the base, raft the river or simply stare in awe from the rim. The entire park is 1,904 square miles in size, with 277 miles of the Colorado River running through it. At its widest point, the north and south rims are 18 miles across, with average elevations of 8,000 feet and 7,000 feet, respectively. The canyon averages a depth of one mile. At its base, 2-billion-year-old rocks are exposed.

The South Rim, open all year, has the greater number of services, including day and overnight mule trips through Xanterra Parks & Resorts, horseback riding through Apache Stables (928-638-2891) and air tours (both fixed-wing and helicopter) through several local companies.

In addition to these tours, there are a variety of museums and facilities on the South Rim. The Kolb Studio in the Village Historic District at the Bright Angel Trailhead features art displays and a bookstore. It was once the home and business of the Kolb brothers, who were pioneering photographers here. The Yavapai Observation Station, one mile east of Market Plaza, contains temporary exhibits about the fossil record at Grand Canyon.

The North Rim, blocked by heavy snows in winter, is open from mid-May to mid-October. Due to the higher elevation, mule trips from the North Rim do not go to the river. Trips range in length from one hour to a full day. For more information, contact Grand Canyon Trail Rides at 435-679-8665.

Fall and spring are the best times for to trek into the canyon, when it's less crowded. Don't plan to hike to the base and back up in one day—changing elevations and temperatures can exhaust hikers quickly. It's best to camp in the canyon overnight (plan on an additional night if hiking from the North Rim). Fifteen main trails provide access to the inner canyon. Make reservations for camping or lodging facilities early.

Rafting the Colorado River through Grand Canyon National Park also requires reservations far in advance of your intended visit. Trips vary in length from 3 to 21 days and can be made through a commercial outfitter, a private river trip or a one-day trip (which may or may not be in Grand Canyon National Park). For one-day whitewater raft trips, contact Hualapai River Runners, 928-769-2119. Half-day smooth-water raft trips are provided by Wilderness River Adventures, 800-992-8022.

Information: Grand Canyon, approximately 50 miles north on Highway 180
(Highway 64) to the South Rim, 928-638-7888; www.nps.gov/grca

WHAT TO SEE AND DO
DRIVE TO CAPE ROYAL
North Rim (Grand Canyon National Park), about 23 miles from Bright Angel
Point over paved road
You'll encounter several good viewpoints along the way—many visitors say the view from here is better than from the South Rim. Archaeology and geology talks are given in summer and fall.

HOTEL
★★GRAND CANYON LODGE
Highway 67, Grand Canyon, 928-638-2611; www.grandcanyonlodgenorth.com/
214 rooms. Closed mid-October-mid-May. Restaurant, bar. $

RESTAURANTS
★★ARIZONA ROOM
South Rim, Grand Canyon Village, 928-638-2631; www.grandcanyonlodges.com
American. Southwestern menu. Lunch, dinner. $$

★★GRAND CANYON LODGE DINING ROOM
AZ 67, Grand Canyon, 928-638-2611; www.grandcanyonnorthrim.com
American menu. Breakfast, lunch, dinner. Reservations required for dinner. Closed November-April. $

★JACOB LAKE INN
Highway 89A and AZ 67, Jacob Lake, 928-643-7232; www.jacoblake.com
American menu. Breakfast, lunch, dinner. $

GOLD CANYON

At the foot of the Superstition Mountains, Gold Canyon is a tiny town with golf courses, cacti and craggy rocks. The community is a popular area for second homes. *Information: www.goldcanyon.net*

HOTEL

★★★GOLD CANYON GOLF RESORT

6100 S. Kings Ranch Road, Gold Canyon, 480-982-9090, 800-827-5281; www.gcgr.com

Located on 3,300 acres in the foothills of the Superstition Mountains, this is a good choice for golfers who don't want to spend a fortune. The resort features a golf school and many scenic holes. The accommodations include suites and private casitas, some with fireplaces or whirlpools. 101 rooms. Two restaurants, bar. Spa. Airport transportation available. Pets accepted. Golf. Fitness center. **$**

GRAND CANYON NATIONAL PARK (SOUTH RIM)

Information: Grand Canyon National Park, approximately 80 miles northwest of Flagstaff via US 180, 928-638-7888; www.nps.gov/grca

WHAT TO SEE AND DO

DRIVES TO VIEWPOINTS

1 Main St., South Rim (Grand Canyon National Park)

The West Rim and East Rim drives out from Grand Canyon Village are both rewarding. Grandview Point and Desert View on the East Rim Drive are especially magnificent. West Rim Drive is closed to private vehicles from early April to early October. Free shuttle buses serve the West Rim and Village area during this period.

GRAND CANYON IMAX THEATRE

Highways 64 and 180, Tusayan, 928-638-2468; www.explorethecanyon.com

Large screen film (35 minutes) highlighting features of the Grand Canyon. March-October, 8:30 a.m.-8:30 p.m.; November-February, 10:30 a.m.-6:30 p.m.; movie is shown hourly on the half hour.

KAIBAB NATIONAL FOREST

800 Sixth St., Williams, 928-638-2443; www.fs.fed.us/r3/kai

More than 1.6 million acres; one area surrounds Williams and includes Sycamore Canyon and Kendrick Mountain wilderness areas and part of National Historic Route 66. A second area is 42 miles north on Highway 180 (Highway 64) near the South Rim of the Grand Canyon; a third area lies north of the Grand Canyon (outstanding views of the canyon from seldom-visited vista points in this area) and includes Kanab Creek and Saddle Mountain wilderness areas, the Kaibab Plateau and the North Rim Parkway National Scenic Byway.

MULE TRIPS INTO THE CANYON
South Rim (Grand Canyon National Park), 928-638-3283;
www.nps.gov/grca/planyourvisit/mule_trips.htm
A number of trips are scheduled, all with guides. There are some limitations. Trips take one, two or three days. Reservations should be made several months in advance (preferably one year prior).

TUSAYAN MUSEUM
Desert View Road, South Rim (Grand Canyon National Park); www.nps.gov/grca
Exhibits on prehistoric man in the Southwest. Excavated pueblo ruin (circa 1185) nearby. Daily 9 a.m.-5 p.m., weather permitting. Ranger-led tours daily 11 a.m.-1:30 p.m.

YAVAPAI OBSERVATION STATION
South Rim (Grand Canyon National Park); www.nps.gov/grca
The station features a small museum, scenic views, geological exhibits and a bookstore. Daily 8 a.m.-8 p.m.

HOTELS
★★BEST WESTERN GRAND CANYON SQUIRE INN
100 Highway 64, Grand Canyon, 928-638-2681, 800-622-6966;
www.grandcanyonsquire.com
250 rooms. Complimentary continental breakfast. Three restaurants, two bars. Children's activity center. Airport transportation available. Pool. Tennis. $

★★BRIGHT ANGEL LODGE
Highway 64, Grand Canyon, 928-638-2631, 888-297-2757;
www.grandcanyonlodges.com/bright-angel-lodge-408.html
89 rooms. Restaurant, bar. Canyon tour service. $

★★★EL TOVAR
On the Canyon rim, 928-638-2631, 888-297-2757;
www.grandcanyonlodges.com/el-tovar-409.html
The premier lodging facility at the Grand Canyon, El Tovar Hotel—named in honor of the Spanish explorer Don Pedro de Tovar, who reported the existence of the Grand Canyon to fellow explorers—opened its doors in 1905 and was said to be the most expensive log house in America. Just 20 feet from the edge of the Canyon's South Rim, the building is charming and rustic. The hotel features a fine dining room, lounge and a gift shop highlighting Native American artists. With so much to do right at your doorstep—hiking, mule rides, train excursions, interpretive walks, cultural activities—El Tovar offers the best of the Grand Canyon, combining turn-of-the-century lodge ambience with the highest standard of service. Advance reservations are recommended, especially for the summer season, which is usually booked up a year in advance. 78 rooms. Restaurant, bar. Airport transportation available. $

★★THE GRAND HOTEL

Highway 64, Grand Canyon, 928-638-3333, 888-634-7263; www.visitgrandcanyon.com
121 rooms. Restaurant, bar. Indoor pool, whirlpool. $

★★QUALITY INN

Highway 64, Grand Canyon, 928-638-2673, 877-424-6423; www.QualityInn.com
232 rooms. High-speed Internet access. Complimentary continental breakfast. Restaurant, bar. Airport transportation available. Pets accepted. Pool. $

★THUNDERBIRD LODGE

On the Canyon rim, 928-638-2631, 888-297-2757; www.grandcanyonlodges.com
55 rooms. Canyon tour service. $

★★YAVAPAI LODGE

Half-mile from the Canyon Rim, 928-638-2631, 888-297-2757;
www.grandcanyonlodges.com
358 rooms. Closed two weeks in mid-November, three weeks in early December, also January-February. Restaurant. $

RESTAURANTS
★★★EL TOVAR DINING ROOM

1 Main St., South Rim, 928-638-2631; www.grandcanyonlodges.com
Considered the premier dining establishment at the Grand Canyon, this restaurant provides a memorable experience, thanks to the spicy regional cuisine and spectacular Canyon views. The atmosphere is casually elegant with native stone fireplaces, Oregon pine-vaulted ceilings, American Indian artwork and Mission-style accents. Diners can select from a well-rounded menu that blends regional flavors and contemporary techniques and offers many vegetarian options. The wine list is extensive. Southwestern menu. Breakfast, lunch, dinner. Children's menu. Reservations recommended. $$

★YIPPEE-EI-O STEAKHOUSE

Highway 64 and Highway 180, Grand Canyon, 928-638-2780
American, Steak menu. Lunch, dinner. Bar. Children's menu. $$

HOLBROOK

This small town has a lot to offer, especially when it comes to the histories of the Navajo, Hopi, Zuni and White Mountain Apache Indian tribes. Stop here on your way to Petrified Forest National Park to learn about these unique tribes.
Information: Chamber of Commerce, 100 E. Arizona St.,
928-524-6558, 800-524-2459; www.ci.holbrook.az.us

WHAT TO SEE AND DO
NAVAJO COUNTY HISTORICAL MUSEUM

100 E. Arizona, Holbrook, 928-524-6558; www.ci.holbrook.az.us
Exhibits on Navajo, Apache, Hopi and Hispanic cultures. Includes petrified forest and dinosaur exhibits. Monday-Friday 8 a.m.-5 p.m., Saturday-Sunday 8 a.m.-4 p.m.

PETRIFIED FOREST NATIONAL PARK

These 93,532 acres include one of the most spectacular displays of petrified wood in the world. The trees of the original forest may have grown in upland areas and then been washed down onto a floodplain by rivers. Subsequently, the trees were buried under sediment and volcanic ash, causing the organic wood to be filled gradually with mineral compounds, especially quartz. The grain, now multicolored by the compounds, is still visible in some specimens.

The visitor center is located at the entrance off Interstate 40 (I-40). The Rainbow Forest Museum (off US 180) depicts the paleontology and geology of the Triassic Era. Service stations and cafeteria are located at the north entrance. Prehistoric Pueblo inhabitants left countless petroglyphs of animals, figures and symbols carved on sandstone throughout the park.

The park contains a portion of the Painted Desert, a colorful area extending 200 miles along the north bank of the Little Colorado River. This highly eroded area of mesas, pinnacles, washes and canyons is part of the Chinle formation, a soft shale, clay and sandstone stratum of the Triassic. The sunlight and clouds passing over this spectacular scenery create an effect of constant, kaleidoscopic change. There are very good viewpoints along the park road.

Picnicking facilities at Rainbow Forest and at Chinle Point on the rim of the Painted Desert; no campgrounds. It is forbidden to take even the smallest piece of petrified wood or any other object from the park. Nearby curio shops sell wood taken from areas outside the park. Daily.

Information: Petrified Forest National Park, 1 Park Road, Holbrook, 928-524-6228; www.nps.gov/pefo

★
★ ★
★ ★
★

SPECIAL EVENTS
NAVAJO COUNTY FAIR AND RODEO
Navajo County Fairgrounds, 404 E. Hopi Drive, Holbrook, 928-524-4757;
www.navajocountyfair.org
Includes livestock judging, a 4-H competition and exhibitors. Mid-September.

OLD WEST CELEBRATION
Navajo County Historic Courthouse, 100 E. Arizona St., Holbrook,
928-524-6558; www.ci.holbrook.az.us
Running, swimming and biking races, a quilt auction, arts and crafts and more. Mid-September.

HOTELS
★★BEST WESTERN ARIZONIAN INN
2508 Navajo Blvd., Holbrook, 928-524-2611, 877-280-7300; www.bestwestern.com
70 rooms. Wireless Internet access. Complimentary continental breakfast. Restaurant. Pets accepted. Pool. $

★HOLIDAY INN EXPRESS

1308 E. Navajo Blvd., Holbrook, 928-524-1466, 888-465-4329; www.holiday-inn.com

59 rooms. Complimentary continental breakfast. Pets accepted. Pool. **$**

RESTAURANT

★★MESA ITALIANA

2318 N. Navajo Blvd., Holbrook, 928-524-6696

Italian menu. Lunch, dinner. Bar. Children's menu. **$$**

HOPI INDIAN RESERVATION

Inside the Navajo Indian Reservation is the 1.5-million-acre Hopi Indian Reservation. The Hopi are pueblo people of Shoshonean ancestry who have lived here for more than 2,000 years in some of the continent's most intriguing towns.

Excellent farmers, the Hopi also herd sheep, as well as craft pottery, silver jewelry, kachina dolls and baskets. Both the Navajo and Hopi are singers and dancers—each in their own style. The Hopi are most famous for their Snake Dance, which may not be viewed by visitors, but there are dozens of other beautiful ceremonies that visitors are allowed to watch. (The photographing, recording or sketching of any events on the reservation is prohibited.)

The Hopi towns are located, for the most part, on three mesas. On the first mesa is Walpi, founded around 1680, one of the most beautiful Hopi pueblos. It is built on the tip of a narrow, steep-walled mesa, along with its companion villages, Sichomovi and Hano, which are inhabited by the Tewa and the Hano. Hanoans speak a Tewa language as well as Hopi. You can drive to Sichomovi and walk along a narrow connecting mesa to Walpi. Only passenger cars are allowed on the mesa; no RVs or trailers. Individuals of Walpi and First Mesa Villages offer Hopi pottery and kachina dolls for sale; inquire locally.

The second mesa has three towns: Mishongnovi, Sipaulovi and Shungopavi, each fascinating in its own way. The Hopi Cultural Center, located on the second mesa, includes a museum and craft shops, a restaurant serving both Hopi and American food and a motel. Reservations (928-734-2401) for May through August should be made at least three months in advance. Near the Cultural Center is a primitive campground.

The third mesa has Oraibi, the oldest Hopi town, and its three off-shoots, Bacavi, Kyakotsmovi and Hotevilla, a town of considerable interest. A restaurant, a small motel and tent and trailer sites can be found at Keams Canyon. There are not many places to stay, so plan your trip carefully. All major roads leading into and across the Navajo and Hopi Reservations are paved.

Information: 928-734-3283; www.hopi.nsn.us

NAVAJO NATIONAL MONUMENT

This monument comprises three scattered areas totaling 600 acres and is surrounded by the Navajo Nation. Each area is the location of a large and remarkable prehistoric cliff dwelling. Two of the ruins are accessible by guided tour.

Headquarters for the monument and the visitor center are near Betatakin, the most accessible of the three cliff dwellings. Guided tours, limited to 25 people (Betatakin tour), are arranged on a first-come, first-served basis (May-September; tours sometimes possible earlier in spring and late in fall; phone for schedule). Hiking distance is five miles round-trip, including a steep 700-foot trail, and takes five to six hours. Betatakin may also be viewed from the Sandal Trail overlook—a 1/2-mile, one-way, self-guided trail. Daily.

The largest and best-preserved ruin, Keet Seel (Memorial Day-Labor Day, phone for schedule), is 8½ miles one-way by foot or horseback from headquarters. A permit is required either way, and reservations can be made up to two months in advance. A primitive campground is available for overnight hikers. The horseback trip takes all day. Horses should be reserved when making reservations (no children under 12 without previous riding experience).

The visitor center has a museum and film program. Daily.

Information: Kayenta, 19 miles southwest of Kayenta on Highway 163, then nine miles north on paved road Highway 564 to visitor center, 928-672-2700; www.nps.gov/nava

KAYENTA

Located in the spectacular Monument Valley, Kayenta's surrounding area offers some of the most memorable sightseeing in the state, including the great tinted monoliths.
Information: City of Kayenta, 928-697-8451; www.kayentaaz.com

WHAT TO SEE AND DO

CRAWLEY'S MONUMENT VALLEY TOURS
Kayenta, 928-697-3463; www.crawleytours.com
Guided tours in backcountry vehicles to Monument Valley, Mystery Valley and Hunt's Mesa. Half- and full-day rates. Sunset tours are also available. Daily.

HOTELS

★★GOULDING'S LODGE
1000 Main St., Monument Valley, 435-727-3231; www.gouldings.com
62 rooms. Restaurant. Pets accepted. Pool. $$

★★HOLIDAY INN
Highways 160 and 163, Kayenta, 928-697-3221, 888-465-4329; www.holiday-inn.com
162 rooms. Restaurant. Pool. $

KINGMAN

The heart of Kingman lies on historic Route 66 and is a convenient stop on the way to the Grand Canyon. Several lakes are nearby with year-round swimming, waterskiing, fishing and boating. To the south are the beautiful Hualapai Mountains. Kingman was once a rich silver and gold mining area and several ghost towns are nearby.

Information: Chamber of Commerce, 120 W. Andy Devine Ave., 928-753-6253; www.kingmanchamber.org

WHAT TO SEE AND DO
BONELLI HOUSE
430 E. Spring St., Kingman, 928-753-3175; www.kingmantourism.org
One of the earliest permanent structures in the city, this restored home is furnished with many original pieces. Monday-Friday 11 a.m.-3 p.m.

MOHAVE MUSEUM OF HISTORY AND ART
400 W. Beale St., Kingman, 928-753-3195; www.mohavemuseum.org
See a portrait collection of U.S. presidents and first ladies at this museum that traces local and state history. Also featured is a turquoise display, a rebuilt 1926 pipe organ, a local artists' gallery and more. Monday-Friday 9 a.m.-5 p.m., Saturday-Sunday 1-5 p.m.

OATMAN
Highway 66, Oatman, 928-768-6222; www.oatmangoldroad.org
In the 1930s, this was the last stop in Arizona before entering the Mojave Desert in California. Created in 1906 as a tent camp, it flourished as a gold mining center until 1942, when Congress declared that gold mining was no longer essential to the war effort. The ghost town has been kept as authentic as possible and several motion pictures have been filmed here. Turquoise and antique shops. Gunfights staged on weekends.

POWERHOUSE VISITOR CENTER
120 W. Route 66, Kingman, 928-753-6106, 866-427-7866; www.kingmantourism.org
Houses the Historic Route 66 Association of Arizona, Tourist Information Center, Carlos Elmer Memorial Photo Gallery and more. Model railroad shop, gift shop, deli. March-November, daily 9 a.m.-6 p.m.; December-February, daily 9 a.m.-5 p.m.

SPECIAL EVENTS
ANDY DEVINE DAYS PRCA RODEO
Mohave County Fairgrounds, 2600 Fairgrounds Blvd., Kingman, 928-757-7919; www.kingmanrodeo.com/kingsmen.html
Sports tournaments, parade and more. Two days in late September.

MOHAVE COUNTY FAIR
Mohave County Fairgrounds, 2600 Fairgrounds Blvd., Kingman, 928-753-2636; www.mcfafairgrounds.org
Annual event featuring a carnival, livestock auctions, 4-H competition and food. First weekend after Labor Day.

HOTEL
★BEST WESTERN A WAYFARER'S INN AND SUITES
2815 E. Andy Devine Ave., Kingman, 928-753-6271, 800-548-5695; www.bestwestern.com
101 rooms. Wireless Internet access. Fitness center. Pets accepted. Pool. $

LAKE HAVASU CITY

This is the center of a year-round resort area on the shores of 45-mile-long Lake Havasu. The London Bridge, imported from England and reassembled here in 1968 as part of a recreational area, connects the mainland city with a three-square-mile island that has a marina, golf course, tennis courts, campgrounds and other recreational facilities.

Information: Lake Havasu City Convention & Visitors Bureau, 314 London Bridge Road, 928-453-3444, 800-242-8278; www.golakehavasu.com

WHAT TO SEE AND DO
LAKE HAVASU STATE PARK
699 London Bridge Road, Lake Havasu City, 928-855-2784; www.pr.state.az.us/Parks/parkhtml/havasu.html

This park occupies 13,000 acres along 23 miles of shoreline. Windsor Beach Unit, two miles north on old Highway 95 (London Bridge Road), has swimming, fishing, boating, hiking and camping; 928-855-2784. Cattail Cove Unit, 15 miles south and a ½-mile west of Highway 95, has swimming, fishing, boating and camping; 928-855-1223. Sunrise-10 p.m.

LONDON BRIDGE RESORT & ENGLISH VILLAGE
1477 Queens Bay, Lake Havasu City, 928-855-0888, 866-331-9231; www.londonbridgeresort.com

This English-style village on 110 acres is home to the world-famous London Bridge. Specialty shops, restaurants, boat rides, nine-hole golf course, accommodations. Village. Daily.

TOPOCK GORGE
Lake Havasu City

Scenic (and steep) volcanic banks along the Colorado River. Migratory birds spend winters here, while herons, cormorants and egrets nest in April and May. Fishing, picnicking.

HOTEL
★★HAMPTON INN
245 London Bridge Road, Lake Havasu City, 928-855-4071, 800-426-7866; www.hamptoninn.com

162 rooms. Restaurant, bar. Pets accepted. Pool. Fitness center. **$**

RESTAURANT
★★SHUGRUE'S
1425 McCulloch Blvd., Lake Havasu City, 928-453-1400; www.shugrues.com

Seafood, steak menu. Lunch, dinner. Bar. Children's menu. **$$**

LITCHFIELD PARK

WHAT TO SEE AND DO
WILDLIFE WORLD ZOO
16501 W. Northern Ave., Litchfield Park, 623-935-9453; www.wildlifeworld.com
You'll see white tigers, African lions, camels and rhinos at this zoo boasting a large collection of exotic animals (about 2,400, representing nearly 400 species). Daily 9 a.m.-5 p.m.

SPECIAL EVENT
WEST VALLEY INVITATIONAL AMERICAN INDIAN ARTS FESTIVAL
The West Valley Fine Arts Council, 200 W. Fairway Drive, Litchfield Park,
623-935-6384; www.wvfac.org
Approximately 200 American Indian craft vendors display their goods. Also includes American Indian dancing and other entertainment. Mid-January.

HOTEL
★★★THE WIGWAM RESORT AND GOLF CLUB
300 Wigwam Blvd., Litchfield Park, 623-935-3811, 800-327-0396;
www.wigwamresort.com
Once a private club for executives of the Goodyear Tire Company, the Wigwam Resort is one of Arizona's best. The rooms and suites highlight authentic regional design with whitewashed wood furniture, slate floors and Mexican ceramic tiles. The property includes award-winning golf courses, nine tennis courts, two pools with a water slide and a spa. Five restaurants and bars have something for everyone. 331 rooms. Three restaurants, two bars. Children's activity center. Spa. Airport transportation available. Pets accepted. Golf. Tennis. Business center. $$$

RESTAURANT
★★★ARIZONA KITCHEN
300 Wigwam East Blvd., Litchfield Park, 623-535-2598; www.wigwamresort.com
This always-packed Southwestern restaurant is a showcase for the fiery culinary techniques and flavors of the region. Using herbs grown on the premises, the kitchen pays homage to local ingredients with signature dishes like smoked corn chowder, grilled sirloin of buffalo with sweet potato pudding and mesquite-dusted Chilean sea bass. The dining room—with adobe fireplace, red brick floors, wood-beamed ceilings and an open kitchen featuring a mesquite wood-fired hearth and grill—is the perfect setting to enjoy it. Southwestern menu. Breakfast, lunch, dinner. Bar. Children's menu. Business casual attire. Reservations recommended. Valet parking. Outdoor seating. $$$

MARBLE CANYON
This section of Grand Canyon National Park has some of the nation's best camping and most captivating scenery. Pitch your tent here and enjoy the view.

WHAT TO SEE AND DO
MARBLE CANYON
Marble Canyon, 928-638-7888; www.nps.gov/grca
Part of Grand Canyon National Park.

HOTEL
★★CLIFF DWELLERS LODGE
HC-67, Marble Canyon, 928-355-2261, 800-962-9755; www.leesferry.com
20 rooms. Restaurant, bar. Pets accepted. $

MCNARY
McNary is in the northeastern section of the Fort Apache Indian Reservation. The White Mountain Apaches have a number of recreation areas on their reservation. Trout fishing, exploring and camping are available.
Information: White Mountain Recreation Enterprise, Whiteriver, 928-338-4385

WHAT TO SEE AND DO
HAWLEY LAKE
White Mountain Apache Indian Reservation, McNary, 12 miles east on Highway 260,
then 11 miles south on Highway 473, 928-335-7511; www.hawleylake.org.uk
With an elevation of 8,200 feet, Hawley Lake is one of the highest lakes in Arizona. Summer activities include fishing, hiking and camping. Cabin rentals are also available. Ice fishing is a popular winter activity.

SUNRISE PARK RESORT
Fort Apache Indian Reservation, Highway 273, Greer,
928-735-7669, 800-772-7669; www.sunriseskipark.com
Resort has two quad, four triple, double chairlift, three rope tows; patrol, school, rentals; cafeteria, restaurants, bars. Sixty-five runs. Snowboarding. November-mid-April, daily. Summer activities include swimming, fishing, canoeing, hiking, horseback riding and tennis. Camping.

MESA
Mesa, Spanish for "table," sits atop a plateau overlooking the Valley of the Sun and is one of the state's largest and fastest-growing cities. Mesa offers year-round golf, tennis, hiking and water sports. It also provides easy access to other Arizona and Southwest attractions and is the home of Arizona State University-Polytechnic Campus.
Information: Convention & Visitors Bureau, 120 N. Center,
480-827-4700, 800-283-6372; www.mesacvb.com

WHAT TO SEE AND DO
ARIZONA MUSEUM FOR YOUTH
35 N. Robson St., Mesa, 480-644-2467; www.arizonamuseumforyouth.com
Fine arts museum with changing hands-on exhibits for children. Tuesday-Saturday 10 a.m.-4 p.m., Sunday noon-4 p.m.

ARIZONA MUSEUM OF NATURAL HISTORY
53 N. MacDonald St., Mesa, 480-644-2230;
www.mesasouthwestmuseum.com/home.aspx
Learn about the Native Americans who lived here, see a replica of a Spanish mission and more as you explore this 80,000-square-foot regional resource. Interactive center for kids. Tuesday-Friday 10 a.m.-5 p.m., Saturday 11 a.m.-5 p.m., Sunday 1-5 p.m.

BOYCE THOMPSON SOUTHWESTERN ARBORETUM

37615 Highway 60, Superior, 520-689-2723; www.ag.arizona.edu/bta

See a large collection of plants from arid parts of the world. Visitor center features biological and historical displays. September-April, daily 8 a.m.-4 p.m.; May-August, daily 6 a.m.-3 p.m.

DOLLY STEAMBOAT CRUISES

Highway 88 Apache Trail, Apache Junction, 480-827-9144; www.dollysteamboat.com

Narrated tours and twilight dinner cruises of Canyon Lake follow the original path of the Salt River. Nature Cruise: daily at noon, 2 p.m. by reservation only, arrangements can be made for 10 a.m. or 4 p.m.; Twilight Dinner Cruise: weekends, call for schedule.

LOST DUTCHMAN STATE PARK

6109 N. Apache Trail, Apache Junction, 480-982-4485;
www.pr.state.az.us/parks/parkhtml/dutchman.html

This 300-acre park in the Superstition Mountains area offers hiking, picnicking and improved camping. Interpretive trails and access to nearby forest service wilderness area. Daily, sunrise-10 p.m.

RIVER TUBING, SALT RIVER RECREATION INC

Tonto National Forest, 1320 N. Bush Highway, Mesa; www.saltrivertubing.com

Go tubing down the Salt River—the fee includes tube rental, parking and shuttle bus service to various points on the river. Early May-September, daily 9 a.m.-7 p.m.

VF OUTLET STORES

2055 S. Power Road, Mesa, 480-984-0697; www.vfoutlet.net

Look for deals at the 25 stores here. Monday-Saturday 10 a.m.-8 p.m., Sunday noon-5 p.m.

SPECIAL EVENTS

CHICAGO CUBS SPRING TRAINING

Hohokam Park, 1235 N. Center St., Mesa, 480-964-4467;
www.cactus-league.com/cubs.html

Watch the Cubs during spring training at exhibition games. Early March-early April.

MESA TERRITORIAL DAY FESTIVAL

Sirrine House, 160 N. Center, Mesa, 480-644-2760; www.mesaaz.gov/home

Come celebrate Arizona's birthday in Old West style. This festival features Western arts and crafts, music, food, games and activities, and historical reenactments. Second Saturday in February.

HOTELS

★★★ARIZONA GOLF RESORT & CONFERENCE CENTER

425 S. Power Road, Mesa, 480-832-3202, 800-528-8282; www.azgolfresort.com

Tropical palms and beautiful lakes surround this East Valley resort occupying 150 acres. Guest suites are arranged in clusters with courtyards, barbecue grills and heated spas. The resort has a golf school and the 14th hole of the championship course requires

NAVAJO INDIAN RESERVATION

The Navajo Nation is the largest Native American tribe and reservation in the United States. The reservation covers more than 25,000 square miles within three states—with the largest portion in northeastern Arizona and the rest in New Mexico and Utah.

More than 400 years ago, the Navajo people (the Dineh) moved into the arid southwestern region of the United States and carved out a way of life that was in harmony with the natural beauty of Arizona, New Mexico and Utah. In the 1800s, westward-moving settlers interrupted this harmonious life. For the Navajo, this conflict resulted in their forced removal from their ancestral land and the "Long Walk" to Fort Sumner, New Mexico. The plan was judged a failure and in 1868, they were allowed to return to their homeland. Coal, oil and uranium have been discovered on the reservation. The income from these resources, which is handled democratically by the tribe, has helped improve the economic and educational situation of its people.

The Navajo continue to practice many of their ancient ceremonies, including the Navajo Fire Dance and the Yei-bi-chei (winter) and Enemy Way Dances (summer). Many ceremonies are associated with curing the sick and are primarily religious in nature. Visitors must obtain permission to view these events—photography, recording and sketching are prohibited.

There are a number of paved roads across the Navajo and Hopi Reservations, as well as some unpaved gravel and dirt roads. During the rainy season (mostly August to September), the unpaved roads are difficult or impassable.

Some of the most spectacular areas in Navajoland are Canyon de Chelly National Monument, Navajo National Monument, Monument Valley Navajo Tribal Park (north of Kayenta) and Four Corners Monument. Accommodations on the reservation are limited; reservations are recommended months in advance.

Information: www.explorenavajo.com

★
★ ★
★
☆

a 175 yard-shot through the trees and over the water. 187 rooms. Wireless Internet access. Two restaurants, bar. Pets accepted. Pool. Golf. Business center. **$**

★★BEST WESTERN DOBSON RANCH INN

1666 S. Dobson Road, Mesa, 480-831-7000, 800-528-1356;
www.dobsonranchinn.com

213 rooms. Wireless Internet access. Complimentary full breakfast. Restaurant, bar. Pets accepted. Fitness center. Pool. **$**

★BEST WESTERN SUPERSTITION SPRINGS INN

1342 S. Power Road, Mesa, 480-641-1164, 800-780-7234; www.bestwestern.com

59 rooms. High-speed Internet access. Complimentary continental breakfast. Pets accepted; fee. Pool. Spa. Fitness center. **$**

★★★HILTON PHOENIX EAST/MESA

1011 W. Holmes Ave., Mesa, 480-833-5555, 800-445-8667;
www.phoenixeastmesa.hilton.com

This newly renovated hotel is centrally located in the East Valley, allowing for easy freeway access to many attractions and business in all directions. Phoenix Sky Harbor airport is 12 miles away. Guest rooms are arranged around the large atrium lobby and are decorated in rich autumn colors with velvety textures. French doors lead to a balcony. Relax by the pool, go horseback riding or a hit the links at one of the nearby courses. The Zuni Bar & Grill serves a breakfast buffet and Sunday brunch. The bar is a good spot to meet friends for one of the micro-brewed beers or tasty margaritas. 260 rooms. High-speed Internet access. Restaurant, two bars. Pool. Business center. Fitness center. **$**

★LA QUINTA INN

6530 E. Superstition Springs Blvd., Mesa, 480-654-1970, 800-642-4271; www.lq.com
107 rooms. Complimentary continental breakfast. Wireless Internet access. Pets accepted. Pool. Fitness center. Pets accepted. **$**

RESTAURANT
★★LANDMARK

809 W. Main St., Mesa, 480-962-4652; www.lmrk.com
American menu. Lunch, dinner. Children's menu. Casual attire. **$$**

PAGE

Page is at the east end of the Glen Canyon Dam, on the Colorado River. The dam, 710 feet high, forms Lake Powell, a part of the Glen Canyon National Recreation Area. The lake, 186 miles long with 1,900 miles of shoreline, is the second-largest man-made lake in the United States. The lake is named for John Wesley Powell, the intrepid and brilliant geologist who lost an arm at the Battle of Shiloh. Powell led an expedition down the Colorado in 1869 and was later director of the United States Geological Survey.

Information: Page/Lake Powell Chamber of Commerce, 697 Vista Ave., Page,
928-645-2741, 888-261-7243; www.cityofpage.org

WHAT TO SEE AND DO
BOAT TRIPS ON LAKE POWELL

Lake Powell Resorts & Marinas, 100 Lakeshore Drive, Page,
928-645-2433, 888-896-3829; www.lakepowell.com

One-hour to one-day trips, some include Rainbow Bridge National Monument. Houseboat and powerboat rentals. Reservations recommended.

GLEN CANYON NATIONAL RECREATION AREA

Highway 89, Page, 928-608-6200; www.nps.gov/glca

More than one million acres, including Lake Powell. Campfire program (Memorial Day-Labor Day). Swimming, waterskiing, fishing, boating, hiking, picnicking, restaurants, lodge, camping. The visitor center on canyon rim, adjacent to Glen Canyon Bridge on Highway 89, has historical exhibits. Ranger station, seven miles north of the dam at Wahweap. Daily.

JOHN WESLEY POWELL MEMORIAL MUSEUM

6 N. Lake Powell Blvd., Page, 928-645-9496, 888-597-6873; www.powellmuseum.org
See a replica of Powell's boat, plus a fluorescent rock collection, Native American artifacts and more. Admission: adults $5, seniors $3, children $, children under 5 free. Monday-Friday 9 a.m.-5 p.m.

RAINBOW BRIDGE NATIONAL MONUMENT

Page, approximately 60 miles northeast in Utah, northwest of Navajo Mountain,
928-608-6200; www.nps.gov/rabr
See the world's largest known natural bridge, a breathtaking phenomenon that attracts more than 300,000 visitors a year.

WILDERNESS RIVER ADVENTURES

2040 E. Frontage Road, Page, 928-645-3296, 800-992-8022;
www.riveradventures.com
Specializes in multiday trips on the Colorado River in Glen Canyon in raft-like neoprene boats. Reservations are required. April-October.

HOTELS
★BEST WESTERN LAKE POWELL

208 N. Lake Powell Blvd., Page, 928-645-5988, 888-794-2888;
www.bestwesternatlakepowell.com
132 rooms. Complimentary continental breakfast. Wireless Internet access. Airport transportation available. Pool. Spa. Fitness center. $

★TRAVELODGE

207 N. Lake Powell Blvd., Page, 928-645-2451, 800-578-7878; www.travelodge.com
132 rooms. High-speed Internet access. Complimentary continental breakfast. Pets accepted; fee. Pool. $

RESTAURANTS
★★BELLA NAPOLI

810 N. Navajo Drive, Page, 928-645-2706
Italian menu. Dinner. Closed January. Casual attire. Reservations recommended. Outdoor seating. $$

★KEN'S OLD WEST

718 Vista Ave., Page, 928-645-5160
Steak menu. Dinner. Closed Sunday-Tuesday, December-February. Bar. Children's menu. Casual attire. Reservations recommended. $$

PARADISE VALLEY

A dozen resorts make this small town one of Arizona's hottest tourist destinations.
Information: www.ci.paradise-valley.az.us

HOTELS

★★★THE HERMOSA INN

5532 N. Palo Cristi Road, Paradise Valley, 602-955-8614, 800-241-1210;
www.hermosainn.com

Built by cowboy artist Lon Megargee as his home and studio, this inn, and its acclaimed onsite restaurant LON's, is a nice alternative to the bigger resorts. Situated on a half acre marked by olive and mesquite trees, towering palms and brilliant flowers, the accommodations range from cozy casitas to huge villas. Rooms feature authentic furnishings and original artwork painted by Megargee some 70 years ago. 35 rooms. Complimentary continental breakfast. Restaurant, bar. Pets accepted, fee. Pool. Tennis. Fitness center. $$

★★★SANCTUARY ON CAMELBACK MOUNTAIN

5700 E. McDonald Drive, Paradise Valley, 480-948-2100, 800-245-2051;
www.sanctuaryoncamelback.com

This boutique hotel overlooking the valley from Camelback Mountain truly is a sanctuary. You won't find typical Southwestern décor here. Casitas are the very essence of desert chic with their spectacular contemporary design. Mountain casitas have wood block floors, glass-tiled dry bars and luxurious bathrooms with travertine marble. The multilevel spa casitas boast floor-to-ceiling windows and walk-in closets, while the spa suites have outdoor soaking tubs in case you just can't bring yourself to walk the short distance to the large infinity-edge pool. Elements restaurant offers New American fare with an Asian influence, served in a contemporary, elegant setting. 98 rooms. Pets accepted. Restaurant. Pool. Fitness room. Tennis. Business center. $$$

RESTAURANTS

★★EL CHORRO LODGE

5550 E. Lincoln Drive, Paradise Valley, 480-948-5170; www.elchorrolodge.com
American menu. Dinner, Sunday brunch. Bar. Casual attire. Valet parking. Outdoor seating. $$$

★★★ELEMENTS

5700 E. McDonald Road, Paradise Valley, 480-607-2300, 800-298-9766;
www.elementsrestaurant.com

Situated on the grounds of the Sanctuary at Camelback Mountain, Elements is a sleek spot that adds a touch of sophistication to leisurely breakfasts, power lunches and romantic dinners. Its clean, minimalist décor features stone and wood accents and expansive floor-to-ceiling windows that offer spectacular views of the sunset over Paradise Valley. The kitchen uses fresh, seasonal ingredients to create the menu of Asian-influenced New American cuisine, which has included dishes such as chilled sesame and lime noodle salad, chili-cured duck breast and braised short ribs with citrus-scented mushrooms. The Jade Bar is a great spot for a drink. American, Asian menu. Breakfast, lunch, dinner, Sunday brunch. Bar. Casual attire. Outdoor seating. $$$

★★★LON'S

5532 N. Palo Cristi Road, Paradise Valley, 602-955-7878; www.lons.com
Built by Southwestern artist Lon Megargee in the 1930s, the inn's adobe design and rustic furnishings are a fitting setting for some of the best American comfort food

in the Phoenix area. The chef grows many herbs, heirloom fruits and vegetables and grains in the onsite garden to use in fresh seasonal specials such as pork tenderloin with prickly pear braised cabbage, green beans and mashed potatoes and roasted lamb with goat cheese herb grits. American menu. Lunch, dinner, Sunday brunch. Bar. Children's menu. Casual attire. Reservations recommended. Outdoor seating. **$$$**

SPA
★★★★THE SANCTUARY SPA AT SANCTUARY ON CAMELBACK MOUNTAIN
5700 E. McDonald Drive, Paradise Valley, 480-948-2100, 800-245-2051; www.sanctuaryoncamelback.com
Originally designed as a tennis club in the 1950s by Frank Lloyd Wright protégé Hiram Hudson Benedict, the resort was completely renovated in 2001. The understated elegance first defined by Benedict is still here. The resort's spa was expanded and seems to include practically every treatment under the sun, from standard facials to acupuncture. The spa menu includes several Asian-inspired treatments including Thai massage and shiatsu. The resort retains its commitment to the championship tennis courts that defined it from the start, but the grounds are also ideal for Yoga and meditation. Guided desert hikes are also available. **$$**

PARKER
Parker is located on the east bank of the Colorado River, about 16 miles south of Parker Dam, which forms Lake Havasu. Popular recreational activities in the area include fishing, boating, jet and waterskiing, golfing, rock hunting and camping.
Information: Chamber of Commerce, 1217 California Ave., 928-669-2174; www.ci.parker.az.us

WHAT TO SEE AND DO
BUCKSKIN MOUNTAIN STATE PARK
5476 Highway 95, Parker, 928-667-3231; www.pr.state.az.us/Parks/parkhtml/buckskin.html
On 1,676 acres, this park features scenic bluffs overlooking the Colorado River. Swimming, fishing, boating; nature trails, hiking; picnicking, camping, riverside cabanas. River Island Unit has boating, picnicking, camping. Daily.

BLUEWATER RESORT & CASINO
11300 Resort Drive, 928-669-7000, 888-243-3360; www.bluewaterfun.com
Bluewater Casino is open 24 hours and includes slots, poker and bingo.

COLORADO RIVER INDIAN TRIBES MUSEUM
Route 1, Parker, 928-669-9211; www.museumofman.org
Exhibits interpret the history of the four Colorado River Tribes: Mohave, Chemehuevi, Navajo and Hopi. You'll find authentic Native American arts and crafts on sale here. Monday-Friday 8 a.m.-5 p.m., Saturday 10 a.m.-3 p.m.

COLORADO RIVER INDIAN TRIBES RESERVATION
11300 Resort Drive, Parker, 928-669-7615; www.critlibrary.com
This reservation spans 278,000 acres in Arizona and California and offers fishing, boating, waterskiing, hunting (tribal permit required) and camping.

ARIZONA ★★★★

LA PAZ COUNTY PARK

7350 Riverside Drive, Parker, 928-667-2069; www.co.la-paz.az.us

A 540-acre park with 4,000 feet of Colorado River beachfront. Swimming, waterskiing, fishing, boating, tennis court, golf course, driving range, picnicking (shelter), playground, camping.

PARKER DAM AND POWER PLANT

Parker, 17 miles north via Highway 95, 760-663-3712

One of the deepest dams in the world—73 percent of its structural height of 320 feet is below the riverbed. Daily.

SPECIAL EVENTS
HOLIDAY LIGHTED BOAT PARADE

Colorado River, Parker

Decorated boats parade on the 11-mile strip to a selected site for trophy presentation; viewing from both sides of the Parker River. Late November.

LA PAZ COUNTY FAIR

Fairgrounds at Four Corners, 13991 Second Ave., Parker, 928-669-8100

Carnival, livestock auction, entertainment and more. Mid-March.

PARKER 400 OFF-ROAD RACE

1217 S. California Ave., Parker

Four hundred miles of desert racing. Late January.

PARKER ENDURO WEEKEND

1 Park Drive, Parker

Longest and oldest boat racing event in the country. May.

PAYSON

Payson, in the heart of the Tonto National Forest, offers numerous outdoor recreational activities in a mild climate.

Information: Chamber of Commerce, 100 W Main St., 928-474-4515; www.ci.payson.az.us

HOTEL
★KOFA INN

1700 S. California Ave., Parker, 928-669-2101, 800-742-6072

41 rooms. Pool. $

WHAT TO SEE AND DO
TONTO NATIONAL FOREST

2324 E. McDowell Road, Phoenix, 602-225-5200; www.fs.fed.us/r3/tonto

This area includes almost three million acres of desert and mountain landscapes. Six lakes along the Salt and Verde rivers offer opportunities for fishing, boating, hiking and camping. Seven wilderness areas are located within the forest's boundaries, providing hiking and bridle trails. The forest also features Tonto Natural Bridge, the largest natural travertine bridge in the world. Scenic attractions include the Apache Trail, Four Peaks, the Mogollon Rim and Sonoran Desert country.

OLD-TIME FIDDLERS CONTEST & FESTIVAL

Rumsey Park, Payson, 928-970-1760

Fiddling contest, storytellers, Irish step-dancers, entertainment, food, arts and crafts and more. Late September.

WORLD'S OLDEST CONTINUOUS PRCA RODEO

Multi-Event Center, 1400 S. Beeline Highway, Payson, 800-672-9766;
www.paysonrimcountry.com

The rodeo features calf roping, bull riding and barrel racing. Third weekend in August.

HOTEL

★★BEST WESTERN PAYSON INN

801 N. Beeline Highway, Payson, 928-474-3241, 800-247-9477; www.bestwestern.com
99 rooms. Complimentary continental breakfast. Restaurant, bar. High-speed Internet access. Pets accepted. Pool. Fitness center. $

PEORIA

One of Phoenix's largest suburbs, Peoria is home to the Challenger Space Center of Arizona, a brand-new performing arts hall and other cultural and educational facilities.

Information: City of Peoria, 8401 W. Monroe St., Peoria, 623-773-7000;
www.peoriaaz.com

WHAT TO SEE AND DO

LAKE PLEASANT REGIONAL PARK

41835 N. Castle Hot Springs Road, Morristown, 928-501-1710;
www.maricopa.gov/parks/lake_pleasant

Go coastal 30 miles north of Phoenix at this man-made reservoir with 114 miles of sun-drenched shoreline. The park has campgrounds for RVs and tents, boat ramps, plenty of picnic tables with grills. Swimming, fishing, and boating. Daily.

PHOENIX

The capital of Arizona lies on flat desert, surrounded by mountains. People come to the Valley of the Sun for the golf, mega-resorts and spas. Phoenix has been getting bigger and better in recent years, with an influx of retirees and new industry. These days, the resorts have grown more contemporary, the spas have constantly made themselves over and the restaurants serve a lot more than Southwestern cuisine.

Information: Greater Phoenix Convention & Visitors Bureau, 50 N. Second St.,
602-254-6500, 877-225-5749; www.visitphoenix.com

WHAT TO SEE AND DO

ANTIQUE GALLERY/CENTRAL ANTIQUES

5037 N. Central Ave., Phoenix, 602-241-1174

More than 150 dealers showcase heirloom-quality antiques in this 30,000-square-foot space. Shop for period furniture, American and English silver, European porcelain and much more. Monday-Saturday 10 a.m.-5:30 p.m., Sunday noon-5 p.m.

ARIZONA CAPITOL MUSEUM

1700 W. Washington St., Phoenix, 602-926-3620; www.lib.az.us/museum

Built in 1899, this stately building first served as the capitol for the territorial government, then as the state capitol after Arizona was admitted to the Union in 1912. The state moved to adjacent office building in the 1970s for more space, and the original structure has operated as a museum since its restoration in 1981. See the House and Senate chambers exactly as they looked during early statehood. Guided tours are offered daily at 10 a.m. and 2 p.m. A landscaped area includes a variety of native trees, shrubs and cacti. Monday-Friday 8 a.m.-5 p.m., Saturday 11 a.m.-4 p.m.

ARIZONA CENTER

400 E. Van Buren St., 602-271-4000; www.arizonacenter.com

This park-like plaza, situated among palm trees, gardens and pools, includes 15 stores and kiosks. Restaurants, bars, 24-screen theater. Monday-Saturday 10 a.m.-9 p.m., Sunday 11 a.m.-5 p.m.

ARIZONA DIAMONDBACKS (MLB)

Bank One Ballpark, 401 E. Jefferson, Phoenix, 602-462-6000; arizona.diamondbacks.mlb.com

Professional baseball team.

ARIZONA MINING AND MINERAL MUSEUM

1502 W. Washington, Phoenix, 602-771-1600, 800-446-4259; www.admmr.state.az.us/musgen.htm

This museum showcases minerals and gems as well as petrified wood. Mining exhibits. Monday-Friday 8 a.m.-5 p.m., Saturday 11 a.m.-4 p.m.

ARIZONA SCIENCE CENTER

600 E. Washington St., Phoenix, 602-716-2000; www.azscience.org

More than 300 hands-on exhibits on topics ranging from geology to healing make learning fun. Gaze up at the stars in the planetarium and stare wide-eyed at science films in the theater with a five-story screen. Daily 10 a.m.-5 p.m.

BILTMORE FASHION PARK

2502 E. Camelback Road, Phoenix, 602-955-1963; www.shopbiltmore.com

Bring your oversized designer handbag to this outdoor shopping area with brick walkways and retailers such as Cartier, Escada and Saks Fifth Avenue. Monday-Wednesday, 10 a.m.-7 p.m., Thursday-Friday 10 a.m.-8 p.m., Saturday 10 a.m.-6 p.m., Sunday noon-6 p.m.

CAMELBACK MOUNTAIN

East McDonald at Tatum Boulevard, Phoenix; www.ci.phoenix.az.us/parks/hikecmlb.html

Its distinctive hump makes this mountain a very visible local landmark—and a popular spot for hiking. Trails wind through desert flora and fauna. The two strenuous summit trails (each approximately 1½ miles) gain more than 1,200 feet in elevation.

Two shorter ones at the base provide much easier trekking, with elevation gains of only 100 and 200 feet. Daily dawn-dusk.

CELEBRITY THEATRE

440 N. 32nd St., Phoenix, 602-267-1600; www.celebritytheatre.com

Some of the entertainment industry's biggest names bring their music and comedy to this theater, where no seat is more than 75 feet from the revolving center stage.

CHAR'S HAS THE BLUES

4631 N. Seventh Ave., Phoenix, 602-230-0205; www.charshastheblues.com

Bands sing the blues every night at this small, no-frills joint. A diverse crowd spans all ages. Daily, doors open at 7:30 p.m.

DESERT BOTANICAL GARDEN

Papago Park, 1201 N. Galvin Parkway, Phoenix, 480-941-1225; www.dgb.org

This 150-acre botanical oasis is home to one of the world's foremost collections of desert plants. Thousands of plants line the $\frac{1}{3}$-mile main trail, including more than half the world's cactus, century plant and aloe species. Music in the Gardens features performances by local bands on Friday evenings from February through June, and Saturday evenings from October through mid-November. Admission: adults $10, seniors $9, students $5, children $4, children under 3 free. October-April, daily 8 a.m.-8 p.m.; May-September, daily 7 a.m.-8 p.m.

ENCANTO PARK AND RECREATION AREA

2605 N. 15th Ave., Phoenix, 602-261-8991; www.enchantedisland.com

Pack up the family and head to this 222-acre park just minutes from downtown. Kids can fish in a small lake, feed ducks in a pond, ride in boats, cool off in the swimming pool and hop aboard a train and eight other rides geared toward 2- to 10-year-olds at the Enchanted Island amusement park. Two public golf courses (18 holes and 9 holes) appeal to an older crowd. Daily.

HALL OF FLAME FIREFIGHTING MUSEUM

6101 E. Van Buren St., Phoenix, 602-275-3473; www.hallofflame.org

Believed to be the largest of its kind in the world, the five galleries at this museum are packed with more than 100 pieces of awe-inspiring firefighting equipment, from antique, hand-drawn pumps dating as far back as the 1700s to snazzy, motorized fire engines. Monday-Saturday 9 a.m.-5 p.m., Sunday noon-4 p.m.

HEARD MUSEUM

2301 N. Central Ave., Phoenix, 602-252-8848; www.heard.org

Immerse yourself in the culture and art of the Southwest at this internationally-acclaimed Native American museum. The 130,000-square-foot museum boasts 10 galleries (and a working-artist studio), all packed with items that attract nearly 250,000 visitors each year. Works include contemporary American Indian fine art, historic Hopi kachina dolls, important Navajo and Zuni jewelry and prize-winning documented Navajo textiles. The Heard also offers artist demonstrations, music and dance performances. Daily 9:30 a.m.-5 p.m.

ARIZONA

★
★
★
★
★

HERITAGE SQUARE

Heritage & Science Park, 115 N. Sixth St., Phoenix, 602-262-5071;
www.ci.phoenix.az.us/parks/heritage.html

Heritage Square is one of three sites that make up Heritage & Science Park. (The other two sites are the Arizona Science Center and Phoenix Museum of History.) Historic Heritage Park has eight turn-of-the-century houses, including the restored 1895 Victorian Rosson House (docent-guided tours: Wednesday-Saturday 10 a.m.-4 p.m., Sunday noon-4 p.m.; closed mid-August-Labor Day; fee) and Arizona Doll & Toy Museum (The Stevens House, Tuesday-Saturday 10 a.m.-4 p.m., Sunday noon-4 p.m.; closed early August-Labor Day). You'll also find the open-air Lath House Pavilion here. Daily.

MYSTERY CASTLE

800 E. Mineral Road, Phoenix, 602-268-1581

This quirky, imaginative 18-room castle made of native stone and found objects was built by Boyce Luther Gulley for his daughter Mary Lou, who often leads tours. October-May, Thursday-Sunday 11 a.m.-4 p.m.

PAPAGO PARK

625 N. Galvan Parkway, Phoenix, 602-261-8318;
www.phoenix.gov/parks/hikepapa.html

This 1,200-acre park with sandstone buttes is flatter than many others in the area, appealing to novice hikers and mountain bikers. (There are more than 10 miles of trails.) Families often come to enjoy its many picnic areas and fishing lagoon, while the golf course lures duffers. The park offers good views of the city, especially at sunset from the Hole-in-the-Rock Archaeological Site, a naturally eroded rock formation. Daily 5 a.m.-11 p.m.

PHOENIX ART MUSEUM

1625 N. Central Ave., Phoenix, 602-257-1222; www.phxart.org

At more than 160,000 square feet, this is one of the largest art museums in the Southwest. There are more than 17,000 works here—about 1,000 of which are on display at any given time, in addition to major traveling exhibits. The museum sponsors Family Sundays every third Sunday of the month for children ages 5-12, which includes imaginative art projects and self-guided explorations of the galleries. Wednesday-Sunday 10 a.m.-5 p.m.; Tuesday 10 a.m.-9 p.m.; closed Monday. Free admission Tuesday 3-9 p.m. First Friday events 6-10 p.m. first Friday of every month.

PHOENIX COYOTES (NHL)

Glendale Arena, 9400 W. Maryland Ave., Glendale, 486-563-7825;
www.phoenixcoyotes.com
Professional hockey team.

PHOENIX INTERNATIONAL RACEWAY

7602 S. Avondale Blvd., Avondale, 602-252-2227; www.phoenixintlraceway.com

If you've seen *Days of Thunder* with Tom Cruise, you've seen this high-octane speedway. Big-name drivers fire up their engines on six weekends throughout the year. More than 100,000 spectators pack the raceway for NASCAR Weekend in late fall. Other events include the Rolex Grand American Sports Car Series and the IRL Indy Car Series. No other speedway in Arizona is open to so many different classes of cars. PIR also hosts plenty of non-racing events, including a large Fourth of July celebration.

PHOENIX MERCURY (WNBA)
America West Arena, 201 E. Jefferson St., Phoenix, 602-252-9622; www.wnba.com/mercury
Women's professional basketball team.

PHOENIX MOUNTAINS PARK
2701 E. Squaw Peak Lane, Phoenix, 602-262-6861; www.ci.phoenix.az.us/parks/hikephx.html
This park offers more than 7,000 acres of unique desert mountain recreational activities. Hiking, horseback riding and picnicking. Daily 5 a.m.-11 p.m. Echo Canyon, located in the park, offers several hiking trails.

PHOENIX MUSEUM OF HISTORY
Heritage & Science Park, 105 N. Fifth St., Phoenix, 602-253-2734; www.pmoh.org
Celebrates more than 2,000 years of Arizona history. Tuesday-Saturday 10 a.m.-5 p.m.; closed Sunday, Monday.

PHOENIX SUNS (NBA)
America West Arena, 201 E. Jefferson, Phoenix, 602-379-7867; www.nba.com/suns
Professional basketball team.

PHOENIX ZOO
Papago Park, 455 N. Galvin Parkway, Phoenix, 602-273-1341; www.phoenixzoo.org
See more than 400 mammals, 500 birds and 500 reptiles and amphibians. The Arabian oryx and desert bighorn sheep are especially popular. The zoo holds special events, educational programs and outdoor recreational activities. Walk, bike (rentals available) or take a train ride around the park. November 5-January 11, daily 9 a.m.-4 p.m.; January 12-May, daily 9 a.m.-5 p.m.; June-September, Monday-Friday 7 a.m.-2 p.m., Saturday-Sunday 7 a.m.-4 p.m.

PIONEER LIVING HISTORY MUSEUM
3901 W. Pioneer Road, Phoenix, 623-465-1052; www.pioneer-arizona.com
Experience city life as pioneers in the Old West did. On these 90 acres celebrating the 1800s, you can belly up to the bar in the saloon, check out the chiseling in the blacksmith shop, eye the vintage fashions in the dress store, say a little prayer in the community church and more. October-May, Wednesday-Sunday 9 a.m.-5 p.m.; June-September, Friday-Sunday 8 a.m.-2 p.m.

PUEBLO GRANDE MUSEUM AND ARCHAEOLOGICAL PARK
4619 E Washington St., Phoenix, 602-495-0901, 602-495-0902, 877-706-4408; www.ci.phoenix.az.us/parks/pueblo.html
At the ruins of a Hohokam village, revisit the past and learn how these prehistoric people lived in Arizona 1,500 years ago. You'll see an old platform mound that the Hohokam probably used for ceremonies or as an administrative center, an excavated

ball court, reproductions of adobe homes and irrigation canals used for farming. Make the rounds of this 102-acre park on your own or take a guided tour on Saturday at 11 a.m. or 1 p.m. or on Sunday at 1:30 p.m. Monday-Saturday 9 a.m.-4:45 p.m., Sunday 1-4:45 p.m.; closed Sunday-Monday from May-September. Free admission Sunday.

ROADRUNNER PARK FARMERS' MARKET
3501 Cactus Road, Phoenix, 623-848-1234;
www.arizonafarmersmarkets.com/pageRoadrunner/roadrunner.htm
Thousands of people come to this outdoor market to stock up on fresh produce grown in the Arizona desert. As many as 60 vendors sell melons, onions, peppers, squash, tomatoes and other fresh-from-the-farm crops. A few sell arts and crafts. Saturday 8 a.m.-noon.

SQUAW PEAK PARK
2701 E. Squaw Peak Lane, Phoenix, 602-262-7901
The views—and the hiking—will take your breath away. The demanding, 1.2-mile trek up the Summit Trail will test you every step of the way. For an easier route, opt for the Circumference Trail. Daily.

VANS SKATEPARK
9617 N. Metro Parkway West, Phoenix, 602-870-8727
Riding areas and obstacles include a street course with birch ramps and a wooden bowl with swimming pool tiles and coping. The park accommodates all skill levels. Sessions for BMX bikers are offered on certain days. Daily 10 a.m.-10 p.m.

SPECIAL EVENTS

ARIZONA OPERA
4600 N. 12th St., Phoenix, 602-266-7464; www.azopera.com
Five operas are held each year at the Phoenix Symphony Hall. October-March, Friday-Sunday.

ARIZONA STATE FAIR
1826 W. McDowell Road, Phoenix, 602-252-6771; www.azstatefair.com
This annual event attracts big crowds. It has everything you'd expect of a good state fair: a busy midway packed with exciting rides and games, high-decibel concerts, gooey cotton candy and other carnival fare, rodeo action, cooking contests and much more. Mid-October-early November.

ARIZONA THEATRE COMPANY
Herberger Theater Center, 222 E. Monroe St., Phoenix, 520-622-2823; 602-257-1222;
www.aztheatreco.org
Professional regional company performs both classic and contemporary works. October-May.

COWBOY ARTISTS OF AMERICA SALE AND EXHIBITION
Phoenix Art Museum, 1625 N. Central Ave., Phoenix, 602-257-1222; www.phxart.org
Members of Cowboy Artists of America—a select group who produce fine Western American art—are considered the most prestigious in the genre. And at this annual

event, they offer more than 100 of their new, never-before-viewed works for sale—some of which command six figures. If that's more than you can wrangle, all the painting, drawings and sculptures remain on exhibit for several weeks so everyone can enjoy them before buyers claim them. Late October-mid-November.

FIRECRACKER SPORTS FESTIVAL
Rose Mofford, Papago and Desert West Complexes, Phoenix, 602-262-6485
About 140 teams from throughout Arizona come to play ball during this annual event, the state's largest and longest-running softball tournament. The action features adult slow pitch and youth (girls) fast pitch in up to 13 divisions. The opening-night party includes a fireworks display. Last weekend in June.

INDIAN FAIR AND MARKET
The Heard Museum, 2301 N. Central Ave., Phoenix, 602-252-8848;
www.heardguild.org/indian-fair/indian-fair.aspx
American Indian artisans, demonstrations, dances, native foods. First weekend in March.

NEW WORKS FESTIVAL
Phoenix Theatre's Little Theatre, 100 E. McDowell Road, Phoenix, 602-258-1974
See plays and musicals staged in their early phases. Actors perform works-in-progress with books in hand and with minimal set decorations. Some get produced as part of Phoenix Theatre's regular season. Late July-mid-August.

PHOENIX SYMPHONY
Symphony Hall, 75 North Second St., Phoenix,
602-495-1999, 800-776-9080; www.phoenixsymphony.org
Annual programming includes classics, chamber orchestra, symphonic pops and family and holiday events.

YAQUI INDIAN EASTER CEREMONIES
Avenida del Yaqui, Yaqui Temple and Ceremonial Grounds, Guadalupe,
520-883-2838; www.guadalupeaz.org
These Lenten celebrations are still a sacred obligation of the Yaqui and represent a unique combination of traditional Yaqui and Catholic customs. Friday-Sunday afternoons from Ash Wednesday to Easter.

HOTELS
★★★ARIZONA BILTMORE RESORT AND SPA
2400 E. Missouri Road, Phoenix, 602-955-6600, 800-950-2575;
www.arizonabiltmore.com
The Arizona Biltmore Resort and Spa opened to great fanfare in 1929. The nice thing about it today is that it's not trying to remain great—it just is. The Frank Lloyd Wright-inspired architecture, as well as the photos of all the presidents and famous people who have stayed here, take you back to another time. Spend your days lounging at one of the eight pools, playing the adjacent golf course or relaxing in the 22,000-square-foot spa. The comfortable rooms have Mission-style furnishings, textiles in calming desert tones and fluffy beds. 738 rooms. High-speed Internet access.

Restaurant, bar. Children. Spa. Airport transportation available. Pets accepted. Pool. Tennis. $$$

★★DOUBLETREE GUEST SUITES PHOENIX GATEWAY CENTER
320 N. 44th St., Phoenix, 602-225-0500, 800-800-3098; www.doubletree.com
242 rooms, all suites. Complimentary full breakfast. Wireless Internet access. Restaurant, bar. Airport transportation available. Pool. Business center. $

★★EMBASSY SUITES HOTEL PHOENIX-BILTMORE
2630 E. Camelback Road, Phoenix, 602-955-3992, 800-362-2779;
www.phoenixbiltmore.embassysuites.com
232 rooms, all suites. Complimentary full breakfast. Wireless Internet access. Restaurant, bar. Pets accepted. Pool. Fitness center. $$

★★EMBASSY SUITES HOTEL PHOENIX-NORTH
2577 W. Greenway Road, Phoenix, 602-375-1777; www.embassysuites.com
314 rooms, all suites. High-speed Internet access. Complimentary full breakfast. Restaurant, bar. Pets accepted. Pool. Tennis. $

★★HILTON PHOENIX AIRPORT
2435 S. 47th St., Phoenix, 480-894-1600, 800-445-8667; www.hilton.com
255 rooms. High-speed Internet access. Restaurant, bar. Airport transportation available. Pool. Business center. Fitness center. $

★★★JW MARRIOTT DESERT RIDGE RESORT AND SPA
5350 E. Marriott Drive, Phoenix, 480-293-5000, 800-835-6206;
www.jwdesertridgeresort.com
This resort has it all: four sun-kissed pools, two 18-hole golf courses designed by Arnold Palmer and Tom Fazio, an eight-court tennis center, miles of hiking trails, a renowned spa and five restaurants. The rooms have balconies and patios. In summer, families can watch favorite movies like *Charlotte's Web* at the pool. 950 rooms. Restaurant, bar. Children's activity center. Spa. Pool. Golf. Tennis. $$$

★★THE LEGACY GOLF RESORT
6808 S. 32nd St., Phoenix, 602-305-5500, 888-828-3673; www.legacygolfresort.com
328 rooms, all suites. High-speed Internet access. Restaurant, bar. Children's activity center. Pool. Golf. Tennis. $$$

★★MARICOPA MANOR BED & BREAKFAST INN
15 W. Pasadena Ave., Phoenix, 602-274-6302, 800-292-6403;
www.maricopamanor.com
Seven rooms, all suites. Complimentary continental breakfast. Wireless Internet access. Airport transportation available. Pool. $

★★★POINTE HILTON SQUAW PEAK RESORT
7677 N. 16th St., Phoenix, 602-997-2626, 800-947-9784; www.pointehilton.com
This sprawling all-suite resort at the base of Squaw Peak is great for families. The nine-acre recreational area includes swimming pools with waterfalls and a huge slide

and an 18-hole miniature golf course. Kids will think they're in heaven after spending a day here and then hitting the old-fashioned ice cream parlor. For adults there's a spa with salon and fitness center, tennis courts, shopping and hikes in the adjacent Phoenix Mountain Preserve. Accommodations range from two-bedroom suites to three-bedroom casitas. 563 rooms, all suites. High-speed Internet access. Two restaurants, three bars. Children's activity center. Spa. Airport transportation available. **$$**

★★★POINTE HILTON TAPATIO CLIFFS RESORT

11111 N. Seventh St., Phoenix, 602-866-7500, 800-947-9784; www.pointehilton.com
This resort is situated among the peaks of the Phoenix North Mountains, offering dramatic views of the city and valley below. The resort boasts its own water playground and a total of eight swimming pools, some with waterfalls. The Lookout Mountain Golf Club is an 18-hole championship course set along the border of an 8,000-acre Sonoran desert park. A full-service spa offers a variety of pampering treatments. The two-room suites all have living rooms and two TVs. 585 rooms, all suites. High-speed Internet access. Restaurant, bar. Children's activity center. Spa. Airport transportation available. Pets accepted. Golf. Tennis. **$$**

★★★POINTE SOUTH MOUNTAIN RESORT

7777 S. Pointe Parkway, Phoenix, 602-438-9000, 877-267-1321;
www.pointesouthmtn.com
This upscale and well-maintained resort offers spacious rooms with high-quality furnishings and an endless list of things to do. The onsite water park is Arizona's largest, boasting an eight-story water slide, wave pool and "river" for tubing. There are also six swimming pools, lighted tennis courts, water and sand volleyball courts, racquetball and croquet, an 18-hole golf course and horseback riding. When you exhaust all that, there's hiking and biking in South Mountain Park next door. 640 rooms. Restaurant, bar. Wireless Internet access. Children's activity center. Spa. Business center. Golf. Tennis. **$$$**

★★★★THE RITZ-CARLTON, PHOENIX

2401 E. Camelback, Phoenix, 602-468-0700, 800-241-3333; www.ritzcarlton.com
The hotel is smack in the middle of the Camelback Corridor, the exclusive shopping, dining and financial district of Phoenix. The rooms, classically decorated with beds topped with luxury linens, all have views of the skyline or the Squaw Peak Mountain Range—and of course, there's the Ritz level of service. Concierges will offers tips on everything from the area's best golf courses to the tastiest cocktail to sip in the lobby lounge. You'll find modern takes on French classics (think steak au poivre with crisp frites) at the hotel's festive Bistro 24. The outdoor pool sparkles and the sundeck area is cooled with hydro-misters. 281 rooms. Wireless Internet access. Restaurant, two bars. Airport transportation available. Fitness center. Pool. Business center. **$$$**

★★★ROYAL PALMS RESORT AND SPA

5200 E. Camelback Road, Phoenix, 602-840-3610, 800-672-6011;
www.royalpalmsresortandspa.com
Constructed in the late 1920s as a private mansion, this hotel brings a bit of the Mediterranean to the Sonoran Desert. Palm trees line the entrance to this hideaway

surrounded by fountains and citrus trees, where lavish casitas and guest rooms have fireplaces and balconies. The dreamy open-air spa has treatment rooms with garden areas and a villa with stone heated tables under overhead showers. T. Cook's is an award-winning restaurant. 119 rooms. Wireless Internet access. Two restaurants, two bars. Spa. Airport transportation available. Pets accepted. Pool. Fitness center. **$$$**

RESTAURANTS
★★★AVANTI OF PHOENIX
2728 E. Thomas Road, Phoenix, 602-956-0900; www.avanti-az.com
A stark, Art Deco-inspired interior of black and white provides the backdrop for this romantic restaurant specializing in fresh pasta with rich sauces. Enjoy piano music in the lounge area Thursday through Saturday. Italian menu. Lunch, dinner. Bar. Business casual attire. Reservations recommended. Valet parking. Outdoor seating. **$$$**

★BABY KAY'S CAJUN KITCHEN
2119 E. Camelback Road, Phoenix, 602-955-0011; www.babykayscajunkitchen.com
Cajun/Creole menu. Lunch, dinner. Closed Sunday. Bar. Casual attire. Outdoor seating. **$$**

★★BARRIO CAFE
2814 N. 16th St., Phoenix, 602-636-0240; www.barriocafe.com
Mexican menu. Lunch, dinner, Sunday bunch. Closed Monday. Bar. Casual attire. Valet parking. **$$$**

★★★BISTRO 24
2401 E. Camelback Road, Phoenix, 602-468-0700; www.ritzcarlton.com
Located within the Ritz-Carlton, Bistro 24 serves classic dishes such as steak au poivre and grilled seafood such as butter-poached halibut. The restaurant is spacious and unpretentious with colorful murals and an outdoor patio, and the service is impeccable. Come for happy hour for half-priced martinis and appetizers. French bistro menu. Breakfast, lunch, dinner, Sunday brunch. Bar. Children's menu. Business casual attire. Reservations recommended. Valet parking. Outdoor seating. **$$$**

★★★CHRISTOPHER'S FERMIER BRASSERIE
2502 E. Camelback Road, Phoenix, 602-522-2344; www.christophersaz.com
You won't see many farmers in this French-influenced spot (the name means "farmer's pub"), strategically positioned in the ritzily revamped Biltmore shopping center. Opened in May 2008, Christopher's aimed to "create a sexy and ultra-chic experience enabling the perfect setting for intimate encounters." That doesn't exactly explain the countrified name. But since the creative wine bar serves some of the best fare in Phoenix, they don't have to. The menu is American with a French twist. Think a foie gras and brioche starter followed by an arugula, pear, and blue cheese salad before a truffle-infused filet mignon or duck confit and fig pizza. And watch it all being prepared a at the bar on the sidelines of the contemporary open kitchen. Decidedly indecisive? For $120/head, groups up to 10 can reserve a private dining area that comes with the nightly tasting menu—just be sure that the chilled white chocolate-

corn husk creation is included with that. American, French menu. Lunch, dinner. Bar. Casual attire. Reservations recommended. Outdoor seating. $$$

★CORONADO CAFÉ

2201 N. Seventh St., Phoenix, 602-258-5149; www.coronadocafe.com

American menu. Lunch, dinner. Closed Sunday. Casual attire. Reservations recommended. $

★★COUP DES TARTES

4626 N. 16th St., Phoenix, 602-212-1082; www.nicetartes.com

American menu. Dinner. Closed Sunday-Monday, also Tuesday in June-August. Casual attire. Reservations recommended. $$

★★FISH MARKET

1720 E. Camelback Road, Phoenix, 602-277-3474; www.thefishmarket.com

Seafood menu. Lunch, dinner. Bar. Children's menu. Casual attire. Reservations recommended. Outdoor seating. $$

★THE FRY BREAD HOUSE

4140 N. Seventh Ave., Phoenix, 602-351-2345

Southwestern menu. Lunch, dinner. Closed Sunday. Children's menu. Casual attire. $

★★HAVANA CAFÉ

4225 E. Camelback Road, Phoenix, 602-952-1991; www.havanacafe-az.com

Cuban menu. Lunch, dinner. Bar. Children's menu. Casual attire. Valet parking. Outdoor seating. $$

★★★LA FONTANELLA

4231 E. Indian School Road, Phoenix, 602-955-1213

The Italian husband-and-wife team who runs this Phoenix gem serves up hearty recipes from their homeland, including fresh pastas and grilled meats. Italian menu. Dinner. Closed two weeks in July. Bar. Casual attire. Reservations recommended. $$$

★MI COCINA, MI PAIS

4221 W. Bell Road, Phoenix, 602-548-7900

Latin American menu. Lunch, dinner. Closed Monday. Children's menu. Casual attire. $$

★★PERSIAN GARDEN

1335 W. Thomas Road, Phoenix, 602-263-1915; www.persiangardencafe.com

Mediterranean, Middle Eastern menu. Lunch, dinner. Closed Sunday, Monday; also late June-early July. Casual attire. $$

★★RUSTLER'S ROOSTE

8383 S. 48th St., Phoenix, 602-431-6474; www.rustlersrooste.com

Steak menu. Dinner. Bar. Children's menu. Casual attire. Valet parking. Outdoor seating. $$

53

ARIZONA

★
★
★
★
★

★★★RUTH'S CHRIS STEAK HOUSE

2201 E. Camelback Road, Phoenix, 602-957-9600; www.ruthschris.com

Born from a single New Orleans restaurant, the chain is a favorite among steak lovers. Aged prime Midwestern beef is broiled at 1,800 degrees and served on a heated plate sizzling in butter with sides such as creamed spinach and au gratin potatoes. Steak menu. Dinner. Bar. Reservations recommended. Valet parking. Outdoor seating. **$$$**

★★SOMA CAFE

10810 N. Tatum Blvd., Phoenix, 602-867-2175; www.somacafe.com

Vegetarian menu. Breakfast, lunch, dinner. Children's menu. Casual attire. Outdoor seating. **$**

★★SOPHIE'S BISTRO

2320 E. Osborn Road, Phoenix, 602-956-8897; www.sophiesbistro.com

French menu. Lunch, dinner. Closed Sunday, Monday. Bar. Casual attire. Reservations recommended. **$$**

★★STEAMERS GENUINE SEAFOOD

2576 E. Camelback Road, Phoenix, 602-956-3631; www.steamersgenuineseafood.com

Seafood menu. Lunch, dinner. Bar. Children's menu. Valet parking. Outdoor seating. **$$$**

★★★T. COOK'S

5200 E. Camelback Road, Phoenix, 602-840-3610, 800-672-6011;
www.royalpalmsresortandspa.com

Located in the Royal Palms Hotel and Spa, this stylish restaurant has deep cherry wood floors, hand-painted Italian frescoes and floor-to-ceiling windows with views of Camelback Mountain. The Mediterranean menu includes dishes such as roast duck with preserved apricots and spiced yogurt and grilled veal flank steak with warm potato salad. Some dishes are made in the restaurant's fireplace. Mediterranean menu. Breakfast, lunch, dinner, Sunday brunch. Bar. Business casual attire. Reservations recommended. Valet parking. Outdoor seating. **$$$**

★★★TARBELL'S

3213 E. Camelback Road, Phoenix, 602-955-8100; www.tarbells.com

Celebrated chef Marc Tarbell—he recently appeared on *Iron Chef*—continues to dazzle with fresh seasonal dishes such as hand-cut pasta with locally made chicken fennel sausage, organic tomatoes and English peas, and double-cut pork chops with Wisconsin cheddar grills, collard greens and wild boar bacon. The sophisticated restaurant features blond wood, white tablecloths and an exhibition kitchen—and somehow maintains a friendly neighborhood feel, perhaps thanks to the large curved bar that's a focal point. American menu. Dinner. Bar. Business casual attire. Reservations recommended. Valet parking. **$$$**

★★TOMASO'S

3225 E. Camelback Road, Phoenix, 602-956-0836; www.tomasos.com

Italian menu. Lunch, dinner. **$$$**

★★★VINCENT ON CAMELBACK

3930 E. Camelback Road, Phoenix, 602-224-0225; www.vincentsoncamelback.com

This intimate restaurant, which combines hearty Southwest flavors with elegant French cuisine, helped build Phoenix's culinary reputation. The flawless waitstaff and enduring menu continue to impress diners. On Friday and Saturday evenings, a pianist performs. French menu. Lunch, dinner. Closed Sunday. Bar. Business casual attire. Reservations recommended. Valet parking. **$$$**

★★THE WILD THAIGER

2631 N. Central Ave., Phoenix, 602-241-8995; www.wildthaiger.com

Thai menu. Lunch, dinner. Bar. Children's menu. Casual attire. Outdoor seating. **$$**

★★★WRIGHT'S

2400 Missouri Road, Phoenix, 602-381-7632; www.arizonabiltmore.com

An homage to Frank Lloyd Wright, this restaurant off the lobby of the Arizona Biltmore reflects the architect's penchant for stark angles and contrasts. Muted Southwestern colors fill the comfortable room and a large paneled window frames excellent views. The American cuisine features the freshest ingredients from boutique farms across the country. The menu changes weekly and includes dishes such as aged buffalo with white cheddar and Yukon purée. Be sure to sample one of the delectable chocolate desserts. American menu. Dinner, Sunday brunch. Bar. Business casual attire. Reservations recommended. Valet parking. Outdoor seating. **$$$**

★★ZEN 32

3160 E. Camelback Road, Phoenix, 602-954-8700; www.zen32.com

Japanese menu. Lunch, dinner. Casual attire. **$$**

SPAS

★★★★ALVADORA SPA AT ROYAL PALMS

5200 E. Camelback Road, Phoenix, 602-840-3610, 800-672-6011;
www.royalpalmshotel.com/phoenix-arizona-spas.php

Inspired by that region's native flowers, herbs and oils, this Mediterranean-style spa brings the outdoors in through its open-air design and plant-inspired therapies. The healing properties of water are a focal point here, whether you're soaking in a bath of grape seeds and herbs or floating in the Watsu pool. Indulge in the Fango mud wrap, a traditional therapy that uses volcanic mud from Italy's northern regions to purify and cleanse skin. The vino therapy facial uses grape leaf extract for intense moisturizing. Enjoy yoga, tai chi, meditation and mat Pilate's classes in the 24-hour fitness center. **$$**

★★★REVIVE SPA AT JW MARRIOTT DESERT RIDGE RESORT

5350 E. Marriott Drive, Phoenix, 480-293-3700, 866-738-4834;
www.jwdesertridgeresort.com

The serenity and beauty of the desert are the true inspirations behind this spa, where outside celestial showers for men and women, private balconies—ideal for outdoor massages—and a rooftop garden with flowing water add to the atmosphere. Indigenous botanicals influence most of Revive's body treatments. Mesquite clay and desert algae body wraps detoxify and purify. Prickly pear and lime-salt body scrubs soften skin. Recharge with a workout in the spacious and well-equipped fitness center.

PIPE SPRING NATIONAL MONUMENT

Located on the Kaibab-Paiute Indian Reservation, the focal point of this monument is a beautifully built sandstone Mormon fort dating to 1870. Several years earlier, Brigham Young had ordered the exploration of this region north of the Grand Canyon. According to legend, rifleman William "Gunlock Bill" Hamblin gave the place its name by shooting the bottom out of a smoking pipe at 50 paces.

The fort, actually a fortified ranch house, was built under the direction of Bishop Anson P. Winsor to protect the families caring for the church's cattle. Cattle drives, headed for the railroad in Cedar City, Utah, began here.

Guide service daily; living history demonstrations June-September. Kaibab Paiute Campground, 1/2 mile north of access road to visitor center.

Information: HC 65, Fredonia, 14 miles west on a spur off Highway 389, 928-643-7105; www.nps.gov/pisp

In addition to cardio machines and free weights, this facility offers several classes, including tai chi, water fitness, golf conditioning, flexibility, yoga and mat Pilates. After a workout, dine on calorie-conscious meals at Revive's Spa Bistro. $$

PRESCOTT

When President Lincoln established the territory of Arizona, Prescott became the capital. In 1867, the capital was moved to Tucson and then back to Prescott in 1877. After much wrangling, it was finally moved to Phoenix in 1889. Tourism and manufacturing are now Prescott's principal occupations. The climate is mild during summer and winter. The Prescott National Forest surrounds the city.

Information: Chamber of Commerce, 117 W. Goodwin St.,
928-445-2000, 800-266-7534; www.prescott.org

WHAT TO SEE AND DO

PRESCOTT NATIONAL FOREST

344 S. Cortez St., Prescott, 928-443-8000; www.fs.fed.us/r3/prescott

Minerals and varied vegetation abound in this forest of more than one million acres. Within the forest are Juniper Mesa, Apache Creek, Granite Mountain, Castle Creek, Woodchute and Cedar Bench wilderness areas, as well as parts of Sycamore Canyon and Pine Mountain wilderness areas. Fishing (Granite Basin, Lynx lakes); hunting, picnicking, camping.

SHARLOT HALL MUSEUM

415 W. Gurley St., Prescott, 928-445-3122; www.sharlot.org

Period houses include the Territorial Governor's Mansion (1864), restored in 1929 by poet-historian Sharlot Hall; Fort Misery (1864); William Bashford house (1877) and John C. Fremont house (1875). Period furnishings. Museum, library, archives. Also on the grounds is the grave of Pauline Weaver. Rose and herb garden. Pioneer schoolhouse. All buildings May-September, Monday-Saturday 10 a.m.-5 p.m., Sunday noon-4 p.m.; October-April, Monday-Saturday 10 a.m.-4 p.m., Sunday noon-4 p.m.

SMOKI MUSEUM

147 N. Arizona St., Prescott, 928-445-1230; www.smokimuseum.org
Native American artifacts, ancient and modern, are on display. Tuesday-Saturday
10 a.m.-4 p.m., Sunday 1-4 p.m.

SPECIAL EVENTS
BLUEGRASS FESTIVAL

Courthouse Plaza, 130 N. Cortez St., Prescott, 928-445-2000;
www.prescottbluegrassfestival.com
Features performances from local bluegrass artists. Late June.

PHIPPEN MUSEUM WESTERN ART SHOW AND SALE

Courthouse Plaza, 130 N. Cortez St., Prescott, 928-778-1385;
www.phippenartmuseum.org
More than 50 artists participate in this event, displaying works of several different
media, including watercolor, sculpture, acrylic and more. Memorial Day weekend.

PRESCOTT FRONTIER DAYS RODEO

848 Rodeo Drive, Prescott, 928-445-3103, 800-358-1888;
www.worldsoldestrodeo.com
Spend a couple of days at the "world's oldest rodeo." Festivities and events are held
throughout the city. There is also a parade and laser show. Late June-July Fourth.

TERRITORIAL PRESCOTT DAYS

Courthouse Plaza, 130 N. Cortez St., Prescott, 928-445-2000
This citywide celebration features an art show, craft demonstrations, old-fashioned
contests and home tours. Early June.

HOTELS
★DAYS INN

7875 E. Highway 69, Prescott Valley, 928-772-8600, 800-329-7466; www.daysinn.com
59 rooms. Complimentary continental breakfast. High-speed Internet access. Pets
accepted. Pool. **$**

★★FOREST VILLAS HOTEL

3645 Lee Circle, Prescott, 928-717-1200, 800-223-3449; www.forestvillas.com
62 rooms. Complimentary continental breakfast. Pool. **$**

★★HASSAYAMPA INN

122 E. Gurley St., Prescott, 928-778-9434, 800-322-1927; www.hassayampainn.com
67 rooms. Complimentary full breakfast. High-speed Internet access. Restaurant,
bar. **$**

SPECIALTY LODGING
PLEASANT STREET INN BED & BREAKFAST

142 S. Pleasant St., Prescott, 928-445-4774, 877-226-7128; www.pleasantbandb.com
Six rooms. Wireless Internet access. Complimentary full breakfast. **$**

RESTAURANTS
★★GURLEY STREET GRILL
230 W. Gurley St., Prescott, 928-445-3388; www.murphysrestaurants.com
American menu. Lunch, dinner. Bar. Children's menu. Casual attire. Outdoor seating. **$$**

★★MURPHY'S
201 N. Cortez, Prescott, 928-445-4044; www.murphysrestaurants.com
American menu. Lunch, dinner, Sunday brunch. Bar. Children's menu. Business casual attire. Reservations recommended. **$$$**

★★PINE CONE INN SUPPER CLUB
1245 White Spar Road, Prescott, 928-445-2970; www.pcisupperclub.com
American menu. Dinner. Closed Monday-Tuesday. Bar. Children's menu. Business casual attire. Reservations recommended. **$$**

SAFFORD
This small town has no shortage of places to play. Opt for a trek up nearby Mount Graham, a hike along Bonita Creek or a day of fishing at Roper Lake.
Information: Graham County Chamber of Commerce, 1111 Thatcher Blvd., Safford, 928-428-2511, 888-837-1841; www.visitgrahamcounty.com

WHAT TO SEE AND DO
ROPER LAKE STATE PARK
101 E. Roper Lake Road, Safford, 928-428-6760; www.azstateparks.com/parks/rola/index.html
This 320-acre park includes a small artificial lake, swimming beach and natural hot springs with tubs for public use. Fishing, boat launch (no gas-powered motors); nature trails, hiking; picnicking (shelter), camping, tent and trailer sites. Daily 6 a.m.-10 p.m.

THE SWIFT TRAIL
504 S. Fifth Ave., Safford, 928-428-4150; www.fs.fed.us/r3/coronado/forest/recreation/scenic_drives/pinaleno_swift.shtml
Highway 366 snakes its way 36 miles southwest from Safford to the high elevations of the Pinaleño Mountains in Coronado National Forest. Five developed campgrounds (mid-April-mid-November, weather permitting); trout fishing at Riggs Flat Lake and in the streams. The upper elevations of Highway 366 are closed mid-November-mid-April.

SPECIAL EVENTS
CINCO DE MAYO BASH
311 S. Central Ave., Safford, 928-428-4920
Mexican-American commemoration of Cinco de Mayo (May Fifth). Entertainment, dancing, world's longest tequila shot chain, games. First weekend in May.

GRAHAM COUNTY FAIR
527 E. Armory Road, Safford, 85546, 928-428-7180
Horse racing, quarter horse racing, race book. The complex also hosts the annual rodeo, Old Time Fiddlers Contest and other events. Mid-October.

HOTEL

★COMFORT INN

450 Entertainment Ave., Safford, 928-348-9400; www.comfortinn.com

88 rooms. Complimentary full breakfast. Wireless Internet access. Pool. Fitness center. Pets accepted. **$**

SAN CARLOS

The San Carlos Apache Indian Reservation covers almost two million acres ranging from desert to pine forests. Many lakes, rivers and ponds offer fishing year-round for trout, bass and catfish. Hunting for small game, large game and waterfowl is also year-round. Apache guides may be hired to lead visitors into the wilderness portions of the reservation. Sunrise ceremonial dances are held from time to time.

Information: San Carlos Recreation & Wildlife Department, San Carlos,
928-475-2343, 888-475-2344; www.scatrwd.com

SCOTTSDALE

Scottsdale is a popular resort destination located on the eastern border of Phoenix. It is renowned for outstanding art galleries, excellent shopping and dining, lush golf courses and abundant recreational activities.

Information: Scottsdale Convention & Visitors Bureau,
Galleria Corporate Centre, 4343 N. Scottsdale Road, Scottsdale,
480-421-1004, 800-782-1117;
www.scottsdalecvb.com

WHAT TO SEE AND DO

ANTIQUE TROVE

2020 N. Scottsdale Road, Scottsdale, 480-947-6074; www.antiquetrove.com

More than 150 dealers sell everything from vintage mink jackets to colonial rockers from the 1940s to claw-foot bathtubs. Prices range from $1 to several thousand. Daily.

CANYON COURSE AT THE PHOENICIAN

6000 E. Camelback Road, Scottsdale, 480-941-8200, 800-888-8234;
www.thephoenician.com

The Canyon is the last in the triumvirate of courses that make the Phoenician a celebrated resort. This nine-hole course can be combined with either of the other two courses (Oasis or Desert) to make a challenging and enjoyable 18-hole trek through the picturesque desert.

CASINO ARIZONA AT SALT RIVER

524 N. 92nd St., Scottsdale; www.casinoaz.com

The Salt River Pima-Maricopa Indian community hit the jackpot when it opened this casino in a prime location off the 101 Freeway on the Valley's east side. They promptly opened a second location just a few miles north, off the same freeway (9700 E. Indian Bend Road). The original funhouse is larger and a notch more upscale with five restaurants—the best being the elegant Cholla Prime Steakhouse. The 250-seat cabaret-style showroom rocks with big-name entertainers. Daily.

COSANTI FOUNDATION

6433 Doubletree Ranch Road, Paradise Valley, 480-948-6145, 800-752-3187;
www.cosanti.com

The famous Paolo Soleri windbells are made and sold here. Self-guided tours daily. Guided tours by reservation only. Daily 9 a.m.-5 p.m.

CRUISE NIGHT AT SCOTTSDALE PAVILIONS

9175 E. Indian Bend Road, Scottsdale, 480-905-9111; www.scottsdalepavilions.com

While Scottsdale Pavilions may be one of the largest and most attractive shopping centers in the country, Saturday nights bring more people to the parking lot than the shops. They come for the hot rods: muscle cars, custom cars, street rods, antique roadsters, vintage trucks, motorcycles and even a few finely tuned imports. Starts about 4 p.m., generally winds down around 8:30 p.m.

DESERT COURSE AT THE PHOENICIAN

6000 E. Camelback Road, Scottsdale, 480-941-8200, 800-888-8234;
www.thephoenician.com

This nine-hole wonder joins two other nine-hole courses (aptly named the "Oasis" and the "Canyon") to earn the swanky Phoenician some major accolades.

GRAYHAWK GOLF CLUB

8620 E. Thompson Peak Parkway, Scottsdale, 480-502-1800; www.grayhawk.com

Grayhawk has two courses: Talon (designed by David Graham and Gary Panks) and Raptor (designed by Tom Fazio). Both are nice, but Talon deserves more attention. Built in the Sonoran Desert, the course features many shots over desert brush or sand, with some water worked in for good measure. The course is good enough to host international-caliber tournaments such as the World Championship of Golf. If your game needs work, schedule some time at the Kostis McCord Learning Center, whose instructors include the two CBS commentators.

IRONWOOD COURSE AT THE WESTIN KIERLAND GOLF RESORT & SPA

15636 Clubgate Drive, Scottsdale, 480-922-9283, 888-625-5144;
www.kierlandresort.com/golf

Designed by Scott Miller (once a designer for Jack Nicklaus), the Ironwood, like the other two nine-hole courses at this resort, offers a beautiful setting for birdies, bogies and maybe even a hole-in-one.

KIERLAND COMMONS

Scottsdale Road and Greenway Parkway, Scottsdale, 480-348-1577;
www.kierlandcommons.com

This 38-acre urban village bills itself as "today's version of yesterday," given its Main Street feel and pedestrian-friendly layout. The well-landscaped streets are lined with more than 50 upscale retailers and restaurants, including Morton's Steak House, News Cafe and P.F. Chang's China Bistro. Monday-Saturday 10 a.m.-9 p.m., Sunday noon-6 p.m.

LEGEND TRAIL GOLF CLUB

9462 E. Legendary Lane, Scottsdale, 480-488-7434; www.legendtrailgc.com

Drive, chip and putt your way through the Sonoran Desert on this picturesque course. Even if you don't quite shoot par, you'll enjoy the gorgeous vistas and desert landscape.

MCCORMICK-STILLMAN RAILROAD PARK

7301 E. Indian Bend Road, Scottsdale, 480-312-2312; www.therailroadpark.com

Kids will enjoy circling around this 30-acre city park aboard the Paradise and Pacific Railroad, a miniature reproduction of a Colorado narrow-gauge railroad. There's also a 1950s carousel and well-equipped playgrounds. Be sure to also tour the Roald Amundsen Pullman Car, used by Herbert Hoover, Franklin Roosevelt, Harry Truman and Dwight Eisenhower. Daily.

MESQUITE COURSE AT THE WESTIN KIERLAND GOLF RESORT & SPA

15636 Clubgate Drive, Scottsdale, 480-922-9283, 888-625-5144;
www.kierlandresort.com/golf

Like its two nine-hole counterparts, this course was designed by Scott Miller (former designer for Jack Nicklaus). The resort offers three 18-hole combinations to challenge and delight duffers of all skill levels.

MONUMENT COURSE AT TROON NORTH GOLF CLUB

10320 E. Dynamite Blvd., Scottsdale, 480-585-5300; www.troonnorthgolf.com

Test your skills in the shadow of Pinnacle Peak at this beautiful desert course.

NORTH COURSE AT TALKING STICK GOLF CLUB

9998 E. Indian Bend Road, Scottsdale, 480-860-2221; www.talkingstickgolfclub.com

This Scottish links course stands ready to challenge golfers with its fairway bunkers, so don't let the gorgeous setting distract you too much.

OASIS COURSE AT THE PHOENICIAN

6000 E. Camelback Road, Scottsdale, 480-423-2450, 800-888-8234;
www.thephoenician.com

The Phoenician has earned praise from national critics and local fans alike. Don't miss an opportunity to swing your clubs at one of three 18-hole combinations, of which the Oasis makes up nine holes.

PINNACLE COURSE AT TROON NORTH GOLF CLUB

10320 E. Dynamite Blvd., Scottsdale, 480-585-5300; www.troonnorthgolf.com

Named for Pinnacle Peak, the course is one of two you'll find at the Troon North Golf Club. After swinging your heart out on the green—and admiring the view—dine at the club's Grille.

RAWHIDE WILD WEST TOWN

5700 W. North Loop Road, Chandler, 480-502-5600, 800-527-1880; www.rawhide.com

Gallop into the Old West at Arizona's largest Western-themed attraction. Roam the range on the stagecoach or train, test your aim in the shooting gallery, ride the mechanical bull, pan for gold, go horseback riding and take in the shows—from stuntmen throwing punches and squaring off in gunfights to performances by American Indian and Mexican dancers. The Steakhouse serves up mesquite-grilled steaks. Browse through the 15 shops. Daily.

SCOTTSDALE CENTER FOR THE ARTS
7380 E. Second St., Scottsdale, 480-994-2787; www.scottsdalearts.org
Offers theater, dance and music. Lectures, outdoor festivals and concerts. Sculpture garden; art exhibits. Daily.

SCOTTSDALE FASHION SQUARE
7014-590 E. Camelback Road, Scottsdale, 480-941-2140; www.fashionsquare.com
The largest shopping destination in the Southwest features more than 225 retailers, including Neiman Marcus, Nordstrom, Louis Vuitton, Sephora and Tiffany & Co. Ten restaurants, food court, movies. Monday-Saturday, 10 a.m.-9 p.m., Sunday 11 a.m.-6 p.m.

TALIESIN WEST
12621 N. Frank Lloyd Wright Blvd., Scottsdale, 480-860-2700;
www.franklloydwright.org
Take a guided tour of this amazing compound and see Frank Lloyd Wright's passion for organic architecture. In the late 1930s, Wright and his apprentices literally built this winter camp out of the Sonoran desert, using rocks and sand they gathered from the rugged terrain. In true Wright fashion, the architect designed the various buildings with terraces, gardens and walkways that link the outdoors with the indoors. Taliesin West still functions as a school for more than 20 architectural students. Daily.

TALKING STICK GOLF CLUB-SOUTH COURSE
9998 E. Indian Bend Road, Scottsdale, 480-860-2221; www.talkingstickgolfclub.com
Unlike its counterpart, which is a Scottish links course, the South Course is a traditional American-style golf course, punctuated with cottonwood and sycamore trees, creeks and lakes.

TOURNAMENT PLAYERS CLUB OF SCOTTSDALE
17020 N. Hayden Road, Scottsdale, 480-585-4334, 888-400-4001; www.tpc.com
Follow in the footsteps of Tiger Woods, Vijay Singh and other big-name golfers and swing into action on the TPC's greens—home of the Phoenix Open. The club has two options: the Stadium Course (the one the pros shoot) and the Desert Course, both open for daily play.

THE WESTIN KIERLAND GOLF RESORT AND SPA-ACACIA COURSE
15636 Clubgate Drive, Scottsdale, 480-922-9285; 480-922-9283;
www.kierlandresort.com/golf
Part of the resort's 27 perfectly manicured holes, the Acacia was created by Scott Miller, who once designed for Jack Nicklaus. Combine these nine holes with Ironwood or Mesquite's nine holes for 18 holes of great golf in one of Arizona's most beautiful resorts.

WESTWORLD OF SCOTTSDALE

16601 N. Pima Road, Scottsdale, 480-312-6802; www.scottsdaleaz.gov/westworld

A 360-acre recreation park, equestrian center, and event facility at the base of the McDowell Mountains. Concerts, sports competitions, special events. Daily.

WILD WEST JEEP TOURS

7127 E. Becker Lane, Scottsdale, 480-922-0144; www.wildwestjeeptours.com

Three- to four-hour guided desert tour. Explore an ancient ruin. Daily.

SPECIAL EVENTS

ARABIAN HORSE SHOW

WestWorld, 16601 N. Pima Road, Scottsdale, 480-515-1500

Arabian horse owners come from all over the world to show their horses. Two weeks in mid-February.

ARTWALK

Downtown Scottsdale, 480-990-3939; www.scottsdalegalleries.com

Locals brag that Scottsdale has more art galleries per capita than most any other U.S. city. To get a taste of this thriving scene, stroll the downtown streets during ArtWalk, a weekly Thursday night tradition for more than 20 years. For two hours, galleries host special exhibits, demonstrations and meet-the-artist receptions complete with wine, champagne and hors d'oeuvres. Thursday evenings.

PARADA DEL SOL & RODEO

Scottsdale, 480-990-3179; www.scottsdalejaycees.com/paradadelsol/art.html

This annual festival is sponsored by the Scottsdale Jaycees and includes a parade, rodeo and live music. Mid-February.

SAFEWAY INTERNATIONAL AT SUPERSTITION MOUNTAIN

Superstition Mountain Golf & Country Club, 3976 S. Ponderosa Drive,
Superstition Mountain, 877-983-3300; www.superstitionmountain.com

Major LPGA Tour golf tournament. Late March.

SAN FRANCISCO GIANTS SPRING TRAINING

Scottsdale Stadium, 7408 E. Osborn Road, Scottsdale,
480-312-2586, 800-225-2277; www.cactus-league.com/giants.html

San Francisco Giants baseball spring training, exhibition games. Early March-early April.

SCOTTSDALE CULINARY FESTIVAL

7309 E. Evans, Scottsdale, 480-945-7193; www.scottsdaleculinaryfestival.org

Indulge in some of the tastiest dishes in the region at this culinary adventure that brings the Southwest's best chefs together. Choose from any of nine individual events ranging from casual to black-tie-only. Proceeds benefit area charities. Mid-April.

ARIZONA

★
★
★
★
★

HOTELS

★★CHAPARRAL SUITES RESORT

5001 N. Scottsdale Road, Scottsdale, 480-949-1414, 800-528-1456;
www.chaparralsuites.com

311 rooms, all suites. Complimentary full breakfast. High-speed Internet access. Restaurant, bar. Airport transportation available. Pet. Fitness center. Pool. Tennis. Business center. **$$**

★COUNTRY INN & SUITES BY CARLSON

10801 N. 89th Place, Scottsdale, 480-314-1200, 888-201-1746; www.countryinns.com
163 rooms. Complimentary continental breakfast. Pets accepted. Pool. High-speed Internet access. Fitness center. **$**

★★★THE FAIRMONT SCOTTSDALE

7575 E. Princess Drive, Scottsdale, 480-585-4848, 800-257-7544; www.fairmont.com
The pink Spanish colonial buildings are spread out over 450 lush acres overlooking Scottsdale and the majestic McDowell Mountains. Golfers come here to play the two championship courses—one of which hosts the PGA Tour's Phoenix Open. The Willow Stream Spa is also a big draw. Kids will love the aquatic recreation area with two water slides. The spacious rooms and suites are a blend of Mediterranean design with Southwestern accents, and offer fantastic views. 650 rooms. Six restaurants, bars. Children's activity center. Spa. Pets accepted. Pool Golf. Tennis. **$$$**

★★★FIRESKY RESORT AND SPA

4925 N. Scottsdale Road, Scottsdale, 480-945-7666, 800-528-7867;
www.fireskyresort.com
A three-story sandstone fireplace flanked by hand-painted adobe walls is the centerpiece of this romantic resort's lobby. A traditional Western theme is reflected in the décor, while the grounds include a sandy beach pool surrounded by palm trees and flowers, as well as cozy fire pits. The convenient location is near restaurants and sports venues and a short drive from the airport. 204 rooms. Wireless Internet access. Restaurant, bar. Spa. Beach. Airport transportation available. Pets accepted. **$$**

★★★★FOUR SEASONS RESORT SCOTTSDALE AT TROON NORTH

10600 E. Crescent Moon Drive, Scottsdale, 480-515-5700, 888-207-9696;
www.fourseasons.com
Located on a 40-acre nature preserve, rooms are spread across 25 Southwestern-style casitas, with views of the stunning desert. Spring for a suite if you can—you'll get a plunge pool, alfresco garden shower and outdoor Kiva fireplace. A veritable mecca for golfers, the resort grants priority tee times at Troon North's two courses, considered among the best in the world. The spa offers desert nectar facials and moonlight massages, plus salon services and a fitness center. Three restaurants reflect the resort's casual elegance. 210 rooms. High-speed Internet access. Restaurant, bar. Children's activity center. Spa. Pets accepted. Pool. Golf. Tennis. **$$$$**

★GAINEY SUITES

7300 E. Gainey Suites Drive, Scottsdale, 480-922-6969, 800-970-4666;
www.gaineysuiteshotel.com

162 rooms, all suites. Complimentary continental breakfast. High-speed Internet access. Pool. Spa. **$$**

★★HILTON GARDEN INN

7324 E. Indian School Road, Scottsdale, 480-481-0400, 877-782-9444;
www.scottsdale.gardeninn.com

199 rooms. High-speed Internet access. Restaurant, bar. Pool. Business center. **$$**

★★★HILTON SCOTTSDALE RESORT AND VILLAS

6333 N. Scottsdale Road, Scottsdale, 480-948-7750, 800-528-3119;
www.scottsdaleresort.hilton.com

Warm shades of gold, blue and apricot complement the resort's natural wood décor, creating a warm and welcoming atmosphere. The villas here just received a total makeover. Galleries, shops and restaurants of Old Town Scottsdale are within easy walking distance or you can take advantage of the hotel's bike rental facility. The resort has three distinct eateries, and Griff's is a nice spot for cocktails and live entertainment. 187 rooms. Three restaurants, three bars. Pets accepted. Pool. Business center. Fitness center. **$**

★★★HOTEL VALLEY HO

6850 E. Main St., Scottsdale, 480-248-2000, 866-882-4484; www.hotelvalleyho.com

A mid-century modern masterpiece, this quirky hotel received a facelift in 2005, which took the property and furnishings back to their 1950s-era Jetsonian glory. Rooms now have plasma TVs, luxury bedding, CD players and Red Flower bath products. The huge outdoor pool has private cabanas for al fresco massages or simply sipping cocktails in private, while the VH Spa offers a full menu of 21st-century treatments, from lomi lomi massages to Tibetan yogic bodywork (a mix of acupressure and massage). Onsite restaurants include the retro-chic Trader Vic's, comfort-food themed Café ZuZu and Oh poolbar. 194 rooms. Restaurant, bar. Pool. Spa. Fitness center. Business center. Wireless Internet access. Pets accepted. **$$**

★★★HYATT REGENCY SCOTTSDALE RESORT AND SPA AT GAINEY RANCH

7500 E. Doubletree Ranch Road, Scottsdale,
480-444-1234, 800-554-9288; www.scottsdale.hyatt.com

Set against the backdrop of the McDowell Mountains, the resort is nestled on 560 acres filled with shimmering pools, trickling fountains and cascading waterfalls. Desert tones and regional furnishings create serene havens in the rooms and suites. The grounds feature championship golf, tennis, a water playground and a camp for kids. 500 rooms. High-speed Internet access. Restaurant, bar. Children's activity center. Spa. Beach. Golf. Tennis. Business center. **$$$$**

★LA QUINTA INN

8888 E. Shea Blvd., Scottsdale, 480-614-5300, 800-642-4271; www.laquinta.com

140 rooms. High-speed Internet access. Complimentary continental breakfast. Pets accepted. Pool. **$**

ARIZONA

★
★
★
★
★

★★★MARRIOTT CAMELBACK INN SPA & GOLF RESORT HOTEL

5402 E. Lincoln Drive, Scottsdale, 480-948-1700, 800-242-2635;
www.camelbackinn.com

Since the 1930s, the Camelback Inn has appealed to travelers seeking the best of the Southwest. This special hideaway is situated on 125 acres in the Sonoran Desert. The pueblo-style casitas feature wood-beamed ceilings, private patios and kitchenettes. Suites have private pools. Set at the base of Mummy Mountain, the spa is a peaceful retreat. Five restaurants satisfy every craving. 453 rooms. High-speed Internet access. Five restaurants, four bars. Children's activity center. Spa. Airport transportation available. Pets accepted. Pool. Golf. Tennis. **$$$**

★★★MARRIOTT SUITES SCOTTSDALE OLD TOWN

7325 E. Third Ave., Scottsdale, 480-945-1550, 888-236-2427; www.marriott.com

Catering mainly to business travelers, this Old Town hotel is close to Scottsdale Road and a large shopping mall. Its 251 suites come equipped with the latest in amenities, and it has plenty of recreational facilities, including a pool and fitness center, to help guests wind down at the end of the day. 251 rooms, all suites. Wireless Internet access. Restaurant, bar. Airport transportation available. Pool. Business center. **$$$**

★★★MILLENNIUM RESORT SCOTTSDALE, MCCORMICK RANCH

7401 N. Scottsdale Road, Scottsdale, 480-948-5050, 800-243-1332;
www.millennium-hotels.com

Situated on a 40-acre lake in the midst of the McCormick Ranch, this hotel's setting attracts couples on romantic getaways, business travelers making the most of the amenities and vacationers looking for a full-service resort experience. Proximity to the lake means easy access to paddle boats and sailboats. The resort also offers volleyball, tennis and swimming. The individually decorated villas include gas fireplaces, laundry facilities and private patios with grills. 175 rooms. High-speed Internet access. Restaurant, two bars. Airport transportation available. Spa. Business center. Pets accepted. Pool. Tennis. **$$**

★★★MONDRIAN HOTEL

7353 E. Indian School Road, Scottsdale, 480-308-1100, 800-697-1791;
www.mondrianscottsdale.com

Following in its older siblings' footsteps, the Mondrian Scottsdale caters to a young and hip clientele, in the style of New York City's Hudson and L.A.'s Mondrian. The white-on-white lobby is accented by modern furniture with sleek, clean lines. The guest rooms continue the stark coolness of the lobby; they are done entirely in black and white, save a single, strategically placed red apple. (The Mondrian is nothing if not striking.) The name Red Bar pretty much speaks for itself. Count on your abode being agreeably appointed with a 42-inch plasma TV, 300-thread count luxury bedding, a European pillow-top mattress with six pillows, Agua bath products by Korres, more than 60 movies on-demand and a deluxe CD sound system with an iPod connection. Need more? Hang in a private pimped-out poolside cabana with flat-screen TVs and passion-inspiring fireplaces when you're looking to impress. Or have dinner at the popular and trendy Asia de Cuba restaurant, which serves up a delicious fusion of Caribbean and Latin American cuisine. 194 rooms, suites. Wireless Internet access. Two restaurant, three bars. Fitness center. Two pools. Jacuzzi. Spa. Business center. **$$**

★★★★THE PHOENICIAN

6000 E. Camelback Road, Scottsdale, 480-941-8200, 800-888-8234;
www.thephoenician.com

This resort, located at the base of Camelback Mountain, is hyper-luxurious. The rooms and suites feature imported Irish linens and oversized bathrooms with Italian marble. But there is no attitude here. Someone is always around to help or steer you toward one of a number of recreational opportunities, including desert hikes. A resort within a resort, the Canyon Suites at the Phoenician offers sprawling, luxuriously decorated rooms and a separate pool with private cabanas. Guests are assigned ambassadors, who arrange everything from in-room aromatherapy baths to chauffeured trips into town in the resort's Mercedes. There's little reason to leave the elegant, comfortable suites (which have DVD players, flat-screen TVs and Italian linen-swathed beds), but the resort's golf courses and full-service spa serve as the primary temptations. 647 rooms. Wireless Internet access. Restaurant, bar. Children's activity center. Spa. Airport transportation available. Pets accepted. Pool. Golf. Tennis. Business center. $$$

★★★RENAISSANCE SCOTTSDALE RESORT

6160 N. Scottsdale Road, Scottsdale, 480-991-1414, 800-309-8138;
www.renaissancehotels.com

The lobby, with its Spanish colonial Monk's Tower, is both the entrance to the resort's many amenities and a buffer against the commotion of busy Scottsdale Road, located next to the Borgata Shopping Center. Lush landscaping with plenty of grass and flowers separates the lobby from the single-story guest rooms and suites. Head to one of two pools for a relaxing swim, play shuffleboard or volleyball, make use of the putting green or jog with your pooch along a trail that includes workout stations. 171 rooms. High-speed Internet access. Restaurant, bar. Pets accepted. Pool. Tennis. Business center. $$

★★★SCOTTSDALE MARRIOTT AT MCDOWELL MOUNTAINS

16770 N. Perimeter Drive, Scottsdale, 480-502-3836, 800-288-6127;
www.scottsdalemarriott.com

This all-suites hotel is located in north Scottsdale. The colorful, attractive public areas and well-furnished guest rooms are designed for both families and the business traveler. Some rooms have views of the TPC-Scottsdale golf course. 270 rooms, all suites. High-speed Internet access. Restaurant, bar. Pets accepted. Pool. Business center. $

★SUMMERFIELD SUITES

4245 N. Drinkwater Blvd., Scottsdale, 480-946-7700, 800-889-6829; www.hyatt.com
164 rooms, all suites. Complimentary full breakfast. High-speed Internet access. Pets accepted. Pool. $$

★★★THE WESTIN KIERLAND RESORT AND SPA

6902 E. Greenway Parkway, Scottsdale, 480-624-1000, 800-937-8461;
www.westin.com/kierlandresort

Located in northeast Phoenix, this handsome boutique-style resort is adjacent to the 38-acre Kierland Commons, where specialty shops and restaurants attract serious shoppers and diners. The spacious rooms and suites feature soothing earth tones and regional furnishings. Everything is at hand here, including two 18-hole golf courses, tennis courts, multiple pools (including a flowing river pool with landscaped waterfall), beach and volleyball courts and six restaurants. The expansive Agave Spa looks to the traditional therapies used by American Indians for inspiration. 732 rooms. Restaurant, bar. Children's activity center. Spa. Beach. Pets accepted. Pool. Golf. Tennis. **$$$**

SPAS

★★★★THE CENTRE FOR WELL-BEING

6000 E. Camelback Road, Scottsdale, 480-941-8200, 800-843-2392;
www.centreforwellbeing.com

This spa is always thinking big, which means services here are on the cutting edge. Want to be more Zen in the real world? Sign up for a private meditation session, where you can learn visualization and other stress-reducing techniques. Have to work 100 hours just to take a week off? The *Jin Shin Jyutsu* utilizes a series of holding techniques to alleviate tension blocked in the body. Tend to overdo it on the golf course? The neuromuscular treatment offers spot relief for injuries. Of course, you'll want to go home looking as great as you feel, and for that there's no shortage of wraps, facials and scrubs. Even the state-of-the-art gym is inviting. **$$**

★★★THE SPA AT CAMELBACK INN

5402 E. Lincoln Drive, Scottsdale, 480-948-1700, 800-582-2169;
www.camelbackspa.com

Following an $8 million facelift, the Spa at Camelback Inn has swapped its old Southwest-style décor for sophisticated chocolate brown woods, flagstone walls and expansive windows to create an inviting, placid retreat. If the gas fireplace in the main relaxation room doesn't soothe your spirit, head outside to the solarium and let the sound of rippling water from a flowing fountain do the trick. Relax in your own private casita, while you choose from the menu of massages, facials and body treatments—many of which draw from Native American techniques and indigenous ingredients. **$$**

★★★★SPA AT FOUR SEASONS RESORT SCOTTSDALE AT TROON NORTH

10600 E. Crescent Moon Drive, Scottsdale, 480-513-5145, 888-207-9696;
www.fourseasons.com

You're guaranteed to relax at this 12,000-square-foot spa. The resort's signature moonlight massage is the perfect way to end the day. You'll also find hot stone massage and facials that feature local, seasonal ingredients, including saguaro blossom, the state flower, as well as the more common green tea and honey. Half-day and full-day packages are available. Full-service salon and fitness center. **$$**

★★★★WILLOW STREAM SPA

7575 E. Princess Drive, Scottsdale, 480-585-2732, 800-908-9540;
www.fairmont.com

The facilities at the Fairmont Scottsdale are top-notch—from championship golf courses to award-winning restaurants—and the spa is no exception. Many of the treatments make use of the Havasupai Waterfall (inspired by the oasis of waterfalls in the Grand Canyon) located on the spa's first floor. The Havasupai Body Oasis treatment combines warm eucalyptus and herbal baths with the healing power of the waterfalls. Other treatments also reflect local surroundings. The Desert Purification features a body mask of cornmeal, clay and oats. An *Ayate* cloth (made from the cactus plant) is then used to exfoliate skin. Or keep it simple with a facial or massage—and hit the beauty salon for a spa pedicure. **$$**

RESTAURANTS

★★ACAPULCO BAY CO.

3030 N. 68th St., Scottsdale, 480-429-1990; www.acapulcobayco.com

Mexican menu. Lunch, dinner. Bar. Children's menu. Casual attire. Reservations recommended. Outdoor seating. **$$**

★★AJO AL'S MEXICAN CAFE

9393 N. 90th St., Scottsdale, 480-860-2611; www.ajoals.com

Southwestern menu. Lunch, dinner, Saturday-Sunday brunch. Bar. Children's menu. Casual attire. **$$**

★★ASIA DE CUBA

7353 East Indian School Road, Mondrian, Scottsdale, 480-308-1131;
www.mondrianscottsdale.com/mondrian_hotel_scottsdale_asiadecuba.asp

Trend whores will eat it up, others may feel their stomachs turn. If you're not into seeing and being seen, you're probably not into Asia de Cuba. The pricey plates are secondary to the stark, white contemporary décor and the crowd who thinks it flatters their figures. But that's not to say you can't get a fine lobster, rack of lamb, or pork roast here. You can, and it'll be an experience unto itself with the unique pairing of Asian and Cuban flavors that has so impressed patrons in London, Los Angeles, New York and San Francisco. We just can't stop staring long enough to chew. Asian, Cuban menu. Breakfast, lunch, dinner. Casual attire. Reservations recommended. Valet parking. $22-$69

★★ATLAS BISTRO

2515 N. Scottsdale Road, Scottsdale, 480-990-2433; www.atlasbistro.com

International menu. Dinner. Closed Sunday-Tuesday. Casual attire. Reservations recommended. **$$$**

★★BLOOM

8877 N. Scottsdale Road, Scottsdale, 480-922-5666; www.foxrc.com

American menu. Lunch, dinner, Saturday-Sunday brunch. Bar. Casual attire. Reservations recommended. Outdoor seating. **$$$**

★THE BREAKFAST CLUB

4400 N. Scottsdale Road, Scottsdale, 480-222-2582; www.thebreakfastclub.us

American menu. Breakfast, lunch. Casual attire. Outdoor seating. **$**

★★★BOURBON STEAK

7575 E. Princess Dr., Scottsdale, 480-513-6002;
www.michaelmina.net/mm_bourbonsteak_scottsdale/

Just another notch on chef Michael Mina's belt, Bourbon Steak Scottsdale has received accolades since it opened in early 2008. This modern American steakhouse takes the classics and improves them. Think three types of beef—certified angus, American kobe and A5 kobe—all prepared with Mina's special touch. He poaches red meat in butter, lamb in olive oil and pork in bacon fat before grilling. You don't have to eat beef here with other options such as whole-fried organic chicken, truffled mac & cheese, Maine lobster pot pie, and tapioca-crusted yellowtail snapper to choose from. Contemporary American steakhouse menu. Dinner, Sunday brunch. Bar. Children's menu. Casual attire. Reservations recommended. Valet parking. Outdoor seating. $$

★★CALLALOO
7051 E. Fifth Ave., Scottsdale, 480-941-1111
Caribbean menu. Dinner. Closed Sunday. Bar. Casual attire. Reservations recommended. $$

★★CHART HOUSE
7255 McCormick Parkway, Scottsdale, 480-951-2250; www.chart-house.com
Seafood menu. Dinner. Bar. Children's menu. Casual attire. Outdoor seating. Reservations recommended. $$$

★CHOMPIE'S
9301 E. Shea Blvd., Scottsdale, 480-860-0475; www.chompies.com
Deli menu. Breakfast, lunch, dinner. Closed holidays. Bar. Children's menu. Casual attire. Outdoor seating. $$

★★★DESEO
6902 E. Greenway Parkway, Scottsdale, 480-624-1030, 480-624-1202, 888-625-5144; www.kierlandresort.com
The open display kitchen is the focal point of this restaurant located in Scottsdale's Westin Keirland Resort. Choose from a variety of mojitos and be sure to order one of the signature ceviches. Other items include foie gras empanadas and Muscovy duck breast with Asian pear and mango. Latin American menu. Dinner. Closed Monday in summer. Bar. Business casual attire. Reservations recommended. Valet parking. Outdoor seating. $$$

★★★DIGESTIF
7114 E. Stetson Dr., Scottsdale, 480-425-9463; www.digestifscottsdale.com
Making the lead sentence of a *Wall Street Journal* article, landing a *Food + Wine* feature article from all the way out West and getting a best-new-restaurant-in-Phoenix award and mentions on local top 10 lists in less than a year has to rank somewhere near the top of the restaurant-success barometer. Why all the buzz? Chef Payton Curry's handmade pasta and housemade charcuterie from locally sourced and house-butchered meat, combined with other local ingredients, are a slam dunk. The inspired cocktail menu includes absinthe, which is served with a sizable production that includes a slotted spoon, sugar cube, and water fountain. Phoenix pastry goddess Tracey Dempsey has also blessed the place with her presence. Her lemon marscapone cheesecake and chocolate raspberry tiramisu are two of many exceedingly generous treats. Italian menu. Lunch, dinner. Bar. Casual attire. Reservations recommended. Valet parking. Two patios. $$

ARIZONA

★
★
★
★
★

★★DRIFT

4341 N. 75th St., Scottsdale, 480-949-8454; www.driftlounge.com
Polynesian menu. Lunch, dinner. Bar. Casual attire. Outdoor seating. **$$**

★★★EDDIE V'S EDGEWATER GRILLE

20715 N. Pima Road, Scottsdale, 480-538-8468; www.eddiev.com
The relaxed lodge-themed interior features murals, black leather chairs, crisp white table linens and brick walls. Diners are entertained nightly by a band or a vocalist. But the main draw here is the food. The Maryland-style all-lump crab cakes are a must for an appetizer, and the bananas Foster makes a memorable end to a meal. Seafood menu. Dinner. Bar. Business casual attire. Reservations recommended. Valet parking. Outdoor seating. **$$$**

★★FARRELLI'S CINEMA SUPPER CLUB

14202 N. Scottsdale Road, Scottsdale, 480-905-7200; www.farrellis.com
Continental menu. Dinner. Bar. Children's menu. Casual attire. Reservations recommended. **$$**

★★FUSION

4441 N. Buckboard Trail, Scottsdale, 480-423-9043
International menu. Lunch, dinner. Children's menu. Casual attire. **$$**

★GRAZIE PIZZERIA & WINE BAR

6952 E. Main St., Scottsdale, 480-663-9797; www.grazie.us
Italian menu. Lunch, dinner. Bar. Casual attire. Reservations recommended. Outdoor seating. **$$**

★★★IL TERRAZZO

6000 E. Camelback Rd., The Phoenician, Scottsdale, 480-423-2530, 800-888-8234;
www.thephoenician.com/pages/terrace/index.html
The Phoenician's American eatery, The Terrace, got a $1 million facelift and an accent. Aiming to capture the rich, indigenous flavors of Italy through classic, upscale cuisine that represents all regions of the country, chef de cuisine Victor Casanova, who most recently served as sous chef at New York's Ocean Grill, offers such dishes as tagliata, a black angus rib cap with wilted spinach and squid ink gnocchi, served with lemon-horseradish gremolata and topped with crispy calamari; and cacciucco (a spicy Tuscan seafood stew with plum tomatoes, Sardinian fregola, squid, clams, shrimp and mussels). The real treats are master baker Ben Hershberger's artisan loaves. Olive walnut sourdough, rosemary and farmer's rye are all baked fresh daily. Paired with The Phoenician's limited-production extra virgin olive oil from Sonoma and 15-year-aged balsamic vinegar, you won't care much about the rest of the meal. Italian menu. Breakfast, lunch, dinner, Sunday brunch. Children's menu. Resort casual attire. Reservations recommended. Valet parking. Outdoor seating. **$$$**

★★JEWEL OF THE CROWN

7373 E. Scottsdale Mall, Scottsdale, 480-949-8000; www.jewelofthecrown.com
Indian menu. Lunch, dinner. Bar. Casual attire. Reservations recommended. Outdoor seating. **$$**

★★★L'ECOLE

8100 E. Camelback Road, Scottsdale, 480-990-3773; www.chefs.edu/about.asp

You can be sure that the food is top-of-the-line at this training ground for the Scottsdale Culinary Institute. The student-operated, full-service restaurant is set in a lovely dining room that is booked weeks in advance. The menu changes based on the student curriculum, but it always offers a nice variety. The outdoor patio has colorful awnings and views of a golf course. French menu. Lunch, dinner. Closed Saturday-Sunday; also two weeks in early July and two weeks in end of December. Business casual attire. Reservations recommended. Outdoor seating. $$

★LOS SOMBREROS

2534 N. Scottsdale Road, Scottsdale, 480-994-1799

Mexican menu. Dinner. Closed Monday. Bar. Casual attire. Outdoor seating. $$

★★★MOSAIC

10600 E. Jomax Road, Scottsdale, 480-563-9600; www.mosaic-restaurant.com

Chef/owner Deborah Knight uses ingredients and cooking techniques from around the world to create her own brand of eclectic cuisine, which has included dishes such as Louisiana spiced prawns, Thai shrimp and coconut soup, and fennel and pesto risotto. Three types of five-course tasting menus are available to suit all tastes (Mosaic, Ocean and Vegetable). Local artwork punctuates the earth-toned dining room with color, and a beautiful, custom-made mosaic floor adds sparkle. International/fusion menu. Dinner. Closed Sunday-Monday; mid-August-late September. Bar. Business casual attire. Reservations recommended. Outdoor seating. $$$

★★NORTH

15024 N. Scottsdale Road, Scottsdale, 480-948-2055;
www.foxrestaurantconcepts.com/north.html

Italian menu. Lunch, dinner. Bar. Casual attire. Reservations recommended. Outdoor seating. $$

★★★PALM COURT

7700 E. McCormick Parkway, Scottsdale, 480-991-9000, 800-548-0293;
www.thescottsdaleresort.com

Although this restaurant is located on the third floor of the main building at the Scottsdale Conference Resort, you'd never know it once you enter the elegant candlelit dinning room, where tuxedo-clad waiters serve lavish French fare. A classical guitarist provides lovely background music during dinner and Sunday brunch sittings. French menu. Breakfast, lunch, dinner, Sunday brunch. Bar. Business casual attire. Reservations recommended. Valet parking. $$$

★★PEPIN

7363 Scottsdale Mall, Scottsdale, 480-990-9026; www.pepinrestaurant.com

Spanish, tapas menu. Lunch, dinner. Closed Monday. Bar. Casual attire. $$$

★QUILTED BEAR

6316 N. Scottsdale Road, Scottsdale, 480-948-7760; www.quiltedbearaz.com

American menu. Breakfast, lunch, dinner. Bar. Children's menu. Casual attire. Outdoor seating. $$

★★RA SUSHI BAR & RESTAURANT

3815 N. Scottsdale Road, Scottsdale, 480-990-9256; www.rasushi.com
Japanese, sushi menu. Lunch, dinner. Bar. Casual attire. Valet parking. Outdoor seating. $$

★★★RANCHO PINOT

6208 N. Scottsdale Blvd., Scottsdale, 480-367-8030; www.ranchopinot.com
Situated within the Lincoln Village Shops, Rancho Pinot offers American cuisine using the best ingredients, many of them from local farms. You might find dishes such as handmade pasta with summer squash, scallions, mint and Parmesan cheese on the menu. Art and Southwestern décor adorn the walls, and an open kitchen allows guests to watch the chef at work. American menu. Dinner. Closed Sunday-Monday in mid-April-mid-October. Bar. Business casual attire. Reservations recommended. Outdoor seating. $$$

★REATA PASS STEAK HOUSE

27500 N. Alma School Parkway, Scottsdale, 480-585-7277; www.reatapass.com
American, Steak menu. Lunch, dinner. Closed Monday. Bar. Children's menu. Casual attire. Outdoor seating. Reservations recommended. $$

★★★REMINGTON'S

7200 N. Scottsdale Road, Scottsdale, 480-951-5101; www.scottsdaleplaza.com
Steak menu. Lunch, dinner. Bar. Business casual attire. Reservations recommended. Valet parking. Outdoor seating. $$$

★★★ROARING FORK

4800 N. Scottsdale Road, Scottsdale, 480-947-0795; www.roaringfork.com
One of the founders of Southwestern cuisine, chef Robert McGrath turns out Western American cooking at this rustic yet refined dining room filled with exposed brick and blond wood. An open display kitchen is featured, with some booths situated across the aisle for great viewing. The adjacent J-Bar is a fun place to congregate for a drink. American menu. Dinner. Bar. Children's menu. Casual attire. Reservations recommended. Valet parking Friday-Saturday. Outdoor seating. $$$

★★SALT CELLAR

550 N. Hayden Road, Scottsdale, 480-947-1963; www.saltcellarrestaurant.com
Seafood menu. Dinner, late-night. Bar. Casual attire. Reservations recommended. $$

★★★SASSI

10455 E. Pinnacle Peak Parkway, Scottsdale, 480-502-9095; www.sassi.biz
New York's famed chef Wade Moises prepared authentic Italian cuisine at this restaurant resembling a Tuscan villa. The extensive wine list offers many delicious complements. A live pianist entertains diners Wednesday through Sunday and is joined by a bass player on the weekends. Italian menu. Dinner. Closed Monday. Bar. Business casual attire. Reservations recommended. Valet parking. Outdoor seating. $$$

★★★SEA SAW

7133 E. Stetson Drive, Scottsdale, 480-481-9463; www.seasaw.net
Japanese, sushi menu. Dinner. Casual attire. Reservations recommended. Valet parking. $$$

73

ARIZONA

★
★
★
★
★

★★SUSHI ON SHEA

7000 E. Shea Blvd., Scottsdale, 480-483-7799; www.sushionshea.com

Japanese menu. Lunch, dinner. Bar. Casual attire. Reservations recommended. Valet parking. Outdoor seating. **$$**

★★★★TALAVERA

*Four Seasons Resort Scottsdale at Troon North, 10600 E. Crescent Moon Drive
Scottsdale, 480-515-5700; www.fourseasons.com*

The surrounding Sonoran Desert is palpable in this new restaurant via rich red love-seats, sand-colored walls and cactus-green chairs, as well as a cozy glass-enclosed fireplace. Opt to dine under the stars on the patio—all the better to behold the craggy Pinnacle Peak and the desert expanse. Start your alfresco dinner with the lobster bisque with pearl onions. For entrées, this steakhouse offers raw choices (Wagyu beef tartare with mustard crème fraîche), Nebraska corn-fed prime cuts, and a list of fish and chicken meals. Go for regional dishes, such as Arizona grass-fed tenderloin with savory chorizo bread pudding. A great steal is the daily three-course tasting menu that changes weekly ($40, $60 with wine pairings), which in the past has included stand-outs such as arugula dotted with pear and Gorgonzola, halibut with tomato and cous-cous, and warm chocolaty cake with caramel ice cream. Steakhouse menu. Dinner. Children's menu. Reservations recommended. Valet parking. Outdoor seating. **$$$$**

★★★TERRACE DINING ROOM

6000 E. Camelback Road, Scottsdale, 480-941-8200; www.thephoenician.com

Situated on the ground floor of the main lobby building at the Phoenician, this restaurant offers a variety of steak and seafood specialties. Guests can enjoy the live jazz music played nightly and at the Sunday and holiday brunches. Steak menu. Breakfast, lunch, dinner, Sunday brunch. Bar. Children's menu. Casual attire. Reservations recommended. Valet parking. Outdoor seating. **$$$**

★★★TRADER VIC'S

6850 E. Main St., Scottsdale, 480-248-2000, 866-882-4484; www.hotelvalleyho.com

This branch of the classic 1950s Polynesian-themed restaurant serves up potent punches in bamboo coolers (and perfect Mai Tais, which they purport to have invented in 1944) plus pu-pu platters of egg rolls and crab Rangoon. Entrées include wok-fried Szechuan prawns and ginger beef, or crispy duck with moo-shu pancakes. The décor takes its cue from the tiki bars of the past (plenty of rattan, a totem here or there) but is updated for the new millennium. Asian Pacific Rim menu. Brunch, dinner. Outdoor seating. Valet parking. **$$**

★★VILLAGE TAVERN

8787 N. Scottsdale Road, Scottsdale, 480-951-6445; www.villagetavern.com

International menu. Lunch, dinner, Sunday brunch. Bar. Children's menu. Casual attire. Reservations recommended. Outdoor seating. **$$**

★★★WINDOWS ON THE GREEN

6000 E. Camelback Road, Scottsdale, 480-941-8200; www.thephoenician.com

Windows on the Green, located near the golf shop at the Phoenician, offers great views from the large picture windows. Dig into grilled Indian bread, Portobello tacos and tortilla-encrusted ahi tuna—or try one of the chef's tapas tastings. Guacamole is prepared tableside. Guests can relax to the sounds of a Spanish guitarist who performs live in the dining room. The bar boasts some unique tequilas and signature margaritas. Southwestern menu. Dinner. Closed Tuesday-Wednesday. Bar. Children's menu. Business casual attire. Reservations recommended. Valet parking. Outdoor seating. **$$$**

★★★ZINC BISTRO
15034 N. Scottsdale Road, Scottsdale, 480-603-0920; www.zincbistroaz.com
A high-energy spot, Zinc Bistro is located in the Kierland Commons shopping center. The Parisian-style space, decorated with a tin ceiling and solid zinc bar, serves up crêpes, omelets, steaks, onion soup and more. French bistro menu. Lunch, dinner. Bar. Casual attire. Outdoor seating. **$$**

★★ZUZU
6850 E. Main St., 480-248-2000, 866-882-4484; www.hotelvalleyho.com
American. Breakfast, lunch, dinner. Reservations recommended. Outdoor seating. **$$**

SEDONA

Known worldwide for the beauty of the surrounding red rocks, Sedona has grown from a pioneer settlement into a favorite film location. This is a resort area with numerous outdoor activities, including hiking, fishing and biking, which can be enjoyed all year. Also an art and shopping destination, Sedona boasts Tlaquepaque, a 4½-acre area of gardens, courtyards, fountains, galleries, shops and restaurants.
Information: Sedona-Oak Creek Canyon Chamber of Commerce, 331 Forest Road, Sedona, 928-282-7722, 800-288-7336; www.sedonachamber.com

WHAT TO SEE AND DO
CHAPEL OF THE HOLY CROSS
780 Chapel Road, Sedona, 928-282-4069; www.chapeloftheholycross.com/store
Chapel perched between two pinnacles of uniquely colored red sandstone. Daily 9 a.m.-5 p.m.

OAK CREEK CANYON
Sedona, 800-288-7336; www.visitsedona.com
A beautiful drive along a spectacular fishing stream, north toward Flagstaff.

RED ROCK JEEP TOURS
270 N. Highway 89A, Sedona, 928-282-6826, 800-848-7728; www.redrockjeep.com
Two-hour back country trips. Daily. Other tours also available.

SLIDE ROCK STATE PARK
6871 N. Highway 89A, Sedona, 928-282-3034; azstateparks.com/Parks/slro/index.html
A 43-acre day-use park on Oak Creek. Swimming, natural sandstone waterslide, fishing, hiking, picnicking. Summer, daily 8 a.m.-7 p.m.; winter, daily 8 a.m.-5 p.m.; fall and spring, daily 8 a.m.-6 p.m.

ARIZONA

★
★
★
★
★

TLAQUEPAQUE
336 Highway 179, Sedona, 928-282-4838; www.tlaq.com
A Spanish-style courtyard, it consists of 40 art galleries and stores. Daily 10 a.m.-5 p.m.

SPECIAL EVENTS
RED ROCK FANTASY OF LIGHTS
Los Abrigados Resort & Spa, 160 Portal Lane, Sedona, 928-282-1777, 800-521-3131; www.redrockfantasy.com
This annual event features kids' activities, concerts, carriage rides and special events. Late November-mid-January.

SEDONA FILM FESTIVAL
Harkins Theatre, 2081 W. Highway 89A, Sedona, 928-282-1177; www.sedonafilmfestival.com
Features independent films and film workshops. Late February.

SEDONA JAZZ ON THE ROCKS
2020 Contractors Road, Sedona, 928-282-1985; www.sedonajazz.com
This extended weekend of entertainment features both local and national jazz acts, and it draws more than 7,500 visitors and music lovers to scenic Sedona each year. Late September.

HOTELS
★★★AMARA CREEKSIDE RESORT
310 N. Highway 89A, Sedona, 928-282-4828, 866-455-6610; www.amararesort.com
Located along the banks of Oak Creek, this chic, contemporary resort features well-appointed rooms and tranquil surroundings with a heated saltwater pool and fire pit. Rooms have pillow-top mattresses, Italian linens and sleek work desks. The new 4,000-square-foot spa offers a wide variety of pampering treatments. 100 rooms. Wireless Internet access. Spa. Restaurant, bar. Airport transportation available. **$$**

★BEST WESTERN ARROYO ROBLE HOTEL & CREEKSIDE VILLAS
400 N. Highway 89A, Sedona, 928-282-4001, 800-773-3662; www.bestwesternsedona.com
65 rooms. Complimentary continental breakfast. High-speed Internet access. Airport transportation available. Tennis. Pool. Whirlpool. Fitness center. **$**

★BEST WESTERN INN OF SEDONA
1200 W. Highway 89A, Sedona, 928-282-3072, 800-292-6344; www.innofsedona.com
110 rooms. Complimentary continental breakfast. Wireless Internet access. Airport transportation available. Pets accepted. Pool. **$**

★★★EL PORTAL SEDONA
95 Portal Lane, Sedona, 928-203-9405, 800-313-0017; www.innsedona.com
This secluded hacienda-style inn is conveniently located in the heart of Sedona near more than 50 shops and restaurants. The 12 luxurious rooms feature Arts and Crafts furnishings, high-beam ceilings, stained glass, whirlpool tubs, cashmere blankets and

Egyptian cotton sheets. After a busy day exploring the area, relax with a delicious meal at the inn's dining room. On Wednesday nights there's a barbecue cookout in the courtyard. 12 rooms. Wireless Internet access. Restaurant. Pets accepted. $$$$

★★★ENCHANTMENT RESORT
525 Boynton Canyon Road, Sedona, 928-282-2900, 800-826-4180; www.enchantmentresort.com

Located within Boynton Canyon, this resort offers spectacular views of the rugged landscape from just about everywhere. This resort is full of Southwestern charm, from the Native American furnishings and decorative accents in the rooms to the regional kick of the sensational dining. Tennis, croquet, swimming and pitch-and-putt golf are some of the activities available for adults, while Camp Coyote entertains young guests with arts and crafts and special programs. The Mii Amo Spa is a destination unto itself with 16 casitas used for treatments. 220 rooms. High-speed Internet access. Restaurant, bar. Spa. Airport transportation available. Tennis. Business center. $$$

★HAMPTON INN
1800 W. Highway 89A, Sedona, 928-282-4700, 800-426-7866; www.hamptoninn.com

56 rooms. Complimentary continental breakfast. Wireless Internet access. Airport transportation available. Pool. Fitness center. $

★★★HILTON SEDONA RESORT AND SPA
90 Ridge Trail Drive, Sedona, 928-284-4040, 877-273-3763; www.hiltonsedona.com

This Southwestern-style resort is located amid the Coconino National Forest. The spacious guest rooms and suites are well decorated and have gas fireplaces, wet bars, sleeper sofas and patios or balconies with views of the Red Rock vistas. There are three pools to choose from, a full-service fitness center, tennis and racquetball and the nearby Sedona Golf Resort, featuring a 71-par championship course. The spa is located steps from the hotel's main building. The property's Grille at ShadowRock features a Southwestern menu, and with its earth tones and soft lighting, is the perfect spot for a romantic dinner. During the day, the restaurant's outdoor patio is a great place to have a hearty breakfast or a light lunch. 219 rooms. High-speed Internet access. Restaurant, bar. Fitness center. Spa. Pets accepted. $$

★★★L'AUBERGE DE SEDONA
301 L'Auberge Lane, Sedona, 928-282-1661, 800-905-5745; www.lauberge.com

This secluded resort offers views of the Red Rock Canyon and Magenta Cliffs. Accommodations include cozy cottages with fireplaces (the staff light a juniper-infused fire nightly) and an inviting lodge. Gourmet dining is an integral part of the experience. L'Auberge Restaurant is noted for its fine French food, special five-course tasting menu and award-winning wine list. The world-class spa will banish every last bit of tension. Enjoy a massage in one of the poolside cabanas. 56 rooms. Wireless Internet access. Restaurant, bar. Airport transportation available. Pool. $$$

★★★LOS ABRIGADOS RESORT AND SPA
160 Portal Lane, Sedona, 928-282-1777, 800-521-3131; www.ilxresorts.com

This Spanish-style stucco and tile-roofed hotel is set among the buttes of Oak Creek Canyon. Rooms are spacious with kitchen facilities and pullout sofas. Activities such

★
★
★
★

as Jeep tours, hiking, biking and helicopter rides are nearby. 182 rooms, all suites. Three restaurants, three bars. Airport transportation available. Pool. Tennis. Pets accepted; fee. $$$

★★RADISSON POCO DIABLO RESORT
1752 S. Highway 179, Sedona, 928-282-7333, 888-201-1718;
www.radisson.com/sedonaaz
138 rooms. Wireless Internet access. Restaurant, bar. Airport transportation available. Spa. Pool. Golf. Tennis. Business center. $$

★SEDONA REAL INN
95 Arroyo Pinon Drive, Sedona, 928-282-1414, 877-299-6016; www.sedonareal.com
89 rooms. Complimentary continental breakfast. High-speed Internet access. Airport transportation available. Pets accepted. Pool. $$

★SOUTHWEST INN AT SEDONA
3250 W. Highway 89A, Sedona, 928-282-3344, 800-483-7422; www.swinn.com
28 rooms. Wireless Internet access. Complimentary continental breakfast. Pool. $$

★★TERRITORIAL HOUSE BED AND BREAKFAST
65 Piki Drive, Sedona, 928-204-2737, 800-801-2737; www.territorialhousebb.com
Four rooms. Complimentary full breakfast. Wireless Internet access. Whirlpool. Airport transportation available. $$

SPECIALTY LODGINGS

ADOBE VILLAGE GRAHAM INN
150 Canyon Circle Drive, Sedona, 928-284-1425, 800-228-1425;
www.sedonasfinest.com
Relax in your own private casita with a king bed and a waterfall shower. 11 rooms. High-speed Internet access. Complimentary full breakfast. Pool. $$$

ALMA DE SEDONA INN
50 Hozoni Drive, Sedona, 928-282-2737, 800-923-2282; www.almadesedona.com
12 rooms. Wireless Internet access. $$

APPLE ORCHARD INN
656 Jordan Road, Sedona, 928-282-5328, 800-663-6968; www.appleorchardbb.com
Personal service awaits guests at this inn with a charming Southwestern atmosphere. It has easily accessible hiking trails with views of Wilson Mountain and Steamboat Rock. Seven rooms. Children over 16 years only. Complimentary full breakfast. Pool. Spa. $$

CANYON VILLA INN OF SEDONA
40 Canyon Circle Drive, Sedona, 928-284-1226, 800-453-1166; www.canyonvilla.com
Charming and intimate, this inn offers views of Sedona's renowned red rock formations. Nearly all of the guest rooms frame unparalleled vistas, with French doors opening onto private patios or decks for even better viewing. Rooms features four-poster beds and floral patterns. 11 rooms. Children over 11 years only. Complimentary full breakfast. Pool. $$$

CASA SEDONA BED AND BREAKFAST

55 Hozoni Drive, Sedona, 928-282-2938, 800-525-3756; www.casasedona.com
16 rooms. Children over 12 years only. Complimentary full breakfast. **$$$**

THE INN ON OAK CREEK

556 Highway 179, Sedona, 928-282-7896, 800-499-7896; www.innonoakcreek.com
This exquisite inn was formerly an art gallery. Family designed and built, it sits on
Oak Creek, near reservations and fantastic shopping. A professional cooking staff
prepares different breakfasts and hors d'oeuvres daily. 11 rooms. Wireless Internet
access. Children over 10 years only. Complimentary full breakfast. Whirlpool. **$$$**

THE LODGE AT SEDONA

125 Kallof Place, Sedona, 928-204-1942, 800-619-4467; www.lodgeatsedona.com
This lodge is situated on 2½ wooded acres with rustic timber and red sandstone décor.
A labyrinth of rocks on a clearing of red earth creates a quiet place to meditate. 14 rooms.
Complimentary full breakfast. Pets accepted. Business center. Fitness center. Pool.
High-speed Internet access. **$$$**

RESTAURANTS

★★COWBOY CLUB

241 N. Highway 89A, Sedona, 928-282-4200; www.cowboyclub.com
American menu. Lunch, dinner. Bar. Children's menu. Casual attire. Reservations
recommended. **$$$**

★★★HEARTLINE CAFÉ

1610 W. Highway 89A, Sedona, 928-282-0785; www.heartlinecafe.com
This intimate, cozy restaurant in a cottage is surrounded by an English garden and
showcases unique daily specials. The menu is creative, with a variety of culinary
influences and vegetarian options. Dishes include smoked mozzarella ravioli and
pistachio-crusted chicken breasts with pomegranate sauce. International menu.
Lunch, dinner. Closed Tuesday in summer. Bar. Casual attire. Reservations recom-
mended. Outdoor seating. **$$$**

★★★L'AUBERGE

301 L'Auberge, Sedona, 928-282-1661; www.lauberge.com
Several separate dining rooms are decorated with imported fabrics, fine china and
walls of green or mocha. A covered porch with large windows offers views of the
creek, and an outdoor patio area is a relaxing choice in good weather. Dine on roasted
pheasant with tomato polenta or silver snapper with coconut bamboo rice. California
menu. Breakfast, lunch, dinner, Sunday brunch. Bar. Business casual attire. Reserva-
tions recommended. Outdoor seating. **$$$**

★★★RENÉ AT TLAQUEPAQUE

336 Highway 179, Sedona, 928-282-9225; www.rene-sedona.com
Located in the Tlaquepaque shopping area, this local favorite has been a mainstay in Sedona since 1977. The menu is varied, offering selections such as tenderloin of venison, grilled ahi tuna salad, sweet potato ravioli and the signature dish,
Colorado rack of lamb. Dine in one of two separate dining areas, where tables are

ARIZONA

★
★
★
★
★

topped with green and white tablecloths and flower-filled vases. Friday and Saturday entertainment includes the sounds of guitar, piano, saxophone and Native American flutes. French menu. Lunch, dinner. Bar. Children's menu. Casual attire. Reservations recommended. Outdoor seating. **$$$**

★★★SHUGRUE'S HILLSIDE GRILL
671 Highway 179, Sedona, 928-282-5300; www.shugrues.com
Great views of the Red Rocks can be seen from the large windows of this modernized, Old World restaurant. Flame-broiled shrimp scampi, whiskey-barbecued duck and herb-grilled rib-eye are among the specialty dishes. Light jazz entertainment is offered nightly, with a pianist and guitarist performing on alternate nights. A nice outdoor seating area offers guests a picturesque dining experience. American menu. Lunch, dinner. Bar. Children's menu. Casual attire. Reservations recommended. Outdoor seating. **$$**

SELIGMAN
Arizona's historic Route 66 begins here, and the tiny town (population about 450) has more Route 66 kitsch than you can imagine. Stop by on your way to the Grand Canyon (about two hours north of here) for a taste of Americana.
Information: Chamber of Commerce, 217 W. Chino Ave., 928-422-3939;
www.seligmanarizona.org

WHAT TO SEE AND DO
GRAND CANYON CAVERNS
Old Route 66, Peach Springs, 928-422-3223; www.gccaverns.com
This natural limestone cavern is 210 feet underground and is the largest dry cavern in the U.S. Take an elevator down (the temperature is around 55 degrees, so bring a sweater). 50-minute guided tours. A 48-room motel is located at the entrance. Restaurant. Summer, daily 9 a.m.-5 p.m.; winter, daily 10 a.m.-5 p.m.

SIERRA VISTA
About 75 miles southeast of Tucson, Sierra Vista is surrounded by mountains—appropriate for a city whose name means "mountain view" in Spanish.
Information: Chamber of Commerce, 21 E. Wilcox, 520-458-6940;
www.sierravistachamber.org

WHAT TO SEE AND DO
CORONADO NATIONAL FOREST
300 W. Congress St., Sierra Vista, 520-388-8300; www.fs.fed.us/r3/coronado
One of the larger sections of the forest lies to the south and west of Fort Huachuca Military Reservation. Picnicking, camping.

CORONADO NATIONAL MEMORIAL
4101 E. Montezuma Canyon Road, Hereford, 520-366-5515; www.nps.gov/coro
Commemorates Francisco Vázquez de Coronado's expedition from 1540 through 1542, when hundreds of soldiers came in search of gold and brought rich Spanish traditions into the area. Daily 8 a.m.-5 p.m.

FORT HUACHUCA

Highway 90, Sierra Vista, 520-538-7111; huachuca-www.army.mil

Founded by the U.S. Army in 1877 to protect settlers and travelers from hostile Apache raids, the fort is now the home of the U.S. Army Intelligence Center, the Information Systems Command and the Electronic Proving Ground. A historical museum is on the "Old Post," Boyd and Grierson avenues (Monday-Friday 9 a.m.-4 p.m., Saturday-Sunday 1-4 p.m.). The historic Old Post area (1885-1895) is typical of frontier post construction and is home to the post's ceremonial cavalry unit; open to public. Directions and visitor's pass at main gate, just west of Sierra Vista. Bronze statue of buffalo soldier.

SPECIALTY LODGING
RAMSEY CANYON INN

29 E. Ramsey Canyon Road, Hereford, 520-378-3010; www.ramseycanyoninn.com

Nine rooms. Children under 16 years cottages only. Complimentary full breakfast. **$$**

RESTAURANT
★★MESQUITE TREE

Highway 92 South and Carr Canyon Road, Sierra Vista, 520-378-2758;
www.mesquitetreerestaurant.com

American, Steak menu. Dinner. Closed Monday. Bar. Children's menu. Outdoor seating. **$$**

TEMPE

Founded as a trading post by the father of former Senator Carl Hayden, this city is now the site of Arizona State University, the state's oldest institution of higher learning.

Information: Chamber of Commerce, 909 E. Apache Blvd., Tempe, 480-967-7891;
www.tempecvb.com

WHAT TO SEE AND DO
ARIZONA HISTORICAL SOCIETY MUSEUM

Papago Park, 1300 N. College Ave., Tempe, 480-929-0292;
www.arizonahistoricalsociety.org

Wander through this regional museum to learn more about 20th-century life in the Salt River Valley. The 28,000 items in its collection include about 14,000 pieces in a country store and 2,800 stage props and sets from the 37-year run of the *Wallace and Ladmo* Show on KPHO Television. Another exhibit focuses on the many ways World War II transformed Arizona. Admission: adults $3, seniors $2, children $2, children under 12 free. Tuesday-Saturday 10 a.m.-4 p.m., Sunday noon-4 p.m.

ARIZONA MILLS

5000 S. Arizona Mills Circle, Tempe, 480-491-7300; www.arizonamills.com

More than 150 stores offer tempting markdowns. Shopping diversions include a large food court, five restaurants, a 24-screen cinema and an IMAX theater. Daily.

ARIZONA STATE UNIVERSITY

University Drive, and Mill Avenue, Tempe, 480-965-9011; www.asu.edu

Established in 1885; 52,000 students. Divided into 13 colleges. Included on the 700-acre main campus are several museums and collections: meteorites; anthropology and geology exhibits; the Charles Trumbull Hayden Library; the Walter Cronkite School of Journalism; and the Daniel Noble Science and Engineering Library. Also on campus is the Grady Gammage Memorial Auditorium, the last major work designed by Frank Lloyd Wright, and the Nelson Fine Arts Center, which features exhibits of American paintings and sculpture.

BIG SURF

1500 N. McClintock, Tempe, 480-947-2477; www.golfland.com
Check out America's original water park, a 20-acre desert oasis with a Polynesian theme. Ride some big ones in the wave pool, whoosh down 16 slippery water slides and more. June-mid-August, daily; late May and mid-late August, weekends; closed rest of year.

NIELS PETERSEN HOUSE MUSEUM

1414 W. Southern Ave., Tempe, 480-350-5151; www.tempe.gov/petersenhouse
Built in 1892 and remodeled in the 1930s. Restoration retains characteristics of both the Victorian era and the 1930s. Half-hour, docent-guided tours available. Tuesday-Thursday, Saturday 10 a.m.-2 p.m.

PHOENIX ROCK GYM

1353 E. University, Tempe, 480-921-8322; www.phoenixrockgym.com
Scale 30-foot walls at Arizona's largest climbing gym. Beginners receive brief video training and a hands-on orientation. Gear is available to rent. Daily.

TEMPE BICYCLE PROGRAM

Tempe, 480-350-2775; www.tempe.gov/tim
This bicycle-friendly city has more than 165 miles of bikeways and most major destinations provide bicycle racks (including some particularly eye-catching ones designed by local artists). City buses are also equipped with racks. Several bicycle shops offer rentals for as little as $15 per day and give free bikeway maps.

TEMPE HISTORICAL MUSEUM

809 E. Southern Ave., Tempe, 480-350-5100; www.tempe.gov/museum
Exhibits relate the history of Tempe from the prehistoric Hohokam to the present, with artifacts, videos and interactive exhibits. Monday-Thursday, Saturday 10 a.m.-5 p.m., Sunday 1-5 p.m.; closed Friday.

TEMPE IMPROVISATION COMEDY THEATRE

930 E. University Drive, Tempe, 480-921-9877; www.symfonee.com/improv/tempe
Check out some of the country's best stand-up comedians. An optional dinner precedes the 8 p.m. shows. Thursday-Sunday.

TEMPE TOWN LAKE

620 N. Mill Ave., Tempe, 480-350-8625; www.tempe.gov/lake
Tempe Town Lake on the Rio Salado, near the Mill Avenue shopping and dining district, is a 224-acre, two-mile waterway that offers rowboats, pedal boats, kayaks and canoes for rent, along with chartered cruises. The nicely renovated 1931 Tempe Beach Park has shaded picnic groves, sandy play areas, a grassy amphitheater and the

popular Splash Playground water park (late April-late September). Take the tour, or simply enjoy the shoreline.

SPECIAL EVENTS

ANAHEIM ANGELS SPRING TRAINING

Tempe Diablo Stadium, 2200 W. Alameda Drive, Tempe, 602-438-9300;
www.cactus-league.com/angels.html

Anaheim Angels baseball spring training, exhibition games. Early March-early April.

TEMPE FESTIVAL OF THE ARTS

Tempe, 480-355-6069; www.tempefestivalofthearts.com

When a three-day event attracts nearly a quarter-million people, you know you need to get there. This street party is a blast—Mill Avenue in downtown Tempe closes to traffic. Buy handmade goods from more than 500 artisans, chow down on tasty food from around the world, quench your thirst with ice-cold beer and rock to live bands. Activities for kids include arts and crafts. It's so fun the party gets crankin' twice a year. Late March and early December.

TOSTITOS FIESTA BOWL

University of Phoenix Stadium, Cardinals Drive, Glendale, 480-350-0911;
www.tostitosfiestabowl.com

College football game. Early January.

TOSTITOS FIESTA BOWL BLOCK PARTY

Tempe Beach Park and Mill Avenue, Tempe, 480-350-0911;
www.tostitosfiestabowl.com

Includes games, rides, entertainment, pep rally, fireworks, food. December 31.

HOTELS

★★★THE BUTTES, A MARRIOTT RESORT

2000 Westcourt Way, Tempe, 602-225-9000, 888-867-7492; www.marriott.com/phxtm

This secluded resort sits atop a bluff overlooking Phoenix and the surrounding mountains. Take a dip in the pool or enjoy one of the four hot tubs carved out of the mountainside, relax in the spa, play some sand volleyball or horseshoes, or get in a game of tennis on the resort's eight courts. The Top of the Rock restaurant is a great spot for dining. This hotel is nonsmoking. 353 rooms. Wireless Internet access. Three restaurants, three bars. Spa. Airport transportation available. **$$**

★COUNTRY INN & SUITES

1660 W. Elliot Road, Tempe, 480-345-8585, 888-201-1746; www.countryinns.com

138 rooms. Complimentary full breakfast. High-speed Internet access. Airport transportation available. Pets accepted. **$**

★★EMBASSY SUITES

4400 S. Rural Road, Tempe, 480-897-7444, 800-362-2779;
www.embassysuitestempe.com

224 rooms, all suites. Complimentary full breakfast. Wireless Internet access. Restaurant, bar. Children's activity center. Airport transportation available. Pool. **$**

ARIZONA

★
★
★
★
☆

★★FIESTA INN RESORT

2100 S. Priest Drive, Tempe, 480-967-1441, 800-501-7590; www.fiestainnresort.com

270 rooms. Wireless Internet access. Restaurant, bar. Airport transportation available. Fitness center. **$**

★HOLIDAY INN EXPRESS

1520 W. Baseline Road, Tempe, 480-831-9800, 800-972-3574; www.hiexpress.com/tempeaz

128 rooms. Complimentary continental breakfast. High-speed Internet access. Airport transportation available. Pets accepted. Pool. **$**

★★SHERATON PHOENIX AIRPORT HOTEL TEMPE

1600 S. 52nd St., Tempe, 480-967-6600, 800-325-3535; www.sheraton.com/phoenixairport

210 rooms. Wireless Internet access. Restaurant, bar. Airport transportation available. Pets accepted. Pool. Business center. Fitness center. **$**

★★TEMPE MISSION PALMS HOTEL

60 E. Fifth St., Tempe, 480-894-1400, 800-547-8705; www.missionpalms.com

303 rooms. High-speed Internet access. Restaurant, bar. Airport transportation available. Fitness center. Pool. Pets accepted. **$$**

RESTAURANTS

★BLUE NILE ETHIOPIAN CUISINE

933 E. University Drive, Tempe, 480-377-1113

Ethiopian/African menu. Lunch, dinner. Closed Monday. Casual attire. Reservations recommended. **$**

★★BYBLOS

3332 S. Mill Ave., Tempe, 480-894-1945; www.amdest.com/az/tempe/br/byblos.html

Mediterranean menu. Lunch, dinner. Closed Monday. Bar. Casual attire. **$$**

★★HOUSE OF TRICKS

114 E. Seventh St., Tempe, 480-968-1114; www.houseoftricks.com

American menu. Lunch, dinner. Closed Sunday; also the last two weeks in July. Bar. Children's menu. Casual attire. Outdoor seating. **$$**

★MACAYO DEPOT CANTINA

300 S. Ash Ave., Tempe, 480-966-6677; www.macayo.com

Mexican menu. Lunch, dinner, late-night. Bar. Children's menu. Casual attire. Outdoor seating. **$**

★★MARCELLO'S PASTA GRILL

1701 E. Warner Road, Tempe, 480-831-0800; www.marcellospastagrill.com

Italian menu. Lunch, dinner. Closed Sunday. Bar. Children's menu. Casual attire. Outdoor seating. **$$**

★
★
★
★
★

★★MICHAEL MONTI'S LA CASA VIEJA

100 S. Mill Ave., Tempe, 480-967-7594; www.montis.com
American menu. Lunch, dinner. Bar. Children's menu. Casual attire. Outdoor seating. **$$**

★SIAMESE CAT

5034 S. Price Road, Tempe, 480-820-0406; www.thesiamesecat.com
Thai menu. Lunch, dinner. Casual attire. Reservations recommended. **$$**

TOMBSTONE

Shortly after Ed Schieffelin discovered silver, Tombstone became a rough-and-tumble town with saloons, bawdy houses and lots of gunfighting. Tombstone's most famous battle was that of the O.K. Corral, between the Earps and the Clantons in 1881. Later, water rose in the mines and could not be pumped out. Fires and other catastrophes occurred, but Tombstone was "the town too tough to die." Now a health and winter resort, it is also a living museum of Arizona frontier life. In 1962, the town was designated a National Historic Landmark.

Information: Tombstone Chamber of Commerce, Tombstone, 888-457-3929;
www.tombstone.org

GUNFIGHTS AND SALOONS

Begin exploring the town on Toughnut Street. At the corner of Third Street, explore the gorgeous Cochise County Courthouse, now a museum and state historic park. Built in 1882, it's a beautiful example of Victorian Neoclassical architecture. Check out the town gallows in the courtyard and browse the bookshop. To the east one block, the Rose Tree Inn Museum at Fourth and Toughnut streets occupies a 1880s home. Inside its courtyard is a century-old rose tree that blooms every April and covers an 8,000-square-foot space. At Fifth and Toughnut streets, stop in to Nellie Cashman's, the oldest restaurant in town (homemade pies are the specialty here).

Follow Third Street north one block to Allen Street, essentially the main drag of historic Tombstone. Stop at the Historama and then next door, see life-size figures in the O.K. Corral, the alleged site of the legendary gunfight between the Earp and Clanton brothers and Doc Holliday.

On the corner of Allen and Fifth streets, the Crystal Palace Saloon has been restored to its 1879 glory, looking every bit the lusty watering hole and gambling den of legend. On the block of Allen between Fifth and Sixth streets, the Prickly Pear Museum is chock-full of military history; on Allen at Sixth, find the famous old Bird Cage Theater Museum. The Pioneer Home Museum, between Eighth and Ninth streets, continues telling the rowdy-days story. From Fifth and Allen, walk north a half-block to the Tombstone Epitaph Museum to see a 1880s printing press and newsroom equipment and buy a copy of the 1881 *Epitaph* report of the O.K. Corral shoot-out.

ARIZONA

★
★
★
★

WHAT TO SEE AND DO
ARIZONA-SONORA DESERT MUSEUM
2021 N. Kinney Road, Tucson, 520-883-2702; www.desertmuseum.org
Live desert creatures: mountain lions, beavers, bighorn sheep, birds, tarantulas, prairie dogs, snakes, otters and many others. Nature trails through labeled desert botanical gardens. Underground earth sciences center with limestone caves; geological, mineral and mining exhibits. Orientation room provides information on natural history of deserts. Admission: adults $9.50-13, children $2.25-4.25, children under 6 free. June-August 7:30 a.m.-10 p.m.; March-May, September: 7:30 a.m.-5 p.m.; October-February: 8:30 a.m.-5 p.m.

BIRD CAGE THEATRE
517 E. Allen St., Tombstone, 520-457-3421, 800-457-3423; www.tombstoneaz.net
Formerly a frontier cabaret (1880s), this landmark was known in its heyday as "the wildest and wickedest nightspot between Basin Street and the Barbary Coast." The upstairs "cages" where feathered girls plied their trade, inspired the song "Only a bird in a gilded cage." Original fixtures and furnishings. Daily 8 a.m.-6 p.m.

BOOTHILL GRAVEYARD
Highway 80, Tombstone, 520-457-3300
About 250 marked graves, many of famous characters, with some unusual epitaphs.

CRYSTAL PALACE SALOON
420 Allen St., Tombstone, 520-457-3611; www.crystalpalacesaloon.com
Restored. Dancing Friday-Sunday evenings. Daily.

O.K. CORRAL
308 Allen St. East, Tombstone, 520-457-3456; www.ok-corral.com
Restored stagecoach office and buildings surrounding the gunfight site; life-size figures; Fly's Photography Gallery (adjacent) has early photos. Daily 9 a.m.-5 p.m.

ROSE TREE INN MUSEUM
118 S. Fourth St., Tombstone, 520-457-3326
Largest rose bush in the world, spreading more than 8,000 square feet; blooms in April. The museum is housed in an 1880 boarding house (the oldest house in town); original furniture, documents. Daily 9 a.m.-5 p.m.

ST. PAUL'S EPISCOPAL CHURCH
19 N. Third St., Tombstone, 520-255-3435; www.1882.org
Oldest Protestant church still in use in the state, built in 1882; original fixtures. Services 10:30 a.m. every Sunday.

TOMBSTONE COURTHOUSE STATE HISTORIC PARK
223 Toughnut St., Tombstone, 520-457-3311;
www.pr.state.az.us/parks/parkhtml/tombstone.html
Victorian building (1882) houses exhibits that recall Tombstone in the turbulent 1880s. Tombstone and Cochise County history. Daily 8 a.m.-5 p.m.

TOMBSTONE EPITAPH MUSEUM

9 S. Fifth St., Tombstone, 520-457-2211; www.tombstone-epitaph.com

The oldest continuously published newspaper in Arizona, founded in 1880; it is now a monthly journal of Western history. Office houses a collection of early printing equipment. Daily 9:30 a.m.-5 p.m.

TOMBSTONE HISTORAMA

308 Allen St. East, Tombstone, 520-457-3456; www.ok-corral.com

A film narrated by Vincent Price tells the story of Tombstone. Daily 9:30 a.m.-4:30 p.m.; half-hourly showings.

TOMBSTONE WESTERN HERITAGE MUSEUM

Sixth St., and Fremont, Tombstone, 520-457-3800; www.thetombstonemuseum.com

This new museum has a great collection of Wyatt Earp memorabilia along with lots of Old West artifacts and cowboy photos. Admission: adults $5, children $3, children under 12 free, family $13. Thursday-Tuesday 9 a.m.-6 p.m.

SPECIAL EVENTS

HELLDORADO

Tombstone, 520-457-3291; www.tombstonevigilantes.com

Three days of Old West reenactments of Tombstone events of the 1880s. Third full weekend in October.

TERRITORIAL DAYS

Fourth and Fremont streets, Tombstone, 520-457-9317, 888-457-3929; www.tombstone.org

Commemorates formal founding of the town. Fire-hose cart races and other events typical of a celebration in Arizona's early days. Second weekend in March.

WILD WEST DAYS AND RENDEZVOUS OF GUNFIGHTERS

O.K. Corral, 308 Allen St. East, Tombstone, 520-457-9465; www.ok-corral.com

This annual event showcases different gunfight reenactment groups from throughout the United States. Activities include costume contests and a parade. Labor Day weekend.

WYATT EARP DAYS

O.K. Corral, 108 W. Allen St. East, Tombstone, 520-457-3434; www.tombstonevigilantes.com

This annual festival is held in honor of the famous lawman. The festivities include a barbecue, gunfights, street entertainment, dances, a chili cook-off and more. Memorial Day weekend.

RESTAURANTS

★LONGHORN

501 E. Allen St., Tombstone, 520-457-3107; www.bignosekate.com

American menu. Breakfast, lunch, dinner. Casual attire. $

117 S. Fifth St., Tombstone, 520-457-2212; www.nelliecashman.freeservers.com
American menu. Breakfast, lunch, dinner. Casual attire. Outdoor seating. **$$**

TUCSON

Tucson offers a rare combination of delightful Western living, colorful desert and mountain scenery and cosmopolitan culture. It is one of several U.S. cities that developed under four flags. The Spanish standard flew first over the Presidio of Tucson, built to withstand Apache attacks in 1776. Later, Tucson flew the flags of Mexico, the Confederate States and finally, the United States. Today, Tucson is a resort area, an educational and copper center, a cotton and cattle market, headquarters for the Coronado National Forest and a place of business for several large industries. The city has many shops, restaurants, resorts and attractions.

Information: Metropolitan Tucson Convention & Visitors Bureau, 100 S. Church Ave., Tucson, 520-624-1817, 800-638-8350; www.visittucson.org

88

ARIZONA

★
★★
★★★
★★★★

SAGUARO NATIONAL PARK

The saguaro cactus that gives this park its name may grow as high as 50 feet and live to be 200 years old. The fluted columns with sharp, tough needles sometimes branch into fantastic shapes. During the rainy season, large saguaros can absorb enough water to sustain themselves during the dry season.

The saguaro's waxy, white blossoms (Arizona's state flower), which open at night and close the following afternoon, bloom in May and June, and the red fruit ripens in July. The Tohono O'Odham people eat this fruit fresh and used it to make jellies, jams and wines.

Wildlife in the park is abundant. Gila woodpeckers and gilded flickers drill nest holes in the saguaro trunks. Once vacated, these holes become home to many other species of birds, including the tiny elf owl. Peccaries (pig-like mammals), coyotes, mule deer and other animals are often seen. Yuccas, agaves, prickly pears, mesquite, paloverde trees and many other desert plants grow here.

The Rincon Mountain District offers nature trails, guided nature walks (winter), eight-mile self-guided drive, mountain hiking, bridle trails, picnicking (no water) and backcountry camping. Stop by the visitor center to check out the museum and see an orientation film.

The Tucson Mountain District offers nature trails, a six-mile self-guided drive, and hiking and bridle trails. Five picnic areas (no water). Visitor center; exhibits, slide program daily.

Information: Rincon Mountain District, 17 miles east of Tucson via Broadway and Old Spanish Trail; Tucson Mountain District, 16 miles west of Tucson via Speedway and Gates Pass Road, 520-733-5153; www.nps.gov/sagu

WHAT TO SEE AND DO
ARIZONA HISTORICAL SOCIETY FORT LOWELL MUSEUM
2900 N. Craycroft Road, Tucson, 520-885-3832; www.arizonahistoricalsociety.org
Reconstruction of commanding officer's quarters. Exhibits, period furniture. Admission: adults $3, seniors $2, children $2, children under 12 free.Wednesday-Saturday 10 a.m.-4 p.m.

ARIZONA HISTORICAL SOCIETY FREMONT HOUSE MUSEUM
151 S. Granada Ave., Tucson, 520-622-0956; www.arizonahistoricalsociety.org
This 19th-century adobe house, once occupied by John C. Fremont's daughter, Elizabeth, when he was territorial governor (1878-1881), has been restored. Special programs all year, including slide shows on Arizona history (Saturday) and walking tours of historic sites (November-March, Saturday; registration in advance). Admission: adults $3, seniors $2, children $2, children under 12 free. Wednesday-Saturday 10 a.m.-4 p.m.

ARIZONA HISTORICAL SOCIETY MUSEUM, LIBRARY, AND ARCHIVES
949 E. Second St., Tucson, 520-628-5774; www.arizonahistoricalsociety.org
Exhibits depicting state history from the Spanish colonial period to present; Arizona mining hall; photography gallery. Admission: adults $5, seniors $4, children $4, children under 12 free. Research library Monday-Friday 10 a.m.-3 p.m., Saturday 10 a.m.-1 p.m.

BIOSPHERE 2
32540 Biosphere Road, Oracle, 520-838-6200; www.bio2.com
An ambitious attempt to learn more about our planet's ecosystems began in September 1991 with the first in a series of missions undertaken inside this 3½-acre, glass-enclosed, self-sustaining model of Earth. (The crew of researchers rely entirely on the air, water and food generated and recycled within the structure.) It contains more than 3,500 species of plants and animals in multiple ecosystems, including a tropical rain forest with an 85-foot-high mountain. Visitors are permitted within the biospherian living areas of the enclosure. Because of variance in research schedule, the biospherian crew may not always be present. Walking tours include multimedia introduction to Biosphere 2. Daily 9 a.m.-4 p.m.

CATALINA STATE PARK
11570 N. Oracle Road, Tucson, 520-628-5798; azstateparks.com/parks/cata/index.html
A 5,500-acre desert park with a vast array of plants and wildlife; bird area (nearly 170 species). Nature and horseback riding trails, hiking, trail access to adjacent Coronado National Forest.

CENTER FOR CREATIVE PHOTOGRAPHY
University of Arizona, 1030 N. Olive Road, Tucson, 520-621-7968;
www.creativephotography.org
This collection of art by more than 2,000 photographers includes the archives of Ansel Adams and Richard Avedon. Gallery: Monday-Friday 9 a.m.-5 p.m., Saturday-Sunday noon-5 p.m.

ARIZONA

★
★
★
★
★

CORONADO NATIONAL FOREST

300 W. Congress St., Tucson, 520-388-8300; www.fs.fed.us/r3/coronado

Mount Lemmon Recreation Area, part of this two-million-acre forest, offers fishing, bird-watching, hiking, horseback riding, picnicking, skiing and camping. Madera Canyon offers recreation facilities and a lodge. Pea Blanca Lake and Recreation Area and the Chiricahua Wilderness area in the southeast corner of the state are part of the 12 areas that make up the forest. The Santa Catalina Ranger District, located in Tucson (520-749-8700), has its headquarters at Sabino Canyon, 12 miles northeast on Sabino Canyon Road; a ¼-mile nature trail begins at the headquarters, as does a shuttle ride almost four miles into Sabino Canyon.

FLANDRAU SCIENCE CENTER & PLANETARIUM

University of Arizona, 1601 E. University Blvd., Tucson, 520-621-7827;
www.gotuasciencecenter.org

Interactive, hands-on science exhibits. Monday-Wednesday 9 a.m.-5 p.m.; Thursday-Saturday 9 a.m.-5 p.m., 7-9 p.m.; Sunday 1-5 p.m.; planetarium shows (limited hours). Nightly telescope viewing: Mid-August-mid-May, Wednesday-Saturday 6:40-10 p.m.; mid-May-mid-August, Wednesday-Saturday 7:30-10 p.m.

INTERNATIONAL WILDLIFE MUSEUM

4800 W. Gates Pass Road, Tucson, 520-629-0100; www.thewildlifemuseum.org

Includes hundreds of wildlife exhibits from around the world; hands-on, interactive computer displays; videos; café. Monday-Friday 9 a.m.-5 p.m., Saturday-Sunday 9 a.m.-6 p.m.

★
★
★
★
★

MOUNT LEMMON SKI VALLEY

10300 Ski Run Road, Mount Lemmon, 520-576-1400; www.fs.fed.us/r3/coronado

Double chairlift, two tows; patrol, school, rentals; snack bar, restaurant. Twenty-one runs, longest run one mile; vertical drop 900 feet. Late December-mid-April, daily. Chairlift operates the rest of the year. Nature trails.

OLD TOWN ARTISANS

201 N. Court Ave., Tucson, 520-623-6024, 800-782-8072; www.oldtownartisans.com

Restored adobe buildings (circa 1850s) in the historic El Presidio neighborhood serve as shops for handcrafted Southwestern and Latin American art. September-May, Monday-Saturday 9:30 a.m.-5:30 p.m., Sunday 11 a.m.-5 p.m.; June-August, Monday-Saturday 10 a.m.-4 p.m., Sunday 11 a.m.-4 p.m.

PIMA AIR & SPACE MUSEUM

6000 E. Valencia Road, Tucson, 520-574-0462; www.pimaair.org

Aviation history exhibits with an outstanding collection of more than 250 aircraft, both military and civilian. Walking tours. Admission: adults $14-16, children $12-13, children under 7 free. Daily 9 a.m.-5 p.m.

REID PARK ZOO

1030 S. Randolph Way, Tucson, 520-881-4753; www.tucsonzoo.org

Picnicking; zoo; rose garden; outdoor performance center. Admission: adults $6, seniors $4, $2, children under 2 free. Daily 9 a.m.-4 p.m.

TITAN MISSILE MUSEUM

1580 W. Duval Mine Road, Sahuarita, 520-625-7736; www.titanmissilemuseum.org

Deactivated Titan II missile on display; UH1F helicopter; other exhibits. A one-hour guided tour begins with a briefing and includes a visit down into the missile silo. The silo may also be viewed from a glass observation area located at the museum level. Daily 9 a.m.-5 p.m.

TOHONO CHUL PARK

7366 N. Paseo del Norte, Tucson, 520-742-6455; www.tohonochulpark.org

A 37-acre preserve with more than 400 species of arid climate plants; nature trails; demonstration garden; geology wall; ethnobotanical garden. Many varieties of wild birds visit the park. Exhibits, galleries, tearoom and gift shops in restored adobe house. Walking tours. Admission: adults $7, seniors $5, children $2, children under 5 free. Daily 8 a.m.-5 p.m.

TUCSON BOTANICAL GARDENS

2150 N. Alvernon Way, Tucson, 520-326-9686; www.tucsonbotanical.org

Gardens include Mediterranean and landscaping plants; native wildflowers; tropical greenhouse; xeriscape/solar demonstration garden. Tours, special events. Picnic area. Daily 8:30 a.m.-4:30 p.m.

TUCSON MOUNTAIN PARK

Ajo Way & Kinney Road, Tucson, 520-883-4200; www.co.pima.az.us

Includes more than 18,000 acres of saguaro cactus and mountain scenery. Picnic facilities.

91

TUCSON MUSEUM OF ART

140 N. Main Ave., Tucson, 520-624-2333; www.tucsonarts.com

Housed in six renovated buildings within the boundaries of El Presidio Historic District (circa 1800). Pre-Columbian, Spanish Colonial and Western artifacts; decorative arts and paintings; art of the Americas; contemporary art and crafts; changing exhibits. Mexican heritage museum; historic presidio room; 6,000-volume art resource library; art school. Tuesday-Saturday 10 a.m.-4 p.m., Sunday noon-4 p.m. Free admission first Sunday of the month.

UNIVERSITY OF ARIZONA

Campbell Avenue and Sixth Street, Tucson, 520-621-5130; www.arizona.edu

Established in 1885; 35,000 students. The 343-acre campus is beautifully landscaped and has handsome buildings. The visitor center, located at University Boulevard and Cherry Avenue, has campus maps and information on attractions and activities. Tours Monday-Saturday.

SPECIAL EVENTS
ARIZONA OPERA

3501 Mountain Ave., Tucson, 520-293-4336; www.azopera.com

Five operas are produced each season. October-March, Friday-Sunday.

ARIZONA THEATRE COMPANY

The Temple of Music and Art, 330 S. Scott Ave., Tucson, 520-622-2823;
www.aztheatreco.org

The State Theatre of Arizona performs both classic and contemporary works. Evening performances Tuesday-Sunday; matinees Wednesday, Saturday-Sunday. September-May.

BASEBALL

Hi Corbett Field, Tucson Electric Park, 2500 E. Ajo Way, Tucson,
520-434-1000, 866-672-1343; www.cactus-league.com

Tucson Electric Park. Chicago White Sox and Arizona Diamondbacks baseball spring training, exhibition games; late February-late March. Also the home of the minor league Tucson Sidewinders; April-September.

CHRYSLER CLASSIC OF TUCSON

Omni Tucson National Golf Resort & Spa, 2727 W. Club Drive, Tucson,
520-571-0400; www.pgatour.com/tournaments/r001

This $3-million tournament features top pros. Late February-early March.

GEM & MINERAL SHOW

Tucson Convention Center, 260 S. Church Ave., Tucson,
520-322-5773, 800-638-8350; www.tgms.org

Displays of minerals; jewelry; lapidary skills; Smithsonian Institution collection. Mid-February.

TUCSON MEET YOURSELF FESTIVAL

El Presidio Park, Tucson, 520-792-4806; www.tucsonmeetyourself.org

Commemorates Tucson's cultural and historic heritage with a torchlight pageant, American Indian dances, children's parade, Mexican fiesta, frontier encampment and other events. October.

TUCSON SYMPHONY ORCHESTRA

Tucson Symphony Center, 2175 N. Sixth Ave., Tucson,
520-882-8585; www.tucsonsymphony.org

The symphony's eight-month season includes classic ensembles, performances by guest artists and special events such as BeatleMania! September-May.

HOTELS

★★★ARIZONA INN

2200 E. Elm St., Tucson, 520-325-1541, 800-933-1093; www.arizonainn.com

This inn was built in 1930 by Arizona Congresswoman Isabella Greenway and is still owned by her family today. Guests who stay here are treated to quiet comfort with spacious, individually decorated rooms and 15 acres of beautifully landscaped lawns and gardens. 95 rooms. Wireless Internet access. Restaurant, bar. Airport transportation available. Pool. Tennis. **$$**

★BEST WESTERN CONTINENTAL INN

8425 N. Cracker Barrel Road, Marana, 520-579-1099, 800-780-7234;
www.bestwestern.com
65 rooms. High-speed Internet access. Complimentary continental breakfast. Pool.
Spa. $

★★BEST WESTERN ROYAL SUN INN AND SUITES

1015 N. Stone Ave., Tucson, 866-293-9454; www.bwroyalsun.com
79 rooms. Complimentary full breakfast. Wireless Internet access. Restaurant, bar.
Airport transportation available. Pool. $

★COUNTRY INN & SUITES BY CARLSON

7411 N. Oracle Road, Tucson, 520-575-9255, 800-456-4000; www.countryinns.com
156 rooms. Complimentary continental breakfast. Airport transportation available.
Pets accepted. Pool. $

★★COURTYARD TUCSON AIRPORT

2505 E. Executive Drive, Tucson, 520-573-0000, 800-321-2211; www.courtyard.com
149 rooms. High-speed Internet access. Restaurant, bar. Airport transportation available. Pool. $

★★DOUBLETREE HOTEL

445 S. Alvernon Way, Tucson, 520-881-4200, 800-222-8733;
www.doubletreehotels.com
295 rooms. High-speed Internet access. Two restaurants, two bars. Airport transportation available. Pets accepted. Pool. Tennis. Fitness center. $

★★EMBASSY SUITES HOTEL TUCSON-WILLIAMS CENTER

5335 E. Broadway Blvd., Tucson, 520-745-2700, 800-362-2779;
www.embassysuites.com
142 rooms, all suites. Complimentary full breakfast. Wireless Internet access. Pool.
Fitness center. $

★HAMPTON INN

6971 S. Tucson Blvd., Tucson, 520-889-5789, 800-426-7866; www.hamptoninn.com
126 rooms. Complimentary continental breakfast. Wireless Internet access. Airport
transportation available. Pool. Fitness center. $

★★★HILTON TUCSON EL CONQUISTADOR GOLF AND TENNIS RESORT

10000 N. Oracle Road, Tucson, 520-544-5000, 800-325-7832;
www.hiltonelconquistador.com
This resort and country club lures visitors with its extensive golf and tennis facilities.
The resort offers 45 holes of golf on three championship courses. There are 16 lighted
tennis courts. Each of the newly remodeled rooms has a patio and balcony. The spa
offers a full range of treatments. 428 rooms. Wireless Internet access. Restaurant, bar.
Children's activity center. Spa. Airport transportation available. Pets accepted. Pool.
Golf. Tennis. Business center. $$

★★★LODGE AT VENTANA CANYON

6200 N. Clubhouse Lane, Tucson, 520-577-1400, 800-828-5701;
www.thelodgeatventanacanyon.com

Located in the foothills of the Santa Catalina Mountains on a 600-acre desert preserve, the Lodge is a peaceful getaway for tennis players, golfers and those in pursuit of nothing more than a day at the pool. Two 18-hole Tom Fazio-designed golf courses wind their way through the landscape of wild brush and giant saguaros, while the resort's tennis pro can help you master your serve on one of 12 hard courts. Rooms have Mission-style furniture, fully-stocked kitchens and old-fashioned freestanding bathtubs. 50 rooms. Restaurant, bar. Pets accepted. Pool. Spa. Fitness center. Golf. Tennis. **$$$$**

★★★LOEWS VENTANA CANYON RESORT

7000 N. Resort Drive, Tucson, 520-299-2020; www.loewshotels.com

Set on 93 acres in the Sonoran Desert, this resort just completed a multimillion dollar room renovation. The new décor offers modern comfort with a Southwestern twist. The two award-winning Tom Fazio-designed 18-hole golf courses challenge duffers. The Spa and Tennis Center offers a full range of treatments as well as a fitness center. Five restaurants and lounges give a taste of every kind of cuisine in a variety of settings, from poolside cafés to refined dining rooms. The Ventana Room delivers artfully presented, elegant cuisine. This intimate and romantic restaurant has floor-to-ceiling windows, which make it the perfect place to dine at sunset. 398 rooms. Pets accepted. Four restaurants, bars. Children's activity center. Fitness room, spa. Outdoor pool, whirlpool. Golf, 36 holes. Tennis. Business center. **$$$**

★★★MARRIOTT TUCSON UNIVERSITY PARK

880 E. Second St., Tucson, 520-792-4100; www.marriotttucson.com

This hotel is a good choice for those visiting the University of Arizona's campus. It's located right at the front gate and features rooms that are specifically designed for business travelers. This hotel is nonsmoking. 267 rooms. Restaurant, bar. Pool. Business center. High-speed Internet access. Fitness center. **$**

★★★OMNI TUCSON NATIONAL GOLF RESORT AND SPA

2727 W. Club Drive, Tucson, 520-297-2271, 888-444-6664; www.omnihotels.com

Located in the foothills of the Santa Catalina Mountains, the Omni Tucson National Golf Resort and Spa has been the home to countless PGA Tours. But there's more than just golf here. There are two pools, four tennis courts, sand volleyball, lots of biking trails and the spa, which boasts 13,000 pleasure-pursuing square feet. Sign up for the terzetto massage, where two therapists perform choreographed massage. The comfortable rooms have a Southwest décor and feature views of the course or mountains. Some rooms also have full kitchens, although most people leave the cooking up to the resort's talented chefs. 167 rooms. Restaurant, bar. Spa. Pets accepted. Pool. Golf. Tennis. Business center. High-speed Internet access. **$**

★★SHERATON TUCSON HOTEL AND SUITES

5151 E. Grant Road, Tucson, 520-323-6262, 800-325-3535; www.sheraton.com

216 rooms. Complimentary continental breakfast. Restaurant, bar. Pets accepted. Pool. High-speed Internet access. **$**

★★★THE WESTIN LA PALOMA RESORT AND SPA

3800 E. Sunrise Drive, Tucson, 520-742-6000, 800-937-8461;
www.westin.com/lapaloma

The large rooms here have warm, golden color schemes and feature patios or balconies and bathrooms with granite countertops and dual sinks. Golfers are drawn to the 27-hole Jack Nicklaus-designed course adjoining the resort. You'll also find tennis, three shimmering pools—one with a 177-foot waterslide—and the Elizabeth Arden Red Door Spa onsite, as well as five restaurants. 487 rooms. Five restaurants, bars. Children's activity center. Spa. Pets accepted. Golf. Tennis. Business center. **$$**

★★★WESTWARD LOOK RESORT

245 E. Ina Road, Tucson, 520-297-1151, 800-722-2500; www.westwardlook.com

The newly renovated Westward Look Resort combines top-notch facilities, gourmet dining and sumptuous spa treatments in a naturally beautiful setting. Set on 80 acres filled with giant cacti and blooming wildflowers, this resort is home to a variety of birds and wildlife. Enjoy horseback riding, onsite tennis, nearby golf—or just the peace and quiet. 244 rooms. Wireless Internet access. Two restaurants, bar. Spa. Airport transportation available. Pets accepted. Tennis. **$$$**

★WINDMILL SUITES AT ST., PHILLIPS PLAZA

4250 N. Campbell Ave., Tucson, 520-577-0007, 800-800-4747; www.windmillinns.com

122 rooms, all suites. Complimentary continental breakfast. Pets accepted. Pool. **$**

SPECIALTY LODGINGS

ADOBE ROSE INN BED AND BREAKFAST

940 N. Olsen Ave., Tucson, 520-318-4644, 800-328-4122; www.aroseinn.com

Seven rooms. Children over 10 years only. Complimentary full breakfast. Pool. Spa. **$**

CATALINA PARK INN

309 E. First St., Tucson, 520-792-4541, 800-792-4885; www.catalinaparkinn.com

Six rooms. Closed mid June-August. Children over 10 years only. Complimentary full breakfast. **$**

TANQUE VERDE GUEST RANCH

14301 E. Speedway Blvd., Tucson, 520-296-6275, 800-234-3833;
www.tanqueverderanch.com

74 rooms. Complimentary full breakfast. High-speed Internet access. Restaurant. Children's activity center. Airport transportation available. Pool. Tennis. Spa. **$$**

WHITE STALLION RANCH

9251 W. Twin Peaks Road, Tucson, 520-297-0252, 888-977-2624; www.wsranch.com

41 rooms. Closed June-August. Complimentary full breakfast. Restaurant, bar. Airport transportation available. Pool. Tennis. Spa. Fitness center. **$$$**

RESTAURANTS

★★CAFÉ POCA COSA

110 E. Pennington, Tucson, 520-622-6400; cafepocacosatucson.com

Mexican menu. Lunch, dinner. Closed Sunday-Monday; mid-July-mid-August. Bar. Casual attire. Reservations recommended. Outdoor seating. **$$**

★★CHAD'S STEAKHOUSE

3001 N. Swan Road, Tucson, 520-881-1802; www.chadssteakhouse.com
Steak menu. Lunch, dinner. Bar. Children's menu. Casual attire. Reservations recommended. **$$**

★DELECTABLES

533 N. Fourth Ave., Tucson, 520-884-9289; www.delectables.com
French bistro menu. Lunch, dinner. Bar. Children's menu. Casual attire. Reservations recommended. Outdoor seating. **$$**

★★EL PARADOR TUCSON

2744 E. Broadway Blvd., Tucson, 520-881-2744, 800-964-5908;
www.elparadortucson.com
Mexican menu. Lunch, dinner, late-night, Sunday brunch. Bar. Children's menu. Casual attire. Reservations recommended. Outdoor seating. **$$**

★★★THE GOLD ROOM

245 E. Ina Road, Tucson, 520-297-1151; www.westwardlook.com
Set at the base of the Catalina Mountains in north central Tucson, the Gold Room features both regional Southwestern fare and traditional American cuisine. Assorted chilies, beans, squash and other produce are cultivated in the chef's onsite garden and are blended into entrées like mesquite-grilled buffalo sirloin with chipotle maple glaze and mesquite-grilled lamb, ostrich and venison with green chile mashed potatoes. Wraparound windows afford spectacular views of the mountains, desert and city. A jazz brunch on Sundays features a weekly changing menu of inspired regional dishes like blue corn pancakes with prickly pear syrup and Sonoran Caesar salad with smoked duck. American menu. Breakfast, lunch, dinner, Sunday brunch. Children's menu. Casual attire. Reservations recommended. Valet parking. Outdoor seating. **$$$**

★★★THE GRILL AT HACIENDA DEL SOL

5601 N. Hacienda del Sol Road, Tucson, 520-299-1501; www.haciendadelsol.com
Rustic Spanish colonial architecture, fine pottery and Mexican art adorn this beautifully restored Tucson landmark. The New American cuisine is complemented by a spectacular wine list and excellent service. The creative menu, which includes dishes like roasted tomato and basil soup with garlic and chèvre croustade, makes this one of Tucson's favorite dining destinations. Jazz musicians perform every Thursday through Sunday. American menu. Dinner, Sunday brunch. Bar. Children's menu. Business casual attire. Reservations recommended. Valet parking. Outdoor seating. **$$$**

★★★JANOS RESTAURANT

3770 E. Sunrise Drive, Tucson, 520-615-6100; www.janos.com
The legendary Janos Wilder presides over this French-inspired Southwestern masterpiece located inside the Westin La Paloma Resort & Spa. The restaurant features both tasting and à la carte menus, which are constantly changing and are inspired by influences from around the world. The emphasis is on ingredients from the region, utilizing an established network of local farmers. The romantic setting features original artwork and views of the valley. Southwestern menu. Dinner. Closed Sunday. Bar. Business casual attire. Reservations recommended. Valet parking. Outdoor seating. **$$$**

ARIZONA

★
★
★
★

★★★KINGFISHER

2564 E. Grant, Tucson, 520-323-7739; www.kingfisherbarandgrill.com

The popular spot serves up dishes like pan-seared Atlantic salmon, spinach tagliatelle and barbecued chicken pasta. There's also a full oyster bar with 15 varieties of oysters. On Mondays and Saturdays, the sounds of jazz and blues can be heard until midnight. American menu. Lunch, dinner, late-night. Bar. Casual attire. Reservations recommended. $$

★★LA FUENTE

1749 N. Oracle Road, Tucson, 520-623-8659; www.lafuenterestaurant.com

Mexican menu. Lunch, dinner, brunch. Bar. Children's menu. Casual attire. Reservations recommended. $$

★★LA PARRILLA SUIZA

2720 N. Oracle Road, Tucson, 520-624-4300; www.laparrillasuiza.com

Mexican menu. Lunch, dinner. Bar. Children's menu. Casual attire. Reservations recommended. $

★LA PLACITA CAFÉ

2950 N. Swan Road, Tucson, 520-881-1150; laplacitatucson.com

Mexican menu. Lunch, dinner. Casual attire. Reservations recommended. Outdoor seating. $$

★★★MCMAHON'S PRIME STEAKHOUSE

2959 N. Swan Road, Tucson, 520-327-7463; www.metrorestaurants.com

This local favorite is a perfect spot for a romantic evening or that special occasion. Original local artwork adorns the walls and a pianist performs nightly. Entrées include filet mignon with Portobello mushrooms, garlic and aged Romano cheese, and New York sirloin with onions, mushrooms, garlic and cracked black pepper. Steak menu. Lunch, dinner. Bar. Children's menu. Business casual attire. Reservations recommended. Valet parking. Outdoor seating. $$$

★MI NIDITO

1813 S. Fourth Ave., Tucson, 520-622-5081

Mexican menu. Lunch, dinner. Closed Monday-Tuesday. Casual attire. $$

★PINNACLE PEAK

6541 E. Tanque Verde Road, Tucson, 520-296-0911; www.traildusttown.com

Steak menu. Dinner. Bar. Children's menu. Casual attire. Outdoor seating. $$

★SERI MELAKA

6133 E. Broadway, Tucson, 520-747-7811; www.serimelaka.com

Pacific-Rim, Malaysian menu. Lunch, dinner. Casual attire. Reservations recommended. $$

★TOHONO CHUL TEA ROOM

7366 N. Paseo del Norte, Tucson, 520-797-1222; www.tohonochulpark.org

American menu. Breakfast, lunch. Children's menu. Casual attire. Outdoor seating. $

★★★★THE VENTANA ROOM

7000 N. Resort Drive, Tucson, 520-615-5494; www.ventanaroom.com

Located in the Loews Ventana Canyon Resort, the Ventana Room is the place to go for panoramic views of the city lights and mountain ranges. The contemporary American cuisine features wild cuts of game, as well as lamb and seafood. A three-, four- or five-course prix fixe menu is offered, and there's a four-course Farmland Degustation, with dishes such as partridge with black truffle or Niman Ranch leg of lamb confit. Maitre'd Kevin Brady oversees the substantial wine list. A chef's table for six is available. French menu. Dinner. Closed Sunday-Monday; also mid-August-mid-September. Bar. Business casual attire. Reservations recommended. Valet parking. $$$$

★★★VINTABLA

2890 E. Skyline Dr., Tucson, 520-577-6210; www.vintabla.com

Come for the outstanding food and first-rate wine list, which received a 2008 *Wine Spectator* Award of Excellence. The food is the oeuvre of executive chef Bruce Yim, whose accomplished career has taken him from Ristorante Harry Cipriani in New York to Wolfgang Puck's Postrio in San Francisco with many notable stops in between, including Vail's Sweet Basil, among others. Here, his menu focuses on small plates (there are entrées for those who want them) that range from a pizzetta with prosciutto, marinated mozzarella, pesto, and onion jam to lamb tartare to shrimp and calamari with Thai chili sauce. Bargain hunters, listen up: The bar and lounge offers a choice of two sliders or shrimp and calamari appetizer with a glass of wine or beer for $10, and you may even be able to avoid contact with the unseasoned servers there. Contemporary American menu. Dinner. Bar. Business casual. $$

SPA

★★★★THE SPA AT OMNI TUCSON NATIONAL

2727 W. Club Drive, Tucson, 520-575-7559; www.tucsonnational.com

The Spa at Omni Tucson National has a tranquil and picturesque location in the foothills of the Santa Catalina Mountains. Whether you have half an hour or an entire day, this spa has something to offer. In 25 minutes, the tension reliever massage works its magic where you are most tense, while the business facial cleanses, tones, exfoliates and hydrates in just under 30 minutes. Other facials include aromatherapy, deep-cleansing, antiaging and deluxe hydration. Body masks smooth rough skin with a variety of ingredients, including seaweed, desert rose clay, rich mud from the Dead Sea, shea butter and aspara, a plant that grows by the beach and is recognized for its calming properties. $$

WICKENBURG

Early Hispanic families who established ranches in the area and traded with the local American Indians first settled Wickenburg. The town was relatively unpopulated until a Prussian named Henry Wickenburg picked up a rock to throw at a stubborn burro and stumbled onto the richest gold find in Arizona, the Vulture Mine. His discovery began a $30 million boom and the birth of a town. Today, Wickenburg is the oldest town north of Tucson and is well known for its area dude ranches.

Information: Chamber of Commerce, Santa Fe Depot, 216 N. Frontier St.,
928-684-5479, 800-942-5242; www.wickenburgchamber.com

WHAT TO SEE AND DO
DESERT CABALLEROS WESTERN MUSEUM
21 N. Frontier St., Wickenburg, 928-624-2272; www.westernmuseum.org
This museum houses a Western art gallery, diorama room, street scene (circa 1915), period rooms, mineral display and Native American exhibit. Admission: adults $7.50, seniors $6, children under 17 free, school groups free. Monday-Saturday 10 a.m.-5 p.m., Sunday noon-4 p.m.

FRONTIER STREET
Wickenburg, 928-684-5479; www.wickenburgchamber.com
Preserved in early 1900s style. Train depot (houses the Chamber of Commerce), brick Hassayampa building (former hotel) and many other historic buildings.

GARCIA LITTLE RED SCHOOLHOUSE
245 N. Tegner St., Wickenburg, 928-684-7473; www.wco.org
This pioneer schoolhouse is on the National Register of Historic Places.

THE JAIL TREE
Tegner Street and Wickenburg Way, Wickenburg, 928-684-5479; www.wickenburgchamber.com
This tree was used from 1863-1890 (until the first jail was built) to chain rowdy prisoners. Friends and relatives visited the prisoners and brought picnic lunches.

OLD 761 SANTA FE STEAM LOCOMOTIVE
Apache and Tegner, Wickenburg, 928-684-5479; www.wickenburgchamber.com
This engine and tender ran the track between Chicago and the West.

SPECIAL EVENTS
BLUEGRASS MUSIC FESTIVAL
Highway 60, Everett Bowman Rodeo Grounds, Wickenburg, 928-684-5479; www.wickenburgchamber.com
Four-Corner States Championship. Contests include mandolin, violin, guitar and banjo. Second full weekend in November.

GOLD RUSH DAYS
Wickenburg, 928-684-5479; www.wickenburgchamber.com
Bonanza days are revived during this large festival, with a chance to pan for gold and keep all you find. Rodeo, contests, food, parade. Second full weekend in February.

SEPTIEMBRE FIESTA
Wickenburg Community Center, 160 N. Valentine St., Wickenburg, 928-684-5479; www.wickenburgchamber.com
This celebration of Hispanic heritage featuring exhibits, arts and crafts, food, dancers and mariachi bands. First Saturday in September.

HOTEL
★★BEST WESTERN RANCHO GRANDE
293 E. Wickenburg Way, Wickenburg, 928-684-5445, 800-854-7235;
www.bwranchogrande.com
78 rooms. Airport transportation available. High-speed Internet access. Pets accepted; fee. Pool. Spa. Tennis. **$**

SPECIALTY LODGINGS
FLYING E RANCH
2801 W. Wickenburg Way, Wickenburg, 928-684-2690, 888-684-2650;
www.flyingeranch.com
Located on a 20,000-acre cattle ranch in the shadow of Vulture Peak, this property offers breakfast cookouts, family-style meals and chuck wagon dinners. 17 rooms. Closed March-October. Pool. Golf. Spa. Tennis. **$$**

RANCHO DE LOS CABALLEROS
1551 S. Vulture Mine Road, Wickenburg, 928-684-5484, 800-684-5030;
www.sunc.com
Experience the Old West at this historic guest ranch and golf club. Dine by campfire. 79 rooms. Closed mid-May-mid-October. Restaurant, bar. Children's activity center. Airport transportation available. Pool. Golf. Spa. Tennis. **$$$$**

WILLCOX

Visit historic downtown Willcox to see the state's oldest operating store amid antique shops, restaurants, boutiques and museums. This little town will give you a flavor of the Old West.
Information: Chamber of Commerce, Cochise Information Center,
1500 N. Circle I Road, Willcox, 520-384-2272, 800-200-2272;
www.willcoxchamber.com

CHIRICAHUA NATIONAL MONUMENT
This national monument features 20 square miles of picturesque natural rock sculptures and deep twisting canyons. The Chiricahua (Cheer-a-CAH-wah) Apaches—Geronimo was one—hunted in this region in the 1870s and 1880s. A visitor's center, about two miles from the entrance, has geological, zoological and historical displays. Daily. At Massai Point Overlook, geologic exhibits explain the volcanic origin of the monument. The road up Bonita Canyon leads to a number of other outlook points. There are also 18 miles of excellent day-use trails to points of special interest. Picnicking and camping sites are located within the national monument. Daily 8 a.m.-4:30 p.m.
Information: 32 miles southeast of Willcox on Highway 186, then three miles east on Highway 181, 520-824-3560; www.nps.gov/chir

WHAT TO SEE AND DO
AMERIND FOUNDATION
2100 N. Amerind Road, Dragoon, 520-586-3666; www.amerind.org
Amerind (short for American Indian) Museum contains one of the finest collections of archaeological and ethnological artifacts in the country. Paintings by Anglo and American Indian artists are on display in the gallery. Picnic area, museum shop. Tuesday-Sunday 10 a.m.-4 p.m.

COCHISE STRONGHOLD
Coronada National Forest, 1500 N. Circle I Road, Willcox, 520-364-3468;
www.cochisestronghold.com
This rugged canyon once sheltered Chiricahua Apache. Unique rock formations provided protection and vantage points. Camping, picnicking, hifking, horseback and history trails. Daily.

FORT BOWIE NATIONAL HISTORIC SITE
3203 S. Old Fort Bowie Road, Bowie, 520-847-2500; www.nps.gov/fobo
On the way to the ruins, you'll see a stage station, post cemetery and Apache Spring. Visitor center daily 8 a.m.-4:30 p.m.

REX ALLEN ARIZONA COWBOY MUSEUM AND COWBOY HALL OF FAME
150 N. Railroad Ave., Willcox, 520-384-4583, 877-234-4111; www.rexallenmuseum.org
This museum is dedicated to Willcox native Rex Allen, the "last of the Silver Screen Cowboys." It details his life from ranch living in Willcox to his radio, TV and movie days. It also has special exhibits on pioneer settlers and ranchers. The Cowboy Hall of Fame pays tribute to real cattle industry heroes. Daily 10 a.m.-4 p.m.

101

SPECIAL EVENTS
REX ALLEN DAYS
Rex Allen Arizona Cowboy Museum and Cowboy Hall of Fame,
150 N. Railroad Ave., Willcox, 520-384-2272; www.willcoxchamber.com
PRCA Rodeo, concert by Rex Allen Jr., parade, country fair, Western dances, softball tournament. First weekend in October.

WINGS OVER WILLCOX/SANDHILL CRANE CELEBRATION
1500 N. Circle I Road, Willcox, 520-384-2272, 800-200-2272;
www.wingsoverwillcox.com
Tours of bird-watching areas, trade shows, seminars, workshops. Third weekend in January.

HOTEL
★★BEST WESTERN PLAZA INN
1100 W. Rex Allen Drive, Willcox, 520-384-3556, 800-262-2649; www.bestwestern.com
91 rooms. Complimentary full breakfast. High-speed Internet access. Restaurant, bar. Pets accepted; fee. Pool. $

ARIZONA

★
★
★
★

WILLIAMS

This town lies at the foot of Bill Williams Mountain (named for an early trapper and guide) and is the principal entrance to the Grand Canyon. It is a resort town in the midst of Kaibab National Forest, which has its headquarters here. There are seven small fishing lakes in the surrounding area.

Information: Williams-Grand Canyon Chamber of Commerce,
200 W. Railroad Ave., Williams, 928-635-4061; www.williamschamber.com

WHAT TO SEE AND DO
GRAND CANYON RAILWAY
233 N. Grand Canyon Blvd., Williams, 800-843-8724; www.thetrain.com
First operated by the Santa Fe Railroad in 1901 as an alternative to the stagecoach, this restored line carries passengers northward aboard authentically refurbished steam locomotives and coaches. Full-day round trips include a 3½-hour layover at the canyon. Museum of railroad history at William's Depot.

SPECIAL EVENTS
BILL WILLIAMS RENDEZVOUS DAYS
Buckskinner's Park, 204 W. Railroad Ave., Williams, 928-635-1418;
www.williamschamber.com
Black powder shoot, carnival, street dances, pioneer arts and crafts. Memorial Day weekend.

LABOR DAY RODEO
200 W. Railroad, Williams, 928-635-1418; www.williamschamber.com
Professional rodeo and Western celebration. Labor Day weekend.

HOTELS
★BEST WESTERN INN OF WILLIAMS
2600 W. Route 66, Williams, 928-635-4400, 800-635-4445; www.bestwestern.com
80 rooms. Complimentary full breakfast. High-speed Internet access. Pool. Spa. Pets accepted; fee. $

★★GRAND CANYON RAILWAY & RESORT
233 N. Grand Canyon Blvd., Williams, 800-843-8724; www.thetrain.com
196 rooms. Restaurant, bar. $

★★GRAND CANYON RAILWAY HOTEL
235 N. Grand Canyon Blvd., Williams, 928-635-4010, 800-843-8724; www.thetrain.com
297 rooms. Restaurant, bar. $

★★HOLIDAY INN
950 N. Grand Canyon Blvd., Williams, 928-635-4114, 888-465-4329;
www.holiday-inn.com
120 rooms. Restaurant, bar. High-speed Internet access. Pets accepted. Pool. $

★
★★
★★
★★

RESTAURANT

★ROD'S STEAK HOUSE

301 E. Route 66, Williams, 928-635-2671; www.rods-steakhouse.com

Steak menu. Lunch, dinner. Closed Sunday; also first two weeks of January. Bar. Children's menu. Casual attire. Reservations recommended. **$$**

WINDOW ROCK

This is the headquarters of the Navajo Nation. The 88-member tribal council, which is democratically elected, meets in an octagonal council building; tribal officials conduct tribal business from Window Rock. Behind the town is a natural bridge that looks like a window. It is in the midst of a colorful group of sandstone formations called "the Window Rock."

Information: Navajoland Tourism Department, Window Rock 928-810-8501; discovernavajo.com

WHAT TO SEE AND DO

CANYON DE CHELLY NATIONAL MONUMENT

Highway 191, Window Rock, 928-674-5500; www.nps.gov/cach

The smooth red sandstone walls of the canyon extend straight up as much as 1,000 feet from the nearly flat sand bottom. When William of Normandy defeated the English at the Battle of Hastings in 1066, the Pueblo had already built apartment houses in these walls. Many ruins are still here. The Navajo came long after the original tenants had abandoned these structures. In 1864, Kit Carson's men drove nearly all the Navajo out of the area, marching them on foot 300 miles to the Bosque Redondo in eastern New Mexico. Since 1868, Navajo have returned to farming, cultivating the orchards and grazing their sheep in the canyon. In 1931, Canyon de Chelly and its tributaries, Canyon del Muerto and Monument Canyon, were designated a national monument. There are more than 60 major ruins—some dating from circa A.D. 300—in these canyons. White House, Antelope House and Mummy Cave are among the most picturesque. Most ruins are inaccessible but can be seen from either the canyon bottom or from the road along the top of the precipitous walls. Two spectacular, 16-mile rim drives can be made by car in any season. Lookout points—sometimes a short distance from the road—are clearly marked. The only self-guided trail (2½ miles round-trip) leads to the canyon floor and White House ruin from White House Overlook. Other hikes can be made only with a National Park Service permit and an authorized Navajo guide. Only four-wheel drive vehicles are allowed in the canyons—and each vehicle must be accompanied by an authorized Navajo guide and requires a National Park Service permit obtainable from a ranger at the visitor center. The visitor center has an archaeological museum and restrooms. Daily.

GUIDED TOURS OF NAVAJOLAND

Window Rock, 928-674-5500; discovernavajo.com

Various organizations and individuals offer walking and driving tours of the area. Fees and tours vary.

NAVAJO NATION MUSEUM

Highway 64 and Loup Road, Window Rock, 928-871-7941;
www.navajonationmuseum.org

Established in 1961 to preserve Navajo history, art, culture and natural history; permanent and temporary exhibits. Literature and Navajo information available. Monday-Tuesday, Thursday-Friday 8 a.m.-5 p.m., Wednesday 8 a.m.-8 p.m., Saturday 9 a.m.-5 p.m.; closed on tribal and other holidays.

NAVAJO NATION ZOOLOGICAL AND BOTANICAL PARK

Tse Bonito Tribal Park, Window Rock, 928-871-6573; www.explorenavajo.com
Features a representative collection of animals and plants of historical or cultural importance to the Navajo people. Daily 8 a.m.-5 p.m.

ST. MICHAEL'S

Highway 264, Window Rock, 928-871-4171; discovernavajo.com
This Catholic mission, established in 1898, has done much for the education and health of the tribe. The original mission building now serves as a museum depicting the history of the area. Memorial Day-Labor Day, Monday-Friday 9 a.m.-5 p.m.

SPECIAL EVENTS
NAVAJO NATION FAIR

Navajo Nation Fairgrounds, Highway 264, Window Rock, 928-871-6478;
www.navajonationfair.com

Dances, ceremonials, rodeo, arts and crafts, educational and commercial exhibits, food, traditional events. Week after Labor Day.

POWWOW AND PRCA RODEO

Navajo Nations Fairgrounds, Highway 264, Window Rock, 928-871-6478;
www.navajonationfair.com
Rodeo, carnival, fireworks, and entertainment. July 4.

WINSLOW

A railroad town, Winslow is also a trade center and convenient stopping point in the midst of a colorful and intriguing area; a miniature painted desert lies to the northeast. The Apache-Sitgreaves National Forests, with the world's largest stand of ponderosa pine, lie about 25 miles to the south.

Information: Chamber of Commerce, 101 E. Second St., Winslow, 928-289-2434;
www.winslowarizona.org

WHAT TO SEE AND DO
HOMOLOVI RUINS STATE PARK

HCR 63, Winslow, 928-289-4106; www.pr.state.az.us/parks/parkhtml/homolovi.html
This park contains six major Anasazi ruins dating from A.D. 1250-1450. The Arizona State Museum conducts occasional excavations in June and July. The park also has trails, a visitor center and interpretive programs. Daily.

★
★
★
★
★

METEOR CRATER

Winslow, 20 miles west on I-40, then five miles south on Meteor Crater Road, 928-289-5898, 800-289-5898; www.meteorcrater.com

Crater is one mile from rim to rim and 560 feet deep. The world's best-preserved meteorite crater was used as a training site for astronauts. Museum, lecture; Astronaut Wall of Fame; telescope on highest point of the crater's rim offers excellent view of surrounding area. Memorial Day-Labor Day, 7 a.m.-7 p.m.; rest of year, 8 a.m.-5 p.m.

OLD TRAILS MUSEUM

212 N. Kinsley Ave., Winslow, 928-289-5861; www.oldtrailsmuseum.org

Operated by the Navajo County Historical Society; exhibits and displays of local history, Native American artifacts and early Americana. March-October, Tuesday-Saturday 1-5 p.m.; rest of year, Tuesday, Thursday-Saturday.

YUMA

The Yuma Crossing, where the Colorado River narrows between the Yuma Territorial Prison and Fort Yuma (one of Arizona's oldest military posts), was made a historic landmark in recognition of its long service as a river crossing. If the scenery looks familiar, it may be because movie producers have used the dunes and desert for location shots. A Marine Corps Air Station and an army proving ground are adjacent to the town.

Information: Convention & Visitors Bureau, 139 S. Fourth Ave., Yuma, 800-293-0071; www.visityuma.com

WHAT TO SEE AND DO

ARIZONA HISTORICAL SOCIETY SANGUINETTI HOUSE

240 Madison Ave., Yuma, 928-782-1841; www.arizonahistoricalsociety.org

This former home of E. F. Sanguinetti, pioneer merchant, is now a division of the Arizona Historical Society, where you can see artifacts from the Arizona Territory, including documents, photographs, furniture and clothing. Gardens and exotic birds surround museum. Historical library open by appointment. Tuesday-Saturday 10 a.m.-4 p.m.

FORT YUMA-QUECHAN MUSEUM

350 Picacho Road, Yuma, 928-572-0661

Part of one of the oldest military posts (1855) associated with the Arizona -Territory. Museum houses tribal relics of southwestern Colorado River Yuman groups. Daily 8 a.m.-noon, 1-5 p.m.

IMPERIAL NATIONAL WILDLIFE REFUGE

100 Red Cloud Mine Road, Yuma, 928-783-3371; www.southwest.fws.gov/refuges/arizona/imperial.html

Bird-watching; photography. Fishing, hunting, hiking.

ARIZONA

★
★
★
★
★

YUMA RIVER TOURS

1920 Arizona Ave., Yuma, 928-783-4400; www.yumarivertours.com

Narrated historical tours on the Colorado River; half- and full-day trips. Sunset dinner cruises. Also jeep tours to sand dunes. Monday-Friday.

YUMA TERRITORIAL PRISON STATE HISTORIC PARK

1 Prison Hill Road, Yuma, 928-783-4771;
www.pr.state.az.us/parks/parkhtml/yuma.html

Remains of 1876 prison; original cellblocks. Southwest artifacts and prison relics. Daily 8 a.m.-5 p.m.

SPECIAL EVENTS
MIDNIGHT AT THE OASIS FESTIVAL

The Ray Kroc Complex, Desert Sun Stadium, 3500 S. Ave. A, Yuma;
www.caballeros.org

This annual event features classic cars and concerts. First full weekend in March.

YUMA COUNTY FAIR

2520 E. 32nd St., Yuma, 928-726-4420; www.yumafair.com

Features carnival rides, live entertainment, food booths and a variety of exhibits. Five days in early April.

HOTELS
★★QUALITY INN

711 E. 32nd St., Yuma, 928-726-4721, 877-424-6423; www.qualityinn.com

80 rooms. Complimentary full breakfast. Wireless Internet access. Restaurant, bar. Pets accepted. Pool. **$**

★★SHILO INN

1550 S. Castle Dome Ave., Yuma, 928-782-9511, 800-222-2244; www.shiloinns.com

134 rooms. Complimentary full breakfast. Restaurant, bar. Airport transportation available. Pets accepted. Pool. **$**

RESTAURANTS
★THE CROSSING

2690 S. Fourth Ave., Yuma, 928-726-5551; www.crossingcatering.com

American menu. Lunch, dinner. Children's menu. Casual attire. Outdoor seating. **$$**

★HUNTER STEAKHOUSE

2355 S. Fourth Ave., Yuma, 928-782-3637

Steak menu. Lunch, dinner. Bar. Children's menu. Casual attire. **$$**

COLORADO

COLORADO'S TERRAIN IS DIVERSE AND SPECTACULARLY BEAUTIFUL—AND ATTRACTS THOSE who want to venture outdoors. Throughout the state there are deep gorges, rainbow-colored canyons, grassy plains, breathtaking alpine mountains and beautiful landmass variations carved by ancient glaciers and erosion. Colorado is the highest state in the Union, with an average elevation of 6,800 feet. It has 53 peaks above 14,000 feet.

Whether you're visiting one of Colorado's booming big cities—Denver, Boulder or Colorado Springs—or heading for the glitz of Vail or Aspen, Colorado beckons people to spend more time outdoors. Hit the slopes, take a river rafting trip or drive up to the famous Pikes Peak. In between, take a trip back in time by visiting historic homes, railroad depots and ghost towns. Colorado has a rich history. When gold was discovered near present-day Denver in 1858, an avalanche of settlers poured into the state. Then, when silver was discovered soon afterward, a new flood came. Mining camps— usually crude tent cities on the rugged slopes of the Rockies—contributed to Colorado's colorful, robust history. Some of these mines still operate, but most of the early mining camps are ghost towns today.

★ **FUN FACTS**

Denver lays claim to the invention of the cheeseburger. The trademark for the term cheeseburger was awarded to Louis Ballast in 1935.

Information: www.colorado.com

ALAMOSA

The settlers who came to the center of the vast San Luis Valley were pleased to find a protected area on the Rio Grande shaded by cottonwood trees, so they named their new home Alamosa, Spanish for "cottonwood." The little town quickly became a rail, agricultural, mining and educational center.

Information: Alamosa County Chamber of Commerce, 300 Chamber Drive, Alamosa, 719-589-3681, 800-258-7597; www.alamosa.org

WHAT TO SEE AND DO
COLE PARK
425 Fourth St., Alamosa, 719-589-3681
See Old Denver and Rio Grande Western narrow-gauge trains on display. Chamber of Commerce located in old train station. Tennis, bicycle trails, picnicking, playgrounds.

CUMBRES & TOLTEC SCENIC RAILROAD
500 S. Terrace Ave., Antonito, 719-376-5483, 888-286-2737; www.cumbrestoltec.com
Take a round-trip excursion to Osier on a 1880s narrow-gauge steam railroad. The route passes through backwoods country and mountain scenery, including Phantom Canyon and the Toltec Gorge. Warm clothing is advised due to sudden weather changes. Memorial Day-mid-October, daily. Also trips to Chama, New Mexico, via the *New Mexico Express* with van return. Reservations recommended.

COLORADO

★
★
★
★
★

FORT GARLAND MUSEUM

29477 Highway 159, Fort Garland, 719-379-3512;
www.coloradohistory.org/hist_sites/ft_Garland/ft_garland.htm

Kit Carson held his last command at this historic Army post (1858-1883), which contains restored officers' quarters and a collection of Hispanic folk art. April-October, daily 9 a.m.-5 p.m.; November-March, Monday and Thursday-Sunday 10 a.m.-4 p.m.; closed Thanksgiving, Christmas and New Year's Day.

SPECIAL EVENTS
EARLY IRON FESTIVAL

Cole Park, 425 Fourth St., Alamosa, 719-589-9170, 888-589-9170;
www.earlyironclub.com

This annual auto show attracts lovers of antique cars and hot rods. Labor Day weekend.

SUNSHINE FESTIVAL

Cole Park, 425 Fifth St., Alamosa, 719-589-3681

Arts, crafts, food booths, bands, horse rides, contests, a pancake breakfast and a parade are all a part of this summer celebration. First full weekend in June.

HOTELS
★★BEST WESTERN ALAMOSA INN

2005 Main St., Alamosa, 719-589-2567, 800-459-5123;
www.bestwestern.com/alamosainn

53 rooms. High-speed Internet access. Complimentary continental breakfast. Restaurant, bar. Airport transportation available. Fitness center. Pool. Pets accepted; fee. **$**

★★INN OF THE RIO GRANDE

333 Santa Fe Ave., Alamosa, 719-589-5833, 800-669-1658; www.innoftherio.com

125 rooms. Restaurant, bar. Airport transportation available. Spa. Fitness center. Pets accepted. **$**

RESTAURANT
★TRUE GRITS STEAKHOUSE

100 Santa Fe Ave., Alamosa, 719-589-9954

Steak menu. Lunch, dinner. Bar. Children's menu. Casual attire. **$$**

ASPEN

The first settlers came here in 1878 in pursuit of silver and named the town for the abundance of aspen trees in the area. They enjoyed prosperity until the silver market crashed in 1893. By World War I, most of the local mining operations had gone bust. Aspen was practically a ghost town for decades until 1946, when developer Walter Paepcke founded the Aspen Skiing Company with the vision of a cerebral, arts-oriented community. In 1950, Aspen hosted the Alpine Skiing World Championship, and the rest is history. Today, Aspen is home to some of the most expensive real estate in the world and draws in the rich and famous with immaculate ski slopes, spectacular shopping and fine dining.

Information: Aspen Chamber Resort Association, 425 Rio Grande Place, Aspen,
970-925-1940, 800-670-0792; www.aspenchamber.org

WHAT TO SEE AND DO
ASHCROFT GHOST TOWN
Castle Creek Road, Aspen, 970-925-3721;
www.aspenhistorysociety.com/ashcroftmuseum
This partially restored ghost town and mining camp features 1880s buildings and a hotel. Guided tours mid-June-early September, daily 11 a.m., 1 p.m. and 3 p.m. Self-guided tours available daily.

ASPEN HIGHLANDS
76 Boomerang Road, Aspen, 970-925-1220, 800-525-6200;
www.aspensnowmass.com/highlands
Three quads, two triple chairlifts; patrol, school, rentals, snowmaking; five restaurants, bar. One hundred twenty-five runs; longest run 3½ miles; vertical drop 3,635 feet. Snowboarding. Shuttle bus service to and from Aspen. Half-day rates. Mid-December-early April, daily.

ASPEN HISTORICAL SOCIETY
620 W. Bleeker St., Aspen, 970-925-3721, 800-925-3721; www.aspenhistory.org
Learn all about Aspen's history. Early June-September and mid-December-mid-April: Tuesday-Friday; rest of year: by appointment.

ASPEN MOUNTAIN
601 E. Dean, Aspen, 970-925-1220, 800-525-6200;
www.aspensnowmass.com/aspenmountain
Three quad, four double chairlifts; gondola; patrol, school, snowmaking; restaurants, bar. Seventy-six runs; longest run 3 miles; vertical drop 3,267 feet. Mid-November-mid-April, daily. Shuttle bus service to Buttermilk, Aspen Highlands and Snowmass.

BLAZING ADVENTURES
407 E. Hyman Ave., Aspen, 970-923-4544, 800-282-7238;
www.blazingadventures.com
Half-day, full-day and overnight river rafting trips on the Arkansas, Roaring Fork, Colorado and Gunnison rivers. Trips range from scenic floats for beginners to exciting runs for experienced rafters. White-water rafting. May-October, reservations required. Transportation to site. Bicycle, jeep and hiking tours are also available.

BUTTERMILK MOUNTAIN
806 W. Hallam, Aspen, 970-925-9000, 888-525-6200;
www.aspensnowmass.com/buttermilk
Two quad, three double chairlifts, surface lift; patrol, school, rentals, snowmaking; cafeteria, restaurants, bar, nursery. Forty-four runs; longest run three miles; vertical drop 2,030 feet. Snowboarding. December-mid-April: daily 9 a.m.-3:30 p.m. Shuttle bus service from Ajax and Snowmass.

INDEPENDENCE PASS
Highway 82 from Highway 24, Aspen, 970-963-4959;
Highway 82 through Independence Pass is a spectacular visual treat, not to mention an adrenaline rush—if you're afraid of heights, opt for another route. The winding road

COLORADO

★
★
★
★
★

between Highway 24 and Aspen is among the nation's highest, reaching 12,095 feet at its rocky summit—and offers beautiful vistas of Colorado's majestic forests and snow-covered peaks at every turn. Stop at the top for the views and a short trail hike. The pass is closed between November and May.

SPECIAL EVENTS
ASPEN MUSIC FESTIVAL
2 Music School Road, Aspen, 970-925-3254, 800-778-5542;
www.aspenmusicfestival.com
Symphonies, chamber music concerts, opera and jazz. June-August.

ASPEN THEATER IN THE PARK
110 E. Hallam St., Aspen, 970-925-9313; www.theatreaspen.org
Performances nightly and afternoons. June-August.

WINTERSKÖL CARNIVAL
Aspen, 800-670-0792; www.aspenchamber.org/
Calendars-Events-Annual-Special-Events-pl1239.cfm
Also known as the Festival of Snow, this annual four-day event features a parade, a torchlight ski procession, contests and more. Mid-January.

HOTELS
★★★ASPEN MEADOWS

845 Meadows Road, Aspen, 970-925-4240, 800-452-4240;
www.aspenmeadowsresort.dolce.com
This 40-acre mountain retreat with its famous Bauhaus design is made of up six buildings and has hosted leaders from around the world since 1949 thanks to its state-of-the art conference facilities. The spacious guest suites include study areas, wet bars and floor-to-ceiling windows with views of the mountains or Roaring Fork River. 98 rooms. Wireless Internet access. Restaurant. Airport transportation available. Pets accepted. Fitness Center. Pool. Tennis. Business center. $$$

ASPEN MOUNTAIN LODGE
311 W. Main St., Aspen, 970-925-7650, 800-362-7736;
www.aspenmountainlodge.com
38 rooms. Closed late April-late May. High-speed Internet access. Complimentary continental breakfast. Pets accepted. Pool. $$

★HOTEL ASPEN
110 W. Main St., Aspen, 970-925-3441, 800-527-7369; www.hotelaspen.com
45 rooms. Complimentary continental breakfast. Wireless Internet access. Pool. Business center. Pets accepted. $$

★★★HOTEL DURANT
122 E. Durant, Aspen, 970-925-8500, 877-438-7268; www.durantaspen.com
Wine and cheese après-ski then a rooftop hot tub and sauna to soak your depleted muscles—that works, but don't expect anything fancy here. At this price, you're

lucky not to be sleeping in a gondola somewhere. Not that these 19 cozy—some more so than others—guest rooms are much better, but you will get a complimentary continental breakfast in the morning. The location and relatively affordable rates are the primary pros here. 19 rooms. Complimentary continental breakfast. Whirlpool. Sauna. $$

★★★HOTEL JEROME
330 E. Main St., Aspen, 970-920-1000, 800-412-7625; www.hoteljerome.com
This downtown hotel was built in 1889 by Jerome B. Wheeler, co-owner of Macy's Department Store, and was one of the first buildings west of the Mississippi River to be fully lit by electricity. The boutique-style rooms here are magnificent, reflecting the hotel's Victorian heritage with carved armoires and beautiful beds. The service is superb: the ski concierge will take care of your every need, and guests are driven to the slopes in luxury SUVs. You also get access to the Aspen Club and Spa, a 77,000-square-foot exercise facility and spa. The dashing J Bar is still one of the hottest places in town. 93 rooms. High-speed Internet access. Two restaurants, two bars. Airport transportation available. Pets accepted. Fitness center. Pool. Business center. Spa. Golf, 18 holes. Tennis. $$$$

★★★HOTEL LENADO
200 S. Aspen St., Aspen, 970-925-6246, 800-321-3457; www.hotellenado.com
Value doesn't get much better than this in a town that's all about boutique and show. Fork over a fair rate (for Aspen) and you'll get a cozy room with a four-poster hickory bed, Bose radio/CD player, down comforter and terry robes. Take advantage of your access to the rooftop deck and hot tub overlooking Aspen Mountain, heated boot lockers and daily ski storage. If that's not enough to make you happy, complimentary hors d'oeuvres and hot apple cider (lemonade in the summer) in the bar after 4 p.m. are sure to hit the spot. 19 rooms. Complimentary full breakfast. Bar. Whirlpool. Pets accepted; fee. $$$$

★★★★★THE LITTLE NELL
675 E. Durant Ave., Aspen, 970-920-4600, 888-843-6355; www.thelittlenell.com
Tucked away at the base of a mountain, the Little Nell provides a perfect location either to hit the slopes or roam the streets in search of Aspen's latest fashions. The rooms and suites are heavenly cocoons with fireplaces, overstuffed furniture and luxurious bathrooms. Some suites feature vaulted ceilings showcasing glorious mountainside views, while others overlook the charming former mining town. Enjoy the well-equipped fitness center and outdoor pool and Jacuzzi. Montagna restaurant is one of the most popular spots in town with its inventive reinterpretation of American cuisine. 92 rooms. Closed late April-mid-May. High-speed Internet access. Three restaurants, two bars. Airport transportation available. Pets accepted. Pool. Spa. Fitness center. Business center. $$$$

★MOLLY GIBSON LODGE
101 W. Main St., Aspen, 970-925-3434, 888-271-2304; www.mollygibson.com
52 rooms. High-speed Internet access. Complimentary continental breakfast. Pool. $$

111

COLORADO

★
★
★
★
★

★★★SKY HOTEL

709 E. Durant Ave., Aspen, 970-925-6760, 800-882-2582; www.theskyhotel.com

Catering to the young and the young at heart, this boutique hotel offers party animals the convenience of being able to stumble upstairs from one of Aspen's trendiest bars, which is but a snowball's throw away from the rest of the city's nightlife. From the evening wine reception to help you "adjust to the altitude" to the plush animal-print terrycloth robe you can throw on when you can't remember where you left your clothes, the Sky Hotel has taken your every vacation need into consideration. The rooms offer amenities including L'Occitane bath products, iPod-compatible clock radios and humidifiers. Furry friends are welcomed with treats and their own beds and bowls in the room. The onsite ski shop will rent you equipment or store yours free of charge. 84 rooms, 6 suites. Wireless Internet access. Restaurant, bar. Airport transportation available. Pets accepted. Pool. Fitness center. **$$$**

★★★★THE ST. REGIS ASPEN RESORT

315 E. Dean St., Aspen, 970-920-3300, 888-454-9005; www.stregis.com/aspen

Located at the base of Aspen Mountain between the gondola and lift, this hotel's upscale, Western atmosphere is the perfect respite from skiing, shopping and warm weather activities such as fly-fishing and white-water rafting. The outdoor pool and accompanying lounge are ideal for whiling away warm afternoons, or you can relax in the lavish spa. Rooms are richly decorated in muted colors with bursts of color and oversized leather furniture. Expect complimentary water bottle service and a humidifier at turndown. The Club Floor offers its own concierge and five complimentary meals throughout the day. Olives Aspen serves Mediterranean-inspired cuisine from renowned chef Todd English, and Whiskey Rocks is a popular gathering place. 199 rooms. Closed late October-mid-November. High-speed Internet access. Restaurant, two bars. Airport transportation available. **$$$$**

SPECIALTY LODGINGS

HEARTHSTONE HOUSE

134 E. Hyman Ave., Aspen,. 970-925-7632, 888-925-7632;
www.hearthstonehouse.com

15 rooms. High-speed Internet access. Complimentary continental breakfast. Spa. **$$**

THE INDEPENDENCE SQUARE

404 S. Galena, Aspen, 970-920-2313, 800-633-0336; www.indysquare.com

25 rooms. Wireless Internet access. Complimentary continental breakfast. Fitness center. **$$**

LITTLE RED SKI HAUS

118 E. Cooper Ave., Aspen, 970-925-3333, 866-630-6119

13 rooms. Complimentary full breakfast. **$$**

RESTAURANTS

★BOOGIE'S DINER

534 E. Cooper Ave., Aspen, 970-925-6610

American menu. Lunch, dinner. Closed mid-April-mid-June. Children's menu. Casual attire. **$$**

★★★CACHE CACHE BISTRO

205 S. Mill St., Aspen, 970-925-3835; www.cachecache.com

Earning accolades from the likes of *The New York Times, Town & Country*, and *InStyle*, not to mention the locals, this eatery has become something of an Aspen institution in the last two decades. Expect the highest-quality food, wine and service from the charming owner Jodi Larner herself, not to get a bargain or a quick seat après-ski. That said, if you're not married to the white-tablecloth experience and don't mind moseying up to the bar, you can relieve your cashed legs and eat Alaskan king crab and foie gras terrine starters. Plus, with the budget-friendly bar menu, you can get out for under $20. French menu. Dinner. Bar. Business casual. Outdoor seating. $$

★★CANTINA

411 E. Main St., Aspen, 970-925-3663; www.cantina-aspen.com

Mexican menu. Lunch, dinner. Bar. Children's menu. Casual attire. Outdoor seating. $$

★★★JIMMY'S AN AMERICAN RESTAURANT & BAR

205 S. Mill St., Aspen, 970-925-6020; www.jimmysaspen.com

Known for both the lively bar and seriously good food, such as the dry-aged rib-eye on the bone, Chesapeake Bay crab cakes and center-cut ahi tuna with herbed rice. The chocolate volcano cake is also a favorite. American menu. Dinner. Bar. Children's menu. Casual attire. Outdoor seating. $$$

★★L'HOSTARIA

620 E. Hyman Ave., Aspen, 970-925-9022; www.hostaria.com

Italian menu. Dinner. Closed mid-April-mid-May. Bar. Children's menu. Casual attire. Reservations recommended. Outdoor seating. $$

★★LA COCINA

308 E. Hopkins, Aspen, 970-925-9714

Mexican menu. Dinner. Closed mid-April-mid-June. Bar. Children's menu. Outdoor seating. $

★★★MATSUHISA ASPEN

303 E. Main St., Aspen, 970-544-6628; www.nobumatsuhisa.com

Renowned chef Nobu Matsuhisa, who has built a mini-empire of restaurants from New York to L.A., gives Aspen a taste of his outstanding, heartfelt Japanese cuisine in this sleek restaurant located 9,000 feet above sea level. The service is polished and prompt, making for a superb experience. Japanese menu. Dinner. Bar. Casual attire. $$$$

★★MEZZALUNA

624 E. Cooper Ave., Aspen, 970-925-5882; www.mezzalunaaspen.com

Italian menu. Lunch, dinner. Casual attire. $$$

★★★MONTAGNA

675 E. Durant Ave., Aspen, 970-920-4600; www.thelittlenell.com

Located in the Little Nell hotel, Montagna is one of the top dining spots in Aspen. With its buttery walls, iron chandeliers and deep picture windows, the restaurant has the feeling of a chic Swiss chalet. The menu, from the pasta with wild boar to the lemon roasted chicken, is outstanding, and the sommelier oversees a 15,000-bottle wine cellar. American menu. Breakfast, lunch, dinner, Sunday brunch. Closed late April-mid-May. Bar. Children's menu. Casual attire. Valet parking. Outdoor seating. **$$$$**

★★★OLIVES

315 E. Dean St., Aspen, 970-920-3300; www.toddenglish.com

Olives, located in the St. Regis and under the direction of star chef Todd English, delivers American cuisine with strong Mediterranean influences. The seasonal menu contains dishes that incorporate local ingredients, such as braised Prince Edward Island mussels, brick-oven-fired oyster flatbread, skillet-seared Rocky Mountain trout and goat cheese gnocchi. The warm dining room with pinewood floors, antique furniture and a Tuscan-influenced exhibition kitchen strikes just the right tone. Mediterranean menu. Lunch, dinner. Children's menu. **$$$**

★★PACIFICA

307 S. Mill St., Aspen, 970-920-9775; www.pacificaaspen.com

American, seafood menu. Lunch, dinner. Bar. Children's menu. Outdoor seating. **$$**

★★★PINE CREEK COOKHOUSE

314 S. Second St., Aspen, 970-925-1044; www.pinecreekcookhouse.com

Dine on warm duck breast salad and wild game kabobs in this cozy cabin located in a scenic valley in the Elk Mountains. Locals like to cycle up Castle Creek road for lunch. American menu. Lunch, dinner. Closed mid-April-mid-June, mid-September-mid-November. Bar. Casual attire. Reservations recommended. Outdoor seating. **$$$**

★★★PINON'S

105 S. Mill St., Aspen, 970-920-2021

A reservation here is one of the most sought-after in town. Hidden away on the second floor of a shop in downtown Aspen, the contemporary restaurant is decorated in a tropical theme and the atmosphere is upbeat and festive. The service is warm and the innovative, seasonal menu delights diners. American menu. Dinner. Closed early April-early June, October-November. Bar. Casual attire. **$$$**

★★★SYZYGY

520 E. Hyman Ave., Aspen, 970-925-3700; www.syzygyrestaurant.com

You might spot a celebrity or two dining at this romantic spot that serves modern American food. Signature dishes include elk tenderloin and vintage beef. The dining room up front boasts spectacular views of Aspen Mountain, while the jazz room in the back features eight intimate booths. American menu. Dinner. Closed mid-April-May. Bar. Children's menu. Casual attire. **$$$**

★★TAKAH SUSHI

320 S. Mill St., Aspen, 970-925-8588, 888-925-8588; www.takahsushi.com

Japanese, sushi menu. Dinner. Closed mid-April-May, late October-late November. Bar. Casual attire. **$$**

★★THE TAVERN
685 E. Durant, Aspen, 970-920-6334
Italian menu. Lunch, dinner. Closed mid-April-mid-May. Bar. Casual attire. Valet parking. Outdoor seating. **$$$**

★★WIENERSTUBE
633 E. Hyman Ave., Aspen, 970-925-3357; www.wienerstube.com
Continental menu. Breakfast, lunch. Closed Monday. Bar. Children's menu. Outdoor seating. **$$**

AURORA
This Denver suburb, Colorado's third-largest city, offers plenty of opportunities to bask in Colorado's sunny weather. Visitors will enjoy Aurora's golf courses, hiking and biking trails, and Aurora Reservoir, where locals fish, swim and even scuba dive.
Information: Aurora Chamber of Commerce, 562 Sable Blvd., Aurora,
303-344-1500; www.aurorachamber.org

HOTELS
★★DOUBLETREE HOTEL
13696 E. Iliff Place, Aurora, 303-337-2800, 800-528-0444; www.doubletree.com
248 rooms. High-speed Internet access. Restaurant, bar. Pool. Business center. Fitness center. **$**

★★RED LION HOTEL DENVER CENTRAL
3200 S. Parker Road, Aurora, 303-695-1700, 888-201-1718; www.redlion.com
478 rooms. Wireless Internet access. Restaurant, bar. Airport transportation available. Pets accepted. Business center. **$**

RESTAURANT
★★LA CUEVA
9742 E. Colfax Ave., Aurora, 303-367-1422; www.lacueva.net
Mexican menu. Lunch, dinner. Closed Sunday. Bar. Children's menu. Casual attire. **$$**

AVON
Avon is the gateway to Beaver Creek/Arrowhead Resort, which is located about two miles south of the town.
Information: 970-748-4060; www.avon.org

WHAT TO SEE AND DO
BEAVER CREEK/ARROWHEAD RESORT
137 Benchmark Road, Avon, 970-476-9090, 800-842-8062;
www.beavercreek.snow.co.
Ten quad, two triple, three double chairlifts; patrol, rentals, snowmaking; cafeteria, restaurants, bar, nursery. Longest run 2¾ miles; vertical drop 4,040 feet. Late November-mid-April, daily. Cross-country trails and rentals, November-April; ice skating, snowmobiling, sleigh rides. Chairlift rides, July-August, daily; September, weekends.

COLORADO RIVER RUNS

Rancho del Rio, 28 miles northwest of Highway 131; 800-826-1081, 970-653-4292; www.coloradoriverruns.com

Raft down the Colorado River. Tours depart from Rancho del Rio (just outside State Bridge) and last two and a half to three hours. Admission: adults $36, children $30. May-September.

HOTELS

★★★BEAVER CREEK LODGE

26 Avondale Lane, Beaver Creek, 970-845-9800, 800-525-7280; www.beavercreeklodge.net

Located at the base of the Beaver Creek Resort, this European-style boutique hotel is close to the Centennial and Strawberry Park chairlifts. Curl up on the leather couch in front of the fireplace in one of the two-room suites, which feature kitchenettes. Condos have state-of-the-art kitchens, laundry facilities and master bedrooms with whirlpool baths. 72 rooms, all suites. Closed mid-April-mid-May, two weeks in November. Wireless Internet access. Restaurant, bar. Ski-in/ski-out. Fitness room. Spa. $$

★★★THE OSPREY AT BEAVER CREEK

10 Elk Track Road, Avon, 970-845-5990, 888-485-4317; www.innatbeavercreek.com

It's all about location here: this ski-in/ski-out is just steps away from the Strawberry Park Express chairlift and is within walking distance of shops and eateries. The cozy guest rooms and suites have mountain lodge décor and offer an array of amenities, including high-speed Internet access, plush robes and ski boot heaters. A complimentary hot breakfast buffet fuels you up for your day on the slopes. 45 rooms. Closed May, October. Complimentary full breakfast. High-speed Internet access. Bar. Ski-in/ski-out. Pool. Fitness center. $$$

★★★PARK HYATT BEAVER CREEK RESORT AND SPA

50 W. Thomas Place, Avon, 970-949-1234, 800-233-1234; www.beavercreek.hyatt.com

This resort showcases Western style at its best. Located at the base of the Gore Mountains, in the heart of the Beaver Creek Village, the ski-in/ski-out resort is a classic mountain lodge, with rooms featuring oversized furniture, comfy quilts and marble bathrooms. Enjoy great service—warmed boots await you in the morning while chocolate chip cookies are available after your run. The Performance Skiing Program helps guests improve their skiing within days. Afterward, visit the newly redesigned spa that focuses on water-based treatments. In the summer, hit the links on the championship golf course. Five restaurants cover all the bases, with family dining spots and intimate bars. 190 rooms. Wireless Internet access. Restaurant, bar. Ski-in/ski-out. Golf. Tennis. Business center. Spa. Fitness center. Pool. $$$

★★★THE PINES LODGE

141 Scott Hill Road, Avon, 970-845-7900, 866-605-7625; www.rockresorts.com

Nestled among towering pines, this resort offers views of the slopes of Beaver Creek Resort. The spacious rooms include refrigerators, marble bathrooms and ski boot heaters. Enjoy the use of a complimentary Volvo during your stay—there's heated underground parking. Other freebies include Internet access and Starbucks coffee in the guest rooms. The friendly service makes this a great place to stay year-round. 60 rooms. High-speed Internet access. Restaurant, bar. Fitness center. Spa. Golf. **$$$**

★★★★THE RITZ-CARLTON BACHELOR GULCH
130 Daybreak Ridge, Avon, 970-748-6200; www.ritzcarlton.com
Rugged meets refined at this resort, located at the base of the mountain at Beaver Creek. From the 10-gallon hat-clad doorman who greets you to the rustic great room, this resort captures the spirit of the Old West while incorporating polished style. The rooms and suites are comfortable and stylish, with leather chairs, dark wood furniture and wood-beamed ceilings. Iron chandeliers and twig furnishings adorn the public spaces. This family-friendly resort offers an abundance of activities, including fly-fishing, a horseshoe pit, two children's play areas, an outdoor pool, golf and of course, skiing. 180 rooms. Wireless Internet access. Two restaurants, bar. Spa. Ski-in/ski-out. Pets accepted. Golf. Tennis. Business center. Fitness center. **$$$$**

SPECIALTY LODGING
WEST BEAVER CREEK LODGE
220 W. Beaver Creek Blvd., Avon, 970-949-9073, 888-795-1061; www.wbclodge.com
This cozy bed and breakfast is a budget-friendly alternative to the area's pricey resorts. All rooms feature rustic beamed ceilings, and larger rooms and condos are available for families and groups. Door-to-door shuttles to Beaver Creek and Vail, onsite ski storage and discounted lift tickets and equipment rentals make this lodge a good choice for families and ski enthusiasts. Nine rooms. Complimentary full breakfast. Restaurant. Wireless Internet access. Spa. **$$**

SPAS
★★★★ALLEGRIA SPA AT PARK HYATT BEAVER CREEK
50 W. Thomas Place, Avon, 970-748-7500, 888-591-1234; www.allegriaspa.com
Aged copper fountains and a crackling fireplace set the mood at this spa inside the Park Hyatt Beaver Creek, which offers a blend of locally- and Eastern-inspired therapies. The three-layer hydration facial is a lifesaver for parched, wind-burned skin. Three feng shui-inspired body treatments incorporate gentle exfoliation, a nourishing body wrap and a rewarding massage into one blissful experience. The body scrubs take their inspiration from the garden. The wild berry and honey scrub, sweet orange and citrus salt glow, and ginger-peach polish render skin supple. The lavender, lemon and Japanese mint hot oil wraps are luxurious ways to hydrate skin. After a day on the slopes, treat your toes to the hot stone and mineral pedicure. **$$**

★★★★THE BACHELOR GULCH SPA AT THE RITZ-CARLTON
130 Daybreak Ridge, Avon, 970-748-6200, 800-576-5582; www.ritzcarlton.com
The Bachelor Gulch Spa captures the essence of its alpine surroundings with polished rock, stout wood and flowing water in its interiors. The rock grotto with a lazy river hot tub is a defining feature, and the fitness rooms have majestic mountain views. The beauty of the outdoors also extends to treatments that utilize ingredients indigenous to the region. Alpine berries, Douglas fir and blue spruce sap are just some of the natural components of the exceptional signature treatments. After a rigorous day on the slopes, there are also plenty of massage options, from the Roaring Rapids, which uses hydrotherapy, or the Four-Hands, where two therapists work out knots. **$$**

RESTAURANT
★★★GROUSE MOUNTAIN GRILL
141 Scott Hill Road, Avon, 970-949-0600; www.grousemountaingrill.com
Located in the Pines Lodge, this elegant, European-style restaurant is the perfect choice for breakfast, lunch or a quiet dinner. The dark wood furnishings, nightly piano music and tables topped with crisp white linens create a warm and cozy atmosphere. The dinner menu focuses on rustic American dishes such as grilled Yukon River salmon with crab bread pudding and cracked mustard sauce, or pretzel-crusted pork chops with orange mustard sauce and balsamic syrup. The warm apple bread pudding is a perfect finish. American menu. Breakfast, lunch, dinner. Closed mid-April-mid-May. Bar. Casual attire. Valet parking. Outdoor seating. $$$

BEAVER CREEK

Beaver Creek's slogan is "not exactly roughing it," a perfect description for this resort town. If you're searching for great skiing, fine dining and luxury in a pristine setting, head to Beaver Creek.
Information: www.beavercreek.snow.com

HOTEL
★★★THE CHARTER AT BEAVER CREEK
120 Offerson Road, Beaver Creek, 970-949-6660, 800-525-2139; www.thecharter.com
This lodge features hotel rooms (as well as one- to five-bedroom condos) that offer guests amenities like plush robes, Aveda bath products and high-speed Internet access. Each condo also includes a fully equipped kitchen, wood-burning fireplace, private bath and TV for each bedroom as well as maid service. 80 rooms. High-speed Internet access. Restaurant, bar. Spa. Ski-in/ski-out. Pool. $$

RESTAURANTS
★★★BEANO'S CABIN
Beaver Creek, 970-949-9090
This log cabin restaurant is located amid the aspen trees on Beaver Creek Mountain. There are a few ways to get here: sleigh, horse-drawn wagon, van or horseback. Regardless of your mode of transport, Beano's is worth the trip. Listen to live music, sit by the crackling fire and enjoy a five-course meal, such as barbecue-glazed boneless veal baby back ribs or gingerbread-crusted Colorado rack of lamb. American menu. Dinner. Closed early April-late June, late September-mid-December. Bar. Children's menu. Casual attire. Reservations recommended. $$$$

★★★★MIRABELLE AT BEAVER CREEK
55 Village Road, Beaver Creek, 970-949-7728; www.mirabelle1.com
Love is in the air at this charming 19th-century cottage in the mountains. Each of the spacious, bright rooms is cozy and warm, while the outdoor porch, lined with colorful potted flowers, is the perfect spot for outdoor dining. The food is just as magical. The kitchen offers sophisticated French food prepared with a modern sensibility. Signature dishes include Colorado lamb chops and roasted elk medallions with fruit compote. The housemade ice cream is the perfect finish. French menu. Dinner. Closed Sunday; also May, November. Bar. Children's menu. Casual attire. Outdoor seating. $$$

★★★SPLENDIDO AT THE CHATEAU
17 Chateau Lane, Beaver Creek, 970-845-8808; www.splendidobeavercreek.com
Locals come to this picturesque, chalet-style dining room tucked into the hills of Beaver Creek to celebrate special occasions and enjoy the wonderful piano music offered nightly. The food is splendid, too. The menu changes nightly, but seasonal signatures have included dishes like sesame-crusted Atlantic salmon with coconut basmati rice and cilantro-lemongrass sauce, and grilled elk loin with braised elk osso bucco. American menu. Dinner. Closed mid-April-mid-June, mid-October-mid-November. Bar. Children's menu. Reservations recommended. Valet parking. $$$

BLACK HAWK
Established as a gold mining town, Black Hawk still attracts visitors in search of riches with its local casino.
Information: www.cityofblackhawk.org

WHAT TO SEE AND DO
BLACK HAWK CASINO BY HYATT
111 Richman St., Black Hawk, 303-567-1234; www.ameristar.com
Once a boom-to-bust mining town, Black Hawk is experiencing a new rush of fortune-seekers thanks to the introduction of limited-stakes gambling in Colorado in 1990. Of the 25 casinos in Black Hawk and nearby Central City, the 55,000-square-foot Black Hawk by Hyatt is by far the largest and most elaborate. The casino boasts more than 1,000 slot machines, 22 poker and blackjack game tables and three restaurants. Daily 8-2 a.m.

BOULDER
Dubbed "the city between the mountains and reality," Boulder benefits from a combination of great beauty and great weather that makes the area ideal for outdoor activity. Its location between the base of the Rocky Mountains and the head of a rich agricultural valley provides an ideal year-round climate, with 300 sunny days annually. More than 30,000 acres of open, unspoiled land and 200 miles of hiking and biking paths make the city an outdoor-lover's paradise. Home to several high-tech companies, the University of Colorado, the National Institute of Standards and Technology and the National Center for Atmospheric Research, Boulder is also sophisticated and artsy, offering a wealth of cultural activities from music to dance, art and one-of-a-kind shops.
Information: Convention & Visitors Bureau, 2440 Pearl St.,
303-442-2911, 800-444-0447; www.bouldercvb.com

COLORADO ★ ★ ★ ★ ★

WHAT TO SEE AND DO
BOULDER CREEK PATH
Boulder, from 55th St. and Pearl Parkway to Boulder Canyon, 303-413-7200;
www.boulderparks-rec.org
This nature and exercise trail runs some 16 miles through the city and into the adjacent mountains, leading past a sculpture garden, a restored steam locomotive and several parks. Daily.

BOULDER HISTORY MUSEUM

Harbeck Bergheim House, 1206 Euclid Ave., Boulder, 303-449-3464;
www.boulderhistorymuseum.org

Learn about the history of Boulder from 1858 to the present. This museum includes 20,000 artifacts, 111,000 photographs and 486,000 documents. Permanent and rotating interpretive exhibits and educational programs. Tuesday-Friday 10 a.m.-5 p.m., Saturday-Sunday noon-4 p.m.

BOULDER MUSEUM OF CONTEMPORARY ART

1750 13th St., Boulder, 303-443-2122; www.bmoca.org

View exhibits of contemporary and regional painting, sculpture and other media, along with changing exhibits featuring local, domestic and international artists. Check out the experimental performance series on Thursdays. Lectures, workshops and special events. Tuesday, Thursday, Friday 11 a.m.-5 p.m., Wednesday 11 a.m.-8 p.m., Saturday 9 a.m.-4 p.m., Sunday noon-3 p.m.

BOULDER RESERVOIR

5565 N. 51 St., Boulder, 303-441-3468; www.bouldercolorado.gov

Swimming beach, Memorial Day-Labor Day, daily; waterskiing, fishing. Boating daily; get a power boat permit at the main gate; boat rentals Memorial Day-Labor Day, daily.

CELESTIAL SEASONINGS FACTORY TOUR

4600 Sleepytime Drive, Boulder, 303-581-1202, 303-530-5300;
www.celestialseasonings.com

This 45-minute tour takes visitors through the beautiful gardens that produce the herbs and botanicals used in the company's teas, with stops in the sinus-clearing Mint Room and the production area, where eight million tea bags are made every day. You can also check out the company's art gallery of original paintings, which decorate their tea boxes, and be among the first to sample some of the company's newest blends. Children must be over 5 to enter the factory. Hourly. Monday-Friday 10 a.m.-4 p.m., Saturday 10 a.m.-3 p.m., Sunday 11 a.m.-3 p.m.

ELDORA MOUNTAIN RESORT

2861 Eldora Ski Road, Nederland, 303-440-8700; www.eldora.com

Two quad, two triple, four double chairlifts; four surface lifts; patrol, school, rentals, snowmaking; cafeteria, bar, nursery. Fifty-three runs; longest run three miles; vertical drop 1,400 feet. Cross-country skiing (27 miles). Mid-November-early April.

LEANIN' TREE MUSEUM OF WESTERN ART

6055 Longbow Drive, Boulder, 303-530-1442, 800-777-8716;
www.leanintreemuseum.com

Check out the original works of art used in many of the greeting cards produced by Leanin' Tree, a major publisher. The museum also features the private collection of paintings and sculptures amassed by Edward P. Trumble, the chairman and founder of Leanin' Tree Inc. Monday-Friday 8 a.m.-5 p.m., Saturday-Sunday 10 a.m.-5 p.m.; closed Thanksgiving Day, Christmas Day and New Year's Day.

MACKY AUDITORIUM CONCERT HALL

Pleasant Street and Macky Drive, Boulder, 303-492-8423; www.colorado.edu/macky

This 2,047-seat auditorium hosts the Boulder Philharmonic Orchestra. Concerts during the academic year.

NATIONAL CENTER FOR ATMOSPHERIC RESEARCH

1850 Table Mesa Drive, Boulder, 303-497-1000; www.ncar.ucar.edu/ncar

Designed by I. M. Pei, the center includes exhibits on global warming, weather, the sun, aviation hazards and supercomputing. There's also a 400-acre nature preserve onsite. Guided tours. Visitor center Monday-Friday 8 a.m.-5 p.m., Saturday-Sunday, holidays 9 a.m.-4 p.m.

PEARL STREET MALL

900 to 1500 Pearl St., Boulder, 303-449-3774; www.boulderdowntown.com

Open year-round, this retail and restaurant district is particularly appealing in the summer with its brick walkways, Victorian storefronts, lush landscaping and parade of colorful personalities. Offering four blocks of mostly upscale restaurants, galleries, bars and boutiques, the mall invites visitors to conclude a day of shopping with a meal at one of its many European-style cafes while taking in the impromptu performances of street musicians, jugglers, artists and mimes.

SOMMERS-BAUSCH OBSERVATORY

2475 Kittridge Loop Drive, Boulder, 303-492-6732; lyra.colorado.edu/sbo

Come here for an evening of stargazing. Weather permitting, school year; closed school holidays. Reservations required on Fridays.

UNIVERSITY OF COLORADO

914 Broadway St., Boulder, 303-492-1411; www.colorado.edu

Many of the buildings on this 786-acre campus, which was established in 1876 and now boasts a student population of 25,000, feature distinctive native sandstone and red-tile. Tours of campus available.

UNIVERSITY OF COLORADO MUSEUM

Henderson Building, 15th and Broadway streets, Boulder, 303-492-6892;
cumuseum.colorado.edu

See relics and artifacts of early human life in the area, plus regional geological, zoological and botanical collections. Changing exhibits. Monday-Friday 9 a.m.-5 p.m., Saturday 9 a.m.-4 p.m., Sunday 10 a.m.-4 p.m.; closed school holidays.

VISTA RIDGE GOLF CLUB

2700 Vista Parkway, Erie, 303-665-1723; www.vistaridgegc.com

This 18-hole Jay Morrish-designed course, occupying more than 200 acres, offers golfers a lot of space to test their skills. The course's gently rolling hills and views of the Rockies take the edge off even the worst shots, while generous fairways make up for ample water hazards.

121

COLORADO

★
★
★
★

SPECIAL EVENTS
BOLDER BOULDER 10K RACE
5500 Central Ave., Boulder, 303-444-7223; www.bolderboulder.com
Join one of the largest road races in the world, with 45,000 runners and more than 100,000 spectators. Live music and entertainment along the route add to the enjoyment of this family-centered celebration. Races begin at 7 a.m., awards at 2:30 p.m. Memorial Day, May.

BOULDER BACH FESTIVAL
University of Colorado, Boulder, Grusin Concert Hall, Boulder, 303-776-9666; www.boulderbachfest.org
Listen to the music of Baroque composer Johann Sebastian Bach. Late January.

COLORADO MUSIC FESTIVAL
Chautauqua Auditorium, 900 Baseline Road, Boulder, 303-449-1397; www.coloradomusicfest.org
Classical music concerts featuring the CMF Chamber Orchestra. Eight weeks in June-August.

COLORADO SHAKESPEARE FESTIVAL
University of Colorado, Mary Rippon Outdoor Theatre, Boulder, 303-492-0554; www.coloradoshakes.org
See three Shakespeare plays in repertory. November-December.

HOTELS
★★COURTYARD BOULDER
4710 Pearl East Circle, Boulder, 303-440-4700, 800-321-2211; www.courtyard.com
149 rooms. High-speed Internet access. Restaurant. Airport transportation available. Pool. **$**

★HAMPTON INN
912 W. Dillon Road, Louisville, 303-666-7700, 800-426-7866; www.hamptoninn.hilton.com
80 rooms. High-speed Internet access. Complimentary continental breakfast. Airport transportation available. Fitness center. Pool. Spa. **$**

★★★HOTEL BOULDERADO
2115 13th St., Boulder, 303-442-4344, 800-433-4344; www.boulderado.com
Boulder was a sleepy little town of 11,000 back in 1905, when the city fathers decided they could move things along by providing the comfort of a first-class hotel. Back then, men worked 24 hours a day stoking the huge coal furnace to keep the hotel evenly heated, and rooms went for $1 per night. Today the hotel has been restored to its original grandeur. You'll feel like you've stepped back in time when you enter the lobby with its stained-glass ceiling, cherry staircase, plush velvet furniture and swirling ceilings fans. 160 rooms. Wireless Internet access. Two restaurants, bar. Airport transportation available. Business center. **$$**

★★★MARRIOTT BOULDER
2660 Canyon Blvd., Boulder, 303-440-8877, 888-238-2178; www.marriott.com
This newly renovated hotel is located at the base on the Flatiron Mountains in downtown Boulder. Rooms feature free Internet and fitness kits. Opting for the Concierge level will get you access to two private rooftop terraces, complimentary continental breakfast and evening appetizers. Take a dip in the outdoor pool or hit the spa. This hotel is nonsmoking. 155 rooms. High-speed Internet access. Restaurant, bar. **$$**

★QUALITY INN & SUITES
2020 Arapahoe Ave., Boulder, 303-449-7550, 888-449-7550;
www.qualityinnboulder.com
46 rooms. High-speed Internet access. Complimentary breakfast buffet. Pool. Fitness center. Pets accepted. **$**

★★★ST. JULIEN HOTEL & SPA
900 Walnut St., Boulder, 720-406-9696, 877-303-0900; www.stjulien.com
Relax at this luxurious yet casual hotel with a 10,000-square-foot spa and fitness center, two-lane infinity pool and outdoor terrace. The elegant rooms feature custom pillow-top beds with fluffy duvets and oversized slate bathrooms with separate showers. They also include complimentary high-speed Internet access, DIRECTV and organic coffee. The martini bar, T-Zero, is an intimate spot for a drink. 211 rooms. Wireless Internet access. Restaurant, bar. **$$**

SPECIALTY LODGINGS
ALPS BOULDER CANYON INN

38619 Boulder Canyon Drive, Boulder, 303-444-5445, 800-414-2577;
www.alpsinn.com
A cross between a luxurious country inn and a cozy bed and breakfast, the Alps caters to those who want to be within 10 minutes of the city but feel a million miles away. Each of the 12 rooms has a wood-burning fireplace, sitting area and some have clawfoot tubs or double Jacuzzis. 12 rooms. Complimentary full breakfast. High-speed Internet access. Spa. **$$**

BRIAR ROSE BED & BREAKFAST
2151 Arapahoe Ave., Boulder, 303-442-3007, 888-786-8440; www.briarrosebb.com
This Victorian-style 1896 house offers cozy rooms with organic cotton sheets and natural bath products. There is also an extended-stay suite with a full kitchen that is rented by the week or the month. The afternoon tea tray, with herbal and black teas, iced tea, lemonade, cider and special shortbread cookies, is a treat. So is the organic breakfast. 10 rooms. Complimentary full breakfast. High-speed Internet access. Airport transportation available. **$**

RESTAURANTS
★★ANTICA ROMA
1308 Pearl St., Boulder, 303-449-1787; www.anticaroma.com
Italian menu. Lunch, dinner. Bar. Children's menu. Outdoor seating. **$$**

★★★★FLAGSTAFF HOUSE RESTAURANT

1138 Flagstaff Road, Boulder, 303-442-4640; www.flagstaffhouse.com

From its perch on Flagstaff Mountain, this restaurant is easily one of the most amazing spots to watch the sunset. And the food here rivals the amazing setting. The upscale and inspired menu changes daily, with plates like beef Wellington dressed up with black truffle sauce and Hawaiian ono with ginger, scallions and soft-shell crabs. The wine list is massive (the restaurant has a 20,000-bottle wine cellar), so enlist the assistance of the attentive sommelier for guidance. The restaurant is owned by the Monette family, which means that you'll be treated to refined service and homegrown hospitality, making dining here a delight from start to finish. If you can, arrive early and have a seat at the stunning mahogany bar for a pre-dinner cocktail. American menu. Dinner. Bar. Business casual attire. Reservations recommended. Valet parking. Outdoor seating. $$$$

★★★THE GREENBRIAR INN

8735 N. Foothills Highway, Boulder, 303-440-7979, 800-253-1474;
www.greenbriarinn.com

Originally built in 1893, this Boulder landmark sits on 20 acres at the mouth of Left Hand Canyon. The atrium room has French doors that open up to the south garden and lawn. The mouthwatering food includes blue crab-crusted beef tournedos and maple cured duck breasts. A champagne brunch is served on Saturday and Sunday. American menu. Dinner, Saturday-Sunday brunch. Closed Monday. Bar. Outdoor seating. $$$

★★★JOHN'S RESTAURANT

2328 Pearl St., Boulder, 303-444-5232; www.johnsrestaurantboulder.com

You'll feel like you're stepping into someone's home when you enter this century-old cottage with lace curtains and white tablecloths. In the spring and summer, windows open to courtyards filled with bright flowers. On the menu, you'll find contemporary dishes from France, Italy, Spain and Scotland, with specialties like smoked Scottish salmon, filet mignon with Stilton cheese and ale sauce, and Italian-style gelato. International menu. Dinner. Closed Sunday-Monday. $$$

★★LAUDISIO

1710 29th St., Boulder, 303-442-1300; www.laudisio.com

Italian menu. Lunch, dinner, Saturday-Sunday brunch. Bar. Outdoor seating. $$$

★★THE MEDITERRANEAN

1002 Walnut St., Boulder, 303-444-5335; www.themedboulder.com

Mediterranean menu. Lunch, dinner. Closed holidays. Bar. Children's menu. Outdoor seating. $$

★★★Q'S

2115 13th St., Boulder, 303-442-4880; www.qsboulder.com

This welcoming, bistro-style restaurant in the Hotel Boulderado offers a spectacular selection of seafood, meat and game. The international wine collection is eclectic and includes small barrel and boutique selections as well as a proprietor's reserve list. The service is delightful and efficient, making dining a pleasure. American menu. Breakfast, lunch, dinner, Saturday-Sunday brunch. Bar. Children's menu. Casual attire. Valet parking. $$$

★ROYAL PEACOCK
5290 Arapahoe Ave., Boulder, 303-447-1409;
www.royalpeacocklounge.com
Indian menu. Lunch, dinner. Outdoor seating. **$$**

BRECKENRIDGE
Born as a mining camp when gold was discovered along the Blue River in 1859, modern Breckenridge wears its rough-and-tumble past like a badge. With 350 historic structures, the town has the largest historic district in Colorado. The population peaked near 10,000 in the 1880s but dwindled to less than 400 in 1960, the year before the town's ski resort opened. Breckenridge now sees more than one million skier visits annually. Located on four interconnected mountains named Peaks 7, 8, 9 and 10, the terrain is revered by skiers but is especially popular with snowboarders. It's more affordable—and rowdier—than Aspen and Vail. During the summer months, outdoor enthusiasts love hiking, mountain biking, fly-fishing, white-water rafting and horseback riding in the surrounding area. The Jack Nicklaus-designed Breckenridge Golf Club offers 27 holes of world-class championship play.
Information: Breckenridge Resort Chamber, 311 S. Ridge St.,
970-453-2913, 888-251-2417; www.breckenridge.com

WHAT TO SEE AND DO
BRECKENRIDGE SKI AREA
Ski Hill Road, Breckenridge, 970-453-5000, 800-789-7669;
www.breckenridge.snow.com
Seven high-speed quad, triple, six double chairlifts; four surface lifts, eight carpet lifts; school, rentals, snowmaking; four cafeterias, five restaurants on mountain, picnic area; four nurseries (from two months old). One-hundred twelve runs on three interconnected mountains; longest run 3½ miles; vertical drop 3,398 feet. Ski mid-November-early May, daily. Cross-country skiing (23 kilometers), heli-skiing, ice skating, snowboarding and sleigh rides. Shuttle bus service. Multiday, half day and off-season rates. Chairlift and alpine slide operate in summer, mid-June-mid-September.

SUMMIT HISTORICAL SOCIETY WALKING TOURS
111 N. Ridge St., Breckenridge, 970-453-9022;
www.summithistorical.org
Tour the historic district, which includes trips to abandoned mines. Late June-August, Tuesday-Saturday 10 a.m.

SPECIAL EVENTS
BACKSTAGE THEATRE
121 S. Ridge St., Breckenridge, 970-453-0199;
www.backstagetheatre.org
See melodramas, musicals and comedies at this hometown performance space. July-Labor Day, mid-December-March.

COLORADO

★
★
★
★
★

BRECKENRIDGE MUSIC FESTIVAL

150 W. Adams, Breckenridge, 970-453-9142; www.breckenridgemusicfestival.com

This eight-week summer celebration includes regular full orchestra performances by Breckenridge's own highly acclaimed National Repertory Orchestra. Performances are held at Riverwalk Center in the heart of downtown Breckenridge, an 800-seat, tented amphitheater. It opens in back to allow lawn seating for an additional 1,500-2,000 symphony lovers who come to picnic and enjoy music under the stars. Most concerts begin at 7:30 p.m. Late June-mid-August.

INTERNATIONAL SNOW SCULPTURE CHAMPIONSHIPS

Riverwalk Center, Breckenridge, 800-936-5573; www.gobreck.com

Sixteen teams from around the world create works of art from 12-foot-tall, 20-ton blocks of artificial snow. Late January-early February.

NO MAN'S LAND DAY CELEBRATION

Breckenridge, 970-453-6018

Breckenridge was mistakenly forgotten in historic treaties when Colorado joined the Union. It became part of Colorado and the United States at a later date. This celebration emphasizes Breckenridge life in the 1880s with a parade, dance and games. Second weekend in August.

ULLR FEST & WORLD CUP FREESTYLE

Breckenridge, 970-453-6018; www.gobreck.com

This annual celebration honors the Norse god of snow with parades, fireworks and a ski competition. Seven days in late January.

★
★
★
★
★

HOTELS

★★★ALLAIRE TIMBERS INN

9511 Highway 9/South Main, Breckenridge, 970-453-7530, 800-624-4904;
www.allairetimbers.com

This charming log cabin bed and breakfast at the south end of Main Street is made from local pine. The innkeepers welcome guests with hearty homemade breakfasts, afternoon snacks and warm hospitality. Take the free shuttle from the inn to several chair lifts. After a day of activity, relax in the sunroom or retreat to the reading loft. 10 rooms. Wireless Internet access. Children over 13 years only. Complimentary full breakfast. $$

★★★BEAVER RUN RESORT AND CONFERENCE CENTER

620 Village Road, Breckenridge, 970-453-6000, 800-265-3560; www.beaverrun.com

This large resort is popular with families in both winter and summer. The suites feature full kitchens and the largest ones sleep up to 10 people. The property includes eight hot tubs and an indoor/outdoor pool, tennis courts and a spa with facials by Dermalogica. There's also a ski school for the kids, as well as miniature golf and a video arcade. 567 rooms. Restaurant, bar. Ski-in/ski-out. Fitness center. Spa. $$

★★★GREAT DIVIDE LODGE

550 Village Road, Breckenridge, 970-547-5550, 888-906-5698;
www.greatdividelodge.com

Located just 50 yards from the base of Peak 9 and two blocks from Main Street, this lodge is excellent for winter or summer vacationing. The large guest rooms come with a wet bar, Starbucks coffee, Nintendo and wireless Internet access. Get around on the free hotel shuttle. 208 rooms. Wireless Internet access. Restaurant, bar. Airport transportation available. Pool. **$$**

★★★SKIWAY LODGE

275 Ski Hill Road, Breckenridge, 970-453-7573, 800-472-1430; www.skiwaylodge.com
Individually designed rooms with mountain views and hearty, homemade breakfasts distinguish this Bavarian-style chalet located just blocks from Main Street. The inn offers ski-in/ski-out access. Nine rooms. Wireless Internet access. Children over 10 years only. Complimentary full breakfast. **$**

SPECIALTY LODGING
BARN ON THE RIVER BED & BREAKFAST

303 N. Main St., Breckenridge, 970-453-2975, 800-795-2975;
www.breckenridge-inn.com
Innkeepers Fred Kinat and Diane Jaynes welcome guests to one of the three historic inns that compose this bed and breakfast. The individually decorated rooms are pleasant and include wireless Internet access, TVs and private balconies or patios. 12 rooms. Closed three weeks in May, last week in October, first two weeks in November. Wireless Internet access. Complimentary full breakfast. Check-in by appointment. Spa. Pets accepted. **$**

RESTAURANTS
★BRECKENRIDGE BREWERY

600 S. Main St., Breckenridge, 970-453-1550; www.breckenridgebrewery.com
American menu. Lunch, dinner, late-night. Bar. Children's menu. Casual attire. Outdoor seating. **$$**

★★CAFE ALPINE

106 E. Adams, Breckenridge, 970-453-8218; www.cafealpine.com
International/Fusion menu. Lunch, dinner. Closed late May. Bar. Children's menu. Casual attire. Reservations recommended. Outdoor seating. **$$$**

★★HEARTHSTONE RESTAURANT

130 S. Ridge St., Breckenridge, 970-453-1148; www.stormrestaurants.com
American menu. Dinner. Bar. Children's menu. Casual attire. Reservations recommended. Outdoor seating. **$$$**

★★MI CASA MEXICAN CANTINA

600 S. Park Ave., Breckenridge, 970-453-2071; www.stormrestaurants.com
Mexican menu. Lunch, dinner. Bar. Children's menu. Casual attire. Outdoor seating. **$$**

★★SALT CREEK

110 E. Lincoln Ave., Breckenridge, 970-453-4949; www.saltcreekbreck.com
Steak menu. Breakfast, lunch, dinner. Closed May. Bar. Children's menu. Casual attire. Outdoor seating. **$$**

★★TOP OF THE WORLD
112 Overlook Drive, Breckenridge, 970-453-9300, 800-736-1607;
www.thelodgeatbreck.com
American menu. Breakfast, dinner. Closed Monday-Tuesday; also May. Bar. Casual attire. Reservations recommended. **$$$**

BROOMFIELD
Broomfield is midway between Denver and Boulder in what is referred to as the technology corridor. The area experienced tremendous growth in the 1990s, much of it focused on technology. The biggest employers include IBM and Sun Microsystems.
Information: www.broomfield.org

WHAT TO SEE AND DO
FLATIRON CROSSING
1 W. Flatiron Circle, Broomfield, 720-887-7467, 866-352-8476;
www.flatironcrossing.com
This architecturally innovative 1.5 million-square-foot retail and entertainment complex located between Denver and Boulder was designed to reflect the natural Flatirons (rock formations), canyons and prairies of its surroundings. The result is a one-of-a-kind visual and shopping experience, with more than 200 stores and numerous restaurants for both indoor and outdoor dining. Daily; closed Easter, Christmas Day.

HOTEL
★★★OMNI INTERLOCKEN RESORT
500 Interlocken Blvd., Broomfield, 303-438-6600, 888-444-6664; www.omnihotels.com
Set against the backdrop of the Rocky Mountains, this 300-acre resort has something for everyone. Golfers needing to brush up on their game head for the L.A.W.s Academy of Golf for its celebrated clinics and courses before hitting the resort's three nine-hole courses. There's a well-equipped fitness center and pool and a full-service spa that offers a variety of treatments. The guest rooms are comfortable and elegant and include amenities like WebTV and high-speed Internet. Three restaurants run the gamut from traditional to pub style. 390 rooms. High-speed Internet access. Three restaurants, bar. Spa. Airport transportation available. Pets accepted. Golf. **$$$**

BUENA VISTA
Lying at the eastern edge of the Collegiate Range and the central Colorado mountain region, Buena Vista is a natural point of departure for treks into the mountains. Within 20 miles you'll find four rivers, 12 peaks with elevations above 14,000 feet and more than 500 mountain lakes and streams.
Information: Chamber of Commerce, 343 S. US 24, 719-395-6612;
www.buenavistacolorado.org

WHAT TO SEE AND DO
ARKANSAS RIVER TOURS
126 S. Main St., Buena, Vista, 719-942-4362, 800-321-4352;
www.arkansasrivertours.com
The upper Arkansas River in South Central Colorado offers some of the most beautiful and challenging rafting experiences in the region. With its long, placid stretches

of scenic wilderness punctuated by plunges through dramatic white-water canyons, the river accommodates all levels of river-rafting thrill-seekers. Experienced rafters won't want to miss an adrenaline-pumping ride through the magnificent Royal George Canyon. Families will love a scenic float through the gently rolling Cottonwood Rapid. Arkansas River Tours is one of several rafting outfitters along Highway 50 offering a variety of outings, from quarter-day trips to multiple-day high-adventure expeditions. Daily; weather permitting.

NOAH'S ARK WHITEWATER RAFTING COMPANY

23910 Highway 285 S, Buena Vista, 719-395-2158; www.noahsark.com
Half-day to three-day trips on the Arkansas River. Mid-May-late August.

WILDERNESS AWARE

12600 Highway 24/285, Buena Vista, 719-395-2112, 800-462-7238; www.inaraft.com
Half-day to 10-day river rafting trips on the Arkansas, Colorado, Dolores, North Platte and Gunnison rivers. May-September.

HOTEL
★BEST WESTERN VISTA INN

733 Highway 24 N., Buena Vista, 719-395-8009, 800-809-3495; www.bestwestern.com
51 rooms. High-speed Internet access. Three hot springs whirlpools. **$**

RESTAURANT
★CASA DEL SOL

333 Highway 24 N., Buena Vista, 719-395-8810
Mexican menu. Lunch, dinner. Closed late May-Labor Day. Children's menu. Casual attire. Outdoor seating. **$**

BURLINGTON

On the eastern edge of Colorado, Burlington is a small town dedicated to preserving its part of Western history.
Information: Chamber of Commerce, 415 15th St., Burlington, 719-346-8652;
www.burlingtoncolo.com

WHAT TO SEE AND DO
KIT CARSON COUNTY CAROUSEL

Fairgrounds, Colorado Avenue and 15th Street, Burlington, 719-346-8652;
www.burlingtoncolo.com
Built in 1905, this restored carousel houses a 1912 Wurlitzer Monster Military Band organ—and rides are only a quarter. Memorial Day-Labor Day, daily 11 a.m.-6 p.m.

OLD TOWN

420 S. 14th St., Burlington, 719-346-7382, 800-288-1334; www.burlingtoncolo.com
This historical village includes 20 buildings that reflect Colorado prairie heritage, plus cancan shows, gunfights and melodramas (summer). A two-day hoedown takes place on Labor Day. Tours. Admission: adult $6, children 12-17 $4, children 3-11 $2, children under 3 free. Memorial Day-Labor Day, Monday-Saturday 9 a.m.-5 p.m., Sunday noon-5 p.m.

SPECIAL EVENT
KIT CARSON COUNTY FAIR & RODEO
Fairgrounds, Colorado Avenue and 15th Street, Burlington, 719-346-0111;
www.kitcarsoncounty.org/~perry/index
This rodeo and livestock exhibition has a 90-year history. Early August.

HOTEL
★AMERICAS BEST VALUE INN-BURLINGTON
2100 Fay St., Burlington, 719-346-5627, 888-315-2378; www.bestvalueinn.com
39 rooms. High-speed Internet access. Complimentary continental breakfast. Pool. **$**

CAÑON CITY
In 1807, Lieutenant Zebulon Pike was one of the first white men to camp on this site, which was long a favored spot of the Ute Indians. Cañon City is located at the mouth of the Royal Gorge and ringed by mountains.
Information: Chamber of Commerce, 403 Royal Gorge Blvd., Cañon City,
719-275-2331, 800-876-7922; www.canoncitychamber.com

WHAT TO SEE AND DO
BUCKSKIN JOE FRONTIER TOWN & RAILWAY
1193 Fremont County Road, Cañon City, 719-275-5149; www.buckskinjoes.com
This Old West theme park includes an old Western town with 30 authentic buildings. Daily gunfights, horse-drawn trolley ride, magic shows and entertainment, plus a 30-minute train ride to the rim of Royal Gorge Railway. Park open March-September, daily. Scenic railway open March-October, daily; November-December, Saturday-Sunday only; closed Thanksgiving, Christmas Eve, Christmas Day.

CAÑON CITY MUNICIPAL MUSEUM
612 Royal Gorge Blvd., Cañon City, 719-276-5279
The complex includes Rudd Cabin, a pioneer log cabin constructed in 1860, and Stone House, built in 1881. Galleries display minerals and rocks, artifacts from the settlement of the Fremont County region and guns. Early May-Labor Day, Tuesday-Sunday; rest of year, Tuesday-Saturday.

DINOSAUR DEPOT MUSEUM
330 Royal Gorge Blvd., Cañon City, 719-269-7150, 800-987-6379;
www.dinosaurdepot.com
Check out an entire Stegosaurus skeleton that was discovered less than 10 miles away. Admission: adult $4, children $2, children age under 3 free. Daily 10 a.m.-4 p.m.; extended summer hours; Wednesday-Sunday only, 10 a.m.-4 p.m. in winter; closed on Thanksgiving, Christmas and New Year's Day.

FREMONT CENTER FOR THE ARTS
505 Macon Ave., Cañon City, 719-275-2790; www.fremontarts.org
This community art center features visual art exhibits and cultural programs. Tuesday-Saturday 10 a.m.-4 p.m.

GARDEN PARK FOSSIL AREA

3170 E. Main St., Cañon City, 719-269-7150; www.dinosaurdepot.com/exhibits.htm

Fossils of well-known species of large dinosaurs have been discovered at this site over the last 120 years, many of which are on exhibit at museums around the country, including the Smithsonian. Fossils of dinosaurs, dinosaur eggs and dinosaur tracks have also been discovered in the Garden Park Fossil Area, along with fossils of rare plants. Daily.

ROYAL GORGE BRIDGE AND PARK

4218 County Road, Cañon City, 719-275-7507, 888-333-5597;
www.royalgorgebridge.com

This magnificent canyon has cliffs rising more than 1,000 feet above the Arkansas River. The Royal Gorge Suspension Bridge, 1,053 feet above the river, is the highest in the world. The Royal Gorge Incline Railway, the world's steepest, takes passengers 1,550 feet down to the bottom of the canyon. A 2,200-foot aerial tramway glides across the spectacular canyon. Daily 10 a.m.-4:30 p.m.

ROYAL GORGE ROUTE

401 Water St., Cañon City, 303-569-1000, 888-724-5748; www.royalgorgeroute.com

Travel by train through the Royal Gorge on two-hour round-trips departing from Cañon City. Summer, daily; call for schedule.

SPECIAL EVENTS
BLOSSOM & MUSIC FESTIVAL

Depot Park, Cañon City, 719-275-2331; www.ccblossomfestival.com

This celebration of springtime features arts and crafts, a parade and a carnival. First weekend in May.

ROYAL GORGE RODEO

1436 S. Fourth St., Cañon City, 719-275-4784;
www.horsestop.net/royalgorgerodeoevents.htm

In addition to the rodeo, the weekend features a Friday night barbecue and Sunday morning pancake breakfast. Late April-Early May.

HOTEL
★★BEST WESTERN ROYAL GORGE

1925 Fremont Drive, Cañon City, 719-275-3377, 800-231-7317; www.bestwestern.com

67 rooms. High-speed internet access. Restaurant, bar. Pool. $

RESTAURANT
★★LE PETIT CHABLIS

512 Royal Gorge Blvd., Cañon City, 719-269-3333

French menu. Lunch, dinner. Closed Sunday-Monday. $

CASCADE

Named for the many waterfalls nearby, Cascade hosts visitors who arrive to visit the popular Pikes Peak.

Information: www.colorado.com/city151

SPECIALTY LODGINGS
BLACK BEAR INN OF PIKES PEAK
5250 Pikes Peak Highway, Cascade, 719-684-0151, 877-732-5232;
www.blackbearinnpikespeak.com
Nine rooms. Children over 8 years only. Complimentary full breakfast. Whirlpool. **$**

EASTHOLME IN THE ROCKIES
4445 Hagerman Ave., Cascade, 719-684-9901, 800-487-6420; www.eastholme.com
Eight rooms. Wireless Internet access. Complimentary full breakfast. Spa. **$**

COLORADO SPRINGS
Fantastic rock formations surround Colorado Springs, located at the foot of Pikes
Peak. General William J. Palmer founded the city as a summer playground and health
resort. The headquarters of Pike National Forest is in Colorado Springs.
Information: Convention & Visitor Bureau, 515 S. Cascade Ave.,
719-635-7506, 877-745-3773; www.experiencecoloradosprings.com

WHAT TO SEE AND DO
BROADMOOR-CHEYENNE MOUNTAIN AREA
1 Lake Ave., Colorado Springs
Broadmoor-Cheyenne Mountain Highway zigzags up the east face of Cheyenne
Mountain with view of plains to the east. The Will Rogers Shrine of the Sun is nearby.
Daily; weather permitting.

CHEYENNE MOUNTAIN ZOOLOGICAL PARK
4250 Cheyenne Mountain Zoo Road, Colorado Springs, 719-633-9925;
www.cmzoo.org
This little gem located on the side of the Cheyenne Mountains in Colorado Springs is
known for its beautiful setting and for the diversity of its animal collection. There are
more than 650 animals here, including many endangered species. Feed the giraffes and
check out the monkeys. Admission includes access to the Will Rogers Shrine of the
Sun. Admission: adults $14.25, children $7.25, children under 2 free. Memorial Day-
Labor Day, daily 9 a.m.-6 p.m.; Labor Day-Memorial Day, daily 9 a.m.-5 p.m.; Thanksgiving Day 9 a.m.-4 p.m., Christmas Eve 9 a.m.-3 p.m., Christmas Day 9 a.m.-4 p.m.

COLORADO SPRINGS FINE ARTS CENTER
30 W. Dale St., Colorado Springs, 719-634-5581; www.csfineartscenter.org
Permanent collections include American Indian and Hispanic art, Guatemalan textiles, 19th- and 20th-century American Western paintings, graphics and sculpture by
Charles M. Russell and other American artists. Admission: adults $10, children, stu-
dents $8.50 children under 4 free. Tuesday-Friday 10 a.m.-5 p.m., Saturday 10 a.m.-
8 p.m., Sunday 10 a.m.-5 p.m.

COLORADO SPRINGS PIONEERS MUSEUM
Former El Paso County Courthouse, 215 S. Tejon St., Colorado Springs,
719-385-5990; www.cspm.org
Learn about the history of the Pikes Peak region. Tuesday-Saturday 10 a.m.-5 p.m.,
Sunday 1-5 p.m. May-October.

EL POMAR CARRIAGE MUSEUM

10 Lake Circle, Colorado Springs, 719-577-7000; www.elpomar.org
An extensive collection of fine carriages, vehicles and Western articles of 1890s located next to Broadmoor Hall. Monday-Saturday 9 a.m.-5 p.m., Sunday 1-5 p.m.

FLYING W RANCH

3330 Chuckwagon Road, Colorado Springs, 719-598-4000, 800-232-3599; www.flyingw.com
A working cattle and horse ranch with chuck-wagon suppers and a Western stage show. More than 12 restored buildings with period furniture. Reservations required. Mid-May-September, daily; rest of year, Friday-Saturday; closed December 25-February.

GARDEN OF THE GODS

1805 N. 30th St., Colorado Springs, 719-634-6666; www.gardenofgods.com
This 1,350-acre park at the base of Pikes Peak is a showcase of geological wonders. It's best known for its outstanding red sandstone formations, including the famous Balanced Rock and Kissing Camels. The park offers eight miles of well-groomed trails to view the geological treasures, plants and wildlife. Take a free guided walking tour or hop on a bus to tour the garden. Other activities include horseback riding (Academy Riding Stables, 719-633-5667) and rock climbing (by permit only). Try to plan a visit at sunrise or sunset, when you'll get a true understanding of where the area gets its name. Memorial Day-Labor Day, daily 8 a.m.-8 p.m.; rest of year, daily 9 a.m.-5 p.m.

GHOST TOWN WILD WEST MUSEUM

400 S. 21st St., Colorado Springs, 719-634-0696; www.ghosttownmuseum.com
This authentic Old West town is housed in an 1899 railroad building and includes a general store, jail, saloon, re-created Victorian home, horseless carriages and buggies and a 1903 Cadillac. Visitors can also have fun with old-time nickelodeons, player pianos, arcade "movies" and a shooting gallery. Admission: adults $6.50, children $4. June-August, Monday-Saturday 9 a.m.-6 p.m., Sunday 11 a.m.-6 p.m.; September-May, Monday-Saturday 10 a.m.-5 p.m., Sunday 11 a.m.-5 p.m.

COLORADO

★
★
★
★
☆

LAKE GEORGE (ELEVEN MILE STATE PARK)

4229 Highway Road, 92, Lake George, 719-748-3401; www.parks.state.co.us/parks/elevenmile
Offering 3,400 surface acres, this reservoir is fully stocked with hungry kokanee salmon, carp, trout and northern pike. A number of local outfitters, such as 11 Mile Sports, Inc. (877-725-3172) can supply the necessary equipment as well as a guide. Daily. Ice fishing in winter.

MAY NATURAL HISTORY MUSEUM

710 Rock Creek Canyon Road, Colorado Springs, 719-576-0450, 800-666-3841; www.maymuseum-camp-rvpark.com
See a collection of more than 8,000 invertebrates from the tropics. Then, check out the Museum of Space Exploration, which includes NASA space photos and movies. Admission: adults $6, children $3. May-October, daily; rest or year by appointment.

MCALLISTER HOUSE MUSEUM

423 N. Cascade Ave., Colorado Springs, 719-635-7925;
www.nscda.org/co/mcallisterhousemuseum.html

This six-room 1873 Gothic-style cottage with Victorian furnishings has an adjacent carriage house. Guided tours. September-April, Thursday-Saturday 10 a.m.-4 p.m.; May-August, Wednesday-Saturday noon-4 p.m.

MUSEUM OF THE AMERICAN NUMISMATIC ASSOCIATION

818 N. Cascade Ave., Colorado Springs, 719-632-2646, 800-367-9723;
www.money.org/moneymus.html

Learn all about the study of currency through the collections of coins, tokens, medals and paper money here. Changing exhibits; library. Admission: free. Tuesday-Friday 9 a.m.-5 p.m., Saturday 10 a.m.-5 p.m., Sunday noon-5 p.m.

OLD COLORADO CITY

West Colorado Ave., between 24th Street to 28th Street, Colorado Springs,
719-577-4112; www.shopoldcoloradocity.com

This renovated historic district features more than 100 quaint shops, art galleries and restaurants. Daily.

PALMER PARK

3650 Maizeland Road, 719-578-6640

Occupying 710 acres on the Austin Bluffs, this park boasts magnificent views from its scenic roads and trails. Picnic areas.

134

PETERSON AIR & SPACE MUSEUM

150 E. Ent Ave., Peterson Air Force Base, 719-556-4915; www.petemuseum.org

Display of 17 historic aircraft from World War I to present, plus exhibits on the history of the Air Force base. Open on restricted basis, call for times. Tuesday-Saturday 9 a.m.-4 p.m., closed Sunday, Monday, Federal Holidays.

PIKE NATIONAL FOREST

1920 Valley Drive, Pueblo, 719-545-8737; www.fs.fed.us/r2/psicc

This massive 1.1 million acres of national land includes world-famous Pikes Peak. Wilkerson Pass (9,507 feet) is 45 miles west on Highway 24, with a visitor information center. Memorial Day-Labor Day.

PIKES PEAK

Pikes Peak Highway, Cascade, 719-385-7325, 800-318-9505;
www.pikespeakcolorado.com

Soaring 14,110 feet, Pikes Peak is the second most visited mountain in the world behind Mt. Fuji. To reach the peak, you can undertake an eight-hour hike or drive an hour up the 19-mile road, the last half of which is unpaved, has no guardrails and contains steep drops (a four-by-four vehicle isn't necessary but weather causes road closures even in the summer). Daily; weather permitting. Closed during annual Hill Climb in July.

PIKES PEAK AUTO HILL CLIMB EDUCATIONAL MUSEUM

135 Manitou Ave., Manitou Springs, 719-685-4400; www.ppihc.com

More than two dozen racecars, plus numerous exhibits on the Pikes Peak race, considered America's second-oldest auto race. Daily, shorter hours in winter.

PIKES PEAK COG RAILWAY

515 Ruxton Ave., Manitou Springs, 719-685-5401, 800-745-3773; www.cograilway.com

The surest bet to the summit of Pikes Peak is the cog railway. Trains usually depart five times daily, rain or shine, but make reservations early. Whenever you go, bundle up: Temperatures are 30-40 degrees cooler at the top. Water and aspirin help alleviate altitude sickness. April-December, daily.

PIKES PEAK MOUNTAIN BIKE TOURS

302 S. 25th St., Colorado Springs, 888-593-3062; www.bikepikespeak.com

Tours vary in length and endurance level, and professional guides provide all the necessary equipment to make your ride safe, comfortable, and most of all, fun. Tour schedules vary; call or visit Web site for schedule.

PRORODEO HALL OF FAME AND MUSEUM OF THE AMERICAN COWBOY

101 ProRodeo Drive, Colorado Springs, 719-528-4764; www.prorodeohalloffame.com

The Hall of Fame pays tribute to giants like nine-time world champion Casey Tibbs, while the museum will help you appreciate the life of a cowboy—try roping one of the dummy steers. The outdoor exhibits include live rodeo animals and a replica rodeo arena. Admission: adults $6, seniors $5, youth $3, children under six free. Daily 9 a.m.-5 p.m.; closed holidays.

135

ROCK LEDGE RANCH HISTORIC SITE

1401 Recreation Way, Colorado Springs, 719-578-6777; www.rockledgeranch.com

This living history program and working ranch demonstrates everyday life in the region. Braille nature trail. June-Labor Day, Wednesday-Sunday 10 a.m.-5 p.m.; Labor Day-December, Saturday 10 a.m.-4 p.m., Sunday noon-4 p.m.

COLORADO

★
★
★
★

SEVEN FALLS

2850 S. Cheyenne Canyon Road, Colorado Springs, 719-632-0765; www.sevenfalls.com

The only completely lighted canyon and waterfall in the world. Best seen from Eagle's Nest, reached by a mountain elevator. Native American dance interpretations occur daily in the summer. Night lighting (summer). Daily 9 a.m.-4:15 p.m.

SHRINE OF THE SUN

4250 Cheyenne Mountain Zoo Road, Colorado Springs, 719-577-7000; www.elpomar.org

This memorial to Will Rogers, who was killed in a plane crash in 1935, is built of Colorado gray-pink granite and steel. Contains memorabilia. Fee for visit is included in zoo admission price. Memorial Day-Labor Day, daily 9 a.m.-5 p.m.; Labor Day-Memorial Day, daily 9 a.m.-4 p.m.

U.S. AIR FORCE ACADEMY

2346 Academy Drive, Colorado Springs, 719-333-2025, 800-955-4438;
www.usafa.af.mil

Established in 1955, the academy has a student population of 4,200 cadets. Cadet Chapel, located on the grounds of the academy, is the city's most famous architectural landmark, with its striking combination of stained glass and 150-foot aluminum spires. Stop by the visitor's center for a free self-guided tour map or to view films and informative exhibits about the Air Force. Also check out the planetarium, which may be offering a special program, and don't miss a chance to see a T-38 and B-52 bomber up close. Call before visiting—the chapel closes for special events, and security events may close the base unexpectedly. Visitors Center: daily 9 a.m.-5 p.m.; Chapel: Monday-Saturday 9 a.m.-5 p.m.

U.S. OLYMPIC TRAINING CENTER

1 Olympic Plaza, Colorado Springs, 719-632-5551, 888-659-8687; www.usoc.org

Tours offer an insider's view of how Olympic-level athletes train. And for most of us, the closest we'll get to a medal are the replicas available in the gift shop. Monday-Saturday 9 a.m.-5 p.m., last tour at 4 p.m., Sunday 11 a.m.-6 p.m.

WORLD FIGURE SKATING HALL OF FAME AND MUSEUM

20 First St., Colorado Springs, 719-635-5200; www.usfsa.org

Exhibits on the history of figure skating include a skate gallery and video collection. Monday-Friday 10 a.m.-4 p.m.; November-April: Saturday 10 a.m.-4 p.m.; May-October: Saturday 10 a.m.-5 p.m.

SPECIAL EVENTS

COLORADO SPRINGS BALLOON CLASSIC

328 Bonfoy Ave., Colorado Springs, 719-471-4833; www.balloonclassic.com

This annual event features more than 100 massive balloons and entertainment. Labor Day weekend.

LITTLE BRITCHES RODEO

5050 Edison Ave., Colorado Springs, 719-389-0333; www.nlbra.com

This annual roping and riding event is one of the oldest junior rodeos in the nation. Late May.

PIKES PEAK INTERNATIONAL HILL CLIMB

1631 Mesa Ave., Colorado Springs, 719-685-4400; www.ppihc.com

The Race to the Clouds has been a part of Colorado Spring's July Fourth celebration since 1916. Spectators of all ages marvel at those who dare steer their racecars, trucks and motorcycles along the final 12.4 miles of Pikes Peak Highway, a gravel route with 156 turns and a 5,000-foot rise in elevation. Vehicles can reach more than 130 mph on straightaways, and there isn't a guardrail in sight. You need to be on the mountain at the crack of dawn to catch the action. Those who don't take advantage of the overnight parking the evening before the race can arrive as early as 4 a.m. to stake out a good spot. The road closes to additional spectators at 8 a.m., so plan to spend the day here. Those who park above the start line won't be able to leave until late afternoon when the race is over. The best views are above the tree line, so dress warmly. Late June, 9:30 a.m.-late afternoon.

PIKES PEAK MARATHON

Colorado Springs, race starts at Memorial Park and ends at Ruxton and Manitou avenues in Manitou Springs, 719-473-2625; www.pikespeakmarathon.org
Late August.

PIKES PEAK OR BUST RODEO

Norris-Penrose Event Center, 1045 W. Rio Grande St., Colorado Springs, 719-635-3547; www.pikespeakorbustrodeo.org
Bareback riding, bull riding, calf roping, steer wrestling and more. Mid-July.

HOTELS
★★THE ACADEMY HOTEL

8110 N. Academy Blvd., Colorado Springs, 719-598-5770, 800-766-8524; www.theacademyhotel.com
200 rooms. Complimentary full breakfast. High-speed Internet access. Restaurant, bar. Airport transportation available. Fitness center. Pool. Pets accepted. **$**

★★ANTLERS HILTON COLORADO SPRINGS

4 S. Cascade Ave., Colorado Springs, 719-955-5600; www.antlers.com
292 rooms. High-speed Internet access. Two restaurants, two bars. **$**

★★★★★THE BROADMOOR

1 Lake Ave., Colorado Springs, 719-634-7711; www.broadmoor.com
Located at the foot of the Rocky Mountains and surrounded by beautiful Cheyenne Lake, the Broadmoor has been one of America's favorite resorts since 1918. This all-season paradise is in Colorado Springs, yet feels a million miles away. The opulent accommodations include rooms with views of the mountains or lake. Activities include a tennis club, three championship golf courses, paddle boating on the lake and horseback riding. Kids will love the "mountain" waterslide. And the world-class spa incorporates indigenous botanicals and pure spring water. The resort includes 15 restaurants, cafés and lounges and several shops. 700 rooms, all suites. High-speed Internet access. Restaurants, bars. Spa. Airport transportation available. Pets accepted. Pool. Golf. Tennis. Business center. Fitness center. **$$$**

★★DOUBLETREE HOTEL

1775 E. Cheyenne Mountain Blvd., Colorado Springs, 719-576-8900, 800-222-8733; www.doubletree.com
299 rooms. High-speed Internet access. Restaurant, bar. Airport transportation available. Pets accepted. Pool. **$**

★DRURY INN

8155 N. Academy Blvd., Colorado Springs, 719-598-2500, 800-325-8300; www.druryhotels.com
118 rooms. Complimentary continental breakfast. High-speed Internet access. Pets accepted. Pool. **$**

★★EMBASSY SUITES

7290 Commerce Center Drive, Colorado Springs, 719-599-9100;
www.embassysuites.com

206 rooms, all suites. Complimentary full breakfast. Wireless Internet access. Restaurant, bar. Children's activity center. Pool. Fitness center. Business center. **$**

★FAIRFIELD INN

2725 Geyser Drive, Colorado Springs, 719-576-1717, 800-228-2800;
www.fairfieldinn.com

84 rooms. Complimentary continental breakfast. Wireless Internet access. Pets accepted. Pool. Fitness center. Business center. **$**

★HOLIDAY INN EXPRESS

1815 Aeroplaza Drive, Colorado Springs, 719-591-6000, 888-465-4329;
www.hiexpress.com/cos-airport

94 rooms. Complimentary continental breakfast. High-speed Internet access. Airport transportation available. Business center. Pool. Fitness center. **$**

SPECIALTY LODGINGS

CHEYENNE CANON INN

2030 W. Cheyenne Blvd., Colorado Springs, 719-633-0625, 800-633-0625;
www.cheyennecanoninn.com

This mission-style mansion, with views of the mountains, offers access to some of the area's best hiking and driving tours. The warm, professional service will ensure your stay is cozy. 10 rooms. Wireless Internet access. Complimentary full breakfast. Whirlpool. Spa. **$$**

HOLDEN HOUSE 1902 BED & BREAKFAST

1102 W. Pikes Peak Ave., Colorado Springs, 719-471-3980, 888-565-3980;
www.holdenhouse.com

Located in a historic home and carriage house dating to 1902, this inn has modern guest rooms with Victorian charm. Enjoy a gourmet breakfast and afternoon wine social. Five rooms. Children not accepted. Complimentary full breakfast. Business center. **$**

OLD TOWN GUEST HOUSE

115 S. 26th St., Colorado Springs, 719-632-9194, 888-375-4210;
www.oldtown-guesthouse.com

This bed and breakfast located in Old Colorado City has all the amenities of a modern hotel, including an elevator to whisk you to your room, where you'll find a TV/DVD player, coffee machine and desk with voice mail. Eight rooms. Children over 12 years only. Complimentary full breakfast. Wireless Internet access. Airport transportation available. **$**

SPA

★★★★THE SPA AT THE BROADMOOR

1 Lake Ave., Colorado Springs, 719-577-5770, 866-686-3965; www.broadmoor.com

With the beautiful scenery of the Rocky Mountains as a backdrop, the Spa at the Broadmoor already has an advantage over other luxury spas. But even without these

★
★
★
★

surroundings, an experience at this two-level lakefront spa is pure bliss. With Venetian chandeliers, earth tones and an overall feeling of serenity, the treatment rooms perfectly set the scene for the spa's luxurious massage therapies and skin treatments. If your Rocky Mountain adventures have left you with aching muscles, the spa's variety of massage therapies will make you feel like new again, while facial therapies such as the calming chamomile facial will get skin glowing. The Junior Ice Cream manicure and pedicure is reserved for those guests ages 11 and under. **$$**

RESTAURANTS
★★★CHARLES COURT
1 Lake Ave., Colorado Springs, 719-577-5733, 806-634-7711; www.broadmoor.com
One of the many restaurants at the luxurious Broadmoor Hotel, Charles Court offers progressive American fare in a relaxed and contemporary setting. In warm weather, you can dine outdoors with lakeside views. The menu features regional Rocky Mountain fare such as Colorado rack of lamb and the signature Charles Court Game Grill. The wine list boasts more than 600 selections from all around the world. For special occasions, opt for the chef's table in the kitchen (four guests minimum). American menu. Breakfast, dinner, Sunday brunch. Bar. Business casual attire. Reservations recommended. Valet parking. Outdoor seating. **$$$**

★★EDELWEISS
34 E. Ramona Ave., Colorado Springs, 719-633-2220; www.edelweissrest.com
German, Continental menu. Lunch, dinner. Bar. Children's menu. Casual attire. Reservations recommended. Outdoor seating. **$$**

★★FAMOUS STEAKHOUSE
31 N. Tejon St., Colorado Springs, 719-227-7333; www.restauranteur.com/famous
Steak menu. Lunch, dinner. Bar. Casual attire. Reservations recommended. **$$$**

★★GIUSEPPE'S OLD DEPOT
10 S. Sierra Madre, Colorado Springs, 719-635-3111; www.giuseppes-depot.com
American menu. Lunch, dinner. Bar. Children's menu. Casual attire. Reservations recommended. **$$**

★IL VICINO
11 S. Tejon St., Colorado Springs, 719-475-9224; www.ilvicino.com
Italian menu. Lunch, dinner, late-night. Bar. Casual attire. Outdoor seating. **$**

★★JAKE AND TELLY'S GREEK DINING
2616 W. Colorado Ave., Colorado Springs, 719-633-0406; www.greekdining.com
Greek menu. Lunch, dinner. Bar. Children's menu. Casual attire. Reservations recommended. Outdoor seating. **$$**

★LA CREPERIE BISTRO
204 N. Tejon, Colorado Springs, 719-632-0984; www.creperiebistro.com
French menu. Breakfast, lunch, dinner. Casual attire. Reservations recommended. Outdoor seating. **$$**

★★LA PETITE MAISON

1015 W. Colorado Ave., Colorado Springs, 719-632-4887; www.lapetitemaisoncs.com
French American menu. Lunch, dinner. Closed Monday. Business casual attire. Reservations recommended. Outdoor seating. **$$$**

★★MACKENZIE'S CHOP HOUSE

128 S. Tejon St., Colorado Springs, 719-635-3536; www.mackenzieschophouse.com
American, seafood, steak menu. Lunch, dinner. Bar. Children's menu. Casual attire. Reservations recommended. Outdoor seating. **$$$**

★OLD CHICAGO PASTA & PIZZA

118 N. Tejon St., Colorado Springs, 719-634-8812; www.oldchicago.com
American, pizza menu. Lunch, dinner, late-night. Bar. Children's menu. Casual attire. Outdoor seating. **$**

★★★★PENROSE ROOM

1 Lake Ave., Colorado Springs, 719-577-5777, 800-634-7711; www.broadmoor.com
Located within the Broadmoor, the sophisticated and recently renovated Penrose Room offers a spectacular dining experience set against magnificent views of Colorado Springs and Cheyenne Mountain. Chef Bertrand Bouquin serves up contemporary continental cuisine influenced by the food of Italy, Spain, Africa and France. The menu changes often and offers prix fixe meals of three, four and seven courses. Favorite appetizers include pistachio-laden warm goat cheese salad, five herbs ravioli and chilled peekytoe crab with cherry relish salad. Entrées include roasted loin of Colorado lamb with purple mustard and slowly cooked halibut in black olive oil. After dinner, enjoy live music and dancing. French menu. Dinner. Closed Sunday. Bar. Children's menu. Jacket required. Reservations recommended. Valet parking. **$$$$**

★★★SUMMIT AT THE BROADMOOR

1 Lake Ave., Colorado Springs, 719-577-5777, 800-634-7711; www.broadmoor.com
At one of the country's premier resorts, Summit fills every bill—from impeccable service to memorable meals to the inventive interior. Chef Bertrand Bouquin was privileged enough to spend time under the tutelage of world-class chefs including Alain Ducasse, Daniel Boulud, and Jean-Pierre Bruneau before coming to Summit to create such chef d'oeuvres as the favored braised beef short ribs with rioja, baby carrots and roasted garlic mashed potatoes. The food is accented by the edgy design, which centers on a turning glass turret of wine bottles—the ultimate wine rack, if you will. American menu. Dinner. Closed Monday. Bar. Business casual attire. Children's menu available. Reservations recommended. Complimentary valet parking. **$$$**

CORTEZ

Originally a trading center for sheep and cattle ranchers, Cortez now accommodates travelers visiting Mesa Verde National Park and oil workers whose business takes them to the nearby Aneth oil field. The semi-desert area 38 miles southwest of Cortez includes the only spot in the nation where one can stand in four states (Colorado, Utah, Arizona, New Mexico) and two Native American nations (Navajo and Ute) at one time. A simple marker located approximately 100 yards from the Four Corners

Highway (Highway 160) indicates the exact place where these areas meet. There are many opportunities for hunting and fishing in the Dolores River valley.

Information: Cortez/Mesa Verde Visitor Info Bureau, 928 E. Main, Cortez, 970-565-3414; www.cortezchamber.org

WHAT TO SEE AND DO
ANASAZI HERITAGE CENTER AND ESCALANTE
27501 Highway 184, Dolores, 970-882-5600; www.co.blm.gov/ahc/index.htm
This museum showcases the Anasazi and other Native American cultures. See exhibits on archaeology and local history. The Escalante site, discovered by a Franciscan friar in 1776, is within a half-mile of the center. This is also the starting point for visits to the Canyons of the Ancients National Monument. March-October, daily 9 a.m.-5 p.m.; November-February, daily 9 a.m.-4 p.m.

HOVENWEEP NATIONAL MONUMENT
McElmo Route, Cortez, 970-562-4282; www.nps.gov/hove
This monument consists of six units of prehistoric ruins—the best preserved is at Square Tower, which includes the remains of pueblos and towers. Self-guided trail (park ranger on duty); visitor area. Daily 8 a.m.-5 p.m.

LOWRY PUEBLO
27501 Highway 184, Cortez, 970-882-5600; www.blm.gov/co/st/en/fo/ahc/ archaeological_sites/lowry_pueblo.html
Part of the Canyons of the Ancients National Monument, the Lowry Pueblo was constructed by the Anasazi (circa 1075) and includes forty excavated rooms. Picnic facilities. No camping. Daily, weather and road conditions permitting.

UTE MOUNTAIN TRIBAL PARK
Highway Junction 160/491 nearCortez, 970-749-1452; www.utemountainute.com/tribalpark.htm
The Ute Mountain Tribe developed this 125,000-acre park on their tribal lands, opening hundreds of largely unexplored 800-year-old Anasazi ruins to the public. Tours begin at the Ute Mountain Visitor Center/Museum, 19 miles south of Cortez via Highway 666 (daily); reservations required. Backpacking trips in summer. Primitive camping available.

SPECIAL EVENTS
MONTEZUMA COUNTY FAIR
Montezuma County Fairgrounds, 30100 Highway 160, Cortez, 970-565-1000; www.co.montezuma.co.us
The fair includes an antique tractor parade, barbecue and carnival. First week in August.

UTE MOUNTAIN ROUND-UP RODEO
Montezuma County Fairgrounds, 30100 Highway 160, Cortez, 970-565-8151
This weeklong extravaganza includes rodeo events as well as a children's "parade"— kids march to businesses downtown and receive treats. Early-mid-June.

141

COLORADO

★
★
★
★
★

HOTELS
★BEST WESTERN TURQUOISE INN & SUITES
535 E. Main St., Cortez, 970-565-3778, 800-547-3376; www.cortezbestwestern.com
77 rooms. High-speed Internet access. Complimentary continental breakfast. Airport transportation available. Pets accepted. Pool. Business center. $

★HOLIDAY INN EXPRESS
2121 E. Main St., Cortez, 970-565-6000, 800-626-5652; www.coloradoholiday.com
100 rooms. High-speed Internet access. Complimentary continental breakfast. Airport transportation available. Pets accepted. Pool. Business center. $

CRAIG
Craig is known for excellent big-game hunting for elk, deer and antelope, as well as bass fishing in Elkhead Reservoir. The Yampa River area draws float-boaters, hikers and wildlife photographers in summer and cross-country skiers in winter.
Information: Greater Craig Area Chamber of Commerce, 360 E. Victory Way, Craig, 970-824-5689, 800-864-4405; www.craig-chamber.com

WHAT TO SEE AND DO
MARCIA
Craig City Park, 341 E. Victory Way, Craig, 970-824-5689
See the private, luxury Pullman railroad car of David Moffat—an important financier and industrialist in late 19th-century Colorado who built many railroads. The car, named for his daughter, is listed on the National Register of Historic Places. Tours are available through the Moffat County Visitors Center.

MUSEUM OF NORTHWEST COLORADO
590 Yampa Ave., Craig, 970-824-6360; www.museumnwco.org
Learn about local history and see wildlife photography. Includes a cowboy and gunfighter collection. Memorabilia from Edwin C. Johnson, governor of Colorado and a U.S. senator, are also on display. Monday-Saturday 9 a.m.-5 p.m.

SAVE OUR SANDROCKS NATURE TRAIL
900 Alta Vista Drive, Craig, 970-824-5689
This sloped, ¾-mile trail provides a view of American Indian petroglyphs on the sandrocks.

HOTEL
★★HOLIDAY INN
300 S. Highway 13, Craig, 970-824-4000, 888-465-4329; www.holiday-inn.com
152 rooms. High-speed Internet access. Restaurant. Pets accepted. Pool. $

CRESTED BUTTE
Crested Butte is a picturesque mining town in the midst of magnificent mountain country. Inquire locally for information on horseback pack trips to Aspen through the West Elk Wilderness. Guided fishing trips are also available on the more than 1,000 miles of streams and rivers within a two-hour drive of Crested Butte.
Information: Crested Butte Visitor Center, Crested Butte, 800-544-4505; www.crestedbutteresort.com

WHAT TO SEE AND DO
CRESTED BUTTE MOUNTAIN RESORT SKI AREA
12 Snowmass Road, Crested Butte, 800-810-7669; www.skicb.com
Four high-speed quad, two triple, three double chairlifts, three surface lifts, two magic carpets; patrol, school, rentals, snowmaking. Longest run 2½ miles; vertical drop 3,062 feet. Multiday, half-day rates. Late November-mid-April, daily. Nineteen miles of groomed cross-country trails, 100 miles of wilderness trails; snowmobiling, sleigh rides.

SPECIALTY LODGING
THE NORDIC INN
14 Treasury Road, Crested Butte, 970-349-5542, 800-542-7669;
www.nordicinncb.com
24 rooms. Closed May. Complimentary continental breakfast. Whirlpool. **$**

RESTAURANTS
★DONITA'S CANTINA
332 Elk Ave., Crested Butte, 970-349-6674
Mexican menu. Dinner. Bar. Children's menu. Casual attire. **$$**

★★LE BOSQUET
Sixth and Belleview, Crested Butte, 970-349-5808
French menu. Dinner. Closed mid-April-mid-May. Bar. Outdoor seating. **$$**

CRIPPLE CREEK 143

At its height, Cripple Creek and the surrounding area produced as much as $25 million in gold in a single year. It was nearly a ghost town when citizens voted to allow legalized gambling in the 1990s. Today it is mostly a gambling and tourist town and has managed to preserve some of its Old West charm.
Information: Chamber of Commerce, 719-689-2169, 877-858-4653;
www.visitcripplecreek.com

★
★★
★★
★

WHAT TO SEE AND DO
CRIPPLE CREEK CASINOS
Cripple Creek, 877-858-4653; www.visitcripple-creek.com
Cripple Creek has nearly 20 limited-stakes ($5 bet limit) casinos along its Victorian storefront main street area. Daily.

CRIPPLE CREEK DISTRICT MUSEUM
Fifth Street and Bennett Avenue, Cripple Creek, 719-689-2634; www.cripple-creek.org
See artifacts of Cripple Creek's glory days including pioneer relics, mining and railroad displays. June-September: daily 10 a.m.-5 p.m.; October-May: Friday-Sunday 10 a.m.-4 p.m.

CRIPPLE CREEK-VICTOR NARROW GAUGE RAILROAD
Fifth Street and Bennett Avenue, Cripple Creek, 719-689-2640
Authentic locomotive and coaches depart from Cripple Creek District Museum. The four-mile round-trip travels past many historic mines. Late May-early October, daily, departs every 45 minutes.

IMPERIAL CASINO HOTEL

123 N. Third St., Cripple Creek, 719-689-7777, 800-235-2922;
www.imperialcasinohotel.com

This 1896 hotel-turned-casino was constructed shortly after the town's great fire and features a variety of slot machines.

MOLLIE KATHLEEN GOLD MINE

Highway 67, Cripple Creek, 719-689-2466, 888-291-5689;
www.goldminetours.com

Descend 1,000 feet on a one-hour guided tour through a gold mine. April-October: daily; tours depart every 10 minutes. Pets not accepted.

VICTOR

Cripple Creek, five miles south on Highway 67, on the southwest side of Pikes Peak,
719-689-2284; www.victorcolorado.com

This "city of mines" actually has streets paved with gold (low-grade ore was used to surface streets in the early days).

SPECIAL EVENTS
DONKEY DERBY DAYS

City Park and Bennett Avenue, Cripple Creek, 719-689-3315;
www.visitcripplecreek.com

Annual series of donkey races includes children's events and a parade. Last full weekend in June.

★
★
★
★
☆

VETERAN'S MEMORIAL RALLY

City Park, Cripple Creek, 719-487-8005

Four-day event honoring veterans. Mid-August.

HOTELS
★★★CARR MANOR

350 E. Carr Ave., Cripple Creek, 719-689-3709; www.carrmanor.com

A night at this boutique hotel, housed in a former 1890's schoolhouse, includes a full breakfast served in the original high school cafeteria. Rooms feature original chalkboards for messages. There's also a small fitness spa. 15 rooms. Closed January-February; also weekdays March-April. Children over 12 years only. Complimentary full breakfast. Wireless Internet access. **$**

★★DOUBLE EAGLE HOTEL & CASINO

442 E. Bennett Ave., Cripple Creek, 719-689-5000, 800-711-7234; www.decasino.com

158 rooms. Complimentary full breakfast. Wireless Internet access. Restaurant, two bars. Casino. $

★★IMPERIAL CASINO HOTEL

123 N. Third St., Cripple Creek, 719-689-7777, 800-235-2922;
www.imperialcasinohotel.com

26 rooms. Restaurant, bar. **$**

SPECIALTY LODGING
VICTOR HOTEL
Fourth Street and Victor Avenue, Victor, 719-689-3553, 800-713-4595;
www.victorhotelcolorado.com
20 rooms. Complimentary continental breakfast. Restaurant. Pets accepted. **$**

RESTAURANT
★★STRATTON DINING ROOM
123 N. Third St., Cripple Creek, 719-689-7777
Breakfast, lunch, dinner. Bar. Valet parking. **$$**

DENVER

The capital of Colorado, nicknamed the "Mile High City" because its official eleva-
tion is exactly one mile above sea level, began as a settlement of gold seekers, many
of them unsuccessful. In its early years, Denver almost lost out to several booming
mountain mining centers in the race to become the state's major city. In 1858, the
community consisted of some 60 raffish cabins, plus Colorado's first saloon. With
the onset of the silver rush in the 1870s, Denver came into its own. By 1890, the
population had topped 100,000. Bolstered by the wealth that poured in from the rich
mines in the Rockies, Denver rapidly became Colorado's economic and cultural cen-
ter. It boomed again after World War II and in the 1990s. Today, with the Great Plains
sweeping away to the east, the foothills of the Rocky Mountains immediately to the
west, and a dry, mild climate (where you'll find 300 days of sunshine), Denver is
a growing city with 2.5 million people in the metropolitan area. A building boom
in the 1990s resulted in a new airport, a downtown baseball park surrounded by a
lively nightlife district dubbed LoDo (lower downtown), new football, basketball and
hockey stadiums, and a redeveloped river valley just west of downtown with an aquar-
ium, amusement park and shopping district. Once economically tied to Colorado's
natural resources, Denver now boasts one of the most diverse economies in the United
States and is a hub for the cable and telecom industries. Parks have long been a point
of civic pride in Denver. The Denver Mountain Park System covers 13,448 acres,
scattered over 380 square miles. The chain begins 15 miles west of the city at Red
Rocks Park, the site of a renowned musical venue, and extends 60 miles to the west to
Summit Lake perched 12,740 feet above sea level.

Information: Denver Metro Convention & Visitors Bureau, 1555 California St.,
303-892-1112, 800-233-6837; www.denver.org

WHAT TO SEE AND DO
16TH STREET MALL
16th Street between Civic Center and Denver Union Station, Denver,
303-534-6161; www.downtowndenver.com
This tree-lined pedestrian promenade of red and gray granite runs through the center
of Denver's downtown shopping district—outdoor cafés, shops, restaurants, hotels,
fountains and plazas line its mile-long walk. European-built shuttle buses offer
transportation from either end of the promenade. Along the mall you'll find Lar-
imer Square. This restoration of the first street in Denver includes a collection of
shops, galleries, nightclubs and restaurants set among Victorian courtyards, gaslights,
arcades and buildings. Carriage rides around square. Daily.

COLORADO

★
★
★
★
★

ANTIQUE ROW

From 300 to 2100 South Broadway, Denver; www.antique-row.com

More than 400 shops along a 14-block stretch of South Broadway sell everything from books to music to vintage Western wear to museum-quality furniture. Take the light rail to Broadway and Interstate 25 (I-25) to begin your tour. Most dealers are located between the 400 and 2000 blocks of South Broadway and the 25 and 27 blocks of East Dakota Avenue. Daily.

ARVADA CENTER FOR THE ARTS & HUMANITIES

6901 Wadsworth Blvd.,Arvada, 720-898-7200; www.arvadacenter.org

Performing arts center with concerts, plays, classes, demonstrations, art galleries and banquet hall. Amphitheater seats 1,200 (June-early September). Historical museum with old cabin and pioneer artifacts. Museum and gallery. Monday-Friday 9 a.m.-6 p.m., Saturday 9 a.m.-5 p.m., Sunday 1-5 p.m.

BOETTCHER CONCERT HALL

1245 Champa St., Denver, 720-865-4220; www.artscomplex.com

The first fully "surround" symphonic hall in the U.S.—all of its 2,630 seats are within 75 feet of the stage. Home of the Colorado Symphony Orchestra (September-early June) and Opera Colorado with performances in the round (May).

BYERS-EVANS HOUSE MUSEUM

1310 Bannock St., Denver, 303-620-4933; www.coloradohistory.org

Restored Victorian house featuring the history of two noted Colorado pioneer families. Guided tours available. Tuesday-Sunday 11 a.m.-3 p.m.

CHARLES C. GATES PLANETARIUM

2001 Colorado Blvd., Denver, 303-322-7009; www.dmns.org

A variety of star and laser light shows are shown here daily. The Phipps IMAX Theater has an immense motion picture system projecting images on screen 4½ stories tall and 6½ stories wide. Located in the Denver Museum of Nature and Science. Daily showings.

CHEESMAN PARK

East Eighth Avenue and Franklin Street, Denver

This park has excellent views of nearby mountain peaks, marked off by dial and pointers. The Congress Park swimming pool is next to it and the Denver Botanical Gardens are also nearby.

THE CHILDREN'S MUSEUM OF DENVER

2121 Children's Museum Drive, Denver, 303-433-7444; www.cmdenver.org

This 24,000-square-foot, two-story hands-on museum allows children to learn and explore the world around them. Exhibits include a year-round ski slope, science center and grocery store. Monday-Friday 9 a.m.-4 p.m., Wednesday until 7:30 p.m., Saturday-Sunday 10 a.m.-5 p.m.

COLORADO AVALANCHE (NHL)

Pepsi Center, 1000 Chopper Circle, Denver, 303-405-1100;
www.coloradoavalanche.com
Professional hockey team.

COLORADO HISTORY MUSEUM

1300 Broadway, Denver, 303-866-3682; www.coloradohistory.org
Permanent and rotating exhibits on the people and history of Colorado, including full-scale mining equipment, American Indian artifacts and photographs and a sod house. Monday-Saturday 10 a.m.-5 p.m., Sunday noon-5 p.m.

COLORADO RAPIDS (MLS)

Dick's Sporting Goods Park, 6000 Victory Way, Commerce City, 303-727-3500;
www.coloradorapids.com
Professional soccer team. Tours. Thursday-Saturday 10 a.m.-3 p.m., every 30 minutes.

COLORADO ROCKIES (MLB)

Coors Field, 2001 Blake St., Denver, 303-762-5437, 800-388-7625;
www.colorado.rockies.mlb.com
Professional baseball team. Tours of Coors Field available; call for fees and schedule.

COLORADO'S OCEAN JOURNEY

700 Water St., Denver, 303-561-4450, 888-561-4450
This world-class 106,500-square-foot aquarium brings visitors face to face with more than 300 species of fish, birds, mammals and invertebrates from around the world. Check out the pool stocked with stingrays. Sunday-Thursday 10 a.m.-10 p.m., Friday-Saturday 10 a.m.-11 p.m.

COMANCHE CROSSING MUSEUM

56060 E. Colfax Ave., Strasburg, 303-622-4322
Experience what is was like to travel via the railways in the late 1800s. This museum includes memorabilia from the completion of the transcontinental railway and includes two buildings on landscaped grounds with period rooms, a restored schoolhouse (circa 1891) and wood-vaned windmill (circa 1880). May-August, daily 1-4 p.m.

DENVER ART MUSEUM

100 W. 14th Ave. Parkway, Denver, 720-865-5000; www.denverartmuseum.org
Houses a collection of art objects representing almost every culture and period, including a fine collection of American Indian art; changing exhibits. Free admission first Saturday of the month. Tuesday-Saturday 10 a.m.-5 p.m., Sunday noon-5 p.m.; closed Monday.

DENVER BOTANIC GARDENS

1005 York St., Denver, 720-865-3500; www.botanicgardens.org
This tropical paradise, which occupies 23 acres about 10 minutes east of downtown, is home to more than 15,000 plant species from around the world. The Conservatory, which holds more than 850 tropical and subtropical plants in an enclosed rainforest setting, is a soothing retreat for midwinter guests. A recent addition is the Cloud

Forest Tree covered with hundreds of orchids and rare tropical plants. There are also alpine, herb, Japanese and wildflower gardens. Children particularly enjoy navigating the mazes in the Secret Path garden and climbing the resident banyan tree. Mid-September-April: daily 9 a.m.-5 p.m.; May-mid-September: Saturday-Tuesday 9 a.m.-8 p.m., Wednesday-Friday 9 a.m.-5 p.m.

DENVER BRONCOS (NFL)
Invesco Field at Mile High, 1701 Bryant St., Denver, 720-258-3333; www.denverbroncos.com
Professional football team. Tours are available; call for fees and schedule.

DENVER FIREFIGHTERS MUSEUM
1326 Tremont Place, Denver, 303-892-1436; www.denverfirefightersmuseum.org
Housed in Fire House No. 1, this museum maintains the atmosphere of a working firehouse, with firefighting equipment from the mid-1800s. Admission: adults $6, seniors and students $5, children under 13 $4. Monday-Saturday 10 a.m.-4 p.m.

DENVER MUSEUM OF NATURE AND SCIENCE
City Park, 2001 Colorado Blvd., Denver, 303-322-7009, 800-925-2250; www.dmns.org
Ninety habitat exhibits from four continents are displayed against natural backgrounds. The Prehistoric Journey exhibit displays dinosaurs in recreated environments. There's also an earth sciences lab, gems and minerals, and a Native American collection. Daily 9 a.m.-5 p.m.

DENVER NUGGETS (NBA)
Pepsi Center, 1000 Chopper Circle, Denver, 803-405-1100; www.nba.com/nuggets
Professional basketball team. Tours of the arena are available.

DENVER PERFORMING ARTS COMPLEX
Speer Boulevard and Arapahoe Street, Denver, 720-865-4220; www.artscomplex.com
One of the most innovative and comprehensive performing arts centers in the county. The addition of the Temple Hoyne Buell Theatre makes it one of the largest under one roof. The complex also contains shops and restaurants.

DENVER PUBLIC LIBRARY
10 W. 14th Ave. Parkway, Denver, 720-865-1111; www.denverlibrary.org
This is the largest public library in the Rocky Mountain region with nearly four million items, including an outstanding Western History collection and Patent Depository Library. Programs, exhibits. Monday-Tuesday 10 a.m.-8 p.m., Thursday-Friday 10 a.m.-6 p.m., Saturday 9 a.m.-5 p.m., Sunday 1-5 p.m.

DENVER ZOO
City Park, 2300 Steele St., Denver, 303-376-4800; www.denverzoo.org
Located in City Park just east of downtown, this 80-acre zoological wonderland is home to more than 4,000 animals representing 700 species. Founded in 1896, the zoo has evolved into one of the nation's premier animal exhibits, noted for its beautiful grounds, innovative combination of outdoor and enclosed habitats and world-class conservation and breeding programs. Don't miss the Primate Panorama, a seven-acre

showcase of rare monkeys and apes. Visit the 22,000-square-foot, glass-enclosed Tropical Discovery and feel what its like to walk into a tropical rain forest complete with caves, cliffs, waterfalls and some of the zoo's most exotic (and dangerous) creatures. The Northern Shores Arctic wildlife habitat provides a nose-to-nose underwater look at swimming polar bears and sea lions. Be sure to check out the feeding schedule posted just inside the zoo's entrance. During evenings throughout December, holiday music and millions of sparkling lights transform the zoo as part of the traditional Wonderlights festival. April-September: daily 9 a.m.-6 p.m.; October-March: daily 10 a.m.-5 p.m.

ELITCH GARDENS

2000 Elitch Circle, Denver, 303-595-4386; www.elitchgardens.com
Located in downtown Denver, this park is best known for its extreme roller coaster rides. Other favorites include a 22-story freefall in the Tower of Doom, white-water rafting and the new Flying Coaster, which simulates the experience of flying. Includes a kiddie park for younger children, the popular Island Kingdom water park and live entertainment nightly. June-August 10 a.m.-10 p.m.; limited and weekend hours May and September.

FORNEY MUSEUM OF TRANSPORTATION

4303 Brighton Blvd., Denver, 303-297-1113; www.forneymuseum.com
This museum houses more than 300 antique cars, carriages, cycles, sleighs, steam locomotives and coaches. One of the most notable permanent exhibits is that of Union Pacific "Big Boy" locomotive X4005, which was involved in a horrific crash in 1953, but has been restored and sits on the museum's grounds. You can also see the "Gold Bug" Kissel automobile owned by Amelia Earhart and Crown Prince Aly Khan's Rolls Royce. Monday-Saturday 10 a.m.-4 p.m.

FOUR MILE HISTORIC PARK

715 S. Forest St., Denver, 720-865-0800; www.fourmilehistoricpark.org
Once a stage stop, this 14-acre living history museum encompasses the oldest house still standing in Denver (circa 1859), plus other outbuildings and farm equipment from the late 1800s. Guides in period costume reenact life on a farmstead. And it's a great place for a picnic. April-September, Wednesday-Friday noon-4 p.m., Saturday-Sunday 10 a.m.-4 p.m.; October-March, Wednesday-Sunday noon-4 p.m.

HALL OF LIFE

2001 Colorado Blvd., Denver, 303-370-6453; www.dmns.org
This health education center has permanent exhibits on genetics, fitness, nutrition and the five senses. Daily 9 a.m.-5 p.m.

THE HELEN BONFILS THEATRE COMPLEX

Denver, 303-572-4466; www.denvercenter.org
Home of the Denver Center Theatre Company. Contains three theaters: the Stage, seating 547 in a circle around a thrust platform; the Space, a theater-in-the-round seating 450; and the Source, a small theater presenting plays by American playwrights. Also contains the Frank Ricketson Theatre, a 195-seat theater available for rental for community activities, classes and festivals.

COLORADO

★
★
★
★
★

HYLAND HILLS WATER WORLD

1800 W. 89th Ave., Federal Heights, 303-427-7873; www.waterworldcolorado.com
Ranked among the nation's largest water parks, this 64-acre aquatic extravaganza is a great time for all ages. Water World's beautifully landscaped grounds include a wave pool the size of a football field, 16 water slides, nine inner-tube rides and a splash pool for tots. Hours vary according to season and weather, so be sure to call ahead. Late May-early September: daily 10 a.m.-6 p.m.

MOLLY BROWN HOUSE MUSEUM

1340 Pennsylvania St., Denver, 303-832-4092; www.mollybrown.org
This museum stands as an enduring tribute to Margaret Molly Brown, the "unsinkable survivor" of the *Titanic*. A spectacular example of Colorado Victorian design, the fully restored 1880s sandstone and lava stone mansion—designed by one of Denver's most famous architects, William Lang—is filled with many of the lavish furnishings and personal possessions of its famous occupant. September-May, Monday-Saturday 10 a.m.-3:30 p.m., Sunday noon-3:30 p.m.; June-August, Monday-Saturday 9 a.m.-4 p.m., Sunday noon-4 p.m.

PEARCE-MCALLISTER COTTAGE

1880 Gaylord St., Denver, 303-322-1053;
www.coloradohistory.org/hist_sites/Pearce/P_Mcallister.htm
This 1899 Dutch Colonial Revival house contains original furnishings. The second floor houses the Denver Museum of Dolls, Toys and Miniatures. Tuesday-Saturday 10 a.m.-4 p.m., Sunday 1-4 p.m.; closed holidays.

150

SAKURA SQUARE

Larimer Street between 19th and 20th streets, Denver
Denver's Japanese Cultural and Trade Center features Asian restaurants, shops, businesses and authentic Japanese gardens. This is also the site of a famed Buddhist Temple.

SKI TRAIN

Union Station, 555 Seventh St., Denver, 303-296-4754; www.skitrain.com
A ride on the Ski Train from downtown Denver to Winter Mountain Ski Resort in Winter Park has been a favorite day trip for skiers, hikers, bikers and family vacationers since 1940. Operating on weekends year-round, the 14-car train takes you on a spectacular 60-mile wilderness ride through the Rockies and across the Continental Divide, climbing 4,000 feet and passing through 28 tunnels before dropping you off at the front entrance of beautiful Winter Park Resort. Tickets are for round-trip, same-day rides only, and reservations are highly recommended. Winter: Saturday-Sunday; June-August: Saturday.

STATE CAPITOL

200 E. Colfax Ave., Denver, 303-866-2604; www.milehighcity.com/capitol
This magnificent edifice overlooking Civic Center Park is a glorious reminder of Denver's opulent past. Designed by architect Elijah Myers in the classical Corinthian style, it was 18 years in the making before its official dedication in 1908. The building is renowned for its exquisite interior details and use of native materials such as

gray granite, white marble, pink Colorado onyx and of course, the gold that covers its dome. Tours include a climb to the dome, 272 feet up, for a spectacular view of the surrounding mountains. Look for the special marker on the steps outside noting that you are, indeed, a mile high. Monday-Friday 7 a.m.-5:30 p.m.

TEMPLE HOYNE BUELL THEATER

1050 13th St., Denver, 303-893-4100; www.denvercenter.org

This 1908 theater—which has hosted operas, political conventions, revivalist meetings and more—is now the stage for Broadway productions and the Colorado Ballet. It's also the home of Colorado Contemporary Dance.

UNIVERSITY OF DENVER

South University Boulevard and East Evans Avenue, Denver, 303-871-2000; www.du.edu

Established in 1864; 8,500 students. Handsome 125-acre main campus with historic buildings dating back to the 1800s. The 33-acre Park Hill campus at Montview Boulevard and Quebec Street is the site of the University of Denver Law School (Lowell Thomas Law Building) and the Lamont School of Music (Houston Fine Arts Center). For a schedule of performances, call 303-871-6400. Campus tours. The University also includes the Chamberlin Observatory, which houses a 20-inch aperture Clark-Saegmuller refractor in use since 1894.

WASHINGTON PARK

Downing Street between East Virginia and East Louisiana avenues, Denver, 303-698-4962

This 165-acre park features a large recreation center with an indoor pool and floral displays, including a replica of George Washington's gardens at Mount Vernon.

SPECIAL EVENTS

CHERRY CREEK ARTS FESTIVAL

Cherry Creek North, on Second and Third avenues between Clayton and Steele streets, 303-355-2787; www.cherryarts.org

Features works by 200 national artists, plus culinary and performing arts. July Fourth weekend.

DENVER FILM FESTIVAL

Starz FilmCenter at the Tivoli, 900 Auraria Parkway, Denver, 303-595-3456; www.denverfilm.org

Movie junkies will get more than their fill of flicks at this 10-day festival, which showcases 175 films, including international feature releases, independent fiction and documentaries, experimental productions and children's programs. All films are shown at the Starz FilmCenter at the Tivoli. Fall.

DENVER LIGHTS AND PARADE OF LIGHTS

Denver, downtown starting at Civic Center Park in front of the City and County Building, 303-478-7878; www.denverparadeoflights.com

From early December through January, downtown Denver is ablaze with what is possibly the largest holiday light show in the world. Locals and tourists drift down

COLORADO

★
★
★
★
★

to Civic Center Park after dark to view the incredible rainbow display covering the buildings. A spectacular Parade of Lights that winds for two miles through Denver's downtown kicks off the holiday season.

THE INTERNATIONAL AT CASTLE PINES GOLF CLUB

8480 E. Orchard Road, Greenwood Village, 303-660-8000; www.golfintl.com

The International is a week-long, world-class golf event that attracts some of the top professional golfers. The Jack Nicklaus-designed course is renowned for the beauty of its pine-strewn mountain setting and the challenge of its terrain. The tournament begins in earnest on Thursday, but spectators are welcome to watch practice rounds as well as the junior and pro-am tournaments held earlier in the week. One week in August.

NATIONAL WESTERN STOCK SHOW, RODEO & HORSE SHOW

National Western Complex, 4655 Humboldt St., Denver, 303-297-1166, 888-551-5004; www.nationalwestern.com

This two-week extravaganza—which includes 600,000 exhibitors and spectators— is packed with nonstop shows and demonstrations, from sheep shearing to steer wrestling. Daily rodeos showcase the horse- and bull-riding skills of some of the best riders in the country before cheering, sellout crowds in the National Western Complex. Other favorites include barrel races, show-horse contests, a junior rodeo (where some of the riders are as young as three years old), Wild West shows and the colorful Mexican Rodeo Extravaganza. Take a break from the action and tour the exhibition hall for demonstrations in wool spinning and goat milking, or walk the grounds to see what a yak looks like up close. Mid-January.

HOTELS

★★★★THE BROWN PALACE HOTEL

321 17th St., Denver, 303-297-3511, 800-321-2599; www.brownpalace.com

Denver's most celebrated and historic hotel, the Brown Palace has hosted presidents, royalty and celebrities since 1892. The elegant lobby features a magnificent stained-glass ceiling that tops off six levels of cast-iron balconies. The luxurious guest rooms have two styles—Victorian or Art Deco. The award-winning Palace Arms restaurant features signature favorites like rack of lamb and pan-roasted veal. Cigar aficionados take to the library-like ambience of the Churchill Bar. Afternoon tea is accompanied by live harp music. And Ellygnton's Sunday brunch is legendary. After a busy day of exploring nearby attractions like the 16th Street Mall and the Museum of Natural History, the full-service spa is the perfect place to unwind with a deep massage, body treatment or facial. 241 rooms. Wireless Internet access. Three restaurants, bar. Spa. Pets accepted. Fitness center. Business center. Pool. $$$

★COMFORT INN DOWNTOWN

401 17th St., Denver, 303-296-0400, 877-424-6423; www.comfortinn.com

231 rooms. Complimentary full breakfast. Wireless Internet access. Pool. Business center. Fitness center. Airport transportation available. Pets accepted. $$

★★★GRAND HYATT

1750 Welton St., Denver, 303-295-1234, 888-591-1234; www.grandhyattdenver.com

The beautiful lobby of this centrally located hotel has a 20-foot sandstone fireplace and cozy seating areas with touches of mahogany, granite and wrought iron. Stay fit with the rooftop tennis courts surrounded by a jogging track, indoor pool and health club. The hotel's restaurant 1876, which is the year Colorado became a state, is a nice spot for dinner. 556 rooms. Complimentary continental breakfast. Wireless Internet access. Restaurant, bar. Pool. Business center. Fitness center. $$$

★★HISTORIC CASTLE MARNE INN

1572 Race St., Denver, 303-331-0621, 800-926-2763; www.castlemarne.com

Nine rooms. Complimentary full breakfast. Wireless Internet access. $$

★★★HOTEL MONACO DENVER

1717 Champa St., Denver, 303-296-1717, 800-990-1303; www.monaco-denver.com

The lobby feels like an elegant, somewhat exotic living room with cushy couches, recessed bookshelves and potted palms. But the scene stealer at this hotel is the domed ceiling, described as a Russian Circus Tent, with diamond shapes in blue, green and gold. The punchy décor carries through to the hallways and guest rooms, with bold, colorful stripes on the walls and very glam black and white ottomans. The rooms also include plush duvet covers, bathroom phones and terrycloth shower curtains. The 24-hour room service is like the cherry on top. 189 rooms. Pets accepted. Wireless Internet access. Restaurant. Spa. Fitness center, Business center. $$$

★★★HOTEL TEATRO

1100 14th St., Denver, 303-228-1100, 888-727-1200; www.hotelteatro.com

Located across from the Denver Center for the Performing Arts, the Hotel Teatro inspires its guests with creative design and contemporary flair. Down comforters, Frette linens, Aveda bath products and Starbucks coffee keep you feeling relaxed, while the staff attends to your every whim. Want someone to draw you an aromatherapy bath? This is the place. Even Fido gets the VIP treatment, with a doggie dish with his name on it and Fiji water. Chef Kevin Taylor, who oversees two restaurants here, is something of a local sensation. 110 rooms. Wireless Internet access. Two restaurants, bar. Pets accepted. Business center. Fitness center. $$$

★★★JET HOTEL

1612 Wazee St., Denver, 303-572-3300, 877-418-2462; www.thejethotel.com

The dimly lit lobby gives you an idea of what you can expect from this ultra-modern boutique hotel. To the right is the open counter of Velocity, where you can get crêpes and organic coffee each morning. To the left, stretching almost the entire length of the lobby, is the futuristic Flow Bar, backlit in soft colors that change every few minutes. Step around a handful of tall, round cocktail tables to get to the inconspicuous reception desk. There are just 19 rooms here, in which standard amenities are anything but. No coffeemakers—just French plunge pots. No ice buckets—only funky insulated pitchers. No clock radios, either. Instead, there's a CD alarm clock with a library of CDs. 19 rooms. Children not allowed. Complimentary continental breakfast. Wireless Internet access. Restaurant, two bars. $$$

★★★JW MARRIOTT DENVER AT CHERRY CREEK

150 Clayton Lane, Denver, 303-316-2700; www.jwmarriottdenver.com

There is plenty to do right outside the doors of this property located just a few miles east of downtown in Cherry Creek. The area is filled with high-end boutiques, art galleries and trendy restaurants. This luxury boutique hotel has modern décor and features comfortable guest rooms with 32-inch flatscreen TVs and minibars—though you may find yourself hanging out in the lobby, which has a waterfall, fireplace and live jazz. Pets are welcomed with sheepskin beds, their own dining menus and designer bowls. 196 rooms. Wireless Internet access. Restaurant, bar. Spa. Whirlpool. Business center. **$$$**

★★★LOEWS DENVER HOTEL

4150 E. Mississippi Ave., Denver, 303-639-1625, 866-563-9792;
www.loewshotels.com

Saying this hotel caters to the entire family is an understatement. Kids get Frisbees, backpacks and games. The hotel also offers a variety of amenities for babies, including tubs, electric bottle warmers and invisible outlet plugs. For mom and dad, there's a menu of comfort items like chenille throws, a pillow menu and CDs. And everyone will appreciate the fitness room and restaurant. 183 rooms. Wireless Internet access. Restaurant, bar. Children's activity center. Fitness center. Business center. **$$**

★★★THE MAGNOLIA HOTEL

818 17th St., Denver, 303-607-9000, 888-915-1110; www.magnoliahoteldenver.com

Many visitors to Denver make the Magnolia their home for extended stays. It's easy to see why. Set back from busy 17th Street, the Magnolia says cozy, from the wing-back chairs and fireplace in its lobby to the full-size kitchens in its suites. Access to a snazzy health club is included with your stay. Upgrading to the Magnolia Club gets you wireless Internet access, access to a nightly cocktail reception and continental breakfast and late-night milk and cookies. Pets are welcome and receive a goodie bag at check-in. 246 rooms. Complimentary continental breakfast. Wireless Internet access. Restaurant, bar. Airport transportation available. **$$$**

★★★MARRIOTT DENVER CITY CENTER

1701 California St., Denver, 303-297-1300, 800-228-9290; www.denvermarriott.com

You'd be hard-pressed to find a better health club in an urban hotel than this one. There is a wide variety of equipment, personal trainers, massage therapy, body treatments and a pool and whirlpool—all of which will come in very handy if you're staying here on business. Located on the first 20 floors of an office building in downtown Denver, this property is within walking distance of Coors Field, as well as several restaurants and shops. 627 rooms. Wireless Internet access. Restaurant, bar. Business center. Fitness center. Pool. **$$$**

★★★OXFORD HOTEL

1600 17th St., Denver, 303-628-5400, 800-228-5838; www.theoxfordhotel.com

Built in 1891, this restored hotel is touted as the city's "oldest grand hotel." The luxurious property is filled with antiques, marble floors, stained glass and beautiful paintings. It's also near many attractions, including Coors Field, the 16th Street Mall, Larimer Square and many shops and galleries. Spend the day getting pampered at the hotel's full-service spa. 80 rooms. Wireless Internet access. Restaurant, bar. Spa. Airport transportation available. Pets accepted. Business center. Fitness center. **$$$**

★★QUEEN ANNE BED AND BREAKFAST

2147-51 Tremont Place, Denver, 303-296-6666, 800-432-4667;
www.queenannebnb.com

14 rooms. Complimentary full breakfast. Wireless Internet access. **$$**

★★★RENAISSANCE DENVER HOTEL

3801 Quebec St., Denver, 303-399-7500; www.denverrenaissance.com

This atrium hotel has Rocky Mountain views and large rooms with mini-refrigerators, free laundry and porches, making it a good choice for families looking for a full-service hotel while trying to stay within a budget, or business travelers who prefer to stay near the airport. (Downtown Denver is about a 10-minute drive.) There's also a pool and exercise facility. 400 rooms. Complimentary continental breakfast. Wireless Internet access. Two restaurants, bar. Airport transportation available. Business center. Pool. Spa. **$$**

★★★THE RITZ-CARLTON DENVER

1881 Curtis St., Denver, 303-312-3800;
www.ritzcarlton.com/en/Properties/Denver/Default.htm

It's the numbers that speak for this Ritz-Carlton's luxury: 400 thread-count Frette linens, 550 square-foot and larger guest rooms, 5-fixture bathrooms, the second branch of Elway's successful steakhouse, and 24-hour room service. Guests will find their rooms hold a number of other treats, including automatic hall light sensors, featherbeds, plush Frette terry robes, flat-panel HD TVs, cappuccino makers, iPod alarm clocks, rain showerheads and Bulgari bath amenities. This outpost of the Ritz was designed with a focus on the state's natural beauty, with red rocks, stones and water features incorporated into the construction. Not that you'll think for a moment that you're camping. 202 rooms, 47 suites. Wireless Internet access. Restaurant, bar. Airport transportation available. Valet parking only. Fitness center. Tennis. Indoor lap pool. Indoor basketball court. Spa. Business Center. Pets accepted.

★★★THE WESTIN TABOR CENTER

1672 Lawrence St., Denver, 303-572-9100, 800-937-8461;
www.starwoodhotels.com

Located in downtown Denver, adjacent to the 16th Street Mall, this hotel boasts some of the largest guest rooms in the city, many with panoramic views of the Rocky Mountains. The signature Heavenly Beds and Baths and nightly wine service ensure a relaxing stay. Get a massage, hit the rooftop pool or whirlpool, work out in the outstanding fitness center (with a personal flatscreen TV on each piece of cardio equipment) or get in a game at the indoor half-basketball court. Afterward, relax in the lobby with Starbucks coffee. 430 rooms. Wireless Internet access. Two restaurants, bar. Pool. Fitness center. Business center. Spa. Pets accepted. **$$$**

155

COLORADO

★
★
★
★

SPECIALTY LODGINGS

CAPITOL HILL MANSION BED & BREAKFAST

1207 Pennsylvania St., Denver, 303-839-5221, 800-839-9329;
www.capitolhillmansion.com

With its ruby sandstone exterior and dramatic entrance, this charming 1891 mansion offers a romantic getaway for couples. The richly decorated inn features rooms with fresh flowers and antique furniture, as well as refrigerators stocked with complimentary water and soft drinks (there's an open kitchen policy, too). Eight rooms. Wireless Internet access. Complimentary full breakfast, Whirlpool. **$**

THE LUMBER BARON INN

2555 W. 37th Ave., Denver, 303-477-8205; www.lumberbaron.com

This place is huge—and there are only five guest rooms. The ground floor consists of a parlor, large dining room and kitchen. Each guest room has a different theme, and they all have separate showers and whirlpool tubs. The entire third-floor is an old ballroom, with 20-foot vaulted ceiling, small kitchen and bathroom, and is used for anything from a romantic dinner for two to the weekly murder mystery dinner hosted by the inn. Five rooms. Pets accepted, some restrictions. Complimentary full breakfast. **$$**

RESTAURANTS

★ANNIE'S CAFE

3100 E. Colfax Ave., Denver, 303-355-8197; www.annies-cafe.com

American menu. Breakfast, lunch, dinner. Children's menu. Casual attire. **$**

★★★BAROLO GRILL

3030 E. Sixth Ave., Denver, 303-393-1040; www.barologrilldenver.com

This upscale Italian farmhouse, named after the famous wine, serves authentic Northern Italian food. The interior is rustic and romantic, with grapevines covering one corner and hand-painted porcelain on display throughout, and the fireplace casts a warm glow. Be sure to ask about the daily tasting menu. And yes, the extensive wine list includes more than Barolo, but why bother? Italian menu. Dinner. Closed Sunday-Monday. Bar. Business casual attire. Reservations recommended. Valet parking. **$$$**

★★BENNY'S

301 E. Seventh Ave., Denver, 303-894-0788; www.bennysrestaurant.com

Mexican menu. Breakfast, lunch, dinner. Bar. Children's menu. Casual attire. Outdoor seating. **$**

★★★THE BROKER RESTAURANT

821 17th St., Denver, 303-292-5065; www.thebrokerrestaurant.com

Located in downtown Denver in what was once the Denver National Bank, the Broker is a fun place to dine. Private parties can take over one of the old boardrooms. The restaurant's centerpiece is a huge bank vault, now a dining room. Go down some stairs and through what seems like it might have been a secret passageway, and you find yourself in the restaurants massive wine cellar, which has a dining table that can seat up to 20—or just two, if you're feeling romantic. Steak menu. Lunch, dinner. Bar. Children's menu. Business casual attire. Reservations recommended. Valet parking. **$$$**

★★BUCKHORN EXCHANGE

1000 Osage St., Denver, 303-534-9505; www.buckhorn.com

Steak menu. Lunch, dinner. Bar. Children's menu. Casual attire. Reservations recommended. Outdoor seating. **$$$**

★★DENVER CHOPHOUSE & BREWERY

1735 19th St., Denver, 303-296-0800; www.chophouse.com

Steak and seafood menu. Microbrewery. Lunch, dinner, brunch. Bar. Outdoor seating. **$$**

★★★ELWAY'S

The Ritz-Carlton, Denver, 1881 Curtis St., Denver, 303-312-3107; www.elways.com

Because it wouldn't be a Colorado vacation without a hearty steak dinner, and Denver wouldn't be Denver without Bronco Hall-of-Famer John Elway, add Elway's to your must-do list. This restaurant is a touchdown all around. The smart décor features a floor-to-ceiling wine wall holding thousands of bottles. The lamb fondue appetizer, Elway's salmon, and the bone-in rib-eye are sure bets. Prices can creep up into the $60 to $70 range per person, though, so go for breakfast or lunch if your vacation budget has left you needing to tighten your belt a little. Try the Bison burger or grilled lamb sandwich. Steak menu. Breakfast, lunch, dinner. Bar. Business casual attire. Reservations recommended. **$$**

★EMPRESS SEAFOOD

2825 W. Alameda Ave., Denver, 303-922-2822

Chinese menu. Lunch, dinner. Bar. **$$**

157

★★★HIGHLANDS GARDEN CAFÉ

3927 W. 32nd Ave., Denver, 303-458-5920; www.highlandsgardencafe.com

This unique Denver mainstay is actually two converted Victorian houses from about 1890. The main dining room is all exposed brick, polished hardwood floors and crisp white tablecloths, but other rooms have a different feel. The country room is painted white and has French doors leading out to the gardens. The eclectic American menu takes advantage of seasonal ingredients. American menu. Lunch, dinner, Sunday brunch. Closed Monday. Outdoor seating. **$$$**

★★★IMPERIAL CHINESE

431 S. Broadway, Denver, 303-698-2800; www.imperialchinese.com

From the giant fish tank at the entrance to the inventive Szechwan, Cantonese and Mandarin menu, this restaurant dazzles. The large dining room is segmented with partitions that provide a sense of privacy. The service is unobtrusive, and the dishes are as eye-catching as they are delicious. Chinese menu. Lunch, dinner. Bar. Casual attire. Reservations recommended. **$$**

★★INDIA'S RESTAURANT

3333 S. Tamarac Drive, Denver, 303-755-4284; www.indiasrestaurant.com

Indian menu. Lunch, dinner. Bar. **$$**

COLORADO

★
★
★
★
★

★JAPON RESTAURANT

1028 S. Gaylord St., Denver, 303-744-0330; www.japonsushi.com
Japanese menu. Lunch, dinner. **$$**

★LAS DELICIAS

439 E. 19th Ave., Denver, 303-839-5675; www.lasdeliciasmexicanrestaurant.com
Mexican menu. Breakfast, lunch, dinner. **$**

★★LE CENTRAL

112 E. Eighth Ave., Denver, 303-863-8094; www.lecentral.com
French menu. Lunch, dinner, brunch. Casual attire. Reservations recommended. **$$**

★★★MORTON'S, THE STEAKHOUSE

1710 Wynkoop St., Denver, 303-825-3353; www.mortons.com
This national chain fits right into the upscale Denver meat-and-potatoes scene. It's very simple here: Order a martini, listen to the server recite the menu, dig in. Go home stuffed. Steak menu. Dinner. Bar. Valet parking. **$$$**

★★★PALACE ARMS

321 17th St., Denver, 303-297-3111, 800-321-2599; www.brownpalace.com
The Palace Arms opened its doors in 1892—and has carried on a tradition of culinary excellence ever since. Located on the ground level of the Brown Palace Hotel, the majestic Palace Arms' dining room has a unique Western charisma, with rich wood, brocade-upholstered seating, wood shutters and antiques. The delicious International cuisine is prepared with regional accents. Taste some of the oldest known blended cognac, which dates back to Napoleonic times. International menu. Dinner. Bar. Children's menu. Business casual attire. Reservations recommended. Valet parking. **$$$**

★★★★RESTAURANT KEVIN TAYLOR

1106 14th St., Denver, 303-640-1012; www.ktrg.net
Located inside the stylish Hotel Teatro and across from the Denver Center for Performing Arts, this 70-seat restaurant brings French style to downtown Denver. Vaulted ceilings are offset with Versailles mirrors and alabaster chandeliers. Chairs are covered in green-and-yellow-striped silk fabric, and tables are topped with yellow Frette linens, Bernardaud china and Christofle silver. Chef Kevin Taylor earns applause for his unpretentious contemporary cuisine. Start with seared Grade A French foie gras, and then try one of the signature dishes such as butter-poached Atlantic salmon, pancetta-roasted pork loin and Colorado lamb sirloin. Top it off with a killer dessert like caramelized pineapple Napoleon. The restaurant features seasonal menus that change every two months, four- and five-course tasting menus and a prix fixe pre-theatre menu. There are also 900 vintages here—ask for a private table in the wine cellar. American, French menu. Dinner. Closed Sunday. Bar. Business casual attire. Reservations recommended. Valet parking. **$$$**

★ROCKY MOUNTAIN DINER

800 18th St., Denver, 303-293-8383; www.rockymountaindiner.com
American menu. Lunch, dinner. Bar. Children's menu. Outdoor seating. **$$**

★★★STRINGS

1700 Humboldt St., Denver, 303-831-7310; www.stringsrestaurant.com

Strings is like no other restaurant in Denver. The locals know it—and so do the scores of celebrities and politicians who have dined here, many of whom have left autographed pictures on the wall. Some love it for the unusual, eclectic cuisine served in the light and airy dining room with an open kitchen. Others are admirers of owner Noel Cunningham, a well-known humanitarian who constantly holds fundraisers at the restaurant to help fight illiteracy and hunger. International menu. Lunch, dinner. Bar. Business casual attire. Reservations recommended. Valet parking. Outdoor seating. $$$

★★3 SONS ITALIAN RESTAURANT

2915 W. 44th Ave, Denver, 303-455-4366; www.threesons.net

Italian menu. Lunch, dinner. Closed Monday. Bar. Children's menu. $$

★★★TUSCANY

4150 E. Mississippi Ave., Denver, 303-639-1600; www.loewshotels.com

Located in the Loews Denver Hotel, Tuscany is decorated in creamy earth tones and luxurious fabrics with soft lighting. Pen-and-ink drawings and paintings of the Tuscan countryside dot the walls, and a central, marble fireplace serves to divide the room. The feeling is contemporary and comfortable, and the restaurant uses only the freshest ingredients to create its outstanding fare paired with wines from the exceptional list. Live music is performed on Wednesday and Thursday evenings. Italian menu. Breakfast, lunch, dinner. Bar. Children's menu. Casual attire. Reservations recommended. Valet parking. $$$

★WAZEE SUPPER CLUB

1600 15th St., Denver, 303-623-9518; www.wazeesupperclub.com

American menu. Lunch, dinner, late-night. Bar. Children's menu. Casual attire. $

★★★WELLSHIRE INN

3333 S. Colorado Blvd., Denver, 303-759-3333; www.wellshireinn.com

The tables at this restaurant are topped with crisp white linens and beautiful china that was created exclusively for the Wellshire and based on the Tudor period, a theme that is richly executed here. Built in 1926 as a clubhouse for the exclusive Wellshire Country Club, the castle-like building fell into disrepair. Today, it has been restored with four intimate dining rooms. Classics like shrimp cocktail and Maryland crab cakes are featured as appetizers, while entrées include steak Oscar, pan-roasted Cornish game hen and grilled North Atlantic salmon. American menu. Lunch, dinner, Sunday brunch. Bar. Children's menu. Business casual attire. Reservations recommended. Outdoor seating. $$$

★ZAIDY'S DELI

121 Adams St., Denver, 303-333-5336; www.zaidysdeli.com

American, deli menu. Breakfast, lunch, dinner. Children's menu. Casual attire. Valet parking. Outdoor seating. $

COLORADO

★
★
★
★
★

SPAS
★★★★THE RITZ-CARLTON SPA, DENVER
1881 Curtis St., Denver, 303-312-3830; www.ritzcarlton.com
Spending the day in the mountains and heading back to the city to rest? Then wind down at this elegant new spa. With eight treatment rooms, including a VIP Suite, the spa is Denver's largest full-service luxury spa. Choose from all manner of treatments, including massage therapies, body treatments, skin care, nail services and makeup application; or skip the slopes and spend the whole day in the spa, indulging in the only-in-Denver Hops n' Honey pedicure, which pays homage to the city's brewery roots; it'll leave your skin fragrant with notes of amber, caramel, oats and honey. And your pampering comes with tastings of three local microbrews (or herbal teas, but c'mon, you're in Denver—drink the beer), just another Rocky Mountain twist.

★★★★THE SPA AT THE BROWN PALACE
321 17th St., Denver, 303-312-8940, 800-321-2599; www.brownpalace.com
An artesian well has supplied the Brown Palace Hotel since it opened in 1892. The soothing natural rock waterfall at its spa's entrance speaks to this history. The Spa at the Brown Palace's six massage, facial and water treatment rooms, separate men's and women's lounges, and private couples' suite are spread over two floors. The facility also has a full-service hair and nail salon. This commitment to guest pampering isn't new—the spa occupies the same space as a spa that opened with the hotel more than a century ago. The treatment menu offers five distinct soaks, and the artesian plunge is 20 minutes of tub time followed by a sea algae masque. **$$**

160
DILLON
After the entire town was moved in the early 1960s to make way for Dillon Lake, a reservoir for the Denver water system, this planned community became a popular resort area in the midst of wonderful mountain scenery.
Information: Summit County Chamber of Commerce, 246 Rainbow Drive, Silverthorne, 800-530-3099; www.summitnet.com

WHAT TO SEE AND DO
COPPER MOUNTAIN RESORT SKI AREA
Interstate 70 and Highway 91, Dillon, 866-841-2481; www.coppercolorado.com
Six-person, four high-speed quad, five triple, five double chairlifts; six surface lifts; patrol, school, rentals, snowmaking; 125 runs; longest run approximately three miles; vertical drop 2,601 feet. November-April, daily. Cross-country skiing. Half-day rates. Athletic club. Summer activities include boating, sailing, rafting, hiking, bicycling, horseback riding, golf. Jeep tours. Chairlift also operates to the summit of the mountain (late June-September, daily).

SUMMIT COUNTY BIKING TOUR
Silverthorne; www.summitcolorado.com/summit-county/biking
The Summit County region in northwest Colorado is a mountain biker's dream with its diverse terrain, spectacular scenery and Wild West heritage. Hundreds of miles of wilderness roads and trails—many left over from the days when miners crisscrossed the land in search of gold and silver—draw cyclists into an unforgettable exploration of Colorado's high country. A ride over the Argentine Pass, at an elevation of more

DINOSAUR NATIONAL MONUMENT

This 325-square-mile monument on the Utah/Colorado border holds one of the largest concentrations of fossilized Jurassic-era dinosaur bones in the world. Visitors can get a close-up view of a quarry wall containing at least 1,500 fossil bones dating back 150 million years. The wall was once part of an ancient riverbed. The monument itself is distinguished by its beautiful landscape of high plateaus and river-carved canyons. Access to the Colorado backcountry section, a land of deeply eroded canyons of the Green and Yampa Rivers, is via the Harper's Corner Road, starting at monument headquarters on Highway 40 (two miles east of Dinosaur). At the end of this 32-mile surfaced road, a one-mile foot trail leads to a promontory overlooking the Green and Yampa rivers.

The entrance to the Dinosaur Quarry section in Utah is at the junction of Highways 40 and 149 in Jensen, Utah (13 miles east of Vernal). Dinosaur Quarry is seven miles north on Highway 149. The Green River campground is about five miles from there. No lodgings are available other than at campgrounds. The visitor's centers and one quarry-section campground are open all year; the remainder are often closed by snow from mid-November-mid-April.

Information: 4545 E. Highway 40, Dinosaur, 435-781-7700; www.nps.gov/dino.

than 13,207 feet, is the ultimate conquest for experienced bikers. Those who want to take it all in without all the huffing and puffing can opt to ride a ski lift up the mountain for some awe-inspiring views of the Ten Mile Range, followed by a breathtaking, one-way plunge back to the valley below. Check out area visitor centers, bike shops and ski resorts for tips and trail maps. March-November.

HOTEL

★BEST WESTERN PTARMIGAN LODGE

652 Lake Dillon Drive, Dillon, 970-468-2341, 800-842-5939; www.bestwestern.com

69 rooms. High-speed Internet access. Complimentary continental breakfast. Bar. Spa. Whirlpool. Pets accepted.$

DURANGO

Will Rogers once said of Durango, "It's out of the way and glad of it." For more than 100 years, this small Western city has profited from its secluded location at the base of the San Juan Mountains. Durango has been the gateway to Colorado's riches for Native Americans, fur traders, miners, prospectors, ranchers and engineers. Founded by the Denver & Rio Grande Railroad, Durango was a rowdy community during its early days. The notorious Stockton-Eskridge gang once engaged local vigilantes in an hourlong gun battle in the main street. In the 1890s, the *Durango Herald-Democrat* was noted for the stinging, often profane, wit of pioneer editor "Dave" Day, who once had 42 libel suits pending against him.

Information: Durango Area Tourism office, 111 S. Camino Del Rio, Durango, 800-525-8855; www.durango.org

COLORADO'S GOLD MINES

The San Juan Skyway is a scenic 236-mile loop out of Durango that ranges over five mountain passes as it wanders through the San Juan Mountains. From Durango, head west on Highway 160 to Hesperus, where you can take a side trip into La Plata Canyon to see mining ruins and a few ghost towns. Continuing west, you'll pass Mesa Verde National Park and come to Highway 145 shortly before Cortez. Head north to the town of Dolores and the Anasazi Heritage Center, which features a large display of artifacts, most more than 1,000 years old. The road now follows the Dolores River, a favorite of trout anglers, and climbs the 10,222-foot-high Lizard Head Pass, named for the imposing rock spire looming overhead.

Descending from the pass, take a short side trip into Telluride, a historic mining town and ski resort nestled in a beautiful box canyon. Follow the San Miguel River valley to Highway 62, and turn north to cross the 8,970-foot Dallas Divide. After passing the historic railroad town of Ridgway and Ridgway State Park, where you might stop for a swim or picnic, turn south on Highway 550 and drive to Ouray, a picturesque old mining town. Continue over the 11,008-foot Red Mountain Pass—there is a monument here dedicated to snowplow operators who died while trying to keep the road open during winter storms. Next stop is Silverton, a small mining town and the northern terminus of the Durango and Silverton Narrow Gauge Railroad. South of Silverton is the 10,910-foot Molas Divide, after which the road almost parallels the rails as they follow the Animas River back to Durango. This tour can be done in one long day by those who want to see only the mountain scenery, but is better over two or three days, with stops at Mesa Verde National Park and the historic towns along the way. Approximately 236 miles.

WHAT TO SEE AND DO
DIAMOND CIRCLE THEATRE
Durango Arts Center, Eighth and Second avenues, Durango, 970-247-3400; www.diamondcirclemelodrama.com
Professional turn-of-the-century melodrama and vaudeville performances. June-September, nightly; closed Sunday. Advance reservations recommended.

DURANGO & SILVERTON NARROW GAUGE RAILROAD
479 Main Ave., Durango, 970-247-2733, 877-872-4607; www.durangotrain.com
This historic Narrow Gauge Railroad, in operation since 1881, links Durango in southwest Colorado with the Victorian-era mining town of Silverton, 45 miles away. A journey on this coal-fired, steam-powered locomotive up the Animas River and through the mountainous wilderness of the San Juan National Forest gives you the chance to relive history while taking in some of the most breathtaking scenery Colorado has to offer. Round-trip travel takes approximately nine hours. Same-day travelers may opt to return by bus; others can stay overnight in historic Silverton with

a return train ride the next day. During the winter season, the train makes a shorter, round-trip journey to and from Cascade Canyon. May-October; shorter routes during the winter months.

DURANGO & SILVERTON NARROW GAUGE RAILROAD MUSEUM
479 Main Ave., Durango, 970-247-2733, 877-872-4607; www.durangotrain.com
Climb aboard a restored railroad car and locomotive, and see exhibits on steam trains, historic photos and railroad art. Hours correspond to the train depot hours.

DURANGO MOUNTAIN RESORT (ALSO KNOWN AS PURGATORY)
1 Skier Place, Durango, 970-247-9000, 800-982-6103; www.ski-purg.com
Quad, four triple, three double chairlifts; patrol, school, rentals; five restaurants, five bars, nursery, lodge, specialty stores. 85 runs; longest run two miles; vertical drop 2,029 feet. Late November-early April. Cross-country skiing. Multiday, half-day rates. Chairlift and alpine slide also operate mid-June-Labor Day.

SAN JUAN NATIONAL FOREST
15 Burnett Court, Durango, 970-247-4874; www.fs.fed.us/r2/sanjuan
This forest consists of nearly two million acres and includes the Weminuche Wilderness, Colorado's largest designated wilderness area, with several peaks topping 14,000 feet. The Colorado Trail begins in Durango and traverses the backcountry all the way to Denver. Recreation includes fishing in high mountain lakes and streams, boating, whitewater rafting, hiking, biking and camping. The San Juan Skyway is a 232-mile auto loop through many of these scenic areas. Daily.

SOUTHERN UTE INDIAN CULTURAL MUSEUM
Southern Ute Indian Reservation, Ignacio, 23 miles southeast via Highways 160 and 172, 970-563-9583; www.southernutemuseum.org
This historical museum contains archival photos, turn-of-the-century Ute clothing, tools and accessories. Multimedia presentation. Monday-Friday 8 a.m.-5 p.m., Saturday 10 a.m.-3 p.m.; closed Sunday.

SPECIAL EVENTS
DURANGO COWBOY GATHERING
Stater Hotel, 699 Main Ave., Durango, 970-382-7494; www.durangocowboygathering.org
This celebration of the American cowboy features several poetry and vocal performances. First weekend in October.

IRON HORSE BICYCLE CLASSIC
346 S. Camino Del Rio, Durango, 970-259-4621; www.ironhorsebicycleclassic.com
Cyclists race the Silverton narrow-gauge train (47 miles). Late May.

SNOWDOWN WINTER CARNIVAL
Durango, 970-247-8163; www.snowdown.org
Winter festival features entertainment, contests, food and more. Late January-February.

COLORADO

★
★
★
★
★

HOTELS

★★★APPLE ORCHARD INN

7758 County Road 203, Durango, 970-247-0751, 800-426-0751;
www.appleorchardinn.com

This lovely inn is just 15 minutes from town and a 20-minute drive to Durango Mountain Resort. The property includes beautiful gardens, trout ponds, waterfalls and streams. All rooms feature featherbeds. Homemade baked goods and jam at breakfast—as well as fresh chocolate chip cookies anytime—make visits extra sweet. Gourmet dinners are also available with a reservation. 10 rooms. Complimentary full breakfast. $$

★BEST WESTERN DURANGO INN AND SUITES

21382 US Highway 160, Durango, 970-247-3251, 800-547-9090; www.durangoinn.com
71 rooms. Wireless Internet access. Complimentary continental breakfast. Restaurant, bar. Pool. $

COLORADO TRAILS RANCH

12161 County Road 240, Durango, 970-247-5055, 877-711-7843;
www.coloradotrails.com

This ranch is on 450 acres adjacent to San Juan National Forest. 15 rooms. Closed October-May. Restaurant. Children's activity center. Airport transportation available. Pool. $$

COUNTRY SUNSHINE BED & BREAKFAST

35130 Highway 550 North, Durango, 970-247-2853, 800-383-2853;
www.countrysunshine.com

Six rooms. Complimentary continental breakfast. Whirlpool. $

★★DOUBLETREE HOTEL

501 Camino Del Rio, Durango, 970-259-6580, 800-222-8733; www.doubletree.com
159 rooms. Restaurant, bar. Airport transportation available. Pets accepted. Fitness center. Pool. $

GENERAL PALMER HOTEL

567 Main Ave., Durango, 970-247-4747, 800-523-3358; www.generalpalmerhotel.com
39 rooms. Complimentary continental breakfast. $$

★★HISTORIC STRATER HOTEL

699 Main Ave., Durango, 800-247-4431; www.strater.com
93 rooms. Wireless Internet access. Complimentary full breakfast. Restaurant, bar. Whirlpool. $

JARVIS SUITE HOTEL

125 W. 10th St., Durango, 970-259-6190, 800-824-1024; www.jarvishoteldurango.com
This restored historic hotel was built in 1888. 21 rooms. Complimentary continental breakfast. Whirlpool. $

★★★LIGHTNER CREEK INN

999 County Road 207, Durango, 970-259-1226, 800-268-9804;
www.lightnercreekinn.com

This inn, built in 1903, resembles a French country manor and offers finely decorated rooms. The mountain getaway feels very secluded but is only five minutes from downtown. Guests are encouraged to make themselves at home here—grab a drink from the kitchen and watch a movie in the living room. Nine rooms. $$

LELAND HOUSE BED & BREAKFAST SUITES

721 E. Second Ave., Durango, 970-385-1920, 800-664-1920; www.leland-house.com

Restored apartment building (circa 1927) with many antiques. 15 rooms. Complimentary full breakfast. Pets accepted. $$

★★★NEW ROCHESTER HOTEL

721 E. Second Ave., Durango, 970-385-1920, 800-664-1920; www.rochesterhotel.com

Built in 1892, this Victorian hotel has been authentically restored and evokes the Old West, and it's only one block from downtown Durango. It bills itself as a "green" hotel—Electra Cruiser bikes are available for guests to get around and all-natural Aveda products are provided. 15 rooms. Complimentary continental breakfast. Pets accepted. $$

TALL TIMBER RESORT

1 Silverton Star Route, Durango, 970-259-4813; www.talltimberresort.com

Accessible exclusively by train or helicopter, Tall Timber Resort is a true getaway. This unique resort rests on 180 private acres rimmed by the San Juan National Forest. There are no televisions, radios or phones to distract from the majestic beauty of crashing waterfalls, majestic evergreens and mesmerizing canyons. Only 30 guests are treated to this singular experience at one time. The resort's two-story, ski condo-like accommodations feature simple, rustic décor with stone fireplaces and faux wood paneling. 10 rooms. Closed late October-May. Restaurant. Pool. $$$$

★★★TAMARRON RESORT

40292 Highway 550 North, Durango, 970-259-2000, 800-982-6103;
www.lodgeattamarron.com

Pine trees surround this scenic resort, located on a 750-acre site in the San Juan Mountains. The property is just a short drive or shuttle from Durango and Purgatory Village and the chairlifts. Accommodations range from studios and lofts to suites, and amenities include golf, tennis and indoor/outdoor pools. 210 rooms. Restaurant, bar. Children's activity center. Spa. Airport transportation available. Pets accepted. Golf. $

WIT'S END GUEST RANCH AND RESORT

254 County Road 500, Bayfield, 970-884-4113, 800-236-9483; www.witsendranch.com

This resort is located in a valley on 550 acres. All cabins are adjacent to a river or pond. 19 rooms. Restaurant, bar. Children's activity center. Spa. $$$$

165

COLORADO

★
★
★
★
★

RESTAURANTS

★★ARIANO'S ITALIAN RESTAURANT
150 E. College Drive, Durango, 970-247-8146
Italian menu. Dinner. Bar. Children's menu. Casual attire. $$

★CARVER BREWING CO.
1022 Main Ave., Durango, 970-259-2545; www.carverbrewing.com
American, Southwestern menu. Breakfast, lunch, dinner. Bar. Children's menu. Casual attire. $

★★★CHEZ GRAND-MÈRE
3 Depot Place, Durango, 970-247-7979; www.chezgrand-mere.com
This restaurant offers a six-course prix fixe French menu that changes nightly. The largest wine list in the region is available here, with bottles from around the world. French menu. Lunch, dinner. $$$

★★FRANCISCO'S
619 Main Ave., Durango, 970-247-4098
Mexican, American menu. Lunch, dinner. Bar. Children's menu. Casual attire. $$

★★THE PALACE RESTAURANT
505 Main Ave., Durango, 970-247-2018; www.palacedurango.com
American menu. Lunch, dinner. Closed Sunday, November-May. Bar. Casual attire. Outdoor seating. $$

★★RED SNAPPER
144 E. Ninth St., Durango, 970-259-3417; www.redsnapperdurango.com
Seafood, steak menu. Dinner. Bar. Children's menu. Casual attire. $$

EDWARDS

Not far from tony Vail Valley and Beaver Creek, Edwards has all of the ski resorts' beauty without the hype. With a charming shopping and dining district, proximity to resorts and plenty of Colorado's natural beauty nearby, Edwards is a good option for visitors looking to spend some time on a Rocky Mountain high.
Information: www.visitedwards.com

HOTELS

★★INN AND SUITES AT RIVERWALK
27 Main St., Edwards, 970-926-0606, 888-926-0606;
www.innandsuitesatriverwalk.com
59 rooms. High-speed Internet access. Two restaurants, bar. $

★★★THE LODGE & SPA AT CORDILLERA
2205 Cordillera Way, Edwards, 970-926-2200, 866-650-7625;
www.cordilleralodge.com
The French-chateau architecture and beautiful mountaintop location make this one of the most exclusive resorts in the area. A lovely rustic style dominates the accommodations, where wood-burning or gas fireplaces add warmth and terraces offer views

of the Vail Valley. The lodge also includes award-winning golf and a full-service spa. Four restaurants feature everything from steaks and seafood to traditional Irish fare at Grouse-on-the-Green, where even the interiors were constructed in Ireland. 55 rooms. Four restaurants, bar. Pool. Golf. Tennis. Business center. **$$**

RESTAURANT
★★★MIRADOR
2205 Cordillera Way, Edwards, 970-926-2200; www.cordilleralodge.com/dining/mirador
Located in the luxurious Lodge & Spa at Cordillera, Mirador features breathtaking views of the Rocky Mountains and an elegant atmosphere. Its innovative menu of regional Colorado fare has won critical acclaim. It's complemented by an impressive wine list. If you'd like to dine privately with a group, you can reserve the 24-seat private dining area or the 12-seat family table in the wine cellar. French menu. Dinner. Bar. Valet parking. Outdoor seating. **$$$**

ENGLEWOOD
Englewood is located in Denver's south metro area and is home to the Denver Technological Center.
Information: Greater Englewood Chamber of Commerce, 3501 S. Broadway, 303-789-4473; www.ci.englewood.co.us

WHAT TO SEE AND DO
FIDDLER'S GREEN AMPHITHEATRE
6350 Greenwood Plaza Blvd.,Greenwood Village, 303-220-7000; www.livenation.com/amphitheatre
Fiddler's Green Amphitheatre, formerly Coors Amphitheatre, is located 15 minutes south of downtown Denver. The park-like setting is an inviting venue for a wide variety of musical performances during the summer months, from marquee names to classical orchestras. Come early to enjoy the mountain sunset. Bring a blanket or tarp (no lawn chairs are allowed) and a picnic, or reserve an indoor seat, purchase dinner from one of the many vendors and watch the acts up close. June-August.

THE MUSEUM OF OUTDOOR ARTS
1000 Englewood Parkway, Englewood, 303-806-0444; www.moaonline.org
Outdoor sculpture garden on 400 acres. Guided tours available. Lunchtime summer performance series (Wednesday). Daily.

HOTELS
★★EMBASSY SUITES
10250 E. Costilla Ave., Centennial, 303-792-0433, 800-654-4810; www.embassysuites.com
236 rooms, all suites. Complimentary full breakfast. Restaurant, bar. Pool. **$**

★HAMPTON INN
9231 E. Arapahoe Road, Greenwood Village, 303-792-9999, 800-426-7866; www.hamptoninn.com
150 rooms. Complimentary continental breakfast. Pets accepted. Pool. **$**

★★★INVERNESS HOTEL AND GOLF CLUB

200 Inverness Drive West, Englewood, 303-799-5800, 800-832-9053;
www.invernesshotel.com

This hotel and conference center, with 60,000 square feet of function space, is the perfect choice for corporate retreats, thanks to naturally lit boardrooms, "fatigue-free" chairs, built-in audiovisual equipment and more. All rooms feature views of the golf course or the Rocky Mountains and suites on the Club Floor have sunken living rooms. The spa offers a variety of treatments. 302 rooms. Restaurant, bar. Airport transportation available. Pool. Golf. Tennis. Business center. $$

★★★SHERATON DENVER TECH CENTER HOTEL

7007 S. Clinton, Greenwood Village, 303-799-6200, 800-325-3535; www.sheraton.com
The spacious guest rooms at this hotel will appeal to both business and leisure travelers. Nearby attractions include the Denver Museum of Natural History, the Denver Zoo and the Coors Brewery. Complimentary shuttle service is provided within a five-mile radius. 262 rooms. Restaurant, bar. Airport transportation available. Pets accepted. Pool. $

ESTES PARK

Estes Park occupies an enviable swath of land at the eastern edge of the Rockies. Many claim that Estes Park offers the quintessential Colorado experience. History certainly would support this. The area has been a vacation destination for thousands of years. Archaeological evidence indicates that Native Americans were drawn here to escape the summer heat. Situated 7,500 feet above sea level, the town's elevation manages to keep summertime temperatures comfortably cool—and also brings an average of 63 inches of snow during the winter months. The snowfall draws hordes of skiers and snowboarders to the area, with a season that typically lasts from November until April. During the warmer months, Estes Park becomes even more crowded. The city's downtown area features an array of shops, restaurants and accommodations, including the Stanley Hotel, constructed nearly 100 years ago in the neoclassical Georgian style—where Stephen King stayed while he was writing *The Shining* in 1973.
Information: Center at the Chamber of Commerce, 500 Big Thompson Ave.,
970-586-4431, 800-378-3708; www.estesparkresort.com

WHAT TO SEE AND DO
AERIAL TRAMWAY
420 Riverside Drive, Estes Park, 970-586-3675
Two cabins suspended from steel cables move up or down Prospect Mountain at 1,400 feet per minute. You get a superb view of the Continental Divide during the trip. Picnic facilities at 8,896-foot summit; panoramic dome shelter; snack bar. Mid-May-mid-September, daily.

BIG THOMPSON CANYON
Estes Park, east on Highway 34
One of the most beautiful canyon drives in the state.

ENOS MILLS ORIGINAL CABIN
6760 Highway 7, Estes Park, 970-586-4706; www.home.earthlink.net/~enosmillscbn

On this family-owned 200-acre nature preserve stands the 1885 cabin of Enos Mills, regarded as the father of Rocky Mountain National Park. In the shadow of Longs Peak, the cabin contains photos, notes and documents of the famed naturalist. Nature guide and self-guided nature trails. Memorial Day-Labor Day, Wednesday-Friday 10 a.m.-3 p.m.; rest of year by appointment.

ESTES PARK AREA HISTORICAL MUSEUM

200 Fourth St., Estes Park, 970-586-6256; www.estesnet.com/museum
Three facilities including a building that served as the headquarters of Rocky Mountain National Park from 1915 to 1923. See exhibits on the history of the park and surrounding area. Gallery: May-October, Monday-Saturday 10 a.m.-5 p.m., Sunday 1-5 p.m.; November-April, Friday-Saturday 10 a.m.-5 p.m., Sunday 1-5 p.m.

FUN CITY AMUSEMENT PARK

455 Prospect Village Drive, Estes Park, 970-586-2828; www.funcityofestes.com
There's plenty of fun here—bumper cars, a 15-lane giant slide and spiral slide, an arcade, miniature golf, two 18-hole golf courses and go-karts. Mid-May-mid-September, daily.

ROOSEVELT NATIONAL FOREST

240 W. Prospect Road, Fort Collins, 970-498-1100; www.fs.fed.us/r2/arnf
On the reserve's more than 780,000 acres of icy streams, mountains and beautiful scenery, visitors can enjoy trout fishing, hiking trails, a winter sports area, picnicking and camping. The Cache la Poudre River, five wilderness areas and the Peak-to-Peak Scenic Byway are all nearby.

SPECIAL EVENTS
ESTES PARK MUSIC FESTIVAL

Performance Park Pavilion, Estes Park, 970-586-9519; www.estesparkmusicfestival.org
Chamber, symphonic and choral concerts. Early June-late August.

HORSE SHOWS

Estes Park, 800-443-7837; www.estes-park.com
Includes an Arabian and Hunter-Jumper horse shows. July-August.

LONGS PEAK SCOTTISH-IRISH HIGHLAND FESTIVAL

Estes Park, 970-586-6308, 800-903-7837; www.scotfest.com
Athletic and dance competitions, arts and crafts shows, magic shows, folk dancing. Weekend after Labor Day.

ROOFTOP RODEO

Stanley Park Fairgrounds, Estes Park, 970-586-6104;
www.estesnet.com/events/rooftoprodeo.htm
Rodeo parade, nightly dances, kids jamboree, steer wrestling, bull riding. Five days in mid-July.

HOTELS
★BEST WESTERN SILVER SADDLE
1260 Big Thompson Ave., Estes Park, 970-586-4476, 800-780-7234;
www.bestwestern.com
55 rooms. Complimentary continental breakfast. High-speed Internet access. Pool. **$**

★BOULDER BROOK ON FALL RIVER
1900 Fall River Road, Estes Park, 970-586-0910, 800-238-0910;
www.boulderbrook.com
16 rooms. Airport transportation available. **$**

★COMFORT INN
1450 Big Thompson Ave., Estes Park, 970-586-2358, 877-424-6423;
www.comfortinn.com
75 rooms. Closed November-April. Complimentary continental breakfast. Wireless Internet access. Pool. Whirlpool. **$**

★★HOLIDAY INN
101 S. St. Vrain Ave., Estes Park, 970-586-2332, 888-465-4329; www.holiday-inn.com
150 rooms. Restaurant, bar. Pool. High-speed Internet access. Fitness center. Whirlpool. Business center. Airport transportation available. Pets accepted. **$**

★PONDEROSA LODGE
1820 Fall River Road, Estes Park, 970-586-4233, 800-628-0512;
www.ponderosa-lodge.com
25 rooms. **$**

★★★STANLEY HOTEL
333 Wonderview Ave., Estes Park, 970-586-3371, 800-976-1377;
www.stanleyhotel.com
The inspiration behind *The Shining*, the Stanley Hotel was built in 1909 by automaker F. O. Stanley and is only six miles from Rocky Mountain National Park. Multimillion dollar renovations have restored the gorgeous white hotel, which occupies 35 acres surrounded by the Rocky Mountains, to its original grandeur. The cozy rooms are classically styled and feature pillow-top mattresses and free wireless Internet. 135 rooms. Wireless Internet access. Restaurant, bar. Pool. Tennis. **$**

SPECIALTY LODGINGS
ASPEN LODGE RANCH
6120 Highway 7, Estes Park, 970-586-8133, 800-332-6867; www.aspenlodge.net
59 rooms. Restaurant (open to the public by reservation), bar. Children's activity center. Airport transportation available. Pool. Tennis. Business center. **$$**

ROMANTIC RIVERSONG INN
1766 Lower Broadview Road, Estes Park, 970-586-4666; www.romanticriversong.com
A gurgling trout stream, gazebo and pond add to the charm of this 1928 bed and breakfast. All rooms are named after wildflowers. Located on 27 acres adjacent to Rocky Mountain National Park, the property offers impressive views. 16 rooms.

COLORADO

★
★
★
★

Children over 12 years only. Complimentary full breakfast. Airport transportation available. $$

RESTAURANTS
★MAMA ROSE'S
338 E. Elkhorn Ave., Estes Park, 970-586-3330, 877-586-3330;
www.mamarosesrestaurant.com
Italian menu. Breakfast, dinner. Closed January-February; also Monday-Wednesday (winter). Bar. Children's menu. Outdoor seating. $$

★★NICKY'S
1360 Fall River Road, Estes Park, 970-586-5377, 866-464-2597; www.nickysresort.com
American menu. Breakfast, lunch, dinner. Bar. Children's menu. Outdoor seating. $$

★★TWIN OWLS STEAKHOUSE
800 MacGregor Ave., Estes Park, 970-586-9344; www.twinowls.net
Steak menu. Dinner. Bar. Children's menu. Casual attire. Reservations recommended. $$

EVERGREEN
This small town, about 45 minutes from downtown Denver, has real mountain charm. At an elevation of about 7,200 feet, Evergreen has cooler summers than Denver and mild winters. Evergreen is home to several beautiful designated open spaces, great for hiking. At Evergreen Lake you can rent canoes and paddleboats in summer and go ice skating or ice fishing in winter.
Information: Evergreen Area Chamber of Commerce, 28065 Hwy 74, Evergreen,
303-674-3412; www.evergreenchamber.org

FLORISSANT FOSSIL BEDS NATIONAL MONUMENT
Florissant Fossil Beds National Monument consists of 6,000 acres once partially covered by a prehistoric lake. Thirty-five million years ago, ash and mudflows from volcanoes in the area buried a forest of redwoods, filling the lake and fossilizing its living organisms. Insects, seeds and leaves of the Eocene Epoch are preserved in perfect detail, along with remarkable samples of standing petrified sequoia stumps. You'll also find nature trails, picnic areas and a restored 19th-century homestead. Guided tours are available. The visitor center is two miles south on Teller County Road 1. Daily.
Information: Florissant, 22 miles west of Manitou Springs on Highway 24;
www.nps.gov/flfo

FORT COLLINS
Founded as a military post in 1864, Fort Collins is a large college town—home to Colorado State University. It's a thriving community these days because of great schools, low crime, jobs in the high-tech field and great outdoor living. Many high-tech companies have moved here, and three microbreweries and Anheuser-Busch are located here as well. Old Town is a historic shopping district with red brick pedestrian

walkways and street lamps. The headquarters for the Roosevelt National Forest and the Arapaho National Forest are also located in Fort Collins.

Information: Fort Collins Convention & Visitors Bureau, 19 Old Town Square, 970-232-3840, 800-274-3678; www.ftcollins.com

WHAT TO SEE AND DO

ANHEUSER-BUSCH BREWERY TOUR

2351 Busch Drive, Fort Collins, 970-490-4691; www.budweisertours.com

The Anheuser-Busch Brewery in Fort Collins produces 2.6 million cans of beer a day. The tour includes an overview of the company's history (which dates back to the mid-1800s), a walking tour of the brewing and control rooms and a visit with the famous Budweiser Clydesdales, housed with their Dalmatian companions in picturesque stables on the beautiful Busch estate. Enjoy complimentary beer tasting at the end of the tour. January-May, Thursday-Monday 10 a.m.-4 p.m.; June-August, daily 9:30 a.m.-4.30 p.m.; September, daily 10 a.m.-4 p.m.; October-December, Thursday-Monday 10 a.m.-4 p.m.

COLORADO STATE UNIVERSITY

Fort Collins, West Laurel and Howes streets, 970-491-4636; www.welcome.colostate.edu

Established in 1870; 24,500 students. Land-grant institution with an 833-acre campus. Pingree Park, adjacent to Rocky Mountain National Park, is the summer campus for the natural resource science education and forestry program.

DISCOVERY SCIENCE CENTER

703 E. Prospect Road, Fort Collins, 970-472-3990; www.dcsm.org

This hands-on science and technology museum features more than 100 educational exhibits. Admission: adults $7.00, children $5.00, seniors $5.50, children under 3 free. Tuesday-Saturday 10 a.m.-5 p.m.

FORT COLLINS MUSEUM

Library Park, 200 Mathews St., Fort Collins, 970-221-6738; www.ci.fort-collins.co.us/museum

Exhibits include a model of the army post, a fine collection of Folsom points and American Indian beadwork, plus displays of historic household, farm, and business items and three historic cabins. Tuesday-Saturday 10 a.m.-5 p.m., Sunday noon-5 p.m.

LINCOLN CENTER

417 W. Magnolia, Fort Collins, 970-221-6735; www.ci.fort-collins.co.us/lctix

Includes a theater for the performing arts, concert hall, sculpture garden, art gallery and display areas with changing exhibits. Daily.

LORY STATE PARK

708 Lodgepole Drive, Bellvue, 970-493-1623; www.parks.state.co.us/Parks/lory

Approximately 2,500 acres near Horsetooth Reservoir. Waterskiing, boating, nature trails, hiking, stables, picnicking. Daily.

HOTELS

★BEST WESTERN KIVA INN

1638 E. Mulberry St., Fort Collins, 970-484-2444, 888-299-5482;
www.bestwestern.com

62 rooms. Complimentary continental breakfast. Pool. Wireless Internet access. Fitness center. Pets accepted. **$**

★★★MARRIOTT FORT COLLINS

350 E. Horsetooth Road, Fort Collins, 970-226-5200, 800-342-4398;
www.marriott.com

Located just three miles from Colorado State University, this hotel is a great place to stay during CSU parents' weekend. Rooms feature new luxury bedding with down comforters and fluffier pillows. Take a swim in the indoor or outdoor pool and hit the gym for a workout. This hotel is nonsmoking. 230 rooms. Restaurant, bar. Pool. Business center. **$**

★★RAMADA INN

3836 E. Mulberry St., Fort Collins, 970-484-4660, 800-272-6232; www.ramada.com
197 rooms. Restaurant, bar. Children's activity center. Pets accepted. Pool. Business center. High-speed Internet access. Fitness center. **$**

SPECIALTY LODGING

PORTER HOUSE BED & BREAKFAST INN

530 Main St., Windsor, 970-686-5793, 888-686-5793; www.porterhouseinn.com
Four rooms. Children over 12 years only. Complimentary full breakfast. Whirlpool. Business center. **$**

FORT MORGAN

The original fort was built in the mid-1860s by "galvanized rebels," former Confederate soldiers who were released from prison on the condition that they move west and fight against Native Americans. The fort protected mail delivery and immigrants traveling along the Overland Trail. About 80 miles from Denver, Fort Morgan today offers opportunities to fish, golf and learn about the nation's westward expansion in the 19th century.

Information: Fort Morgan Area Chamber of Commerce, 300 Main St.,
970-867-6702, 800-354-8660; www.fortmorganchamber.org

GEORGETOWN

Georgetown is named for George Griffith, who discovered gold in this valley in 1859 and opened up the area to other gold seekers. The area around Georgetown has produced almost $200 million worth of gold, silver, copper, lead and zinc. Numerous 19th-century structures remain standing.

Information: Town of Georgetown Visitor Information, 800-472-8230;
www.georgetowncolorado.com

COLORADO

★
★
★
★
★

WHAT TO SEE AND DO
GEORGETOWN LOOP HISTORIC MINING AND RAILROAD PARK
Georgetown, 888-456-6777; www.georgetownlooprr.com
The reconstructed Georgetown Loop Railroad was used in the late 1800s for shipping ore and was hailed as an engineering marvel. It now carries visitors on a scenic 6½-mile trip, which includes a stop at the mine area for tours. The train leaves from Devil's Gate Viaduct (west on Interstate 70 to exit 228, then a half mile south on Old US 6) or Silver Plume (I-70, exit 226). Five or six round-trips per day. Late May-early October, daily.

HAMILL HOUSE MUSEUM
305 Argentine St., Georgetown, 303-569-2840;
www.historicgeorgetown.org/houses/hamill.htm
Early Gothic Revival house acquired by William A. Hamill, Colorado silver magnate and state senator, with period furnishings. Partially restored carriage house and office. Late May-September, daily; rest of year, by appointment.

HOTEL DE PARIS MUSEUM
409 Sixth St., Georgetown, 303-569-2311; www.hoteldeparismuseum.org
This internationally known hostelry was built in 1875 and is elaborately decorated with original furnishings. Admission: adults $4, seniors and AAA members $3, students $2, children under 6 free. Memorial Day-Labor Day, daily 10 a.m.-4:30 p.m.; May, September-December, Saturday-Sunday noon-4 p.m.

LOVELAND SKI AREA
Loveland Pass, Georgetown, 303-569-3203, 800-736-3754; www.skiloveland.com
Three quad, two triple, four double chairlifts, Poma lift, Mighty-mite; patrol, school, rentals, snowmaking; cafeteria, restaurants, bars; nursery; 60 runs; longest run two miles; vertical drop 2,410 feet. Mid-October-mid-May, Monday-Friday 9 a.m.-4 p.m., Saturday-Sunday 8:30 a.m.-4 p.m.

SPECIAL EVENT
GEORGETOWN CHRISTMAS MARKET
Sixth Street, Georgetown, 303-569-2405, 303-569-2888;
www.georgetowncolorado.com
For a delightful old-fashioned Christmas experience, visit the little Victorian hamlet of Georgetown during the first two weekends in December. The streets and shops come alive with holiday lights, music, dancing and strolling carolers. Early December.

SPECIALTY LODGING
NORTH FORK
55395 Highway 285, Shawnee, 303-838-9873, 800-843-7895;
www.northforkranch.com
Six rooms. Closed mid-September-mid-May. Restaurant. Children's activity center. Airport transportation available. Pool. **$$**

COLORADO

★
★
★
★

RESTAURANT
★HAPPY COOKER
412 Sixth St., Georgetown, 303-569-3166
American menu. Breakfast, lunch. Children's menu. Outdoor seating. **$**

GLENWOOD SPRINGS

Doc Holliday, the famous gunman, died here in 1887. Today, Glenwood Springs is a popular year-round health spa destination, thanks to its famous hot springs. The town is located between Aspen and Vail on the forested banks of the Colorado River and is the gateway to White River National Forest. Excellent game and fishing country surrounds Glenwood Springs, and camping areas are sprinkled throughout the region. The nearby town offers museums, art galleries, specialty shops and restaurants in a relaxed, Western-style setting.

Information: Chamber Resort Association, 1102 Grand Ave.,

970-945-6589, 888-445-3696; www.glenscape.com

WHAT TO SEE AND DO
GLENWOOD HOT SPRINGS POOL
Hot Springs Lodge and Pool, 415 Sixth St., Glenwood Springs,

970-945-6571, 800-537-7946; www.hotspringspool.com

For centuries, visitors have traveled to the hot springs in Colorado to soak in their soothing—and many say healing—mineral-rich waters. Today, those same legendary springs feed this hot spring pool—the world's largest. The main pool, more than two blocks long, circulates 3.5 million gallons of naturally heated, spring-fed water each day. The complex includes lap lanes, a shallow play area, diving area, two water slides (summer only) and a therapy pool. Late May-early September, daily 7:30 a.m.-10 p.m.; early September-late May, daily 9 a.m.-10 p.m.

SCENIC DRIVES
Glenwood Springs, on Highway 133, visit Redstone, Marble and Maroon peaks;
Interstate 70 provides access to Lookout Mountain and Glenwood Canyon
Just a two-mile hike from the road, you'll find beautiful Hanging Lake and Bridal Veil Falls. The marble quarries in the Crystal River Valley are the source of stones for the Lincoln Memorial in Washington, D.C. and the Tomb of the Unknown Soldier in Arlington National Cemetery.

SUNLIGHT MOUNTAIN RESORT
10901 County Road 117, Glenwood Springs, 970-945-7491, 800-445-7931;
www.sunlightmtn.com
Triple, two double chairlifts; surface tow; patrol, school, rentals; cafeteria, bar; nursery. 67 runs; longest run 2½ miles; vertical drop 2,010 feet. Snowmobiling half-day rates. Late November-early April, daily. Also cross-country touring center, 10 miles.

WHITE RIVER NATIONAL FOREST
900 Grand Avenue, Glenwood Springs, 970-945-2521; www.fs.fed.us/r2/whiteriver
More than 2,500,000 acres in the heart of the Colorado Rocky Mountains. Recreation at 70 developed sites with boat ramps, picnicking, campgrounds and observation points; Holy Cross, Flat Tops, Eagles Nest, Maroon Bells-Snowmass, Raggeds,

Collegiate Peaks and Hunter-Frying Pan wildernesses. (Check with local ranger for information before entering wildernesses or any backcountry areas.) Many streams and lakes with trout fishing; large deer and elk populations. Dillon, Green Mountain and Ruedi reservoirs.

SPECIAL EVENTS
GARFIELD COUNTY FAIR & RODEO
Garfield County Fairgrounds, 1001 Railroad Ave., Rifle, 970-625-5922; www.garfieldcountyfair.com
Mid-August.

STRAWBERRY DAYS FESTIVAL
Sayre Park, Glenwood Springs, 970-945-6589; www.strawberrydaysfestival.com
Arts and crafts fair, rodeo, parade. Third weekend in June.

HOTELS
★BEST WESTERN ANTLERS
171 W. Sixth St., Glenwood Springs, 970-945-8535, 800-626-0609; www.bestwestern.com
99 rooms. Complimentary continental breakfast. High-speed Internet access. Pool. $

★HOT SPRINGS LODGE
415 E. Sixth St., Glenwood Springs, 970-945-6571, 800-537-7946; www.hotspringspool.com
107 rooms. Complimentary continental breakfast. Airport transportation available. Pool. $

RESTAURANTS
★★FLORINDO'S
721 Grand Ave., Glenwood Springs, 970-945-1245
Italian menu. Dinner. Bar. Children's menu. Casual attire. $$

★LOS DESPERADOS
55 Mel Rey Road, Glenwood Springs, 970-945-6878
Mexican menu. Lunch, dinner. Bar. Children's menu. Casual attire. Outdoor seating. $

★★RIVER'S RESTAURANT
2525 S. Grand Ave., Glenwood Springs, 970-928-8813; www.theriversrestaurant.com
American menu. Dinner, Sunday brunch. Bar. Children's menu. Casual attire. Outdoor seating. $$

GOLDEN
Not surprisingly, Golden was founded during Colorado's gold rush. A mere 15 miles from downtown Denver, Golden has done a good job preserving its small-town charm.
Information: Greater Golden Chamber of Commerce, 1010 Washington Ave., 303-279-3113, 800-590-3113; www.goldencochamber.org

WHAT TO SEE AND DO

ASTOR HOUSE HOTEL MUSEUM
822 12th St., Golden, 303-278-3557; www.astorhousemuseum.org
The first stone hotel west of the Mississippi, the Astor House was built in 1867. Period furnishings. Self-guided and guided tours (reservations required). Tuesday-Saturday 10 a.m.-4:30 p.m.

BUFFALO BILL MUSEUM & GRAVE
987-1/2 Lookout Mountain Road, Golden, 303-526-0744; www.buffalobill.org
Lookout Mountain is the final resting place of the man who virtually defined the spirit of the Wild West: William F. "Buffalo Bill" Cody, whose life included stints as a cattle driver, fur trapper, gold miner, Pony Express rider and scout for the U.S. Cavalry. He became world famous with his traveling Buffalo Bill's Wild West Show. At the Buffalo Bill Museum & Grave, Cody still draws crowds who come to see the museum's Western artifacts collection, take advantage of the beautiful hilltop vistas and pay homage to this legendary Western hero. May-October: daily 9 a.m.-5 p.m.; November-April: Tuesday-Sunday 9 a.m.-4 p.m.

COLORADO RAILROAD MUSEUM
17155 W. Fourth Ave., Golden, 303-279-4591, 800-365-6263; www.crrm.org
This 1880s-style railroad depot houses memorabilia and an operating model railroad. More than 50 historic locomotives and cars from Colorado railroads are displayed outside. Daily 9 a.m.-5 p.m.

COLORADO SCHOOL OF MINES
1500 Illinois St., Golden, 303-273-3000, 800-446-9488; www.mines.edu
World-renowned institution devoted exclusively to the education of mineral, energy and material engineers and applied scientists. Tours of campus.

COORS BREWERY TOUR
13th and Ford streets, Golden, 303-277-2337, 866-812-2337; www.coors.com
For a fun, free factory tour, visit Coors Brewing Company—the nation's third-largest brewer—to see how beer is made. The 40-minute walking tour reviews the malting, brewing and packaging processes and ends with a free sampling in the hospitality room (proper ID required). Visitors under 18 must be accompanied by an adult. Monday-Saturday 10 a.m.-4 p.m.

GOLDEN GATE CANYON STATE PARK
Crawford Gulch Road, Golden, 303-582-3707;
www.parks.state.co.us/goldengatecanyon
On 12,000 acres. Nature and hiking trails, cross-country skiing, snowshoeing, biking, horseback riding, ice skating, picnicking, camping. Visitor center. Panorama Point Overlook provides a 100-mile view of the Continental Divide. Daily.

GOLDEN PIONEER MUSEUM
923 10th St., Golden, 303-278-7151; www.goldenpioneermuseum.com
This museum houses more than 4,000 items dating from Golden's days as the territorial capital, including household articles, clothing, furniture, mining, military and

COLORADO

★
★
★
★
★

ranching equipment. Monday-Saturday 10 a.m.-4:30 p.m.; Memorial Day-Labor Day: Sunday 11 a.m.-5 p.m.

HERITAGE SQUARE

18301 W. Colfax Ave., Golden, 303-279-2789; www.heritagesquare.info

Heritage Square family entertainment park is reminiscent of a 1870s Colorado mining town with its Old West streetscapes and Victorian façades. In addition to specialty shops, restaurants, museums and a theater, there are amusement rides, a waterslide, a 70-foot bungee tower, go-karts and a miniature golf course. Heritage Square is also home to Colorado's longest Alpine slide. Winter, Monday-Saturday 10 a.m.-5 p.m., Sunday noon-5 p.m.; summer, Monday-Saturday 10 a.m.-8 p.m., Sunday noon-8 p.m.

LARIAT TRAIL

Golden, also known as Lookout Mountain Road, trail begins west of
Sixth Avenue at 19th Street, 720-971-9649; www.lariatloop.org

Leads to Denver Mountain Parks. Lookout Mountain (five miles west off Highway 6) is the nearest peak.

SPECIAL EVENT
BUFFALO BILL DAYS

Golden, 303-279-8141; www.buffalobilldays.com

Held in honor of "Buffalo Bill" Cody, this event features a parade, golf tournament, children's rides and games, a car show, food and arts and crafts. July.

HOTELS
★LA QUINTA INN

3301 Youngfield Service Road, Golden, 303-279-5565, 800-642-4271;
www.laquinta.com

129 rooms. Complimentary continental breakfast. Pets accepted. Pool. High-speed Internet access. **$**

★★★MARRIOTT DENVER WEST

1717 Denver West Blvd., Golden, 303-279-9100, 888-238-1803; www.marriott.com

Rooms at this hotel feature new Revive bedding and high-speed Internet access. The renovated health club is stocked with cutting-edge equipment. The sports bar has 37 flatscreen high-def TVs. This hotel is nonsmoking. 305 rooms. High-speed Internet access. Restaurant, bar. **$**

★★TABLE MOUNTAIN INN

1310 Washington Ave., Golden, 303-277-9898, 800-762-9898;
www.tablemountaininn.com

74 rooms. Restaurant, bar. Airport transportation available. **$**

RESTAURANTS
★★CHART HOUSE

25908 Genesee Trail Road, Golden, 303-526-9813; www.chart-house.com

American menu. Dinner. Bar. Children's menu. **$$**

★★SIMMS LANDING

11911 W. Sixth Ave., Golden, 303-237-0465; www.simmslandingrestaurant.com
Seafood menu. Lunch, dinner, Sunday brunch. Bar. Children's menu. Business casual
attire. Reservations recommended. Outdoor seating. **$$**

★★TABLE MOUNTAIN INN

1310 Washington Ave., Golden, 303-216-8040; www.tablemountaininn.com
Southwestern menu. Breakfast, lunch, dinner, Sunday brunch. Bar. Children's menu.
Outdoor seating. **$$**

GRANBY

The Arapaho National Recreation Area, developed by the Department of Interior as
part of the Colorado-Big Thompson Reclamation Project, is northeast of Granby.
Several national forests, lakes and big-game hunting grounds are within easy reach.
Two ski areas are also nearby.

Information: Greater Granby Area Chamber of Commerce,
970-887-2311, 800-325-1661; www.granbychamber.com

WHAT TO SEE AND DO

ARAPAHO NATIONAL RECREATION AREA

9 Ten Mile Drive, Granby, 970-887-4100; www.fs.fed.us/r2/arnf
The area includes Shadow Mountain and several lakes. Boating, fishing, hunting,
camping, picnicking, horseback riding. Daily.

BUDGET TACKLE

255 E. Agate Ave., Granby, 970-887-9344
Rent ice-fishing equipment, get advice on techniques and request directions to the
best places to fish.

GRAND ADVENTURE BALLOON TOURS

127 Fourth St., Granby, 970-887-1340; www.grandadventureballoon.com
Take a sunrise hot air balloon flight over the Rockies from the Winter Park/Fraser
Valley area.

SILVERCREEK SKI AREA

1000 Village Road, Granby
Two triple, double chairlifts; Poma lift; patrol, school, rentals, snowmaking; conces-
sion, cafeteria, bar; nursery; day-lodge. 22 runs; longest run 1½ miles; vertical drop
1,000 feet. December-mid-April. Snowboarding, sleigh rides. Health club.

SPECIALITY LODGINGS

C LAZY U RANCH

3640 Highway 125, Granby, 970-887-3344; www.clazyu.com
Since the 1940s, C Lazy U Ranch has offered families a taste of life on a Western
ranch. Enjoy the beautiful Colorado countryside—there are no televisions or telephones here to distract you. The horsemanship program is the centerpiece of the
ranch—upon arrival, you're matched with a horse for the duration of your stay. The
guest rooms are decorated with a distinctively Western décor, and nearly all have

fireplaces. Meals are served family style and there's a fireside singalong afterward. 40 rooms. Closed mid-February-mid-May, early October-mid-December. Complimentary full breakfast. Wireless Internet access. Two bars. Children's activity center. Airport transportation available. **$**

DROWSY WATER RANCH
County Road 219, Granby, 970-725-3456, 800-845-2292; www.drowsywater.com
17 rooms. Closed mid-September-May. Children's activity center. Pool. **$$**

RESTAURANT
★LONGBRANCH & SCHATZI'S PIZZA
165 E. Agate Ave., Granby, 970-887-2209
German menu. Lunch, dinner. Closed early April-mid-May and early November-mid-December. Bar. Children's menu. Casual attire. Reservations recommended. **$$**

GRAND JUNCTION
Grand Junction's name stems from its location at the junction of the Colorado and Gunnison rivers. The altitude and warm climate combine to provide a rich agricultural area, which produces peaches, pears and grapes for the local wine industry. The city serves as a trade and tourist center for Western Colorado and Eastern Utah, as well as a gateway to two national parks, six national forests and seven million acres of public land.
Information: Visitor & Convention Bureau, 740 Horizon Drive, 800-962-2547; www.visitgrandjunction.com

WHAT TO SEE AND DO
ADVENTURE BOUND RIVER EXPEDITIONS
2392 H. Road, Grand Junction, 970-245-5428, 800-423-4668; www.raft-colorado.com
Two- to five-day whitewater rafting trips on the Colorado, Green and Yampa rivers.

CROSS ORCHARDS HISTORIC FARM
3073 F Road, Grand Junction, 970-434-9814; www.wcmuseum.org/crossorchards.htm
Costumed guides interpret the social and agricultural heritage of Western Colorado. Restored buildings and equipment on display; narrow gauge railroad exhibit and country store. Demonstrations, special events. Admission: adults $4, seniors $3, children $2.50 and family groups $10. May-October, Tuesday-Saturday 9 a.m.-4 p.m.

MUSEUM OF WESTERN COLORADO
462 Ute Ave., Grand Junction, 970-242-0971, 888-488-3466; www.wcmuseum.org
Features exhibits on regional, social and natural history of the Western Slope, plus a collection of small weapons and wildlife exhibits. Admission: adults $5.50-$12, seniors $4.50-$10, children $3-$8 and family groups $16. Tuesday-Saturday 10 a.m.-3 p.m. Tours by appointment.

RABBIT VALLEY TRAIL THROUGH TIME

2815 H. Road, Grand Junction, 970-244-3000;
www.blm.gov/co/st/en/fo/mcnca/recreation/camping/rabbitvalley.html
This 1½-mile self-guided walking trail takes you through a paleontologically significant area where you can see fossilized flora and fauna from the Jurassic Age. No pets allowed. Daily.

RIGGS HILL

South Broadway and Meadows Way, Grand Junction, 970-241-9210
A ¾-mile, self-guided walking trail in an area where the bones of the Brachiosaurus dinosaur were discovered in 1900. Daily.

SPECIAL EVENTS

COLORADO MOUNTAIN WINEFEST

2785 Highway 50, Grand Junction, 970-464-0111, 800-704-3667;
www.coloradowinefest.com
Wine tastings, outdoor events. Late September.

COLORADO STAMPEDE

Grand Junction
Rodeo. Third week in June.

HOTELS

★BEST WESTERN SANDMAN MOTEL

708 Horizon Drive, Grand Junction, 970-243-4150; www.bestwestern.com
80 rooms. High-speed Internet access. Airport transportation available. Pets accepted. Pool. $

★★DOUBLETREE HOTEL GRAND JUNCTION

743 Horizon Drive, Grand Junction, 970-241-8888; www.doubletree.com
273 rooms. Restaurant, bar. Pool. Tennis. High-speed Internet access. Business center. Fitness center. Airport transportation available. $

★★GRAND VISTA HOTEL

2790 Crossroads Blvd., Grand Junction, 970-241-8411, 800-800-7796;
www.grandvistahotel.com
158 rooms. Restaurant, bar. Airport transportation available. Pets. Pool. Fitness center. $

★★HOLIDAY INN

755 Horizon Drive, Grand Junction, 970-243-6790, 888-489-9796;
www.holiday-inn.com
292 rooms. High-speed Internet access. Restaurant, bar. Airport transportation available. Pets. Exercise. Swim. $

RESTAURANTS
★★FAR EAST RESTAURANT
1530 North Ave., Grand Junction, 970-242-8131
Chinese, American menu. Lunch, dinner. Bar. Children's menu. $

★STARVIN' ARVIN'S
752 Horizon Drive, Grand Junction, 970-241-0430
American menu. Breakfast, lunch, dinner. Bar. Children's menu. $

★★WINERY RESTAURANT
620 Main St., Grand Junction, 970-242-4100; www.thewineryrestaurant.net
American menu. Dinner. Bar. $$

GRAND LAKE
Grand Lake is on the northern shore of the largest glacial lake in Colorado. As one of the state's oldest resort villages, Grand Lake boasts the world's highest yacht club, a full range of water recreation and horseback riding and pack trips on mountain trails. Grand Lake is at the terminus of Trail Ridge Road at the west entrance to Rocky Mountain National Park.

Information: Grand Lake Area Chamber of Commerce, West Portal Road and Highway 34, 970-627-3402, 800-531-1019; www.grandlakechamber.com

SPECIAL EVENTS

BUFFALO BARBECUE & WESTERN WEEK CELEBRATION
Grand Lake, 970-627-3402
Parade, food; Spirit Lake Mountain Man rendezvous. Third week in July.

LIPTON CUP SAILING REGATTA
Grand Lake, 970-627-3402; www.grandlakechamber.com
Early August.

ROCKY MOUNTAIN REPERTORY THEATRE
Community Building, Town Square, Grand Lake, 970-627-3421, 970-627-5087; www.rockymountainrep.com
Three musicals change nightly, Monday-Saturday. Reservations advised. Late June-late August.

WINTER CARNIVAL
Grand Lake, 970-627-3372; www.winter-carnival.com/contact
Ice skating, snowmobiling, snow sculptures, ice fishing derby, ice-golf tournament. February.

SPECIALTY LODGING
SPIRIT MOUNTAIN RANCH BED & BREAKFAST
3863 County Road 41, Grand Lake, 970-887-3551; www.spiritmtnranch.com
Four rooms. Children over 10 years only. Complimentary full breakfast. $$

RESTAURANTS

★★★CAROLINE'S CUISINE

9921 Highway 34, Grand Lake, 970-627-8125, 800-627-9636;
www.sodaspringsranch.com

At this cozy restaurant, large windows offer views of either the mountain or the hills, and the bistro-style menu includes steak frites and roasted duck. French, American menu. Dinner. Closed two weeks in April and two weeks in November. Bar. Children's menu. Outdoor seating. $$

★E. G.'S GARDEN GRILL

1000 Grand Ave., Grand Lake, 970-627-8404

American menu. Lunch, dinner. Bar. Children's menu. Outdoor seating. $$

WHAT TO SEE AND DO

GREAT SAND DUNES FOUR-WHEEL DRIVE TOUR

5400 Highway 150, Great Sand Dunes National Monument, 719-378-2222

This 12-mile, two-hour round-trip tour through the Great Sand Dunes National Monument features spectacular scenery and includes stops for short hikes on the dunes. May-October, daily.

GREELEY

Horace Greeley conceived of "Union Colony" as a Utopian agricultural settlement similar to the successful experiment at Oneida, New York. The town was founded by Nathan Meeker, agricultural editor of Greeley's *New York Tribune*. Thanks to irrigation, the region today is rich and fertile and sustains a thriving community.

Information: Greeley Convention & Visitors Bureau, 902 Seventh Ave.,
970-352-3567, 800-449-3866; www.greeleycvb.com

WHAT TO SEE AND DO

CENTENNIAL VILLAGE

14th Avenue and A Street, Greeley, 970-350-9220;
www.greeleygov.com/museums/centennialvillage.aspx

Restored buildings with period furnishing show the growth of Greeley and Weld County from 1860 to 1920. Tours, lectures, special events. April-October, Tuesday-Sunday.

FORT VASQUEZ

13412 Highway 85, Greeley, 970-785-2832; www.coloradohistory.org

This reconstructed adobe trading post of the 1830s contains exhibits of Colorado's fur trading and trapping industries, the Plains Indians and archaeology of the fort. Memorial Day-Labor Day, Monday-Saturday 9:30 a.m.-4:30 p.m., Sunday 1-4:30 p.m.; Labor Day-Memorial Day, Wednesday-Saturday 9:30 a.m.-4:30 p.m., Sunday 1-4:30 p.m.

MARIANI ART GALLERY

1819 Eighth Ave., Greeley, 970-351-2184

This art gallery features faculty, student and special exhibitions. Multipurpose University Center.

MEEKER HOME

1324 Ninth Ave., Greeley, 970-350-9220;
www.greeleygov.com/museums/meekerhome.aspx
The 1870 house of city founder Nathan Meeker contains many of his belongings, as well as other historical mementos. May-September, Wednesday-Friday 1-4 p.m.

UNIVERSITY OF NORTHERN COLORADO

1862 10th Ave., Greeley, 970-351-2097; www.unco.edu
Established in 1889; 10,800 students. On the 236-acre campus is the James A. Michener Library, Colorado's largest university library. Collection includes materials owned by Michener while he was writing the book *Centennial.*

SPECIAL EVENT
GREELEY INDEPENDENCE STAMPEDE

600 N. 14th Ave., Greeley, 970-356-2855, 800-982-2855; www.greeleystampede.org
This weeklong celebration includes nightly country and western concerts by top-name entertainers and culminates in a rodeo. Also includes a bull-fighting event, demolition derby and carnival. Fees vary per event. Late June-early July.

SPECIALTY LODGING
SOD BUSTER INN

1221 Ninth Ave., Greeley, 970-392-1221, 866-501-8667; www.thesodbusterinn.com
10 rooms. Complimentary full breakfast.

184 GUNNISON

With 2,000 miles of trout-fishing streams and Colorado's largest lake within easy driving range, Gunnison has long been noted as an excellent fishing center.
Information: Gunnison Country Chamber of Commerce, 500 E. Tomichi Ave.,
970-641-1501; www.gunnison-co.com

WHAT TO SEE AND DO
ALPINE TUNNEL

500 E. Tomichi Ave., Gunnison, 36 miles northeast via Highway 50
Completed in 1881 and abandoned in 1910, this railroad tunnel—nearly 12,000 feet above sea level—is 1,771 feet long. July-October.

CURECANTI NATIONAL RECREATION AREA

102 Elk Creek, Gunnison, 970-641-2337; www.nps.gov/cure
This area includes Blue Mesa, Morrow Point and Crystal reservoirs. Elk Creek Marinas, Inc., offers boat tours on Morrow Point Lake (Memorial Day-Labor Day, daily; 970-641-0402 for reservations). Blue Mesa Lake has water-skiing, windsurfing, fishing, boating; picnicking, camping. The Elk Creek visitor center is 16 miles west (mid-April-October, daily).

GUNNISON NATIONAL FOREST

216 N. Colorado St., Gunnison, 970-641-0471; www.fs.fed.us/r2/gmug
This forest contains 27 peaks. Activities include fishing, hiking, picnicking and camping. Includes West Elk Wilderness and portions of the Maroon Bells-Snowmass, Collegiate Peaks, La Garita and Raggeds wilderness areas.

TAYLOR PARK RESERVOIR

216 N. Colorado St., Gunnison, 970-641-2922

The road runs through this 20-mile canyon. Fishing, boating, hunting, camping. Memorial Day-September, daily.

SPECIAL EVENT
CATTLEMEN'S DAYS, RODEO AND COUNTY FAIR

275 S. Spruce, Gunnison, 970-641-4160; www.visitgunnison.com

The oldest rodeo in Colorado. Mid-July.

HOTELS
★★BEST WESTERN VISTA INN

733 E. Highway 24, Gunnison, 970-641-1131, 800-641-1131; www.bestwestern.com

52 rooms. High-speed Internet access. Restaurant. Airport transportation available. Pool. $

★HOLIDAY INN EXPRESS

910 E. Tomichi Ave., Gunnison, 970-641-1288, 888-465-4329; www.holiday-inn.com

107 rooms. Complimentary continental breakfast. Airport transportation available. Pool. $

RESTAURANT
★★TROUGH

37550 Highway 50, Gunnison, 970-641-3724

American menu. Dinner. Bar. Children's menu. Casual attire. $$

KEYSTONE

This tiny town is best known for its skiing and scenic setting, so strap on your sticks and enjoy.

Information: www.keystone.snow.com

WHAT TO SEE AND DO
KEYSTONE RESORT SKI AREA

1254 Soda Ridge Road, Keystone, 800-344-8878; www.keystone.snow.com

Four ski mountains (Arapahoe Basin, Keystone, North Peak and the Outback). Patrol, school, rentals. Snowmaking at Keystone, North Peak and the Outback. Late October-early May. Cross-country skiing, night skiing, ice skating, snowmobiling and sleigh rides. Shuttle bus service. Combination and half-day ski rates; package plans. Summer activities include boating, rafting and gondola rides, plus golf, tennis, horseback riding, bicycling and jeep riding.

HOTEL
★★★KEYSTONE LODGE & SPA

22101 Highway 6, Keystone, 970-496-3000, 888-455-7625;
www.keystonelodge.rockresorts.com

Keystone Lodge is a perfect Rocky Mountain getaway, thanks to a variety of activities, comfortable accommodations and enjoyable dining. The guest rooms and suites are the picture of mountain chic, with large windows framing unforgettable views of snow-capped peaks and the Snake River. You'll never be at a loss for something to do, with an onsite ice-skating rink, BMW driving tours, nearby skiing and golf and a complete fitness center. After an action-packed day, the RockResorts Spa offers a variety of soothing treatments. The dining is superb, from the elegant French dining at Champeaux to the prime cuts Bighorn Steakhouse. 152 rooms. Wireless Internet access. Pool. Fitness center. Business center. Spa. $$$

SPECIALTY LODGING
SKI TIP LODGE
764 Montezuma Road, Keystone, 877-753-9786; www.skitiplodge.com
11 rooms. Complimentary full breakfast. Restaurant, bar. Tennis. $

RESTAURANT
★★★SKI TIP LODGE
764 Montezuma Road, Keystone, 800-354-4386; www.skitiplodge.com
This charming bed and breakfast has been served American regional cuisine for more than 50 years. Dinner. Bar. Children's menu. $$$

LAKEWOOD
Lakewood is a suburban community west of Denver.
Information: City of Lakewood, 480 S. Allison Pkwy., 303-987-7000; www.lakewood.org

WHAT TO SEE AND DO
BEAR CREEK LAKE PARK
15600 W. Morrison Road, Morrison, 303-697-6159; www.ci.lakewood.co.us/comres/page.cfm?ID=43&BearCreekLakePark
Approximately 2,600 acres. Waterskiing school, fishing, boating; hiking, bicycle trails, picnicking, camping. Archery. View of downtown Denver from Mount Carbon. Daily.

COLORADO MILLS
14500 W. Colfax Ave., Lakewood, 303-384-3000; www.coloradomills.com
This brand-new 1.2-million-square-foot state-of-the-art retail and entertainment complex is just 10 minutes from downtown Denver, and brings a vast array of value-oriented stores, restaurants and entertainment venues together. Movie theaters, shops, restaurants, an interactive play area for kids and a 40,000-square-foot ESPN X Games Skatepark for older kids form the core of the entertainment center. Monday-Saturday 10 a.m.-9 p.m., Sunday 11 a.m.-6 p.m.

CROWN HILL PARK
West 26th Avenue and Kipling Street, Lakewood, 303-271-5925; www.jeffco.us/openspace/openspace_T56_R7.htm
This 242-acre nature preserve includes Crown Hill Lake and a wildlife pond. Fishing, hiking, bicycle, bridle trails. Daily.

★
★
★
★
★

LAKEWOOD'S HERITAGE CENTER

801 Yarrow St., Lakewood, 303-987-7850;
www.ci.lakewood.co.us/comres/page.cfm?ID=17&LakewoodsHeritageCenter
This 127-acre park includes nature, art and historical exhibits. Turn-of-the-century farm; one-room schoolhouse; vintage farm machinery; Barn Gallery with permanent and changing exhibits, interpretive displays. Lectures, workshops. visitor center. Admission: adults $5, seniors $4, children $3, children under 3 free. Tuesday-Saturday 10 a.m.-4 p.m.

HOTELS

★HAMPTON INN

3605 S. Wadsworth Blvd., Lakewood, 303-989-6900, 800-426-7866;
www.hamptoninn.com
150 rooms. Complimentary continental breakfast. Pool. Business center. Fitness center. $

★★HOLIDAY INN

7390 W. Hampden Ave., Lakewood, 303-980-9200, 888-565-6159;
www.holiday-inn.com
188 rooms. Restaurant, bar. Pets accepted. Pool. $

★★★SHERATON DENVER WEST HOTEL

360 Union Blvd., Lakewood, 303-987-2000, 800-325-3535; www.sheraton.com
Adjacent to the Denver Federal Center, this hotel is a perfect launching pad to explore nearby attractions, including Coors Brewery and Red Rocks Concert Amphitheater. The 10,000-square-foot health club includes a heated indoor lap pool and the spa offers a variety of relaxing treatments. The rooms are warm and cozy in deep maroons and traditional décor. And even dogs get the Sheraton Sweet Sleeper beds. 242 rooms. High-speed Internet access. Business center. Pool. Spa. Fitness center. $$

RESTAURANTS

★★★240 UNION

240 Union Blvd., Lakewood, 303-989-3562; www.240union.com
This contemporary American grille with a large open kitchen is known for having some of the best seafood in the Denver area. Other favorites include wood-fired oven pizzas, New York strip steak with forest mushrooms and short ribs with garlic mashed potatoes. The wine list features a number of good selections, and desserts like key lime pie and chocolate mousse are very tempting. American menu. Lunch, dinner. Bar. Business casual attire. Reservations recommended. $$

★CASA BONITA OF DENVER

6715 W. Colfax Ave., Lakewood, 303-232-5115; www.casabonitadenver.com
Mexican menu. Lunch, dinner. Bar. Children's menu. Casual attire. $$

LEADVILLE

Located just below the timberline, Leadville's high altitude contributes to its reputation for excellent skiing, cool summers and beautiful fall colors. First a rich gold camp, then an even richer silver camp, the town boasts a lusty, brawling past in which millionaires were made and destroyed in a single day, a barrel of whiskey could net $1,500 and thousands of dollars could be won and lost in a card game in the town's saloons and smoky gambling halls. Leadville's lively history is intertwined with the lives of Horace Tabor and his two wives, Augusta and Elizabeth Doe, whose rags-to-riches-to-rags story is the basis of the American opera *The Ballad of Baby Doe*. The "unsinkable" Molly Brown (of *Titanic* fame) made her fortune here, as did David May, Charles Boettcher, Charles Dow and Meyer Guggenheim. Until 1950, Leadville was a decaying mining town. However, a burst of civic enthusiasm has led to the rebirth of many attractions that date back to the town's glory days, including several museums and a Victorian downtown area.

Information: Greater Leadville Area Chamber of Commerce, 809 Harrison Ave., 719-486-3900, 888-532-3845; www.leadvilleusa.com

WHAT TO SEE AND DO
EARTH RUNS SILVER
Fox Theater, 115 West Sixth St., Leadville, 719-486-3900
Video presentation featuring Leadville's legendary mining camp with music and narration. Daily.

HEALY HOUSE-DEXTER CABIN
912 Harrison Ave., Leadville, 719-486-0487;
www.coloradohistory.org/hist_sites/healyhouse/h_house.htm
The restored Healy House, built in 1878, contains many fine Victorian-era furnishings. Dexter Cabin, built by early mining millionaire James V. Dexter to entertain wealthy gentlemen, looks like an ordinary two-room miner's cabin from the outside but is surprisingly luxurious. Memorial Day-Labor Day, daily.

HERITAGE MUSEUM AND GALLERY
Ninth Street and Harrison Avenue, Leadville, 719-486-1878
Learn all about local history at this museum, which houses Victorian costumes, memorabilia of mining days and changing exhibits of American art. Mid-May-October, daily.

LEADVILLE, COLORADO & SOUTHERN RAILROAD TRAIN TOUR
326 E. Seventh St., Leadville, 719-486-3936, 866-386-3936; www.leadville-train.com
Depart from the old depot for a 23-mile round trip scenic ride following the headwaters of the Arkansas River through the Rocky Mountains. Memorial Day-October, daily.

THE MATCHLESS MINE
East Seventh Street, Leadville, 719-486-1899; www.matchlessmine.com
When Horace Tabor died in 1899, his last words to his wife were "hold on to the Matchless," which produced as much as $100,000 a month in its bonanza days. Faithful to his wish and ever hopeful, the once fabulously rich Baby Doe lived on in poverty in the little cabin next to the mine for 36 years, where she was found frozen to death in 1935. The cabin is now a museum. June-Labor Day, daily.

NATIONAL MINING HALL OF FAME AND MUSEUM

120 W. Ninth St., Leadville, 719-486-1229; www.mininghalloffame.org

This Museum is dedicated to those who have made significant contributions to the industry. It includes history and technology exhibits of the mining industry. May-October, daily; rest of year, Monday-Friday.

SKI COOPER

Highway 24, Leadville, 800-707-6114; www.skicooper.com

Triple, double chairlift; Poma lift, T-bar; patrol, school, rentals; snowcat tours; cafeteria, nursery; 26 runs; longest run 1½ miles; vertical drop 1,200 feet. Groomed cross-country skiing (15 miles). Late November-early April, daily.

TABOR OPERA HOUSE

308 Harrison Ave., Leadville, 719-486-8409; www.taboroperahouse.net

Now a museum, this 1879 theater played host to the Metropolitan Opera, the Chicago Symphony and most of the famous actors and actresses of the period. Their photos line the corridors. Many of the original furnishings, scenery and the dressing areas are still in use and on display. Summer shows. Memorial Day-September, daily.

SPECIAL EVENTS
BOOM DAYS & BURRO RACE

Leadville, 719-486-3900, 888-532-3845; www.leadvilleboomdays.com

Celebrates the town's 1880s Old West heritage with mining skill competitions, gunslingers, a parade and the 21-mile International Pack Burro Race. Early August.

CRYSTAL CARNIVAL WEEKEND

Harrison Ave., Leadville, 719-486-0739; www.colorado.com/events

This event does not actually include a carnival. Instead, it features a skijoring competition in which dogs draw a person on skis over a snowy obstacle course. First full weekend of March.

VICTORIAN HOME TOUR AND BRUNCH

Leadville, 888-532-3845

Locals and visitors dress in Victorian fashions and tour the town's historic Victorian homes decorated brightly and cheerfully for Christmas. First Saturday in December.

★
★
★
★
★

SPECIALTY LODGINGS
ICE PALACE INN BED & BREAKFAST

813 Spruce St., Leadville, 719-486-8272, 800-754-2840; www.icepalaceinn.com

Five rooms. Complimentary full breakfast. **$**

THE LEADVILLE INN

127 E. Eighth St., Leadville, 719-966-4770; www.leadvilleinn.com

This stately 15-room Victorian mansion was built in the 1800s and has been an inn since 1999. Nine rooms. Complimentary full breakfast. Pets accepted. **$$**

RESTAURANT
★★★TENNESSEE PASS COOKHOUSE
1892 Highway 25, Leadville, 719-486-8114; www.tennesseepass.com
This ski-oriented dining room serves one prix fixe meal nightly with entrées ordered 24 hours in advance. American menu. Lunch, dinner. Reservations recommended. $$$

LONGMONT
Considered one of the top small communities in the country, Longmont has found its own place in the spotlight outside the shadow of Boulder, its better-known neighbor.
Information: Chamber of Commerce, 528 Main St., 303-776-5295;
www.longmontchamber.org

WHAT TO SEE AND DO
LONGMONT MUSEUM
400 Quail Road, Longmont, 303-651-8374; www.ci.longmont.co.us/museum
Changing and special exhibits on art, history, space and science; permanent exhibits on the history of Longmont and the St. Vrain Valley. Tuesday-Saturday 9 a.m.-5 p.m., Wednesday until 8 p.m, Sunday 1-5 p.m.; closed Monday, holidays.

SPECIAL EVENTS
BOULDER COUNTY FAIR AND RODEO
Longmont, 303-441-3927
Fairgrounds. Nine days in early August.

RHYTHM ON THE RIVER
Roger's Grove, Hover Street. and Boston Avenue, Longmont, 303-776-5295;
www.ci.longmont.co.us/rotr
This annual festival honors Roger Jones, who preserved this riverside grove for generations to enjoy. Activities include music, an art show and children's activities. Early July.

HOTEL
★★RADISSON HOTEL
1900 Ken Pratt Blvd., Longmont, 303-776-2000, 888-201-1718; www.radisson.com
210 rooms. Wireless Internet access. Restaurant, two bars. Pets accepted. Pool. $

LOVELAND
In recent years, more than 300,000 Valentines have been re-mailed annually by the Loveland post office, stamped in red with the "Sweetheart Town's" cachet, a different valentine verse each year.
Information: Visitor Center/Chamber of Commerce, 5400 Stone Creek Circle,
970-667-6311, 800-258-1278; www.loveland.org

WHAT TO SEE AND DO
BOYD LAKE STATE PARK
3720 N. Country Road, Loveland, 970-669-1739;
www.parks.state.co.us/parks/boydlake
Swimming, waterskiing, fishing, boating; picnicking, camping. Daily.

SPECIAL EVENT
LARIMER COUNTY FAIR AND RODEO
The Ranch, Crossroads Boulevard and Fairgrounds Avenue, Loveland,
970-619-4000; www.larimercountyfair.org
The fair includes a carnival, parade, PRCA rodeo and other activities. Mid-August.

SPECIALTY LODGING
CATTAIL CREEK INN BED & BREAKFAST
2665 Abarr Drive, Loveland, 970-667-7600; www.cattailcreekinn.com
Located on the Cattail Creek Golf Course, this luxury inn offers views of Lake Loveland and the Rocky Mountains. The open guest rooms have cherry woodwork and ceiling fans. Delicious breakfasts include dishes such as Belgian pecan waffles with sautéed peaches. Eight rooms. Children over 14 years only. Complimentary full breakfast. **$**

SYLVAN DALE GUEST RANCH
2939 N. County Road 31 D, Loveland, 970-667-3915, 877-667-3999;
www.sylvandale.com
This dude ranch, owned and operated by the Jessup family, was established in the 1920s and is still a working cattle and horse ranch. Located in a river valley at the mouth of Colorado's Big Thompson Canyon, the ranch has more than 3,000 acres to enjoy, with elevations ranging up to 7,500 feet. 23 rooms. Complimentary full breakfast. Restaurant (public by reservation). Children's activity center. Airport transportation available. Pool. **$**

LYONS
In the foothills of the Rocky Mountains, this small town is known for the beautiful red cliffs that surround it.
Information: Chamber of Commerce, 303-823-5215, 877-596-6726;
www.lyons-colorado.com

SPECIAL EVENT
GOOD OLD DAYS CELEBRATION
350 Broadway Ave., Lyons, 303-823-5215;
www.lyons-colorado.com/goodolddays/schedule.htm
Parade, flea market, craft fair, food. Last weekend in June.

SPECIALTY LODGING
PEACEFUL VALLEY RANCH
475 Peaceful Valley Road, Lyons, 303-747-2881, 800-955-6343;
www.peacefulvalley.com
52 rooms. Restaurant. Children's activity center. Airport transportation available. **$$**

RESTAURANTS
★ANDREA'S HOMESTEAD CAFE
216 E. Main St., Lyons, 303-823-5000; www.andreashomesteadcafe.com
German menu. Breakfast, lunch, dinner, brunch. Closed Wednesday. Bar. Children's menu. Casual attire. Reservations recommended. **$$**

★★★BLACK BEAR INN

42 E. Main St., Lyons, 303-823-6812; www.blackbearinn.com

Since 1977, owners Hans and Annalies Wyppler have welcomed guests to their cozy Alpine-style restaurant with hearty dishes such as roasted duck and pork schnitzel. American menu. Lunch, dinner. Closed Monday-Tuesday; also January-mid-February. Bar. Outdoor seating. $$$

★★★LA CHAUMIÈRE

Highway 36, Lyons, 303-823-6521; www.lachaumiere-restaurant.com

This charming French restaurant offers friendly service and a simple but delicious menu of French cuisine. The menu changes with the seasons, but you might see filet mignon with red wine sauce, stuffed quail with wild mushrooms and a port wine demi-glaze. One mainstay is the chef's award-winning Maryland crab soup. The tranquil mountain setting adds to the relaxing atmosphere. French menu. Dinner. Closed Monday. Children's menu. $$

MANITOU SPRINGS

Nestled at the foot of Pikes Peak, only seven miles west of downtown Colorado Springs, Manitou Springs is one of the state's definitive—and most accessible—mountain communities. The many mineral springs gave nearby Colorado Springs its name. The natives, attributing supernatural powers to the waters (Manitou is an American Indian word for "Great Spirit"), once marked off the surrounding area as a sanctuary. Today, the town is a National Historic District and a popular tourist resort. Manitou Avenue has many artists' studios, restaurants and boutiques.

Information: Chamber of Commerce, 354 Manitou Ave.,
719-685-5089, 800-642-2567; www.manitousprings.org

WHAT TO SEE AND DO
CAVE OF THE WINDS

Cave of the Winds Road, Manitou Springs, 719-685-5444; www.caveofthewinds.com

This fascinating 45-minute guided tour—which goes through underground passageways filled with beautiful stalactites, stalagmites and flowstone formations created millions of years ago—leaves every 15 minutes and includes a laser light show with music. Summer, 9 a.m.-9 p.m.; winter, 10 a.m.-5 p.m.

IRON SPRINGS MELODRAMA DINNER THEATER

444 Ruxton Ave., Manitou Springs, 719-685-5104;
www.pikes-peak.com

Dinner theater featuring a traditional "olio" show. Named for the mineral-rich water beneath the ground. Monday-Saturday.

MANITOU CLIFF DWELLINGS MUSEUM

Highway 24 W., Manitou Springs, 719-685-5242, 800-354-9971;
www.cliffdwellingsmuseum.com

See the architecture of the cliff-dwelling natives, circa 1100-1300. American Indian dancing June-August. March-November, daily.

MIRAMONT CASTLE MUSEUM

9 Capitol Hill Ave., Manitou Springs, 719-685-1011; www.miramontcastle.org

A 46-room, four-story Victorian house (circa 1895) featuring nine styles of architecture, a miniatures and doll collection, a tea room, a soda fountain and gardens. Admission: adults $6, seniors $5.50, children $2, children under 6 free. Tuesday-Sunday.

HOTELS

★AMERICAS BEST VALUE INN VILLA MOTEL

481 Manitou Ave., Manitou Springs, 719-685-5492, 888-315-2378; www.villamotel.com

47 rooms. Pool. $

★★★THE CLIFF HOUSE AT PIKES PEAK

306 Canon Ave., Manitou Springs, 719-685-3000, 888-212-7000;
www.thecliffhouse.com

Built in 1873—before Colorado was even a state—this hotel has retained every charming detail of the Victorian age while adding modern touches. Each room is different and may include a gas fireplace, steam shower and towel warmers. Galleries, shops, restaurants and museums surround the hotel, and bicycles are available for rent. The dining room and wine cellar repeatedly win national awards. 55 rooms. Complimentary full breakfast. Wireless Internet access. Restaurant. $$$

★★★RED CRAGS BED & BREAKFAST INN

302 El Paso Blvd., Manitou Springs, 719-685-1920, 800-721-2248; www.redcrags.com

Housed in an 1884 mansion that was originally built as a clinic, this charming and elegant inn, surrounded by the Rocky Mountains, has high ceilings, hardwood floors and beautiful antiques. In-room fireplaces provide a romantic atmosphere. All rooms also have plasma TVs. Eight rooms. Children over 10 years only. Complimentary full breakfast. $$

★★★ROCKLEDGE COUNTRY INN

328 El Paso Blvd., Manitou Springs, 719-685-4515, 888-685-4515;
www.rockledgeinn.com

Situated atop a hill and surrounded by lush juniper and pine trees, the Rockledge Country Inn is located at the foot of Pikes Peak and has a beautiful view of the Rocky Mountains. Built in 1912, the inn is built in an Arts and Crafts style. The living room has leather couches, a marble fireplace and a grand piano. And there's plenty on hand here, from bike rentals to hiking trails to croquet. Five rooms. Children over 8 years permitted. Complimentary full breakfast. Wireless Internet access. $$

RESTAURANTS

★★★BRIARHURST MANOR

404 Manitou Ave., Manitou Springs, 719-685-1864, 877-685-1448; www.briarhurst.com

Located in a pink sandstone Tudor manor house built in 1876 by the founder of Manitou Springs, this elegant fine-dining restaurant's kitchen is headed up by executive chef Lawrence "Chip" Johnson, who uses homegrown vegetables and herbs in his recipes. Menu items include artisan cheeses, crusted lamb chops, Sicilian pheasant and

193

COLORADO

★
★
★
★
★

black hollow wild boar. The dessert sampler is the perfect ending to a delicious meal. American menu. Dinner. Closed Monday-Tuesday in January-March. Bar. Children's menu. Business casual attire. Reservations recommended. Outdoor seating. **$$$**

★★★THE CLIFF HOUSE DINING ROOM

306 Canon Ave., Manitou Springs, 719-685-3000, 888-212-7000;
www.thecliffhouse.com

Located in the historic Cliff House hotel, this elegant dining room serves up new American cooking presented with flair. Look for dishes like Rocky Mountain red trout almondine, or vanilla-marinated pork tenderloin. The ingredients in each dish are fresh and local, and the restaurant has more than 700 bottles of wine to accompany them. American menu. Breakfast, lunch, dinner. **$$**

★★★CRAFTWOOD INN

404 El Paso Blvd., Manitou Springs, 719-685-9000; www.craftwood.com

This romantic restaurant located in a 1912 Tudor manor house serves Southwestern-influenced cuisine. The focus is on steaks, elk, pheasant, venison, quail and seafood. When in season, the kitchen also uses Colorado vegetables and produce. Dining here is an adventure. Dishes include antelope with Porcini mushroom sauce, and Colorado blue cheese and pheasant with smoked Gouda baked in a phyllo crust. American menu. Dinner. Bar. Outdoor seating. **$$$**

★★MISSION BELL INN

178 Crystal Park Road, Manitou Springs, 719-685-9089; www.missionbellinn.com

Mexican menu. Dinner. Closed first three weeks of January; Monday and Tuesday in winter. Children's menu. Casual attire. Outdoor seating. **$$**

MESA VERDE NATIONAL PARK

In the far southwest corner of Colorado exists the largest—and arguably the most interesting—archaeological preserve in the nation. Mesa Verde National Park, with 52,000 acres encompassing 4,000 known archaeological sites, is a treasure trove of ancestral Pueblo cultural artifacts, including the magnificent Anasazi cliff dwellings. Constructed in the 13th century, these huge, elaborate stone villages built into the canyon walls are spellbinding. To fully appreciate their significance, first take a walk through the park's Chapin Mesa Museum for a historical overview. A visit to the actual sites can be physically challenging but is well worth the effort. Several of the sites can be explored year-round, free of charge; others require tickets for ranger-guided tours in summer months only. Tour tickets can be purchased at the park's Far View Visitor Center. Daily.

Information: Mesa Verde, eight miles east of Cortez, 36 miles west of Durango on Highway 160 to park entrance, then 15 miles south to visitor center, 970-529-4465; www.nps.gov/meve

★★STAGECOACH INN
702 Manitou Ave., Manitou Springs, 719-685-9400; www.stagecoachinn.com
American menu. Lunch, dinner. Bar. Children's menu. Casual attire. Reservations recommended (summer). Outdoor seating. **$$**

WHAT TO SEE AND DO
CHAPIN MESA ARCHEOLOGICAL MUSEUM
Mesa Verde National Park, 21 miles south of park entrance, 970-529-4465;
www.nps.gov/meve
Learn the story of the Mesa Verde people though arts, crafts, industries. Daily.

CLIFF DWELLING TOURS
Mesa Verde National Park, 970-529-4465; www.nps.gov/meve
The cliff dwellings can be entered only while rangers are on duty. During the summer, five cliff dwellings may be visited at specific hours. During the winter there are trips to Spruce Tree House only, weather permitting. Obtain daily tickets for Cliff Palace, Balcony House and Long House tours at Far View Visitor Center. Balcony House tours are limited to 50 people, Cliff Palace tours are limited to the first 60 and Long House tours are limited to 40 people.

MESA TOP LOOP AND CLIFF PALACE LOOP
Mesa Verde National Park, enter at crossroads near museum, 970-529-4465;
www.nps.gov/meve
Two six-mile, self-guided loops afford visits to 10 excavated mesa-top sites illustrating 700 years of architectural development; views of 20 to 30 cliff dwellings from canyon rim vantage points. Daily; closed during heavy snowfalls.

PARK POINT FIRE LOOKOUT
Mesa Verde National Park, halfway between the park entrance and headquarters,
970-529-4465; www.nps.gov/meve
From an elevation of 8,572 feet, enjoy spectacular views of the entire Four Corners area of Colorado, Arizona, New Mexico and Utah. The access road is closed in winter.

HOTEL
★★FAR VIEW LODGE IN MESA VERDE
1 Navajo Hill, Mesa Verde National Park, 866-875-8456;
www.nationalparkreservations.com/mesaverde.htm
150 rooms. Closed late October-mid-April. Restaurant, bar. Pets accepted. **$**

MONTE VISTA
Located in the heart of the high-altitude San Luis Valley, Monte Vista means "mountain view" in Spanish.
Information: Monte Vista Chamber of Commerce, 1035 Park Ave.,
719-852-2731, 800-562-7085; www.monte-vista.org

★
★★
★★
★

WHAT TO SEE AND DO
MONTE VISTA NATIONAL WILDLIFE REFUGE
9383 El Rancho Lane, Alamosa, 719-589-4021; www.fws.gov/alamosa
Created as a nesting, migration and wintering habitat for waterfowl and other migratory birds. Marked visitor tour road.

SPECIAL EVENTS
MONTE VISTA CRANE FESTIVAL
Ski-Hi Park, 2345 Sherman Ave., Monte Vista, 719-852-2731; www.cranefest.com
Tour this refuge to view cranes and other wildlife. Arts, crafts, workshops. Mid-March.

SKI-HI STAMPEDE
Ski-Hi Park, 2345 Sherman Ave., Monte Vista, 719-852-2055; www.skihistampede.com
Rodeo, carnival, arts and crafts show, street parade, barbecue, Western dances. Last weekend in July.

HOTEL
★★BEST WESTERN MOVIE MANOR
2830 W. Highway 160, Monte Vista, 719-852-5921, 800-771-9468;
www.bestwestern.com
59 rooms. Restaurant, bar. Pets accepted. $

SPECIALTY LODGING
PECOSA INN
1519 Grand Ave., Monte Vista, 719-852-0612, 888-732-6724; www.pecosainn.com
44 rooms. Complimentary continental breakfast. Pets accepted. Pool. $

MONTROSE
Montrose is a trading center for a rich mining, agricultural and recreational area in the Uncompahgre Valley. Several fishing areas are nearby, including the Gunnison River east of town and Buckhorn Lakes southeast.
Information: Montrose Chamber of Commerce, 1519 E. Main St.,
970-249-5000, 800-923-5515; www.montrosechamber.com

WHAT TO SEE AND DO
BLACK CANYON OF THE GUNNISON NATIONAL MONUMENT
102 Elk Creek, Gunnison, 970-641-2337; www.nps.gov/blca
Within this monument, 12 of the most spectacular miles of the rugged gorge of the Gunnison River slice down to a maximum depth of 2,660 feet. At one point, the river channel is only 40 feet wide. The narrowest width between the north and south rims at the top is 1,100 feet. The combination of dark, weathered rock and lack of sunlight due to the narrowness of the canyon give the monument its name. The spectacular scenery includes pine trees—some more than 800 years old. There are scenic drives along the south rim (the road is plowed to Gunnison Point in winter) and the north rim (approximately May-October). There are also hiking areas and concessions

(June-Labor Day). The visitor center is located at Gunnison Point on the south rim. A descent into the canyon requires a free hiking permit from the visitor center. Cross-country skiing is open in winter from Gunnison Point to High Point.

MONTROSE COUNTY HISTORICAL MUSEUM
Depot Building, 21 N. Rio Grande, Montrose, 970-249-2085
Collections of antique farm machinery; archaeological artifacts; pioneer cabin with family items; tool collection; early electrical equipment; Montrose newspapers 1896-1940. May-September, daily.

SCENIC DRIVE, OWL CREEK PASS
Montrose, 23 miles south on Highway 550 to the left-hand turnoff for Owl Creek Pass, marked by a U.S. Forest Service sign, then east seven miles along Cow Creek to Debbie's Park
A scene with Debbie Reynolds from *How the West Was Won* was filmed in the meadow here. Go up the Owl Creek Pass (at 10,114 feet). Fifteen miles from the pass is Silver Jack Reservoir, an area with good fishing and scenic hiking trails. About 20 miles north, the road joins Highway 50 at Cimarron.

HOTEL
★★BEST WESTERN RED ARROW
1702 E. Main St., Montrose, 970-249-9641, 800-468-9323; www.bestwestern.com/redarrow
59 rooms. Restaurant. Airport transportation available. Pets accepted. $

RESTAURANT
★WHOLE ENCHILADA
44 S. Grand Ave., Montrose, 970-249-1881
Mexican menu. Lunch, dinner. Closed Sunday. Bar. Casual attire. Outdoor seating. $

MORRISON
This tiny town has played a big role in paleontologists' search for dinosaur bones. In the late 19th century, scientists found fossil remains of a Stegosaurus and an Apatosaurus in and around Morrison, and recent discoveries include preserved adult Stegosaurus tracks.
Information: www.town.morrison.co.us

WHAT TO SEE AND DO
RED ROCKS PARK AND AMPHITHEATER
18300 W. Alameda Parkway, Morrison, 720-865-2494; www.redrocksonline.com
Red Rocks Amphitheater is located in the majestic 816-acre Red Rocks Park, 15 miles west of Denver. Two 300-foot sandstone monoliths serve as stadium walls for this open-air arena. During the summer months, the 8,000-seat amphitheater, with its perfect acoustical conditions, awe-inspiring beauty and panoramic view of Denver, serves as a stunning stage for performers ranging from chart-topping rock bands to world-renowned symphony orchestras.

COLORADO ★★★

RESTAURANT
★★★THE FORT
19192 Highway 8, Morrison, 303-697-4771; www.thefort.com

Sam Arnold's popular, kitschy restaurant has been serving buffalo steaks for 30 years. The menu also features other game, such as elk chops, as well as beef and seafood. The adobe re-creation of the historic Bent's Fort is reason enough to check out this restaurant. American menu. Dinner. Bar. Children's menu. Business casual attire. Reservations recommended. Outdoor seating. **$$$**

OURAY

Ouray's location in a natural basin surrounded by the majestic 12,000- to 14,000-foot peaks of the San Juan Mountains has made it a nice spot for visitors. Ouray, named for a Ute chief, is reached by the magnificent Million Dollar Highway section of the San Juan Skyway, which was blasted from sheer cliff walls high above the Uncompahgre River.

Information: Ouray Chamber Resort Association, 970-325-4746, 800-228-1876; www.ouraycolorado.com

WHAT TO SEE AND DO
BACHELOR-SYRACUSE MINE TOUR
1222 County Road 14, Ouray, 970-325-0220, 888-227-4585; www.bachelorsyracusemine.com

This mine has been in continuous operation since 1884. Guided tours are aboard a mine train that advances 3,350 feet horizontally into Gold Hill (mine temperature 47°F) where you can see mining equipment, visit work areas and learn how explosives are used. Gold panning. Late May-September, daily.

BEAR CREEK FALLS
1230 Main, Ouray, 970-325-4746; www.ouraycolorado.com
An observational point lets you take in the 227-foot falls.

BOX CANON FALLS PARK
Highway 550, Ouray, 970-325-7080; www.ouraycolorado.com/boxcanyon
Canyon Creek has cut a natural canyon 20 feet wide and 400 feet deep. Take the stairs and a suspended bridge to the floor of the canyon, where you can see the thundering falls. Daily.

HOT SPRINGS POOL
Ouray City Park, 1220 Highway 50, Ouray, 970-325-7073; www.cityofouray.com
Outdoor, million-gallon pool fed by natural mineral hot springs (sulphur-free). Bathhouse; spa. Daily)

SPECIAL EVENT
ARTISTS' ALPINE HOLIDAY & FESTIVAL
1230 Main St., Ouray, 970-325-4746; www.ouraycolorado.com
Each year, artists from across the country come to Ouray to enter their work in this juried art show. One week in mid-August.

★
★
★
★
☆

IMOGENE PASS MOUNTAIN MARATHON
100 Fifth St., Ouray, 970-728-0251; www.imogenerun.com
The 18-mile course, which follows an old mining trail, starts at Ouray's 7,800-foot elevation, crosses over Imogene Pass (13,114 feet) and ends at Main Street, Telluride (8,800 feet).

HOTELS
★BOX CANYON LODGE & HOT SPRING
45 Third Ave., Ouray, 970-325-4981, 800-327-5080; www.boxcanyonouray.com
38 rooms. Wireless Internet access. Pool. **$**

★COMFORT INN
191 Fifth Ave., Ouray, 970-325-7203, 800-438-5713; www.ouraycomfortinn.com
33 rooms. Wireless Internet access. Complimentary continental breakfast. Whirlpool. Pets accepted. **$**

★★★ST. ELMO HOTEL
426 Main St., Ouray, 970-325-4951; www.stelmohotel.com
The guest rooms at this restored 1898 hotel are individually decorated in Victorian style and feature period antiques. Enjoy a wine and cheese social hour every afternoon in the parlor and a full breakfast every morning in the sun room. Nine rooms. Complimentary continental breakfast. Restaurant. Whirlpool. **$**

SPECIALTY LODGING
CHINA CLIPPER INN
525 Second St., Ouray, 970-325-0565, 800-315-0565; www.chinaclipperinn.com
Each guest room has a view of the magnificent San Juan Mountains. Winter guests receive half-price coupons to the nearby million-gallon natural Hot Springs Pool. 12 rooms. Wireless Internet access. Children over 15 years only. Complimentary continental breakfast. Whirlpool. **$**

RESTAURANTS
★★BON TON
426 Main St., Ouray, 970-325-4951; www.stelmohotel.com
American, Italian menu. Dinner. Bar. Children's menu. Casual attire. Outdoor seating. **$$$**

★BUEN TIEMPO
515 Main St., Ouray, 970-325-4544; www.stelmohotel.com
Mexican menu. Lunch, dinner. Bar. Children's menu. Casual attire. Outdoor seating. **$$**

PAGOSA SPRINGS
People come here for the remarkable mineral springs. The town is surrounded by the San Juan National Forest, and deer and elk hunting are popular activities.
Information: Pagosa Springs Chamber of Commerce, 402 San Juan St.,
970-264-2360, 800-252-2204; www.pagosa-springs.com

WHAT TO SEE AND DO
CHIMNEY ROCK ARCHAEOLOGICAL AREA
180 N. Pagosa Blvd., Pagosa Springs, 970-883-5359; www.chimneyrockco.org
This area features twin pinnacles, held sacred by the Anasazi. The Fire Tower offers a spectacular view of nearby ruins. Four guided scheduled tours daily.

FRED HARMAN ART MUSEUM
85 Harman Park Drive, Pagosa Springs, 970-731-5785; www.harmanartmuseum.com
See original paintings by Fred Harman—best known for his famous Red Ryder and Little Beaver comic strip. Rodeo, movie and Western memorabilia. Admission: adults $4, children under 6 $.50. Monday-Saturday 10:30 a.m.-5 p.m., Sunday noon-4 p.m.; Winter, Monday-Friday 10:30 a.m.-5 p.m.

ROCKY MOUNTAIN WILDLIFE PARK
4821 Highway 84, Pagosa Springs, 970-264-5546; www.alldurango.com/wildlife
Exhibits animals indigenous to the area, plus wildlife museum and photography displays. Summer, daily 9 a.m.-6 p.m.; Winter, daily noon-4 p.m.

TREASURE MOUNTAIN
Pagosa Springs
Begin at the Wolf Creek Pass, just east of summit marked where Continental Divide Trail winds southward and connects with the Treasure Mountain Trail. Legend states that in 1790, 300 men mined five million dollars in gold and melted it into bars but were forced to leave it behind. The gold has never been found.

WOLF CREEK PASS
Pagosa Springs, 20 miles northeast on Highways 160 and 84
Take a scenic drive across the Continental Divide. The eastern approach is through the Rio Grande National Forest, the western approach through the San Juan National Forest. The best time to drive through is September, when you'll see spectacular views of the aspens changing color. Drive takes approximately one hour.

WOLF CREEK SKI AREA
Pagosa Springs, 20 miles northeast of Highways 160 and 84, 970-264-5639;
www.wolfcreekski.com
Two triple, two double chairlifts; Poma lift; patrol, school, rentals; cafeteria, restaurant, bar, day lodge; 50 runs; longest run two miles; vertical drop 1,604 feet. Shuttle bus service. Early November-April, daily.

HOTELS
★★BEST VALUE HIGH COUNTRY LODGE
3821 E. Highway 160, Pagosa Springs, 800-862-3707; www.highcountrylodge.com
35 rooms. Complimentary continental breakfast. Restaurant. Whirlpool. Pets accepted. **$**

★★PAGOSA LODGE
3505 W. Highway 160, Pagosa Springs,
970-731-4141, 800-523-7704; www.pagosalodge.com
101 rooms. High-speed Internet access. Restaurant, bar. Airport transportation available. Pool. Fitness center. $

RESTAURANT
★★TEQUILA'S
439 San Juan St., Pagosa Springs, 970-264-9989
Mexican menu. Lunch, dinner. Children's menu. Casual attire. Outdoor seating. $

PUEBLO
Pueblo began as a crossroad for Native Americans, Spaniards and fur traders. When the Rio Grande Railroad reached here in 1872, Pueblo was the leading center for steel and coal production west of the Mississippi. Today, Pueblo is a major transportation and industrial center—more than half of all goods manufactured in Colorado are produced in Pueblo.
Information: Chamber of Commerce, 302 N. Santa Fe Ave.,
719-542-1704, 800-233-3446; www.pueblo.org

WHAT TO SEE AND DO
EL PUEBLO MUSEUM
301 N. Union, Pueblo, 719-583-0453; www.coloradohistory.org
Check out this full-size replica of Old Fort Pueblo, which served as a base for fur traders and other settlers from 1842-1855. Daily.

LAKE PUEBLO STATE PARK
640 Pueblo Reservoir Road, Pueblo, 719-561-9320;
www.parks.state.co.us
Swimming, water-skiing, boating, hiking, camping. Daily.

MINERAL PALACE PARK
1500 N. Santa Fe, Pueblo
In addition to a pool, this park has a rose garden and green house. The Pueblo Art Guild Gallery, which showcases the work of local artists, is also here. Saturday-Sunday; closed December-February.

PUEBLO WEISBROD AIRCRAFT MUSEUM
Pueblo Memorial Airport, 31001 Magnuson Ave., Pueblo, 719-948-9219;
www.pwam.org
This outdoor museum features static aircraft displays. Adjacent is the B-24 Aircraft Memorial Museum, with indoor displays of the history of the B-24 bomber. Guided tours. Monday-Saturday 10 a.m.-4 p.m., Sunday 1-4 p.m.

COLORADO

★
★
★
★
★

ROSEMOUNT VICTORIAN HOUSE MUSEUM

419 W. 14th St., Pueblo, 719-545-5290; www.rosemount.org

This 37-room mansion contains original Victorian furnishings and the McClelland Collection of World Curiosities. Tuesday-Sunday; closed in January.

SAN ISABEL NATIONAL FOREST

2840 Kachina Drive, Pueblo, 719-553-1400,
www.sangres.com/nationalforests/sanisabel

This forest, spread over 1,109,782 acres, offers camping and two winter sports areas, Monarch and Ski Cooper. In the southern part of the forest is the Spanish Peaks National Natural Landmark. Collegiate Peaks, Mount Massive and Holy Cross Wilderness areas are also within the forest, as well as four wilderness study areas. Colorado's highest peak, Mount Elbert (14,433 feet), is within the forest south of Leadville.

SANGRE DE CRISTO ARTS AND CONFERENCE CENTER

210 N. Santa Fe Ave., Pueblo, 719-295-7200; www.sdc-arts.org

The four art galleries here include the Francis King Collection of Western Art, currently on permanent display. Children's museum, workshops, dance studios, theater. Monday-Saturday.

SPECIAL EVENT
COLORADO STATE FAIR

Fairgrounds, 1001 Beulah Ave., Pueblo, 719-561-8484, 800-876-4567;
www.coloradostatefair.com

Annual event includes rodeo, grandstand and amphitheater entertainment, agricultural and technological displays, arts and crafts and a carnival. August-September.

HOTELS
★LA QUINTA INN & SUITES

4801 N. Elizabeth St., Pueblo, 719-542-3500; www.laquinta.com

101 rooms. Complimentary continental breakfast. High-speed Internet access. Airport transportation available. Pets accepted. Pool. $

★★★MARRIOTT PUEBLO CONVENTION CENTER

110 W. First St., Pueblo, 719-542-3200, 800-228-9290; www.marriott.com

This hotel is connected to the convention center downtown and is surrounded by beautiful landscaping. Guest rooms feature modern furnishings and include microwaves and ergonomic desk chairs. The restaurant offers western fare. This hotel is nonsmoking. 164 rooms. High-speed Internet access. Restaurant, bar. Pets accepted. Pool. Business center. $$

SPECIALTY LODGING
ABRIENDO INN

300 W. Abriendo Ave., Pueblo, 719-544-2703; www.abriendoinn.com

Located just south of downtown, this inn is decorated with antiques and period furniture. Wake up to a gourmet breakfast and enjoy refreshments in the afternoon. Relax on the large front porch that overlooks the lovely residential area surrounding the inn or soak in your in-room whirlpool. 10 rooms. Wireless Internet access. Complimentary full breakfast. Whirlpool. $

ROCKY MOUNTAIN NATIONAL PARK

Straddling the Continental Divide, the 415-square-mile park contains a staggering profusion of peaks, upland meadows, sheer canyons, glacial streams and lakes. Dominating the scene is Longs Peak, with its east face towering 14,255 feet above sea level. The park's forests and meadows provide sanctuary for more than 750 varieties of wildflowers, 260 species of birds and such indigenous mammals as deer, wapiti (American elk), bighorn sheep and beaver. There are five campgrounds, two of which take reservations from May to early September. Some attractions are not accessible during the winter months.

Information: Rocky Mountain National Park, 1000 US Highway 36, Estes Park, 970-586-1206; www.nps.gov/romo

RESTAURANTS

★★GIACOMO'S RISTORANTE

910 Highway 50 W., Pueblo City, 719-546-0949

Italian menu. Lunch, dinner. Bar. Children's menu. Casual attire. Reservations recommended. Outdoor seating. $$

★★★LA RENAISSANCE

217 E. Routt Ave., Pueblo, 719-543-6367; www.larenaissancerestaurant.com

This award-winning restaurant was originally built in 1886 as a Presbyterian church and still includes the pews and stained-glass windows. It's an interesting atmosphere for dining, and the food is superb, from lobster tail to prime rib. American menu. Dinner. Closed Sunday. Bar. Casual attire. Reservations recommended. $$

★THE LAUGHING CROW

5200 Nature Center Road, Pueblo, 719-549-2009

American, Mexican menu. Breakfast, lunch, dinner. Children's menu. Casual attire. Reservations recommended. Outdoor seating. $

SALIDA

Located on the eastern slope of the Rocky Mountains, Salida is surrounded by San Isabel National Forest. A pleasant climate makes it ideal for recreational activities throughout the year, including river rafting, fishing, mountain biking, hiking and hunting.

Information: Heart of the Rockies Chamber of Commerce, 406 W. U.S. 50, 719-539-2068, 877-772-5432; www.salidachamber.org

WHAT TO SEE AND DO

ANGEL OF SHAVANO

Salida

Every spring, the snow melts on the 14,239-foot slopes of Mount Shavano leaving an outline called "the Angel."

ARKANSAS HEADWATERS STATE RECREATION AREA

307 W. Sackett Ave., Salida, 719-539-7289;
www.parks.State.co.us/Parks/arkansasheadwaters

This outstanding waterway cuts its way through rugged canyons for 148 miles, from Leadville to Pueblo, making it one of the world's premier places for kayaking and white-water rafting. Fishing, boating, hiking, bridle trails, picnicking, camping. Daily.

JEEP TOURS

Chamber of Commerce, 406 W. Rainbow Blvd., Salida, 719-539-4789, 888-996-7669

Outfitters offer half-hour, half-day and full-day trail rides. Fishing, hunting, photography and pack trips. Contact Chamber of Commerce for details.

MONARCH SCENIC TRAM

Chamber of Commerce, 406 W. Rainbow Blvd., Salida, 719-539-4789, 888-996-7669

This trip to an observatory at 12,000 feet offer panoramic views of Rocky Mountains. May-September, daily.

MONARCH SKI & SNOWBOARD AREA

1 Powder Place, Monarch, 719-539-3573, 888-996-7669; www.skimoarch.com

Four double chairlifts; patrol, school, rentals; 63 runs; longest run one mile; vertical drop 1,170 feet. Multiday, half-day rates. Mid-November-mid-April, daily. Cross-country skiing.

MOUNTAIN SPIRIT WINERY

16150 County Road 220, Salida, 719-539-1175, 888-679-4637;
www.mountainspiritwinery.com

Family-operated boutique winery. Five acres with apple orchard, homestead, tours and tastings. Memorial Day-Labor Day, Monday-Saturday 10 a.m.-5 p.m.

SALIDA MUSEUM

406 Highway 50, Salida, 719-539-2068, 877-772-5432;
www.salidachamber.org/museum

Museum features a mineral display, American Indian artifacts, an early pioneer household display and mining and railroad displays. Late May-early September, daily.

TENDERFOOT DRIVE

Salida, west on Highway 291

This spiral drive encircling Mount Tenderfoot offers view of the surrounding mountain area and the upper Arkansas Valley.

SPECIAL EVENTS
ARTWALK

Downtown Historic District, 406 W. Rainbow Blvd., Salida, 877-772-5432;
www.salidaartwalk.org

Local artists, craftspeople and entertainers display artwork to celebrate Colorado's largest historic district. Last weekend in June.

CHRISTMAS MOUNTAIN USA
406 W. Rainbow Blvd., Salida, 719-539-2068; www.salidachamber.org
This three-day event kicks off the holiday season. More than 3,500 lights outline a 700-foot Christmas tree on Tenderfoot Mountain. Parade. Day after Thanksgiving.

FIBARK WHITEWATER FESTIVAL
240 N. F St., Salida, 719-539-6918; www.fibark.com
International experts compete in a 26-mile kayak race. Other events include slalom, raft, foot and bicycle races. Father's Day weekend.

NEW OLD-FASHIONED CHAFFEE COUNTY FAIR
10165 County Road 120, Poncha Springs, 719-539-6151; www.chaffeecounty.org
This annual event features a rodeo, live entertainment, arts and crafts, food, a beer garden, livestock auctions, tractor-pull contests and much more. Late July-early August.

SPECIALTY LODGING
TUDOR ROSE BED & BREAKFAST
6720 County Road 104, Salida, 719-539-2002, 800-379-0889; www.thetudorrose.com
Six rooms. Wireless Internet access. Children over 10 years only. Complimentary full breakfast. Whirlpool. Pets accepted. $

RESTAURANTS
★★COUNTRY BOUNTY
413 W. Highway 50, Salida, 719-539-3546; www.countrybounty.net
American menu. Breakfast, lunch, dinner. Children's menu. Casual attire. $

★WINDMILL
720 E. Rainbow Blvd., Salida, 719-539-3594
American menu. Lunch, dinner. Bar. Children's menu. Casual attire. $

SILVERTON
Situated in the San Juan Mountains, Silverton is nicknamed "the mining town that never quits." The last mine in Silverton closed in 1991. Since then, tourists have discovered the natural beauty, historic ghost towns and many recreational opportunities of the area.
Information: Silverton Chamber of Commerce, Highway 550 and Greene Street, 110, 970-387-5654, 800-752-4494; www.silvertoncolorado.com

WHAT TO SEE AND DO
CIRCLE JEEP TOUR
414 Greene St., Silverton, 970-387-5654, 800-752-4494; www.silvertoncolorado.com
Take in the history of the area, including information on mines and ghost towns, on a jeep tour.

OLD HUNDRED GOLD MINE TOUR
721 County Road 4 A, Silverton, 970-387-5444, 800-872-3009; www.minetour.com
Learn all about the methods of hard rock mining. This guided one-hour tour of an underground mine offers views of the equipment and crystal pockets. Memorial Day-September, daily.

RED MOUNTAIN PASS
Silverton, Highway 550 between Ouray and Silverton
Stretching through the towering San Juan Mountains, the 23-mile stretch of Highway 550 between Ouray and Silverton passes through some of Colorado's wildest country. The road rises to 11,075 feet to cross the Red Mountain Pass, a favorite spot for hikers, rock climbers, mountain bikers and backcountry ski enthusiasts. Along the way you'll see numerous gorges and falls, as well as abandoned log cabins and mining equipment.

SAN JUAN COUNTY HISTORICAL SOCIETY MUSEUM
1315 Snowden, Silverton
Located in an old three-story jail, this museum showcases mining and railroad artifacts from Silverton's early days. Memorial Day-mid-October, daily.

SPECIAL EVENT
GREAT WESTERN ROCKY MOUNTAIN BRASS BAND CONCERTS
Silverton, 800-752-4494; www.silvertoncolorado.com
Nationally recognized musicians—and Silverton's own brass band—perform concerts throughout the weekend. Mid-August.

HOTEL
★★WYMAN HOTEL
1371 Greene St., Silverton, 970-387-5372, 800-609-7845; www.thewyman.com
17 rooms. Wireless Internet access. Closed late March-early May, mid-October-mid-December. Complimentary continental breakfast. Restaurant. Pets accepted. $

SPECIALTY LODGING
ALMA HOUSE BED AND BREAKFAST
220 E. 10th St., Silverton, 970-387-5336, 800-267-5336; www.innoftherockies.com
Nine rooms. Whirlpool. Complimentary full breakfast. Pets accepted. $

SNOWMASS VILLAGE
Snowmass Village, only eight miles from Aspen, is best known as the location of Snowmass Ski Area, a popular winter resort. (The village is located at the base of the ski area.) There's also much to do in summer, including swimming (there are 50 outdoor heated pools and hot tubs), rafting, hiking, horseback riding, golf, tennis, hot air balloon rides and free outdoor concerts. The village includes more than 20 restaurants. A free shuttle bus runs throughout the village.
Information: Snowmass Resort Association, 104 A Gateway Center, 970-923-2000, 800-766-9627; www.snowmassvillage.com

WHAT TO SEE AND DO
ASPEN SNOWMASS SKIING COMPANY
40 Carriage Way, Snowmass Village, 970-923-1220; www.aspensnowmass.com
Seven quad, two triple, six double chairlifts; two platter pulls; patrol, school, rentals, snowmaking; restaurants, bar, nursery. 91 runs; longest run five miles, vertical drop 4,406 feet. Cross-country skiing (50 miles). Shuttle bus service from Aspen. Late November-mid-April, daily.

BICYCLE TRIPS AND JEEP TRIPS

48 Snowmass Village Mall, Snowmass Village, 970-923-4544, 800-282-7238; www.blazingadventures.com

Throughout the Snowmass/Aspen area. Transportation and equipment provided. June-September.

HOTELS

★★★SILVERTREE HOTEL SNOWMASS VILLAGE

100 Elbert Lane, Snowmass Village, 970-923-3520, 800-837-4255; www.silvertreehotel.com

This year-round mountain resort offers ski-in/ski-out access, two heated pools and a fitness center with a steam room and massage services. Family-style suites are available. 260 rooms. Restaurant. Children's activity center. Airport transportation available. Fitness center. Pets accepted. Business center. $$$

★★★SNOWMASS CLUB

0239 Snowmass Club Circle, Snowmass Village, 970-923-5600, 800-525-0710; www.snowmassclub.com

This year-round resort is located in the Elk Mountain range area and offers one-, two- and three-bedroom villas with daily maid service. All of the villas have full kitchens and high-speed Internet access, and most feature a fireplace, deck with barbecue grill and laundry. The 19,000-square-foot health club includes four pools, spa services and dozens of fitness classes. (There are also private residences here.) Brother's Grille serves everything from barbecue to New York-style cuisine. 55 rooms. High-speed Internet access. Restaurant. Children's activity center. Spa. Airport transportation available. Golf. Tennis. Business center. $$$$

★★STONEBRIDGE INN

300 Carriage Way, Snowmass Village, 970-923-2420, 800-213-3214; www.stonebridgeinn.com

92 rooms. Closed mid-April-May. Complimentary continental breakfast. Restaurant. Airport transportation available. Wireless Internet access. $$

★★WILDWOOD LODGE

100 Elbert Lane, Snowmass Village, 970-923-3520, 800-837-4255; www.silvertreehotel.com

140 rooms. Closed early April-May. Complimentary continental breakfast. Restaurant. Children's activity center. Airport transportation available. Pets accepted. Pool. $$

RESTAURANTS

★★★KRABLOONIK

4250 Divide Road, Snowmass Village, 970-923-3953; www.krabloonik.com

Celebrate the dog days of winter at this log restaurant with ski-in access and large picture windows framing the mountain views. More than 200 sled dogs live in the kennel next door—take a sled ride after a lunch of wild mushroom soup, fresh baked bread and smoked meat from the onsite smokehouse. (No lunch during summer.) At night, the sunken fire pit keeps everyone warm and toasty. American, seafood menu. Lunch, dinner. Closed mid-April-May, October-Thanksgiving. Children's menu. Casual attire. Reservations recommended. $$$

★★★SAGE

239 Snowmass Circle, Snowmass Village, 970-923-0923; www.snowmassclub.com

Located in the Snowmass Club, this restaurant offers simple classics with fresh ingredients. In the summer, the patio is a lovely spot for lunch, thanks to unobstructed views of Mount Daly. American menu. Breakfast, lunch, dinner. Bar. Children's menu. Valet parking. Outdoor seating. $$$

STEAMBOAT SPRINGS

In 1913, Norwegian Carl Howelsen introduced ski jumping here. Since then, 10 national ski-jumping records have been set on Steamboat Springs' Howelsen Hill. The area has produced 47 winter Olympians. Summer activities include camping, fishing, hot air ballooning, horseback riding, hiking, bicycling, river rafting, canoeing and llama trekking. One of the largest elk herds in North America ranges near the town. There are more than 100 natural hot springs in the area.

Information: Steamboat Ski Resort Corporation, 2305 Mt. Werner Circle,
970-879-6111, 800-922-2722; www.steamboat.com

WHAT TO SEE AND DO

HOWELSEN HILL SKI COMPLEX

245 Howelsen Parkway, Steamboat Springs, 970-879-8499

International ski jump complex includes a double chairlift, Poma lift, rope tow, five ski-jumping hills; patrol; ice skating, snowboarding. Evening skiing available. December-March, daily.

ROUTT NATIONAL FOREST

925 Weiss Drive, Steamboat Springs, 970-879-1722; www.fs.fed.us/r2/mbr/

Includes the 139,898-acre Mount Zirkel Wilderness. Fishing, hunting, winter sports area, hiking, picnicking, camping.

STEAMBOAT

2305 Mount Werner Circle, Steamboat Springs, 970-879-6111, 800-922-2722;
www.steamboat.com

High-speed gondola; four high-speed quad (two covered), quad, six triple, seven double chairlifts; two surface tows; patrol, school, rentals, snowmaking; cafeterias, restaurants, bars, nursery; 142 runs; longest run more than three miles; vertical drop 3,668 feet. Snowboarding. Cross-country skiing (14 miles). Multiday, half-day rates. Late November-early April, daily. Gondola also operates mid-June-mid-September. Daily, fee.

STEAMBOAT LAKE STATE PARK

61105 Routt County Road 129, Steamboat Springs, 970-879-3922;
www.parks.state.co.uss

Swimming, water-skiing, fishing, boating, picnicking, camping. Daily.

STRAWBERRY PARK NATURAL HOT SPRINGS

44200 County Road 36, Steamboat Springs, 970-879-0342;
www.strawberryhotsprings.com

Mineral springs feed four pools (water cooled from 160 F to 105 F). Changing area, picnicking, camping, cabins. Daily. Sunday-Thursday 10 a.m.-10.30 p.m., Friday-Saturday 10 a.m.-midnight.

STEAMBOAT SPRINGS HEALTH & RECREATION ASSOCIATION
136 Lincoln Ave., Steamboat Springs, 970-879-1828; www.sshra.org
Three hot pools fed by 103-degree mineral water. Lap pool, saunas, exercise classes, massage, weight room, tennis courts (summer). Daily.

TREAD OF PIONEERS MUSEUM
800 Oak St., Steamboat Springs, 970-879-2214; www.treadofpioneers.org
Check out the permanent ski exhibit tracing the evolution of skiing and a Victorian house with period furnishings and pioneer and cattle-ranching artifacts. Admission: adults $5, seniors $4 children. Tuesday-Saturday 11 a.m.-5 p.m.

SPECIAL EVENTS
COWBOY ROUNDUP DAYS
Steamboat Springs
Rodeos, parade, entertainment. July Fourth weekend.

ROCKY MOUNTAIN MUSTANG ROUND-UP
1255 S. Lincoln Ave., Steamboat Springs, 970-879-0880; www.steamboatchamber.com
Car fanatics will enjoy this parade of more than 350 Ford Mustangs. Timed driving event. Mid-June.

WINTER CARNIVAL
Steamboat Springs
Snow and ski competitions, parade. Early February.

HOTELS
★FAIRFIELD INN BY MARRIOTT
3200 S. Lincoln Ave., Steamboat Springs, 970-870-9000, 800-325-3535; www.fairfieldinn.com
66 rooms. Pets accepted. High-speed Internet access. Complimentary continental breakfast. Business center. **$**

★HAMPTON INN & SUITES
725 S. Lincoln Ave., Steamboat Springs, 970-871-8900; www.hamptoninn.com
68 rooms. Business center. Fitness center. Pool. **$**

★★PTARMIGAN INN
2304 Après Ski Way, Steamboat Springs, 970-879-1730, 800-538-7519; www.steamboat-lodging.com
77 rooms. Closed early April-late May. Restaurant, bar. Pets accepted. Pool. **$**

★★★SHERATON STEAMBOAT SPRINGS RESORT AND CONFERENCE CENTER

2200 Village Inn Court, Steamboat Springs, 970-879-8000, 800-325-3535; www.starwoodhotels.com

This hotel is a great choice for families and business travelers—it's the only conference hotel in the area with ski-in/ski-out access. After a day on the slopes, enjoy the rooftop hot tubs or get a massage at the spa. The elegant and comfortable rooms include Sweet Sleeper beds. Ask for a slope view room. The resort has boutiques and an art gallery. 213 rooms. Closed mid-April-May, fall season. Restaurant, bar. Children's activity center. Spa. Golf. High-speed Internet access. $$

★★★THE STEAMBOAT GRAND RESORT HOTEL

2300 Mount Werner Circle, Steamboat Springs, 970-871-5500, 877-366-2628; www.steamboatgrand.com

The accommodations here range from studios to private residences with Alder cabinets and granite countertops. The spa offers a wide variety of treatments, from hot stone massage to herbal hibernation body wraps. The fitness center has lots of equipment but, more importantly, a eucalyptus steam room, perfect after a day on the slopes. The Cabin restaurant has an extensive wine list and serves Midwestern beef aged at least 30 days in controlled cellars and native Colorado game. 327 rooms. Restaurant, bar. Fitness center. Pool. Spa. $$$

SPECIALTY LODGINGS

THE HOME RANCH

54880 Rou County Road 129, Clark, 970-879-1780; www.homeranch.com

The Home Ranch makes everyone feel at home. Situated in the Elk River Valley with the majestic Rocky Mountains in the distance, the ranch is only 18 miles from Steamboat Springs and offers an authentic guest ranch experience. Activities are plentiful, with more than 12 miles of snow-covered trails for snowshoeing and cross-country skiing in winter, and mountain biking and hiking in summer. But horsemanship is the focus here. Cattle-working and stockmanship lessons are offered in addition to general riding. The Western-style rooms in the main lodge are convenient to the pool and dining room. There are also eight cabins for those desiring more privacy. The family-style meals in the restaurant are memorable. After dinner, listen to the sounds of the Ranch Hand Band. Eight rooms. Closed late October-mid-December, late March-late May. Restaurant. Children's activity center. Airport transportation available. $$$

VISTA VERDE RANCH

31100 Seehouse Road, Steamboat Springs, 970-879-3858, 800-526-7433; www.vistaverde.com

Situated on 500 acres in the Rocky Mountains, this wonderful ranch is fun for the whole family. The cozy accommodations range from lodge rooms to private cabins and feature furnishings handcrafted by the ranch's very own woodworker. There are plenty of activities on the property, from backcountry skiing and sleigh rides to fly-fishing, hot air ballooning and hiking, though horseback riding is the most popular activity at the ranch (instruction is available for both kids and adults). Afterward, feast on gourmet meals in the rustic dining room. 12 rooms. Closed late September-late December, late March-early June. Restaurant. Children's activity center. Airport transportation available. $$$

RESTAURANTS

★★ANTARES

57 1/2 Eighth St., Steamboat Springs, 970-879-9939

American menu. Dinner. Closed mid-April-early June. Bar. Children's menu. Casual attire. $$$

★★★L'APOGEE

911 Lincoln Ave., Steamboat Springs, 970-879-1919; www.lapogee.com

Housed in a former saddlery store, L'Apogee has become local favorite. The interesting American menu features favorites like dry-aged New York strip steak and filet mignon, as well as less traditional dishes such as marinated and baked tofu served with shiitake mushrooms and bok choy. The large wine cellar is filled with many reasonably priced choices from around the world. American menu. Dinner. Bar. Children's menu. Casual attire. Outdoor seating. $$$

★★LA MONTANA

2500 Village Drive, Steamboat Springs, 970-879-5800; www.la-montana.com

Southwestern, Mexican menu. Dinner. Closed mid-April-early June. Bar. Children's menu. Casual attire. Outdoor seating. $$

★★ORE HOUSE AT THE PINE GROVE

1465 Pine Grove Road, Steamboat Springs, 970-879-1190, 800-280-8310; www.orehouseatthepinegrove.com

American menu. Dinner. Closed mid-April-mid-May. Bar. Children's menu. Casual attire. Outdoor seating. $$$

★TUGBOAT GRILL & PUB

1860 Mt Werner Road, Steamboat Springs, 970-879-7070

American menu. Lunch, dinner. Closed mid-April-early June. Bar. Children's menu. Casual attire. Outdoor seating. $

★WINONA'S DELI-BAKERY

617 Lincoln Ave., Steamboat Springs, 970-879-2483

American menu. Breakfast, lunch. Children's menu. Casual attire. Outdoor seating. $

STERLING

Sterling is known as the "City of Living Trees" because of the unique carved trees found throughout town.

Information: Logan County Chamber of Commerce, 109 N. Front St., 970-522-5070, 800-522-5070; www.sterlingcolo.com

WHAT TO SEE AND DO

OVERLAND TRAIL MUSEUM

210533 CR 26.5, Sterling, 970-522-3895

This village of seven buildings includes collections of American Indian artifacts, cattle brands, farm machinery, archaeological and paleontological exhibits, a one-room schoolhouse, a fire engine and more. Park and picnic area. April-October, daily; rest of year, Tuesday-Saturday.

HOTELS

★BEST WESTERN SUNDOWNER
125 Overland Trail St., Sterling, 970-522-6265; www.bestwestern.com
58 rooms. High-speed Internet access. Complimentary continental breakfast. Pets accepted. Spa. Fitness center. **$**

★★RAMADA
22140 E. Highway 6, Sterling, 970-522-2625, 800-272-6232; www.ramada.com
100 rooms. Wireless Internet access. Restaurant, bar. Pool. Whirlpool. Fitness center. Pets accepted. **$**

SPECIALTY LODGING

PIONEER TRAILS LODGE
47490 Weld County Road 155, Stoneham, 970-735-2426;
www.bbonline.com/co/elkecho
This large log bed and breakfast offers guest rooms with a quiet atmosphere. Watch more than 500 head of elk and a small buffalo herd from the deck. Four rooms. Complimentary full breakfast. **$**

RESTAURANT

★T. J. BUMMER'S
203 Broadway St., Sterling, 970-522-8397
American menu. Breakfast, lunch, dinner. Closed holidays. Children's menu. **$$**

TELLURIDE

Gray granite and red sandstone mountains surround this mining town, named for the tellurium ore containing precious metals found in the area. Telluride, proud of its bonanza past, has not changed its façade. Because of its remoteness and small size, Telluride is a favorite getaway spot for celebrities. Summer activities include fly-fishing, mountain biking, river rafting, hiking, Jeep trips, horseback riding and camping, as well as many annual events and festivals from May to October.
Information: Telluride Visitor Services, 666 W. Colorado Ave.,
970-728-4431, 888-605-2578; www.telluride.com

WHAT TO SEE AND DO

BEAR CREEK TRAIL
South end of Pine Street, Telluride
This two-mile canyon walk features a view of a tiered waterfall. May-October.

BRIDAL VEIL FALLS
Telluride, 2½ miles east on Highway 145
See the highest waterfall in Colorado.

TELLURIDE GONDOLA
Aspen and San Juan, Telluride
Passengers are transported from downtown Telluride to Mount Village. Early June-early October and late November-mid-April, daily.

TELLURIDE HISTORICAL MUSEUM

201 W. Gregory Ave., Telluride, 970-728-3344; www.telluridemuseum.org
Built in 1893 as the community hospital, this historic building houses artifacts, historic photos and exhibits that show what Telluride was like in its Wild West days. Tuesday-Saturday 11 a.m.-5 p.m., Sunday 1-5 p.m.

TELLURIDE SKI RESORT

565 Mountain Village Blvd., Telluride, 800-778-8581; www.tellurideskiresort.com
Three-stage gondola; seven quad, two triple, two double chairlifts; two surface lift; patrol, school, rentals; restaurants, nursery. 92 runs; longest run 4½ miles; vertical drop 3,530 feet. Thanksgiving-early April, daily. Cross-country skiing, heli-skiing, ice skating, snowmobiling, sleigh rides. Shuttle bus service and two in-town chairlifts.

SPECIAL EVENTS
BALLOON FESTIVAL

Colorado Avenue, Telluride, 970-728-4769; www.tellurideballoonfestival.com
See the balloons launch in the morning, or come in the evening to see them lined up on Colorado Avenue. Early June.

JAZZ CELEBRATION

Town Park, Telluride, 970-728-7009; www.telluridejazz.com
After the daytime concerts with the San Juan Mountains as a backdrop, several of the musicians can be found in the Main Street saloons mingling with visitors and fans. Early August.

MOUNTAIN FILM FESTIVAL

109 E. Colorado Ave., Telluride, 970-728-4123; www.mountainfilm.org
In addition to showing films, the Mountain Film Festival is a unique conglomeration of filmmakers, authors, political activists and other thinkers who host seminars and symposiums throughout the weekend. These highbrow hosts discuss the films with the public and discuss how they relate to the festival's theme. Late May.

TELLURIDE BLUEGRASS FESTIVAL

Telluride; www.bluegrass.com/telluride
Thousands of music lovers come to Telluride for what many agree is the nation's premier bluegrass festival. The festival draws top bluegrass and folk performers. But the best part might be the spontaneous jams that break out in the wee hours at local drinking spots. The festival includes amateur competitions and workshops and is a favorite destination for campers seeking high-spirited fun in a natural setting. Mid-June.

HOTELS
★★★HOTEL COLUMBIA

300 W. San Juan Ave., Telluride, 970-728-0660, 800-201-9505;
www.columbiatelluride.com
Situated on the San Miguel River at the base of the Telluride Ski Resort, this hotel feels more like a small inn, with only 21 Victorian-style rooms, each with a gas fireplace. (Columbia was Telluride's original name.) Spring for the penthouse—it has a steam shower and two-person jetted tub surrounded by windows overlooking

COLORADO

★
★
★
★
★

the mountains and river. 21 rooms. Restaurant, bar. Fitness room. Pets accepted. Spa. High-speed Internet access. **$$**

★★★THE PEAKS RESORT & GOLDEN DOOR SPA

136 Country Club Drive, Telluride, 866-282-4557, 800-789-2220;
www.thepeaksresort.com

This is the perfect home for outdoor enthusiasts who like to rough it a bit outdoors—and live it up indoors. Situated on top of the mountain, Peaks Resort is a skier's heaven with ski-in/ski-out access and a ski valet who will warm and tune your equipment. The guest rooms and suites are cocoons of luxury, with huge picture windows with plantation shutters, fluffy duvets and glass-enclosed showers with separate tubs. Suites boast leather furniture and stone fireplaces. The centerpiece of this first-class resort is the Golden Door Spa, an outpost of the legendary California destination spa featuring a variety of restorative treatments. There's even a doggie spa for your pooch. If you're here in summer, challenge yourself on one of the country's highest golf courses. 174 rooms. High-speed Internet access. Closed mid-April-mid-May, mid-October-mid-November. Restaurant, bar. Children's activity center. Spa. Ski-in/ski-out. Airport transportation available. Fitness cener. Pets accepted. **$$$**

★★★NEW SHERIDAN HOTEL

231 W. Colorado Ave., Telluride, 970-728-4351, 800-200-1891; www.newsheridan.com

Built in 1891, this hotel is located in the heart of Telluride. Many of the elegant guest rooms feature mountain views and separate sitting rooms. Warm up with a hearty gourmet breakfast and then relax in the afternoon with a complimentary glass of Pine Ridge wine at the New Sheridan Bar. 28 rooms. Closed mid-April-mid-May. Complimentary continental breakfast. Restaurant. Whirlpool. **$$**

SPECIALTY LODGING

THE SAN SOPHIA INN AND CONDOMINIUMS

330 W. Pacific Ave., Telluride, 970-728-3001, 800-537-4781; www.sansophia.com

The interior of this romantic inn is Victorian-meets-Southwestern, with stained and etched glass and period furnishings. You can choose to stay in a standard guest room or in one of the private residences. After a day on the slopes—there's ski-in/ski-out access—the Gazebo-covered hot tub with views of Bear Creek beckons. You won't go hungry here, from the treats (like Rocky Mountain toffee) handed out at check-in to the full breakfast to the cocktail hour, where you can sample wines from around the world and nibble on appetizers such as brie and red grape quesadillas. 16 rooms. Closed April, November. Children over 9 years only. Complimentary full breakfast. Whirlpool. **$**

RESTAURANTS

★★★ALLRED'S

2 Coonskin Ridge, Telluride, 970-728-7474; www.allredsrestaurant.com

At more than 10,000 feet above sea level, Allred's offers mountain views to complement its delicious culinary creations. The menu is made up of regional Colorado cuisine with international accents such as free-range chicken breast with creamy polenta, Manchego, spinach and roasted peppers and elk short loin with summer squash and braised figs. If you're looking for a special treat, reserve the Chef's Table (for four to six guests), where you'll be treated to a five-course, chef-prepared menu with the option to pair wines with each course. American menu. Dinner. Closed mid-April-mid-June, late September-mid-December. Bar. Children's menu. Casual attire. Reservations recommended. $$$

★★★COSMOPOLITAN
300 W. San Juan, Telluride, 970-728-1292; www.cosmotelluride.com
Housed in the luxurious Hotel Columbia, Cosmopolitan is an elegant restaurant where fresh ingredients and flavors from around the world are blended together to create an innovative contemporary American menu. Dishes, which change on a weekly basis, have included creations such as crispy Asian short rib roll with kimchee, black bean sauce and mango sauce and a grilled vegetable open calzone with goat cheese, parmesan and basil. French, American menu. Dinner. Closed mid-April-mid-May and the last week in October. Bar. Children's menu. Casual attire. Reservations recommended. $$

★★FLORADORA
103 W. Colorado Ave., Telluride, 970-728-8884
Southwestern, American menu. Lunch, dinner. Bar. Children's menu. $$

VAIL
Built to resemble a Bavarian village, Vail is the world's largest single-mountain ski resort. Known for having vast and varied terrain for every skill level of skier or snowboarder, Vail often tops ski resort lists and gets rave reviews for its legendary powder. Summer has also emerged as a prime recreation season on Vail Mountain, with mountain biking being the sport of choice. Today, ski conglomerate Vail Resorts owns numerous ski resorts in Colorado, including Beaver Creek, Breckenridge and Arapahoe Basin, and many passes work at all the properties.
Information: Vail Valley Tourism & Convention Bureau, 100 E. Meadow Drive, 970-476-1000, 800-525-3875; www.vail.com

WHAT TO SEE AND DO
COLORADO SKI MUSEUM & SKI HALL OF FAME
In Vail Village Transportation Center, 231 S. Frontage Road E., Vail, 970-476-1876; www.skimuseum.net
Learn everything you ever wanted to know about skiing. The museum traces the history of skiing in Colorado back more than 120 years. Memorial Day-late September and late November-mid April, Tuesday-Sunday.

GERALD R. FORD AMPHITHEATER VILAR PAVILION/BETTY FORD ALPINE GARDENS
Ford Park and the Betty Ford Alpine Gardens, Vail, 970-845-8497, 888-920-2797; www.vvf.org
Enjoy top-notch entertainment under Vail's crystal-clear starlit skies at this open-air theater surrounded by the Betty Ford Alpine Gardens—a public botanical garden with more than 500 varieties of wildflowers and alpine plants. Performances throughout the summer normally include classical music, rock and roll, jazz, ballet, contemporary dance and children's theater. June-August.

VAIL SKI RESORT

137 Benchmark Road, Avon, 970-476-9090, 800-503-8748; www.vail.com

Gondola; 14 high-speed quad, seven fixed-grip quad, three triple, five double chair-lifts; ten surface lifts; patrol, school, rentals, snowmaking; cafeterias, restaurants, bars, nursery. Longest run four miles; vertical drop 3,450 feet. Late November-mid-April, daily. Cross-country trails, rentals November-April; ice skating, snowmobiling, sleigh rides. Gondola and Vista Bahn June-August, daily; May and -September, weekends.

SPECIAL EVENT
TASTE OF VAIL

Vail, 970-926-5665; www.tasteofvail.com

This unique food festival combines tastings, competitions and cooking seminars. Sample premium desserts, or watch the annual bartender mix-off. Listen to winemakers talk about their craft—and then taste the fruits of their labor. Past demonstrations have explained how to pair wine with Japanese cuisine. Early April.

HOTELS
★★HOTEL GASTHOF GRAMSHAMMER

231 E. Gore Creek Drive, Vail, 970-476-5626, 800-610-7374; www.pepis.com

34 rooms. Closed mid April-June. Complimentary continental breakfast. High-speed Internet access. Restaurant, bar. Fitness center. Spa. $

★★LION SQUARE LODGE

660 W. Lionshead Place, Vail, 970-476-2281, 800-525-1943; www.lionsquare.com

108 rooms. High-speed Internet access. Restaurant. Children's activity center. Pool. $$

★★★THE LODGE AT VAIL

174 E. Gore Creek Drive, Vail, 970-476-5011, 877-528-7625; www.rockresorts.com

This lodge perfectly marries the charm of an alpine inn with the amenities of a world-class resort. The individually decorated rooms are the ideal blend between Western style and European elegance. Located at the base of Vail Mountain, the lift—as well as boutiques and shops of Vail Village—are just steps away. Mickey's Piano Bar is a great spot for a drink. 145 rooms. Wireless Internet access. Restaurant, bar. Children. Whirlpool. Ski-in/ski-out. Pool. $$$

★★★MARRIOTT VAIL MOUNTAIN RESORT

715 W. Lionshead Circle, Vail, 970-476-4444, 800-648-0720; www.marriott.com

This newly renovated hotel is in a great location at the base of Vail Mountain near the lift and many boutiques and restaurants. The rustic guest rooms contain wood furnishings and marble and granite baths. Privately owned condos are also available. The new Golden Leaf Spa offers body wraps and massages. The full-service retail shop has rental equipment. This hotel is nonsmoking. 344 rooms. Restaurant, bar. Spa. Fitness center. $$

★SAVORY INN

2405 Elliott Road, Vail, 970-476-1304, 866-754-8245; www.savoryinn.com

12 rooms. Closed mid-April-mid-May. Complimentary full breakfast. Whirlpool. $$

★★SITZMARK LODGE

183 Gore Creek Drive, Vail, 970-476-5001, 888-476-5001; www.sitzmarklodge.com

35 rooms. Complimentary continental breakfast. Wireless Internet access. Restaurant, bar. Ski-in/ski-out. Swim. **$**

★★★SONNENALP RESORT OF VAIL

20 Vail Road, Vail, 970-476-5656, 800-654-8312; www.sonnenalp.com

This charming family-owned and -operated resort recalls the Bavarian countryside. Located in Vail Village within walking distance of the ski lift, it's a natural choice for winter sports lovers while the 18-hole championship golf course and European style makes it a treasure any time of the year. A variety of dishes—from contemporary American to ski favorites such as fondue at the Swiss Chalet—promise to keep your stomach happy. The King's Club fireside lounge is perfect for live entertainment and après ski, serving everything from burgers to caviar. 127 rooms, all suites. High-speed Internet access. Restaurant, bar. Spa. **$$$**

★★★VAIL CASCADE RESORT & SPA

1300 Westhaven Drive, Vail, 970-476-7111, 800-282-4183; www.vailcascade.com

Located on Gore Creek at the base of Vail Mountain, this European-style alpine village contains a combination of standard guest rooms, condominiums and private residences. This huge property boasts the largest athletic facility in the Vail Valley, a shopping arcade, two movie theaters, a beauty shop, two outdoor pools and five whirlpools. Camp Cascade keeps kids entertained throughout the day. 292 rooms. Restaurant, bar. Children's activity center. Spa. Ski-in/ski-out. Fitness center. High-speed Internet access. **$$**

★★VAIL MOUNTAIN LODGE & SPA

352 E. Meadow Drive, Vail, 970-476-0700, 866-476-0700; www.vailmountainlodge.com

28 rooms. Complimentary full breakfast. High-speed Internet access. Restaurant, bar. Spa. Whirlpool. **$$**

★★VAIL'S MOUNTAIN HAUS

292 E. Meadow Drive, Vail, 970-476-2434, 800-237-0922; www.mountainhaus.com

75 rooms. Complimentary continental breakfast. High-speed Internet access. Restaurant, bar. Spa. Pool. Fitness center. **$$$**

SPECIALTY LODGING
GALATYN LODGE

365 Vail Valley Drive, Vail, 970-479-2418, 800-943-7322; www.vail.net/galatyn

15 rooms. High-speed Internet access. **$$**

RESTAURANTS
★BLU'S

193 E. Gore Creek Drive, Vail, 970-476-3113; www.blusrestaurant.com

American menu. Breakfast, lunch, dinner. Bar. Children's menu. Casual attire. Outdoor seating. **$$**

COLORADO

★
★
★
★

★★GOLDEN EAGLE INN

118 Beaver Creek Place, Vail, 970-949-1940; www.thegoldeneagleinn.com

American menu. Lunch, dinner. Bar. Children's menu. Casual attire. Outdoor seating. Reservations recommended. **$$**

★★LANCELOT RESTAURANT

201 E. Gore Creek Drive, Vail, 970-476-5828; www.lancelotinn.com

Seafood, steak menu. Lunch, dinner. Closed April-Memorial Day weekend. Bar. Casual attire. Reservations recommended. Valet parking. Outdoor seating. **$$$**

★★★LEFT BANK

183 Gore Creek Drive, Vail, 970-476-3696; www.leftbankvail.com

As the name suggests, this restaurant serves classic French cuisine in a friendly, casual atmosphere in the heart of the Village. The restaurant serves all the classics from escargot to steak au poivre. Start off with a Kir Royale. French, Mediterranean menu. Dinner. Closed Wednesday; two weeks in March-April and two weeks in fall. Bar. Casual attire. Reservations recommended. **$$$**

★★MONTAUK SEAFOOD GRILL

549 W. Lionshead Circle, Vail, 970-476-2601; www.montaukseafoodgrill.com

Seafood menu. Dinner. Casual attire. Reservations recommended. **$$$**

★★★RESTAURANT KELLY LIKEN

12 Vail Road, Vail, 970-479-0175; www.kellyliken.com

The warm burgundy and champagne colors, custom-made furniture, slate and glass tile floors and hand-blown glass chandelier create an elegant and romantic atmosphere. And Kelly Liken is *the* chef in Vail. Liken uses a majority of locally produced and cultivated products for the seasonal American menu, including elk carpaccio, potato-crusted trout and Colorado lamb. American menu. Dinner. Closed mid-April-mid-May. Bar. Children's menu. Business casual attire. Reservations recommended. Valet parking. **$$$**

★★★SWEET BASIL

193 E. Gore Creek Drive, Vail, 970-476-0125; www.sweetbasil-vail.com

This contemporary American restaurant has been a local favorite since it opened in 1977. Understated modern décor with cherry wood accents and colorful artwork provides a comfortable setting in which to enjoy the inventive menu. The culinary adventure begins with starters like Dungeness crab and avocado salad and inside-out French onion soup with Gruyère, white cheddar and caramelized onions. Entrées might include pumpkin-crusted New England sea scallops, grilled Niman Ranch pork chops with sweet potato pie and dry-aged, Kansas City strip steak with Colorado russet potato puree. An award-winning wine list complements all menu selections, and a number of desserts can provide the perfect ending. American menu. Lunch, dinner, brunch. Bar. Business casual attire. Reservations recommended. Outdoor seating. **$$$$**

★★★THE WILDFLOWER

174 Gore Creek Drive, Vail, 877-528-7625; www.lodgeatvail.rockresorts.com

If you're searching for a memorable dining experience, head to the Wildflower, a beautiful restaurant located inside the Lodge at Vail. Filled with baskets of wildflowers and massive floral arrangements, the room boasts wonderful views and tables lined with country-style floral linens. The restaurant features a delicious and innovative selection of seafood, game and poultry (such as Nebraska ostrich), accented with global flavors like lemongrass, curry and chilies, and local fruits and vegetables, including herbs grown in the Wildflower's garden. An extensive and reasonably priced wine list concentrates on Italy and matches the distinctive menu. American menu. Lunch, dinner. Closed Monday. Bar. Business casual attire. Reservations recommended. Outdoor seating. $$$$

WINTER PARK

Winter Park is located in the Arapaho National Forest on the western slope of Berthoud Pass, one of the nation's highest and oldest ski areas. It is an easy 90-minute drive from Denver, or a two-hour ride on the popular weekend Ski Train. In addition to its many winter activities, Winter Park is gaining a reputation as a year-round recreational area with dozens of activities available during the spring, summer and fall. Winter Park, Granby and Hot Sulphur Springs are part of the Sulphur Ranger District of the Arapho and Roosevelt National forests.

Information: Winter Park/Fraser Valley Chamber of Commerce, 800-903-7275; www.winterpark-info.com

WHAT TO SEE AND DO

DEVIL'S THUMB RANCH

3530 County Road 83, Tabernash, 800-933-4339; www.devilsthumbranch.com
Set on 3,700 acres at the foot of the Continental Divide, Devil's Thumb Ranch is a year-round resort with an abundance of activities in every season. In summer, visitors enjoy fly-fishing, horseback riding, river rafting, hiking, bird/nature walks and inflatable kayaking. Winter brings opportunities for cross-country skiing, sleigh rides, winter horseback riding, ice skating and snowshoeing.

DOG SLED RIDES

505 Zerex, Fraser, 970-726-8326; www.dogsledrides.com/winterpark
Thirty-minute, one-hour and two-hour rides on a sled pulled by eight Siberian and Alaskan huskies. Guides give talks on wildlife, trees and mountains.

FRASER RIVER TRAIL

Winter Park, one mile southeast off Highway 40, 970-726-4118; www.allwinterpark.com
This wide, flat, five-mile trail runs between the Winter Park Resort and the towns of Winter Park and Fraser, and is a haven for walkers, bikers and in-line skaters who want to enjoy the scenery without worrying about crosswalks or traffic lights. The route between Winter Park and Fraser has picnic tables.

MONARCH STABLES AND WAGON RIDES

1400 County Road 5, Fraser, 970-726-5376; www.winterpark-info.com
Horse-drawn wagon rides, playground, petting zoo, pony rides, volleyball and horseshoes.

POLE CREEK GOLF CLUB

6827 County Road 51, Tabernash, 970-887-9195, 800-511-5076;
www.polecreekgolf.com

The *Rocky Mountain News* ranked this 27-hole course the best mountain golf course. It is also the only nationally ranked course open to the public.

WINTER PARK RESORT

239 Winter Park Drive, Winter Park, 970-726-5514, 800-979-0332;
www.skiwinterpark.com

In winter, skiers make full use of the resort's eight high-speed quad, five triple and seven double chairlifts and 143 runs—longest is five miles, vertical drop 2,610 feet. Patrol, school, equipment rentals and snowmaking; cafeterias, restaurants and bars. NASTAR and coin-operated racecourses. Mid-November-mid-April, daily. In summer, the Zephyr Express chairlift takes mountain bikers and their bikes to the top of a summit where they can access the resort's 50-mile network of interconnected trails. Colorado's longest Alpine Slide takes riders on heavy-duty plastic sleds equipped with hand-held brakes 3,030 feet down the side of a mountain. An outdoor climbing wall, bungee jumping, disc golf (18 holes that wrap around the top of Winter Park Mountain) and miniature golf are also available.

HOTEL
★★GASTHAUS EICHLER HOTEL

78786 Highway 40, Winter Park, 970-726-5133, 800-543-3899;
www.gasthauseichler.com

15 rooms. Restaurant, bar. Whirlpool. **$$**

RESTAURANTS
★★DENO'S MOUNTAIN BISTRO

78911 Highway 40, Winter Park, 970-726-5332; www.denosmountainbistro.com
American menu. Lunch, dinner. Bar. Children's menu. Casual attire. Outdoor seating. **$**

★★DEZELEY'S

78786 Highway 40, Winter Park, 970-726-5133; www.gasthauseichler.com
German, American menu. Breakfast, lunch, dinner. Bar. Children's menu. Casual attire. Outdoor seating. **$$**

★★★DINING ROOM AT SUNSPOT

239 Winter Park Drive, Winter Park, 970-726-1446
The upscale dining room at the Winter Park Ski Resort can be reached only by chairlift—and it's worth the trip. The restaurant has the feel of a mountain lodge, built with logs from Grand County. The windows are eight feet high, so you have magnificent views of the Continental Divide. It is a glorious setting to enjoy the satisfying American menu. American menu. Lunch, dinner. Closed May-October. Bar. Children's menu. Reservations recommended. **$$$**

★★RANDI'S IRISH SALOON

78521 Highway 40, Winter Park, 970-726-1172
Irish menu. Breakfast, lunch, dinner. Bar. Children's menu. Outdoor seating. **$**

NEVADA

THERE'S MORE TO NEVADA THAN LAS VEGAS AND GAMBLING. NEVADA ALSO HAS A RICH HISTORY, magnificent scenery and some of the wildest desert country on the continent. You'll find large mountain peaks and beautiful lakes, including Lake Tahoe. Ghost towns hint at earlier days filled with fabulous gold and silver streaks that made men millionaires overnight.

Nevada became part of U.S. territory after the Mexican-American War in 1846. It became a state in 1864 (for a while, it was part of Utah). Gold was found along the Carson River in Dayton Valley in May of 1850. A decade later, the fabulous Comstock Lode (silver and gold ore) was discovered. The gold rush was on, and Virginia City mushroomed into a town of 20,000.

Unregulated gambling (called "gaming" here) was common in these early mining towns but was outlawed in 1909. It was legalized in 1931, when construction on the Hoover Dam began and there was a population boom. This was also the same year residency requirements for obtaining a divorce were relaxed. The government owns much of the land in Nevada, and the area about one hour northwest of Las Vegas has been the site of much nuclear testing.

Las Vegas keeps reinventing itself. These days, it's perhaps known for being home to some of the best dining in the country as much as it is for gambling. You'll also find some of the best shopping and spas.

Information: www.travelnevada.com

★
★
★
★
★

BOULDER CITY

A mere 20 miles from Las Vegas, Boulder City is also a world away from the bright lights of Sin City. This quiet town is a haven for visitors seeking thrills outside the casinos. Its proximity to Lake Mead National Recreation Area makes it a perfect spot to rest after a day of fishing, swimming, hiking and sightseeing in one of the Southwest's most beautiful playgrounds.

Information: www.bcnv.org

WHAT TO SEE AND DO
HOOVER DAM
Highway 93, Boulder City, 702-494-2517, 866-730-9097; www.usbr.gov/lc/hooverdam/
It took 6.6 million tons of concrete—enough to pave a highway between New York and San Francisco—to stop the mighty Colorado River at Hoover Dam, which was completed in 1935 and is now a National Historic Landmark. Check out the visitor center where you can watch a short film that tells the story of the dam's construction in Black Canyon. An elevator plunges 500 feet down the canyon wall, depositing passengers in a tunnel that leads to the power plant and its eight enormous generators. The observation deck takes in both sides of the dam, including Lake Mead and the Colorado River. Parking. Daily 9 a.m.-6 p.m.

SCENIC NEVADA

This tour from Reno, which can be accomplished over one or two days, combines the scenic beauty and recreational opportunities of Lake Tahoe with historic sites from Nevada's mining days. From Reno, go south on Highway 395 to Highway 431 (the Mount Rose Scenic Byway), which heads west and southwest as it climbs to an 8,911-foot pass and then drops down to Lake Tahoe, providing splendid panoramic views of the lake. Continue on Highway 431 to Highway 28 and Incline Village, a good base from which to enjoy the beach, swimming, fishing and the spectacular views at Lake Tahoe Nevada State Park. The beach at the park's Sand Harbor section is delightful—and also very popular. If you're looking for a little more seclusion, opt for Memorial Point and Hidden Beach. Those visiting from late July through August might want to experience the Lake Tahoe Shakespeare Festival, with shows at an outdoor theater at Sand Harbor. Also in Incline Village is the Ponderosa Ranch, a Western theme park where the popular television series *Bonanza* was filmed from 1959 to 1973.

From Incline Village, continue south on Highway 28 along Lake Tahoe's eastern shore, and then take Highway 50 east to Carson City. Part of the Lake Tahoe Scenic Byway, this route offers panoramic views of the lake and nearby mountains. Carson City, Nevada's capital, is roughly the halfway point of this tour and is a good spot to spend the night. Founded in 1858, Carson City features numerous historic sites, including the handsome state capitol, built in 1871 with a dome of silver. Attractions also include the 1864 Bowers Mansion, built of granite and furnished with many original pieces; the Warren Engine Company No. 1 Fire Museum, where you'll see a variety of historic firefighting equipment; and the Nevada State Railroad Museum, with three steam locomotives and numerous freight and passenger cars.

Now head northeast on Highway 50 to Highway 341, which you follow north to picturesque Virginia City, a historic mining town that had its heyday in the 1870s. Beautifully restored, Virginia City today offers a glimpse into its opulent and sometimes wicked past with historic buildings, a mine and a working steam train. To see the epitome of 19th-century extravagance, stop at the Castle, an 1868 Victorian mansion known for its marble fireplaces, crystal chandeliers and silver doorknobs. Other attractions include Piper's Opera House, which hosted the major stars of the late 1800s, and the Mackay Mansion, built in 1860 as the headquarters of mining magnate John Mackay. To return to Reno, take Highway 341 north to Highway 395 north. Approximately 100 miles.

LAKE MEAD CRUISES

Lake Mead Marina, 480 Lakeshore Road, Boulder City, 702-293-6180; www.lakemeadcruises.com

Paddle wheelers take you on a 90-minute sightseeing cruise to the Hoover Dam. Breakfast and dinner cruises available. Casual dress recommended. Daily.

LAKE MEAD NATIONAL RECREATION AREA

601 Nevada Highway, Boulder City, 702-293-8906; www.nps.gov/lame

Lake Mead was formed when Hoover Dam was completed in 1935. Located 30 miles from the Strip, visitors come here for boating and fishing. You can catch trout, bass and bluegill. Several marinas around the lake and on neighboring Lake Mojave offer rentals, everything from kayaks to houseboats that sleep up to 14 people (because of the great demand for the latter, call six months prior to your visit). Hikers can take in the desert basins, steep canyons, rainbow-hued rocks and wildlife including bighorn sheep in the recreation area surrounding the lake. Open 24 hours; visitors center 8:30 a.m.-4:30 p.m.

CARSON CITY

The state capital is situated near the edge of the forested eastern slope of the Sierra Nevada in Eagle Valley. A Ranger District office of the Humboldt-Toiyabe National Forest is located here.

Information: Carson City Convention and Visitors Bureau, 1900 S. Carson St., 775-687-7410, 800-638-2321; www.carson-city.org

WHAT TO SEE AND DO

BOWERS MANSION

4005 Highway, 775-849-0201

The Bowers, Nevada's first millionaires, built this $200,000 granite house with the profits from a gold and silver mine. Half-hour guided tours of 16 rooms with many original furnishings. Memorial Day-Labor Day, daily 11 a.m.-4:30 p.m.

CHILDREN'S MUSEUM OF NORTHERN NEVADA

813 N. Carson St., Carson City, 775-884-2226; www.cmnn.org

This excellent kids' museum provides 8,000 square feet of education and playground-style fun. A grocery store, arts and crafts station, and a walk-in kaleidoscope are among the permanent exhibits. Daily 10 a.m.-4:30 p.m.

NEVADA STATE MUSEUM

600 N. Carson St., Carson City, 775-687-4810; www.nevadaculture.org

The former site of the U.S. Mint contains varied exhibits showcasing Nevada's natural history and anthropology, including life-size displays of a Nevada ghost town and an American Indian camp. A 300-foot mine tunnel with displays runs beneath the building. Daily 8:30 a.m.-4:30 p.m.

NEVADA STATE RAILROAD MUSEUM

2180 S. Carson St., Carson City, 775-687-6953; www.nsrm-friends.org

This museum houses more than 600 pieces of railroad equipment. It also exhibits 50 freight and passenger cars, as well as five steam locomotives that once belonged to the Virginia and Truckee railroad. Also houses pictorial history gallery and artifacts of the famed Bonanza Road. Daily 8:30 a.m.-4:30 p.m.

STATE CAPITOL

101 N. Carson St., Carson City, 775-684-5700; www.nv.gov

Large Classical Revival structure with Doric columns and a silver dome. Houses portraits of past Nevada governors. Self-guided tours. Daily 8 a.m.-5 p.m.

★
★
★
★
★

MINING AND MONEY IN CARSON CITY

A walking tour of Carson City offers a good viewpoint for investigating the heady days of the Old West's 19th-century mining boom. Start at the Nevada State Museum (600 N. Carson St.), which served as a U.S. Mint from 1870 to 1895 and pressed more than $50 million in coinage during that span. Opened as a museum a half-century after the mint closed, the building houses a collection of archaeological finds, dioramas, Indian baskets and an antique and operational coin press.

Next, head two blocks north on Carson Street to the Children's Museum of Northern Nevada (813 N. Carson St.), the area's best attraction for kids. You'll pass through Carson City's primary casino district in the vicinity of Spear and Telegraph streets. The casinos house the majority of the restaurants in downtown Carson City, so this is a good opportunity to grab a bite to eat. Continuing south on Carson Street for three blocks, the quarried sandstone Nevada State Capitol (just east of the intersection of Carson and Second streets) is the cornerstone of a beautifully landscaped plaza that is also home to the state's supreme court, legislative building and library and archives building.

Just southeast of the capitol plaza on Stewart Street is the Warren Engine Company No. 1 Museum (777 S. Stewart St.), with exhibits, photographs and memorabilia detailing the oldest continuously operating firefighting company in the West. From here, it is just a block north on Stewart Street to Fifth Street; take Fifth west to Nevada Street and walk three blocks north to King Street, on which you'll want to go west once again. At 449 West King Street is the Brewery Arts Center, a showcase for the work of local artists in the former Carson Brewing Company building, which was built in 1864 and is currently on the National Historic Register. The Arts Center is in the heart of Carson City's most historic neighborhood.

NEVADA

★
★ ★
★ ★
★

STATE LIBRARY BUILDING

100 N. Stewart, Carson City, 775-684-3360; www.nevadaculture.org

Files of Nevada newspapers and books about the state. Monday-Friday 8 a.m.-5 p.m.

WARREN ENGINE COMPANY NO. 1 FIRE MUSEUM

777 S. Stewart St., Carson City, 775-887-2210; www.visitcarsoncity.com

See the old photographs, antique fire-fighting equipment, the state's first fire truck (restored), an 1847 four-wheel cart and more. Children under 18 must be accompanied by an adult.

SPECIAL EVENT
NEVADA DAY CELEBRATION

Carson Street and Highway 50 East, Carson City, 775-882-2600, 866-683-2948; www.nevadaday.com

Commemorates Nevada's admission to the Union. Grand Ball, parades, exhibits. Four days in late October.

HOTEL
★HARDMAN HOUSE PARK INN
917 N. Carson St., Carson City, 775-882-7744, 800-626-0793
62 rooms. **$**

RESTAURANT
★★ADELE'S
1112 N. Carson St., Carson City, 775-882-3353; www.adelesrestaurantandlounge.com
American menu. Lunch, dinner, late-night. Closed Sunday. Bar. Business casual attire. Valet parking. Outdoor seating. **$$**

CRYSTAL BAY
On the California-Nevada state line, Crystal Bay sits on the north rim of Lake Tahoe, overlooking its namesake bay. (Swim from one state to another at Cal-Neva Resort's pool.)

HOTELS
★★CAL NEVA
2 Stateline Road, Crystal Bay, 800-233-5551, 800-225-6382; www.calnevaresort.com
220 rooms. Restaurant, bar. Casino. Tennis. Pool. Spa. Fitness center. **$**

★★TAHOE BILTMORE LODGE AND CASINO
5 Highway 28, Crystal Bay, 775-831-0660, 800-245-8667; www.tahoebiltmore.com
92 rooms. Complimentary full breakfast, Two restaurants, bar. Casino. Pets accepted. Pool. Spa.

ELKO
Located on the Humboldt River, Elko is the center of a large ranching area. Originally a stopping point for wagon trains headed for the West Coast, its main sources of revenue today include tourism, gold mining and gaming.
Information: Elko Chamber of Commerce, 1405 Idaho St.,
775-738-7135, 800-428-7143; www.elkonevada.com

WHAT TO SEE AND DO
NORTHEASTERN NEVADA MUSEUM
1515 Idaho St., Elko, 775-738-3418; www.museum-elko.us
Three galleries feature art, historical, American Indian and nature exhibits of the area. See pioneer vehicles and an original 1860 Pony Express cabin. Tuesday-Sunday 9 a.m.-5 p.m.

SPECIAL EVENTS
COUNTRY FAIR AND LIVESTOCK SHOW
13th and Cedar streets, Elko, 775-738-7135
Horse racing. Four days on Labor Day weekend.

COWBOY POETRY GATHERING
501 Railroad St., Elko, 775-738-7135
Working cowboys and cowgirls participate in storytelling and verse. Demonstrations; music. Last full week in January.

NATIONAL BASQUE FESTIVAL

Basque House at Golf Course Road and Cedar Street, Elko, 775-738-7135

Contests in weightlifting, sheep hooking and other skills of mountaineers are accompanied with dancing and a feast. Weekend early in July.

HOTELS

★★HIGH DESERT INN

3015 E. Idaho St., Elko, 775-738-8425, 888-394-8303

170 rooms. Restaurant, bar. Airport transportation available. Pets accepted. Pool. **$**

★★RED LION

2065 E. Idaho St., Elko, 775-738-2111, 800-733-5466; www.redlion.com

223 rooms. High-speed Internet access. Restaurant, bar. Airport transportation available. Casino. Pool. Pets accepted. Business center. Fitness center. **$**

ELY

Although founded in 1868 as a silver mining camp, Ely's growth began in 1906 with the arrival of the Nevada Northern Railroad, which facilitated the development of large-scale copper mining in 1907. Gold and silver are still mined in Ely. The seat of White Pine County, it is the shopping and recreational center of a vast ranching and mining area. The city is surrounded by mountains and offers winter skiing, deer hunting and trout fishing. Its high elevation provides a cool, sunny climate.

Information: White Pine Chamber of Commerce, 636 Aultman St., 775-289-8877; www.whitepinechamber.com

WHAT TO SEE AND DO

NEVADA NORTHERN RAILWAY MUSEUM

1100 Ave., A, Ely, 866-407-8326; www.nevadanorthernrailway.net

Located in the historic Nevada Northern Railway Depot.

WARD CHARCOAL OVENS STATE HISTORIC PARK

Highway 6/50/93 and Cave Valley Road, Ely, 775-728-4460; www.parks.nv.gov/ww.htm

Includes six stone beehive charcoal ovens used during the 1870 mining boom.

WHITE PINE PUBLIC MUSEUM

2000 Aultman St., Ely, 775-289-4710; www.wpmuseum.org

See a 1905 stagecoach, as well as early-day relics and mementos; mineral display. Daily.

SPECIAL EVENT

PONY EXPRESS DAYS

Highway 50 and Pony Express Trail, Ely, 775-289-8877

Pari-mutuel betting. Last two weekends in August.

HOTEL

★★RAMADA INN & COPPER QUEEN CASINO

805 Great Basin Blvd., Ely, 775-289-4884, 800-851-9526; www.ramada.com

65 rooms. High-speed Internet access. Complimentary continental breakfast. Restaurant, bar. Airport transportation available. Casino. Business center. Pool. Fitness center. Pets accepted. **$**

FALLON

Fallon is one of the westernmost cities on what is often called "the Loneliest Road in America," a segment of Route 50 that runs through Nevada and is known for its relative seclusion.

Information: Fallon Chamber of Commerce, 85 N. Taylor St., 775-423-2544;
www.fallonchamber.com

WHAT TO SEE AND DO

LAHONTAN STATE RECREATION AREA

16799 Lahontan Dam, Fallon, 775-867-3500; www.parks.nv.gov/lah.htm
Approximately 30,000 acres with a 16-mile-long reservoir. Water sports, fishing, boating (launching, ramps), picnicking, camping.

SPECIAL EVENTS

ALL INDIAN RODEO

65 S. Maine St., Fallon, 775-423-2544
Rodeo events, parade, powwow, Native American dances, arts, games. Third weekend in July.

FALLON AIR SHOW

Fallon Naval Air Station, 4755 Pasture Road, Fallon, 775-426-2880;
www.fallontourism.com
Part of the state's "Aerial Triple Crown," this event includes military exhibition flying, civilian aerobatics, aircraft displays and a Blue Angels Demonstration Team. Ground events and static displays of vintage and modern aircraft. Late spring-early summer.

NEVADA

★
★
★
★
★

GREAT BASIN NATIONAL PARK

Established as a national park in 1986, Great Basin consists of 77,092 acres of diverse scenic, ecologic and geologic attractions. It includes Lehman Caves (formerly Lehman Caves National Monument), Wheeler Peak, a glacier and Lexington Arch, a natural limestone arch more than six stories tall.

Of particular interest is Lehman Caves, a large limestone solution cavern. The cave contains numerous limestone formations, including shields and helictites.

The 12-mile Wheeler Peak Scenic Drive reaches to the 10,000-foot elevation mark of Wheeler Peak. From there, you can hike to the summit. Backcountry hiking and camping are permitted. The Lexington Arch is located at the south end of the park. Camping is allowed at three campgrounds located along the Wheeler Peak Scenic Drive: the Wheeler Peak Campground, the Upper Lehman Creek Campground and the Lower Lehman Campground. Baker Creek Campground is located approximately five miles from park headquarters. Picnic facilities are available near park headquarters.
Information: Five miles west of Baker on Highway 488, 775-234-7331; www.nps.gov/grba

HOTELS

★COMFORT INN

1830 W. Williams Ave., Fallon, 775-423-5554, 877-424-6423; www.comfortinn.com
82 rooms. Wireless Internet access. Complimentary continental breakfast. Restaurant. Pool. Whirlpool. Business center. Pets accepted. $

★SUPER 8

855 W. Williams Ave., Fallon, 775-423-6031; www.super8.com
75 rooms. High-speed Internet access. Restaurant, bar. Casino. Pool. Fitness center. Business center. Pets accepted. $

HENDERSON

The fastest growing city in Nevada, Henderson has become the third-largest city in the state, thanks to its proximity to Las Vegas. Many of the area's swankiest resorts are actually in Henderson.
Information: Henderson Chamber of Commerce, 590 S. Boulder Highway,
702-565-8951; www.hendersonchamber.com

WHAT TO SEE AND DO

CLARK COUNTY HERITAGE MUSEUM

1830 S. Boulder Highway, Henderson, 702-455-7955; www.co.clark.nv.us
Learn all about the history of southern Nevada. You'll see replicas of Native American dwellings, historic houses and businesses from the early 20th century, a ghost town, vintage automobiles, a 1932 train depot, old photos of the Strip and more. A detailed timeline charts the region's evolution from prehistoric times. Daily 9 a.m.-4:30 p.m.

ETHEL M. CHOCOLATES FACTORY & CACTUS GARDEN

2 Cactus Garden Drive, Henderson, 702-435-2655, 888-627-0990; www.ethelm.com
Take the self-guided tour of this factory, where everything from chewy caramels to crunchy nut clusters roll off the assembly line. Daily 8:30 a.m.-6 p.m.

GALLERIA AT SUNSET

1300 W. Sunset Road, Henderson, 702-434-0202; www.galleriaatsunset.com
This mall has 140 shops and restaurants. There is also a free rock climbing wall. Monday-Saturday 10 a.m.-9 p.m., Sunday 11 a.m.-7 p.m.

MONTELAGO VILLAGE

1600 Lake Las Vegas, Henderson, 702-564-4700, 866-564-4799;
www.montelagovillage.com
Escape to this charming development reminiscent of a centuries-old seaside village. About 35 unique shops and restaurants line the cobblestone streets of MonteLago, which borders the Ritz-Carlton Las Vegas. Retailers offer everything from fine art and custom-made jewelry to women's apparel and handcrafted home furnishings.

REFLECTION BAY GOLF CLUB

1605 Lake Las Vegas Parkway, Henderson, 702-740-4653, 877-698-4653;
www.lakelasvegas.com
Designed by golf great Jack Nicklaus, the public, par-72 resort course follows the rugged desert contours with the final holes along the shore of the 320-acre man-made

★
★★
★★
★

Lake Las Vegas. Arroyo-meets-grass flora, maddening bunkers and interesting (and frustrating) water features make the course memorable. Afterward, kick back at the Mediterranean-style clubhouse with patio dining under a colonnade. Winter 7 a.m.-dusk, summer 6:30 a.m.-dusk.

RIO SECCO GOLF CLUB
2851 Grand Hills Drive, Henderson, 702-777-2400; www.riosecco.net
Rio Secco is an expensive course, but its variety makes it well worth playing. The course is essentially divided into thirds, with six holes in small canyons, six on plateaus with views of the local skyline and six built to resemble the Nevada desert. The course is more than 7,300 yards long, so be prepared to swing for the fences. Number 9 is a long par-5 with bunkers surrounding the green. Make the turn facing the city and count yourself lucky if you've played 8 and 9 (back-to-back par-fives measuring 1,150 yards combined) at one or two over.

SPECIAL EVENT
HERITAGE PARADE AND FESTIVAL
Henderson Events Plaza, 200 S. Water St., Henderson, 702-565-8951;
www.visithenderson.com
This annual festival is one of the largest in Henderson. It lasts nine days and features food, a carnival, appraisal fair and more. Late April.

HOTELS
★★★GREEN VALLEY RANCH RESORT AND SPA
2300 Paseo Verde Parkway, Henderson, 702-617-7777, 866-782-9487;
www.greenvalleyranchresort.com
The Mediterranean-style Green Valley Ranch Resort and Spa is a peaceful escape, but there's still plenty of action when the mood strikes. The elegant rooms come with in-room martini bars. There are seven restaurants, and the Whiskey Bar is a great spot to gather with friends. The Whiskey also has a large patio, which goes out to a pool, café and amphitheater used for live concerts. The spa has a dizzying array of treatments, including 20 different kinds of massage therapies. 490 rooms. Wireless Internet access. Seven restaurants, four bars. Spa. Beach. Airport transportation available. Pets accepted. **$$$**

★★★★THE RITZ-CARLTON LAKE LAS VEGAS
1610 Lake Las Vegas Parkway, Henderson, 702-567-4700; www.ritzcarlton.com
Exchange the over-the-top glitz of the Las Vegas strip for the serenity of the Mediterranean-inspired Ritz-Carlton on Lake Las Vegas. A 35-minute ride from the Strip, the resort is nestled in a valley surrounded by low-lying desert mountains. A replica of Florence's Ponte Vecchio extends across the 320-acre lake, and singing gondoliers take guests on a romantic trip under the bridge. After playing the tables at the nearby MonteLago Village Resort, wind down with a massage in one of 22 treatment rooms at the resort spa or a round of golf on one of two championship golf courses. Guests can dine at the Medici Café and Terrace, which overlooks the resort's Florentine gardens or have a cocktail in the Firenze Lobby Lounge. 349 rooms. Wireless Internet access. Restaurant, bar. Spa. Pets accepted. Golf. Tennis. Business center. Fitness center. Pool. Whirlpool. **$$**

★★SUNSET STATION HOTEL
1301 W. Sunset Road, Henderson, 702-547-7777, 888-786-7389;
www.sunsetstation.com

457 rooms. Wireless Internet access. Eight restaurants, four bars. Airport transportation available. Casino. Business center. Fitness center. Pool. **$**

SPA
★★★★RITZ-CARLTON SPA LAKE LAS VEGAS
1610 Lake Las Vegas Parkway, Henderson, 702-567-4700, 800-241-3333;
www.ritzcarlton.com

This Mediterranean-influenced, 30,000-square-foot facility is a sanctuary from the hot desert sun. Treatment rooms are luxurious and spacious—several have outdoor terraces that overlook the lake, and some are designed exclusively for couples. The La Culla treatment includes an array of body and facial treatments, accompanied by music and other sounds and aromatherapy. The signature facial uses an exclusive marine concentrate. The spa facilities include a complete fitness center, movement studio for yoga and Pilates, full-service salon and a boutique. Nutritional and wellness counseling, physician-directed cosmetic dermatology and extensive recreations programs and activities are available.

INCLINE VILLAGE
Swanky and affluent, Incline Village sits on the north rim of Lake Tahoe. It derives its name from the Great Incline Tramway built by loggers in 1878, but today the town is primarily a haven for those seeking outdoor fun.

Information: Lake Tahoe Incline Village/Crystal Bay Visitors Bureau,969 Tahoe Blvd.,
Incline Village, 775-832-1606; www.gotahoe.com

WHAT TO SEE AND DO
DIAMOND PEAK SKI RESORT
1210 Ski Way, Incline Village, 775-832-1177; www.diamondpeak.com

Three quads, three double chairlifts; patrol, school, rentals, snowmaking. Thirty runs; longest run approximately 2½ miles; vertical drop 1,840 feet. Mid-December-mid-April, daily.

LAKE TAHOE NEVADA STATE PARK
2005 Highway 28, Incline Village, 775-831-0494; www.parks.nv.gov/lt.htm

Approximately 14,200 acres on the eastern shore of beautiful Lake Tahoe. Gently sloping sandy beach, swimming, fishing, boating (ramp), hiking, mountain biking, cross-country skiing. No camping. Daily.

SPECIAL EVENTS
LAKE TAHOE SHAKESPEARE FESTIVAL
Sand Harbor State Park, 948 Incline Way, Incline Village,
775-832-1616, 800-747-4697; www.laketahoeshakespeare.com

This event has grown into one of the premier Shakespeare festivals in the West. The troupe performs nightly from mid-July to late August in a natural amphitheater on the water's edge at Sand Harbor. A food court serves tasty fare from several outstanding local eateries, as well as beer and wine. Mid-July-late August.

LAKE TAHOE WINTER GAMES FESTIVAL
Diamond Peak Ski Resort, 1210 Ski Way, Incline Village,
775-832-1177; www.diamondpeak.com
Early March.

HOTEL
★★★HYATT REGENCY LAKE TAHOE RESORT & CASINO
1111 Country Club Drive, Incline Village, 775-832-1234; www.hyatt.com
This resort is a top pick for rustic, luxury accommodations on the North Shore of Lake Tahoe. It's not on a mountain but the resort will shuttle you to the slopes. Spa services are offered through the fitness center. The hotel also houses a small but charming old-style casino, a private hotel beach and a destination restaurant with arguably one of the best dining views of the lake. 422 rooms. Four restaurants, bar. Children's activity center. Spa. Casino. Pool. Business center. Fitness center. $$

LAS VEGAS
Plan a visit to Vegas these days and you'll still see "world wonders," glitzy showgirls and plenty of dice-throwing. But today's version of Las Vegas is more haute. The kitsch has been toned down a bit and world-class spas, more refined accommodations and some of the country's best restaurants have moved in. In the last few years, Las Vegas has morphed into one of the top cities for dining in the country.

You'll still hear plenty of ding, ding, ding all day long. But today it's as much about the pool—as in which resort has the best one—championship golf and Cirque du Soleil. Check out one of the best aquariums (at Mandalay Bay) and browse the collection at the Guggenheim Museum.

And bring your hiking shoes! You'll find numerous canyons, valleys and man-made lakes around the city. Enjoy spectacular scenery and a wide range of recreational activities, including hiking, swimming, fishing, biking, boating, horseback riding, rock climbing, camping and whitewater rafting.
Information: Las Vegas Convention/Visitors Authority, Convention Center,
3150 Paradise Road, 702-892-0711; www.lasvegas24hours.com

WHAT TO SEE AND DO
A PERMANENT TRIBUTE TO HEROES
New York-New York Hotel and Casino, 3790 Las Vegas Blvd. S., Las Vegas,
800-689-1797; www.nynyhotelcasino.com
This memorial of September 11, 2001 includes display cases showing some of the thousands of T-shirts, notes and other mementos left by mourning tourists in the months following the terror attacks.

ADVENTUREDOME
Circus Circus Hotel and Casino, 2880 Las Vegas Blvd. S., Las Vegas,
702-794-3939, 866-634-8894; www.adventuredome.com
Escape the heat at the country's largest indoor theme park, where you'll find more than 15 exciting rides, including the Canyon Blaster, a double-loop, double-corkscrew roller coaster and the Rim Runner, which includes a slide down a 60-foot waterfall. A carnival midway and clown shows add to the fun. Monday-Thursday 10 a.m.-6 p.m.; Friday-Saturday 10 a.m.- midnight; Sunday 10 a.m.-8 p.m.

AIR PLAY
Tropicana Hotel and Casino, 3801 Las Vegas Blvd. S., Las Vegas, 702-739-2222;
www.tropicanalv.com
Step inside the Tropicana to glimpse a performance by acrobats, aerialists, jugglers and singers to a variety of music. The 20-minute show takes place just below the famous Tiffany glass ceiling on a stage that was set up atop a bank of slot machines. Daily at 11 a.m., 1, 3, 5, 7 and 9 p.m.

ART ENCOUNTER
3979 Spring Mountain Road, Las Vegas, 702-227-0220, 800-395-2996;
www.artencounter.com
More than 100 artists display oils, watercolors, jewelry, pottery, sculpture and more in a wide variety of styles. Tuesday-Friday 10 a.m.-6 p.m., Saturday and Monday noon-5 p.m.

BADLANDS GOLF CLUB
9119 Alta Drive, Las Vegas, 702-363-0754; www.badlandsgc.com
Designed by Chi Chi Rodriguez and Johnny Miller. Badlands is an example of an increasing trend of three sets of nine holes, offering different combinations of courses. The three nines (Diablo, Desperado and Outlaw) are markedly different. The Outlaw course is more forgiving than the other two, which are the usual tournament 18.

BALI HAI GOLF CLUB
5160 Las Vegas Blvd. S., Las Vegas, 888-427-6678; www.balihaigolfclub.com
The white-sand bunkers here complement the traditional architecture of the clubhouse, which contains Cili, an exclusive Vegas eatery. The signature hole is the 16th, a par-3 with an island green.

BELLAGIO CASINO
Bellagio, 3600 Las Vegas Blvd. S., Las Vegas, 702-693-7111, 888-987-3456;
www.bellagiolasvegas.com
Where other Vegas casinos cram in the tables and pour on the flash, Bellagio makes a more soothing pitch for your money. Tables are well spaced and slot machines ding at lower volume levels. Daily, 24 hours.

BELLAGIO CONSERVATORY AND BOTANICAL GARDENS
Bellagio, 3600 Las Vegas Blvd. S., Las Vegas, 702-693-7111, 888-987-3456;
www.bellagiolasvegas.com
Take a leisurely stroll through the 90,000-square-foot conservatory at the Bellagio to see thousands of gorgeous plants and colorful blooms, including orchids and other exotics that are painstakingly maintained by 140 horticulturists. Daily, 24 hours.

BELLAGIO GALLERY OF FINE ART
Bellagio, 3600 Las Vegas Blvd. S., Las Vegas, 702-693-7871, 877-957-9777;
www.bellagiolasvegas.com
The Bellagio Gallery of Fine Art mounts rotating exhibitions on subjects ranging from Fabergé eggs to Calder mobiles to Andy Warhol's celebrity silk screens. Admission: adults $15, Nevada residents $12, seniors $12, students, teachers, Military with valid ID $10. Sunday-Thursday 10 a.m.-6 p.m., Friday-Saturday 10 a.m.-9 p.m.

BONNIE SPRINGS OLD NEVADA

1 Gunfighter Lane, Blue Diamond, 702-875-4191; www.bonniesprings.com

Experience what life was like in the Wild West at this replica of a mining town complete with stagecoaches, saloons, simulated gunfights and more. Summer, daily 10:30 a.m.-6 p.m.; winter, daily 10:30 a.m.-5 p.m.

BOULEVARD MALL

3528 S. Maryland Parkway, Las Vegas, 702-732-8949; www.blvdmall.com

Shop at the more than 150 stores including Macy's, Victoria's Secret and Gap. Monday-Saturday 10 a.m.-9 p.m., Sunday 11 a.m.-6 p.m.

BROADACRES SWAP MEET

2930 Las Vegas Blvd. N., Las Vegas, 702-642-3777; www.broadacresswapmeet.com

Up to 1,000 vendors hawk new and used merchandise that's priced to *sell*. Friday 6 a.m.-3 p.m., Saturday-Sunday 6 a.m.-4 p.m.

CONEY ISLAND EMPORIUM

New York-New York Hotel and Casino, 3790 Las Vegas Blvd. S., Las Vegas, 702-736-4100; www.coneyislandemporium.com

This 32,000-square-foot emporium is a replica of the famed Coney Island in New York and includes more than 20 midway-style games and hundreds of arcade games. Kids will enjoy laser tag, bumper cars (which are bright yellow cabs) and racing in Daytona-style driving stimulators. Sunday-Thursday 8 a.m.-midnight, Friday-Saturday 8-2 a.m.

COTTONWOOD VALLEY

Las Vegas, on State Route 160 at about mile marker 17

Pedal your way across the desert in one of the most popular cycling areas in the Las Vegas Valley. Several trails snake their way through the rugged but beautiful terrain. Trail maps are available at kiosks in the area.

CREATIVE COOKING SCHOOL

7385 W. Sahara Ave., Las Vegas, 702-562-3900; www.creativecookingschool.com

The city's first cooking school, opened by chef-author Catherine Margles, offers demonstrations and hands-on lessons. Also includes children's classes.

DANNY GANS SHOW

Mirage Hotel and Casino, 3400 Las Vegas Blvd. S., Las Vegas, 702-792-7777, 800-963-9634; www.mirage.com

This singer-impressionist never disappoints with his dead-on mimicking of your favorite artists, making his award-winning show one of the hottest on the Strip.

DESERT FOX TOURS

6265 Dean Martin Road, Las Vegas, 702-361-0676; www.vegashummertours.com

If you're the adventurous type, go off-road in a Hummer and see the desert in all its rugged glory. Various tours last from three to six hours and take you to Red Rock National Conservation Area, the Valley of Fire, or a gold mine and ghost town.

DESERT PINES GOLF CLUB

3415 E. Bonanza Road, Las Vegas, 888-427-6678; www.desertpinesgolfclub.com

Desert Pines strives to emulate the seaside designs found in the Carolinas. Pine trees line most of the narrow fairways, and several ponds can increase a score in short order. The Desert Pines golf center is comprehensive, even offering target areas shaped like famous holes such as the 17th island green at Sawgrass and the second hole at Pinehurst.

EIFFEL TOWER EXPERIENCE

Paris Las Vegas, 3655 Las Vegas Blvd. S., Las Vegas, 877-603-4386;
www.parislasvegas.com

See this 50-story half-scale replica of the Eiffel Tower. A glass elevator whisks tourists up 460 feet for panoramic views of the mountain-ringed valley by day and the neon canyon by night. The 11th-floor restaurant Eiffel Tower serves classic French food. Daily 10-1 a.m.

FANTASTIC INDOOR SWAP MEET

1717 S. Decatur Blvd., Las Vegas, 702-877-0087; www.fantasticindoorswapmeet.com

Locals flock to this giant indoor swap meet in search of bargains. The 700 shops are packed with merchandise from car accessories to perfume. Open Friday, Saturday and Sunday 10 a.m.-6 p.m.

FASHION SHOW MALL

3200 Las Vegas Blvd. S., Las Vegas, 702-784-7000; www.thefashionshow.com

Most of the nation's major department stores anchor the vast two-story Fashion Show Mall. Monday-Saturday 10 a.m.-9 p.m., Sunday 11 a.m.-7 p.m.

NEVADA

★ ★ ★ ★ ★

FLAMINGO WILDLIFE HABITAT

Flamingo Las Vegas, 3555 Las Vegas Blvd. S., Las Vegas, 702-733-3111;
www.flamingolv.com

Walk through this 1½-acre birdhouse and you'll see Chilean flamingos, crowned cranes, swans, African penguins, pheasants, quail and more. Daily, 24 hours.

FLOYD LAMB PARK

9200 Tule Springs Road, Las Vegas, 702-229-6297

This pleasant 2,000-acre park has four small fishing lakes, tree-shaded picnic areas with tables and grills, a walking/bicycle path, volleyball courts and horseshoe pits. No overnight camping.

FLYAWAY INDOOR SKYDIVING

200 Convention Center Drive, Las Vegas, 702-731-4768, 877-545-8093;
www.flyawayindoorskydiving.com

This vertical wind tunnel simulates the freefall experience of skydiving. The column of air is 12 feet across and up to 22 feet high, with vertical airspeeds of up to 120 mph. Your experience begins with a 20-minute training class and a 15-minute equipment preparation and concludes with a three-minute flight session. Daily 10 a.m.-7 p.m.

FOLIES BERGERE

Tropicana Hotel and Casino, 3801 Las Vegas Blvd. S., Las Vegas,
702-739-2222, 888-826-8767; www.tropicanalv.com

This daring cabaret show debuted on the Strip in 1959 and has been packing in audiences ever since, making it Sin City's longest-running production show. The 90-minute extravaganza features vocalists, acrobats, adagio artists, a juggler and showgirls. All-ages shows (no nudity) are held weekdays at 7:30 p.m. Monday, Wednesday, Thursday and Saturday at 7:30 and 10 p.m.; Tuesday and Friday 8:30 p.m.

FORUM SHOPS AT CAESARS PALACE

Caesars Palace, 3500 Las Vegas Blvd. S., Las Vegas, 702-893-4800;
www.caesarspalace.com

With piazzas, fountains and an ever-changing (painted) sky overhead, the Forum Shops offers a taste of Rome. Time your visit to catch one of the hourly shows at the Festival Fountain, where the statues of Bacchus, Venus, Apollo and Mars come to life in an animatronic bacchanal (there's also a similar show at the other end of the mall involving Atlas). Stores scale toward luxury retailers like Gucci and Fendi, but also include Gap, FAO Schwarz and Niketown. Several good restaurants include Wolfgang Puck's Spago and Chinois. Monday-Thursday 10 a.m.-11 p.m., Friday-Saturday 10 a.m.–midnight.

FOUNTAINS OF BELLAGIO

Bellagio, 3600 Las Vegas Blvd. S., Las Vegas, 702-693-7111;
www.bellagiolasvegas.com

A Busby Berkeley chorus line with water cannons subbing for gams, the Fountains of the Bellagio perform daily to a roster of tunes ranging from campy to operatic. The razzle-dazzle really roils after dark, when 4,500 lights dramatize the 1,000-nozzle, 27-million-gallon performances. Crowds tend to stake out spots along the wall ringing the hotel-fronting lake several minutes before every evening show. It goes off every 15 minutes between 8 p.m. and midnight and every half-hour before 8 p.m. Monday-Friday 3-8 p.m. show every half-hour, 8 p.m.-midnight.

FREMONT STREET EXPERIENCE

425 Fremont St., Las Vegas, 702-678-5600; www.vegasexperience.com

This light and sound show broadcast on a 90-foot-high canopy over a 4½-block stretch of Fremont Street was built in 1995. Embedded with 12 million lights and 218 speakers, the overhead show synchronizes music and colored-light-derived images in six-minute shows. Each computerized performance per night is different, keying off various musical styles from calypso to disco to country-western. Hourly shows from dusk to midnight.

GAMBLERS GENERAL STORE

800 S. Main St., Las Vegas, 702-382-9903, 800-322-2447;
www.gamblersgeneralstore.com

Wares range from portable poker chip sets and playing cards to roulette wheels, slot machines and raffle drums—all shippable. Daily 9 a.m.-6 p.m.

GAMEWORKS LAS VEGAS

3785 Las Vegas Blvd. S., Las Vegas, 702-432-4263; www.gameworks.com

Over 300 video and virtual reality games as well as a 75-foot climbing wall entertain the clan, while the adults-only bar offers pool tables and live music. The kitchen serves casual fare. Sunday-Thursday 10 a.m.-midnight; Friday-Saturday 10-1 a.m.

GRAND CANAL SHOPPES AT THE VENETIAN

The Venetian Resort Hotel Casino, 3355 Las Vegas Blvd. S., Las Vegas,
702-414-1000, 877-883-6423; www.venetian.com

A 1,200-foot-long replica of the Grand Canal bisects the Grand Canal Shoppes. Venetian bridges, arches and arcades dress up the mall, where you can scoop up Burberry and Jimmy Choo. Stop at Il Prato or Ripa de Monti for Venetian paper goods, carnival masks and Murano glass. Grab at bite at the food court or in one of the full-service restaurants, many with patio seating. Sunday-Thursday10 a.m.-11 p.m., Friday-Saturday 10 a.m.-midnight.

GUGGENHEIM HERMITAGE MUSEUM

The Venetian, 3355 Las Vegas Blvd. S., Las Vegas, 702-414-2440;
www.guggenheimlasvegas.org

A venue for rotating exhibitions, the Guggenheim Hermitage is actually managed by a trio of museums, including the New York Guggenheim, Russia's Hermitage and the Kunsthistorisches Museum in Vienna. Daily 9:30 a.m.-8:30 p.m.

HARD ROCK MEMORABILIA TOUR

Hard Rock Hotel Casino, 4455 Paradise Road, Las Vegas,
702-693-5000, 800-693-7625; www.hardrockhotel.com

This is the largest exhibition of rock memorabilia ever assembled in one place. Shuttles depart from the Harley-Davidson Cafe, Fashion Show Mall and Caesars Palace between 10 a.m. and 7 p.m. daily.

IMPERIAL PALACE AUTO COLLECTION

Imperial Palace Hotel & Casino, 3535 Las Vegas Blvd., Las Vegas, 702-731-3311;
www.autocollections.com

The Auto Collection housed on the fifth floor of the parking lot at Imperial Palace showcases some 170-plus vintage cars (some of which are for sale). Models range from historic autos to muscle cars and late-model luxury brands. See a 1962 red Alfa Romeo Spider, 1954 Chevy Bel Air convertible and 1929 Duesenberg sedan, along with vintage car parts and jukeboxes. Admission: adults $8.95, seniors $5, children $5, children under 3 free. Daily 10 a.m.-6 p.m.

KING TUT'S TOMB AND MUSEUM

Luxor Hotel & Casino, 3900 Las Vegas Blvd. S., Las Vegas, 888-777-0188;
www.luxor.com

Explore an exact replica of King Tut's tomb and see hundreds of reproductions of the eye-popping treasures found in the original. 15-minute self-guided tour. Daily 10 a.m.-11 p.m.

LANCE BURTON: MASTER MAGICIAN

Monte Carlo Resort and Casino, 3770 Las Vegas Blvd. S., Las Vegas,
702-730-7160, 877-386-8224; www.lanceburton.com

Since 1996, this world-champion magician has been mesmerizing audiences five nights a week with impressive illusions that defy logic. Smoke effects, pyrotechnics and even a live bird named Elvis make up this entertaining 90-minute spectacle. To perform his sleight-of-hand tricks, Burton often enlists the help of kids on stage. Admission: Main Floor-Mezzanine $72.55, Balcony $66.50. Tuesday and Saturday 7 and 10 p.m., Wednesday, Thursday and Friday 7 p.m.

LAS VEGAS 51S

Cashman Fields, 850 Las Vegas Blvd. N., Las Vegas, 702-386-7200; www.lv51.com

A farm team of the L.A. Dodgers, the 51s play at Cashman Field, which seats more than 9,000 fans.

LAS VEGAS ART MUSEUM

Sahara West Library/Fine Arts Museum, 9600 W. Sahara Ave., Las Vegas,
702-360-8000; www.lasvegasartmuseum.org

An affiliate of the Smithsonian, this museum serves primarily as a venue for traveling shows. Admission: adults $6, seniors $5, students $3, children under 12 free. Tuesday-Saturday 10 a.m.-5 p.m., Sunday 1-5 p.m.

LAS VEGAS CONVENTION CENTER

3150 Paradise Road, Las Vegas, 702-892-0711; www.lasvegas24hours.com

This facility occupies 3.2-million square feet, making it the largest single-level convention center in the country.

LAS VEGAS HARLEY-DAVIDSON/BUELL

2605 S. Eastern Ave., Las Vegas, 702-431-8500, 888-218-0744; www.lvhd.com

This Harley dealership ranks as the world's largest. Either buy one of the flashy two-wheelers or rent one. The dealership offers shuttle service from some area hotels. Monday-Friday 7:30 a.m.-6 p.m., Saturday 9 a.m.-6 p.m., Sunday 10 a.m.-5 p.m.

LAS VEGAS MINI GRAN PRIX

1401 N. Rainbow Blvd., Las Vegas, 702-259-7000; www.lvmgp.com

Three tracks feature go-karts, sprint carts and Grand Prix cars, so take your pick. The smallest drivers can maneuver kiddie carts around the fourth track. There's also a large arcade and amusement rides, including a roller coaster and a 90-foot slide. Sunday-Thursday 10 a.m.-10 p.m.; Friday-Saturday 10 a.m.-11 p.m.

LAS VEGAS MOTOR SPEEDWAY

7000 Las Vegas Blvd. N., Las Vegas, 800-644-4444; www.lvms.com

Competitive events occur most weekends and include short-track programs as well as motocross, dragway and marquee races like NASCAR Nextel Cup races. Also includes a driving school with classes such as the popular Richard Petty Driving Experience and CART Driving 101.

LAS VEGAS NATURAL HISTORY MUSEUM

900 Las Vegas Blvd. N., Las Vegas, 702-384-3466; www.lvnhm.org

Exhibits focus on wildlife and plants from Africa and other parts of the world, as well as Nevada's Mojave Desert. Kids will love the Dinosaur Gallery and Marine Life, a 3,000-gallon reef tank where shark feedings take place several times a week at 2 p.m. Admission: adults $8, seniors and students $7, children 3-11 $4. Daily 9 a.m.-4 p.m.

LAS VEGAS OUTLET CENTER

7400 Las Vegas Blvd. S., Las Vegas, 702-896-5599; www.premiumoutlets.com

This outlet mall now boasts 155 shops and two food courts (with plans to expand) and includes Tommy Hilfiger, Calvin Klein and Bose. Monday-Saturday 10 a.m.-9 p.m., Sunday 10 a.m.-8 p.m.

LAS VEGAS SKI AND SNOWBOARD RESORT

Highway 156, Las Vegas, 702-385-2754; www.skilasvegas.com

Choose from 11 different ski runs at this alpine resort, just 45 minutes from the city in the Spring Mountain Range, in Mount Charleston's Lee Canyon. A half-pipe and terrain park challenge snowboarders. Thanksgiving-Easter, daily 9 a.m.-4 p.m.

LAS VEGAS SOARING CENTER

23600 S. Las Vegas Blvd., Jean, 702-874-1010; www.soaringcenter.net

Soar above the desert in a towplane or sailplane. Daily 9 a.m.-sunset.

LASER QUEST

7361 W. Lake Mead Blvd., Las Vegas, 702-243-8881; www.laserquest.com

People of all ages come to play, snake through labyrinths and use laser pistols to take their best shots and tag other players wearing vests with laser-sensitive targets. Shots can even be ricocheted off mirrored reflecting paper hanging on the walls. Tuesday-Thursday 6-9 p.m., Friday 4-11 p.m., Saturday noon-11 p.m., Sunday noon-6 p.m.

LE BOULEVARD DISTRICT

Paris Las Vegas, 3655 Las Vegas Blvd. S., Las Vegas, 877-603-4386;
www.parislasvegas.com

Go on a French-style spending spree in this 31,500-square-foot shopping district that transports you overseas to the City of Light. The cobblestone streets and winding alleyways will make you feel like you're in Paris. Buy French wines, cheese and treats at La Cave.

LEFT OF CENTER ART GALLERY AND STUDIO

2207 W. Gowan, North Las Vegas, 702-647-7378; www.leftofcenterart.org

Local and national artists display artwork that typically touches on social issues at this 3,6000-square-foot gallery in an industrial part of town. Resident artists also present workshops and gallery talks and teach classes. Tuesday-Friday 1-6 p.m., Saturday 10 a.m.-2 p.m.

LION HABITAT

MGM Grand, 3799 Las Vegas Blvd. S., Las Vegas, 702-891-1111; www.mgmgrand.com
During the day, you can see lions up close at the sky-lit habitat surrounded by waterfalls, acacia trees and a pond at the MGM. There's even a see-through tunnel that allows you to see the lions' pad from above and below. Feline expert Keith Evans brings up to six big cats to the Strip daily from his ranch 12 miles away. Daily 11 a.m.-10 p.m.

MADAME TUSSAUDS LAS VEGAS

The Venetian Resort Hotel Casino, 3377 Las Vegas Blvd. S., Las Vegas,
702-862-7800; www.venetian.com
See more than 100 wax figures of celebrities, from Barbara Streisand to Harrison Ford. Daily; varies by season.

MANHATTAN EXPRESS

New York-New York Hotel and Casino, 3790 Las Vegas Blvd. S., Las Vegas,
702-740-6969; www.nynyhotelcasino.com
Looping around the faux Big Apple skyline, New York-New York's Manhattan Express roller coaster looks tame enough from street level. But when you're buckled into one of its yellow cab cars, its a streaker, climbing 16 stories, dropping 12 and reaching 67 miles per hour through somersaults, barrel rolls and a twisting dive. Sunday-Thursday 11 a.m.-11 p.m., Friday-Saturday 10:30 a.m.-midnight.

MARJORIE BARRICK MUSEUM OF NATURAL HISTORY

4505 S. Maryland Parkway, Las Vegas, 702-895-3381; www.hrc.nevada.edu/museum
Exhibits of the biology, geology and archaeology of the Las Vegas area, including live desert animals. Monday-Friday 8 a.m.-4:45 p.m., Saturday 10 a.m.-2 p.m.

MASQUERADE SHOW IN THE SKY

Rio All-Suite Hotel and Casino, 3700 W. Flamingo Road, Las Vegas,
702-777-7776, 866-746-7671; www.playrio.com
This unique and exciting show is modeled after Brazil's Carnivale. The show features state-of-the-art floats suspended from the ceiling that parade above the casino floor. Performers wear exotic masks and colorful costumes. Audience members can take part in the parade, ride a float and wear a costume. Thursday-Monday at 3, 4, 5, 6:30, 7:30, 8:30 and 9:30 p.m.

MIRACLE MILE SHOPS

Aladdin Resort & Casino, 3663 Las Vegas Blvd. S., Las Vegas,
702-866-0710, 888-800-8284; www.miraclemileshopslv.com
Modeled after a North African bazaar with Moroccan archways, mosaic tiles and fountain courtyards, this circular center includes 130 shops and 14 restaurants. Sunday-Thursday 10 a.m.-11 p.m., Friday-Saturday 10 a.m.-midnight.

MYSTERE BY CIRQUE DU SOLEIL

Treasure Island, 3300 Las Vegas Blvd. S., Las Vegas,
702-894-7111, 800-392-1999; www.treasureisland.com

Cirque du Soleil has taken up permanent residence at Treasure Island with *Mystere*. Monday-Wednesday, Saturday 7:30 and 9:30 p.m., Sunday 4:30 and 7 p.m.

NEON MUSEUM

Third and Fremont Streets, Las Vegas, 702-387-6366; www.neonmuseum.org

In an effort to preserve the outrageous neon signs for which the city is famed, this museum currently consists of 10 vintage ads, refurbished and remounted in two outdoor galleries located on the Third Street cul-de-sac and the intersection of Fremont Street and Las Vegas Boulevard. The neon signs, including Dots Flowers (from 1949) and the Nevada Motel (1950) almost seem quaint beside today's more elaborately evolved wattage. Daily, 24 hours. $3 adults and teens, $2 children 6-12, children under 6 admitted free.

NEVADA STATE MUSEUM AND HISTORICAL SOCIETY

Lorenzi Park, 700 Twin Lakes Drive, Las Vegas, 702-486-5205;
www.nevadaculture.org/docs/museums/lv/vegas.htm

The Nevada State Museum and Historical Society delivers a mix of natural and human history. Prehistory galleries mount a reconstructed Columbian mammoth and Pacific horse as well as an ichthyosaur fossil. Regional coverage includes gangster Bugsy Siegel's involvement in the Flamingo hotel. Though the museum primarily draws school groups, its sylvan lakeside setting in Lorenzi Park offers an incentive to visit. Daily 9 a.m.-5 p.m.

NEVADA TEST SITE HISTORY CENTER

755 E. Flamingo Road, Las Vegas, 702-794-5161; www.ntshf.org

At this center, learn more about the role this site played in strengthening the country's defense and increase your overall knowledge of the U.S. nuclear testing program, from 1950 to the present. You'll see exhibits on Camp Desert Rock, experiments done to try building a nuclear rocket for manned flight to Mars, as well as other interesting topics. Monday-Saturday 9 a.m., Sunday 1-5 p.m.

O BY CIRQUE DU SOLEIL

Bellagio, 3600 Las Vegas Blvd. S., Las Vegas, 702-693-7722, 888-488-7111;
www.bellagiolasvegas.com

The inventive French Canadian troop Cirque du Soleil takes their acrobatic choreography to the pool in a theater built specifically for the aquatic show. Wednesday-Sunday 7:30 and 10:30 p.m.; closed Monday-Tuesday.

PAINTED DESERT GOLF CLUB

5555 Painted Mirage Road, Las Vegas, 702-645-2570; www.painteddesertgc.com

Painted Desert is one of the older desert-style golf courses in Vegas, and it makes a deliberate effort to be playable by almost everyone, even on a bad day. The course is meticulously maintained. Eight of the nine par-fours measure less than 400 yards, so if your approach shots are good, you have a nice chance of making some birdies while enjoying the course's namesake feature.

RED ROCK CANYON NATIONAL CONSERVATION AREA

1000 Scenic Drive, Las Vegas, 702-515-5350; www.nv.blm.gov/redrockcanyon

As the days wear on in Vegas and the trilling of slot machines wears you down, head to the red-rock boulders and pinnacles that form the western view from Strip hotel windows. Although it's only 10 miles from the city limits, Red Rock Canyon feels farther away. The 13-mile-loop through the conservation area on a one-way road takes you to many entertaining features, including several trailhead stops for day hikes and almost certain photo opportunities with the assertive wild burros who thrive there. Thirty miles of Mojave Desert trails take hikers deep into the petrified sand dunes, past ancient pictographs and mysterious waterfalls. Scenic drive: winter 6 a.m.-5 p.m., spring and fall 6 a.m.-7 p.m., summer 6 a.m.-8 p.m.; visitor center, winter 8 a.m.-4:30 p.m., summer 8 a.m.-5:30 p.m.

RED ROOSTER ANTIQUE MALL

1109 Western Ave., Las Vegas, 702-382-5253

Housed in a former soda pop bottling plant, this is the oldest antique mall in town. Goods constantly change, but regulars check the warehouse-sized space frequently for old signs, vintage Vegas memorabilia and 1950s modern furniture. You'll find more than 50 antique and collectible dealers here. Daily 10 a.m.-6 p.m.

RHODES RANCH GOLF CLUB

20 Rhodes Ranch Parkway, Las Vegas, 702-740-4114; www.rhodesranch.com

Tucked into the southwest corner of the Las Vegas Valley, the Ted Robinson-designed Rhodes Ranch course is the center of a 1,500-acre planned community. Open to the public, the well-groomed 162-acre course spreads over multiple elevations with city, plateau and mountain views plus ample water features. Course management claims three of Robinson's best par-threes. Winter 7 a.m.-dusk, summer 6 a.m.-dusk.

ROYAL LINKS GOLF CLUB

5995 E. Vegas Valley Drive, Las Vegas, 702-450-8123, 888-427-6678; www.royallinksgolfclub.com

Royal Links does its best to create the atmosphere of a traditional Scottish or Irish course. Each hole was inspired by one on which the British Open is contested each year. Designs were taken from Royal Troon, Prestwick and Royal Birkdale, among others. The club suggests that you let the caddies on staff carry your bag to get the full British Isles golf experience right here in the states.

SCENIC AIRLINES

2705 Airport Drive, North Las Vegas, 702-638-3300, 800-634-6801; www.scenic.com

Board one of this company's twin-engine planes for a bird's-eye view of the glorious Grand Canyon. More than 20 different tours are offered, ranging from one hour to three days of sightseeing. Depending on which tour you choose, you'll also see other popular natural attractions, such as Bryce Canyon, the Hoover Dam, Lake Mead, Monument Valley and the Valley of Fire. On some tours, you'll also spend some time exploring on foot or in a boat. Plane wings are up high, so no aerial views are obstructed, and oversized panoramic windows give you an even better look at what's down below.

241

NEVADA

★ ★ ★ ★ ★

SHADOW CREEK GOLF CLUB

5400 Losee Road, North Las Vegas, 866-260-0069; www.shadowcreek.com

Probably the most exclusive course in town, a tee time here will cost $500 and you might find yourself playing behind George Clooney or Michael Jordan. The views of the surrounding mountains are breathtaking. (Because it's so pricey, the course isn't crowded.) Pine trees make for an interesting site in the Nevada desert, as do crystal-clear lagoons and streams along holes like the signature 15th, which runs toward the mountains.

SHARK REEF AT MANDALAY BAY

Mandalay Bay Resort and Casino, 3950 Las Vegas Blvd. S., Las Vegas, 702-632-7777; www.mandalaybay.com

This aquarium houses more than 2,000 animals, including the great hammerhead shark, the only one in a closed-system aquarium in the world. Its residence is a 1.6-million-gallon tank, the third largest in North America. Other remarkable exhibits include 5 of the 12 golden crocodiles in captivity in the world as well as an Asian water monitor and green sea turtles, all of which are endangered species. Admission: adults $16.95, children 12 and under $10.95, children 4 and under free. Sunday-Thursday 10 a.m.-8 p.m., last admission at 7 p.m, Friday-Saturday 10 a.m.-10 p.m., last admission at 9 p.m.

SIENA GOLF CLUB

10575 Siena Monte Ave., Las Vegas, 702-341-9200, 888-689-6469; www.sienagolfclub.com

Sienna has a lot of bunkers. The sand is nearly omnipresent, but it's only a problem on the back nine, which features doglegs and blind shots that stand in contrast to the long, straight holes of the front side. Siena is more of a risk-reward course than it is a course for playing target golf. You could go for an adventurous shot in many places, but by the end of the day, the sand traps may have you thinking twice before you play such brazen golf.

SIRENS OF TI

Treasure Island, 3300 Las Vegas Blvd. S., Las Vegas, 702-894-7111; www.treasureisland.com

The sailors of the *HMS Britannia* challenge pirates offloading their stolen booty from the *Hispaniola* in this animatronic spectacle staged outside Treasure Island. The show has recently been updated, bringing new innovations in lighting and pyrotechnics and adding a sexy new twist. Women now battle it out with the renegade pirates in a more adult interpretation of this popular attraction. Join the crowds that cluster around the ships well before show time for best viewing. Daily at 7, 8:30, 10 and 11:30 p.m.

SOUTHERN NEVADA ZOOLOGICAL-BOTANICAL PARK

1775 N. Rancho Drive, Las Vegas, 702-647-4685; www.lasvegaszoo.org

This park, with 150 species of animals and plants, is home to the last family of Barbary apes in this country and the very rare Bali Mynah birds. You'll also see endangered cats, chimpanzees, eagles, emus, ostriches, venomous reptiles native to southern Nevada and wallabies. Those interested in botany will appreciate the endangered cycads and rare bamboos. Half-day and full-day eco-desert tours are also available. Daily 9 a.m.-5 p.m.

SPEED—THE RIDE

NASCAR Cafe, Sahara Hotel & Casino, 2535 Las Vegas Blvd. S., Las Vegas, 702-737-2111; www.saharavegas.com/content/NASCAR

This 70-mph thrill ride begins inside the NASCAR Cafe and propels you over its first hill with electromagnetic force. It then travels through a loop and shoots up a 224-foot tower before dropping backward down the same track. Sunday-Thursday10 a.m.-midnight, Friday-Saturday 10-1 a.m.

SPORTS BOOK AT THE MIRAGE HOTEL AND CASINO

Mirage Hotel and Casino, 3400 Las Vegas Blvd. S., Las Vegas, 702-791-7111; www.mirage.com

Most casinos have one, but sports books are shrinking in newer hotels. The Mirage boasts a 10,000-square-foot sports betting palace. Big events, including the Super Bowl, the Kentucky Derby and the NBA Finals, are predictably jammed. Daily.

SPORTS HALL OF FAME

Las Vegas Club Casino and Hotel, 18 E. Fremont St., Las Vegas, 702-385-1664, 800-634-6532; www.vegasclubcasino.net

Hardcore sports fans won't want to miss a visit to this championship attraction, which is packed with memorabilia connected to some of the sports world's biggest names. The all-star collection includes Michael Jordan's autographed University of North Carolina basketball jersey, 10 autographed NFL footballs, prized photos of boxing greats such as Muhammad Ali and Joe Louis, and many more noteworthy items. The hotel showcases all the memorabilia in the long hallways that connect its two towers. Daily, 24 hours.

STALLION MOUNTAIN COUNTRY CLUB

5500 E. Flamingo Road, Las Vegas, 702-450-8077; www.stallionmountaincc.com

A private 54-hole facility, Stallion Mountain follows the lead of several other courses in the area and gives its three tracks the names Secretariat, Man o'War and Citation, after the legendary Triple Crown winning thoroughbreds. Secretariat is the course to play if you have to choose just one. It plays at the foot of Sunrise Mountain, and each hole has a name that suggests something about the tracks layout (including Forced Carry and Entrapment). The course is fairly difficult and pricey.

STAR TREK: THE EXPERIENCE

Las Vegas Hilton, 3000 Paradise Road, Las Vegas, 702-697-8717, 888-462-6535; www.startrekexp.com

Trekkies will love this sci-fi immersion. Get beamed up to the Starship *Enterprise*. The 22-minute tour Turbo-lifts you to the Shuttlebay to board a four-minute sound-and-motion simulator ride through space. Disembark at the History of the Future Museum filled with props and costumes from the various Star Trek series. Quarks, the canteen based on the café aboard *Deep Space Nine*, gives you your fill of "hamborgers" and glop on a stick. Daily 11 a.m.-11 p.m.

243

NEVADA

★
★
★
★
☆

STRATOSPHERE TOWER THRILL RIDES

Stratosphere Hotel and Casino, 2900 Las Vegas Blvd. S., Las Vegas,
702-380-7777, 800-998-6937; www.stratospherehotel.com

Go 1,149 feet to the top of the tallest freestanding building west of the Mississippi and then get tossed 160 feet at 45 mph. Or ride the X-Scream and let a mechanical arm dangle you off the side like a cruel seesaw. The roller coaster is much tamer but will give you some of the best aerial views of Vegas. Sunday-Thursday 10-1 a.m., Friday-Saturday 10-2 a.m.

SUNDANCE HELICOPTER TOURS

5596 Haven St., Las Vegas, 800-653-1881; www.helicoptour.com

Take a seat in one of Sundance's choppers for a breathtaking, bird's-eye view of the majestic Grand Canyon. On some of the more expensive tours, you'll descend below the canyon rim and even land for a scenic boat ride along the Colorado River, followed by a picnic lunch and champagne toasts. For a lot less money, you can fly over the Strip to see the city's trump card from high above the nonstop action.

SUNSET PARK

2601 E. Sunset Road, Las Vegas, 702-455-8200;
www.sunsetcities.com/sunset-park/index.html

When you feel like getting out of those windowless casinos, head to this 320-acre park. Shoot some hoops on one of the basketball courts, play a round of disc golf, get in a game of tennis or volleyball, go swimming and much more. The park has ample picnic facilities. Daily 7 a.m.-11 p.m.

THE SECRET GARDEN OF SIEGFRIED & ROY

Mirage Hotel and Casino, 3400 Las Vegas Blvd. S., Las Vegas, 702-791-7111;
www.miragehabitat.com

Besides stunningly beautiful royal white tigers, you'll see an Asian elephant, a black panther, heterozygous tigers, a snow leopard, white lions and more wild creatures. Use one of the free listening wands to learn about each animal from the famed duo themselves. Also visit the 2.5-million-gallon Dolphin Habitat, where Atlantic bottlenose dolphins will charm you with their playfulness. Daily 10 a.m.-7 p.m.

THOMAS & MACK CENTER

4505 S. Maryland Parkway., Las Vegas, 702-895-3761; www.unlvtickets.com

This 18,500-seat events center features concerts, ice shows, rodeos and sporting events.

TOURNAMENT PLAYERS CLUB AT THE CANYONS

9851 Canyon Run Driv., Las Vegas, 702-256-2000; www.tpc.com/canyons

Codesigned by PGA legend Raymond Floyd, the Canyons features short fairways and rough that's consistent but tough. The course hosts the Las Vegas Senior Classic on the PGA's Champions Tour each year. There are fairway bunkers on many holes to penalize golfers for hitting errant tee shots, and the greens make it challenging to get your approach shots close enough to have consistent birdie opportunities. It's a difficult course, but one that shouldn't be missed.

UNIVERSITY OF NEVADA, LAS VEGAS

4505 S. Maryland Parkway., Las Vegas, 702-895-3011; www.unlv.edu

Established in 1957; 19,500 students. Campus tours arranged in advance. On campus is the Artemus W. Ham Concert Hall. This 1,900-seat theater features the Charles Vanda Master Series of symphony, opera and ballet. Jazz and popular music concerts are also performed here.

UNLV PERFORMING ARTS CENTER

University of Nevada Las Vegas, 4505 S. Maryland Parkway, Las Vegas,
702-895-2787; www.pac.unlv.edu

Performers as diverse as Herbie Hancock, Yo-Yo Ma, the Shanghai Ballet, Regina Carter and André Watts have all played here. In addition to classical musicians, jazz players and world dance troops, the center hosts lectures by visiting authors such as John Irving and journalists such as Cokie Roberts. The UNLV departments of theater and performing arts also mount shows on the several stages here.

UNLV SPORTS

Las Vegas, 702-739-3267; unlvrebels.cstv.com

A perennial contender in the NCAA's basketball tourney each March, the Runnin' Rebels' basketball team is the oldest team in a town that lacks deep roots. Football games come with pageantry from marching bands to tailgating parties. Basketball, November-March; football, August-November.

VIA BELLAGIO

Bellagio, 3600 Las Vegas Blvd. S., Las Vegas, 702-693-7111;
www.bellagiolasvegas.com

The sky-lit Via Bellagio provides fittingly luxe surroundings for high-end designer shops, including Giorgio Armani, Gucci, Prada, Chanel, Yves Saint Laurent, Hermes and Fred Leighton. Daily 11 a.m.-midnight.

XERISCAPE

4505 S. Maryland Parkway, Las Vegas, 702-895-1421

This 1½-acre garden proves that a landscape featuring desert plants can be a real eye-pleaser. You'll get lost in the serene setting as you wander the many paved pathways and cross over the wooden bridges scattered across the grounds. Many of the plants are indigenous to North America's four desert regions, while others were introduced from Australia, the Mediterranean, Mexico and South America. Daily 24 hours.

SPECIAL EVENTS
BOXING AT CAESARS PALACE

Caesars Palace, 3570 Las Vegas Blvd. S., Las Vegas, 702-731-7110, 877-427-7243;
www.caesarspalace.com

Nowhere is the sport of boxing cheered more vigorously than in Las Vegas, where bouts are often sponsored by Caesars Palace. Key title match-ups range from featherweight to heavyweight. Major boxing event weekends tend to flood Las Vegas with Saturday night visitors, making both beds and tickets hard to come by without advance planning.

MICHELIN CHAMPIONSHIP AT LAS VEGAS (LAS VEGAS INVITATIONAL)

Tournament Players Club at Summerlin, 1700 Village Center Circle, Las Vegas,
702-873-1010; www.pgatour.com/tournaments/r047/index.html

Host of the PGA event since 1992, the Tournament Players' Club at Summerlin was designed by architect Bobby Weed with input from player/consultant Fuzzy Zoeller. In addition to offering elevation changes and a variety of challenges, the course was built to accommodate spectators with natural amphitheaters and clear sightlines to the tees. October.

NATIONAL FINALS RODEO

Thomas & Mack Center, 4505 S. Maryland Parkway, Las Vegas,
719-593-8840, 888-388-3267; www.prorodeo.com

For 10 days in December, the Old West rides into Las Vegas with a round up of events, including bull riding, calf roping, barrel racing and steer wrestling. Only the top 15 money winners per event on the Professional Rodeo Cowboys Association competitive circuit earn the right to compete in this championship event, vying for millions in prize money. Despite being somewhat of a novelty act, this rodeo is one of the most sought-after tickets in Vegas. Ten days in early December.

WORLD SERIES OF POKER

Las Vegas, 702-382-1600; www.worldseriesofpoker.com

The number of competitors in this tournament has increased dramatically from fewer than 100 in the early days to more than 7,000 in recent years. The prize money has climbed proportionately to $20 million, more than $7.5 million of which the champion pocketed in 2005. A wide variety of games are played, and anyone age 21 or older can enter the competition, which continues for five suspenseful, nerve-wracking weeks. May-July.

HOTELS

★★ALEXIS PARK ALL-SUITE RESORT

375 E. Harmon Ave., Las Vegas, 702-796-3300, 800-582-2228; www.alexispark.com

495 rooms, all suites. High-speed Internet access. Restaurant, bar. Spa. Fitness Center. Business center. $

★★★BALLY'S LAS VEGAS

3645 Las Vegas Blvd., Las Vegas, 877-603-4390; www.ballyslv.com

A neon-lit tunnel ushers you from the heart of the Strip into Bally's. At more than 500 square feet each, the rooms are spacious and comfortable. The pool and spa are small compared to newer hotels, but Bally's is a good value in a prime location for those who still equate Vegas with showgirls. 2,814 rooms. High-speed Internet access. Eleven restaurants, five bars. Spa. Casino. Tennis. Golf. Pool. $$

★★★★BELLAGIO

3600 Las Vegas Blvd. S., Las Vegas, 702-693-7111, 888-987-6667;
www.bellagiolasvegas.com

A fantastic casino is only the beginning at this all-encompassing hotel, with a beautifully landscaped pool, arcade of fine shopping and a set of celebrity-chef restaurants. Visitors will gaze with awe at the exotic botanical gardens and magnificent hand-blown glass flowers by renowned artist Dale Chihuly in the lobby. Of course, the star of the show is the eight-acre man-made lake, where the popular fountain and light show takes place every half-hour. The Bellagio is also home to Cirque du Soleil's *O*, a mesmerizing aquatic performance. The rooms have luxurious fabrics and Italian marble. The only downside here is that you have to go through the casino to get everywhere. But then again, that's the point. 3,933 rooms. Wireless Internet access. Twelve restaurants, five bars. Spa. Casino. Shopping. **$$**

★★★CAESARS PALACE

3570 Las Vegas Blvd. S., Las Vegas, 702-731-7110, 866-227-5938;
www.caesarspalace.com
The Roman-themed Caesars was the Strip's first megaresort when it opened in 1966, and it remains one of the top hotels, mostly because it's always changing and challenging competitors to keep up. The hotel's swimming deck, modeled on Pompeii, surrounds the three pools. The lavish rooms have couches and marble bathrooms and a variety of suites are offered, some with high ceilings and whirlpool tubs. Prepare to spend at the Forum Shops. 3300 rooms. Wireless Internet access. Ten restaurants, eight bars. Spa. Airport transportation available. Casino. Business center. **$$**

★★CLARION HOTEL

325 E. Flamingo Road, Las Vegas, 702-732-9100, 800-424-6423;
www.clarionhotel.com
150 rooms. Restaurant, bar. Pool. Wireless Internet access. Fitness center. **$**

★★COURTYARD LAS VEGAS CONVENTION CENTER

3275 Paradise Road, Las Vegas, 702-791-3600, 800-661-1064; www.courtyard.com
149 rooms. High-speed Internet access. Restaurant. Pets not accepted; service animals allowed for persons with disabilities. **$$**

★★EMBASSY SUITES HOTEL LAS VEGAS

4315 Swenson St., Las Vegas, 702-795-2800, 800-362-2779;
www.embassysuites.com
220 rooms, all suites. High-speed Internet access. Restaurant, bar. Pool. Fitness center. **$$**

★FAIRFIELD INN

3850 Paradise Road, Las Vegas, 702-791-0899, 800-228-2800; www.fairfieldinn.com
129 rooms. Wireless Internet access. Pool. Fitness center. **$**

★FIESTA RANCHO STATION CASINO HOTEL

2400 N. Rancho Driv., Las Vegas, 702-631-7000, 888-899-7770; www.fiestacasino.com
100 rooms. High-speed Internet access. Five restaurants, two bars. Casino. Pool. **$**

★★FITZGERALDS HOTEL CASINO

301 Fremont St., Las Vegas, 702-388-2400, 800-274-5825;
www.fitzgeraldslasvegas.com
638 rooms. High-speed Internet access. Three restaurants, two bars. Casino. Pool. **$**

★★FLAMINGO LAS VEGAS

3555 Las Vegas Blvd. S., Las Vegas, 702-733-3111, 888-902-9929;
www.lv-flamingo.com

3,642 rooms. Wireless Internet access. Seven restaurants, seven bars. Spa. Airport transportation available. Casino. Pets accepted. Fitness center. Pool. **$$**

★★★★FOUR SEASONS HOTEL LAS VEGAS

3960 Las Vegas Blvd. S., Las Vegas, 702-632-5000, 877-632-5000;
www.fourseasons.com

The Four Seasons Hotel is a palatial refuge in glittering Las Vegas. Located on the southern tip of the Strip on the top floors of the Mandalay Bay Resort tower, it's close to the action but also provides a welcome respite when you need it. The sumptuous rooms at this non-gaming hotel have floor-to-ceiling windows overlooking the city. The glorious pool is a lush oasis with its swaying palm trees and attentive poolside service. The sublime spa offers innovated treatments. Steak lovers will enjoy Charlie Palmer Steak while the sun-filled Verandah offers a casual dining alternative. 424 rooms. High-speed Internet access. Two restaurants, bar. Spa. Fitness center. Pool. **$$$**

★★★GOLDEN NUGGET HOTEL AND CASINO

129 E. Fremont St., Las Vegas, 702-385-7111, 800-846-5336; www.goldennugget.com
This downtown hotel is the best of the bunch. You get Strip-style amenities, including a cabana-ringed pool with a 200,000-gallon shark tank and full-service spa, at discount prices, since everything is cheaper downtown, including the gambling minimums. Still, the Nugget upholds elegant standards with a marble-trimmed lobby just off raucous Fremont Street, and the rooms are comfortable and modern. The International Beer Bar pours 40 foreign brands while Zax serves an eclectic menu that includes everything from sushi to tostadas. 1915 rooms. High-speed wireless Internet access. Five restaurants, four bars. Spa. Casino. Pool. Golf. **$$**

★★★HARD ROCK HOTEL CASINO

4455 Paradise Road, Las Vegas, 702-693-5000, 800-473-7625;
www.hardrockhotel.com

A youthful party atmosphere prevails in the memorabilia-strewn complex. About a mile off the Strip, Hard Rock generates its own fun, particularly when a big act is booked at the Joint concert hall. That's when the swim-up blackjack tables by the pool really fill up and it's harder to nab at table at Nobu, the celebrated sushi spot. Rooms feature French doors that open to views of the Strip or mountains (try to get one facing the city), Bose stereos and bathrooms with stainless-steel sinks. Simon Kitchen and Bar—the chef has won *Iron Chef*—is a great spot for dining. 647 rooms. Wireless Internet access. Five restaurants, two bars. Spa. Casino., Pool. **$$**

★★★HARRAH'S HOTEL & CASINO LAS VEGAS

3475 Las Vegas Blvd. S., Las Vegas, 800-214-9110; www.harrahslasvegas.com
The gaming powerhouse Harrah's runs this Strip hotel, where the emphasis is on the casino. The carnival theme spills out to an outdoor plaza that features entertainers, trinket vendors and snack booths. Spacious but rather bland rooms are lodged in a 35-story tower behind the gaming floor, although guests spend most of their time at the many tables, Olympic-size swimming pool, boutique spa and seven eateries.

Entertainer Rita Rudner performs at the showroom here. 2,526 rooms. High-speed Internet access. Seven restaurants, four bars. Spa. Casino. Pool. $

★★★JW MARRIOTT LAS VEGAS RESORT & SPA
221 N. Rampart Blvd., Las Vegas, 702-869-7777, 877-869-8777; www.marriott.com
Fifteen minutes from the Strip, the JW Marriott Las Vegas Resort offers a tranquil alternative to the neon lights. Set on 50 acres of lush tropical gardens against the backdrop of the Red Rock Mountains, this resort is lavish and comfortable. Guest rooms include marble-paved entries, premium bedding and oversized bathrooms. The shimmering pool is an inviting spot to enjoy the warm weather while eight championship courses lure golfers away from their lounge chairs. The deluxe European-style spa is the perfect retreat while those who prefer blackjack to body treatments head for a nearby casino. 545 rooms. High-speed Internet access. Restaurant, bar. Spa. Pool. Golf. Casino. $$$$

★LA QUINTA INN
3970 Paradise Road, Las Vegas, 702-796-9000, 800-531-5900; www.laquinta.com
285 rooms. Complimentary continental breakfast. Airport transportation available. Pets accepted. High-speed Internet access $

★★LAS VEGAS CLUB HOTEL
18 E. Fremont St., Las Vegas, 702-385-1664, 800-634-6532; www.playlv.com
408 rooms. Restaurant, bar. Casino. Pool. High-speed Internet access. $

★★★LAS VEGAS HILTON
3000 Paradise Road, Las Vegas, 702-732-5111, 888-732-7117; www.lvhilton.com
This popular, family-friendly Las Vegas destination is adjacent to the Convention Center. Set on 80 lushly landscaped acres, this 30-story hotel has more than a dozen restaurants, a spa and an enormous sports book. The theater—everyone from Barry Manilow to Tony Bennett plays here—is one of the great old showrooms. 3,000 rooms. High-speed Internet access. Fifteen restaurants, nine bars. Spa. Casino. Tennis. Fitness center. $$

★★★LUXOR HOTEL & CASINO
3900 Las Vegas Blvd. S., Las Vegas, 702-262-4444, 888-777-0188; www.luxor.com
This big, shiny Vegas wonder certainly stands out on the Strip. Allegedly the light beam on top of the pyramid can be seen from outer space. "Inclinators" transport you to your room in the main tower where you'll find an Egyptian motif and a sloping wall, a constant reminder that you are, in fact, staying in a pyramid. Rooms in the tower next door are newer and don't require inclinators. King Tutankhamun's Tomb and Museum, a replica of the King Tut's tomb, is a lot of fun. Kids will love the arcade floor. 4,407 rooms. Restaurant, bar. Spa. Casino. Wireless Internet access. Pool. Golf. $

★★MAIN STREET STATION
200 N. Main St., Las Vegas, 702-387-1896, 800-465-0711; www.mainstreetcasino.com
406 rooms. Wireless Internet access. Two restaurants, two bars. Airport transportation available. Casino. Pool. $

★★★MANDALAY BAY RESORT AND CASINO

3950 Las Vegas Blvd. S., Las Vegas, 702-632-7777, 877-632-7800;
www.mandalaybay.com

Even in over-the-top Las Vegas, Mandalay Bay exceeds expectations. Located at the southern end of the Strip, this all-encompassing resort has rooms with a tropical flavor, and the casino is a paradise of lush foliage and flowing water. The resort is known for its Shark Reef aquarium. There's also a variety of entertainment, from live music to Broadway-style shows, as well as 13 restaurants. The more affordable but still luxurious rooms in the main hotel have comfortable beds and slate bathrooms. 3,215 rooms. Thirteen restaurants, bar. Spa. Beach. Casino. Golf. Fitness center. **$$**

★★★MARRIOTT SUITES LAS VEGAS

325 Convention Center Drive, Las Vegas, 702-650-2000, 800-228-9290;
www.marriott.com

Adjacent to the Las Vegas Convention Center and near the famous Las Vegas Strip, this is a good choice for business travelers. Rooms feature multiple data ports and workstations. And after a long day of conventions, you can hit the pool or fitness center. 278 rooms, all suites. Restaurant, bar. Airport transportation available. High-speed Internet access. **$**

★★★MGM GRAND HOTEL & CASINO

3799 Las Vegas Blvd. S., Las Vegas, 702-891-7777, 877-880-0880;
www.mgmgrand.com

The largest hotel on the Strip (and perhaps the world—this place is *huge*), the MGM Grand virtually pulses with Las Vegas energy. The Art Deco rooms are nice—but you're not likely to ever be in them, as there's so much to see and do here. In the casino, lions roam about a glassed-in habitat with waterfalls. The outdoor pool includes a current-fed river and the spa specializes in cutting-edge treatments. MGM eateries Nobhill Tavern and Craftsteak are some of the best in the city. Big-name headliners like Cher and David Copperfield often play the MGM, and the French act *Le Femme* updates the showgirl revue. The party crowd crows for the dance club Studio 54 and the lounge Tabu. For a more luxurious experience, check into the ultrachic Skylofts at MGM Grand (a boutique hotel-within-the-hotel offering contemporary, full-service lofts perched on the top levels of the building) or the Signature at MGM Grand (modern junior suites with their own separate entrance). 5,018 rooms. Wireless Internet access. Nineteen restaurants, seven bars. Children's activity center. Spa. Airport transportation available. Casino. **$$**

★★★MIRAGE HOTEL AND CASINO

3400 Las Vegas Blvd. S., Las Vegas, 702-791-7111, 800-456-4564; www.mirage.com

The Strip-side volcano—which erupts every hour at night—marks the Mirage and its exotic theme. A huge aquarium serves as the backdrop for the registration desk, the route to room elevators passes through a cascade of jungle foliage and a lavish pool deck is ringed by towering palms. Though Siegfried & Roy are no longer here, you can see their animals in the garden. The elegant and cheerful rooms feature spacious, marble-trimmed baths. 3,323 rooms. Wireless Internet access. Ten restaurants, three bars. Spa. Casino. Golf. Pool. **$**

★★★MONTE CARLO RESORT AND CASINO

3770 Las Vegas Blvd. S., Las Vegas, 702-730-7777, 888-529-4828;
www.montecarlo.com

Modeled on the sophisticated European republic of Monaco, this resort on the Strip is relatively toned down in comparison to its neighbor Bellagio. Its quiet opulence, with marble floors and chandeliers, is its chief asset and a significant contrast to the party set. But the Monte Carlo couldn't claim a piece of Strip real estate without its considerable amenities: four pools, including a lazy river and a wave pool, a luxurious spa and seven eateries. Standard rooms are bright and attractively furnished in cherry wood and Italian marble and granite. Crowd-pleasing magician Lance Burton is the house entertainer. 3,002 rooms. Wireless Internet access. Four restaurants, bar. Spa. Indoor pool. Casino. Tennis. Business center. Fitness center. Golf. $$

★★★NEW YORK-NEW YORK HOTEL AND CASINO

3790 Las Vegas Blvd. S., Las Vegas, 800-689-1797, 866-815-4365;
www.nynyhotelcasino.com

With its Manhattan skyline façade, New York-New York does a cheerful imitation of the Big Apple. The main-floor casino mimics Central Park with trees, bridges and brooks while Coney Island beckons guests with carnival games and the thrilling Manhattan Express roller coaster. Even the rooms are cramped—another ode to the city that never sleeps? The pool is a relatively straightforward affair relative to others on the strip. Il Fornaio does fine Italian. 2,034 rooms. High-speed Internet access. Eight restaurants, two bars. Spa. Airport transportation available. Casino. Business center. Pool. $

★★ORLEANS CASINO & HOTEL

4500 W. Tropicana Ave., Las Vegas, 702-365-7111, 800-675-3267;
www.orleanscasino.com

1,886 rooms. High-speed Internet access. Restaurant, bar. Children's activity center. Spa. Casino. Business center. Fitness center. $$

★★PALACE STATION HOTEL

2411 W. Sahara Ave., Las Vegas, 702-367-2411, 800-634-3101;
www.palacestation.com

1,021 rooms. Restaurant, bar. Casino. Wireless Internet access. Golf. Pool. Business center. Fitness center. $

★★★THE PALMS

4321 W. Flamingo Road, Las Vegas, 702-942-7777, 866-942-7777; www.palms.com

It's like a party in the lobby of this boutique hotel. The rooftop Ghost Bar and the swanky 9 restaurant attract a lively crowd. The pool is also a scene and there's 95,000 square feet of gaming action. For a little quiet, there's a 14-screen movie theater. The inviting rooms have supremely comfortable beds, although the hotel is known for its suites, from the 1960s-style bachelor and bachelorette rooms to the *Real World: Las Vegas* residence. 710 rooms. Wireless Internet access. Eight restaurants, bar. Spa. Outdoor pool, whirlpool. Business center. Casino. $$$

★★★★ THE PALAZZO RESORT HOTEL CASINO

3325 Las Vegas Blvd. South, Las Vegas, 702-607-7777; www.palazzolasvegas.com

One of the newest kids on the block—if a megaresort with more than 3,000 rooms can be considered a kid—this sister property of the Venetian opened in January 2008 at an estimated cost of $1.9 billion. The guest rooms in the 50-story tower start at 720-square-feet and are decorated in a contemporary Italian style complete with remote-controlled Roman shades, Egyptian linens from Anichini and curtains to block out that searing desert sun. The Shoppes at Palazzo has more than 50 stores. Not in the mood for shopping? Then head to the many restaurants on the premises— celebrity chefs such as Mario Batali, Wolfgang Puck, Emeril Lagasse and Charlie Trotter have all opened signature restaurants here. 3,066 rooms, all suites. Wireless Internet access. Restaurant, bar. Airport transportation available. Fitness center. Pool. Spa. Business center. $$

★★★PARIS LAS VEGAS

3655 Las Vegas Blvd. S., Las Vegas, 877-603-4386; www.parislasvegas.com

A half-scale model of the Eiffel Tower is the landmark attraction at Paris Las Vegas. There's also the "Arc de Triomphe" and costumed landscape painters fronting the Strip-side pavilion. The scene continues inside, where three legs of the Eiffel rest in the casino and a cobblestone street winds its way through the shopping arcade. Rooms underscore the theme with French fabrics and custom furniture. Request a Strip view to see the dancing Bellagio fountains across the street. Most of the restaurants here are French, including the charming Mon Ami Gabi, which features outdoor dining on a terrace overlooking the Las Vegas Boulevard. 2,916 rooms, Restaurants, bar. Casino. Business center. Spa. Golf. Pool. $$

★★★PLANET HOLLYWOOD RESORT & CASINO

3667 Las Vegas Blvd. S., Las Vegas, 702-785-5555, 866-919-7472;
www.planethollywood.com

This resort may have a Los Angeles theme, but the experience is pure [Las] Vegas. The glitzy, nightclub-like casino features 100,000 square feet of gaming space with more than 90 gaming tables, 2,800 slots and poker room with daily tournaments. It may not be Rodeo Drive but the Miracle Mile offers 170 shops. Mandara Spa can undo the stress of an all-night gambling spree with its selection of relaxing massages, facials, aroma stone therapies and body wraps. After a busy day, guests can retire to luxurious rooms fit for a movie star that feature deluxe amenities like marble baths with separate showers and tubs and 27-inch televisions. For a night away from the gambling table, guests can take in a show like *Stomp Out Loud.* 2,567 rooms. Wireless Internet access. Six restaurants, four bars. Spa. Casino. Fitness center. Pool. Golf. $$

★★★RED ROCK CASINO, RESORT & SPA

11011 W. Charleston Blvd., Las Vegas, 702-797-7777, 866-767-7773;
www.redrocklasvegas.com

An upbeat, contemporary retreat off the Strip, this resort and casino offers an upscale experience away from the crowds. Rooms are crisp and modern with flatscreen TVs, iPod stations and luxury linens. The 10 different restaurants serve up everything from fresh oysters to Mexican cuisine. The adventure spa offers a unique opportunity to get outdoors and experience the Red Rock country beyond Las Vegas, with hiking, rock climbing, horseback riding and more. 828 rooms. Pets accepted; some restrictions. Wireless Internet access. Nine restaurants, four bars. Children's activity center. Spa. Airport transportation available. Casino. Pool. Golf. $$

★★★RIO ALL-SUITE HOTEL AND CASINO

3700 W. Flamingo Road, Las Vegas, 866-746-7671; www.playrio.com
The all-suite Rio furnishes spacious rooms with sitting areas and floor-to-ceiling views of the Strip. There are better rooms in Vegas, but if you want a celebratory atmosphere, this is it. A carnival parades above the casino floor seven times a day. Rosemary's restaurant is acclaimed by local gourmets. You won't find waterfalls and Roman statues out by the pool, but there are four of them to choose from. 2,522 rooms, all suites. High-speed Internet access. 13 restaurants, five bars. Spa. Casino. Swimming. Golf. Fitness center. Business center. $$$

★★SAHARA HOTEL & CASINO

2535 Las Vegas Blvd. S., Las Vegas, 702-737-2654, 866-382-8884; www.saharavegas.com
1,720 rooms. High-speed Internet access. Five restaurants, four bars. Casino. Pool. Business center. Spa. $

★★SANTA FE STATION HOTEL

4949 N. Rancho Drive, Las Vegas, 702-658-4900, 866-767-7771; www.stationcasinos.com
200 rooms. Twelve restaurants, four bars. Whirlpool. Casino. Pool. Golf. Spa. $

★★★★ THE SIGNATURE AT MGM GRAND LAS VEGAS

145 E. Harmon Ave., Las Vegas, 877-612-2121; www.signaturemgmgrand.com
Get away from it all while remaining in the heart of it. That's the idea behind this seductive all-suite retreat within the palatial MGM Grand. There's no gaming or smoking in these three towers, but with a 24-hour concierge, exclusive private pool and dining options, there's plenty of service. Of course, you can always head over to the MGM Grand to catch a show, try your luck at the casino or bliss out at the spa. 1,728 suites. Wireless Internet access. Restaurant, bar. Fitness center. Pool. Business center. $$$

★★SILVERTON HOTEL CASINO

3333 Blue Diamond Road, Las Vegas, 702-263-7777, 866-946-4373; www.silvertoncasino.com
300 rooms. Two restaurants, three bars. Casino. Pool. $

★★ST. TROPEZ ALL-SUITE HOTEL

455 E. Harmon Ave., Las Vegas, 702-369-5400, 800-666-5400; www.sttropezlasvegas.com
149 rooms, all suites. Complimentary continental breakfast. Wireless Internet access. Restaurant, bar. Fitness room. Pool. Whirlpool. Airport transportation available. Pets accepted. $

NEVADA

★ ★ ★ ★

★★★★★THE TOWER SUITES AT WYNN LAS VEGAS

3131 Las Vegas Blvd. S., Las Vegas, 702-770-7100, 877-321-9966;
www.wynnlasvegas.com

As if the regular guest rooms at the ultraposh Wynn resort weren't luxurious enough, the 50-story Wynn features refined, apartment-like Tower Suites located in their own tower that raise the bar for luxury resorts. Upon arrival, guests are whisked up in private elevators to the suites, which overlook either the city lights or the Wynn Country Club—the only golf course on the Strip. With a private gated entrance, priority access to high-stakes tables and slots in the 111,000-square-foot casino, and access to an exclusive pool, guests are given the star treatment. Ranging in size from 640 to nearly 2,000 square feet, the refined rooms have the feel of an intimate residence. Suites feature replicas of artwork from Steve Wynn's impressive collection, floor-to-ceiling windows covered by sleek, electronic draperies and 42-inch flatscreen LCD televisions (not to mention a 13-inch version int he marble bathroom). A restful night's sleep is guaranteed on the signature Wynn bed, with pillow-top mattresses and 320-count European linens. Tableau, the restaurant in the Tower and Suites, turns out impeccable American cuisine. (Dinner is served to all hotel guests, but breakfast and lunch are reserved for suites-only customers). 653 rooms. Wireless Internet Access. Restaurant, bar. Spa. Casino. Golf. Pool. Business center. $$$$

★★★TREASURE ISLAND (TI)

3300 Las Vegas Blvd. S., Las Vegas, 702-894-7111, 800-288-7206;
www.treasureisland.com

The South Seas pirate theme of Treasure Island—now known simply at TI—makes it appealing for families. The sinking of a British frigate in the *Sirens of TI* show outside the hotel draws crowds here every night (as does Cirque du Soleil's show *Mystere*). The hotel has modern, urban décor. Done in beige and gold hues, the spacious guest rooms provide a tranquil respite from the theme of the place. However, the pool area follows the penchant for themes with a tropical one, complete with tiki accents and outdoor dining. 2,665 rooms. Wireless Internet access. Eight restaurants, four bars. Spa. Casino. Golf. Pool. Shopping. $$

★★★ TRUMP INTERNATIONAL HOTEL & TOWER LAS VEGAS

2000 Fashion Show Drive, Las Vegas, 702-982-0000, 877-878-6711;
www.trumplasvegashotel.com

Trump International Hotel & Tower Las Vegas has The Donald's signature gold gilding written all over it—as evidenced by the 24-karat gold glass windows that wrap around the 64-story building. Located just off the Strip and adjacent to the Fashion Show Mall, the non-gaming Trump is another jewel in a neighborhood that also houses the Wynn. The condominium suites feature floor-to-ceiling windows offering panoramic views of the city, custom-designed furnishings in warm earth tones that play off the white duvets, and a marble bathroom with separate shower and jet-stream tub. Not only is the refrigerator custom-stocked, but each guest is assigned a Trump Attaché to make sure every whim is granted. Or if you're too tired to head to the hotel's restaurant DJT, request an in-room chef to prepare a meal in your personal kitchen, which has appliances by Sub-Zero, Wolf and Bosch. End the day by unwinding at The Spa at Trump. 1,282 rooms, all suites. Wireless Internet access. Restaurant, bar. Fitness center. Pool. Spa. Business center. Pets accepted. **$$**

★★★★THE VENETIAN RESORT HOTEL CASINO

3355 Las Vegas Blvd. S., Las Vegas, 702-414-1000, 877-883-6423; www.venetian.com
From the masterfully re-created Venetian landmark buildings to the frescoed ceilings and gilded details, the Venetian faithfully mimics the splendor that is Venice in the heart of the Las Vegas Strip. Guests walk down winding alleys and glide past ornate architecture in gondolas. (In fact, you can take a gondola ride with a singing gondolier.) From the moment you enter through the Doge's Palace and walk through the lobby to the casino and its frescoes, you'll be impressed. The suites are large and luxurious, with sunken living rooms and walk-in closets. Some of the biggest names in American cuisine operate award-winning restaurants here. The Venetian's Guggenheim showcases rotating exhibits while the Canyon Ranch Spa offers the same pampering treatments as the famed spa in Arizona. The Grand Canal Shoppes is a *Who's Who* of designers, from Chanel to Jimmy Choo. 4,027 rooms, all suites. 19 restaurants, six bars. Spa. Casino. Pool. Golf. Business center. **$$**

★★★THE WESTIN CASUARINA HOTEL & SPA

160 E. Flamingo Road, Las Vegas, 702-836-5900, 866-837-4215; www.westin.com
Comfortable accommodations with numerous business amenities, a large casino and an ideal location near the Strip and convention center make the Westin an ideal destination for both corporate and leisure travelers. This hotel caters to the modern traveler in both look and feel, and the rooms and suites show off a stylish contemporary design. Westin signature amenities, including the comfortable Heavenly Bed and soothing Heavenly Bath, are among the many pluses of a visit to this hotel. The hotel's own Starbucks is a perk. 826 rooms. Restaurant, bar. Spa. Casino. Pets accepted. High-speed Internet access. Pool. Fitness center. **$**

★★★★WYNN LAS VEGAS

3131 Las Vegas Blvd. S., Las Vegas, 702-770-7100, 888-320-9966;
www.wynnlasvegas.com
You won't find any world wonders or replicas here. This is the haute version of Las Vegas. The rooms, with deep orange walls, impressive art work and richly appointed couches, are decorated to make you feel like you're staying in someone's apartment in London or Manhattan. Here you can open the drapes with the push of a button and soak in the tub while watching the flatscreen LCD in the bathroom. On the main level there are two spacious pools, a European-style bathing pool and the Cabana Bar, where you can play poolside blackjack in season. (Guests of the suites enjoy two quieter pools.) Then there's the championship golf course and the boutiques. Shops include Manolo Blahnik, Dior, Louis Vuitton and Oscar de la Renta. There's even a Ferrari dealership, and some of the country's most revered chefs—including Daniel Boulud, Alessandro Stratta and Paul Bartolotta—have opened restaurants here. 2,716 rooms. 18 restaurants, bars. Spa. Casino. Pool. Golf. High-speed Internet access. **$$$$**

RESTAURANTS

★★★★★ALEX

3131 Las Vegas Blvd. S., Las Vegas, 702-248-3463, 888-352-3463;
www.wynnlasvegas.com

Famed chef Alessandro Stratta has brought his sumptuous French cuisine to this stunning restaurant at the Wynn, which has a grand hourglass-shaped staircase, chandeliers and mahogany furniture. The artfully presented dishes might include Robiola cheese agnolotti with black truffles and aged Parmigiano or the Dover sole with a potato crust, artichokes and tomato confit. Desserts by pastry chef Jenifer Witte are just as imaginative and special. Request one of two private seating areas overlooking a private courtyard or reserve the popular chef's table. French menu. Dinner. Thursday-Monday. Bar. Reservations recommended. Valet parking. Outdoor seating. $$$$

★★★ALIZE

4321 W. Flamingo Road, Las Vegas, 702-951-7000; www.alizelv.com

This refined French restaurant is located on the top floor of the Palms Casino Resort. Diners will enjoy a 280-degree view through the floor-to-ceiling windows as they indulge in the French creations of chef/owner André Rochat. Dishes include pan-seared Muscovy duck with peach and foie gras tart, and grilled milk-fed veal chop with artichoke, morel and Gruyère cannelloni. The two-story-high wine tower provides plenty of choices for the perfect dinner pairing. A jacket isn't required, but jeans are discouraged. French menu. Dinner. Bar. Business casual attire. Reservations recommended. Valet parking. Casual Attire. $$$

★★ALL AMERICAN BAR & GRILLE

Rio Hotel & Casino, 3700 W. Flamingo Road, Las Vegas,
702-777-7923; www.harrahs.com

American, Pan-Asian, Tex-Mex menu. Lunch, dinner. Bar. Casual attire. Valet parking. $$$

★★AMERICA

3790 Las Vegas Blvd. S., Las Vegas, 702-740-6451; www.nynyhotelcasino.com

American menu. Breakfast, lunch, dinner, late-night. Open 24 hours. $$

★★★AQUAKNOX

3355 S. Las Vegas Blvd. S., Las Vegas, 702-414-3772; www.venetian.com

The Venetian's Restaurant Row offers an eatery to satisfy every culinary craving, with AquaKnox, sibling to the popular Dallas eatery, positioned to please seafood-seeking diners. A raw bar is stocked with oysters and stone crab claws. Other offerings include caviar, grilled lobster with drawn herb butter and butternut squash soup with duck confit. The exhibition kitchen provides a bustling focal point for the sleek dining room, which also includes a water-encased walk-in wine cellar. Seafood menu. Bar. Casual attire. Dinner. Reservations recommended. Valet parking. $$$

★★★★AUREOLE

3950 Las Vegas Blvd. S., Las Vegas, 702-632-7401; www.aureolerestaurant.com

A branch of chef Charlie Palmer's New York original, Aureole wows patrons with its centerpiece four-story wine tower. Be sure to order a bottle just to see the catsuit-clad climber, suspended by ropes, locate your vintage. The extensive wine list complements Palmer's seasonal contemporary American cuisine, typified by dishes such as Peking duck with foie gras ravioli and roast pheasant with sweet potato gnocchi. The modern but romantic room, with encircling booths, sets the stage for event dining at Mandalay Bay. American menu. Dinner. Bar. Reservations recommended. Valet parking. $$$

★★★BED AND BREAKFAST RISTORANTE

Venetian, 3355 Las Vegas Blvd. S., 702-266-9977; www.venetian.com

It used to be you could only find celebrity chef Mario Batali's restaurants in New York City, but he's expanded to Las Vegas with a few new restaurants. B&B Ristorante (the other "B" being his partner, Joe Bastianich) is a small space where you might be bumping elbows with your neighbors, but the coziness adds to the jovial atmosphere. Batali's cuisine is simple, rustic Italian with a fine-dining edge. In an Italian trattoria such as this one, charcuterie should definitely be on your radar, as some come from Batali's father's popular salumeria Salumi in Seattle, and others are made fresh in house by executive chef Zach Allen. More adventurous options, including the light and airy lambs' brain Francobolli (they're said to sell more of this dish in Las Vegas than they do in New York), and a pasta tasting menu is available for those who can't choose. The wine list, featuring mostly the Bastianich label, is extensive, especially as far as—you guessed it—Italian wines. Italian menu. Dinner. Bar. Casual attire. Reservations recommended. Valet parking. $$$

★★★BARTOLOTTA RISTORANTE DI MARE

3131 Las Vegas Blvd. S., Las Vegas, 702-248-3463, 888-352-3463;
www.wynnlasvegas.com

Guests will feel like they've escaped to Italy when visiting Bartolotta. The dining room is a grand, two-story space with enchanting views of the lake through floor-to-ceiling windows and magnificent frescos. Chef Paul Bartolotta, whose previous efforts earned him a nod from the James Beard Foundation, insists that all seafood be flown in fresh from Europe and Italy the day before. Appetizers include regional favorites like tiny clams with garlic white wine and warm seafood salad. Don't miss such stunners as the seafood risotto and linguine with clams in a white wine garlic sauce.Italian, seafood menu. Dinner. Bar. Business casual attire. Reservations recommended. Valet parking. Outdoor seating. $$$$

★★BLUE AGAVE

4321 W. Flamingo Road, Las Vegas, 702-942-7777;
www.thepalmslasvegas.com

Latin American menu., Lunch, dinner. Bar. Casual attire. Valet parking. $$

NEVADA

★
★
★
★
★

★★★BOUCHON

3355 Las Vegas Blvd. S., Las Vegas, 702-414-6200;
www.bouchonbistro.com

Star chef Thomas Keller has brought delicious French bistro fare—"bouchon" describes a particular style of French café—to this sophisticated restaurant in the Venezia Tower of the Venetian Resort Hotel Casino. The beautiful interior, by famed designer Adam D. Tihany, sets a romantic mood with an impressive French pewter bar, colorful mosaic flooring, deep blue velvet banquettes, antique light fixtures and truly gorgeous hand-painted mural. The restaurant is open for breakfast and dinner, and offers classic bistro dishes such as steak frites, roasted chicken, pot de crème and profiteroles. French bistro menu. Breakfast, lunch (afternoon oyster bar), dinner, Saturday-Sunday brunch. Bar. Business casual attire. Jacket required. Reservations recommended. Valet parking. Outdoor seating. **$$$**

★★★★BRADLEY OGDEN

3570 Las Vegas Blvd. S., Las Vegas, 877-346-4642;
www.caesarspalace.com

Bradley Ogden's eponymous restaurant at Caesars Palace—his first outside of California—is a sure bet. Although this modern Las Vegas location is a world away from the farms and ranches Ogden depends on when preparing his innovative take on American cuisine, no expense is spared in bringing it all in. Dishes include oak-grilled lamb rack with fava beans and cumin spaetzle, and hot and cold foie gras with kumquats. American menu. Dinner Wednesday-Sunday, Bar. Business casual attire. Reservations recommended. Valet parking. **$$$$**

★BUFFET AT BELLAGIO

3600 Las Vegas Blvd. S., Las Vegas, 702-693-7111; www.bellagio.com
American and International menu. Breakfast (Monday-Friday), lunch (Monday-Friday), dinner (Sunday–Thursday). Bar. Children's menu. Casual attire. **$$**

★★BUZIO'S

3700 W. Flamingo Road, Las Vegas, 702-777-7923; www.playrio.com
American, Seafood menu. Dinner (Wednesday-Sunday). Bar. Casual attire. Outdoor seating. Reservations recommended. **$$$**

★★★CARNEVINO

3325 Las Vegas Blvd. S., Palazzo Hotel, Las Vegas, 702-789-4141;
www.carnevino.com

The first steakhouse venture of the ubiquitous restaurateur duo, Mario Batali and Joe Bastianich, CarneVino opened in January 2008. With Batali protégé Zach Allen at the helm as executive chef, the restaurant's focus is on high-quality American meat and an international wine list. The menu lists details such as that CarneVino "buys the best organic, free-range veal from Marshal Farms in Pennsylvania" and that their beef "is often beyond regular USDA prime standards for marbling and flavor and is hormone and antibiotic free." So go ahead and relish every bite of that 12-ounce filet. Italian steakhouse menu. Lunch, dinner. Bar. Casual attire. Reservations recommended. Valet parking. $33-$75.

★CATHAY HOUSE

5300 W. Spring Mountain Road, Las Vegas, 702-876-3838;
www.cathayhouse.com

Chinese menu. Lunch, dinner. Bar. Casual attire. $$

★★★CHINOIS

3500 Las Vegas Blvd. S., Las Vegas, 702-737-9700; www.wolfgangpuck.com

This spin-off of chef Wolfgang Puck's acclaimed Chinois in Santa Monica, located in the Forum Shops at Caesars Palace, features similar Asian-fusion fare. The broad menu includes sushi and sashimi, dim sum, wok-fried meat and vegetable recipes such as kung pao chicken, and Asian noodle dishes such as pad Thai. Asian menu. Lunch, dinner. Bar. Children's menu. Casual attire. Valet parking, Reservations recommended. $$$

★★★THE COUNTRY CLUB

3131 Las Vegas Blvd. S., Las Vegas, 702-248-3463, 888-352-3463;
www.wynnlasvegas.com

Executive chef Rene Lenger brings his culinary talents from New York City to the Wynn at this hideaway overlooking the championship golf course. He knows the desires of a steak lover and his menu does not disappoint. Lenger compliments the superb cuts of meat with tasty appetizers such as jumbo lump crab cake, Maine lobster bisque and green and white asparagus salad with prosciutto di Parma and lemon aioli. Sides include truffle cream spinach and buttermilk onion rings. Several fish dishes are also offered. Steak menu. Breakfast, lunch (Monday-Friday), dinner, Saturday-Sunday brunch. Bar. Business casual attire. Reservations recommended. Valet parking. Outdoor seating. $$$$

★★★CRAFTSTEAK

3799 Las Vegas Blvd. S., Las Vegas, 702-891-7318; www.mgmgrand.com

After earning the James Beard Foundation's 2002 best new restaurant nod for Craft in New York, chef Tom Colicchio—you might know him as a judge on Bravo's *Top Chef*—spun off this version in the MGM Grand. With an emphasis on top-shelf ingredients from boutique farms and artisanal producers, the à la carte menu incorporates fish, shellfish, poultry, veal, lamb and pork as well as steak. A raw bar, generous salads and a roster of veggies supplement the main items. Many dishes are served in small skillets or pots that facilitate sharing. The handsome room features generous circular booths and open sightlines for spotting the celebrities who frequently dine here. Steak menu. Dinner. Bar. Business casual attire. Reservations recommended. $$$$

★★★CUT

Palazzo Las Vegas, 3325 Las Vegas Blvd. S., 702-607-6300;
www.palazzolasvegas.com

Wolfgang Puck's latest venture is a steakhouse at the Palazzo, and some are saying it's the best new steakhouse in Las Vegas. The 160-seat metallic dining room manages to feel simultaneously industrial and warm thanks to well-chosen appointments and color schemes. In the adjacent bar, guests can enjoy custom cocktails and the

NEVADA

★
★
★
★

smaller "Rough Cuts" bar menu. The classic steakhouse menu is definitely given the Puck treatment. It features both Nebraska corn-fed and pure Japanese Wagyu beef, and innovative and fascinating dishes such as rotisserie duckling with a lavender and thyme-honey gastrique allow the chef's true talents to shine through. Other hits from the menu include the "Indian-spiced" Kobe short ribs, slow cooked for eight hours and finished with puree of curried cauliflower. Steak menu. Dinner. Bar. Casual attire. Reservations recommended. $$$$

★★★DANIEL BOULUD BRASSERIE

3131 Las Vegas Blvd. S., Las Vegas, 702-248-3463, 888-352-3463;
www.wynnlasvegas.com

Daniel Boulud Brasserie provides diners with a modern and romantic dining experience. The room is divided into intimate sections with antique farmhouse windows and a kitchen that is encased in dark, tinted glass. Chef Daniel Boulud and chef Philippe Rispoli provide a diverse menu including dishes for two, à la carte items and a prix fixe option. A selection of recipes including cheeses and seafood are prepared in the restaurant's brick oven. Specialty dishes include the steak au poivre, wild mushroom paté with homemade pickles and a roasted chicken with tarragon jus. The cocoa-crusted profiteroles with rocky road ice cream and bittersweet chocolate are heavenly. American, French menu. Dinner. Bar. Business casual attire. Reservations recommended. Valet parking. Outdoor seating. $$$$

★★★DELMONICO STEAKHOUSE

3355 Las Vegas Blvd. S., Las Vegas, 702-414-3737; www.emerils.com

Exuberant New Orleans chef Emeril Lagasse is behind this meat-centric dining room in the Venetian Resort Hotel and Casino, a sequel to the Crescent City original. Luxe appointments—a baby grand piano, French doors and linen-topped tables—make this a seductive affair of indulgence. All the steakhouse standards make the menu, along with specialties such as Creole-marinated rack of lamb, châteaubriand for two and charred sirloin. Cajun/Creole menu. Lunch, dinner. Bar. Casual attire. Reservations recommended. Valet parking. $$$

★★★DJT

Trump International Hotel & Tower,2000 Fashion Show Drive, Las Vegas,
702-476-7358; www.trumplasvegashotel.com

It's all about the art of the meal at this handsome restaurant inside Trump International Hotel & Tower. The dining room, with rich colors and intimate seating, recalls the glamour of the 1930s. Upscale and sophisticated contemporary American cuisine blends flavors and cooking styles from France, Asia and the Mediterranean. Even if you can't make a deal like a Trump, you can eat like one—Ivanka's caviar breakfast and the Donald's favorite ice cream sundae are among the selections on the menu. American menu. Breakfast, dinner, Sunday brunch. Closed Monday. Bar. Reservations recommended. Valet parking. $$$

★★EMBERS

3535 Las Vegas Blvd. S., Las Vegas, 702-731-3311; www.imperialpalace.com

Steak, seafood menu. Dinner. Bar. Casual attire. $$

★★★EMERIL'S NEW ORLEANS FISH HOUSE

3799 Las Vegas Blvd. S., Las Vegas, 702-891-7374; www.emerils.com

Big Easy chef Emeril Lagasse runs this Louisiana kitchen at the MGM Grand. Wrought-iron gates, a stone courtyard and French doors evoke historic New Orleans. But the star is the bold food for which the gregarious chef is renowned. Creole-spiced lobster, pecan-roasted redfish and cedar plank steak exemplify Emeril's use of big flavors. Finish off with the swoonworthy banana cream pie. Seafood, Cajun menu. Lunch, dinner. Bar. Business casual attire. Reservations recommended. Valet parking. **$$**

★★★ENOTECA SAN MARCO

3355 Las Vegas Blvd. S., The Venetian Las Vegas, 702-266-9969; www.enotecasanmarco.com

Yet another success in the Bastianich-Batali empire—which includes Babbo, Lupa, Otto and others in New York—Enoteca San Marco excels in serving casual dishes, like small plates and pizzas, made for sharing. There are, of course, more substantial entrées and pastas as well—for those who didn't learn how in kindergarten. The laidback atmosphere is as appropriate for a long, leisurely lunch as it is for a friendly, informal dinner. Very similar to the menu at Otto in New York, this restaurant is best sampled with a slightly adventurous spirit and an appreciation for the quality ingredients and simple Italian cooking that has won Batali so many fans. Italian menu. Lunch, dinner. Bar. Casual attire. $19-$24.

★★FERRARO'S

5900 W. Flamingo Road, Las Vegas, 702-364-5300; www.ferraroslasvegas.com

Italian, seafood menu. Lunch, dinner. Bar. Children's menu. Casual attire. **$$$**

★★★FIAMMA TRATTORIA & BAR

3799 Las Vegas Blvd. S., Las Vegas, 702-891-7600; www.mgmgrand.com

With a fun, vibrant atmosphere, FiAMMA Trattoria & Bar in the MGM Grand is a good choice for those looking for a night out with friends. The setting is contemporary Italian, and the décor is warm, with rich, dark wood floors, modern furniture and copper-toned lighting. The Italian cuisine features such specialties as ravioli, brasato and branzino. Italian menu. Dinner. Bar. Business casual attire. Reservations recommended. Valet parking. **$$$**

★★FIORE STEAKHOUSE

3700 W. Flamingo Road, Las Vegas, 702-777-7702; www.harrahs.com

Steak menu. Dinner. Bar. Business casual attire. Reservations recommended. Valet parking. **$$$**

★★GARDUNO'S

4321 W. Flamingo Road, Las Vegas, 702-942-7777; www.thepalmslasvegas.com

Mexican menu. Lunch, dinner, Sunday brunch. Bar. Children's menu. Casual attire. Outdoor seating. **$$$**

★★HAMADA OF JAPAN

365 E. Flamingo Road, Las Vegas, 702-733-3005; www.hamadaofjapan.com

Japanese menu. Lunch, dinner. Bar. Casual attire. Valet parking. **$$$**

★★IL FORNAIO

3790 Las Vegas Blvd. S., Las Vegas, 702-650-6500; www.ilfornaio.com
Italian menu. Breakfast, lunch, dinner. Bar. Casual attire. Valet parking. **$$$**

★★★JASMINE

3600 Las Vegas Blvd. S., Las Vegas, 702-693-8166; www.bellagiolasvegas.com
No expense was spared to entice famed chef Philip Lo to create a new restaurant for the Bellagio. Lo, renowned for his contemporary takes on traditional Cantonese and Szechuan dishes, does not disappoint, providing such favorites as Imperial Peking duck and caramelized pork tenderloin with pineapples and bell pepper. The décor is not the traditional take on a Chinese restaurant, but rather an exploration of Victorian Hong Kong with such touches as high ceilings, chintz curtains, crystal chandeliers and windows that overlook the famed Bellagio fountains. Chinese menu. Dinner, late-night. Bar. Business casual attire. Reservations recommended. **$$$**

★★★★★JOËL ROBUCHON AT THE MANSION

3799 Las Vegas Blvd. S., Las Vegas, 702-891-7925; www.mgmgrand.com
Foodies everywhere salivated when they heard of Joël Robuchon's arrival in Sin City. His first of three restaurants in North America, Joël Robuchon at the Mansion, located in the MGM Grand, is a superluxe temple of haute cuisine, showcasing the signature cooking style that earned him a reputation as one of the world's greatest chefs. The menu, which reflects simplicity and a respect for fine ingredients, includes signature dishes like crispy amadai snapper with pistachio oil, truffled langoustine ravioli with diced cabbage and scallops in a ginger bouillon with baby leeks. Additional highlights include the bread cart (which showcases nearly two dozen different kinds of breads baked fresh daily) and a petit four cart with fanciful confections. The intimate Art Deco space has 17-foot ceilings and features cream-colored walls, black lacquered furniture and a black-and-white tiled entrance lit by a stunning crystal chandelier. The knowledge and grace demonstrated by the staff almost seems invisible. You'll remember a meal here for years to come. French menu. Dinner. Bar. Children's menu. Jacket required. Reservations recommended. Valet parking. Outdoor seating, Formal attire. **$$$$**

★★★KOI

3667 Las Vegas Blvd. S., Planet Hollywood, Las Vegas,
720-454-4555; www.koirestaurant.com
This might be the best sushi spot to try with that certain someone you met last night, if anyone did dinner dates in Vegas. Trendy, sexy design meets dim, dim, dim lighting and decent Japanese food. Specialties include miso-bronzed black cod and grilled skirt steak with crispy fried onions and sesame sauce. The fish is fresh considering its land-locked desert location, but you're paying for its plane ticket with your bill. Japanese menu. Dinner. Bar. Casual attire. Reservations recommended. Valet parking. $50

★★★L'ATELIER DE JOËL ROBUCHON

3799 Las Vegas Blvd. S., Las Vegas, 702-891-7358; www.mgmgrand.com
Las Vegas is synonymous with show-stopping performances, but where can you watch a world-famous French chef work his magic? L'Atelier de Joël Robuchon at the MGM Grand lets diners do just that. The legendary chef's casual counterpart to his more formal restaurant (also inside the MGM Grand) offers a unique approach to fine

dining where you can grab a seat at the counter and prepare to be dazzled by the food and the show. Steak tartar and miniature lamb chops are the chef's signature dishes, but expect anything and everything. Friendly, knowledgeable service complements the spirited atmosphere. French menu. Dinner, Business casual. $$

★★★LE CIRQUE

3600 Las Vegas Blvd. S., Las Vegas, 702-693-8135, 866-259-7111; www.bellagiolasvegas.com

The iconic New York restaurant has made it to Las Vegas at the Bellagio. Like the New York City original, this Le Cirque is a shining jewel of a restaurant, awash in bold colors and warm fabrics, with a bright, silk-tented ceiling that brings a festive big-top feel to the sumptuous dining room. The show-stopping French fare includes braised rabbit with riesling and fava beans, and the Le Cirque lobster salad with black truffle dressing. French menu. Dinner, late-night. Bar. Reservations recommended. Valet parking. Business casual attire. $$$

★★★LILLIE'S NOODLE HOUSE

129 E. Fremont St., Las Vegas, 702-385-7111; www.goldennugget.com

Presenting traditional Cantonese and Szechwan favorites, Lillie's, with its tranquil and refined atmosphere, is a nice break from the onslaught of sights and sounds that is Las Vegas. Specialties include Mongolian beef and stir-fried lobster. Chinese, pan-Asian menu. Dinner. Bar. Casual attire. Reservations recommended. $$$

★★★LUXOR STEAKHOUSE

3900 Las Vegas Blvd. S., Las Vegas, 702-262-4852; www.luxor.com

World-class cuisine is served in a luxurious, cherry wood dining room. Start with the roasted Hudson Valley foie gras or Maryland crab cake before cutting into the mouth-watering aged prime beef, filet mignon or Maine lobster. French menu. Dinner. Bar. Business casual attire. Reservations recommended. $$$

★★MAYFLOWER CUISINIER

4750 W. Sahara Ave., Las Vegas, 702-870-8432; www.mayflowercuisinier.com

Chinese menu. Lunch (Monday-Friday), dinner. Closed Sunday. Bar. Outdoor seating. $$

★★★★MICHAEL MINA

3600 Las Vegas Blvd. S., Las Vegas, 702-693-7223, 877-234-6358; www.bellagiolasvegas.com

This luxurious, contemporary dining room, bathed in creamy neutral tones and golden light, is just past the botanical gardens at the Bellagio. The menu here is in the care of a talented group of chefs trained and transported from San Francisco, who create innovate seafood dishes with Californian ingredients. The menu is extensive and offers á la carte selections in addition to a pair of five-course tasting menus, one vegetarian and one seasonal. Classic dishes include savory black mussel soufflé with saffron and chardonnay cream and Maine lobster pot pie. The wine list focuses on American producers and contains some gems from small vineyards. Seafood menu. Dinner, late-night. Bar. Reservations recommended. Valet parking. Business casual attire. $$$

★
★
★
★
★

★★MING'S TABLE

3475 Las Vegas Blvd. S., Las Vegas, 800-214-9110; www.harrahslasvegas.com

Asian menu. Lunch, dinner. Closed Monday-Tuesday. Bar. Casual attire. Reservations recommended. **$$$**

★★★★MIX RESTAURANT

3950 Las Vegas Blvd., Las Vegas, 702-632-9500; www.mandalaybay.com

It was only a matter of time before culinary mastermind Alain Ducasse took his place on the Strip. And in classic Ducasse style, the result is nothing less than grand. Located on the 64th floor of the hotel at Mandalay Bay, Mix is something of a futuristic fantasy. The light and airy, Patrick Jouin-designed interior features a 24-foot, $500,000 champagne-bubble chandelier consisting of more than 15,000 glass spheres, massive floor-to-ceiling windows that offer spectacular 360-degree views of Las Vegas, and tables with white faux leather-covered chairs. The staff inside the $2 million open kitchen turns out Ducasse's classic French cuisine, but with a contemporary twist. Dishes include duck foie gras with date-apricot chutney and beef tenderloin Rossini with potato galette and black truffle sauce. The extensive wine collection, consisting of approximately 7,000 bottles, lines an entire wall at the dining room's entrance. French, American menu. Dinner. Bar. Business casual attire. Reservations recommended. Valet parking. **$$$**

★★★NOBHILL TAVERN

3799 S. Las Vegas Blvd., Las Vegas, 702-891-7337; www.mgmgrand.com

Chef Michael Mina of San Francisco teamed with hot designer Tony Chi to create a snug city-by-the-Bay-inspired eatery in Sin City's MGM Grand. Named for the ritzy San Fran enclave, Nobhill Tavern conjures California cuisine with its fresh-baked sourdough bread, organic produce, natural meats, locally caught sand dabs and a heaping raw bar. Don't miss the whipped potatoes, which come in a chorus of flavors from leek to cheese. Glass-walled booths oppose the bar, which dispenses the applause-worthy house Cable Car martini. American menu. Dinner. Bar. Business casual attire. Reservations recommended. Valet parking. **$$$**

★★★NOBU

4455 Paradise Road, Las Vegas, 702-693-5000; www.hardrockhotel.com

The Zen-like décor of Nobu at the Hard Rock Hotel, with its bamboo-lined walls and seaweed-toned banquettes, brings a sense of calm to the otherwise frenetic pace of Las Vegas. This mini empire, which began with the original Nobu in New York's Tribeca, is known for spicy sashimi and creative dishes like miso-marinated black cod. Japanese menu. Dinner. Bar. Jacket required. Reservations recommended. Valet parking. **$$**

★★★OKADA

3131 Las Vegas Blvd. S., Las Vegas, 702-248-3463, 888-352-3463;
www.wynnlasvegas.com

Steve Wynn commissioned architectural firm Hirsch Bedner to create a contemporary Japanese design—clean lines, Japanese characters and traditional gardens—for his new restaurant, Okada. The design is a metaphor for chef Masa Ishizawa's modern take on Japanese cuisine with a French flair. Signature dishes include red miso bouillabaisse, braised *Kurobuta* short ribs with fingerling potatoes and organic chicken with ginger-caramel broth. There's also sushi and sashimi and a selection of marinated vegetables, fish and poultry bites that are grilled over Japanese charcoal in a process known as *robatayaki*. Japanese menu. Dinner. Bar. Business casual attire. Reservations recommended. Valet parking. Outdoor seating. **$$$$**

★★OLIVES

3600 S. Las Vegas Blvd., Las Vegas, 702-693-7223, 877-234-6358;
www.bellagiolasvegas.com
Italian, Mediterranean menu. Lunch, dinner, late-night. Bar. Casual attire. Outdoor seating. **$$$**

★★OSTERIA DEL CIRCO

3600 S. Las Vegas Blvd., Las Vegas, 702-693-8150; www.osteriadelcirco.com
Italian menu. dinner. Bar. Business casual attire. **$$**

★★★THE PALM

3500 Las Vegas Blvd. S., Las Vegas, 702-732-7256; www.thepalm.com
A destination eatery in the Forum Shops at Caesars Palace, the Palm steakhouse is a branch of the New York power eatery. The woody surroundings lend a clubby feel to the dining room, which specializes in healthy portions of meat supplemented by à la carte vegetables and potatoes. Lunches of salads, pastas and the house burger make this a more affordable midday option. Local notables like mayor Oscar Goodman and tennis pro Andre Agassi have been spotted dining here, as have many others; celebrity cartoon caricatures adorn the walls. Steak menu. Lunch, dinner, late-night. Bar. Business casual attire. Reservations recommended. Valet Parking. **$$**

★★PEARL

3799 Las Vegas Blvd. S., Las Vegas, 702-891-7380; www.mgmgrand.com
Chinese menu. Dinner. Business casual attire. Reservations recommended. **$$$**

★★★★PICASSO

3600 Las Vegas Blvd. S., Las Vegas, 702-693-7223, 866-259-7111;
www.bellagiolasvegas.com
Considered by many to be the most popular of Las Vegas restaurants, Picasso impresses with its ambience and food. Gold and red surround the dining room like holiday wrapping paper, drawing attention to authentic oil paintings and ceramics of the master artist. Chef Julian Serrano's French-Mediterranean cuisine more than competes for similar accolades. The prix-fixe menu changes daily, but certain favorites may often be available, including poached oysters, roasted ruby red shrimp or sautéed center cut filet of swordfish, all of which are artfully presented. French, Spanish menu. Dinner. Closed Tuesday. Bar. Business casual, no shorts. Reservations recommended. Valet parking. Outdoor seating. **$$$$**

★★PINOT BRASSERIE

3355 S. Las Vegas Blvd., Las Vegas, 702-414-8888; www.patinagroup.com
California bistro, French menu. Breakfast, lunch, dinner. Bar. Business casual attire. Reservations recommended. Valet parking. Outdoor seating. **$$$**

★★POSTRIO

3377 Las Vegas Blvd. S., Las Vegas, 702-796-1110; www.wolfgangpuck.com
American, Asian, Meditteranean menu. Dinner. Bar. Children's menu. Casual attire and formal. Reservations recommended. Valet parking. **$$**

★★★PRIME

3600 Las Vegas Blvd. S., Las Vegas, 702-693-7223, 877-234-6358;
www.bellagiolasvegas.com
Modeled after a 1930s speakeasy, Prime—with its plush drapery and powder blue marble—sets the stage for famed chef Robert Moore Vongerichten's modern steakhouse. The aged steaks are nice, but order the veal chop with kumquat-pineapple chutney and caramelized cauliflower, or the seared tuna au poivre with wasabi-mashed potatoes. Sides include gingered sweet potatoes, truffled mashed potatoes and roasted root vegetables. Prime manages one of the most impressive wine collections in the city, focusing on hearty reds from California and Bordeaux. Steak menu. Dinner, late-night. Bar. Reservations recommended. Valet parking. Business casual attire. **$$$**

★★RED 8

3131 Las Vegas Blvd. S., Las Vegas, 702-248-3463, 888-352-3463;
www.wynnlasvegas.com
Chinese menu. Lunch, dinner. Bar. Casual attire. Valet parking. **$$$**

★★★RESTAURANT CHARLIE

Palazzo Las Vegas, 3325 Las Vegas Blvd. S., 702-607-6336; www.palazzolasvegas.com
Charlie Trotter has long been known as one of the chefs who helped define contemporary American cuisine at his eponymous Chicago restaurant. Restaurant Charlie, at the Palazzo, is Trotter's second attempt on the Vegas culinary stage since his first restaurant at MGM Grand in the early 1990s. The main dining room, with its high ceilings and contemporary, clean lines, is almost churchlike in its silence and reverence. The menu is seafood-centric, with hints of further Asian influence interspersed with French technique, such as the sea bream, served with a bright addition of lemon, chile and cilantro, or the slow-poached Artic char enhanced by sunchokes and a rich but delicate trout roe and shiso vinaigrette. Bar Charlie, his "restaurant within a restaurant," looks like a sushi bar lined with Japanese chefs, but rest assured, you're not getting a rainbow roll here. The narrow room is serene and calm, and features Japanese-style *kaiseki* dining as either an eight- or 14-course tasting menu of some of the most divine sushi and sashimi done in what can only be described as the style of Trotter. Seafood menu. Dinner. Bar. Business casual attire. Reservations recommended. Valet parking. Credit cards accepted. **$$$$**

★★★★RESTAURANT GUY SAVOY

3570 Las Vegas Blvd. S., Las Vegas, 877-346-4642; www.caesarspalace.com
Perfect for a romantic dinner or a night out with friends, Restaurant Guy Savoy offers a fine-dining experience in a chic atmosphere with dark wood lattice, dramatic high ceilings and contemporary art. The creative French cuisine includes specialties such as artichoke black truffle soup, crispy sea bass with delicate spices and butter-roasted veal sweetbreads. Restaurant Guy Savoy is located in Caesars Palace on the second floor of the Augustus Tower. French menu. Dinner. Closed Monday-Tuesday. Bar. Business casual attire. Reservations recommended. Valet parking. **$$$$**

★SAM WOO BBQ

4215 Spring Mountain Road, Las Vegas, 702-368-7628
Chinese menu. Breakfast, lunch, dinner. Casual attire. $

★★SAMBA BRAZILIAN STEAKHOUSE

3400 Las Vegas Blvd. S., Las Vegas, 866-339-4566; www.mirage.com
Brazilian menu, Latin American menu. Dinner. Reservations recommended. Casual
attire. $$$

★★SHANGHAI LILLY

3950 Las Vegas Blvd. S., Las Vegas, 702-632-7409; www.mandalaybay.com
Shanghai Lilly's upscale Chinese cuisine is dished up on Limoges china and strikes
a refined note in the often party-hearty Mandalay Bay Resort and Casino. Despite its
location near the gaming floor, the elegant restaurant, designed by the celebrated Tony
Chi, does its best to conjure tranquility. A water wall leads guests into the dining room,
where three-story ceilings create a grand stage while sheer curtain-draped booths
serve those seeking intimacy. Cantonese, Szechwan and Hong Kong specialties fea-
ture authentic indulgences like braised shark's fin, abalone with sea cucumber, lobster
sashimi and Peking duck. Chinese menu. Dinner. Reservations recommended. $$

★★★SMITH & WOLLENSKY

3767 Las Vegas Blvd. S., Las Vegas, 702-862-4100; www.smithandwollensky.com
This Las Vegas outpost of the growing Manhattan-based chain re-creates the atmo-
sphere of the original, right down to the chalkboards listing daily specials. Steak menu.
Lunch, dinner. Bar. Casual attire. Valet parking. Reservations recommended. $$$

★SPICE MARKET BUFFET

3667 Las Vegas Blvd. S., Las Vegas, 702-785-5555;
www.planethollywoodresort.com
International menu. Breakfast, lunch, dinner, brunch. $$

★★THE STEAK HOUSE

2880 Las Vegas Blvd. S., Las Vegas, 702-794-3767; www.circuscircus.com
Steak menu. Dinner, Sunday brunch. Bar. Valet parking. Casual attire. $$$

★★★STRATTA

Wynn Las Vegas, 3131 Las Vegas Blvd. S., Las Vegas, 702-770-3463;
www.wynnlasvegas.com
Chef Alessandro Stratta's second restaurant at the Wynn (formerly known as Corsa
Cucina) is his more casual concept of rustic, regional Italian fare. Red-backed chairs,
an open-fire hearth and a clear view into the kitchen create an atmosphere that is
laid-back and welcoming. The restaurant's lounge is a smart place to meet for drinks,
and the location makes it an ideal spot to grab a bite before or after catching a show at
Wynn. The wood-fired pizzas are great noshes, and the pastas definitely have enough
variety to make everyone in your group happy. For a more substantial meal, the osso
bucco with saffron risotto and gremolata is heavenly. Italian menu. Dinner. Bar. Busi-
ness casual attire. Reservations recommended. Valet parking. $$$

★★★SW STEAKHOUSE

3131 Las Vegas Blvd. S., Las Vegas, 702-248-3463, 888-352-3463;
www.wynnlasvegas.com

European sophistication comes to the traditional steakhouse thanks to award-winning chef David Walzog at the Wynn Las Vegas. The entrance and ambiance is as grand as the menu. Guests descend on a winding escalator that leads to a foyer filled with plush couches and a captivating bar. The menu offers both traditional cuts of beef, such as bone-in rib-eye, New York strip and veal chop, as well as creative dishes, such as wild French sea bass, lobster bouillabaisse and roast duck breast l'orange. Steak menu. Dinner. Bar. Business casual attire. Reservations recommended. Valet parking. Outdoor seating. **$$$$**

★★★STRIP HOUSE

3667 Las Vegas Blvd S., Planet Hollywood Resort, Las Vegas, 702-737-5200;
www.planethollywoodresort.com/din_strip_house.php

This celebrated New York steakhouse headed out to Vegas and fit right in. Consider its name for starters. Then consider that it serves rich, decadent meals made for celebrating—not to mention for curing and preventing hangovers. If a bone-in rib-eye and crisp goose-fat potatoes won't do it, what will? Possibly the 24-layer chocolate cake—either way, you have to try it. Steakhouse menu. Dinner. Bar. Casual attire. Reservations recommended. Valet parking. **$$$**

★★★TABLEAU

3131 Las Vegas Blvd. S., Las Vegas, 702-248-3463, 888-352-3463;
www.wynnlasvegas.com

This signature restaurant at the Wynn, with an atrium setting that highlights poolside views, features the American cuisine of chef Mark LoRusso. Start with the Dungeness crab ravioli or Hamachi carpaccio before digging into Colorado rack of lamb with goat cheese soufflé or the organic roasted chicken with corn pudding and summer truffles. The chef's tasting menu (available in a fantastic vegetarian version) changes often. Don't miss Sunday brunch, when you can indulge in blueberry and lemon ricotta pancakes or Kobe short ribs and eggs. American menu. Breakfast, lunch, dinner, Saturday-Sunday brunch. Bar. Casual attire. Reservations recommended. Valet parking. Outdoor seating. **$$$$**

★★★TAO

3355 Las Vegas Blvd., Las Vegas, 702-388-8338; www.taorestaurant.com

This super-swanky fusion restaurant is massive. Occupying 40,000 square feet, Tao attracts visitors who want to dine, party or chill out—or all of the above. The focal point is the 20-foot-high Buddha that towers above the infinity pool. This is a place to come with a group. Chef Sam Hazen's menu is meant for sharing. While you can order a fresh and traditional selection of sushi and sashimi, the focus here is on new interpretations of old favorites. Seaweed salad is replaced by mango and truffle salad with wasabi caviar, egg rolls give way to spicy lobster rolls with black caviar. Other highlights include grilled rare yellowfin tuna, Hoisin chicken for two and the 12-ounce grilled Kobe rib-eye with yuzu cilantro butter. Pan-Asian menu. Dinner. Bar. Business casual attire. Reservations recommended. Valet Parking. **$$$**

★★★TOP OF THE WORLD

2000 Las Vegas Blvd. S., Las Vegas, 702-380-7711; www.stratospherehotel.com

Located atop the Stratosphere Hotel Tower, the circular room revolves once every 80 minutes, offering 360-degree nighttime views of Vegas. Few scenery-centric restaurants push the culinary envelope, and Top of the World is no exception, though it does a nice job with steaks and continental classics like lobster bisque. The mini chocolate stratosphere, which serves two, is a decadent dessert. American, seafood menu. Lunch, dinner. Business casual attire. Bar. Reservations recommended. Valet parking. $$$

★★★VALENTINO

3355 Las Vegas Blvd., S., Las Vegas, 702-414-3000; www.valentinolv.com

Restaurateur Piero Selvaggio's restaurant, Valentino, is a Vegas replica of his Angelino original. Chef Luciano Pellegrini hails from Italy, where he learned to create the authentic, rustic fare that makes the intimate Valentino a worthy destination. The bilingual menu includes classic à la carte choices such as carpaccio and lasagna, as well as several seasonal five-course tasting menus that delve into delicacies like quail paired with foie gras and oysters accented with caviar. The vast 24,000-bottle wine cellar also distinguishes itself among the numerous dining venues at the Venetian. Italian menu. Dinner, late-night. Bar. Casual attire. Reservations recommended. $$$$

★★★THE VERANDAH

3960 Las Vegas Blvd. S., Las Vegas, 702-632-5000; www.fourseasons.com

Discreetly hidden just off the Las Vegas Strip, the Four Seasons Hotel houses this equally discreet restaurant and patio. Overlooking the palm-flanked pool, the Verandah serves as the hotel's all-day restaurant, serving breakfast, lunch, dinner and afternoon tea in a casual but stylish setting. Selections are eclectic and include ahi sashimi, crab Napoleon, seared salmon and beef tenderloin with foie gras sauce. American menu. Breakfast, lunch, dinner. Bar. Casual attire. Outdoor seating. Reservations recommended. $$$

★★VIVA MERCADOS

3553 S. Rainbow Blvd., Las Vegas, 702-871-8826; www.vivamercadoslv.com

Mexican menu. Lunch, dinner. Bar. Children's menu. Casual attire. Reservations recommended. $

★★VOODOO STEAK & LOUNGE

3700 W. Flamingo Road, Las Vegas, 702-777-7923; www.harrahs.com

American, Cajun/Creole menu. Dinner. Bar. Business casual attire. Reservations recommended. Valet parking. $$$$

★★★WING LEI

3131 Las Vegas Blvd. S., Las Vegas, 702-248-3463, 888-352-3463;
www.wynnlasvegas.com

East meets West at chef Richard Chen's restaurant at the Wynn. While at the acclaimed Shanghai Terrace restaurant in Chicago, Chen helped create the concept of reverse fusion in which Western ingredients are used to create traditional Chinese dishes.

NEVADA

★
★
★
★
★

Signature favorites include pan-seared crab cake, lobster dan dan noodle, steamed stuffed poussin and braised veal shank. The restaurant offers an à la carte menu, five-course Peking duck prix fixe menu and a chef's Signature Menu. This is a popular group restaurant and fills up quickly, so make reservations well in advance. Chinese menu. Dinner. Bar. Children's menu. Business casual attire. Reservations recommended. Valet parking. **$$$$**

★★WOLFGANG PUCK CAFE
3799 Las Vegas Blvd. S., Las Vegas, 702-891-7777; www.mgmgrand.com
International menu. Lunch, dinner. Bar. Casual attire, Reservations recommended **$$**

SPAS
★★★THE BATHHOUSE AT THEHOTEL
3950 Las Vegas Blvd. S., Las Vegas, 702-632-7777; www.mandalaybay.com
This spa consistently delivers the unexpected. The Bathhouse at THEhotel at Mandalay Bay Resort has attracted international accolades for its striking interior. The entranceway's gray slate walls and marble floors establish instant, understated drama. The 12 treatment rooms include a redwood sauna, a eucalyptus steam room, several cold and hot plunge pools and a coed relaxation area. The exhaustive spa menu is as creative as it is endless, with everything from massage to reflexology, facials and body treatments. Ingredients in the intensely fresh herbal skincare line the spa uses, Eminence Organics of Hungary, are so fragrant you can almost taste the apple, grape and lime extracts. Advanced reservations available. **$$**

★★★CANYON RANCH SPACLUB AT THE VENETIAN
3355 Las Vegas Blvd. S., Las Vegas, 702-414-3606, 877-220-2688;
www.canyonranch.com
For years, Canyon Ranch has been the gold standard in the spa industry, known for its innovative approach to healthy living. The focus here is on fitness, nutrition and stress management. This 65,000-square-foot facility has the largest fitness center on the Las Vegas Strip and includes cutting-edge fitness classes, state-of-the-art equipment and a 40-foot rock-climbing wall. After a vigorous workout, reward yourself with one of the spa's massages (from neuromuscular therapy to Thai) or body treatments. There's also a full-service salon. **$$**

★★★QUA BATHS AND SPA
3570 Las Vegas Blvd. S., Las Vegas, 702-731-7110, 866-782-0655;
www.harrahs.com/qua
It's hard to believe people come to Las Vegas to relax, but the QUA Baths and Spa at Caesars Palace offer a transcendent experience. Roman baths are the focal point (they call it "social spa-ing"), but Vichy showers, chakra balancing, couples rituals and an Arctic Ice Room—where snowflakes fall from the ceiling—are what set the spa apart. Treatments range from practical to sensual, and water's healing properties are worked into many of the spa's services. The facility features an incredible 51 treatment rooms, including 35 massage suites, seven facial rooms, a Men's Zone plus Barber Spa, two hydrotherapy tubs and his and hers tea lounges, so you'll never get wound up waiting to unwind. **$$**

★★★★THE SPA AT FOUR SEASONS HOTEL LAS VEGAS

3960 Las Vegas Blvd. S., Las Vegas, 702-632-5000, 800-819-5053;
www.fourseasons.com

A Buddhist goddess greets visitors at this Asian-inspired spa. Try the 80-minute JAMU massage, which blends Indian, Chinese and European styles and techniques (including acupressure and skin rolling) with essential oils to work out every last kink. Other treatments include Balinese foot washes, aromatherapy scalp massages and reflexology. There are a variety of herbal wraps, salt glows and European facials. **$$**

★★★THE SPA AT RED ROCK

11011 W. Charleston Blvd., Las Vegas, 702-797-7777; www.redrocklasvegas.com

While not turning its back totally on Las Vegas's neon strip, the Spa at Red Rock instead looks out and up to the commanding sandstone cliffs that give their name to the Red Rock Casino, Resort and Spa. There are 20 treatment rooms and several alfresco private cabanas where you can experience everything from massage to champagne pedicures. The Adventure Spa (a spa within a spa) offers indoor rock climbing, rafting down the Colorado River below Hoover Dam, mountain biking over wild horse trails in the high desert or hiking up to bubbling hot springs. Reservations recommended. **$$**

★★★★ THE SPA AT TRUMP

Trump International Hotel & Tower Las Vegas,2000 Fashion Show Drive, Las Vegas,
702-476-8000; www.trumplasvegashotel.com

The Spa at Trump International Hotel & Tower is among Vegas' newest, most intimate and, of course, swankiest refuges. A spa attaché guides you through 11,000 square feet of Eucalyptus steam-laden space to help discern your signature intention: Calm, Balance, Purify, Heal or Revitalize. Special gemstone-infused oil massages are meant to heal internally and externally—we'll take rubies, emeralds, sapphires and diamonds in *any* form. For long-lasting benefits, sample the Dermalucent with LED skin rejuvenation; or a hotel-exclusive Ultimate Kate facial, which combines the above treatment with a pressure point massage and foot rub. Late-night partiers flock to the Morning-After Eye Cure (to refresh before starting the cycle again). Of course, The Donald wouldn't open a spa without some kind of service for luscious locks, so try an Espresso Yourself hair treatment for damage control.

★★★★★THE SPA AT THE WYNN LAS VEGAS

3131 Las Vegas Blvd. S., Las Vegas, 702-770-3900, 877-321-9966;
www.wynnlasvegas.com

The décor of this spa is grand, and the waiting room—adorned with fireplaces—feels plush and regal. The gorgeous Jacuzzi room harkens to a mermaid's lair, with its lily pad-covered walls inset with stones, Deluge showers that simulate waterfalls and a central soaking bath. Exotic Asian- and Middle Eastern-inspired treatments are signatures here, but the real attraction is the ultra-indulgent 80-minute Good Luck Ritual, one of the most comprehensive treatments on the Strip. Based on the five elements of feng shui, the service addresses every needy area of your body with heated Thai herbs, verbena and peppermint foot treatment, 50-minute intense customized-for-your-tension massage and wild lime botanical scalp massage. Male estheticians are plentiful here, so make sure to specify if you have a gender preference.

★★★★SPA BELLAGIO AT BELLAGIO

3600 Las Vegas Blvd. S., Las Vegas, 702-693-7472, 888-987-3456; www.bellagio.com
This Roman-style spa is the height of luxury, even in over-the-top Las Vegas. The facility includes a redwood sauna, eucalyptus steam room and cold plunge pools. The staff attends to your every whim. You'll feel pampered as you sip a latte served in Bernardaud china that fits perfectly into the armrest of a pedicure chair. Try a lemon-ginger stone or deluxe scalp massage. Hot toe voodoo can be added to any massage and is a wonderfully relaxing treatment in which warm stones are placed between your toes to re-energize tired feet. The lemon-ginger scrub is another fantastic treatment for rough skin. Facials target common problems, such as sun damage, dehydration and wrinkles, and eye and lip treatments can be added to these services. Hydrotherapy services include thalasso seaweed baths, revitalizing mineral baths and aromatic Moor mud baths. Reservations recommended. **$$**

LAUGHLIN

This resort community offers a pleasant change of pace from the glitz of Las Vegas. In many ways, it resembles Las Vegas in its earlier days. Hotels and casinos line the Colorado River, and some provide ferry service to and from parking facilities on the Arizona side. Laughlin offers other diversions such as fishing, waterskiing and swimming in nearby Lake Mohave.

Information: Laughlin Visitor Information Center, 1555 Casino Drive, 702-298-3321, 800-452-8445; www.visitlaughlin.com

SPECIAL EVENT
LAUGHLIN RIVER DAYS

1585, Casino Drive, Laughlin, 702-298-2214; www.laughlinchambers.com
APBA Powerboat racing on a 1½-mile course. Early June.

HOTELS
★★★AQUARIUS CASINO RESORT

1900 S. Casino Drive, Laughlin, 702-298-5111, 888-662-5825; www.aquariuscasinoresort.com
The largest resort on the Colorado River, this enormous property offers activities for every member of the family. Visitors will enjoy the 2,000-seat showroom, 3,300-seat outdoor amphitheater and 60,000-square-foot casino. 1,912 rooms. Restaurant, bar. Spa. Airport transportation available. Casino. Tennis. Fitness center. Pool. Business center. **$**

★★DON LAUGHLIN'S RIVERSIDE RESORT

1650 Casino Drive, Laughlin, 702-298-2535, 800-227-3849; www.riversideresort.com
1,404 rooms. Restaurant, bar. Airport transportation available. Casino. Movie theaters. Car Museum. **$**

★★★GOLDEN NUGGET

2300 S. Casino Drive, Laughlin, 702-298-7111, 800-955-7278; www.goldennugget.com/laughlin

This resort is like a tropical paradise in the desert. A jungle theme is carried from the rain-forest-inspired lobby to the tropical themed rooms. Tarzan's Night Club completes the illusion. 300 rooms. Restaurant, bar. Outdoor pool. Airport transportation available. Casino. Golf $

★★RIVER PALMS
2700 S. Casino Drive, Laughlin, 800-835-7904; www.rvrpalm.com
1,003 rooms. Restaurant, bar. Spa. Airport transportation available. Pool. $

MINDEN
This small town is located just minutes from beautiful Lake Tahoe.
Information: www.townofminden.com

HOTEL
★★CARSON VALLEY INN HOTEL CASINO
1627 US 395 N., Minden, 775-782-9711, 800-321-6983; www.cvinn.com
152 rooms. Restaurant, bar. Children's activity center. Casino. Wireless Internet access. Pool. Golf. Spa. Fitness center. $

PRIMM
Forty miles south of Las Vegas, Primm is primarily a gaming destination, especially for gamers from Southern California on their way to Las Vegas.

WHAT TO SEE AND DO
FASHION OUTLETS OF LAS VEGAS
Interstate 15 S., Primm, 702-874-1400; www.fashionoutletlasvegas.com
Located about 30 miles south of Las Vegas, the nearly 100 retailers here include Burberry, Coach, Kenneth Cole New York, Polo Ralph Lauren Factory Store and Versace. The mall offers daily shuttle service from the MGM Grand Hotel & Casino. Daily, 10 a.m.-8 p.m.

HOTEL
★★PRIMM VALLEY RESORT & CASINO
31900 S. Las Vegas Blvd., Primm, 702-386-7867, 860-386-7867;
www.primmvalleyresort.com
624 rooms. Two restaurants, two bars. Casino. Pool. $

RENO
Reno, "the biggest little city in the world," is renowned as a gambling and vacation center. Between the steep slopes of the Sierra and the low eastern hills, Reno spills across the Truckee Meadows. The neon lights of the nightclubs, gambling casinos and bars give it a glitter that belies its many quiet acres of fine houses, churches and schools. The surrounding area is popular for sailing, boating, horseback riding and deer and duck hunting. The downtown Riverwalk along the Truckee's banks is loaded with coffee shops, art galleries, chic eateries, eclectic boutiques, antique stores, salons and theaters.
Information: Chamber of Commerce, 1 E. First St., Reno, 775-337-3030;
www.reno-sparkschamber.org

WHAT TO SEE AND DO

ANIMAL ARK

1265 Deerlodge Road, Reno, 775-970-3111; www.animalark.org

Tucked in the forested hills north of Reno, Animal Ark is not a zoo, but a sanctuary for animals that cannot be returned to the wild. Many were disabled or orphaned, and others were unwanted exotic pets. The residents include big cats (tigers, snow leopards and cougars), gray wolves, black bears and a few reptiles and birds. Each has a name and is presented as an "ambassador" for its species. April-October, Tuesday-Sunday 10 a.m.-4:30 p.m.

FLEISCHMANN PLANETARIUM AND SCIENCE CENTER

1650 N. Virginia St., Reno, 775-784-4811; www.planetarium.unr.edu

This facility projects public shows on the inside of its 30-foot dome. The museum here also houses all four of the meteorites that have landed in Nevada (including a massive specimen that weighs more than a ton) and scales rigged to reflect the gravity on Jupiter or a neutron star. On cloudless Friday nights, guests can peer through telescopes with members of the Astronomical Society of Nevada.

GREAT BASIN ADVENTURE

Rancho San Rafael Regional Park, 1595 N. Sierra St., Reno, 775-785-4064; www.maycenter.com

Part of the Wilbur D. May Center in Rancho San Rafael Regional Park, Great Basin Adventure consists of several attractions designed to educate and entertain kids. At Wilbur's Farm, pint-sized visitors can take a pony ride or explore the 1½-acre petting zoo. Guests can pan for gold at a replica mine building, with faux mine shafts that double as slides and displays on minerals and the area's mining history. Tuesday-Saturday 10 a.m.-5 p.m., Sunday noon-5 p.m.

HUMBOLDT-TOIYABE NATIONAL FOREST

1200 Franklin Way, Sparks, 775-331-6444; www.fs.fed.us/r4htnf

At 6.3 million acres, this is the largest national forest in the lower 48 states. It extends across Nevada from the California border in a scattershot pattern, comprising 10 ranger districts that encompass meadows, mountains, deserts and canyons. Just northwest of the Reno city limits, Peavine Mountain is crisscrossed by a number of old mining roads now reserved for hikers and mountain bikers. Other Humboldt-Toiyabe highlights include scenic Lamoille Canyon and the Ruby Mountains, southeast of Elko; the rugged, isolated Toiyabe Range, near the geographic center of Nevada; and Boundary Peak, the state's highest point at 13,143 feet, southeast of Reno on the California-Nevada border. Open Monday-Friday.

MEADOWOOD MALL

5000 Meadowood Mall Circle, Reno, 775-827-8451, www.simon.com

The most contemporary shopping center in the region, this is actually the city's most-visited tourist attraction.

MOUNT ROSE SKI AREA

22222 Mt. Rose Highway, Reno, 775-849-0704, 800-754-7673; www.mtrose.com

Of all the ski resorts in the Reno-Tahoe area, Mount Rose has the highest base elevation (a precipitous 7,900 feet above sea level), making it the best bet for late-season skiing. Eight lifts, including two six-person, high-speed chairlifts, take skiers and snowboarders to the 9,700-foot summit to 1,200 acres of terrain nearly evenly split among skill levels (20 percent beginner, 30 percent intermediate and 40 percent advanced) and a pair of snowboarding parks. Located northwest of Lake Tahoe, Mount Rose is also known for its excellent beginners' program. There are no on-mountain accommodations. Mid-November-mid-April, daily.

NATIONAL AUTOMOBILE MUSEUM (THE HARRAH COLLECTION)

10 Lake St. S., Reno, 775-333-9300; www.automuseum.org

The brainchild of car collector and gaming titan Bill Harrah, this excellent facility covers more than a century of automotive history in detail. Four galleries house the museum's collection of more than 200 cars: The first gallery details the late 19th and early 20th century (complete with a blacksmith's shop, the garage of the day); the second covers 1914 to 1931; the third, 1932 to 1954; and the fourth, 1954 to modern day. The Masterpiece Circle Gallery in the fourth gallery also accommodates temporary themed exhibits on subjects ranging from Porsches to pickup trucks. The oldest car in the museum dates from 1892, and there are a number of collector's trophies (such as the 1949 Mercury Coupe driven by James Dean in *Rebel Without a Cause*) and one-of-a-kind oddities (the steam-powered 1977 Steamin' Demon). Monday-Saturday 9:30 a.m.-5:30 p.m., Sunday 10 a.m.-4 p.m.

275

NEVADA HISTORICAL SOCIETY MUSEUM

1650 N. Virginia St., Reno, 775-688-1190; www.nevadaculture.org

Founded in 1904, this is both Nevada's oldest museum and one of its best. On permanent display is "Nevada: Prisms and Perspectives," which examines the Silver State's five biggest historical stories: the Native American perspective, the mining boom, the neon-lit story of gaming, transportation and the "Federal Presence" (the federal government owns 87 percent of Nevada's land). Monday-Saturday 10 a.m.-5 p.m.

NEVADA MUSEUM OF ART

160 W. Liberty St., Reno, 775-329-3333; www.nevadaart.org

The only nationally accredited art museum in the entire state, the Nevada Museum of Art would be a top-notch facility no matter where it was located. Perhaps the most distinctive architectural specimen in all of artsy Reno, the curved, sweeping structure is a work of art in and of itself: modern (it opened in 2003) and monolithic (60,000 square feet), evoking the image of the legendary Black Rock of the Nevada desert. The collection housed within is equally impressive, broken into five different themes: contemporary art, contemporary landscape photography (one of the best of its kind anywhere), regional art, American art from 1900 to 1945, and the E. L. Weigand Collection, American art with a work-ethic theme. Tuesday-Wednesday, Friday-Sunday 10 a.m.-5 p.m., Thursday 10 a.m.-8 p.m.; Galleries closed Mondays and national holidays.

RENO ARCH

Virginia St., downtown Reno

In 1926, Reno commemorated the completion of the first transcontinental highway in North America, which ran through the city en route to San Francisco, with an arch that traverses Virginia Street downtown. Three years later, locals adopted the tagline "the biggest little city in the world" and added it to the landmark. The arch has since been replaced twice, in 1964 and in 1987.

RENO-SPARKS THEATER COALITION

528 W. First St., Reno, 775-786-2278; www.theatercoalition.org

Consisting of more than 20 separate companies in the Reno-Sparks area, this organization is a cooperative effort to market a varied slate of theater, dance and other performing arts. Member troupes range from the avant-garde to the kid-friendly, and the Coalition puts together an up-to-date events schedule for all of them.

SIERRA SAFARI ZOO

10200 N. Virginia St., Reno, 775-677-1101; www.sierrasafarizoo.org

The largest zoo in Nevada, Sierra Safari is home to 150 animals representing more than 40 species. The majority of the animals were selected for the rugged Reno climate, including a Siberian tiger and a number of other felines, but there are also tropical birds, a few reptiles and a number of primates. A petting zoo and a picnic area are onsite. April-October, daily 10 a.m.-5 p.m.

UNIVERSITY OF NEVADA, RENO

1664 N. Virginia St., Reno, 775-784-1110; www.unr.edu

Established in 1874; 12,000 students. The campus covers 200 acres on a plateau overlooking the Truckee Meadows, in the shadow of the Sierra Nevada Mountains. Opened in Elko, it was moved to Reno and reopened in 1885. Nevada enrolled 16,336 students in fall 2005. Tours of campus.

W. M. KECK EARTH SCIENCES AND ENGINEERING MUSEUM

Mackay School of Mines Building, 1664 N. Virginia St., Reno, 775-784-4528;
www.mines.unr.edu/museum

Located in the Mackay School of Mines Building, the Keck Museum focuses on the state's mining history. The collection of specimens originated from Nevada's most renowned mining districts—the Comstock Lode, Tonopah and Goldfield—but exotic minerals from all over the world share the space. Rounding out the museum are displays of fossils, vintage mining equipment and a collection of fine silver donated by the family of mining tycoon John Mackay. Monday-Friday 9 a.m.-4 p.m.

SPECIAL EVENTS
ARTOWN FESTIVAL

Reno, 775-322-1538; www.renoisartown.com

Held annually in July (with a newer holiday counterpart in November and December), Reno's Artown Festival is a monthlong extravaganza that includes more than 200 events and exhibitions and 1,000 artists in all—making it the largest arts festival in the United States. Not surprisingly, it has won its fair share of national acclaim since it launched in 1996. The artists span the disciplines of ballet, opera, theater, film and the visual arts.

There are flamenco dancers, comedy troupes and internationally known performers of all stripes not to mention myriad gallery openings and historical tours. Multiple downtown venues host various aspects of the festival. Wingfield Park is the setting of an outdoor film every week. "Rollin' on the River" is a weekly concert series. Mondays are family nights, with entertainment ranging from science experiments to storytelling. July.

ELDORADO GREAT ITALIAN FESTIVAL
Fourth and Virginia streets, Reno, 775-786-5700, 800-879-8879;
www.eldoradoreno.com
Put on by the Eldorado Hotel and Casino, the two-day event includes several buffets, a farmers market and live entertainment. But the contests, including a spaghetti sauce cook-off, gelato-eating contest for kids and a grape-stomping competition, are the real attraction. Early October.

ELDORADO'S GREAT BBQ, BREW AND BLUES
North Virginia Street, Reno, 775-786-5700, 800-879-8879;
www.eldoradoreno.com
This street fair focuses on the three staples in its name: tangy barbecue, ice-cold beer and a pair of stages featuring nonstop blues. The participating breweries hail from Nevada, California and Oregon. Only those 21 years old and older are admitted. Last weekend in June.

HOT AUGUST NIGHTS
1425 E. Greg St., Sparks, 775-356-1956; www.hotaugustnights.net
This retro event pays homage to the 1950s and 1960s. Highlights include a series of concerts by nostalgia acts (past performers have included Chuck Berry, the Turtles, and Jan and Dean) and a classic car parade. There are street dances and sock hops, and casinos get in on the action by awarding a classic car or two to a few lucky winners. Early August.

NATIONAL CHAMPIONSHIP AIR RACES
Reno Stead Field, Reno, 775-972-6663; www.airrace.org
Races (classes include Biplane, Formula One, Unlimited, Jet, Sport and T-6), demonstrations and fly-bys. Four days in mid-September.

NEVADA OPERA
Pioneer Center for the Performing Arts, 100 S. Virginia St., Reno, 775-786-4046;
www.nevadaopera.org
Founded in 1967, the Nevada Opera stages several noteworthy operas each year in its fall/spring calendar. Recent productions have included *La Traviata* and *Aida*.

NEVADA STATE FAIR
1350 N. Wells Ave., Reno, 775-688-5767; www.nvstatefair.com
A Reno area tradition since 1874, the Nevada State Fair features rodeo events, livestock competitions and a carnival midway. The event also includes a kid-oriented science festival, an aerial motorcycle stunt show and contests for the best homemade pies, cookies and salsa. Late August.

NEVADA

★
★
★
★
★

RENO BASQUE FESTIVAL

Wingfield Park, Reno, 775-762-3577

Basques from Northern Spain and Southern France immigrated to Nevada's Great Basin in the early 20th century to herd sheep, and they have been a visible part of the Reno community ever since. The Reno Basque Festival started in 1959 with the goal of preserving Basque culture in the United States. Today, it's one of the largest events of its kind in the country, kicked off by a parade that snakes around downtown before coming to a stop at Wingfield Park along the Truckee River. From there, the festival takes over with food, dancing, singing and athletic competitions. Basque cuisine available for sampling includes sheepherder bread, Basque beans, lamb stew and other hearty staples, and there's also a market. Crowds gather for the traditional games: soka tira (a Basque tug-of-war), woodcutting and weightlifting. Late July.

RENO FILM FESTIVAL

925 Riverside Drive, Reno, 775-334-6707; www.renofilmfestival.com

Drawing a handful of celebrities to downtown Reno every November, this film festival screens Hollywood productions, independent features, world premieres and retrospective revivals. Movies are shown at various downtown venues (casinos, museums and theaters), and there are also a number of film-related workshops, demonstrations and lectures. Early November.

RENO JAZZ FESTIVAL

University of Nevada, Reno, 775-784-4046; www.unr.edu

Held on the University of Nevada at Reno campus since 1963, this three-day event is one of the biggest of its kind, drawing hundreds of school bands (junior high to college) from Nevada, California, Oregon, Idaho and Washington. The top bands and soloists play at a concluding encore performance, and the first two nights are highlighted by sets from nationally known jazz artists. Late April.

RENO PHILHARMONIC ORCHESTRA

925 Riverside Drive, Reno, 775-323-6393; www.renophilharmonic.com

Reno's symphony orchestra plays a September-to-April Master Classics Series (as well as a July 4th pops concert) at a number of venues in town, with Pioneer Center for the Performing Arts serving as its home stage. The orchestra plays works from composers such as Mozart, Beethoven, Copland and Gershwin. A free one-hour lecture is given immediately before each concert.

RENO RODEO

Reno Livestock Events Center, 1350 N. Wells Ave., Reno,
775-329-3877, 800-225-2277; www.renorodeo.com

Known as the wildest, richest rodeo in the west—with a total purse in excess of $1 million—the Reno Rodeo has been a big event since its inaugural year in 1919. Includes bull riding, barrel racing and roping events. Late June.

HOTELS

★★★ATLANTIS CASINO RESORT

3800 S. Virginia St., Reno, 775-825-4700, 800-723-6500;
www.atlantiscasino.com

Located about three miles south of downtown, Atlantis is among Reno's top resorts, with several smoke-free gaming areas in the glass-enclosed casinos, a top-notch business center and a dizzying array of rooms. A highlight is the spa, which offers a variety of treatments using Ahava and Dermalogica products. The Sky Terrace has sushi and oyster bars. 973 rooms. Restaurant, bar. Spa. Airport transportation available. Casino. Pets accepted. $

★★BEST WESTERN AIRPORT PLAZA HOTEL

1981 Terminal Way, Reno, 775-348-6370, 800-648-3525; www.bestwestern.com
269 rooms. Restaurant, bar. Airport transportation available. Casino. Fitness center. Pets accepted. Pool. High-speed Internet access. $

★★★ELDORADO HOTEL AND CASINO

345 N. Virginia St., Reno, 800-879-8879; www.eldoradoreno.com
Of the casinos in downtown Reno, Eldorado attracts the youngest crowd, thanks to its myriad nightspots, which include a microbrewery with live rock and blues, a martini/ piano bar and BuBinga, a popular dance club with DJs and live bands. Eldorado has some of the best-looking hotel rooms in town. 817 rooms. Ten restaurants, bar. Airport transportation available. Casino. $

★★★HARRAH'S HOTEL RENO

219 N. Center St., Reno, 775-786-3232; www.harrahs.com
Located downtown next to the Reno Arch, Harrah's Reno is one of the glitziest casinos in the city, a distinction it has held since opening in the early 1960s. The casino is immense and diverse, featuring 1,300 slot machines, table games of all kinds and a sports book. Accommodations come in the form of nearly 1,000 sleek hotel rooms, ranging from standard rooms to skyline suites. There are seven restaurants, including the renowned Steak House at Harrah's Reno. Entertainers work the crowd onstage at Sammy's Showroom, named after Sammy Davis, Jr., who performed here 40 times. 928 rooms. Seven restaurants, bar. Airport transportation available. Casino. Pets accepted. Pool. Spa. Golf. $

★LA QUINTA INN

4001 Market St., Reno, 775-348-6100, 800-531-5900; www.laquinta.com
130 rooms. Complimentary continental breakfast. Airport transportation available. Pets accepted. High-speed Internet access. $

★★★PEPPERMILL HOTEL AND CASINO RENO

2707 S. Virginia St., Reno, 775-826-2121, 800-648-6992; www.peppermillreno.com
Consistently ranked one of the best casinos in the city, Peppermill's flagship resort is a fixture in the entertainment district near the airport, about two miles south of downtown. The slick property features 2,000 slot machines, the full spectrum of table gaming, poker and sports betting, plus nightly live entertainment in the swanky cabaret and the more intimate piano lounge. In addition to seven restaurants, the resort boasts a dozen

NEVADA

★
★
★
★

nightspots, including Oceano, with large aquariums, and the domed-shaped Romanza. 1635 rooms. Seven restaurant, bars. Airport transportation available. Casino. Pool. Spa. Fitness center. Business center. Wireless Internet access. $

★★★SIENA HOTEL SPA CASINO
1 S. Lake St., Reno, 775-327-4362, 877-743-6233; www.sienareno.com
Designed to resemble a Tuscan village, this comprehensive resort, located along the banks of the Truckee River, includes a 23,000-square-foot casino and a full-service spa with a variety of treatments. The bright and comfortable rooms include custom fabrics reflecting the sun-drenched palette of Tuscany and have views of the mountains or river. Among the three restaurants, Lexie's offers view of the water. 214 rooms. Three restaurants, bars. Spa. Casino. High-speed Internet access. $

★★★SILVER LEGACY RESORT CASINO RENO
407 N. Virginia St., Reno, 775-325-7401, 800-687-7733; www.silverlegacyreno.com
This Victorian-themed resort has a steel and brass dome and a façade designed to resemble an 1890s storefront. Beyond the gaming—2,000 slots, table games, sports book and a keno lounge—there's a comedy club and a rum bar with dueling pianos. And the showroom attracts big-name entertainers. 1,720 rooms. Restaurant, bar. Airport transportation available. Pool. Spa. Business center. Wireless Internet access. $

RESTAURANTS
★★BRICKS RESTAURANT AND WINE BAR
1695 S. Virginia St., Reno, 775-786-2277

American menu. Lunch, dinner. Closed Sunday. Bar. $$

★★FAMOUS MURPHY'S
3127 S. Virginia St., Reno, 775-827-4111; www.famousmurphys.com
Seafood, steak menu. Lunch, dinner. Closed Sunday. Bar. Children's menu. Reservations recommended. $$

★★PALAIS DE JADE
960 W. Moana Lane, Reno, 775-827-5233; www.palaisdejadereno.com
Chinese menu. Lunch, dinner. Bar. $$

★★RAPSCALLION
1555 S. Wells Ave., Reno, 775-323-1211, 877-932-3700; www.rapscallion.com
Seafood menu. Dinner, Sunday brunch. Bar. Outdoor seating. Reservations recommended. $$

★★WASHOE GRILL
4201 W. Fourth St., Reno, 775-786-1323; www.washoesteakhouse.com
Seafood, steak menu. Dinner. Bar. Reservations recommended. $$$

SOUTH LAKE TAHOE
With more than 300 sunny days a year and a mountain playground that can make any outdoor enthusiast grin, this small town on Lake Tahoe has plenty to offer.
Information: www.tahoeinfo.com

WHAT TO SEE AND DO
FACTORY STORES AT THE Y
Highways 50 and 89, South Lake Tahoe; 775-783-8872; www.shopthe-y.com
This small group of factory stores includes Adidas and Izod. Daily 10 a.m.-6 p.m.

SPECIAL EVENTS
VALHALLA WINTER MICROBREW FESTIVAL
Horizon Casino, 50 Highway 50, South Lake Tahoe, 530-542-4166
Held at the Horizon Casino, this annual fundraiser for the Valhalla Arts and Music Festival gives attendees the chance to sample 120 microbrews from Nevada and Northern California. Mid-February.

SPARKS
Located in the Truckee Meadows of northern Nevada, Sparks is close to Reno. Its desert climate makes it a perfect destination if you want to recreate outdoors and enjoy some of Reno's high-stakes fun.
Information: www.ci.sparks.nv.us

WHAT TO SEE AND DO
SPARKS HERITAGE MUSEUM
820 Victorian Ave., Sparks, 775-355-1144
Housed in a former courthouse, the museum's exhibits follow Sparks' progression from a train depot to a mining hub to a municipality of more than 80,000 people. Highlights include a vintage model train set and a pump-powered antique player piano. Tuesday-Friday 11 a.m.-4 p.m., Saturday-Sunday 1-4 p.m.

WILD ISLAND FAMILY ADVENTURE PARK
250 Wild Island Court, Sparks, 775-359-2927; www.wildisland.com
Primarily known as a summer water park, Wild Island is now a year-round facility with the 2003 addition of Coconut Bowl, a state-of-the-art 20-lane bowling alley, and the surprisingly chic Smokin' Marlin Grill. The water park is huge, with a wave pool, tubing river and myriad slides. Hours vary by attraction and season.

SPECIAL EVENTS
BEST OF THE WEST RIB COOK-OFF
John Ascuaga's Nugget Casino Resort,1100 Nugget Ave., Sparks, 775-356-3428;
www.nuggetribcookoff.com
Nearly 300,000 barbecue lovers flock to this annual event. In recent years, about 150,000 pounds of ribs have been consumed at this five-day cook-off where two dozen of the West's most revered barbecue pros (all of whom are invited) compete for the first-prize trophy. There is also a lineup of live entertainment on numerous outdoor stages. Labor Day weekend.

SPARKS HOMETOWNE FARMERS MARKET
Victorian Square, Sparks, 775-353-2291; www.ci.sparks.nv.us
Every Thursday evening between June and August, more than 100 vendors gather and offer everything from rhubarb to pastries to tacos. Also includes cooking demonstrations, kids' area, and home and garden vendors.

HOTEL
★★★JOHN ASCUAGA'S NUGGET
1100 Nugget Ave., Sparks, 775-356-3300, 800-648-1177; www.janugget.com
An anchor in downtown Sparks, the Nugget has been one of the top resorts in the Reno area since it opened in 1955. It's a few miles outside of downtown Reno, but right on the doorstep of Victorian Square, the site of numerous special events. The casino is loaded with all of the standards: slots, table games, poker room and sports book. The Celebrity Showroom is the place to go for fabulous entertainment. The hotel itself is a landmark, with a pair of 29-story towers flanking the casino, and a slate of amenities that includes everything from an arcade to a wedding chapel. 1,407 rooms. Eight restaurants, bars. Airport transportation available. Casino. Exercise. Pool. Spa. Business center. Wireless Internet access. **$**

STATELINE
This area is best known for its famous high-rise casino/hotels, cabarets and fine dining, but as an integral part of Tahoe's "south shore," it is also appreciated for its spectacular natural beauty. Alpine beaches and Sierra forests afford visitors an endless variety of year-round recreation. There are several excellent public golf courses in the area.

HOTELS
★HORIZON CASINO RESORT
50 Highway 50, Stateline, 775-588-6211, 800-648-3322; www.horizoncasino.com
539 rooms. Restaurant, bar. Casino. Exercise. Pool. **$**

★★LAKESIDE INN AND CASINO
168 Highway 50, Stateline, 775-588-7777, 800-624-7980; www.lakesideinn.com
124 rooms. Restaurant, bar. Casino. Pool. **$**

★★★HARRAH'S LAKE TAHOE
15 Highway 50, Stateline, 775-588-6611, 800-427-7247; www.harrahstahoe.com
This property offers 18,000 square feet of function space and plenty of recreation options for leisure visitors. Shop at the Galleria, swim in the glass-domed pool and, of course, hit the casino. 532 rooms. Restaurant, bar. Casino. Pets accepted. Pool. Spa. **$**

★★★HARVEY'S LAKE TAHOE
Stateline Ave., Stateline, 775-588-2411, 800-427-8397; www.harveys.com
Most rooms at this resort, the first built in South Lake Tahoe, have a view of Lake Tahoe or the Sierra Nevada mountains. The resort offers a variety of ski packages in the winter and the outdoor arena draws top music guests (including Beyoncé and Diana Krall) in the summer. 740 rooms. Restaurant, bar. Airport transportation available. Casino. Pool. Fitness center. **$**

RESTAURANTS
★★CHART HOUSE
392 Kingsbury Grade, Stateline, 775-588-6276; www.chart-house.com

American menu. Dinner. Bar. Children's menu. Outdoor seating. Reservations recommended. **$$$**

★★★FRIDAY'S STATION STEAK & SEAFOOD GRILL

15 Highway 50, Stateline, 775-588-6611; www.harrahs.com
The view of the lake from this restaurant, located on the 18th floor, is truly breathtaking. Several steak and seafood combos are offered, such as filet mignon and Alaskan king crab or blackened shrimp. Seafood, steak menu. Dinner. Reservations recommended. Bar. **$$$**

★★★SAGE ROOM

Highway 50, Stateline, 775-588-2411; www.harrahs.com
Since 1947, the Sage Room Steak House has been world-renowned for its old Western ambience and fine cuisine. Dine among the works of Russell and Remington while enjoying traditional steak house dining highlighted by tableside flambé service. Top off your meal with the Sage Room's famous bananas Foster. American menu. Dinner. Bar. Valet parking. **$$$**

★★★SUMMIT

15 Highway 50, Stateline, 775-588-6611; www.harrahs.com
Located on the 16th and 17th floors of Harrah's, this restaurant has stunning views and sophisticated cuisine. Try the filet mignon with truffled parsnip purée or pistachio-encrusted rack of lamb. American menu. Dinner. Bar. Valet parking. **$$$$**

TONOPAH

In the hills of the San Antonio Mountains, Tonopah is located about halfway between Reno and Las Vegas. Visitors will enjoy roaming Tonopah's historic streets, taking in the scenic vistas and exploring nearby ghost towns.
Information: Chamber of Commerce, 301 Brougher St., 775-482-3558; www.tonopahnevada.com

WHAT TO SEE AND DO
MINING MUSEUM AND PARK

520 McCulloch Ave., Tonopah, 775-482-9274; www.tonopahnevada.com
If you're into rock collecting, this historic mining park has a rich variety of minerals. Daily.

HOTELS
★BEST WESTERN HI-DESERT INN

320 Main St., Tonopah, 775-482-3511, 877-286-2208; www.bestwestern.com
89 rooms. Complimentary full breakfast. Pets accepted. Pool. High-speed Internet access. **$**

★★STATION HOUSE HOTEL AND CASINO

1137 S. Main St., Tonopah, 775-482-9777, 866-611-9777; www.tonopahstation.com
75 rooms. Restaurant, bar. Casino. Pets accepted. **$**

★
★
★
★
☆

VIRGINIA CITY

Nevada's most famous mining town once had a population of about 35,000 people and was one of the richest cities in North America. Its dazzling career coincided with the life of the Comstock Lode, which yielded more than $1 billion worth of silver and gold. In the 1870s, Virginia City had four banks, six churches, 110 saloons, an opera house, numerous theaters and the only elevator between Chicago and San Francisco. Great fortunes, including those of Hearst and Mackay, were founded here.

Virginia City is perched on the side of Mount Davidson, where a diagonal slit marks the Comstock Lode. The site is beautiful and the air is so clear that the blue and purple masses of the Stillwater Range can be seen 120 miles away. Visitors can tour mines and old mansions, some of which have been restored (Easter week, Memorial Day-October, daily); visit several museums and saloons (daily); stroll through the local shops; and ride on the steam-powered V&T Railroad (May-September).

Information: Chamber of Commerce, 86 South C. St., 775-847-7500; www.virginiacity-nv.org

WHAT TO SEE AND DO
THE CASTLE
70 South B St., Virginia City

Built by Robert N. Graves, a mine superintendent of the Empire Mine, the building was patterned after a castle in Normandy, France. Filled with international riches and original furnishings. Memorial Day weekend-October; daily.

WINNEMUCCA

Originally called French Ford, the town was renamed for the last great chief of the Paiutes, who ruled the area. Winnemucca was first settled by a Frenchman who set up a trading post. Many Basques live here.

Information: Winnemucca visitors Authority, 50 W. Winnemucca Blvd., 775-623-5071; www.winnemucca.nv.us

WHAT TO SEE AND DO
HUMBOLDT MUSEUM
175 W. Jungo Road, Winnemucca, 775-623-2912

Historical museum features American Indian artifacts; pioneers' home items; antique auto display; old country store and more. Monday-Saturday.

HOTELS
★BEST WESTERN GOLD COUNTRY INN
921 W. Winnemucca Blvd., Winnemucca, 775-623-6999, 800-346-5306; www.bestwestern.com

71 rooms. Airport transportation available. Pets accepted. Complimentary continental breakfast. High-speed Internet access. Business center. Pool. $

★DAYS INN
511 W. Winnemucca Blvd., Winnemucca, 775-623-3661, 800-329-7466; www.daysinn.com

50 rooms. Pets accepted. Pool. High-speed Internet access. Complimentary continental breakfast. Fitness center. Spa. $

★★RED LION

741 W. Winnemucca Blvd., Winnemucca, 775-623-2565, 800-733-5466;
www.redlion.com

105 rooms. Restaurant, bar. Airport transportation available. Casino. Pets accepted. Pool. High-speed Internet access. Fitness center. Business center. **$**

RESTAURANT

★ORMACHEA'S

180 Melarky St., Winnemucca, 775-623-3455

Basque, American menu. Dinner. Closed Monday. Bar. Children's menu. **$$**

285

NEVADA

★
★
★
★
★

NEW MEXICO

NEW MEXICO IS A LAND OF CONTRASTS. ITS HISTORY DATES BACK FAR BEFORE THE FIRST Spanish explorers arrived in 1540 in search of gold. One day you might be on a Native American reservation, the next you may be taking in the many art galleries and restaurants in Santa Fe.

New Mexico was first occupied by Native Americans and had been a territory of Spain and then Mexico before becoming a state in 1912. Today, it still has the highest percentage of Hispanic Americans and the second-highest population of Native Americans, making for a unique culture.

The landscape ranges from desert in the south to forest and mountain country with clear streams and snow in the north. The Sangre de Cristo (Blood of Christ) Mountains run north and south along the east side of the Rio Grand in the north. There are many national parks in New Mexico and several reservations, which are popular with tourists. The government built the Los Alamos Research Center during World War II, where the atomic bomb was developed and first detonated in the desert in 1954. There are atomic museums in Albuquerque. Experiments near Roswell caused some people to believe that a UFO landed here after headlines reported that a "flying disk" was found. The government said this was a research balloon, but this hasn't stopped speculation of a cover-up, although this has never been proven. The capital, Santa Fe, has a large artistic community. There are many art galleries and museums, including one honoring Georgia O'Keefe.

Information: www.newmexico.org

FUN FACTS

One out of four workers in New Mexico works directly for the federal government.

Santa Fe, at 7,000 feet, is the highest capital in the U.S.

ALAMOGORDO

Alamogordo is a popular tourist destination because of its proximity to Mescalero Apache Indian Reservation, Lincoln National Forest and White Sands National Monument. A branch of New Mexico State University is located here. Surrounded by desert and mountains, the first atomic bomb was set off nearby.

Information: Chamber of Commerce, 1301 N. White Sands Blvd.,
505-437-6120, 888-843-3441; www.alamogordo.com

WHAT TO SEE AND DO
ALAMEDA PARK ZOO
1321 N. White Sands Blvd., Alamogordo, 505-439-4290
Built in 1898, this is the oldest zoo in the Southwest. It has 300 native and exotic animals. Daily 9 a.m.-5 p.m.

LINCOLN NATIONAL FOREST

3463 Las Palomas Road, Alamogordo, 505-434-7200; www.fs.fed.us/r3/lincoln

This forest is known as the birthplace of Smokey Bear. Fishing, hunting, picnicking, camping, wild cave tours and winter sports in the Sacramento, Capitan and Guadalupe mountains. Backpack in the White Mountain Capitan Wildernesses. Camping.

NEW MEXICO MUSEUM OF SPACE HISTORY

Highway 2001, Alamogordo, 575-437-2840, 877-333-6589; www.nmspacemuseum.org

This museum features space-related artifacts and exhibits and an IMAX theater. Daily 9 a.m.-5 p.m.

OLIVER LEE STATE PARK

409 Dog Canyon Road, Alamogordo, 505-437-8284;
www.emnrd.state.nm.us/PRD/oliverlee.htm

Mountain climbers, photographers and history buffs will enjoy this state park, the site of at least five major battles. The box canyon is protected by a 2,000-foot bluff. Also includes Frenchy's Place, a substantial rock house with miles of stone fence. Hiking, camping. Visitor center, museum, tours of restored Lee Ranch House.

THREE RIVERS PETROGLYPH SITE

County Road B-30, Three Rivers, 505-525-4300; www.blm.gov

Twenty-thousand rock carvings were made here between A.D. 900-1400 by the Jornada Branch of the Mogollon Indian Culture. Semidesert terrain includes interpretive signs, a reconstructed prehistoric village, six picnic sites and tent and trailer sites.

WHITE SANDS NATIONAL MONUMENT

These shifting, dazzling-white dunes are a challenge to plants and animals. Here, lizards and mice are white like the sand, helping them blend in with the background. (Similarly, mice are black in the black lava area only a few miles north.)

Plants elongate their stems up to 30 feet so that they can keep their leaves and flowers above the sand. When the sands recede, the plants are sometimes left on elevated pillars of hardened gypsum bound together by their roots. Even an ancient two-wheeled Spanish cart was laid bare when the sands shifted.

Beach sand is usually silica, but White Sands National Monument sand is gypsum, from which plaster of Paris is made. Dunes often rise to 60 feet; White Sands is the largest gypsum dune field in the world.

White Sands National Monument encloses 143,732 acres of this remarkable area. The visitor center has exhibits concerning the dunes and how they were formed. Daily. Evening programs and guided nature walks in the dunes area are conducted Memorial Day-mid-August. Picnic area with shaded tables and grills (no water); primitive backpackers' campsite (by permit only).

Information: Highway 70, Alamogordo, 505-679-2599;
www.nps.gov/whsa

TOY TRAIN DEPOT

1991 N. White Sands Blvd., Alamogordo, 888-207-3564;
www.toytraindepot.homestead.com

More than 1,200 feet of model railroad track and hundreds of model and toy trains are on display in this five-room, 100-year-old train depot, as well as a two-mile outdoor miniature railroad track.

SPECIAL EVENT
TRINITY SITE TOUR

1301 N. White Sands Blvd., Alamogordo, 505-437-6120, 888-843-3441;
www.alamogordo.com/activites/trinity.html

Visit the site of the first atomic bomb explosion, open to the public twice a year. First Saturday in April and October, 9 a.m.-2 p.m.

HOTEL
★BEST WESTERN DESERT AIRE HOTEL

1021 S. White Sands Blvd., Alamogordo, 505-437-2110; www.bestwestern.com

92 rooms. High-speed Internet access. Complimentary continental breakfast. Pets accepted. Pool. Spa. $

NEW MEXICO

★
★ ★
★ ★
★

THE NATIVE AMERICAN INFLUENCE

Native Americans occupied New Mexico for centuries before the arrival of Europeans. The exploring Spaniards called them Pueblo Indians because their tightly clustered communities were not unlike Spanish pueblos, or villages. The Apache and Navajo, who arrived in New Mexico after the Pueblo people, were seminomadic wanderers. The Navajo eventually adopted many of the Pueblo ways, although their society is less structured than that of the Pueblo. The main Navajo reservation straddles New Mexico and Arizona. The Apache, living closer to the Plains Indians, remained more nomadic.

The 19 Pueblo groups have close-knit communal societies and cultures, even though they speak six different languages. Their pueblos are unique places to visit. In centuries-old dwellings, craftspeople make and sell a variety of wares. Religious ceremonies, which include many dances and songs, are quite striking and not to be missed.

Tourists are welcome at all reservations in New Mexico on most days, although there are various restrictions. Because the religious ceremonies are sacred, photography is generally prohibited. This may also be true of certain sacred areas of the pueblo (in a few cases, the entire pueblo). Sometimes permission to photograph or draw is needed and fees may be required. The ancient culture and traditions of these people hold great meaning; visitors should be as respectful of them as they would be of their own. Questions should be directed to the pueblo governor or representative at the tribal office.

More can be learned about New Mexico's Native Americans and their origins at the many museums and sites in Santa Fe, the visitor center at Bandelier National Monument and the Indian Pueblo Cultural Center.

ALBUQUERQUE

In 1706, Don Francisco Cuervo y Valdes, then-governor of New Mexico, moved 30 families from Bernalillo to a spot some 15 miles south on the Rio Grande where the pasturage was better.

Catholic missionaries began to build churches in the area and inadvertently brought diseases that afflicted the Pueblo Indians. The settlers fought with the Native Americans for many years, but Albuquerque now celebrates the cultural heritage of groups like the Pueblo, the Anasazi and other tribes. By 1790, the population had grown to almost 6,000 (a very large town for New Mexico at the time). Today, Albuquerque is the largest city in New Mexico.

Albuquerque was an important U.S. military outpost from 1846 to 1870. In 1880, when a landowner near the Old Town refused to sell, the Santa Fe Railroad chose a route two miles east, forming a new town called New Albuquerque. It wasn't long before the new town had enveloped what is still called "Old Town," now a popular tourist shopping area.

Surrounded by mountains, Albuquerque continues to grow. The largest industry is Sandia National Laboratories, a laboratory engaged in solar and nuclear research and the testing and development of nuclear weapons.

Dry air and plenty of sunshine (more than 75 percent of the time) have earned Albuquerque a reputation as a health center. Adding to that reputation is the Lovelace Medical Center (similar to the Mayo Clinic in Rochester, Minnesota), which gave the first United States astronauts their qualifying examinations. The University of New Mexico is also located in Albuquerque.

Local attractions such as the annual Albuquerque Balloon Fiesta and several nearby vineyards make it a place for all to visit and enjoy. The culture is an active one and the people of Albuquerque enjoy as many outdoor activities as they can fit into their schedules.

Information: Convention & Visitors Bureau, 20 First Plaza N.W., 505-842-9918, 800-284-2282; www.abqcvb.org

WHAT TO SEE AND DO
ALBUQUERQUE BIOLOGICAL PARK
903 10th St. S.W., Albuquerque, 505-764-6200; www.cabq.gov/biopark
This biological park consists of the Albuquerque Aquarium, the Rio Grande Botanic Garden and the Rio Grande Zoo. The aquarium features a shark tank, eel tunnel and shrimp boat. The botanic garden displays formal walled gardens and a glass conservatory. The zoo exhibits include koalas, polar bears, sea lions and shows. Daily 9 a.m.-5 p.m., until 6 p.m. summer weekends and holidays.

ALBUQUERQUE LITTLE THEATRE
224 San Pasquale Ave. S.W., Albuquerque, 505-242-4750;
www.albuquerquelittletheatre.org
This historic community theater troupe stages Broadway productions. September-May.

ALBUQUERQUE MUSEUM

2000 Mountain Road N.W., Albuquerque, 505-243-7255; www.cabq.gov/museum
Located in a solar-heated building across from the New Mexico Museum of Natural History and Science, this museum showcases regional art and history. Tuesday-Sunday 9 a.m.-5 p.m.

CIBOLA NATIONAL FOREST

2113 Osuna Road N.E., Albuquerque, 505-346-3900; www.fs.fed.us/r3/cibola
This forest has more than 1.5-million acres and stretches throughout Central New Mexico. The park includes Mount Taylor (11,301 feet), several mountain ranges and four wilderness areas: Sandia Mountain (where you'll see bighorn sheep), Manzano Mountain, Apache Kid and Withington. Scenic drives.

CORONADO STATE MONUMENT

485 Kuaua Road, Bernalillo, 505-867-5351
Francisco Vásquez de Coronado is said to have camped near this excavated pueblo in 1540 on his famous quest for the seven golden cities of Cibola. Reconstructed, painted kiva; visitor center devoted to Southwestern culture and the Spanish influence on the area. Wednesday-Monday 8:30 a.m.-4:30 p.m.

FINE ARTS CENTER, UNIVERISTY OF NEW MEXICO

Central Avenue and Stanford Drive, Albuquerque, 505-277-4001; www.unm.edu
Houses the University Art Museum, which features more than 23,000 pieces in its collection. Tuesday-Friday 9 a.m.-4 p.m., Sunday 1-4 p.m.; the Fine Arts Library, which contains the Southwest Music Archives; the Rodey Theatre; and Popejoy Hall, home of the New Mexico Symphony Orchestra and host of the Best of Broadway International Theatre seasons of plays, dance and music.

INDIAN PUEBLO CULTURAL CENTER

2401 12th St. N.W., Albuquerque, 505-843-7270, 866-855-7902;
www.indianpueblo.org
Owned and operated by the 19 pueblos of New Mexico, exhibits in the museum tell the story of the Pueblo culture. The gallery showcases handcrafted art; Native American dance and craft demonstrations (weekends). Restaurant. Daily 9 a.m.-5 p.m.; closed major holidays.

JONSON GALLERY

1909 Las Lomas Road N.E., Albuquerque, 505-277-4967; www.unm.edu/~jonsong
This gallery, owned by the University of New Mexico and part of its art museums, houses the archives and work of modernist painter Raymond Jonson (1891-1982) and a few works by his contemporaries. Tuesday-Friday 10 a.m.-4 p.m.

MAXWELL MUSEUM OF ANTHROPOLOGY

1 University of New Mexico, Albuquerque, 505-277-4405; www.unm.edu/~maxwell
Permanent and changing exhibits of early man and Native American cultures with an emphasis on the Southwest. Tuesday-Friday 9 a.m.-4 p.m., Saturday 10 a.m.-4 p.m.

MUSEUM OF GEOLOGY AND INSTITUTE OF METEORITICS METEORITE MUSEUM

Northrop Hall, 200 Yale Blvd. N.E., Albuquerque, 505-277-4204

The Museum of Geology contains numerous samples of ancient plants, minerals, rocks and animals while the meteorite museum has a major collection of more than 550 meteorites. Monday-Friday 7:30 a.m.-4:30 p.m.

NATIONAL ATOMIC MUSEUM

1905 Mountain Road N.W., Albuquerque, 505-245-2137; www.atomicmuseum.com

This nuclear energy science center, the nation's only such museum, features exhibits depicting the history of the atomic age, including the Manhattan Project, the Cold War and the development of nuclear medicine. See replicas of Little Boy and Fat Man, the world's first two atomic weapons deployed in Japan in World War II, as well as B-52 and B-29 aircraft. Guided tours and audiovisual presentations are offered. Daily 9 a.m.-5 p.m.; closed holidays.

NEW MEXICO MUSEUM OF NATURAL HISTORY AND SCIENCE

1801 Mountain Road N.W., Albuquerque, 505-841-2800; www.museums.state.nm.us/nmmnh

Those interested in dinosaurs, fossils and volcanoes will love this museum, with exhibits on botany, geology, paleontology and zoology. The LodeStar Astronomy Center gives museumgoers a view of the heavens in its observatory. Daily 9 a.m.-5 p.m.; closed Thanksgiving Day, Christmas Day, New Years Day and nonholiday Mondays in September and January.

OLD TOWN

Old Town and Romero roads, Albuquerque

The original settlement is one block north of Central Avenue, the city's main street, at Rio Grande Boulevard. Old Town Plaza retains a lovely Spanish flavor with many interesting shops and restaurants.

PETROGLYPH NATIONAL MONUMENT

6001 Unser Blvd., Albuquerque, 505-899-0205; www.nps.gov/petr

This park contains concentrated groups of rock drawings experts believe ancestors of the Pueblo carved on lava formations. Three hiking trails wind along the 17-mile escarpment. Daily 8 a.m.-5 p.m.

RIO GRANDE NATURE CENTER STATE PARK

2901 Candelaria Road N.W., Albuquerque, 505-344-7240; www.emnrd.state.nm.us/prd/RGNC.htm

The highlight here is a glass-enclosed observation room overlooking a three-acre pond that is home to birds and other wildlife; interpretive displays on the wildlife of the bosque (cottonwood groves) along the Rio Grande; two miles of nature trails. Guided hikes, hands-on activities. Daily 8 a.m.-5 p.m.

RIO GRANDE ZOO

903 10th St. S.W., Albuquerque, 505-764-6200; www.cabq.gov/biopark/zoo

More than 1,200 exotic animals; rain forest, reptile house, white tigers and more. Daily 9 a.m.-5 p.m., until 6 p.m. weekends in summer.

SANDIA PEAK AERIAL TRAMWAY

Albuquerque, five miles northeast of city limits via Interstate 25 and Tramway Road,
505-856-7325; www.sandiapeak.com

The tram travels almost three miles up the west slope of the Sandia Mountains to 10,378 feet, with amazing 11,000-square-mile views. Hiking trail; restaurant at summit and Mexican grill at base. Memorial Day-Labor Day, daily 9 a.m.-9 p.m.; shorter hours rest of year; closed two weeks in April and two weeks in October.

SANDIA PEAK TRAMWAY SKI AREA

Albuquerque, in Cibola National Forest, Crest Scenic Byway, Sandia Mountains,
505-856-7325; www.sandiapeak.com

Four double chairlifts, surface lift; patrol, school, rentals, snowmaking. Aerial tramway on the west side of the mountain meets lifts at the top. Longest run is more than 2½ miles; vertical drop 1,700 feet. Mid-December-March, daily. Chairlift also operates July-Labor Day. Friday-Sunday.

TELEPHONE PIONEER MUSEUM

110 Fourth St. N.W., Albuquerque, 505-842-2937

Displays trace the development of the telephone from 1876 to the present. More than 400 types of telephones, plus switchboards, early equipment and old telephone directories. Monday-Friday 10 a.m.-2 p.m.; weekends by appointment.

UNIVERSITY OF NEW MEXICO

Central Avenue and University Boulevard, Albuquerque,
505-277-1989, 800-225-5866; www.unm.edu

Established 1889; 25,000 students. This campus has both Spanish and Pueblo architectural influences. It is one of the largest universities in the Southwest.

SPECIAL EVENTS
ALBUQUERQUE INTERNATIONAL BALLOON FIESTA

Balloon Fiesta Park, North Albuquerque, 505-821-1000, 888-422-7277; www.aibf.org

As many as 100,000 people attend this annual event, the largest of its kind in the world. Attendees can catch their own balloon rides from Rainbow Ryders Inc. (505-823-1111). First Saturday in October through the following Sunday.

FOUNDERS DAY

Old Town, Albuquerque, 505-768-3556; www.cabq.gov

Celebrates the city's founding in 1706 with traditional New Mexican festivities. Late April.

INDIAN PUEBLO CULTURAL CENTER

2401, 12th St., Albuquerque, 505-843-7270; www.indianpueblo.org

Traditional Native American dances, races, contests. Late May-mid-June.

MUSICAL THEATER SOUTHWEST

2401 Ross Ave. S.E., Albuquerque, 505-265-9119; www.musicaltheatresw.com

This troupe produces five Broadway-style musicals each season at the historic Hiland Theater in the Frank A. Peloso Performing Arts Center.

NEW MEXICO ARTS & CRAFTS FAIR

303 Romero St. N.W., Albuquerque, 505-884-9043; www.nmartsandcraftsfair.org

Exhibits and demonstrations by more than 200 craftsworkers representing Spanish, Native American and other North American cultures. Artists sell their wares, which range from paintings to sculpture to jewelry. Last weekend in June.

NEW MEXICO STATE FAIR

Expo New Mexico State Fairgrounds, 300 San Pedro Blvd., Albuquerque, 505-265-3976; www.exponm.com

Horse shows and racing, rodeo, midway, flea market; entertainment. September.

NEW MEXICO SYMPHONY ORCHESTRA

University of New Mexico, Popejoy Hall, 4407 Menaul Blvd., Albuquerque, 505-881-9590, 800-251-6676; www.nmso.org

September-May.

SANTA ANA FEAST DAY

Santa Ana and Taos Pueblos, Albuquerque; www.santaana.org

Corn dance. Late July.

TAOS PUEBLO DANCES

Taos Pueblo, Albuquerque, 505-758-1028; www.taospueblo.com

Several Native American dances are held throughout the year. For a schedule of annual dances, contact the pueblo.

HOTELS

★★BEST WESTERN RIO GRANDE INN

1015 Rio Grande Blvd. N.W., Albuquerque, 505-843-9500, 800-959-4726; www.riograndeinn.com

173 rooms. Restaurant, bar. High-speed Internet access. Business center. Fitness center. Pool. $

★★COURTYARD ALBUQUERQUE AIRPORT

1920 S. Yale Blvd., Albuquerque, 505-843-6600, 800-321-2211; www.marriott.com

150 rooms. Wireless Internet access. Restaurant, bar. Airport transportation available. Pool. $

★★DOUBLETREE HOTEL

201 Marquette Ave. N.W., Albuquerque, 505-247-3344; www.albuquerque.doubletree.com

295 rooms. High-speed Internet access. Restaurant, bar. Pool. Business center. Fitness center. $$

★★★HILTON ALBUQUERQUE

1901 University Blvd. N.E., Albuquerque, 505-884-2500, 800-274-6835; www.hilton.com

With its arched doorways, Native American rugs and local art, this hotel on 14 acres near the university fits right in. Guests will enjoy the indoor and outdoor heated pools, sauna and lighted tennis courts. Accommodations feature sliding glass doors and balconies with great view of the high desert. 261 rooms. High-speed Internet access. Two restaurants, bar. Pool. Fitness center. Business center. **$**

★★★HOTEL ALBUQUERQUE AT OLD TOWN

800 Rio Grande Blvd. N.W., Albuquerque, 505-843-6300, 800-237-2133;
www.buynewmexico.com

With its large, open lobby and tiled floors, this property offers a casual yet elegant environment. Located in historic Old Town across from the New Mexico Museum of Natural History, it is close to more than 200 specialty stores. All guest rooms feature furniture made by local artists. 188 rooms. High-speed Internet access. Two restaurants, bar. Pets accepted. Pool. Spa. Business center. **$**

★HOMEWOOD SUITES BY HILTON ALBUQUERQUE

7101 Arvada Ave. N.E., Albuquerque, 505-881-7300; www.homewoodsuites.com

151 rooms, all suites. Business center. Fitness Room. Pool. Complimentary breakfas. High-speed Internet access. **$**

★★★HYATT REGENCY ALBUQUERQUE

330 Tijeras N.W., Albuquerque, 505-842-1234, 800-233-1234; www.hyatt.com

Adjacent to the convention center, this 22-story tower is centrally located near Old Town and the Rio Grande Zoo and is only five miles from the airport. One of the city's newest high-rise hotels, the property offers a health club, sauna and outdoor pool. Business rooms include separate work areas and dual line phones. All rooms have a warm Southwestern décor and views of the city or mountains. 395 rooms. High-speed Internet access. Restaurant, two bars. Fitness center. Pool. Business center. **$$**

MCM ELEGANTE

2020 Menaul Blvd. N.E., Albuquerque, 505-884-2511;
www.mcmelegantealbuquerque.com

360 rooms. Restaurant, bar. Airport transportation available. Pets accepted. Pool. Fitness center. **$**

SPECIALTY LODGINGS

CASAS DE SUENOS OLD TOWN BED & BREAKFAST INN

310 Rio Grande Blvd. S.W., Albuquerque, 505-247-4560, 800-655-7002;
www.casasdesuenos.com

Situated in the valley of the Sandia Mountains just three blocks from the Historic Old Town Area, this inn features the art of local talents. Beautiful guest rooms offer private baths, private entrances, televisions and VCRs. Enjoy a full breakfast in the sunny garden room featuring such dishes as Southwestern frittatas. 21 rooms. Complimentary full breakfast. Wireless Internet access. Pets accepted. **$**

HACIENDA ANTIGUA BED & BREAKFAST

6708 Tierra Drive N.W., Albuquerque, 505-345-5399, 800-201-2986;
www.haciendaantigua.com

Built on the famous Camino Real, this 200-year-old adobe inn is conveniently located in the North Valley area. The warm property features traditional kiva fireplaces and antique furnishings in the guest rooms. Eight rooms. Complimentary full breakfast. Pets accepted. Pool. **$$**

MAUGER BED & BREAKFAST INN

701 Roma Ave. N.W., Albuquerque, 505-242-8755, 800-719-9189;
www.maugerbb.com

This warm bed and breakfast is centrally located near the business district and Old Town. The suites in this restored Queen Anne house include fresh flowers, antique furniture, private baths and data ports. 10 rooms. Complimentary full breakfast. Pets accepted. Wireless Internet access. Spa. **$**

RESTAURANTS

★66 DINER

1405 Central Ave. N.E., Albuquerque, 505-247-1421; www.66diner.com

American, Southwestern menu. Breakfast, lunch, dinner. Children's menu. Casual attire. **$**

★★ANTIQUITY

112 Romero St. N.W., Albuquerque, 505-247-3545; www.themenupage.com

American, Southwestern menu. Dinner. Casual attire. Reservations recommended. **$$**

★★★ARTICHOKE CAFÉ

424 Central St., Albuquerque, 505-243-0200; www.artichokecafe.com

This pleasant eatery, which has tables set with beautiful fresh flowers, serves a mix of French, Italian and creative American cuisine. Dishes include steamed artichokes with three dipping sauces, or housemade pumpkin ravioli and scallops wrapped in prosciutto. American menu. Lunch, dinner. Casual attire. Reservations recommended. **$$**

★★BARRY'S OASIS

4451 Osuna Road N.E., Albuquerque, 505-884-2324; www.barrysoasis.com

Mediterranean menu. Lunch, dinner. Casual attire. Reservations recommended. **$**

★CHRISTY MAE'S

1400 San Pedro Drive N.E., Albuquerque, 505-255-4740; www.christymaes.com

American menu. Lunch, dinner. Closed Sunday. Children's menu. Casual attire. **$**

★COOPERAGE

7220 Lomas Blvd. N.E., Albuquerque, 505-255-1657

American menu. Lunch, dinner. Bar. Casual attire. **$$**

★GARDUNO'S OF MEXICO

10551 Montgomery Blvd. N.E., Albuquerque, 505-298-5000;
www.gardunosrestaurants.com

Mexican menu. Lunch, dinner, Sunday brunch. Bar. Children's menu. Casual attire. Outdoor seating. **$$**

★★HIGH NOON

425 San Felipe St. N.W., Albuquerque, 505-765-1455; www.999dine.com

Southwestern, steak menu. Lunch, dinner. Bar. Children's menu. Casual attire. **$$**

★LA HACIENDA DINING ROOM

302 San Felipe St. N.W., Albuquerque, 505-243-3131

Southwestern menu. Lunch, dinner. Bar. Children's menu. Casual attire. Outdoor seating. **$$**

★★★SCALO NOB HILL

3500 Central Ave. S.E., Albuquerque, 505-255-8782; www.scalonobhill.com

Chef Enrique Guerrero has taken over the kitchen of this Northern Italian grill with dining areas on several levels. He's already brought back favorites such as chicken cooked under a brick. American menu. Lunch, dinner. Closed Monday. Bar. Casual attire. Reservations recommended. Outdoor seating. **$$**

★★TROMBINO'S BISTRO ITALIANO

5415 Academy Blvd. N.E., Albuquerque, 505-821-5974

Italian menu. Lunch, dinner, brunch. Closed Super Bowl Sunday. Bar. Children's menu. **$$**

ANGEL FIRE

This is a family resort area high in the Sangre de Cristo Mountains of Northern New Mexico.

Information: Chamber of Commerce, 505-377-6661, 800-446-8117;
www.angelfirechamber.org

WHAT TO SEE AND DO

ANGEL FIRE SKI RESORT

10 Miller Lane, Angel Fire, 575-377-6401, 800-633-7463; www.angelfireresort.com

Resort has two high-speed quad, three double chairlifts; patrol, school, rentals; 70 runs, longest run more than three miles; vertical drop 2,077 feet. Thanksgiving-March, daily. Nordic center, snowmobiling. Summer resort includes fishing, boating, 18-hole golf, tennis, mountain biking, riding stables. Conference center year round.

CIMARRON CANYON STATE PARK

29519 Highway 64, Eagle Nest, 505-377-6271

This region of high mountains and deep canyons has scenic 200-foot palisades; winding mountain stream has excellent trout fishing; state wildlife area. Hiking, rock climbing, wildlife viewing, winter sports, camping. Daily.

EAGLE NEST LAKE

Highway 64, Angel Fire, www.eaglenestlake.org

This 2,200-acre lake offers year-round fishing for rainbow trout and Kokanee salmon (fishing license required).

VIETNAM VETERANS STATE PARK MEMORIAL

Highway 64, Angel Fire, 505-377-6900; www.angelfirememorial.com

This beautiful, gracefully designed building stands on a hillside overlooking Moreno Valley and the Sangre de Cristo Mountains. Chapel. Daily.

★
★
★
★
★

ARTESIA

Artesia was named for the vast underground water supplies that once rushed up through drilled wells and are now used to irrigate the area's farmland. The first underground school in the United States, Abo Elementary School, was built here for safety from the radiation effects of fallout. Artesia is also the home of the Federal Law Enforcement Training Center. The area offers wild turkey, deer, bear and upland game for hunting enthusiasts.

Information: Chamber of Commerce, 107 N. First St., 505-746-2744, 800-658-6251; www.artesiachamber.com

WHAT TO SEE AND DO
HISTORICAL MUSEUM AND ART CENTER
503 and 505 W. Richardson Ave., Artesia, 505-748-2390
Pioneer and Native American artifacts; changing art exhibits. Tuesday-Saturday.

HOTELS
★★BEST WESTERN PECOS INN MOTEL
2209 W. Main St., Artesia, 505-748-3324; www.bestwestern.com
82 rooms. Restaurant, bar. Pool. Complimentary full breakfast. Free parking. Free high-speed Internet access. Fitness center. $

HERITAGE INN
209 W. Main St., Artesia, 505-748-2552, 866-207-0222; www.artesiaheritageinn.com
11 rooms. Complimentary continental breakfast. Wireless Internet access. Pets accepted. $

RESTAURANT
★★LA FONDA
210 W. Main St., Artesia, 505-746-9377; www.hi-nm.com/?cat=5
Mexican menu. Lunch, dinner. Casual attire. $

AZTEC

Aztec is the seat of San Juan County, a fruit-growing and cattle-grazing area. This town is filled with history. Architectural and historic commentary for walking tours may be obtained at the Aztec Museum.

Information: Chamber of Commerce, 110 N. Ash, 505-334-9551; www.aztecnm.com

WHAT TO SEE AND DO
AZTEC MUSEUM AND PIONEER VILLAGE
125 N. Main St., Aztec, 505-334-9829
The main museum here houses authentic pioneer artifacts, including mineral and fossil displays, household items, farm and ranch tools and Native American artifacts. Also includes the Oil Field Museum with 1920s cable tool oil rig, oil well pumping unit and more. Also here is Pioneer Village, which features 12 reconstructed buildings, including doctor's and sheriff's offices, blacksmith shop and foundry, 1880 pioneer cabin, general store and post office, original Aztec jail and church. Admission: adults $3, children $1, children under 12 free. Wednesday-Saturday 10 a.m.-4 p.m.

AZTEC RUINS NATIONAL MONUMENT

Aztec Ruins Road, Aztec, 505-334-6174; www.nps.gov/azru

These are actually ancient Pueblo ruins, dating back to the 11th to 13th centuries, that were misnamed by early settlers in the 1800s. The partially excavated pueblo contains nearly 450 rooms, with its plaza dominated by the Great Kiva (48 feet in diameter). Instructive museum; interpretive programs in summer. Self-guided tours; trail guide available at visitor center for the ¼-mile trail. Daily.

NAVAJO LAKE STATE PARK

Aztec, 18 miles east via Highway 173, 505-632-2278;
www.emnrd.state.nm.us/PRD/navajo.htm

Surrounded by sandstone mesas and stands of piñon and juniper, the reservoir extends 35 miles upstream into Colorado, totaling 15,000 surface acres of water. Daily.

PINE RIVER SITE

Aztec

Swimming, waterskiing, fishing (panfish, catfish, bass, salmon and trout), boating (ramps, rentals, marina); picnicking (fireplaces), camping. Visitor center with interpretive displays.

SAN JUAN RIVER RECREATION AREA

Aztec, below the dam
Fishing (trout); camping.

SIMS MESA SITE

Aztec, east side
Boat ramp; camping.

HOTEL
★STEP BACK INN

123 W. Aztec Blvd., Aztec, 505-334-1200, 800-334-1255
39 rooms. Complimentary continental breakfast. **$**

BERNALILLO

Located in the Rio Grande Valley, midway between Santa Fe and Albuquerque, Bernalillo is an area rich in history. Camino del Pueblo, the city's main street, is part of the famed Route 66.

Information: 243 Camino del Pueblo, 505-867-8687, 800-252-0191

SPECIALTY LODGING
LA HACIENDA GRANDE

21 Barros Road, Bernalillo, 505-867-1887, 800-353-1887; www.lahaciendagrande.com
This bed and breakfast, a Spanish hacienda built in the 1750s, has cathedral ceilings, an open-air center courtyard, a kiva-warmed sitting room and a brick kitchen. Six rooms. Complimentary full breakfast. Pets accepted. **$**

RESTAURANTS
★★★PRAIRIE STAR
288 Prairie Star Road, Bernalillo, 505-867-3327; www.santaanagolf.com
This casual fine-dining restaurant in the Santa Ana Golf Club specializes in game and has stunning views of the Sandia Mountains. American menu. Dinner. Closed Monday. Bar. Children's menu. Casual attire. Reservations recommended. Outdoor seating. **$$**

★RANGE CAFÉ AND BAKERY
925 Camino del Pueblo, Bernalillo, 505-867-1700; www.rangecafe.com
Southwestern menu. Breakfast, lunch, dinner. Bar. Children's menu. Casual attire. **$$**

CAPITAN
Capitan, a village in Lincoln County, is known as the birthplace of Smokey Bear. In 1950, a badly burned bear was rescued from a large forest fire in the Capitan Mountains. The bear was named "Smokey" and was used as the mascot for the U.S. Forest Service. He was sent to the National Zoo in Washington DC, where he spent 26 years. After he died, he was returned here and buried in Smokey Bear Historical State Park.

Information: www.villageofcapitan.com

WHAT TO SEE AND DO
SMOKEY BEAR HISTORICAL STATE PARK
118 Smokey Bear Blvd., (Highway 380), Capitan, 505-354-2748;
www.emnrd.state.nm.us/fd/SmokeyBear/SmokeyBearPark.htm
Commemorates the history and development of the national symbol of forest fire prevention. The original Smokey, who was orphaned by a fire raging in the Lincoln National Forests, is buried here within sight of the mountain where he was found. Fire prevention exhibit, film. Admission: adults $2, children $1, children under 7 free. Daily 9 a.m.-5 p.m.

SMOKEY BEAR MUSEUM
102 Smokey Bear Blvd., Capitan, 575-354-2298
Features 1950s memorabilia of famed fire-fighting bear, whose real-life counterpart was found in the nearby Capitan Mountains. Daily.

NEW MEXICO

★
★
★
★
☆

CAPULIN VOLCANO NATIONAL MONUMENT
This dormant volcano last erupted approximately 10,000 years ago. The strikingly symmetrical cinder cone rises more than 1,500 feet from plains, with a crater one mile in circumference and 415 feet deep. Visitors can spiral completely around the mountain on paved road to rim (Daily); five states can be seen on clear days. Picnic area. Visitor center with exhibits of geology, flora and fauna of the area. Daily. Uniformed personnel on duty at the crater rim (summer only).
Information: 29 miles east on Highway 64/87 to Capulin, then 3½ miles north, 505-278-2201; www.nps.gov/cavo

HOTEL
★SMOKEY BEAR MOTEL
316 Smokey Bear Blvd., Capitan, 505-354-2257, 800-766-5392;
www.smokeybearmotel.com
Nine rooms. **$**

CARLSBAD
On the lovely Pecos River, Carlsbad is an excellent place to get out and explore, thanks to nearby Carlsbad Caverns and the Guadalupe Mountains National Park.
Information: Convention & Visitors Bureau, 302 S. Canal St., Carlsbad,
505-887-6516, 800-221-1224; www.carlsbadchamber.com

WHAT TO SEE AND DO
CARLSBAD MUSEUM & ART CENTER
Halagueno Park, 418 W. Fox St., Carlsbad, 505-887-0276; www.nmculture.org
Showcases Pueblo pottery, art and meteorite remains; pioneer and Apache relics; bird carvings by Jack Drake; mineral exhibits and more. Summer: Monday-Saturday 10 a.m.-6 p.m.; winter, Monday-Saturday 10 a.m.-5 p.m.

LAKE CARLSBAD WATER RECREATION AREA
Carlsbad, off Green Street on the Pecos River, 575-887-2702
Swimming, water sports, fishing, boating; tennis, golf, picnic area.

LIVING DESERT ZOO AND GARDENS STATE PARK
1504 Miehls Drive, Carlsbad, 505-887-5516;
www.emnrd.state.nm.us/PRD/livingdesert.htm
This 1,100-acre park is an indoor/outdoor living museum of the Chihuahuan Desert's plants and animals. The Desert Arboretum has an extensive cactus collection and the zoo has more than 60 animal species native to the region, including mountain lions, bear, wolf, elk, bison and an extensive aviary. Summer: daily 8 a.m.-8 p.m.; winter: daily 9 a.m.-5 p.m.

SITTING BULL FALLS
Carlsbad, 11 miles northwest on Highway 285 to Highway 137, then 30 miles
southwest, in Lincoln National Forest, 505-885-4181, 800-221-122

HOTELS
★★BEST WESTERN STEVENS INN
1829 S. Canal St., Carlsbad, 505-887-2851; www.bestwestern.com
220 rooms. High-speed Internet access. Complimentary full breakfast. Restaurant, bar. Pets accepted. Pool. Fitness center. **$**

★★HOLIDAY INN
2210 W. Pierce St., Carlsbad, 505-234-1252, 888-465-4329; www.holiday-inn.com
100 rooms. Complimentary full breakfast. Restaurant, bar. Pool. High-speed Internet access. Fitness center. **$**

CARLSBAD CAVERNS NATIONAL PARK

One of the largest and most remarkable in the world, this cavern extends approximately 30 miles and extends as deep as 1,037 feet below the surface. It was once known as Bat Cave because of the spectacular bat flights, still a daily occurrence at sunset during the warmer months.

Cowboy and guano miner Jim White first explored and guided people through the caverns in the early 1900s, later working for the National Park Service as the Chief Park Ranger. Carlsbad Cave National Monument was established in 1923 and in 1930 the area was enlarged and designated a national park. The park contains 46,755 acres and more than 80 caves. Carlsbad Cavern was formed by the dissolving action of acidic water in the Tansill and Capitan limestones of the Permian age. When an uplift drained the cavern, mineral-laden water dripping from the ceiling formed the stalactites and stalagmites.

The main cavern has two self-guided routes, a Ranger-guided Kings Palace tour and several "off-trail" trips. The "Cavern Guide," an audio tour rented at the visitor center, enhances self-guided tours with interpretations of the caverns, interviews and historic re-creations. Tours are also available in two backcountry caves: Slaughter Canyon Cave and Spider Cave. All guided tours require reservations.

Bat flight programs are held each evening during the summer at the cavern entrance amphitheater.

Information: 727A Carlsbad Caverns Highway, Carlsbad, 505-785-2232; www.nps.gov/cave

CEDAR CREST

Located 20 miles outside of Albuquerque, Cedar Crest is a small town off of Highway 40.

Information: 12480 N. Highway 14B-163, Cedar Crest; www.eastmountainchamber.com

WHAT TO SEE AND DO
MUSEUM OF ARCHAEOLOGY AND MATERIAL CULTURE

22 Calvary Road, Cedar Crest, 505-281-2005

Highlights 12,000 years of Native American history and archaeological artifacts. Turquoise mining exhibit. May-November 1; daily noon-7 p.m.

SPECIALTY LODGING
ELAINE'S, A BED & BREAKFAST

72 Showline Road, Cedar Crest, 505-281-2467, 800-821-3092; www.elainesbnb.com

Set in a beautiful log cabin within easy distance of golfing, hiking, skiing, bird watching and more. Five rooms. Free wireless Internet access. $

CERRILLOS

Cerrillos, which means "Little Hills" in Spanish, is one of this region's traditional villages. Thanks to its preserved historic buildings, visitors can imagine they're in the Wild West as they stroll the town's tree-lined streets.

Information: www.newmexico.org

CHACO CULTURE NATIONAL HISTORICAL PARK

From A.D. 900 to 1150, Chaco Canyon was a major center of Anasazi culture. A prehistoric roadway system, which included stairways carved into sandstone cliffs, extends for hundreds of miles in all directions. Ancient roads up to 30 feet wide represent the most developed and extensive road network of this period north of Central America. Researchers speculate that Chaco Canyon was the center of a vast, complex and interdependent civilization in the American Southwest.

There are five self-guided trails with tours conducted Memorial Day-Labor Day, as well as evening campfire programs in summer. Visitor center has museum. Daily. Camping.

Information: Nageezi, from Highway 44, 25 miles south on country road 7900; three miles south of Nageezi Trading Post; from Interstate 40, 60 miles north of Thoreau on Highway 57. Check road conditions locally; may be extremely difficult when wet; www.nps.gov/chcu

WHAT TO SEE AND DO
BROKEN SADDLE RIDING COMPANY
56 Vicksville Road, Cerrillos, 505-424-7774; www.brokensaddle.com

Explore the desert backcountry surrounding the historic mining town of Cerrillos on smooth riding Missouri Foxtrotters and Tennessee Walkers. Broken Saddle Riding Company offers morning, afternoon and sunset rides catering to all riding levels and private rides by appointment. Excursions can include any number of scenic and historic areas surrounding the town of Cerrillos, including old mining areas, ghost towns and beautifully scenic desert terrain. Monthly full-moon rides are also offered. By appointment.

CERRILLOS TURQUOISE MINING MUSEUM
17 Waldo St., Cerrillos, 505-438-3008

Celebrates the mining legacy of this area with a collection of mineral samples that are breathtaking. Daily.

SPECIALTY LODGING
HIGH FEATHER RANCH BED & BREAKFAST
29 High Feather Ranch, Cerrillos, 505-424-1333, 800-757-4410;
www.highfeatherranch-bnb.com

This architecturally stunning ranch on 65 private acres features luxurious accommodations and a full gourmet breakfast. Three rooms. $$

CHAMA

Like many of New Mexico's towns, Chama began in the mid-1800s, when explorers discovered gold and silver in the surrounding hills and streams. The precious metals ran out, but the area's natural beauty is prize enough. Chama sits at the base of the Cumbres Pass in the San Juan Mountains.

Information: www.chamanewmexico.com

★
★
★
★
★

WHAT TO SEE AND DO
CUMBRES & TOLTEC SCENIC RAILROAD, NEW MEXICO EXPRESS
500 S. Terrace Ave., Chama, 888-286-2737; www.cumbrestoltec.com
Take a round-trip excursion to Osier, Colo., on an 1880s narrow-gauge steam railroad. The route passes through backwoods country and features spectacular mountain scenery. Trips to Antonito, Colo., are also available with van return. Reservations are recommended. Memorial Day-mid-October, daily.

EL VADO LAKE STATE PARK
Chama, 15 miles south on Highway 84 to Tierra Amarilla, then 13 miles southwest on Highway 112, 575-588-7247; www.emnrd.state.nm.us/PRD/elvado.htm
This park features an irrigation lake with fishing, ice fishing, boating (dock, ramps); hiking trail connects to Heron Lake, picnicking, playground, camping. Daily.

HERON LAKE STATE PARK
640 Highway 95, Chama, 505-588-7470; www.emnrd.state.nm.us/PRD/heron.htm
This region, with tall ponderosa pines, offers swimming, fishing (trout, salmon), ice fishing, boating (ramp, dock); hiking, winter sports, picnicking, camping. Daily.

CIMARRON
This historic Southwestern town was part of Lucien B. Maxwell's land holdings on the Santa Fe Trail. The St. James Hotel (1872), where Buffalo Bill Cody held his Wild West Shows, old jail (1872) and several other historic buildings still stand.
Information: Chamber of Commerce, 505-376-2417, 888-376-2417; www.cimarronnm.com

WHAT TO SEE AND DO
PHILMONT SCOUT RANCH
17 Deer Run Road, Cimarron, 575-376-2281; www.scouting.org/philmont
A 138,000-acre camp for some 20,000 Boy Scouts. Villa Philmonte, former summer home of ranch's benefactor, offers tours (mid-June-mid-August, daily; rest of year, call for schedule; fee). Ernest Thompson Seton Memorial Library and Philmont Museum includes several thousand drawings, paintings and Native American artifacts (Monday-Friday). Kit Carson Museum (seven miles south of headquarters; mid-June-August, daily). Camp also has buffalo, deer, elk, bear and antelope.

SPECIAL EVENTS
CIMARRON DAYS
Village Park Highway 64, Cimarron, 505-376-2417; www.cimarronnm.com/cimarron_days.htm
Crafts, entertainment. Labor Day weekend.

MAVERICK CLUB RODEO
Maverick Club Arena, Cimarron, 505-376-2417; www.cimarronnm.com/mavrodeo.htm
Rodeo for working cowboys. Parade, dance. July 4.

NEW MEXICO

★ ★ ★ ★ ★

CASA DEL GAVILAN

Highway 21 S., Cimarron, 505-376-2246, 800-428-4526; www.casadelgavilan.com

Nestled in the Sangre de Cristo Mountains, this Southwestern adobe inn built in 1912 is away from it all. Relax in the library or on the porch while sipping tea or wine, or go hiking in the trails behind the inn. Five rooms. Complimentary full breakfast. **$**

CLOUDCROFT

Cloudcroft has one of the highest golf courses in North America, but this is also a recreation area for nongolfers. It is located at the crest of the Sacramento Mountains in the Lincoln National Forest, among fir, spruce, pine and aspen trees. The area is popular with writers, photographers and artists. Several art schools conduct summer workshops here. There are also many miles of horseback trails through the mountains and skiing, snowmobiling and skating in winter. Several campgrounds are located in the surrounding forest. During the day temperatures seldom reach 80 F, and nights are always crisp and cool.

Information: Chamber of Commerce, 505-682-2733, 866-874-4447;
www.cloudcroft.net

WHAT TO SEE AND DO

SACRAMENTO MOUNTAINS HISTORICAL MUSEUM

1000 Highway 82, Cloudcroft, 505-682-2932;
www.cloudcroftmuseum.com/contact.htm

Exhibits depict life from 1880 to 1910 in the Sacramento Mountains area. Monday, Tuesday, Friday-Sunday.

SKI CLOUDCROFT

1920 Highway 82, East of Cloudcroft, Cloudcroft, 575-682-2333;
www.skicloudcroft.net

Double chairlift, beginner tows; patrol, school, rentals, snowmaking, lodge, snack bar, cafeteria, restaurant. Vertical drop 700 feet. Mid-December-mid-March, daily. Snowboarding. Elevations of 8,350-9,050 feet.

HOTEL

★★★THE LODGE RESORT AND SPA

1 Corona Place, Cloudcroft, 505-682-2566, 800-395-6343; www.thelodgeresort.com

This historic 1899 building is surrounded by 215,000 acres of the Lincoln National Forest and features a challenging golf course, full-service spa and lawn games including croquet, horseshoes and volleyball. Individually appointed rooms are decorated with antiques. 59 rooms. High-speed Internet access. Restaurant, bar. Children's activity center. Spa. Pets accepted. Pool. Golf. Business center. Fitness center. **$$**

CLOVIS

A mid-sized city in Eastern New Mexico, Clovis calls itself the gateway to the Land of Enchantment.

Information: Chamber of Commerce, 105 E. Grand Ave.,
575-763-3435, 800-261-7656; www.clovisnm.org

WHAT TO SEE AND DO
CLOVIS DEPOT MODEL TRAIN MUSEUM
221 W. First St., Clovis, 505-762-0066, 888-762-0064; www.clovisdepot.com
Built in 1907 by the Atchison, Topeka and Santa Fe Railway, the Depot has been restored to its condition in the 1950s era, and features working model train layouts, railroad memorabilia, historical displays and an operating telegraph station. Real train operations along one of the busiest rail lines in the U.S. can be viewed from a platform.

HILLCREST PARK AND ZOO
1201 Sycamore and 10th streets, Clovis, 575-769-7873
Second-largest zoo in New Mexico with more than 500 animals, most of which are exhibited in natural environments. Informational programs. Also includes a park with amusement rides, outdoor and indoor swimming pool, golf course, picnic areas and sunken garden.

SPECIAL EVENT
PIONEER DAYS & PRCA RODEO
1002 W. McDonald, Clovis, 575-763-3435
Parade, Little Buckaroo Rodeo. First week in June.

RESTAURANTS
★GUADALAJARA CAFÉ
916 L Casillas St., Clovis, 505-769-9965
Mexican menu. Lunch, dinner. Closed Sunday. Children's menu. Casual attire. Outdoor seating. **$**

★LEAL'S MEXICAN RESTAURANT
2115 N. Prince St., Clovis, 505-763-9069; www.lealsmexicanfoods.com
Mexican menu. Lunch, dinner. Children's menu. Casual attire. **$$**

CORRALES
Part of the Albuquerque metro area, Corrales grew up as an agricultural center and it's striving to preserve its rural lifestyle in the midst of the area's growth. It is home to Rancho de Corrales, a bar that locals claim is haunted.
Information: 4324 Corrales Road, 505-897-0502; www.corrales-nm.org

SPECIALTY LODGING
CHOCOLATE TURTLE BED & BREAKFAST
1098 W. Meadowlark Lane, Corrales, 505-898-1800, 877-298-1800;
www.chocolateturtleblo.com
Guests can relish the beautiful view of the mountains while enjoying the homemade chocolates and gourmet breakfasts. Four rooms. Wireless Internet access. Children over 6 years only. Complimentary full breakfast. **$**

DEMING

The old Butterfield Trail, route of an early stagecoach line to California, passed through about 12 miles north of here; there is a marker on Highway 180. Hunting enthusiasts will find deer, antelope, ibex, bear and blue quail plentiful in the surrounding mountains.

Information: Chamber of Commerce, 800 E. Pine St., Deming,
505-546-2674, 800-848-4955; www.cityofdeming.org

WHAT TO SEE AND DO
DEMING-LUNA MIMBRES MUSEUM
301 S. Silver St., Deming, 505-546-2382

See mining, military, ranching, railroad, Native American and Hispanic artifacts of the Southwest. Includes Mimbres pottery, Indian baskets, chuckwagon with equipment, quilt room gems and minerals and more. Musical center; art gallery. Daily.

ROCK HUNTING
Deming Gem and Mineral Society, Raymond Reed Blvd. next to Southwestern
NM Fairgrounds, 4335 Salvador Road S.E. Deming, 575-546-2674

Check out the jasper, onyx, nodules and many other types of semiprecious stones found in the area.

ROCKHOUND STATE PARK
Highway 143, Deming, 575-546-6182; www.emnrd.state.nm.us/prd/Rockhound.htm

This 1,000-acre park is on the rugged western slope of the Little Florida Mountains and has an abundance of agate, geodes and other semiprecious stones for collectors (limit 15 lbs). Display of polished stones. Hiking, picnicking, playground, camping. Daily.

SPECIAL EVENTS
OLD WEST GUN SHOW
4335 Salvador Road S.E., Deming, 800-848-4955

Western artifacts, jewelry, military equipment, guns, ammunition. Third weekends in February and August.

ROCKHOUND ROUNDUP
4335 Salvador Road S.E., Deming, 800-848-4955

Guided field trips for agate, geodes, candy rock, marble and honey onyx attract more than 6,000 participants. Auctions; exhibitions; demonstrations. Mid-March.

SOUTHWESTERN NEW MEXICO STATE FAIR
Deming, Done Ana Country Fairgrounds, 505-524-8602; www.snmstatefair.com

Livestock shows, midway, parade. Early-mid-October.

HOTEL
★★HOLIDAY INN
Interstate 10 E., Deming, 505-546-2661, 888-465-4329; www.holiday-inn.com

120 rooms. Restaurant. Airport transportation available. Pets accepted. Pool. Business center. Fitness center. High-speed Internet access. **$**

★
★★
★★★
★★
★

EL MORRO NATIONAL MONUMENT (INSCRIPTION ROCK)

The towering cliff that served as the guest book of New Mexico is located here on the ancient trail taken by the conquistadores from Santa Fe to Zuni. Don Juan de Oñate carved his name here in 1605; scores of other Spaniards and Americans added their names to the cliff at later dates. The rock is pale buff Zuni sandstone. The cliff, 200 feet high, has pueblo ruins on its top and pre-Columbian petroglyphs. Visitor center and museum. Daily. Trail, picnic facilities. Primitive camping.

Information: El Morro National Monument, from Interstate 40, 43 miles southwest of Grants off Highway 53, 505-783-4226; www.nps.gov/elmo

DULCE

This small town is the headquarters of the Jicarilla Apache Reservation. Folks who believe in UFOs and extraterrestrials contend that Dulce houses an underground hub populated by aliens.

Information: 800-477-0149; www.chamavalley.com

WHAT TO SEE AND DO

JICARILLA APACHE INDIAN RESERVATION

Seneca Drive, Dulce, 505-759-3242; www.jicarillaonline.com

The Jicarilla Apaches came from a group that migrated from southwestern Canada several centuries ago. The reservation is at an elevation of 6,500 to 8,500 feet and has excellent fishing and boating.

ESPAÑOLA

First settled 700 years ago by the Pueblo, then by Don Juan de Oñate in 1598, Española was claimed by the United States in 1846. Espãnola is situated between Taos and Santa Fe.

Information: Española Valley Chamber of Commerce, 710 Paseo de Onate,
505-753-2831; www.espanolanmchamber.com

WHAT TO SEE AND DO

FLORENCE HAWLEY ELLIS MUSEUM OF ANTHROPOLOGY

Mile Post 224, Highway 84, Española, 505-685-4333, 877-804-4678;
www.ghostranch.org

Exhibits of Native American/Spanish history. Memorial Day-Labor Day, Tuesday-Sunday; rest of year, Tuesday-Saturday; closed December.

RUTH HALL MUSEUM OF PALEONTOLOGY

Mile Post 224, US-84, Española, 505-685-4333, 877-804-4678

Exhibits on Triassic animals and Coelophysis, the New Mexico state fossil. Memorial Day-Labor Day, Tuesday-Sunday; rest of year, Tuesday-Saturday.

SPECIAL EVENTS
FIESTA DEL VALLE DE ESPAÑOLA
Española

Celebrates the establishment of New Mexico's first Spanish settlement in 1598. Torch relay, vespers, candlelight procession, street dancing, arts and crafts, food, entertainment, parade. Second week in July.

SAINTE CLAIRE FEAST DAY
One Kee St., Santa Clara Pueblo, Española, 505-753-7326; www.espanolaonline.com

Dancing, food, market. Mid-August.

SAN JUAN FEAST DAY
Española, San Juan Pueblo, 505-852-4400, 800-793-4955; www.espanolaonline.com/events.htm

Dancing, food, carnival. Late June.

TRI-CULTURAL ARTS FESTIVAL
Northern New Mexico Community College, 921 Paseo de Onte Road, Española

Features local artisans and their works, including potters, weavers, woodworkers, photographers, painters, singers and dancers. Usually first weekend in October.

WHITE-WATER RAFTING RACE
Española, 800-222-7238

Canoe, kayak and raft experts challenge 14 miles of white water below Pilar. Mother's Day.

HOTEL
★★★RANCHO DE SAN JUAN COUNTRY INN
Highway 285, Española, 505-753-6818; www.ranchodesanjuan.com

Situated between Taos and Santa Fe, this inn boasts numerous tranquil spots spread over its 225 scenic acres. Designed in the Spanish tradition, the décor is both rustic and refined with wildflower-filled courtyards, exposed beams, tile floors and Southwestern art and antiques. Rooms feature views of the colorful mountains and river valley. The elegant rooms are adorned with local art and warmed by wood-burning fireplaces; the bathrooms have granite countertops and marble showers. The award-winning restaurant is a gem. 17 rooms. Children over 12 years only. Complimentary full breakfast. Restaurant. Spa. **$$**

RESTAURANTS
★★EL PARAGUA
603 Santa Cruz Road, Española, 505-753-3211, 800-929-8226; www.elparagua.com

Southwestern menu. Lunch, dinner. Bar. Children's menu. Casual attire. Reservations recommended. **$$**

★★★RANCHO DE SAN JUAN
Highway 285, Española, 505-753-6818; www.ranchodesanjuan.com

The elegant, cheerful dining room of this inn overlooks the Ojo Caliente River Valley and the Jemez Mountains. The tranquil setting is the perfect backdrop for chef/owner

John H. Johnson's Southwest-inspired international cuisine, including dishes such as roasted coriander quail and coconut-crusted white shrimp. Each dish on the daily-changing prix fixe menu is artistically prepared and as stunning as the patio sunsets. International menu. Dinner. Closed Sunday-Monday; also January. Bar. Casual attire. Reservations recommended. Outdoor seating. $$$

FARMINGTON

The Navajos call it Totah, the meeting place at the convergence of three rivers in the colorful land of the Navajo, Ute, Apache and Pueblo. Once the home of the ancient Anasazi, Farmington is now the largest city in the Four Corners area and supplies much of the energy to the Southwest. From Farmington, visitors may explore Mesa Verde, Chaco Canyon and the Salmon and Aztec ruins. You can enjoy some of the best year-round fishing in the state at Navajo Lake State Park and in the San Juan River. And there are many shops offering traditional Native American crafts in the immediate area—baskets, jewelry, pottery, rugs and sand paintings. Obtain a list of local art galleries and trading posts at the Convention and Visitors Bureau.

Information: Visitors Burea, 3041 E. Main St., Farmington,
505-326-7602, 800-448-1240; www.farmingtonnm.org

WHAT TO SEE AND DO
BISTI BADLANDS
Highway 371, Farmington, 505-599-8900
A federally protected wilderness area of strange geologic formations; large petrified logs and other fossils are scattered among numerous scenic landforms. No vehicles permitted beyond boundary.

FOUR CORNERS MONUMENT
Navajo Reservation, Farmington, 64 miles northwest via Highway 64,
Highway 504, Highway 160, 928-871-6647; www.navajonationparks.org
Only point in the country common to four states: Arizona, Colorado, New Mexico and Utah.

SPECIAL EVENTS
BLACK RIVER TRADERS
Lions Wilderness Park Amphitheater, Pinon Hills and College boulevards, Farmington,
505-326-7602
Historical drama about the Southwest's multicultural heritage presented in an outdoor amphitheater. Contact Convention and Visitors Bureau for schedule. Mid-June-mid-August.

CONNIE MACK WORLD SERIES BASEBALL TOURNAMENT
Ricketts Park, 1101 Fairgrounds Road, Farmington
Annual 17-game series involves teams from all over the U.S. and Puerto Rico. August.

FARMINGTON INVITATIONAL BALLOON RALLY
3041 E. Main St., Farmington, 800-448-1240
Hare and hound races; competitions. Memorial Day weekend.

SAN JUAN COUNTY FAIR

41 Road 5568, Farmington

Parade; rodeo; fiddler contest; chili cook-off; exhibits. Mid-late August.

TOTAH FESTIVAL

200 W. Arrington, Farmington

Fine arts displays and juried show. Rug auction; powwow. Labor Day weekend.

HOTELS

★★BEST WESTERN INN & SUITES

700 Scott Ave., Farmington, 505-327-5221; www.bestwestern.com

192 rooms. Complimentary full breakfast. Restaurant, bar. Pets accepted. Pool. Business center. Fitness center. High-speed Internet access. Spa. **$**

★COMFORT INN

555 Scott Ave., Farmington, 505-325-2626, 800-341-1495; www.comfortinn.com

60 rooms. Complimentary continental breakfast. High-speed Internet access. Pets accepted. Pool. Business center. **$**

SPECIALTY LODGINGS

CASA BLANCA

505 E. La Plata St., Farmington, 505-327-6503, 800-550-6503;
www.4cornersbandb.com

This mission-style house built in the 1950s features manicured lawns and gardens on a bluff overlooking Farmington and the San Juan River. Rooms have hand-crafted furniture, Navajo rugs and Guatemalan textiles. Four rooms. Complimentary full breakfast. Airport transportation available. **$**

RESTAURANT

★CLANCY'S PUB

2703 E. 20th St., Farmington, 505-325-8176; www.clancys.net

Mexican, American menu. Lunch, dinner. Bar. Children's menu. Casual attire. Outdoor seating. **$**

GRANTS

More than half of the known domestic reserves of uranium ore are found in this area. About four miles east, Interstate 40 (I-40/Route 66) crosses one of the most recent lava flows in the continental United States. Native American pottery has been found under the lava, which first flowed about four million years ago from Mount Taylor to the north. Lava also flowed less than 1,100 years ago from fissures that today are near the highway. The lava is sharp and hard; heavy shoes are advisable for walking on it.

Information: Chamber of Commerce, 100 N. Iron St., Grants,
505-287-4802, 800-748-2142; www.grants.org

WHAT TO SEE AND DO

CASAMERO PUEBLO RUINS

Grants, 505-761-8700

The Chaco Anasazi occupied Casamero Pueblo between A.D. 1000 and 1125 as a community building that served a number of nearby farmsteads. It was used for social and religious activities aimed at uniting individual families into a cohesive community. Casamero is included on the World Heritage List.

EL MALPAIS NATIONAL MONUMENT AND NATIONAL CONSERVATION AREA

123 East Roosevelt Ave., Grants, 505-783-4774; www.nps.gov/elma

These two areas total 376,000 acres of volcanic formations and sandstone canyons. Monument features splatter cones and a 17-mile-long system of lava tubes. The Conservation area, which surrounds the monument, includes La Ventana Natural Arch, one of the state's largest freestanding natural arches; Cebolla and West Malpais wildernesses; and numerous Anasazi ruins. The Sandstone Bluffs Overlook, off Highway 117, offers an excellent view of the lava-filled valley and surrounding area. Facilities include hiking, bicycling, scenic drives, primitive camping (acquire Backcountry Permit at information center or ranger station). Lava is rough; caution is advised. Most of the lava tubes are accessible only by hiking trails; check with the information center in Grants before attempting any hikes. Monument, conservation area, daily. Information center and visitor facility on Highway 117. Daily.

ICE CAVE AND BANDERA VOLCANO

Highway 53, 28 miles southwest of Grants, 888-423-2283; www.icecaves.com

See an example of volcanic activity and hike on lava trails. The ice cave is part of a collapsed lava tube. The temperature never rises above 31 degrees, but reflected sunlight creates beautiful scenery. A historic trading post displays and sells artifacts and American Indian artwork. Daily 8 a.m.-one hour before sunset.

NEW MEXICO MINING MUSEUM

100 N. Iron Ave., Grants, 505-287-4802, 800-748-2142; www.grants.org

This is the only underground uranium mining museum in the world. Native American artifacts and relics; native mineral display. Monday-Saturday.

HOTEL

★★BEST WESTERN INN & SUITES

1501 E. Santa Fe Ave., Grants, 505-287-7901, 800-528-1234; www.bestwestern.com

126 rooms. Complimentary full breakfast. High-speed Internet access. Restaurant, bar. Fitness center. Pool. Pets accepted. $

JEMEZ SPRINGS

Nestled among red rock mesas, the village is named for its hot springs.

Information: www.jemezsprings.org

WHAT TO SEE AND DO

JEMEZ STATE MONUMENT

18160 State Road 4, Jemez Springs, 505-829-3530

This stabilized Spanish mission, built in 1621 by Franciscan missionaries, sits next to a prehistoric pueblo. Self-guided bilingual trail. Visitor center has anthropology and archaeology exhibits. Picnicking. Daily.

SPECIALTY LODGINGS
CANON DEL RIO RIVERSIDE INN
16445 Highway 4, Jemez Springs, 505-829-4377, 575-829-4377;
www.canondelrio.com
Located near the village of Jemez Springs, this five-acre property has beautiful natural landscaping. Each guest room has a Native American tribal name and motif. A fine art gallery is located on the premises. Six rooms. Closed January. Complimentary full breakfast. Whirlpool. Children 12 and older. $

JEMEZ MOUNTAIN INN
Highway 4, Jemez Springs, 505-829-3926, 888-819-1075; www.jemezmtninn.com
Located within walking distance of local restaurants, sights and attractions, this completely remodeled turn-of-the-century inn has six individually decorated rooms. $

LAS CRUCES
In 1830 a group of people from Taos were traveling on the Spanish highway El Camino Real. They camped here and were massacred by the Apache. They were buried under a field of crosses; hence the name Las Cruces ("the crosses"). Situated in the vast farming area of the fertile lower Rio Grande Valley, this region is especially noted for its homegrown green chiles. There are ghost mining towns, extinct volcanoes, frontier forts, mountains and pecan orchards in the area.
Information: Convention & Visitors Bureau, 211 N. Water St.,
575-541-2444, 800-343-7827; www.lascrucescvb.org

WHAT TO SEE AND DO
BRANIGAN CULTURAL CENTER
501 N. Main St., Las Cruces, 505-541-2155; www.las-cruces.org
Located at the north end of the Downtown Mall, this complex includes the Las Cruces Museum of Fine Art & Culture and the Bicentennial Log Cabin Museum, Monday-Friday 10 a.m.-4 p.m., Saturday 9 a.m.-1 p.m.; closed Sunday.

NEW MEXICO FARM AND RANCH HERITAGE MUSEUM
4100 Dripping Springs Road, Las Cruces, 505-522-4100; www.frhm.org
Interactive 47-acre museum that brings to life Mexico's 3,000-year history and farming and ranching life. Hands-on exhibits including plowing, blacksmithing and cow-milking. Outdoor animal and plant life. Monday-Saturday 9 a.m.-5 p.m., Sunday noon-5 p.m.

NEW MEXICO STATE UNIVERSITY
University Avenue, Las Cruces, 505-646-0111, 800-662-6678; www.nmsu.edu
Established in 1888; 15,500 students. The 950-acre campus includes a history museum (Tuesday-Sunday), art gallery and an 18-hole public golf course.

WHITE SANDS MISSILE RANGE
Las Cruces, 20 miles east on Highway 70, 575-678-1134; www.wsmr.army.mil
The range where missiles are tested is closed to the public but visitors are welcome at the outdoor missile park and museum. Missile Park: daily 8 a.m.-4 p.m. Museum: Monday-Friday 8 a.m.-4:30 p.m.

THE WILD WEST

This two- to three-day tour from Las Cruces offers a combination of scenic wonders, hiking and fishing opportunities and a glimpse into the old West. From Las Cruces, head northeast on Highway 70 to White Sands National Monument, a seemingly endless expanse of sparkling white gypsum dunes. You'll drive past the dunes along a 16-mile scenic drive, which also provides access to the monument's four hiking trails. Or just take off on foot into the dunes, where kids will have endless hours of fun sliding down the mountains of sand on plastic saucers (available at the monument's gift shop). Visiting the monument is best either early or late in the day, when the dunes display mysterious and often surreal shadows.

Continue northeast on Highway 70 to Alamogordo, a good spot to spend the night. Attractions here include the Space Center, where you can test your skills as a pilot in a Space Shuttle simulator, explore the International Space Hall of Fame and visit the Toy Train Depot, which has a fascinating collection of toy trains—some dating from the 1800s. About 12 miles south of Alamogordo via Highway 54 is Oliver Lee Memorial State Park, with a short, pleasant nature trail along a shaded stream, plus a rugged hiking trail that climbs up the side of a mountain and offers spectacular views. The park also includes the ruins of a pioneer cabin and a museum that tells the story of the site's violent past.

From Alamogordo, go north on Highway 54 to Tularosa, where you can visit Tularosa Vineyards. Then head east on Highway 70 up into the Sacramento Mountains to the resort community of Ruidoso, whose name (Spanish for "noisy") comes from the babbling Ruidoso Creek. Surrounded by the Lincoln National Forest, this picturesque town is a good base for hiking. Head east out of Ruidoso Downs to Hondo and then turn back to the northwest on Highway 380, which leads to Lincoln. This genuine Wild West town, which is preserved as a state monument, was the site of a jail break by famed outlaw Billy the Kid. Continue west on Highway 380 to the town of Capitan for a visit to Smokey Bear Historical State Park, with exhibits and the grave of the orphaned bear cub who was found in a forest fire near here and became a symbol of forest fire prevention. Leaving Capitan, drive west on Highway 380 to the town of Carrizozo and cross Highway 54. Continue four miles to Valley of Fires National Recreation Site, where a short trail provides close-up views of numerous jet-black lava formations. Return to Carrizozo and head south on Highway 54 to the turnoff to Three Rivers Petroglyph Site, one of the best places in the Southwest to see prehistoric rock art. An easy trail meanders along a hillside where there are thousands of images, ranging from geometric patterns to handprints to a variety of animals (some pierced by arrows or spears) created by the Mogollon people at least 1,000 years ago. To return to Las Cruces, take Highway 54 south through Tularosa and Alamogordo; turn southwest on Highway 70. *Approximately 349 miles.*

NEW MEXICO

★ ★ ★ ★ ★

SPECIAL EVENT
WHOLE ENCHILADA FIESTA
Downtown Mall, Main and Las Cruces streets, Las Cruces, 505-526-1938;
www.enchiladafiesta.com
Street dancing, entertainment, parade, crafts, food including world's largest enchilada. Last weekend in September.

HOTELS
★★BEST WESTERN MESILLA VALLEY INN
901 Avenida De Mesilla, Las Cruces, 505-524-8603, 800-327-3314;
www.mesillavalleyinn.com
160 rooms. Restaurant, bar. Pets accepted. Pool. Wireless Internet access. Whirlpool. Spa.

★FAIRFIELD INN
2101 Summit Court, Las Cruces, 505-522-6840; www.fairfieldinn.com
78 rooms. Complimentary continental breakfast. High-speed Internet access. Pool. $

★★★HOTEL ENCANTO DE LAS CRUCES
705 S. Telshor Blvd., Las Cruces, 575-522-4300; www.sterlinghotels.com
This hotel is minutes from New Mexico State University, Las Cruces International Airport, White Sands Missile Range and Historic Old Mesilla. Activities such as golfing, bowling, horseback riding and fishing are nearby. All of the guest rooms feature a warm Southwestern style. 203 rooms. High-speed Internet access. Restaurant, bar. Pets accepted. Pool. Fitness center. $$

★★RAMADA PALMS DE LAS CRUCES
201 E. University Ave., Las Cruces, 505-526-4411; www.ramada.com
114 rooms. Restaurant, bar. Airport transportation available. Pets accepted. Business center. Complimentary continental breakfast. High-speed Internet access. Fitness center. Pool. $

SPECIALTY LODGING
LUNDEEN INN OF THE ARTS
618 S. Alameda Blvd., Las Cruces, 505-526-3326, 888-526-3326;
www.innofthearts.com
This 100-year old inn includes a pair of two-story guest houses connected by a great room with dark wood floors, a tin ceiling, antique furniture and an impressive art collection. Seven rooms. Complimentary full breakfast. Pets accepted. Fitness center. $

RESTAURANT
★★★MESON DE MESILLA
1803 Avenida de Mesilla, Las Cruces, 505-525-9212; www.mesondemesilla.com
This romantic restaurant in an adobe-style bed and breakfast combines continental cuisine with Italian and Southwestern accents for an unusual and delicious menu. French menu. Dinner. Closed Monday. Bar. Casual attire. Reservations recommended. $$$

314

LAS VEGAS

Las Vegas was once a stopover on the old Santa Fe Trail. The town prospered as a shipping point and after the arrival of the railroad in 1879 it began an active period of building and rebuilding. There are 918 historic buildings (1846-1938) here as a result. Las Vegas is home to New Mexico Highlands University and Armand Hammer United World College of the American West.

Information: Las Vegas-San Miguel Chamber of Commerce, 503 Sixth St.,
505-425-8631, 800-832-5947; www.lasvegasnewmexico.com

WHAT TO SEE AND DO

CITY OF LAS VEGAS MUSEUM AND ROUGH RIDERS' MEMORIAL COLLECTION

Municipal Building, 727 Grand Ave., Las Vegas, 505-454-1401;
www.lasvegasmuseum.org

See artifacts and memorabilia from the Spanish-American War and turn-of-the-century northern New Mexico life. May-October, daily; November-April, Monday-Friday.

LAS VEGAS NATIONAL WILDLIFE REFUGE

Storrie Project, Las Vegas, two miles east via Highway 104, then four miles
south via Highway 281, 505-425-3581; www.fws.gov

See all kinds of wildlife, including migratory water fowl. Nature trails. Daily; some areas Monday-Friday.

STORRIE LAKE STATE PARK

Las Vegas, four miles north on Highway 518, 505-425-7278;
www.emnrd.state.nm.us/PRD/storrielake.htm

Swimming, waterskiing, fishing, boating, windsurfing, picnicking, playground, camping. Daily.

HOTELS

★COMFORT INN

2500 N. Grand Ave., Las Vegas, 505-425-1100, 877-424-6423; www.comfortinn.com

101 rooms. Complimentary continental breakfast. Pets accepted. Pool. Business center. Fitness center. $

★★PLAZA HOTEL

230 Plaza, Las Vegas, 505-425-3591, 800-328-1882; www.plazahotel-nm.com

54 rooms. Complimentary continental breakfast. Wireless Internet access. Restaurant, bar. Pets accepted. Business center. $

LINCOLN

This small town, only about 60 miles west of Roswell, was once the home of Billy the Kid.

Information: www.ruidosonow.com

CASA DE PATRON BED & BREAKFAST INN
Highway 380 East, Lincoln, 505-653-4676; www.casapatron.com
This inn, built in 1860, was the home of Juan Patron, the youngest Speaker of the House in the Territorial Legislature. Legendary figures such as Billy the Kid and Pat Garrett are said to have spent the night here. Seven rooms. Complimentary continental breakfast. $

LOS ALAMOS
Nestled on high mesas between the Rio Grande Valley floor and the Jemez Mountain peaks, Los Alamos offers spectacular views and outdoor activities. The city was originally the site of a boys' school. It was acquired by the government in 1942 to develop the first atomic bomb. In 1967, the city property was turned over to Los Alamos County. The scientific laboratory, where research continues, remains a classified installation.

Information: Los Alamos County Chamber of Commerce, 109 Central Park Square, 505-662-8105, 800-444-0707; www.losalamoschamber.com

WHAT TO SEE AND DO
BRADBURY SCIENCE MUSEUM
15th Street and Central Avenue, Los Alamos, 505-667-4444; www.lanl.gov
Displays artifacts relating to the history of the laboratory and the atomic bomb. Exhibits on modern nuclear weapons, life sciences, materials sciences, computers, particle accelerators, geothermal, fusion and fission energy sources. Daily.

FULLER LODGE ART CENTER AND GALLERY
2132 Central Ave., Los Alamos, 505-662-9331; www.artfulnm.org
This historic log building is the setting for changing exhibits featuring arts and crafts of northern New Mexico. Monday-Saturday.

LOS ALAMOS HISTORICAL MUSEUM
Fuller Lodge Cultural Center, 1921 Juniper, Los Alamos, 505-662-6272;
www.losalamoshistory.org
See artifacts, photos, other material tracing local history from prehistoric to present times; exhibit on the Manhattan Project. Daily.

PAJARITO MOUNTAIN SKI AREA
397 Camp May Road, Los Alamos, 505-662-5725; www.skipajarito.com
Despite being a small resort (280 acres), Pajarito offers some excellent and challenging terrain, making it a well-kept secret for local ski buffs. Friday-Sunday, 9 a.m.-4 p.m.; closed Monday-Thursday.

HOTEL
★BEST WESTERN HILLTOP HOUSE HOTEL
400 Trinity Drive, Los Alamos, 505-662-2441, 800-462-0936; www.bestwestern.com
92 rooms. Complimentary full breakfast. High-speed Internet access. Bar. Pets accepted. Pool. $

BANDELIER NATIONAL MONUMENT

A major portion of this 32,000-acre area is designated wilderness. The most accessible part is in Frijoles Canyon, which features cave dwellings carved from the soft volcanic turf and houses built out from the cliffs. There's also a great circular pueblo ruin (Tyuonyi) on the floor of the canyon. These houses and caves were occupied from about A.D. 1150 to 1550. The depletion of resources forced residents to abandon the area. Some of the modern pueblos along the Rio Grande are related to the prehistoric Anasazi people of the canyon and the surrounding mesa country. There is a paved one-mile self-guided trail to walk and view these sites. The monument is named after Adolph Bandelier, ethnologist and author of the novel, *The Delight Makers*, which used Frijoles Canyon as its locale.

There are 70 miles of trails (free permits required for overnight trips; pets not accepted on the trails). Visitor center with exhibits depicting the culture of the pueblo region, ranger-guided tours (summer), campfire programs (Memorial Day-Labor Day). Campground (March-November, daily).

Information: Los Alamos, six miles southwest on Highway 502, then six miles southeast on Highway 4 to turnoff sign, 505-672-0343; www.nps.gov/band

SPECIALTY LODGING
ASHLEY HOTEL & SUITES

2175 Trinity Drive, Los Alamos, 505-662-7211, 800-745-9910;
www.ashleyhotelandsuites.com
116 rooms. Complimentary full breakfast. Wireless Internet access. Pets accepted. $

RATON

Raton is at the southern foot of the famous Raton Pass, on the original Santa Fe Trail (the main road to Denver, now Interstate 25). The road over the pass is a masterpiece of engineering and the view from several points is magnificent.
Information: Chamber & Economic Development Council, 100 Clayton Road,
505-445-3689, 800-638-6161; www.raton.info

WHAT TO SEE AND DO
SUGARITE CANYON STATE PARK

Sugarite Canyon, Raton, 575-445-5607; www.emnrd.state.nm.us/PRD/sugarite.htm
This park contains 3,600 acres on the New Mexico side and offers fishing, ice fishing, boating (oars or electric motors only) and tubing; cross-country skiing, ice skating, riding trails (no rentals); picnicking, camping. Visitor center. May-September, daily; rest of year by appointment.

HOTEL
★★BEST WESTERN SANDS

300 Clayton Road, Raton, 505-445-2737, 800-518-2581; www.bestwestern.com
50 rooms. Restaurant. High-speed Internet access. Pets accepted. Pool. $

RED RIVER

This was a gold-mining boomtown with a population of 3,000 in the early days of the 20th century. Today it is a summer vacation and winter ski center. Trout fishing, hunting (deer, elk and small game), snowmobiling, horseback riding and backpacking are all popular.

Information: Chamber of Commerce, Main Street, 575-754-2366, 800-348-6444; www.redrivernewmex.com

WHAT TO SEE AND DO
RED RIVER SKI AREA
400 Pioneer Road, Red River, 505-754-2223; redriverskiarea.com

Two triple, three double chairlifts, surface tow; patrol, school, rentals; snowmaking. Fifty-seven runs, longest run more than 2½ miles; vertical drop 1,600 feet. Thanksgiving-late March, daily. Chairlift also operates Memorial Day-Labor Day. Daily.

SPECIAL EVENTS
ENCHANTED CIRCLE CENTURY BIKE TOUR
100 E. Main, Red River

Nearly 1,000 cyclists participate in a 100-mile tour around the Enchanted Circle (Red River, Angel Fire, Taos, Questa). September.

MARDI GRAS IN THE MOUNTAINS
Red River

Ski slope parades, Cajun food. February.

HOTELS
★★ALPINE LODGE
417 W. Main, Red River, 575-754-2952, 800-252-2333; www.thealpinelodge.com

45 rooms. Restaurant, bar. $

★BEST WESTERN RIVER'S EDGE
301 W. River St., Red River, 505-754-1766, 877-600-9990; www.bestwestern.com

30 rooms. Complimentary continental breakfast. High-speed Internet access. Pets accepted. $

RESTAURANT
★★SUNDANCE
401 E. High St., Red River, 505-754-2971; www.redrivernm.com/sundance/sr_food.html

Mexican menu. Dinner. Closed April-mid-May. Children's menu. $

ROSWELL

Did a UFO crash here in 1947? That has been the question for decades. The government maintains that materials recovered were from a top-secret research balloon. UFO proponents believe it was wreckage of an alien spacecraft and that the military has been covering it up. You decide.

Information: Chamber of Commerce, 131 W. Second St., 505-623-5695; www.roswellnm.org

WHAT TO SEE AND DO

BITTER LAKE NATIONAL WILDLIFE REFUGE

4067 Bitter Lakes Road, Roswell, 505-622-6755;
www.fws.gov/southwest/refuges/newmex/bitterlake
Wildlife observation, auto tour. Daily.

BOTTOMLESS LAKES STATE PARK

Roswell, 10 miles east on Highway 380, then six miles south on Highway 409,
575-624-6058; www.emnrd.state.nm.us/PRD/bottomless.htm
Bordered by high red bluffs, seven small lakes were formed when circulating underground water formed caverns that collapsed into sinkholes. Headquarters at Cottonwood Lake has displays and a network of trails. Beach and swimming at Lea Lake only; some lakes have fishing (trout), paddleboat rentals; picnicking, camping. Daily.

DEXTER NATIONAL FISH HATCHERY AND TECHNOLOGY CENTER

7116 Hatchery Road, Roswell, 575-734-5910
This facility is the U.S. Fish and Wildlife Service's primary center for the study and culture of endangered fish species of the American Southwest. Daily. Visitor center, April-October.

HISTORICAL CENTER FOR SOUTHEAST NEW MEXICO

200 N. Lea, Roswell, 575-622-8333
See turn-of-the-century furnishings, communications exhibits and more; research library and archives. Daily, afternoons; Friday, by appointment.

INTERNATIONAL UFO MUSEUM & RESEARCH CENTER

114 N. Main St., Roswell, 505-625-9495, 800-822-3545; www.iufomrc.org
Check out the exhibits here on various aspects of UFO phenomena; video viewing room. Daily 9 a.m.-5 p.m.

NEW MEXICO MILITARY INSTITUTE

101 W. College Blvd., Roswell, 575-622-6250, 800-421-5376; www.nmmi.edu
Established in 1891; 1,000 cadets. State-supported high school and junior college. Alumni Memorial Chapel, near the entrance, has beautiful windows. Also here is the General Douglas L. McBride Military Museum with an interpretation of 20th-century American military history. Tuesday-Friday. Occasional marching formations and parades. Tours.

ROSWELL MUSEUM AND ART CENTER

100 W. 11th St., Roswell, 575-624-6744; www.roswellmuseum.org
Southwest arts collection including Georgia O'Keeffe, Peter Hurd, Henriette Wyeth; Native American, Mexican-American and western arts. Robert H. Goddard's early liquid-fueled rocketry experiments. Monday-Saturday, also Sunday and holiday afternoons.

SPRING RIVER PARK & ZOO
1306 E. College Blvd., Roswell, 575-624-6760
Zoo and children's zoo area; small lake with fishing for children 11 and under only; miniature train; antique wooden horse carousel. Picnicking, playground. Daily.

SPECIAL EVENTS
EASTERN NEW MEXICO STATE FAIR AND RODEO
Fair Park, 2500 N. Main St., Roswell, 505-623-9411; www.enmsf.com
The oldest and second-largest fair in New Mexico, with rodeos, carnival, a demolition derby, antique tractor shows and pulls, motocross shows and other entertainment. September-October.

UFO ENCOUNTERS FESTIVAL
International UFO Museum & Research Center, 114 Main St., Roswell,
505-625-9495; www.iufomrc.org
UFO Expo trade show, alien chase, alien parade, costume contest, guest speeches. July Fourth weekend.

HOTELS
★★BEST WESTERN SALLY PORT INN & SUITES
2000 N. Main St., Roswell, 505-622-6430; www.bestwestern.com
124 rooms. Complimentary continental breakfast. High-speed Internet access. Fitness center. Restaurant, bar. Pool. $

★RAMADA
2803 W. Second St., Roswell, 505-623-9440, 800-272-6232; www.ramada.com
58 rooms. Complimentary continental breakfast. High-speed Internet access. Fitness center. Pets accepted. Pool. $

RESTAURANT
★EL TORO BRAVO
102 S. Main St., Roswell, 575-622-9280
Mexican menu. Lunch, dinner. Children's menu. Casual attire. $

RUIDOSO
This resort town in the Sierra Blanca Mountains, surrounded by the trees of the Lincoln National Forests, has seen spectacular growth. It is a year-round resort with skiing in winter and fishing and horseback riding in summer. If you're planning to visit in the summer, secure confirmed reservations before leaving home. The forested mountain slopes and streams are idyllic, the air is clear and cool and there are many interesting things to do.
Information: Ruidoso Valley Chamber of Commerce, 720 Sudderth Drive,
505-257-7395, 877-784-3676; www.ruidoso.net

WHAT TO SEE AND DO
HUBBARD MUSEUM OF THE AMERICAN WEST
841 Highway 70 West, Ruidoso Downs, 575-378-4142; www.hubbardmuseum.org
Western-themed exhibits relating to horses and pioneer life. Daily.

LINCOLN STATE MONUMENT

Ruidoso, 30 miles east on Highway 70, then 10 miles northwest on Highway 380

Lincoln was the site of the infamous Lincoln County War and a hangout of Billy the Kid. Several properties have been restored, including the Old Lincoln County Courthouse and the mercantile store of John Tunstall. Guided tours (summer, reservations required). Daily.

OLD DOWLIN MILL

Sudderth 641, Ruidoso, 575-257-2811

A 20-foot waterwheel still drives a mill more than 100 years old.

SKI APACHE RESORT

Highway 532, Ruidoso, 505-464-3600; www.skiapache.com

Resort has four-passenger gondola; two quad, five triple, one double chairlift; surface lift; patrol, school, rentals. Fifty-five runs, longest run more than two miles; vertical drop 1,800 feet. Thanksgiving-Easter, daily.

THE SPENCER THEATER FOR THE PERFORMING ARTS

108 Spencer Road, Airport Highway 220, Alto, 575-336-4800, 888-818-7872;
www.spencertheater.com

This stunning $22 million structure was created from 450 tons of Spanish limestone; breathtaking blown glass installations by Seattle artist Dale Chihuly are inside. Tours Tuesday, Thursday.

SPECIAL EVENTS

ASPENFEST

Ruidoso, 505-257-7395, 877-784-3676; www.ruidosonow.com/aspenfest

Includes motorcycle convention, official state chili cook-off, arts and crafts. Early October.

HORSE RACING

Ruidoso Downs, 1461 Highway 70 West, 573-378-4431; www.ruidownsracing.com

Thoroughbred and quarter horse racing; pari-mutuel betting. Home of All-American Futurity, the world's richest quarter horse race (Labor Day); All-American Derby and All-American Gold Cup. Thursday-Sunday and holidays. Early May-Labor Day.

RUIDOSO ART FESTIVAL

Paradise Canyon Road and Sudderth Drive, Ruidoso, 505-257-7395;
www.ruidosonow.com/artfestival

More than 125 artists exhibits displaying painting, drawings, photography, glass, porcelain, woodwork, jewelry, pottery and sculpture. Last full weekend in July.

SMOKEY BEAR STAMPEDE

8 Fifth St., Ruidoso

Fireworks, music festival, parade, dances, barbecue. Early July.

NEW MEXICO

★
★
★
★

HOTEL
★SWISS CHALET INN
1451 Mechem Drive, Ruidoso, 505-258-3333; www.sciruidoso.com
82 rooms. Complimentary continental breakfast Bar. Pets accepted. Pool. **$**

SANTA FE

This picturesque city, the oldest capital in the United States, is set at the base of the Sangre de Cristo Mountains. A few miles south, these mountains taper down from a height of 13,000 feet to a rolling plain, marking the end of the North American Rockies. Because of the altitude, the climate is cool and bracing. There's much to do and see here all year.

Don Pedro de Peralta, who laid out the plaza and built the Palace of the Governors in 1610, founded Santa Fe. In 1680, the Pueblo revolted and drove the Spanish out. In 1692, led by General Don Diego de Vargas, the Spanish made a peaceful reentry. The opening of the Santa Fe Trail followed Mexico's independence from Spain in 1821. In 1846, General Stephen Watts Kearny led U.S. troops into the town without resistance and hoisted the American flag. During the Civil War, Confederate forces occupied the town for two weeks before they were driven out.

In addition to its own attractions, Santa Fe is also the center of a colorful area, which can be reached by car. It is in the midst of Pueblo country. The Pueblos, farmers for centuries, are also extremely gifted craftworkers and painters. Their pottery, basketry and jewelry are especially beautiful. At various times during the year, especially on the saint's day of their particular pueblo, they present dramatic ceremonial dances. Visitors are usually welcome.

Information: Convention & Visitors Bureau, 505-955-6200, 800-777-2489; www.santafe.org

WHAT TO SEE AND DO
ATALAYA MOUNTAIN HIKING TRAIL
St. John's College, 1160 Camino Cruz Blanca, Santa Fe
The Atalaya Mountain Trail, accessible from the parking lot at St. John's College, is one of the most popular and easily accessible hiking trails in Santa Fe. Hikers have the option of taking the longer route (Trail 174), which is approximately seven miles round-trip, or parking further up near the Ponderosa Ridge development and doing a 4.6-mile loop (Trail 170). Both trails eventually join and take you toward the top of Atalaya Mountain, a 9,121-foot peak. The first few miles of the trail are relatively easy, but it becomes increasingly steep and strenuous as you near the summit, which offers great views of the Rio Grande valley and the city below.

CANYON ROAD TOUR
Canyon Road, Santa Fe
Many artists live on this thoroughfare and there is no better way to savor the unique character of Santa Fe than to travel along its narrow, picturesque old streets, which includes the famous Camino del Monte Sol. Stop in the Cristo Rey Church, the largest adobe structure in the U.S., with beautiful ancient stone *reredos* (altar screens). Monday-Friday.

CATHEDRAL OF ST. FRANCIS
Santa Fe Plaza, 231 Cathedral Place, Santa Fe, 505-982-5619

SANTA FE'S ART AND ARCHITECTURE

Every visitor's exploration of Santa Fe begins at the Plaza, plotted when the town was built in 1610. A square block planted with trees and grass, it's a great place to take in the city. Lining the Plaza on the east, south and west are art galleries, Native American jewelry shops, boutiques and restaurants. Facing the Plaza on the north is the Palace of the Governors, the first stop on your walking tour. Sheltered along the porch that spans the front of the block-long, pueblo-style building, you'll find dozens of craft and art vendors from nearby pueblos.

One block west along Palace Avenue, the Museum of Fine Arts was built in 1917 and represents the Pueblo Revival style of architecture, also called Santa Fe style. Continue west on Palace another block, turning north on Grant Avenue one block, then west on Johnson Street one block. Stop inside the relatively new Georgia O'Keeffe Museum to see the world's largest collection of her work.

Next, head to the Catron Building, which forms the east wall of the Plaza. Inside this building are several art galleries and stores. At the building's southern end, anchoring the southeast corner of the Plaza, is La Fonda, the oldest hotel in Santa Fe. The lobby's art is worth a look and the rooftop bar is a favorite gathering place. From the Plaza, walk south two blocks on Old Santa Fe Trail to Loretto Chapel. Now walk east on Water Street one block to Cathedral Place, turning left (north) on Cathedral one block to the magnificent St. Francis Cathedral, built over several years in the later 1800s. Directly across the street, see the Institute of American Indian Arts Museum. Back on Palace, Sena Plaza is on the north side of the street. Inside the lovely, flower-filled courtyard, you'll find a 19th-century hacienda filled with art galleries, shops and a restaurant.

This French Romanesque cathedral was built in 1869 under the direction of Archbishop Jean-Baptiste Lamy, the first archbishop of Sante Fe (the novel *Death Comes for the Archbishop* is based on his life). Also here is La Conquistadora Chapel, said to be the country's oldest shrine to the Virgin Mary. Daily 8 a.m.-5:45 p.m., except during mass. Tours in summer.

COLLEGE OF SANTA FE

1600 St., Michael's Drive, Santa Fe, 505-473-6133, 800-456-2673; www.csf.edu

Established in 1947; 1,400 students. Includes the Greer Garson Theatre Center, Garson Communications Center and Fogelson Library.

CROSS OF THE MARTYRS

Paseo de la Loma, 545 Canyon Road, Santa Fe, 505-983-2567;
www.historicsantafe.org/popcross.html

This large, hilltop cross weighs 76 tons, stands 25 feet tall and honors the memory of more than 20 Franciscan priests and numerous Spanish colonists who were killed during the 1680 Pueblo Revolt against Spanish dominion. Dedicated in 1920, this cross shouldn't be confused with the newer one at nearby Fort Marcy Park. Vistas from the old cross include those of the Sangre de Cristos mountain range immediately northeast, the Jemez about 40 miles west and the Sandias, 50 miles south near Albuquerque.

EL RANCHO DE LAS GOLONDRINAS

334 Los Pinos Road, Santa Fe, 505-471-2261; www.golondrinas.org

This living history museum is set in a 200-acre rural valley and depicts Spanish Colonial life in New Mexico from 1700-1900. It was once a stop on El Camino Real and is one of the most historic ranches in the Southwest. Original colonial buildings date from the 18th century. Special festivals offer visitors a glimpse of the music, dance, clothing, crafts and celebrations of Spanish Colonial New Mexico. June-September: Wednesday-Sunday 10 a.m.-4 p.m.

FEDERAL COURT HOUSE

Federal Place and Paseo De Peralta, Santa Fe

A monument to American frontiersman Kit Carson stands in front of the courthouse.

GEORGIA O'KEEFFE MUSEUM

217 Johnson St., Santa Fe, 505-946-1000; www.okeeffemuseum.org

One of the most important American artists of the 20th century, Georgia O'Keeffe lived and worked at Ghost Ranch near Abiqui for much of her career, drawing inspiration from the colors and forms of the surrounding desert environment. This museum houses the world's largest permanent collection of her artwork and is also dedicated to the study of American Modernism, displaying special exhibits of many of her contemporaries. November-June, Monday-Tuesday, Thursday, Saturday-Sunday 10 a.m.-5 p.m., Friday 10 a.m.-8 p.m.; daily rest of year.

HYDE MEMORIAL STATE PARK

740 Hyde Park Road, Santa Fe, 505-983-7175;
www.emnrd.state.nm.us/PRD/Hyde.htm

Perched 8,500 feet up in the Sangre de Cristo Mountains near the Santa Fe Ski Basin, this state park serves as a base camp for backpackers and skiers in the Santa Fe National Forests. Cross-country skiing, rentals, picnicking, camping. Daily.

HYDE PARK HIKING/BIKING TRAILS

Santa Fe, eight miles northeast via Hyde Park Road

One of the closest hiking opportunities to Santa Fe is available in the Hyde Park area on the road to the ski basin. From the Hyde Park parking lot, you can access a loop covering three different trails offering easy hiking that's popular with dog walkers and locals on weekends. The loop consists of switchbacks, moderate grades and creek crossings and has good views of the mixed conifer forest. If you come during the fall, you can view the spectacularly colorful changing of the Aspen leaves. Start with the common trailhead at the far side of the parking lot. Look for the Borrego Trail (150), Bear Wallow Trail (182) and Winsor Trail (254) markings. A loop covering all three is about four miles long.

INSTITUTE OF AMERICAN INDIAN ARTS MUSEUM

108 Cathedral Place, Santa Fe, 505-983-8900; www.iaiancad.org

The Institute of American Indian Arts, established in 1962, runs a college in south Santa Fe in addition to a museum just off the Plaza. The museum is the only one in the country dedicated solely to collecting and exhibiting contemporary Native American art, much of it produced by the staff and faculty of the college. June-September, daily 9 a.m.-5 p.m.; October-May, daily 10 a.m.-5 p.m.

KOKOPELLI RAFTING ADVENTURES

551 W. Cordova Road, Santa Fe, 505-983-3734, 800-879-9035; www.kokopelliraft.com
Kokopelli Rafting offers a full range of white-water rafting trips to the Rio Grande and Rio Chama rivers, as well as sea kayaking trips to Cochiti and Abiqui lakes and Big Bend National Park in Texas. Excursions include half-day, full-day, overnight and two- to eight-day wilderness expeditions. Transportation from Santa Fe included. April-September.

LAS COSAS SCHOOL OF COOKING

DeVargas Center, 181 Paseo de Peralta, Santa Fe, 877-229-7184;
www.lascosascooking.com
Located within a store stocked with gourmet kitchen tools and elegant tableware, this cooking center offers hands-on culinary education experiences that fill a morning or evening. Taught by school director John Vollertsen and chefs from New Mexico's leading restaurants, the classes cover a wide range of topics. Classes usually start at 10 a.m. and 6 p.m.

LENSIC PERFORMING ARTS CENTER

211 W. San Francisco St., Santa Fe, 505-988-1234; www.lensic.com
The Lensic Theater is one of Santa Fe's historical and architectural gems, reopened after a full restoration in 2001. The structure was first built in 1931 in a Moorish/ Spanish Renaissance style and has always been Santa Fe's premiere theater space, having played host to celebrities such as Roy Rogers and Judy Garland over the years. Since reopening, it has provided a constantly changing schedule of theater, symphony and performing arts events.

LORETTO CHAPEL

207 Old Santa Fe Trail, Santa Fe, 505-982-0092; www.lorettochapel.com
Modeled after St. Chapelle Cathedral in Paris, this chapel, built in 1873, was the first Gothic building built west of the Mississippi. The chapel itself is not particularly impressive, but what draws countless tourists is the miraculous stairway, a two-story spiral wooden staircase built without any nails or central supports that seems to defy engineering logic. Summer, Monday-Saturday 9 a.m.-6 p.m., Sunday 10:30 a.m.-5 p.m.; winter, Monday-Saturday 9 a.m.-5 p.m., Sunday 10:30 a.m.-5 p.m.

MUSEUM OF FINE ARTS

107 W. Palace Ave., Santa Fe, 505-476-5072; www.museumofnewmexico.org
Designed by Isaac Hamilton Rapp in 1917, the museum is one of Santa Fe's earliest Pueblo revival structures and its oldest art museum. It contains more than 20,000 holdings, with an emphasis on Southwest regional art and the artists of Santa Fe and Taos from the early 20th century. The St. Francis Auditorium inside the museum also presents lectures, musical events, plays and various other performances. Free admission on Friday evenings. Tuesday-Sunday 10 a.m.-5 p.m., Friday 5-8 p.m.

MUSEUM OF INDIAN ARTS AND CULTURE

710 Camino Lejo, Santa Fe, 505-476-1250; www.indianartsandculture.org

When the Spanish arrived in the Southwest in the 16th century, they found many sprawling towns and villages, which they referred to as pueblos, a name that is still used to identify Native American communities here. The Museum of Indian Arts and Culture houses an extensive collection of historic and contemporary Pueblo art from throughout the Southwest. The highlight is an excellent interpretive section where you can encounter Pueblo cultures from the viewpoint and narrative of modern-day natives and exhibit designers. The museum itself is housed in a large, adobe-style building that blends architecturally into the surroundings and also houses many outstanding examples of Pueblo textiles, pottery, jewelry, contemporary paintings and other rotating exhibits. Tuesday-Sunday10 a.m.-5 p.m.

MUSEUM OF INTERNATIONAL FOLK ART

706 Camino Lejo, Santa Fe, 505-476-1200; www.moifa.org

The Museum of International Folk Art, first opened in 1953, contains more than 130,000 objects, billing itself as the world's largest folk museum dedicated to the study of traditional cultural art. Much of the massive collection was acquired when the late Italian immigrant and architect/designer Alexander Girard donated his 106,000-object collection of toys, figurines, figurative ceramics, miniatures and religious/ceremonial art, which he had collected from more than 100 countries around the world. This is a rich museum experience and can easily take several hours to explore. Two museum shops offer a wide variety of folk-oriented books, clothing and jewelry to choose from. Tuesday-Sunday 10 a.m.-5 p.m.

★
★
★
★
★

MUSEUM OF SPANISH COLONIAL ART

750 Camino Lejo, Santa Fe, 505-982-2226; www.spanishcolonial.org

This small museum, housed in a building designed in 1930 by famous local architect John Gaw Meem, holds some 3,000 objects showcasing traditional Hispanic art in New Mexico dating from conquest to present day. The collection includes many early works in wood, tin and other local materials, as well as numerous works by contemporary New Mexican artists. The galleries are open Tuesday-Sunday 10 a.m.-5 p.m.

OLDEST HOUSE

De Vargas Street and Old Santa Fe Trail, Santa Fe

It is believed that Native Americans built this structure more than 800 years ago.

PALACE OF THE GOVERNORS

105 Palace Ave., Santa Fe, 505-476-5100; www.palaceofthegovernors.org

Built in 1610, this is the oldest public building in continuous use in the U.S. It was the seat of government in New Mexico for more than 300 years. Lew Wallace, governor of the territory (1878-1881), wrote part of *Ben Hur* here in 1880. It is now a major museum of Southwestern history. The Palace, Museum of Fine Arts, Museum of Indian Arts and Culture, Museum of International Folk Art and state monuments all make up the Museum of New Mexico. Free admission Friday evenings. Tours. Monday-Saturday 10:15 a.m.-noon, Tuesday-Sunday 10 a.m.-5 p.m., Friday 5-8 p.m.

PLAZA

100 Old Santa Fe Trail, Santa Fe

The Santa Fe Plaza, steeped in a rich history, has been a focal point for commerce and social activities in Santa Fe since the early 17th century. The area is marked by a central tree-lined park surrounded by some of Santa Fe's most important historical landmarks, many of which hail from Spanish colonial times. The most important landmark is the Palace of the Governors. Native American artists from nearby Pueblos sell handmade artwork in front of the Palace and various museums, shops and dining establishments surround the Plaza, making it the top tourist destination in Santa Fe. Numerous festivals and activities are held throughout the year.

SAN ILDEFONSO PUEBLO

Santa Fe, 16 miles north on Highway 84, 285, then six miles west on Highway 502, 505-455-2273

This pueblo is famous for its beautiful surroundings and its black, red and polychrome pottery made famous by Maria Poveka Martinez. Daily; closed winter weekends; visitors must register at the visitor center. Various festivals take place here throughout the year. The circular structure with the staircase leading up to its rim is a *kiva* or ceremonial chamber. There are two shops in the pueblo plaza and a tribal museum adjoins the governor's office.

SAN MIGUEL MISSION

401 Old Santa Fe Trail, Santa Fe, 505-983-3974

Built in the early 1600s, this is the oldest church in the U.S. still in use. Construction was overseen by Fray Alonso de Benavidez, along with a group of Tlaxcala Indians from Mexico, who did most of the work. The original adobe still remains beneath the stucco walls and the interior has been restored along with Santa Fe's oldest wooden *reredos* (altar screen). Church services are still held on Sundays. Sunday 1-4:30 p.m.; summer, Monday-Saturday 9 a.m.-4:30 p.m.; winter, Monday-Saturday 10 a.m.-4 p.m.

SANTA FE CHILDREN'S MUSEUM

1050 Old Pecos Trail, Santa Fe, 505-989-8359; www.santafechildrensmuseum.org

The hands-on exhibits invite kids to make magnetic structures, route water streams, create paintings, illustrate cartoon movies, discover plants on a greenhouse scavenger hunt, scale an 18-foot-high climbing wall, use an old-fashioned pitcher pump and weave beads and fabric on a loom. Local artists and scientists make appearances. Wednesday-Saturday 10 a.m.-5 p.m., Sunday noon-5 p.m.

SANTA FE FASHION OUTLETS

8380 Cerrillos Road, Santa Fe, 505-474-4000; www.fashionoutletssantafe.com

This is New Mexico's only outlet center. More than 40 stores include Bose, Brooks Brothers and more. Daily

SANTA FE NATIONAL FOREST

1474 Rodeo Road, Santa Fe, 505-438-7840; www.fs.fed.us/r3/sfe

This forest covers more than 1.5 million acres. Fishing is excellent in the Pecos and Jemez rivers and tributary streams and hiking trails are close to unusual geologic formations. You'll find hot springs in the Jemez Mountains. Four wilderness areas within the forest total more than 300,000 acres. Campgrounds are provided by the Forest Service at more than 40 locations.

SANTA FE RAFTING COMPANY

1000 Cerrillos Road, Santa Fe, 505-988-4914, 888-988-4914; www.santaferafting.com
The Rio Grande and Rio Chama rivers north of Santa Fe provide excellent opportunities for river running and white-water rafting. Santa Fe Rafting Company offers several rafting trips including half-day, full-day and multi-day camping excursions, some of which include a boxed lunch. The biggest rapids are found on their Taos Box full-day trip, open to anyone over age 12. All trips include roundtrip transportation from Santa Fe. April-September.

SANTA FE SCHOOL OF COOKING

116 W. San Francisco St., Santa Fe, 505-983-4511, 800-982-4688; www.santafeschoolofcooking.com
Sign up for classes offered several times weekly in traditional and contemporary Southwestern cuisine. Culinary tours involve classes with nationally renowned chefs and trips to local farms and wineries.

SANTA FE SOUTHERN RAILWAY

410 S. Guadalupe St., Santa Fe, 505-989-8600, 888-989-8600; www.sfsr.com
Several scenic train rides in restored vintage cars are offered to the public, following the original high desert route to and from Lamy. The rides range from short scenic roundtrips to longer outings that include picnics, barbecues and various holiday-themed events, such as the Halloween Highball Train and New Year's Eve Party Train. The start of the route is housed in the old Santa Fe Depot, where you can view vintage railcars and shop for gifts and memorabilia in the original mission-style train depot.

SANTA FE TRAIL MUSEUM

614 Maxwell Ave., Springer, 505-483-2682
The Santa Fe Trail Museum displays artifacts and exhibits about pioneer life on and around the trail from 1880 to 1949. Open daily 9 a.m.-4 p.m., summer only.

SENA PLAZA AND PRINCE PLAZA

Washington and East Palace avenues, Santa Fe
Both plazas include small shops and old houses, built behind portals and around central patios.

SHIDONI BRONZE FOUNDRY AND GALLERY

1508 Bishop's Lodge Road, Santa Fe, 505-988-8001; www.shidoni.com
A fantastic resource for art collectors and sculptors, Shidoni consists of a bronze foundry, art gallery and outdoor sculpture garden set in an eight-acre apple orchard. Artists from around the country come to work at Shidoni's 14,000-square-foot foundry, open to the general public for self-guided tours. Explore the lovely sculpture garden during daylight hours or shop for works of bronze and metal in the adjacent gallery. Gallery: Monday-Saturday 9 a.m.-5 p.m. Foundry: Monday-Friday noon-1 p.m., Saturday 9 a.m.-5 p.m.

SHONA SOL SCULPTURE GARDEN

Turquoise Trail, Highway 14, Santa Fe, 505-473-5611

See exhibits of some of the world's finest stone sculptors, whose work is also shown around the world. Open weekends 10 a.m.-6 p.m.

SKI SANTA FE

2209 Brothers Road, Santa Fe, 505-982-4429; www.skisantafe.com

World-class skiing and snowboarding in the majestic Sangre de Cristo Mountains is only a 20-minute drive from the downtown Santa Fe Plaza. Ski Santa Fe is a family-owned resort catering to skiers and snowboarders of all levels. In addition to great views of the city, the 12,075-foot summit offers six lifts and 67 runs (20 percent easy, 40 percent more difficult, 40 percent most difficult), with a total of 660 acres of terrain. The longest run is three miles and the mountain offers a vertical drop of 1,725 feet. The average yearly snowfall is 225 inches. A PSIA-certified ski school offers group and private lessons for adults and children and there are restaurants, rental shops and a clothing boutique onsite. The Chipmunk Corner offers activities and lessons for children ages 4-9. Late November-early April, daily.

STATE CAPITOL

Old Santa Fe Trail at Paseo de Peralta, Santa Fe, 505-986-4589

This round building in modified Territorial style is intended to resemble a Zia Sun symbol. Mid-May-August, Monday-Saturday 8 a.m.-7 p.m.; September-mid-May, Monday-Friday 8 a.m.-7 p.m.

TEN THOUSAND WAVES

3451, Hyde Park Road, Santa Fe, 505-982-9304; www.tenthousandwaves.com

This exquisite Japanese-themed spa and bathhouse is a genuine treat. Located in a unique Zen-like setting in the Sangre de Cristo Mountains, Ten Thousand Waves offers soothing hot tubs, massages, facials, herbal wraps and other spa treatments. Includes coed public hot tubs (where clothing is optional before 8:15 p.m.), a women-only tub, secluded private tubs and large private tubs that can accommodate up to 20. All the tubs are clean and chlorine-free and amenities such as kimonos, towels, sandals, lotion and lockers are provided for you. Be sure to call ahead for reservations, especially for massage services. Daily.

TURQUOISE TRAIL

South from Santa Fe on Interstate 25, Highway 14 south toward Madrid;
www.turquoisetrail.org

Undeniably the most interesting path between Albuquerque and Santa Fe, this poetically named route is the 50-mile reach of New Mexico 14 that parallels Interstate 25 north from Interstate 40 and is a National Scenic Byway. Cutting a course along the backside of the Sandias just north of Albuquerque, the trail winds through a rolling countryside of sumptuous, cactus-lined hills populated by tiny burgs. Along the way, watch for crumbling rock houses, ancient family cemeteries and long-abandoned ranch houses and barns. Stops include the town of Golden, where the first discovery of gold west of the Mississippi was made and where a silver boom once employed more than 1,200 workers, and Madrid (pronounced MAD-rid), once rich in coal mines but today the refuge of artists whose galleries and shops have become lucrative businesses.

NEW MEXICO ★ ★ ★ ★ ☆

The wonderful Mine Shaft Tavern offers burgers, buffalo steaks and cold beer, along with live entertainment on weekends.

WHEELWRIGHT MUSEUM

704 Camino Lejo, Santa Fe, 505-982-4636, 800-607-4636; www.wheelwright.org

Founded in 1937 by Mary Cabot Wheelwright and Navajo singer/medicine man Hastiin Klah to help preserve Navajo art and traditions, the Wheelwright now devotes itself to hosting major exhibits of Native American artists from tribes throughout North America. The Case Trading Post in the basement sells pottery, jewelry, textiles, books, prints and other gift items. Monday-Saturday 10 a.m.-5 p.m., Sunday 1-5 p.m.

SPECIAL EVENTS

CHRISTMAS EVE CANYON ROAD WALK

Santa Fe Plaza, Canyon Road, Santa Fe, 800-777-2489

This major Santa Fe tradition is not to be missed. Adorned with thousands of *farolitos* (paper bag lanterns), the streets and homes around Canyon Road play host to a unique and colorful festival each Christmas Eve. Thousands of pedestrians stroll up and down the streets while singing Christmas carols, lighting bonfires and enjoying hot apple cider. December 24.

EIGHT NORTHERN PUEBLOS ARTS & CRAFTS SHOW

San Juan Pueblo, Santa Fe, 505-747-1593

This annual festival features traditional and contemporary American Indian art at more than 500 booths. Approximately 1,500 artists attend and have their work judged for prizes before being displayed for sale. Third weekend in July.

FIESTA AT SANTO DOMINGO PUEBLO

Santo Domingo Pueblo, Santa Fe, 505-465-2214

This is probably the largest and most famous of the Rio Grande pueblo fiestas. Includes a corn dance. Early August.

INDIAN MARKET

Santa Fe Plaza, Santa Fe, 505-983-5220; www.swaia.org/indianmrkt.html

Buyers and collectors from all over the world come to the largest and oldest Native American arts show and market in the world. More than 1,200 artists from 100 North American tribes participate in the show, with around 600 outdoor booths set up in the middle of the ancient Santa Fe Plaza. The market is a great opportunity to meet the artists and buy directly. Numerous outdoor booths sell food. The event draws an estimated 100,000 visitors to Santa Fe during the weekend. Late August.

INTERNATIONAL FOLK ART MARKET

Milner Plaza, Camino Lejo, Santa Fe, 505-476-1189; www.folkartmarket.org

This new two-day event brings together 75 master folk artists from Bangladesh to Zimbabwe in a celebration of color, music and cuisine. Includes everything from textiles to woodblock prints to ceramics and sculptures. In addition to shopping for works to take home, visitors can attend demonstrations and lectures, tour local folk art collections, bid on works at an auction and participate in children's activities. Mid-July.

INVITATIONAL ANTIQUE INDIAN ART SHOW
Sweeney Center, 201 W. Marcy, Santa Fe
This large show attracts dealers, collectors and museum curators. Includes pre-1935 items. Two days in mid-August.

MOUNTAIN MAN RENDEZVOUS AND FESTIVAL
105 W. Palace Ave., Santa Fe, 505-476-5100; www.santafe.org
Costumed mountain men ride into town on horseback for the Museum of New Mexico's annual buffalo roast, part of a large gathering of trappers and traders from the pre-1840 wilderness. Participants sell primitive equipment, tools and trinkets and compete in period survival skills such as knife and tomahawk throwing, muzzleloader rifle shooting and cannon firing. Early August.

RODEO DE SANTA FE
Santa Fe Rodeo Grounds, Santa Fe, 505-471-4300; www.rodeodesantafe.org
The Santa Fe rodeo offers a chance to see real cowboys and bucking broncos in action. Various professional competitions and public exhibitions are put on during the brief summer season. Rodeo events generally happen during evening and weekend matinee hours. A downtown rodeo parade takes place in mid-June at the start of the season.

SANTA FE CHAMBER MUSIC FESTIVAL
St. Francis Auditorium, Museum of Fine Arts and the Lensic Performing
Arts Center, Santa Fe, 505-983-2075, 888-221-9836; www.sfcmf.org
Since the first season of the festival in 1973, this artistic tradition has grown into a major event consisting of more than 80 performances, open rehearsals, concert previews and roundtable discussions with composers and musicians during the annual summer season. Performances are frequently heard on National Public Radio. July-August.

SANTA FE FIESTA
Santa Fe Plaza, Santa Fe, 505-988-7575; www.santafefiesta.org
This ancient folk festival dating back to 1712 features historical pageantry, religious observances, arts and crafts shows and street dancing. It also celebrates the reconquest of Santa Fe by Don Diego de Vargas in 1692. First weekend in September.

SANTA FE OPERA
Highways 84/285, Santa Fe, 505-986-5900, 800-280-4654; www.santafeopera.org
Founded in 1957, this opera company presents one of the world's most famous and respected opera festivals each summer. The company stages five works per season, including two classics, a lesser-known work by a well-known composer, a Richard Strauss offering and a world premiere or new American staging. What's more, the Santa Fe Opera performs in a gorgeous hilltop amphitheater. Designed by Polshek & Partners of New York, who refurbished Carnegie Hall in Manhattan, the Opera incorporates bold, swooping lines with excellent sight lines and is known for superb acoustics. Backstage tours early July-late August: Monday-Saturday at 1 p.m. Performances begin between 8 and 9 p.m.

SANTA FE PRO MUSICA

Lensic Performing Arts Center, 211 W. San Francisco St., Santa Fe,
505-988-4640, 800-960-6680; www.santafepromusica.com

This chamber orchestra and ensemble performs classical and contemporary music. A performance of *Messiah* takes place during Christmas season. Mozart Festival in February. September-May.

SANTA FE SYMPHONY AND CHORUS

Lensic Performing Arts Center, 211 W. San Francisco St., Santa Fe,
505-983-1414, 800-480-1319; www.sf-symphony.org

Santa Fe's orchestral company presents works in classical and jazz music, as well as specialty programs that may include the music of Spain and Mexico. The season generally runs from early October-Memorial Day, with matinée and evening performances at the Lensic Performing Arts Center. Early October-late May.

SANTA FE STAGES

Lensic Performing Arts Center, Santa Fe, 505-982-6680; www.santafestages.org

With presentations offered primarily at the wonderfully renovated and historic Lensic Performing Arts Center, Santa Fe Stages hosts a season of dance, music and theater with national appeal. The season typically begins before Memorial Day and ends in late September and may offer Irish folk dance, classical ballet, opera, jazz, drama, comedy and cabaret. Late May-late September.

SANTA FE WINE AND CHILE FIESTA

551 W. Cordova Road, Santa Fe, 505-438-8060; www.santafewineandchile.org

Begun in 1991, this wildly popular festival honoring the best in food and drink brings in some 2,000 appreciative fans from around the state and across the country. Roughly 30 local restaurants and 90 wineries from around the globe team up with a half-dozen or so of America's top celebrity chefs and cookbook authors to present a culinary extravaganza in a variety of venues around town. Includes wine seminars, cooking demonstrations, special vintners lunches and dinners and the gastronomic circus called the Grand Tasting, staged in mammoth tents on the Santa Fe Opera grounds. Late September.

SPANISH MARKET

Museum of Spanish Colonial Art, 750 Camino Lejo, Santa Fe, 505-982-2226;
www.spanishmarket.org

The rich and colorful Hispanic art traditions of Northern New Mexico are celebrated twice a year during Spanish Market, the oldest and largest exhibition and sale of traditional Hispanic art in the U.S. The smaller winter market in December is held indoors in the Sweeney Convention Center (201 W. Marcy St.), while the larger summer market occupies the entire Santa Fe Plaza for one weekend in July. As many as 300 vendors sell and display *santos* (carved saints), hide paintings, textiles, furniture, jewelry, tinwork, basketry, pottery, bonework and other locally produced handicrafts reflecting the unique and deeply religious traditional art that still flourishes in this part of New Mexico. Sponsored by the Spanish Colonial Arts Society. December and late July.

TESUQUE PUEBLO FLEA MARKET

Highway 84/285, Santa Fe, 505-670-2599; www.tesuquepueblofleamarket.com

You'll find hundreds of vendors offering antiques, gems, jewelry, pottery, rugs and folk art, all at very competitive prices, at this flea market. Plan on devoting a couple of hours to browse all the various treasures and myriad of vendor booths stretching for several acres.

ZOZOBRA FESTIVAL

Fort Marcy Park, 490 Washington Ave., Santa Fe, 505-660-1965; www.zozobra.com

Each year on the Thursday before Labor Day, the Kiwanis Club of Santa Fe hosts the burning of Zozobra, a 50-foot effigy of Old Man Gloom, whose passing is designed to dispel the hardships and travails of the previous year. Zozobra started in 1924 as part of the Fiesta's celebration when a local artist conceived a ritual based on a Yaqui Indian celebration from Mexico. Over the years, Zozobra caught on and the crowd sizes have grown, making it Santa Fe's largest and most colorful festival. Lasting for several hours, as many as 60,000 visitors crowd into a large grassy field in Fort Marcy Park to listen to live bands, watch spectacular fireworks displays and cheer the ritual burning. The celebration continues through the Labor Day weekend with booths and activities set up in the nearby plaza. Thursday before Labor Day.

HOTELS

★★★BISHOP'S LODGE

1297 Bishop's Lodge Road, Santa Fe, 505-983-6377, 800-419-0492; www.bishopslodge.com

This lodge is a Santa Fe treasure. The historic resort dates back to 1918 and its beloved chapel, listed on the National Register of Historic Places, remains a popular site for weddings. This resort is vintage chic, with rooms decorated either in an old Sante Fe style or with more modern décor. The ShaNah spa is influenced by Native American traditions—each treatment begins with a soothing drumming and blessing. Modern American cuisine is the focus at the lodge's restaurant. 88 rooms. Restaurant, bar. Children's activity center. Spa. Pets accepted. Tennis. $$$

★COMFORT INN SANTA FE

4312 Cerrillos Road, Santa Fe, 505-474-7330, 877-424-6423; www.comfortinn.com

83 rooms. Complimentary continental breakfast. Wireless Internet access. Pets accepted. Pool. $

★★★ELDORADO HOTEL

309 W. San Francisco St., Santa Fe, 505-988-4455, 800-955-4455; www.eldoradohotel.com

The Pueblo Revival-style building is one of Santa Fe's largest and most important landmarks. Its lobby and interiors are lavishly decorated with an extensive collection of original Southwest art. Rooms have private balconies and kiva fireplaces. The lobby lounge is a great spot for snacking, people-watching and enjoying live entertainment. Sunday brunch is a local favorite. 219 rooms. High-speed Internet access. Two restaurants, bar. Pets accepted. Pool. Business center. Fitness center. $$$

★★GALISTEO INN

9 La Vega, Galisteo, 866-404-8200; www.galisteoinn.com

11 rooms. Children over 10 years only. Complimentary continental breakfast. Restaurant, bar. Wireless Internet access. Pool. $$

★★★HILTON SANTA FE

100 Sandoval St., Santa Fe, 505-986-2811, 800-336-3676; www.hiltonofsantafe.com

Located just two blocks from the historic Plaza, this hotel is in a 380-year-old family estate, and takes up an entire city block. The hotel has the city's largest pool. Guest rooms feature locally handcrafted furnishings. 157 rooms. Three restaurants, bar. High-speed Internet access. Airport transportation available. Pets accepted. $$

★★HOTEL PLAZA REAL

125 Washington Ave., Santa Fe, 505-988-4900, 877-901-7666; www.sterlinghotels.com

56 rooms. Restaurant, bar. Pets accepted. $$

★★HOTEL SANTA FE

1501 Paseo De Peralta, Santa Fe, 800-825-9876; www.hotelsantafe.com

129 rooms. Restaurant, bar. Airport transportation available. Pets accepted. Pool. $$

★★HOTEL ST. FRANCIS

210 Don Gaspar Ave., Santa Fe, 505-983-5700, 800-529-5700;
www.hotelstfrancis.com

82 rooms. Wireless Internet access. Fitness room. Restaurant, two bars. $$

★★★HYATT REGENCY TAMAYA RESORT & SPA

1300 Tamaya Trail, Santa Ana Peublo, 505-867-1234, 800-554-9288;
www.tamaya.hyatt.com

Located on 500 acres of unspoiled desert, the Hyatt Regency Tamaya Resort & Spa has striking views of the Sandia Mountains. The property blends right in with its Pueblo-style buildings and open-air courtyards and includes punches of turquoise and bright oranges throughout the public and private spaces. Golf, tennis and hot air ballooning are among the activities available at this family-friendly resort, where programs for kids are available. The restaurants are a showcase of Southwestern flavors, offering sophisticated takes on local favorites. 350 rooms. High-speed Internet access. Five restaurants, two bars. Children's activity center. Spa. Airport transportation available. Pets accepted. $$

★★★INN AND SPA AT LORETTO

211 Old Santa Fe Trail, Santa Fe, 505-988-5531, 800-727-5531; www.hotelloretto.com

Built in 1975, this boutique hotel, which rests at the end of the Sante Fe Trail, is a re-creation of an ancient adobe. Rooms feature a charming Southwestern motif with hand-carved furniture and Native American art. The property includes a heated pool and 12 specialty stores, including many art galleries. 134 rooms. Restaurant, bar. Spa. Fitness room. Pool. $$

★★★★INN OF THE ANASAZI, A ROSEWOOD HOTEL

113 Washington Ave., Santa Fe, 505-988-3030; www.innoftheanasazi.com

Located just off the historic Plaza, the inn was designed to resemble the traditional dwellings of the Anasazi. Enormous handcrafted doors open to a world of authentic artwork, carvings and textiles synonymous with the Southwest. The lobby sets a sense of place for arriving guests with its rough-hewn tables, leather furnishings, unique objects and huge cactus plants in terra-cotta pots. The region's integrity is maintained in the guest rooms, where fireplaces and four-poster beds rest under ceilings of *vigas* and *latillas* and bathrooms are stocked with toiletries made locally with native cedar extract. The restaurant earns praise for honoring the area's culinary heritage. 58 rooms. Restaurant, bar. Pets accepted. Wireless Internet access. Fitness room. $$$

★★★INN OF THE GOVERNORS
101 W. Alameda, Santa Fe, 800-234-4534; www.innofthegovernors.com

Discerning travelers know this inn as one of Santa Fe's best. First-rate service and amenities are the draw, and guests are treated to a complimentary full breakfast each morning, a friendly and helpful concierge and a heated outdoor pool with poolside service. Rooms are decorated Southwestern style and feature handcrafted furniture, Spanish artwork, fireplaces and French doors that open to a patio. Amenities include wireless Internet access, feather pillows, down comforters and plush towels and robes. The rustic Del Charro Saloon, a popular gathering place for locals and tourists alike, offers cocktails and a full bar menu, including what many say are the best burgers in town. 100 rooms. Wireless Internet access. Complimentary full breakfast. Restaurant, bar. Pool. $$

★★★LA POSADA DE SANTA FE
330 E. Palace Ave., Santa Fe, 505-986-0000, 866-331-7625; www.rockresorts.com

Nestled on six lush acres, La Posada effortlessly blends past and present. The original Staab House, dating to 1870, is the focal point of the resort. The lovely rooms and suites are scattered throughout the gardens in a village setting. Rich colors mix with Spanish colonial and old-world style and every amenity has been added. The fantastic Avanyu Spa features Native American-themed treatments using local ingredients. Fuego Restaurant is a standout for its innovative food with Spanish and Mexican inflections, while the historic Staab House is an inviting setting for American classics. 157 rooms. Restaurant, bar. Spa. Fitness room. Pool. $$$

★LA QUINTA INN
4298 Cerrillos Road, Santa Fe, 505-471-1142; www.laquinta.com

130 rooms. Complimentary continental breakfast. Pets accepted. Pool. $

★★★SUNRISE SPRINGS
242 Los Pinos Road, Santa Fe, 505-471-3600, 800-955-0028; www.sunrisesprings.com

Get your chakras in order at Santa Fe's Zen-chic Sunrise Springs. This eco-conscious resort proves that it's easy being green with biodynamic gardens, organic produce and locally harvested spa products. It's all about peace and tranquility at this 70-acre property, where trickling ponds provide background music for meditation and Yoga. Sunrise Springs takes its cues from the East for its activity menu, offering tai chi, Raku ceramics and Yoga, as well as traditional tea ceremonies in its authentic Japanese tea house, but the guestrooms and casitas are definitively Southwestern. The spa, the centerpiece of the resort, blends ancient traditions with native therapies in its treatments. 56 rooms. Spa. Restaurant. $$

SPECIALTY LODGINGS

ADOBE ABODE

202 Chapelle St., Santa Fe, 505-983-3133; www.adobeabode.com

Built in 1905 as officer quarters for Fort Marcy, this property offers guests a unique stay in one of its finely decorated rooms. Visitors will enjoy the complimentary sherry and Santa Fe cookies in the afternoon. Six rooms. Complimentary full breakfast. **$**

EL FAROLITO BED & BREAKFAST

514 Galisteo St., Santa Fe, 505-988-1631, 888-634-8782; www.farolito.com

Eight rooms. **$$**

EL REY INN

1862 Cerrillos Road, Santa Fe, 505-982-1931, 800-521-1349;
www.elreyinnsantafe.com

About two miles from downtown, this adobe-style inn (1936) is well kept, with a cozy atmosphere and friendly staff. 86 rooms. Complimentary continental breakfast. Swim. **$**

GUADALUPE INN

604 Agua Fria St., Santa Fe, 505-989-7422; www.guadalupeinn.com

This is a quiet inn offering rooms with unique décor. Local artists display their work in the rooms and many pieces are for sale. 12 rooms. Complimentary full breakfast. **$**

INN OF THE TURQUOISE BEAR

342 E. Buena Vista, Santa Fe, 505-983-0798, 800-396-4104; www.turquoisebear.com

10 rooms. Complimentary continental breakfast. Pets accepted. **$$$**

INN ON THE ALAMEDA

303 E. Alameda, Santa Fe, 505-984-2121, 888-984-2121; www.inn-alameda.com

Tucked unassumingly behind adobe walls near the start of Canyon Road, this inn offers all the comforts of a luxury hotel, but has the quiet elegance of a smaller bed and breakfast with lovely gardens and sheltered courtyards. 69 rooms. Complimentary continental breakfast. Bar. Two whirlpools. Pets accepted. **$$**

INN ON THE PASEO

630 Paseo de Peralta, Santa Fe, 505-984-8200, 800-457-9045;
www.innonthepaseo.com

Located on the Paseo de Peralta in the heart of downtown Santa Fe, this recently renovated inn offers a relaxing Southwest experience. Guest rooms feature down comforters, patchwork quilts and private baths. The breakfast buffet is served on the sundeck. 18 rooms. Complimentary full breakfast. **$**

WATER STREET INN

427 W. Water St., Santa Fe, 505-984-1193, 800-646-6752; www.waterstreetinn.com

Located just two blocks from Santa Fe's historic Plaza, this inn features Southwestern décor with art and photography lining its walls. Spacious brick-floored guest rooms have private baths, cable TV and decks/patios. The courtyard offers a sundeck with great views. 12 rooms. Complimentary continental breakfast. Whirlpool. Pets accepted. **$$**

RESTAURANTS
★★AMAYA AT HOTEL SANTA FE
1501 Paseo de Peralta, Santa Fe, 800-825-9876; www.hotelsantafe.com
Southwestern menu. Breakfast, lunch, dinner. Bar. Children's menu. Casual attire. Outdoor seating. **$$$**

★★★THE ANASAZI
113 Washington Ave., Santa Fe, 505-988-3236; www.innoftheanasazi.com
The creators of the memorable cuisine at this Plaza mainstay like to point out that the Navajo definition of Anasazi has come to embody an ancient wisdom that is "synonymous with the art of living harmoniously and peacefully with our environment." That philosophy is translated in the petroglyph-inspired art on the walls. Executive chef Tom Kerpon devotes himself finding inventive uses for organic, locally grown products in dishes such as grilled basil-marinated opah with green chile risotto, buffalo osso bucco and grilled corn, tortilla and lime soup. Southwestern menu. Breakfast, lunch, dinner, Sunday brunch. Bar. Children's menu. Casual attire. Valet parking. **$$$**

★★ANDIAMO
322 Garfield St., Santa Fe, 505-995-9595; www.andiamoonline.com
Italian menu. Dinner. Children's menu. Casual attire. Outdoor seating. **$$**

★BLUE CORN CAFÉ & BREWERY
133 Water St., Santa Fe, 505-984-1800; www.bluecorncafe.com
Southwestern menu. Lunch, dinner. Bar. Children's menu. Casual attire. Outdoor seating. **$$**

★★★BLUE HERON
242 Los Pinos Road, Santa Fe, 505-471-3600, 800-955-0028; www.sunrisesprings.com
Housed at the unique, eco-friendly Sunrise Springs resort, this restaurant is equally green, serving only fresh, organic ingredients, many of them picked daily from the onsite gardens. Dishes are straightforward and delicious, from the grilled basil salmon with brown rice to the chile-rubbed filet mignon with goat cheese chile relleno. The wine list features organic wines and fine sakes. Southwestern menu. Brunch, lunch, dinner. **$$**

★★CAFE PARIS
31 Burro Alley, Santa Fe, 505-986-1688; www.cafeparisnm.com
French menu. Breakfast, lunch, dinner. Closed Monday. Casual attire. Reservations recommended. Outdoor seating. **$$**

★★CAFE PASQUAL'S
121 Don Gaspar, Santa Fe, 505-983-9340; www.pasquals.com
Southwestern menu. Breakfast, lunch, dinner. Children's menu. Casual attire. Reservations recommended. **$$$**

★★CELEBRATIONS

613 Canyon Road, Santa Fe, 505-989-8904

American menu. Breakfast, lunch, dinner, Sunday brunch. Children's menu. Casual attire. Reservations recommended. Outdoor seating. **$$**

★CHOW'S CUISINE BISTRO

720 St., Michaels Drive, Santa Fe, 505-471-7120; www.mychows.com

Chinese menu. Lunch, dinner. Closed Sunday. Casual attire. **$$**

★★★THE COMPOUND RESTAURANT

653 Canyon Road, Santa Fe, 505-982-4353; www.compoundrestaurant.com

The setting of this landmark restaurant is casual yet elegant, with minimalist décor, neutral tones and white-clothed tables. Patios surrounded by flower gardens and a marble fountain make for a relaxing outdoor dining experience. The contemporary American menu features specialties such as grilled beef tenderloin and tuna tartar topped with Osetra caviar and preserved lemon. The warm bittersweet liquid chocolate cake is a star dessert. Guests can also choose from an extensive wine list, featuring rare and French wines. American menu. Lunch, dinner. Bar. Business casual attire. Reservations recommended. Outdoor seating. **$$**

★★★COYOTE CAFE

132 W. Water St., Santa Fe, 505-983-1615; www.coyotecafe.com

Famed cookbook author and Southwestern cuisine pioneer Mark Miller has enjoyed nothing but success at this super-cool restaurant decorated with folk art and located just a block off the Plaza. Although the menu changes seasonally, regulars know they'll find a whimsical mingling of the cuisines of New Mexico, Mexico, Cuba and Spain. Look for chile-glazed beef short ribs with corn dumplings, pecan wood-roasted quail and halibut in a mango-habanero blend. The rooftop Cantina is a festive spot. Southwestern menu. Dinner. Bar. Children's menu. Casual attire. Reservations recommended. Outdoor seating. **$$$**

★★EL FAROL

808 Canyon Road, Santa Fe, 505-983-9912; www.elfarolsf.com

Spanish menu. Lunch, dinner. Bar. Casual attire. Reservations recommended. Outdoor seating. **$$$**

★★EL MESÓN—LA COCINA DE ESPAÑA

213 Washington Ave., Santa Fe, 505-983-6756; www.elmeson-santafe.com

Spanish, tapas menu. Dinner. Closed Sunday-Monday. Bar. Children's menu. Casual attire. **$$**

★★GABRIEL'S

Four Banana Lane, Santa Fe, 505-455-7000; www.restauranteur.com/gabriels

Southwestern menu. Lunch, dinner. Closed late November-late December. Bar. Casual attire. Reservations recommended. Outdoor seating. **$$**

★★★★GERONIMO

724 Canyon Road, Santa Fe, 505-982-1500; www.geronimorestaurant.com

Housed in a restored 250-year-old landmark adobe building, Geronimo (the name of the restaurant is an ode to the hacienda's original owner, Geronimo Lopez) offers robust Southwestern-spiked global fusion fare in a stunning and cozy space. Owners Cliff Skoglund and Chris Harvey treat each guest like family. The interior is like a Georgia O'Keeffe painting come to life, with its wood-burning cove-style fireplace, tall chocolate-and-garnet-leather seating and local Native American-style artwork decorating the walls. The food is remarkable, fusing the distinct culinary influences of Asia, the Southwest and the Mediterranean. Vibrant flavors, bright colors and top-notch seasonal and regional ingredients come together in such dishes as Maryland soft-shell tempura crabs with soba noodle and Asian pear salad, or mesquite-grilled New York strip steak with French onion tart and polenta fries with green pepper corn and mustard sauce. When it's warm outside, sit on the patio for prime Canyon Road people-watching. International menu. Lunch, dinner, Sunday brunch. Bar. Casual attire. Reservations recommended. Valet parking. Outdoor seating. **$$$**

★★IL PIATTO

95 W. Marcy St., Santa Fe, 505-984-1091; www.ilpiattorestaurant.com

Italian menu. Lunch, dinner. Bar. Children's menu. Casual attire. Reservations recommended. Outdoor seating. **$$**

★★INDIA PALACE

227 Don Gaspar Ave., Santa Fe, 505-986-5859; www.indiapalace.com

Indian menu. Lunch, dinner. Children's menu. Casual attire. Outdoor seating. **$$**

★★★JULIAN'S

221 Shelby St., Santa Fe, 505-988-2355; www.juliansofsantafe.com

Officially called Julian's Cucina d'Italia, this bistro has long been a favorite for romantic dining in a neighborhood cluster of high-end shops and galleries. Two fireplaces warm the old adobe room, where owner-executive chef Wayne Gustafson treats guest to creative versions of authentic dishes, such as the antipasto of oysters baked with Parmesan and the pasta shells stuffed with snails, prosciutto, garlic butter and pesto. Signature entrées include osso bucco Milanese with saffron risotto and shrimp sautéed with tomatoes and graced with fresh basil and mascarpone. Italian menu. Dinner. Bar. Casual attire. Outdoor seating. **$$$**

★★★LAS FUENTES AT BISHOP'S LODGE

1297 Bishop's Lodge Road, Santa Fe, 505-983-6377, 800-419-0492;
www.bishopslodge.com

Executive chef Alfonso Ramirez brings an explosion of Nuevo Latino cuisine to the Bishop's Lodge at this inviting restaurant. Favorite dishes include seared plantain-crusted salmon with fennel and chipotle juice and swordfish marinated with chile guajillo. Spa cuisine choices include gazpacho with roasted cumin seeds and Cuban black bean soup. American, Southwestern menu. Breakfast, lunch, dinner, Sunday brunch. Bar. Children's menu. Outdoor seating. Spa. **$$$**

★★MARIA'S NEW MEXICAN KITCHEN

555 W. Cordova Road, Santa Fe, 505-983-7929; www.marias-santafe.com

Southwestern menu. Lunch, dinner. Bar. Children's menu. Casual attire. Reservations recommended. Outdoor seating. **$$**

★★★THE OLD HOUSE RESTAURANT

309 W. San Francisco St., Santa Fe, 505-988-4455, 800-955-4455;
www.eldoradohotel.com

Chef Charles Kassels is known for introducing unexpected flavors into otherwise everyday items. Witness his roasted pork tenderloin, accompanied by sweet potatoes puréed with oranges that he's preserved for nine days, or his duck confit and foie gras in puff pastry with pistachios and cherry-celery compote. Take a moment to look up and take in the candlelit stucco room, part of one of the city's oldest buildings, which is adorned with Mexican folk art and bold, oversized paintings. Southwestern menu. Dinner. Bar. Business casual attire. Reservations recommended. Valet parking. **$$$**

★★ORE HOUSE ON THE PLAZA

50 Lincoln Ave., Santa Fe, 505-983-8687; www.orehouseontheplaza.com

Southwestern, steak menu. Lunch, dinner. Bar. Children's menu. Casual attire. Outdoor seating. **$$**

★★OSTERIA D'ASSISI

58 S. Federal Place, Santa Fe, 505-986-5858; www.osteriadassisi.net

Italian menu. Lunch, dinner. Bar. Children's menu. Casual attire. Reservations recommended. Outdoor seating. **$$$**

★★THE PINK ADOBE

406 Old Santa Fe Trail, Santa Fe, 505-983-7712; www.thepinkadobe.com

Southwestern menu. Lunch, dinner. Bar. Children's menu. Casual attire. Reservations recommended. Outdoor seating. **$$$**

★PLAZA

54 Lincoln Ave., Santa Fe, 505-982-1664; www.thefamousplazacafe.com

Southwestern menu. Breakfast, lunch, dinner. Children's menu. Casual attire. **$$**

★★PRANZO ITALIAN GRILL

540 Montezuma, Santa Fe, 505-984-2645; www.pranzosantafe.com

Italian menu. Lunch, dinner, late-night. Bar. Children's menu. Casual attire. Reservations recommended. **$$**

★★RISTRA

548 Agua Fria St., Santa Fe, 505-982-8608; www.ristrarestaurant.com

French, Southwestern menu. Dinner. Casual attire. Reservations recommended. Outdoor seating. **$$$**

★★SAN MARCOS CAFE

3877 NM 14, Santa Fe, 505-471-9298

Southwestern menu. Breakfast, lunch. **$**

★★★SANTACAFÉ

231 Washington Ave., Santa Fe, 505-984-1788; www.santacafe.com

Situated a block from the Plaza in the restored Padre Gallegos House, Santacafé offers simple but exquisite dishes such as a salad of blood oranges and grapefruit with fennel and celeriac remoullade, shrimp-spinach dumplings in a tahini sauce, filet mignon with persillade and green chile mashed potatoes or roasted free-range chicken with quinoa and a cranberry-chipotle chutney. Patio dining in warmer weather is divine. American, Pan-Asian, Southwestern menu. Lunch, dinner, Sunday brunch. Bar. Children's menu. Casual attire. Reservations recommended. Outdoor seating. **$$$**

★THE SHED

113 1/2 E. Palace Ave., Santa Fe, 505-982-9030; www.sfshed.com

Southwestern menu. Lunch, dinner. Closed Sunday. Bar. Children's menu. Casual attire. Reservations recommended. Outdoor seating. **$$**

★★SHOHKO CAFÉ

321 Johnson St., Santa Fe, 505-982-9708; www.shohkocafe.com

Japanese menu. Lunch, dinner. Casual attire. Reservations recommended. **$$**

★STEAKSMITH AT EL GANCHO

104 B Old Las Vegas Highway, Santa Fe, 505-988-3333; www.santafesteaksmith.com

Steak menu. Dinner. Bar. Children's menu. Casual attire. **$$$**

★★TOMASITA'S

500 S. Guadalupe, Santa Fe, 505-983-5721

Southwestern menu. Lunch, dinner. Closed Sunday. Bar. Children's menu. Casual attire. Outdoor seating. **$$**

★★★TRATTORIA NOSTRANI

304 Johnson St., Santa Fe, 505-983-3800; www.trattorianostrani.com

Guests can dine in one of four semiprivate dining rooms at Trattoria Nostrani, a northern Italian restaurant housed in an 1883 territorial-style house. The casual yet elegant interior retains much of its historical ambience, with tin ceilings and adobe archways. Tempting entrées include filet mignon with Tuscan vegetable ragu and fried potatoes; stuffed chicken with sweet Italian sausage, Fontina and Asiago; and ravioli with black pepper and Pecorino Toscano. More than 400 wines are offered on the extensive European wine list and a knowledgeable staff will assist in selecting the perfect one. Italian menu. Dinner. Closed Sunday. Casual attire. Reservations recommended. **$$$**

★★VANESSIE OF SANTA FE

434 W. San Francisco St., Santa Fe, 505-982-9966; www.vanessiesantafe.com

American menu. Dinner. Bar. Casual attire. Reservations recommended. **$$**

SANTA ROSA

In grama-grass country on the Pecos River, Santa Rosa has several natural and manmade lakes.

Information: Santa Rosa Chamber of Commerce, 141 S. Fifth St., 505-472-3404; www.santarosanm.org

WHAT TO SEE AND DO

BILLY THE KID MUSEUM

1435 E. Sumner Ave., Fort Sumner, 575-355-2380;
www.billythekidmuseumfortsumner.com

Contains 60,000 items, including relics of the Old West, Billy the Kid and Old Fort Sumner. Admission: adults $5.00, seniors $4.00, children $3.00, children under 7 free. Summer, daily 8.30 a.m.-5 p.m.; winter, Monday-Saturday 8:30 a.m.-5 p.m.

BLUE HOLE

Blue Hole Road, Santa Rosa; www.santarosanm.org
This clear blue lake in a rock setting is fed by natural artesian spring; scuba diving.

FORT SUMNER STATE MONUMENT

RR 1, Fort Sumner, 575-355-2573
Original site of the Bosque Redondo, where the U.S. Army held thousands of Navajo and Mescalero Apache captive from 1863-1868. The military established Fort Sumner to oversee the containment. Visitor center has exhibits relating to the period. Monday, Wednesday-Sunday.

GRZELACHOWSKI TERRITORIAL HOUSE

Santa Rosa
Billy the Kid visited this store and mercantile built in 1800 frequently. Daily, mid-morning-early evening.

PUERTA DE LUNA

Puerta de Luna
Founded in approximately 1862, this Spanish-American town of 250 people holds to old customs in living and working.

SANTA ROSA DAM AND LAKE

Highway 91, Santa Rosa, 505-472-3115;
www.spa.usace.army.mil/recreation/sr/location.htm
An irrigation pool is often available for recreation. Fishing, boating; nature trails; camping. Daily.

SUMNER LAKE STATE PARK

Santa Rosa, three miles east on Highways 54/66, then 32 miles south on Highway 84, near Fort Sumner, 575-355-2541; www.emnrd.state.nm.us/prd/SumnerLake.htm
An irrigation dam created this 4,500-surface-acre reservoir. Swimming, fishing (bass, crappie, channel catfish); camping. Daily.

SPECIAL EVENTS

OLD FORT DAYS

Santa Rosa, Fort Sumner, downtown and County Fairgrounds
Parade, rodeo, bank robbery, barbecue, contests, exhibits. Second week in June.

SANTA ROSA DAY CELEBRATION

Santa Rosa

Sports events, contests, exhibits. Memorial Day weekend.

HOTEL

★BEST WESTERN ADOBE INN

1501 Historic Route 66 St., Santa Rosa, 505-472-3446; www.bestwestern.com

58 rooms. Complimentary continental breakfast. High-speed Internet access. Pets accepted. Pool. $

SILVER CITY

The rich gold and silver ores in the foothills of the Mogollon Mountains are running low, but copper mining has now become important to the economy. Cattle ranching thrives on the plains. The forested mountain slopes to the north are the habitat of turkey, deer, elk and bear and the streams and lakes provide excellent trout fishing.

Information: Chamber of Commerce, 201 N. Hudson, 505-538-3785, 800-548-9378; www.silvercity.org

WHAT TO SEE AND DO

GILA CLIFF DWELLINGS NATIONAL MONUMENT

Silver City, 44 miles north on Highway 15, 505-536-9461; www.nps.gov/gicl

More than 40 rooms in six caves are accessible by a one-mile hiking trail. The Mogollon circa 1300 occupied the caves. Self-guided tour; camping. Forest naturalists conduct programs Memorial Day-Labor Day. Admission: adult $3, children under 16 free, family $10. Ruins and visitor center, daily.

GILA NATIONAL FOREST

Silver City, surrounds town on all borders except on the southeast, 505-388-8201; www.fs.fed.us/r3/gila

The Gila National Forest covers about three million acres. Blue Range Wilderness and Aldo Leopold Wilderness are within its borders. Hunting, backpacking, horseback riding. Also includes several lakes (Quemado, Roberts, Snow) ideal for fishing, boating and camping.

PHELPS DODGE COPPER MINE

Silver City, seven miles northeast on Highway 15, 575-538-5331

This historic mining town is home to forts and other historic buildings.

SILVER CITY MUSEUM

312 W. Broadway, Silver City, 505-538-5921, 877-777-7947; www.silvercitymuseum.org

This museum is located in the restored 1881 house of H. B. Ailman, owner of a rich silver mine. Includes Victorian antiques and furnishings; artifacts; memorabilia from mining town of Tyrone. Admission: $3. Tuesday-Sunday; closed Monday.

WESTERN NEW MEXICO UNIVERSITY MUSEUM

In Fleming Hall, 1000 College Ave., Silver City, 575-538-6386; www.wnmu.edu

This museum depicts the contributions of Native American, Hispanic, African American and European cultures to the history of region; largest display of Mimbres pottery in the nation; photography, archive and mineral collections. Daily.

SPECIAL EVENT
FRONTIER DAYS
Silver City
Parade, dances, exhibits, food. Western dress desired. July Fourth.

HOTELS
★COMFORT INN
1060 E. Highway 180, Silver City, 505-534-1883; www.comfortinn.com
92 rooms. Complimentary continental breakfast. Pets accepted. $

★★COPPER MANOR MOTEL
710 Silver Heights Blvd., Silver City, 575-538-5392; www.coppermanor.com
68 rooms. Complimentary continental breakfast. Restaurant. Pets accepted. Pool. $

RESTAURANT
★★BUCKHORN SALOON AND OPERA HOUSE
32 Main St., Pinos Altos, 575-538-9911
Steak menu. Dinner. Closed Sunday. Bar. Casual attire. Reservations recommended. $$

SOCORRO

Socorro is located in the Rio Grande Valley. Originally a Piro Indian town, Socorro had a Franciscan mission as early as 1598. It is the home of a very large astronomy observatory (where parts of the movie *Contact*, starring Jodie Foster, were filmed). *Information: Socorro County Chamber of Commerce, 101 Plaza, 505-835-0424; www.socorro-nm.com*

WHAT TO SEE AND DO
MINERAL MUSEUM
801 Leroy Place, Socorro, 505-835-5140; geoinfo.nmt.edu/museum
See more than 12,000 mineral specimens from around the world. Free rockhounding and prospecting information. Monday-Saturday.

NATIONAL RADIO ASTRONOMY OBSERVATORY
1003 Lopez Ville Road, Socorro, 505-835-7000; www.nrao.edu
The main component here is the VLA (Very Large Array), a radio telescope that consists of 27 separate antennas situated along three arms of railroad track. The VLA is used to investigate all kinds of astronomical topics. Self-guided walking tour of grounds and visitor center. Daily.

OLD SAN MIGUEL MISSION
403 El Camino Real Northwest, Socorro, 505-835-1620; www.sdc.org/~smiguel
This restored 17th-century mission has carved ceiling beams and corbels and walls that are five feet thick. Daily. Artifacts on display in church office (building south of church). Monday-Friday.

SALINAS PUEBLO MISSIONS NATIONAL MONUMENT

This monument was established to explore European-Native American contact and the resulting cultural changes. The stabilized ruins of the massive 17th-century missions are basically unaltered, preserving the original design and construction. All three units are open and feature wayside exhibits, trails and picnic areas. Monument Headquarters, one block west of Highway 55 on Highway 60 in Mountainair, has an audiovisual presentation and an exhibit depicting the Salinas story. There are three units of this monument:

Gran Quivira. The massive walls of the 17th-century San Buenaventura Mission (begun in 1659 but never completed) are here, as well as San Isidro Church (circa 1639) and 21 pueblo mounds, two of which have been excavated. A self-guided trail and museum/visitor center combine to vividly portray Native American life over the past 1,000 years. Various factors led to the desertion of the pueblo and the mission around 1671. Tompiro Indians occupied this and the Ab site. 25 miles southeast of Mountainair on Highway 55, 505-847-2770.

Ab. Contains ruins of the mission church of San Gregorio de Ab (circa 1622), built by Native Americans under the direction of Franciscan priests. This is the only early church in New Mexico with 40-foot buttressed curtain walls—a style typical of medieval European architecture. The pueblo adjacent to the church was abandoned around 1673 because of drought, disease and Apache uprisings. The Ab and others from the Salinas jurisdiction eventually moved south with the Spanish to El Paso del Norte, where they established the pueblo of Ysleta del Sur and other towns still in existence today. There are self-guided trails throughout the mission compound and pueblo mounds. Nine miles west of Mountainair on Highway 60, then ¾-mile north on Highway, 505-847-2400.

Quarai. Encompasses the ruins of the Mission de la Pursima Concepción de Cuarac, other Spanish structures and unexcavated American Indian mounds, all built of red sandstone. Built about 1630, it was abandoned along with the pueblo about 1677, most likely for the same reasons. Unlike the other two, Tiwa-speaking people occupied this site. Much of the history is related to the Spanish-Indian cultural conflict. The church ruins have been excavated and it is the most complete church in the monument. The visitor center has a museum and interpretive displays. Eight miles north of Mountainair on Highway 55, then one mile west on a county road from Punta.

Information: Socorro, approximately 75 miles southeast of Albuquerque via Interstate 40, Highway 337, 505-847-2290; www.nps.gov/sapu

HOTELS
★BEST WESTERN SOCORRO
1100 N. California St., Socorro, 575-838-0556; www.bestwestern.com
120 rooms. Complimentary continental breakfast. Pets accepted. Pool. High-speed Internet access. Fitness center. Children activities center. Business center. **$**

★ECONO LODGE SOCORRO
713 California St. N.W., Socorro, 505-835-1500, 877-424-6423; www.econolodge.com
66 rooms. Complimentary continental breakfast. Restaurant. Pets accepted. Pool. **$**

TAOS
As early as 1615, a handful of Spanish colonists settled in this area. In 1617 a church was built. After the Pueblo Rebellion of 1680, the town was a farming center plagued by Apache raids and disagreements with the Taos Indians and the government of Santa Fe. The first artists came in 1898; since then it has flourished as an art colony. Many people come here for the clear air, magnificent surroundings and exciting and congenial atmosphere.

Taos is actually three towns: the Spanish-American settlement into which Anglos have infiltrated, which is Taos proper; Taos Pueblo, two and a half miles north; and Ranchos de Taos, four miles south. Many farming communities and fishing resorts can be found in the surrounding mountains. Taos Ski Valley, 19 miles northeast, is a popular spot for winter sports. The town has a few famous residents, including Julia Roberts, Val Kilmer and Donald Rumsfeld.

Information: Taos County Chamber of Commerce, 1139 Paseo Del Pueblo Sur, 505-758-3873, 800-732-8267; www.taos.org

WHAT TO SEE AND DO
CARSON NATIONAL FOREST
208 Cruz Alta Road, Taos, 575-758-6200; www.fs.fed.us/r3/carson
This forest occupies 1½ million acres and includes Wheeler Peak, New Mexico's highest mountain at 13,161 feet. Lots of small mountain lakes and streams provide good fishing. There's also hunting, hiking, winter sports, picnicking, camping. Daily.

ERNEST L. BLUMENSCHEIN HOME
222 Ledoux St., Taos, 575-758-0505; www.taosmuseums.org/blumenschein.php
This restored adobe house includes furnishings and exhibits of paintings by the Blumenschein family and other early Taos artists. May-October: daily 9 a.m.-5 p.m.; call for winter hours. Combination tickets to seven Taos museums available.

FORT BURGWIN RESEARCH CENTER
6580 Highway 518, Taos, 505-758-8322; www.smu.edu/taos
The First Dragoons of the U.S. Calvary (1852-1860) occupied this restored fort. Summer lecture series, music and theater performances. Operated by Southern Methodist University. Schedule varies.

GOVERNOR BENT HOUSE MUSEUM AND GALLERY

117 Bent St., Taos, 505-758-2376; www.laplaza.org/art/museums_bent.php3

Visit the home of New Mexico's first American territorial governor (and the scene of his death in 1847). Includes Bent family possessions, Native American artifacts, Western American art. Summer, daily 9 a.m.-5 p.m.; winter, daily 10 a.m.-4 p.m.

HACIENDA DE LOS MARTINEZ

708 Ranchitos Road, Taos, 505-758-0505; www.taoshistoricmuseums.com

Contains early Spanish Colonial hacienda with period furnishings; 21 rooms, two large patios. Early Taos, Spanish culture exhibits. Used as a fortress during raids. Living museum demonstrations. Summer, daily 9 a.m.-5 p.m., call for winter hours. Combination tickets to seven Taos museums available.

HARWOOD MUSEUM OF ART

238 Ledoux St., Taos, 505-758-9826; www.harwoodmuseum.org

Founded in 1923, this museum features paintings, drawings, prints, sculptures and photographs by artists of Taos from 1800 to the present. Tuesday-Saturday 10 a.m.-5 p.m., Sunday noon-5 p.m.; closed Monday. Combination tickets to seven Taos museums available.

KIT CARSON HOME AND MUSEUM

113 Kit Carson Road, Taos, 505-758-4945; www.kitcarsonhome.com

Restored 1825 home of the famous frontiersman with artifacts, including a gun exhibit. Summer: daily 9 a.m.-5 p.m., call for winter hours.

KIT CARSON PARK

211 Paseo del Pueblo Norte, Taos, 575-758-8234

This 25-acre park includes a bicycle/walking path, picnic tables, a playground and a sand volleyball pit. No camping. The graves of Kit Carson and his family are also here. Daily.

ORILLA VERDE RECREATION AREA

Highway 570 and Highway 68, Taos, 505-758-8851;
www.blm.gov/nm/st/en/prog/recreation/taos/orilla_verde.html

This park runs along the banks of the Rio Grande, offering some of the finest trout fishing in the state; white-water rafting through deep chasm north of park. Hiking, picnicking. Spectacular views. Daily.

RANCHOS DE TAOS

60 Ranchos Plaza Road, Taos, 575-758-2754

This adobe-housed farming and ranching center has one of the most beautiful churches in the Southwest—the San Francisco de Asis Church. Its huge buttresses and twin bell towers only suggest the beauty of its interior. Monday-Saturday 9 a.m.-4 p.m.

RIO GRANDE GORGE BRIDGE

Taos, 12 miles northwest on Highway 64

This bridge is 650 feet above the Rio Grande; observation platforms, picnic and parking areas.

NEW MEXICO

★ ★ ★ ★ ★

SIPAPU SKI & SUMMER RESORT

Highway 518, three miles west of Tres Ritos, 800-587-2240; www.sipapunm.com

Area has two triple chairlifts, two Pomalifts; patrol, school, rentals, snowmaking; 39 runs, the longest two miles; vertical drop 1,055 feet. Mid-December-March, daily. Cross-country skiing on forest roads and trails. Snowboarding.

TAOS PUEBLO

Taos, 505-758-1028; www.taospueblo.com

With a full-time population of 150, this is one of the most famous Native American pueblos and has been continuously inhabited for more than 1,000 years. Within the pueblo is a double apartment house. The north and south buildings, separated by a river, are five stories tall and form a unique communal dwelling. Small buildings and corrals are scattered around these impressive architectural masterpieces. The residents here live without modern utilities such as electricity and plumbing and get their drinking water from the river. The people are independent, conservative and devout in their religious observances. Fees are charged for parking and photography permits. Photographs of individual Native Americans may be taken only with their consent. Daily 8 a.m.-4 p.m.; closed for special occasions in spring.

TAOS SKI VALLEY

103A Suton Place, Taos Ski Valley, 866-968-7386; www.skitaos.org

Area has 12 chairlifts, two surface lifts; patrol, school, rentals; cafeteria, restaurants, bar; nursery, lodges. Longest run more than four miles; vertical drop 2,612 feet. November-April, daily.

SPECIAL EVENTS

ANNUAL POW WOW

Taos Pueblo, Taos, 505-758-1028; www.taospueblopowwow.com

Intertribal dancers from throughout U.S., Canada and Mexico participate in this competition. Second weekend in July.

CHAMBER MUSIC FESTIVAL

145 Paseo del Pueblo, Taos, 505-776-2388; www.taosschoolofmusic.com

Mid-June-early August.

FIESTAS DE TAOS

Taos Plaza, Taos, 505-741-0909; www.fiestasdetaos.com

This traditional festival honoring the patron saints of Taos includes a candlelight procession, parade, crafts, food and entertainment. Late July.

SAN GERONIMO EVE SUNDOWN DANCE

Taos Pueblo, Taos, 505-758-1028; www.taospueblo.com/calendar.php

See a traditional men's dance, which is followed the next day by San Geronimo Feast Day, with intertribal dancing, trade fair, pole climb and foot races. Last weekend in September.

SPRING ARTS FESTIVAL

Taos, 505-758-3873, 800-732-8267; www.taoschamber.com

This three-week festival celebrates the visual, performing and literary arts. May.

TAOS ARTS FESTIVAL

Taos, 505-758-1028; www.taosguide.com

Arts and crafts exhibitions, music, plays, poetry readings. Mid-September-early October.

TAOS PUEBLO DANCES

Taos Pueblo, Albuquerque, 505-758-1028; www.taospueblo.com

Several Native American dances are held throughout the year. For a schedule of annual dances, contact the pueblo.

TAOS PUEBLO DEER OR *MATACHINES* DANCE

Taos Pueblo, Taos, 505-758-1028; www.taospueblo.com

Symbolic animal dance or ancient Montezuma dance. December 25.

TAOS RODEO

County Fairgrounds, Taos, 800-348-0696; www.taosvacationguide.com

Late June or early July.

YULETIDE IN TAOS

Taos, 800-348-0696; www.taosvacationguide.com

The celebration includes area *farolito* (paper bag lantern) tours, food and craft fairs, art events and dance performances. Late November-late December.

HOTELS

★COMFORT INN

1500 Paseo Del Pueblo Sur, Taos, 505-751-1555; www.comfortinn.com

60 rooms. Complimentary continental breakfast. Pool. $

★★★EL MONTE SAGRADO

317 Kit Carson Road, Taos, 505-758-3502, 800-828-8264; www.elmontesagrado.com

El Monte Sagrado speaks to the naturalist in all travelers. This unique resort, tucked away in magical Taos, celebrates the natural beauty of New Mexico while highlighting its rich Native American heritage. The themed guestrooms and suites, which proudly display local and international artwork, are seductive retreats. Taos, well known for its world-class skiing, is a year-round playground, offering everything from rock climbing and fly fishing to llama trekking and mountain biking. Closer to home, El Monte Sagrado features a world-class spa, with a focus on renewal of body and mind. The award-winning De La Tierra restaurant is a feast for the eyes and the palate. 36 rooms. Spa. Pool. Fitness room. Wireless Internet access. Business center. $$$$

★HAMPTON INN

1515 Paseo Del Pueblo Sur, Taos, 505-737-5700; www.hamptoninn.com

71 rooms. Complimentary continental breakfast. Pool. Fitness center. Business center. $

★★★THE HISTORIC TAOS INN

125 Paseo Del Pueblo Norte, Taos, 505-758-2233, 888-518-8267; www.taosinn.com

This historic inn offers a comfortable Old West atmosphere and modern amenities. Guests will enjoy the outdoor heated pool and greenhouse whirlpool. The unique guest rooms feature Southwestern décor and many offer kiva fireplaces. Be sure to dine at the acclaimed Doc Martin's Restaurant. 36 rooms. Restaurant, bar. Pool. $

★★★SAGEBRUSH INN

1508 Paseo Del Pueblo Sur, Taos, 505-758-2254, 800-428-3626;
www.sagebrushinn.com

Built in 1929, this 100-room adobe inn houses a large collection of paintings, Native American rugs and other regional art. The most recent addition, an 18,000-square-foot conference center, features hand-hewn *vigas* and fireplaces. Visitors will enjoy the outdoor pool and two whirlpools. Guest rooms feature have handmade furniture. 100 rooms. Complimentary full breakfast. Restaurant, bar. Pets accepted. Pool. $

SPECIALTY LODGINGS

ADOBE AND STARS INN

584 Highway 150, Taos, 505-776-2776, 800-211-7076; www.taosadobe.com

Located near the Historic Taos Plaza and the Taos Ski Valley, this Southwestern inn offers panoramic views of the Sangre de Cristo Mountains. Guest rooms feature kiva fireplaces, private baths with terra-cotta tile and ceiling fans. Eight rooms. Complimentary full breakfast. Pets accepted. Wireless Internet access. $

AUSTING HAUS BED & BREAKFAST

1282 Highway 150, Taos Ski Valley, 505-776-2649, 800-748-2932;
www.austinghaus.net

This newly remodeled inn was constructed of oak-pegged heavy timbers with beams exposed inside and out. 45 rooms. Closed mid-April-mid-May. Complimentary continental breakfast. Restaurant. Whirlpool. Pets accepted. $

CASA DE LAS CHIMENEAS

405 Cordoba Road, Taos, 505-758-4777, 877-758-4777; www.visit-taos.com

True to its Spanish name (the House of Chimneys), all guest rooms in this bed and breakfast have kiva fireplaces as well as brass and wooden beds, private entrances and baths, down pillows and electric blankets or down comforters. Guests will enjoy the inn's formal gardens and courtyards, fountains and whirlpool. Nine rooms. Complimentary full breakfast. Reservation recommended. $$

CASA EUROPA INN

840 Upper Ranchitos Road, Taos, 505-758-9798, 888-758-9798;
www.casaeuropanm.com

Set on six acres of land, this 17th-century Pueblo-style inn offers a soothing experience and beautiful views. The flowered courtyards feature a fountain, as well as a sauna and whirlpool. The spacious guest rooms offer private bathrooms, desks and fans. Seven rooms. Complimentary full breakfast. $

HACIENDA DEL SOL

109 Mabel Dodge Lane, Taos, 505-758-0287, 866-333-4459;
www.taoshaciendadelsol.com
This inn consists of three adobe buildings set on 1.2 acres overlooking the Taos
Mountains. The romantic guest rooms feature thick adobe walls, original artwork and
corner fireplaces. 11 rooms. Complimentary full breakfast. **$$**

INN ON LA LOMA PLAZA

315 Ranchitos Road, Taos, 505-758-1717, 800-530-3040; www.vacationtaos.com
This restored historic inn offers mountain views and spacious gardens. Visitors will
enjoy the large whirlpool and can take advantage of complimentary spa, tennis and
health club privileges nearby. Guest rooms feature private baths, fireplaces, phones,
televisions, robes and slippers. Seven rooms. Complimentary full breakfast. Spa.
Pool. Tennis. Wireless Internet access. **$**

LA POSADA DE TAOS

309 Juanita Lane, Taos, 505-758-8164, 800-645-4803; www.laposadadetaos.com
Six rooms. Complimentary full breakfast. Wireless Internet access. **$**

SALSA DEL SALTO BED & BREAKFAST INN

543 Highway 150, Anoyo Seco, 505-776-2422, 800-530-3097; www.bandbtaos.com
With the inn conveniently located close to Taos Ski Valley and Taos, guests will have
the option of skiing or shopping. After a game of tennis, you can enjoy the mountain
view from the whirlpool. 10 rooms. Children over 6 years only. Complimentary full
breakfast. Tennis. Wireless Internet access. **$**

SAN GERONIMO LODGE

1101 Witt Road, Taos, 505-751-3776, 800-894-4119; www.sangeronimolodge.com
18 rooms. Complimentary full breakfast. Pool. Pets accepted. **$**

TOUCHSTONE INN & SPA

110 Mabel Dodge Lane, Taos, 505-758-0192, 800-758-0192; www.touchstoneinn.com
This quiet, historic bed and breakfast is nestled among the trees on the edge of Taos
Pueblo Lands. 10 rooms. Complimentary full breakfast. No children under 12. Spa. **$**

RESTAURANTS
★★APPLE TREE

123 Bent St., Taos, 505-758-1900; www.appletreerestaurant.com
American, Southwestern menu. Lunch, dinner, Sunday brunch. Children's menu.
Business casual attire. Reservations recommended. Outdoor seating. **$$**

★★★DE LA TIERRA

317 Kit Carson Road, Taos, 505-758-3502, 800-828-8267; www.elmontesagrado.com
From its one-of-a-kind décor to its sensational cuisine, De la Tierra, tucked inside
Taos' striking El Monte Sagrado resort, practically begs for special occasions. Tower-
ing ceilings capped by an enormous wrought iron chandelier, high-backed, tapestry-
covered chairs and soft, golden lighting make this dining room exude pure seduction.
Chef Ruben Tanuz's signature style puts a Southwestern spin on an internationally

influenced menu. Everything from mustard-crusted elk, rack of lamb with sage bread pudding, grilled salmon with spinach enchiladas, and molasses-marinated grilled quail is given his unique stamp. Southwestern/American menu. Breakfast, lunch, dinner. Reservations recommended. $$$

★★★DOC MARTIN'S
125 Paseo Del Pueblo, Taos, 505-758-1977; www.taosinn.com
Chef Zippy White serves organic Southwestern cuisine in an adobe setting. Specialties include chipotle shrimp on corn cakes and Southwestern lacquered duck. The wine list is one of the best in the area. American, Southwestern menu. Breakfast, lunch, dinner, Sunday brunch. Bar. Children's menu. Casual attire. Reservations recommended. Outdoor seating. $$$

★★★LAMBERT'S OF TAOS
309 Paseo Del Pueblo Sur, Taos, 505-758-1009; www.lambertsoftaos.com
Zeke and Tina Lambert came to Taos years ago on their honeymoon and never left. This restaurant serves contemporary cuisine. The produce is local when possible and all the sauces are made from scratch. Dishes include grilled lamb tenderloin with warm lentil salad and New Mexico feta cheese or fillet of beef on potato cake with grilled spinach and horseradish cream. The extensive wine list is primarily from California. American menu. Dinner. Bar. Children's menu. Casual attire. Reservations recommended. Outdoor seating. $$$

★★OGELVIE'S TAOS BAR AND GRILLE
103 E. Plaza, Taos, 505-758-8866; www.ogelvies.com
American, Southwestern menu. Lunch, dinner. Bar. Children's menu. Casual attire. Outdoor seating. $$

★★★OLD BLINKING LIGHT
Mile Marker One, Ski Valley Road, Taos, 505-776-8787; www.oldblinkinglight.com
American, Southwestern menu. Dinner. Bar. Children's menu. Casual attire. Outdoor seating. $$

★★STAKEOUT GRILL AND BAR
101 Stakeout Drive, Taos, 505-758-2042; www.stakeoutrestaurant.com
Seafood, steak menu. Dinner. Closed November. Bar. Children's menu. Casual attire. Outdoor seating. May-October. $$

TRUTH OR CONSEQUENCES

Formerly called "Hot Springs" for the warm mineral springs nearby, the town changed its name in 1950 to celebrate the tenth anniversary of Ralph Edwards' radio program, *Truth or Consequences*.

In the early 1500s, the Spanish Conquistadores came through this area and legends of lost Spanish gold mines and treasures in the Caballo Mountains persist today. There are numerous ghost towns and old mining camps in the area.

Information: Truth or Consequences/Sierra County Chamber of Commerce,
400 W. Fourth St., 575-894-3536; www.truthorconsequencesnm.net

WHAT TO SEE AND DO
CABALLO LAKE STATE PARK
Truth or Consequences, 18 miles south on Interstate 25, 575-743-3942;
www.emnrd.state.nm.us/prd/caballo.htm
The Caballo Mountains form a backdrop for this lake. Swimming, windsurfing, water-skiing, fishing, boating (ramp); hiking, picnicking, playground, camping. Daily.

GERONIMO SPRINGS MUSEUM
211 Main St., Truth or Consequences, 505-894-6600;
www.geronimospringsmuseum.com
See exhibits of Mimbres pottery, fossils and photographs, as well as articles on local history. Gift shop (Monday-Saturday).

HOTELS
★BEST WESTERN HOT SPRINGS MOTOR INN
2270 N. Date St., Truth or Consequences, 505-894-6665; www.bestwestern.com
40 rooms. Pets accepted. Pool. Wireless Internet access. $

★★★ELEPHANT BUTTE INN & SPA
401 Highway 195, Elephant Butte, 575-744-5431; www.elephantbutteinn.com
This hotel provides a tranquil getaway in Elephant Butte—it overlooks Elephant Butte Lake and features an onsite spa, where you can get a soothing full-body wrap to calm sunburned skin in addition to great massages. Rooms are comfortable and well-equipped as well, featuring desks, refrigerators and microwaves. To further relax in this desert oasis, head for the pool, where you can sun or swim a few laps before heading to the restaurant Ivory Tusk for some New Mexican fare. 47 rooms. Complimentary continental breakfast. Restaurant, bar. Pets accepted. Pool. $

RESTAURANT
★★LOS ARCOS STEAK HOUSE
1400 N. Date St., Truth or Consequences, 575-894-6200
American menu. Dinner. Bar. Children's menu. Casual attire. Outdoor seating. $$

TUCUMCARI
Tucumcari is a convenient stopping point between Amarillo, Texas, and Albuquerque. Tucumcari Mountain (4,957 feet) is to the south.
Information: Tucumcari/Quay County Chamber of Commerce, 404 W. Route 66,
575-461-1694; www.tucumcarinm.com

WHAT TO SEE AND DO
TUCUMCARI HISTORICAL MUSEUM
416 S. Adams St., Tucumcari, 575-461-4201;
www.cityoftucumcari.com/html/tucumcari_historical_museum.html
See Western Americana, Native American artifacts, gems, minerals, rocks, fossils and more. Summer, Monday-Saturday 8 a.m.-6 p.m.; Winter, Monday-Friday 8 a.m.-5 p.m.

ROUTE 66 FESTIVAL

404 W. Tumcari Blvd., Tucumcari

Rodeo, car show, parade, arts and crafts, entertainment. July.

HOTELS

★COMFORT INN

2800 E. Tucumcari Blvd., Tucumcari, 505-461-4094, 877-424-6423;
www.comfortinn.com

59 rooms. High-speed Internet access. Complimentary continental breakfast. Pet. Pool. **$**

★★HOLIDAY INN

2624 S. Adams St., Tucumcari, 505-461-3333, 888-465-4329; www.holiday-inn.com

100 rooms. Complimentary full breakfast. Restaurant, bar. Pool. Fitness center. High-speed Internet access. **$**

ZUNI PUEBLO

Thirty-nine miles south of Gallup, via Highway 602 and west on Highway 53, is one of Coronado's "Seven Cities of Cibola." Fray Marcos de Niza reported that these cities were built of gold. When looking down on the Zuni pueblo from a distant hilltop at sunset, it does seem to have a golden glow.

The people here make beautiful jewelry, beadwork and pottery. They also have a furniture and woodworking center with colorful and uniquely painted and carved items. Ashiwi Awan Museum and Heritage Center displays historical photos and exhibits. The pueblo, built mainly of stone, is one story high. The old Zuni mission church has been restored and its interior painted with murals of Zuni traditional figures. A tribal permit is required for photography; certain rules must be observed.

354

NEW MEXICO

★
★
★
★

UTAH

UTAH'S NATURAL DIVERSITY HAS MADE IT A STATE OF MAGNIFICENT BEAUTY, WITH MORE than 3,000 lakes, miles of mountains, acres of forests and large expanses of desert. In northern Utah, the grandeur of the Wasatch Range, one of the most rugged mountain ranges in the United States, cuts across the state north to south. The Uinta Range, capped by the white peaks of ancient glaciers, is the only major North American range that runs east to west. In the western third of the state is the Great Basin. Lake Bonneville extended over much of western Utah leaving behind the Great Salt Lake, Utah Lake and Sevier Lake. To the east and west extends the Red Plateau. This red rock country, renowned for its brilliant coloring and fantastic rock formations, is home to one of the largest concentrations of national parks and monuments. Utah is definitely the place for those who love the western outdoors and can appreciate the awesome accomplishments of the pioneers who developed it.

This natural diversity created an environment inhospitable to early settlers. Although various groups explored much of the state, it took the determination and perseverance of a band of religious fugitives, members of the Church of Jesus Christ of Latter-Day Saints, to settle the land permanently.

Brigham Young, leader of the Mormons, once remarked, "If there is a place on this earth that nobody else wants, that's the place I am hunting for." On July 24, 1847, on entering the forbidding land surrounding the Great Salt Lake, Young exclaimed, "This is the place!" The determined settlers immediately began to plow the unfriendly soil and build dams for irrigation. During 1847, as many as 1,637 Mormons came to Utah, and by the time the railroad made its way here, more than 6,000 had settled in the state. Before his death in 1877, 30 years after entering the Salt Lake Valley, Brigham Young had directed the founding of more than 350 communities.

The LDS church undoubtedly had the greatest influence on the state, developing towns in an orderly fashion with wide streets, planting straight rows of poplar trees to provide wind breaks and introducing irrigation throughout the desert regions. But the church members were not the only settlers. In the latter part of the 19th century, the West's fabled pioneer era erupted. The gold rush of 1849-1850 sent gold seekers pouring through Utah on their way to California.

The arrival of the Pony Express in Salt Lake City in 1860 brought more immigrants, and when the mining boom hit the state in the 1870s and 1880s, Utah's mining towns appeared almost overnight. In 1900, the population was 277,000. It now stands at more than 1.7 million, with more than 75 percent living within 50 miles of Salt Lake City. The LDS church continues to play an important role and close to 60 percent of the state's population are members.

Information: www.utah.com

 FUN FACTS

Rainbow Bridge, nature's abstract sculpture carved of solid sandstone, is the world's largest natural-rock span. It stands 275 feet wide and 209 feet high.

Kanab is known as Utah's Little Hollywood because a large number of motion pictures are filmed in the area.

ALTA

Founded around silver mines in the 1870s, Alta was notorious for constant shoot-outs in its 26 saloons. With the opening of Utah's first ski resort in 1937, the town became the center of a noted resort. Unusual wildflowers are found in Albion Basin.
Information: 801-742-3522; www.townofalta.com

WHAT TO SEE AND DO
ALTA SKI AREA
Highway 210, Little Cottonwood Canyon Alta, 801-359-1078; www.alta.com
Two quad, two triple, three double chairlifts; four rope tows; patrol, school, rentals, snowmaking. Longest run 3.5 miles, vertical drop 2,020 feet. Half-day rates. No snowboarding. Mid-November-April, daily.

HOTELS
★ALTA LODGE
10230 East State Highway 210, Alta, 801-742-3500, 800-707-2582;
www.altalodge.com
57 rooms. Closed mid-late October, May. Wireless Internet access. Restaurant, bar. Children's activity center. Whirlpool. Ski-in/ski-out. Tennis. $

★★★ALTA'S RUSTLER LODGE
10380 Highway 210, Alta, 801-742-2200, 888-532-2582; www.rustlerlodge.com
With its ski-in/ski-out access to all of Alta's lift base facilities and a full-service ski shop onsite, the Rustler Lodge is all about the slopes. A complimentary shuttle takes

ARCHES NATIONAL PARK

This natural landscape of giant stone arches, pinnacles, spires, fins and windows was once the bed of an ancient sea. Over time, erosion laid bare the skeletal structure of the earth, making this 114-square-mile area a spectacular outdoor museum. This wilderness, which contains the greatest density of natural arches in the world, was named a national monument in 1929 and a national park in 1971. More than 2,000 arches have been cataloged, ranging in size from three feet wide to the 105-foot-high, 306-foot-wide Landscape Arch. The arches, other rock formations and views of the Colorado River canyon (with the peaks of the La Sal Mountains in the distance) can be reached by car, but hiking is the best way to explore. Petroglyphs from the primitive peoples who roamed this section of Utah from A.D. 700-1200 can be seen at the Delicate Arch trailhead.

Hiking, rock climbing or camping in isolated sections should not be undertaken unless first reported to a park ranger at the visitor center (check locally for hours). Twenty-four miles of paved roads are open year-round. Graded and dirt roads should not be attempted in wet weather. Devils Garden Campground, 18 miles north of the visitor center off Highway 191, provides 52 individual and two group campsites (year-round; fee; water available only March-mid-October).
Information: Five miles northwest of Moab on Highway 191 to paved entrance road. 435-719-2299; www.nps.gov/arch

guests wherever they want to go in Alta and Snowbird. The new business center offers wireless Internet access for those who need to get some work done between runs. The lodge also has a steam room and offers manicures, pedicures and other spa treatments. The children's programs will keep kids occupied. 85 rooms. Closed May-October. Wireless internet access. Business center. Restaurant, bar. Ski-in/ski-out. Exercise. Pool. Skiing. Fitness room. $$$

BEAVER

The seat of Beaver County, this town is a national historic district with more than 200 houses of varied architectural styles and periods. Butch Cassidy was born here in 1866.

Information: Beaver County Travel Council, 405 Main St., 435-438-5438; www.beaverutah.net

SPECIAL EVENT
PIONEER DAY CELEBRATION AND PARADE
Beaver, 435-438-5438

Features a parade, entertainment and horse racing, along with other events. Late July.

HOTELS
★BEST WESTERN BUTCH CASSIDY INN
161 S Main St., Beaver, 435-438-2438, 800-780-7234; www.bestwestern.com

35 rooms. Complimentary continental breakfast. High-speed Internet access. Pets accepted. Pool. $

★QUALITY INN
781 W. 1800 S., Beaver, 435-438-5426; www.qualityinn.com

52 rooms. Pets accepted. Pool. Wireless Internet access. Complimentary continental breakfast. $

BLANDING

The city is a gateway to hunting and fishing grounds and national monuments. The sites can be explored by jeep or horseback along the many trails, or by boat through the waters of Glen Canyon National Recreation Area. A Pueblo ruin, inhabited between A.D. 800 and A.D. 1200, is now a state park within the city limits.

Information: San Juan County Visitor Center, 117 S. Main St., Monticello, 435-587-3235, 800-574-4386; www.southeastutah.org

WHAT TO SEE AND DO
EDGE OF THE CEDARS STATE PARK
660 W. 400 North, Blanding, 435-678-2238; www.utah.com/stateparks/edge_of_cedars.htm

This park sits on the site of a pre-Columbian Pueblo Indian ruin. You'll find excavated remnants of ancient dwellings and ceremonial chambers fashioned by the ancient Pueblo people, as well as artifacts and pictographs. Visitor center. Daily; hours vary by season.

NATURAL BRIDGES NATIONAL MONUMENT

This 7,439-acre area of colorful, fantastically eroded terrain was made a national monument in 1908. It features three natural bridges (formed through erosion by water), all with Hopi names. Sipapu, a 268-foot span, and Kachina, a 204-foot span, are both in White Canyon, a major tributary gorge of the Colorado River. Owachomo, a 180-foot span, is near Armstrong Canyon, which joins White Canyon. Sipapu is the second-largest natural bridge in the world. From 2,000 to 650 years ago, the ancestral Puebloan people lived in this area, leaving behind cliff dwelling ruins and pictographs that visitors can view today. The major attraction is Bridge View Drive, a nine-mile-loop road open daily from early morning to 30 minutes past sunset, providing views of the three bridges from rim overlooks. There are also hiking trails to each bridge within the canyon.

The park also has a visitor center (Daily 8 a.m.-5 p.m.) and primitive campground with 13 tent and trailer sites (all year). Car and passenger ferry service across Lake Powell is available.

Information: Blanding, four miles south on Highway 191, then 36 miles west on Highway 95, then four miles north on Highway 275, 435-692-1234; www.nps.gov/nabr

GLEN CANYON NATIONAL RECREATION AREA/LAKE POWELL

Blanding, four miles south on Highway 191, then 85 miles west on Highways 95 and 276, 928-608-6200; www.nps.gov/glca

More than 1.2 million acres of recreational bliss, Glen Canyon National Recreation Area is an ideal place for backcountry exploration or fun in Lake Powell.

HOVENWEEP NATIONAL MONUMENT

Blanding, 970-562-4282; www.nps.gov/hove

The monument consists of six units of prehistoric ruins; the best preserved are the remains of pueblos (small cliff dwellings) and towers at Square Tower. Self-guided trail; park ranger on duty; visitor center. April–September, daily 8 a.m.-6 p.m.; October-March 8 a.m.-5 p.m.

BLUFF

Bluff's dramatic location between the sandstone cliffs along the San Juan River, its Anasazi ruins among the canyon walls and its Mormon pioneer past all combine to make it an interesting stop along scenic Highway 163 between the Grand Canyon and Mesa Verde national parks.

Information: San Juan County Visitor Center, 117 S. Main St., Monticello, 435-587-3235, 800-574-4386; www.bluffutah.org

WHAT TO SEE AND DO

TOURS OF THE BIG COUNTRY

Highway 191, Bluff, 435-672-2281; www.bluffutah.org/recapturelodge

Naturalist-guided walking and four-wheel-drive tours include trips to Monument Valley, the Navajo Reservation and more. Also includes llama rentals. Half-day, full-day and overnight trips. Year-round.

WILD RIVERS EXPEDITIONS
101 Main St., Bluff, 800-422-7654; www.riversandruins.com

This tour company, in business since 1957, arranges fun and educational single-day and multiday trips on the archaeologically rich San Juan River, framed by dramatic red rock formations and fossil beds. Licensed guides, many of whom are archaeologists, geologists or of Navajo descent, conduct the tours, interpreting the native ruins and rock art found along the journey. Reserve well in advance. March-mid-November.

SPECIAL EVENT
UTAH NAVAJO FAIR
Bluff, 435-651-3755; www.southeastutah.com/en/events

Traditional song and dance, food, crafts and a rodeo. Mid-September.

BRIGHAM CITY

Renamed for Brigham Young in 1877 when he made his last public address here, this community, situated at the base of the towering Wasatch Mountains, was first known as Box Elder because of the many trees of that type that grew in the area. Main Street, which runs through the center of this city, is still lined with these leafy trees.

Information: Chamber of Commerce, 6 N. Main St., 435-723-3931;
www.bcareachamber.com, www.brighamcity.utah.gov

WHAT TO SEE AND DO
BRIGHAM CITY MUSEUM-GALLERY
24 N. 300 W. Brigham City, 435-723-6769;
www.brighamcity.utah.govt

Displays include furniture, clothing, books, photographs and documents reflecting the history of the Brigham City area since 1851. Also showcases rotating art exhibits. Tuesday-Friday 11 a.m.-6 p.m., Saturday 1-5 p.m.; closed Sunday-Monday.

GOLDEN SPIKE NATIONAL HISTORIC SITE
Brigham City, 32 miles west via Highways 13 and 83, 435-471-2209;
www.nps.gov/gosp

This is the site where America's first transcontinental railroad was completed when the Central Pacific and Union Pacific lines met on May 10, 1869. At the visitor center, you'll find movies and exhibits. There's also a self-guided auto tour along the old railroad bed. The summer interpretive program includes presentations and operating replicas of steam locomotives (May-early October). Daily 9 a.m.-5 p.m.

TABERNACLE
251 S. Main St., Brigham City, 435-723-5376; www.ldsces.org

The Box Elder tabernacle, one of the most architecturally interesting buildings in Utah, has been in continuous use since 1881. Gutted by fire and rebuilt in the late 1890s, it was restored in the late 1980s. Guided tours are given in the summer months.

UTAH

★
★
★
★
★

SPECIAL EVENTS
DRIVING OF THE GOLDEN SPIKE
Brigham City, 435-471-2209
The reenactment of the driving of the golden spike (the ceremonial nail driven to mark the completion of a railroad) takes place at the site where the Central Pacific and Union Pacific railroads met in 1869. Locomotive replicas are used. Mid-May.

PEACH DAYS CELEBRATION
Brigham City; www.boxelder.org/tourism/events
Parade, arts and crafts, carnival, car show, entertainment. First weekend after Labor Day.

HOTEL
★CRYSTAL INN, A RODEWAY INN
480 Westland Drive, Brigham City, 435-723-0440, 877-462-7978; www.crystalinns.com
30 rooms. Pets accepted. Business center. Pool. Fitness center. Wireless Internet access. $

BRYCE CANYON NATIONAL PARK

Bryce Canyon is a 56-square-mile area of colorful, fantastic cliffs created by millions of years of erosion. Towering rocks worn down into odd, sculptured shapes stand grouped in striking sequences. The Paiute, who once lived nearby, called this "the place where red rocks stand like men in a bowl-shaped canyon." Although labeled as a canyon, Bryce is actually a series of "breaks" in 12 large amphitheaters—some plunging as deep as 1,000 feet into the multicolored limestone. The formations appear to change color as the sunlight strikes from different angles and seem incandescent in the late afternoon. The famous Pink Cliffs were carved from the Claron Formation; shades of red, orange, white, gray, purple, brown and soft yellow appear in the strata. The park road follows 17 miles along the eastern edge of the Paunsaugunt Plateau, where the natural amphitheaters are spread out below. Plateaus covered with evergreens and valleys filled with sagebrush stretch into the distance.

The visitor center at the entrance station has information about the park, including orientation shows, geologic displays and detailed maps. The park is open 24 hours a day year-round; in winter, the park road is open to most viewpoints. Lodging is also available from April to October.

Information: Panguitch, seven miles south on Highway 89, then 17 miles southeast, on Highway 12 to Highway 63, three miles to entrance, 435-834-5322; www.nps.gov/brca

WHAT TO SEE AND DO
CAMPING
Bryce Canyon
Camping is available at the North Campground (year-round), east of park headquarters; Sunset Campground, two miles south of park headquarters. Fourteen-day limit at both sites; fireplaces, picnic tables, restrooms, water available. April-October.

HOTEL
★★BEST WESTERN RUBY'S INN
1000 Highway 63, Bryce Canyon, 435-834-5341, 866-866-6616; www.rubysinn.com
368 rooms. Restaurant. Pets accepted. Pool. $

RESTAURANT

★FOSTER'S STEAK HOUSE

1150 Highway 12, Bryce, 435-834-5227; www.fostersmotel.com

Steak menu. Breakfast, lunch, dinner. Children's menu. Casual attire. **$$**

CEDAR CITY

In 1852, Cedar City produced the first iron made west of the Mississippi. The blast furnace operation was not successful, however, and stock-raising soon overshadowed it. A branch line of the Union Pacific entered the region in 1923 and helped develop the area. Now a tourist center because of its proximity to Bryce Canyon and Zion national parks, Cedar City takes pride in its abundant natural wonders. Streams and lakes have rainbow trout and the Markagunt Plateau provides deer and mountain lion hunting. Headquarters and a Ranger District office of the Dixie National Forest are located here.

Information: Chamber of Commerce, 581 N. Main St., Cedar City, 84720,
435-586-4484; www.cedarcity.org

WHAT TO SEE AND DO

DIXIE NATIONAL FOREST

1789 N. Wedgewood Lane, Cedar City, 435-865-3700; www.fs.fed.us/dxnf

This two-million-acre forest provides opportunities for camping, fishing, hiking, mountain biking and winter sports. Daily.

IRON MISSION STATE PARK

635 N. Main, Cedar City, 435-586-9290;
www.stateparks.utah.gov/stateparks/parks/iron-mission

The museum at the park is dedicated to the first pioneer iron foundry west of the Rockies and features an extensive collection of horse-drawn vehicles and wagons from Utah pioneer days. Daily.

SOUTHERN UTAH UNIVERSITY

351 W. Center, Cedar City, 435-586-5432; www.suu.edu

Established in 1897; 7,000 students. Braithwaite Fine Arts Gallery, Monday-Saturday.

SPECIAL EVENTS

RENAISSANCE FAIR

City Park, Cedar City; www.umrf.net

Entertainment, food and games, all in the style of the Renaissance. Held in conjunction with opening of Utah Shakespearean Festival. Early July.

UTAH SHAKESPEAREAN FESTIVAL

Southern Utah University Campus, 351 W. Center St., Cedar City,
435-586-7884; www.bard.org

Shakespeare is presented on an outdoor stage (a replica of 16th-century Tiring House) and 750-seat indoor facility. Monday-Saturday evenings; preplay activities. Children over five years only; babysitting at festival grounds. Late June-early October.

UTAH

★
★
★
★
★

CEDAR BREAKS NATIONAL MONUMENT

Cedar Breaks National Monument's major formation is a spectacular, multicolored, natural amphitheater created by the same forces that sculpted Utah's other rock formations. The amphitheater, shaped like an enormous coliseum, is 2,000 feet deep and more than three miles in diameter. It is carved out of the Markagunt Plateau and is surrounded by Dixie National Forest. Cedar Breaks, at an elevation of more than 10,000 feet, was established as a national monument in 1933. It derives its name from the surrounding cedar trees; "breaks" means "badlands." Although similar to Bryce Canyon National Park, the formations here are fewer but more vivid and varied in color. Young lava beds, resulting from small volcanic eruptions and cracks in the earth's surface, surround the Breaks area. The heavy forests include bristlecone pines, one of the oldest trees on earth. As soon as the snow melts, wildflowers bloom profusely and continue to bloom throughout the summer.

Rim Drive, a five-mile scenic road through the Cedar Breaks High Country, provides views of the monument's formations from four different overlooks. The area is open late May through mid-October, weather permitting. Point Supreme Campground, two miles north of south entrance, provides 30 tent and trailer sites (mid-June-mid-September). The visitor center offers geological exhibits (June-mid-October, daily); interpretive activities (mid-June-Labor Day).

Information: Cedar City, 23 miles east of Cedar City via Highway 14, 435-586-0787; www.nps.gov/cebr

UTAH SUMMER GAMES

351 W. Center St., Cedar City, 435-865-8421; www.utahsummergames.org
Olympic-style athletic events for amateur athletes. June.

HOTELS

★ABBEY INN

940 W. 200 N. Cedar City, 435-586-9966, 800-325-5411; www.abbeyinncedar.com
Eight rooms. Complimentary full breakfast. Airport transportation available. Pool. Spa. Sundeck. Wireless Internet access. $

★BEST WESTERN TOWN AND COUNTRY INN

189 N. Main St., Cedar City, 435-586-9900, 800-493-0062; www.bwtowncountry.com
157 rooms. High-speed Internet access. Complimentary deluxe breakfast. Pool. $

FILLMORE

Fillmore, the seat of Millard County and Utah's territorial capital until 1856, is today a trading center for the surrounding farm and livestock region. It is a popular hunting and fishing area.

Information: City of Fillmore, 75 W. Center, 435-743-5233; www.millardcounty.com

WHAT TO SEE AND DO
TERRITORIAL STATEHOUSE STATE PARK
50 W. Capitol Ave., Fillmore, 435-743-5316;
www.utah.com/stateparks/territorial_house.htm
Utah's first territorial capitol, built in the 1850s of red sandstone, is now a museum with an extensive collection of pioneer furnishings Native American artifacts and early documents. There's also a lovely rose garden. Monday-Saturday.

HOTEL
★★BEST WESTERN PARADISE INN AND RESORT
905 N. Main, Fillmore, 435-743-6895; www.bestwestern.com
78 rooms. Restaurant, bar. Pets accepted. Pool. High-speed Internet access. $

GARDEN CITY
This small resort town on the western shore of Bear Lake offers many water-based activities.
Information: Bear Lake Convention and Visitors Bureau, 208-945-2333, 800-448-2327;
www.bearlake.org

WHAT TO SEE AND DO
BEAR LAKE
Garden City
Covering 71,000 acres on the border of Utah and Idaho, this body of water is the state's second-largest freshwater lake. Approximately 20 miles long and 200 feet deep, it offers good fishing for mackinaw, rainbow trout and the rare Bonneville cisco. Boat rentals at several resorts.

BEAR LAKE STATE PARK
1030 N. Bear Lake Road, Garden City, 435-946-3343;
www.utah.com/stateparks/bear_lake.htm
Three park areas include State Marina on the west shore of the lake, Rendezvous Beach on the south shore and Eastside area on the east shore. Swimming, beach, waterskiing, fishing, ice fishing, boating (ramp, dock), sailing; hiking, mountain biking, cross-country skiing, snowmobiling, picnicking, tent and trailer sites. Visitor center. Daily.

BEAVER MOUNTAIN SKI AREA
40000 E. Highway 89, Garden City, 435-753- 4822; www.skithebeav.com
Three double chairlifts, two surface lifts; patrol, school, rentals; day lodge, cafeteria. Twenty-two runs; vertical drop 1,600 feet. Half-day rates. December-early April, daily.

GREEN RIVER
This tiny town (fewer than 1,000 people live here) in eastern Utah is named for the river that winds through much of Utah (and the town itself).
Information: Green River Travel Council, 885 E. Main St., 435-564-3526

WHAT TO SEE AND DO
GOBLIN VALLEY STATE PARK
450 S. Green River Blvd., Green River, 435-564-3633;
www.utah.com/stateparks/goblin_valley.htm
This mile-wide basin is filled with intricately eroded sandstone formations. Hiking, camping. Daily.

JOHN WESLEY POWELL RIVER HISTORY MUSEUM
1765 E. Main St., Green River, 435-564-3427; www.jwprhm.com
This 20,000-square-foot museum sits on the banks of the Green River and contains exhibits exploring the geology and geography of area; auditorium with 20-minute multimedia presentation; river runner Hall of Fame. Green River Visitor Center. Daily.

HOTELS
★BEST WESTERN RIVER TERRACE MOTEL
1740 E. Main St., Green River, 435-564-3401; www.bestwestern.com
50 rooms. Pool. High-speed Internet access. $

★HOLIDAY INN EXPRESS
1845 E. Main St., Green River, 435-564-4439; www.hiexpress.com
60 rooms. Complimentary continental breakfast. Pets accepted. Pool. High-speed Internet access. $

RESTAURANT
★TAMARISK
870 E. Main St., Green River, 435-564-8109
American menu. Breakfast, lunch, dinner. Children's menu. Casual attire. $

HEBER CITY
Located in a fertile, mountain-ringed valley, Heber City is the bedroom community for Orem, Provo, Park City and Salt Lake City. Unusual crater mineral springs, called hot pots, are located four miles west near Midway. Mount Timpanogos, one of the most impressive mountains in the state, is to the southwest in the Wasatch Range.
Information: Heber Valley Chamber of Commerce, 475 N. Main St., 435-654-3666;
www.hebervalleycc.org

WHAT TO SEE AND DO
HEBER VALLEY RAILROAD
450 S. 600 W., Heber City, 435-654-5601, 800-888-7499; www.hebervalleyrr.org
A 100-year-old steam-powered excursion train takes passengers through the farmlands of Heber Valley, along the shore of Deer Creek Lake and into Provo Canyon on various one-hour to four-hour trips. Restored coaches and open-air cars. Special trips some Friday, Saturday evenings. Reservations required. May-mid-October, Tuesday-Sunday; mid-October-November, schedule varies; December-April, Monday-Saturday.

WASATCH MOUNTAIN STATE PARK

Heber City, two miles northwest off Highway 224, 435-654-1791;
www.stateparks.utah.gov/stateparks/parks/wasatch

This park occupies approximately 25,000 acres in Heber Valley and offers fishing, hiking, 36-hole golf, snowmobiling, cross-country skiing, picnicking and camping. Visitor center. Daily.

SPECIAL EVENT
WASATCH COUNTY FAIR

2843 S. Daniels Road, Heber City; www.co.wasatch.ut.us/fair

Parades, exhibits, country market, livestock shows, rodeos, dancing. First weekend in August.

HOTEL
★HOLIDAY INN EXPRESS

1268 S. Main St., Heber City, 435-654-9990, 800-465-4329; www.holiday-inn.com

75 rooms. Pool. Whirlpool. High-speed Internet access. Complimentary full breakfast. $

SPECIALTY LODGING
THE SUNDOWNER INN BED AND BREAKFAST

425 Moulton Lane, Heber City, 435-654-4200, 866-455-4200;
www.thesundownerinn.com

Nine rooms. Complimentary full breakfast. $$

TIMPANOGOS CAVE NATIONAL MONUMENT

UTAH

★
★
★
★
★

Timpanogos Cave National Monument consists of three small, beautifully decorated underground chambers within limestone beds. The cave entrance is on the northern slope of Mount Timpanogos. A filigree of colorful crystal formations covers much of the cave's interior, where stalactites and stalagmites are common. But what makes Timpanogos unique is its large number of helictites—formations that appear to defy gravity as they grow outward from the walls of the cave. The temperature in Timpanogos Cave is a constant 45 F, and the interior is electrically lighted.

The cave's headquarters are located on Highway 92, eight miles east of American Fork. There is picnicking at Swinging Bridge Picnic Area, ¼ mile from the headquarters. The cave entrance is 1½ miles from headquarters via a paved trail with a vertical rise of 1,065 feet. Allow three to five hours for a guided tour. Tours limited to 20 people (late May-early-September, daily). Purchase tickets in advance by calling 801-756-5238 or stopping at the visitor center. Monday-Friday 8 a.m.-4:30 p.m. Information: Heber City, 26 miles south of Salt Lake City on I-15, then 10 miles east on Highway 92, 801-756-5238; www.nps.gov/tica

KANAB

Since 1922, more than 200 Hollywood productions have used the sand dunes, canyons and lakes surrounding Kanab as their settings. Some movie-set towns can still be seen. Kanab is within a 1½-hour drive from the north rim of the Grand Canyon, Zion and Bryce Canyon national parks, Cedar Breaks and Pipe Spring national monuments and Glen Canyon National Recreation Area.

Information: Kane County Office of Tourism, 78 S. 100 E.,
435-644-5033, 800-733-5263; www.kaneutah.com

WHAT TO SEE AND DO
CORAL PINK SAND DUNES STATE PARK
Yellow jacket and Hancock Roads, Kanab, 435-648-2800;
www.stateparks.utah.gov/stateparks/parks/coral-pink
Includes six square miles of very colorful, windswept sand hills. Hiking, picnicking, tent and trailer sites. Off-highway vehicles allowed; exploring, photography. Daily.

HOTEL
★★PARRY LODGE
89 E. Center St., Kanab, 435-644-2601, 888-289-1722; www.parrylodge.com
89 rooms. Complimentary full breakfast. Restaurant. Pets accepted. Pool. $

RESTAURANT
★HOUSTON'S TRAILS' END
32 E. Center St., Kanab, 435-644-2488; www.houstons.net
American menu. Breakfast, lunch, dinner. Closed mid-December-mid-March. Children's menu. Casual attire. $

LAKE POWELL

Lake Powell is the second largest man-made lake in the United States, with more than 1,900 miles of shoreline. The lake is named for John Wesley Powell, the one-armed explorer who, in 1869, successfully navigated the Colorado River through Glen Canyon and the Grand Canyon and later became director of the U.S. Geological Survey.

Information: www.lakepowell.com

WHAT TO SEE AND DO
BOAT TRIPS ON LAKE POWELL
Bullfrog Marina, Highway 276, Lake Powell, 435-684-3000; www.lakepowell.com
Trips include the Canyon Explorer tour (2½ hours) and the half-day and all-day Rainbow Bridge tours. (Due to the current level of the lake, these tours involve a 1¼-mile hike to see the monument.) Visitors can also take wilderness float trips and rent houseboats and powerboats. Reservations are advised. Daily.

GLEN CANYON NATIONAL RECREATION AREA (BULLFROG MARINA)
Highway 276, Lake Powell, 435-684-3010; www.lakepowell.com
Additional access and recreational activities are available at Hite Marina, at the north end of lake. This boasts more than a million acres with year-round recreation area, including swimming, fishing, boating, boat tours and trips, boat rentals; picnicking, camping, tent and trailer sites, lodgings. April-October, daily.

RAINBOW BRIDGE NATIONAL MONUMENT

Rainbow Bridge, which rises from the eastern shore of Lake Powell, is the largest natural rock bridge in the world. It was named a national monument in 1910. This natural bridge stands 290 feet tall, spans 275 feet and stretches 33 feet wide at the top. One of the natural wonders of the world, Rainbow Bridge is higher than the nation's capitol dome and nearly as long as a football field. The monument is predominantly salmon pink in color, modified by streaks of iron oxide and manganese. In the light of the late afternoon Sunday, the bridge is a brilliant sight. American Indians consider the area a sacred place; legend holds that the bridge is a rainbow turned to stone.

The easiest way to reach Rainbow Bridge is a half-day round-trip boat ride across Lake Powell from Page, Arizona, or a full-day round-trip boat ride from Bullfrog and Halls Crossing marinas. The bridge also can be reached on foot or horseback via the Rainbow Trail through the Navajo Indian Reservation. Fuel and camp supplies are available at Dangling Rope Marina, accessible by boat only, 10 miles south down lake.

Information: Rainbow Bridge National Monument, 928-608-6200; www.nps.gov/rabr

LOGAN

Situated in the center of beautiful Cache Valley, Logan is surrounded by snowcapped mountains and is home to Utah State University.

Information: City of Logan, 255 N. Main, 435-716-9000; www.loganutah.org

WHAT TO SEE AND DO

DAUGHTERS OF THE UTAH PIONEERS MUSEUM

160 N. Main, Logan, 435-752-5139; www.dupinternational.org/histDep.html
Exhibits depict Utah's past. Monday-Friday.

HYRUM STATE PARK

405 W. 300 S. Logan, 435-245-6866; www.stateparks.utah.gov/stateparks/parks/hyrum
A 450-acre reservoir with beach swimming, waterskiing, fishing, ice fishing, boating (ramp, dock), sailing; picnicking, camping. Year-round. Summer, 6 a.m.-10 p.m.; winter, 8 a.m.-5 p.m.

MORMON TABERNACLE

50 N. Main St., Logan, 435-755-5598
A gray limestone example of an early Mormon building. Genealogy library. Monday-Friday.

MORMON TEMPLE

175 N. 300 E. Logan, 435-752-3611
The site for this massive, castellated limestone structure was chosen by Brigham Young, who broke ground here in 1877. Grounds are open all year, but the temple is closed to the general public.

UTAH

★
★★
★★
★★
★

UTAH STATE UNIVERSITY

1400 Old Main Hill, Logan, 435-797-1000; www.usu.edu

Established in 1888; 20,100 students. On campus is the Nora Eccles Harrison Museum of Art. Monday-Friday.

WASATCH-CACHE NATIONAL FOREST, LOGAN CANYON

1500 E. Highway 89, Logan, 435-755-3620; www.fs.fed.us/r4/uwc

This national forest offers fishing, backcountry trails, hunting, winter sports, picnicking and camping. Daily.

WILLOW PARK ZOO

419 W. 700 S. Logan, 435-716-9265; www.loganutah.org

This small but attractive zoo has shady grounds and especially good bird-watching of migratory species, with more than 100 captive species and 80 species of wild birds visiting and nesting at the zoo. Daily 9 a.m.-dusk.

SPECIAL EVENTS
CACHE COUNTY FAIR

400 S. 500 W., Logan

Rodeo, horse races, exhibits. Early August.

UTAH FESTIVAL OPERA COMPANY

59 S. 100 W., Logan

July-August.

HOTELS
★★BEST WESTERN BAUGH MOTEL

153 S. Main St., Logan, 435-752-5220, 800-462-4154; www.bestwestern.com

76 rooms. Complimentary continental breakfast. Restaurant. Pool. High-speed Internet access. **$**

★COMFORT INN

447 N. Main St., Logan, 435-752-9141, 866-537-6459; www.choicehotels.com

83 rooms. Complimentary continental breakfast. Exercise. Pool. High-speed Internet access. **$**

SPECIALTY LODGING
THE ANNIVERSARY INN

169 E. Center St., Logan, 435-752-3443, 800-324-4152; www.anniversaryinn.com

Each room or suite at this charming inn has its own theme, from the Pyramids of Egypt to Aphrodite's Court to Lost in Space. Most have jetted tubs, and some have fireplaces and big-screen TVs. 20 rooms. No children allowed. Whirlpool. **$$**

RESTAURANTS
★BLUEBIRD

19 N. Main St., Logan, 435-752-3155

American menu. Lunch, dinner. Closed Sunday. Children's menu. Casual attire. **$**

★THE COPPER MILL

55 N. Main St., Logan, 435-752-0647
American menu. Lunch, dinner. **$**

★★LE NONNE

129 N. Main St., Logan, 435-752-9577
Italian menu. Lunch, dinner. Closed Monday. **$$**

MIDWAY

This town recalls its Swiss roots with Swiss architecture and an annual festival that celebrates the town's heritage. Less than an hour's drive from Salt Lake, Midway is near Wasatch Mountain State Park.

Information: 75 N. 100 W., 435-654-3227; www.midwaycityut.org

SPECIAL EVENT

SWISS DAYS

Midway Town Square; www.midwayswissdays.com
Old country games, activities, costumes. Friday and Saturday before Labor Day.

HOTELS

★★★THE BLUE BOAR INN

1235 Warm Springs Road, Midway, 435-654-1400, 888-650-1400;
www.theblueboarinn.com

The blissful quiet of this remote location is perfect for visitors who want to get away from it all, yet stay in relatively close proximity to the slopes and nightlife of the ski resorts of Deer Valley, the Canyons and Sundance. During summer months, nearby fly-fishing and 54 holes of golf entertain guests. Decorated in a unique Austrian-influenced style, the guest rooms feature amusing themes inspired by famous authors and poets. From the handmade willow bed of the Robert Frost to the English cottage style of the William Butler Yeats and the exotic flavor of the Rudyard Kipling, each room attempts to capture its namesake's distinctive personality. While the chandeliers are crafted of antlers and the furnishings are indicative of the region, the restaurant is a showpiece of fresh American cuisine. 12 rooms. Complimentary full breakfast. Restaurant, bar. Business center. **$$**

★★★HOMESTEAD RESORT

700 N. Homestead Drive, Midway, 435-654-1102, 888-327-7220;
www.homesteadresort.com

Surrounded by lush gardens and the Wasatch Mountains, this historic country resort on 200 acres welcomes guests with Western hospitality. Quaint cottages make up the majority of the accommodations, which include traditional and historic rooms, executive suites and condos that accommodate large groups. Amenities include an Aveda spa, adventure center with billiards, board games, video library and more, championship golf course and a crater in which guests can float in the crystal-clear, 90-plus-degree mineral waters. The resort also rents cross-country skis and snowshoes and provides transportation to nearby Deer Valley's Jordanelle Express Gondola. 144 rooms. Restaurant, bar. Children's activity center. Spa. Golf. Tennis. Business center. **$$**

★★★INN ON THE CREEK
375 Rainbow Lane, Midway, 435-654-0892, 800-654-0892; www.innoncreek.com

Picturesque landscaping and hot springs surround this luxurious full-service inn. Located at the base of the Wasatch Mountains in Heber Valley, the inn is near popular ski resorts and golf courses. Guests can choose from rooms in the main inn or luxury chalets. All are spacious and tastefully decorated, and most rooms feature fireplaces and balconies or private decks. The spa offers a variety of services, including massages, facials, pedicures and manicures. The inn's restaurant, which serves American-French cuisine, utilizes garden vegetables and herbs, and has an extensive wine selection. 40 rooms. Restaurant, bar. $$

RESTAURANTS
★★★THE BLUE BOAR INN RESTAURANT
1235 Warm Springs Road, Midway, 435-654-1400, 888-650-1400;
www.theblueboarinn.com

Well worth the 20-minute drive from Park City, this charming Tyrolean chalet offers some of the best New American cuisine in Utah. The menu changes periodically to capture the best produce and fresh seafood available, but you might see entrées like grilled Copper River salmon or broiled range-fed veal chop with rustic French bread, creamed spinach and morels. American menu. Lunch, dinner, Sunday brunch. Bar. Casual attire. Outdoor seating. $$$

★★★SIMON'S FINE DINING
700 N. Homestead Drive, Midway, 435-654-1102, 800-327-7220;
www.homesteadresort.com

Dine on delicious Western cuisine in an elegant country setting, either inside the dining room by the fireplace or outside on the deck, with beautiful views of the valley. American menu. Dinner, Sunday brunch. Closed Monday-Tuesday. Bar. Children's menu. Casual attire. Outdoor seating. $$

MOAB
The first attempt to settle this valley was made in 1855, but Moab, named after an isolated area in the Bible, was not permanently settled until 1880. Situated on the Colorado River at the foot of the La Sal Mountains, Moab was a sleepy agricultural town until after World War II, when uranium and oil exploration created a boom. Today, tourism and moviemaking help make it a thriving community. Headquarters for Canyonlands and Arches national parks are located here.

Information: Moab Area Travel Council, 435-259-8825, 800-635-6622;
www.discovermoab.com

WHAT TO SEE AND DO
ADRIFT ADVENTURES
378 N. Main St., Moab, 435-259-8594, 800-874-4483; www.adrift.net

Oar, paddle and motorized trips available; one to seven days. Jeep tours and horseback rides are also offered. Early April-late October.

CANYON VOYAGES ADVENTURE COMPANY

211 N. Main St., Moab, 435-259-6007, 800-733-6007; www.canyonvoyages.com
Kayaking, white-water rafting, canoeing, biking or four-wheel drive tours. Early April-October.

CANYONLANDS BY NIGHT

1861 S. Highway 191, Moab, 435-259-2628, 800-394-9978;
www.canyonlandsbynight.com
This two-hour boat trip with sound-and-light presentation highlights the history of area. April-mid-October, daily, leaves at sundown, weather permitting. Reservations required.

CANYONLANDS FIELD INSTITUTE

1320 S. Highway 191, Moab, 435-259-7750, 800-860-5262;
www.canyonlandsfieldinst.org
Adult and family-oriented educational seminars and trips feature geology, natural and cultural history, endangered species and Southwestern literature. Many programs use Canyonlands and Arches national parks as outdoor classrooms. Monday-Friday.

DAN O'LAURIE CANYON COUNTRY MUSEUM

118 E. Center St., Moab, 435-259-7985; www.discovermoab.com
See exhibits on local history, archaeology, geology, uranium and minerals of the area. Walking tour information. Summer, Monday-Friday 10 a.m.-6 p.m., Saturday-Sunday noon-6 p.m.; winter, Monday-Friday 10 a.m.-3 p.m., Saturday-Sunday noon-5 p.m.

DEAD HORSE POINT STATE PARK

313 State Road, Moab, 435-259-2614, 800-322-3770;
www.stateparks.utah.gov/parks/dead-horse
This island mesa offers views of the La Sal Mountains, Canyonlands National Park and the Colorado River. Visitor center, museum. Daily 6 a.m.-10 p.m.

UTAH

★
★
★
★
★

HOLE 'N THE ROCK

11037 S. Highway 191, Moab, 435-686-2250; www.moab-utah.com/holeintherock
See a 5,000-square-foot home carved into huge sandstone rock. Picnic area with stone tables and benches. Tours. Daily 8 a.m.-dusk.

MANTI-LA SAL NATIONAL FOREST, LA SAL DIVISION

599 W. Price River Drive, Price, 435-637-2817; www.fs.fed.us/r4/mantilasal
The land here is similar in color and beauty to some parts of the Grand Canyon and also includes high mountains nearing 13,000 feet, as well as pine and spruce forests. Swimming, fishing; hiking, hunting.

PACK CREEK RANCH TRAIL RIDES

La Sal Mountain Loop Road, Moab, 435-259-5505; www.packcreekranch.com
Go horseback riding through the foothills of the La Sal Mountains. Guided tours for small groups; reservations required. March-October; upon availability.

REDTAIL AVIATION SCENIC AIR TOURS

North Highway 191, Moab, 435-259-7421, 800-842-9251; www.moab-utah.com/redtail
Offers flights over Canyonlands National Park and various other tours. All-year.

RIM TOURS

1233 S. Highway 191, Moab, 435-259-5223, 800-626-7335; www.rimtours.com
Guided mountain bike tours in canyon country and the Colorado Rockies. Vehicle support for camping tours. Daily and overnight trips; combination bicycle/river trips available.

SHERI GRIFFITH RIVER EXPEDITIONS

2231 S. Highway 191 Moab, 435-259-8229, 800-332-2439; www.griffithexp.com
Take your pick and ride oar boats, motorized rafts, paddleboats or inflatable kayak for one- to five-day trips. Instruction available. May-October.

TAG-A-LONG EXPEDITIONS

452 N. Main St., Moab, 435-259-8946, 800-453-3292; www.tagalong.com
Choose from one- to seven-day white-water rafting trips on the Green and Colorado rivers; jet boat trips on the Colorado River; and jet boat trips and four-wheel-drive tours into Canyonlands National Park. Winter four-wheel drive tours, November-February. One-day jet boat trips with cultural performing arts programs are offered part of the year as well. April-mid-October.

TEX'S RIVERWAYS

691 N. 500 W., Moab, 435-259-5101; www.texsriverways.com
Flatwater canoe trips, four to 10 days. Confluence pick-ups available, jet boat cruises. March-October.

SPECIAL EVENTS
BUTCH CASSIDY DAYS PRCA RODEO

Moab, 800-635-6622
Second weekend in June.

JEEP SAFARI

Moab, 435-259-7625
This event, sponsored by Red Rock Four Wheelers, offers 30 different trails. Easter week and weekend.

MOAB MUSIC FESTIVAL

58 E. 300 S. Moab, 435-259-7003; www.moabmusicfest.org
This festival features classical music performed in natural settings throughout southeastern Utah. First two weeks in September.

HOTELS
★★BEST WESTERN CANYONLANDS INN

16 S. Main St., Moab, 435-259-5167; www.bestwestern.com
77 rooms. Complimentary continental breakfast. Pool. Fitness center. High-speed Internet access. **$**

★★BEST WESTERN GREENWELL INN

105 S. Main St., Moab, 435-259-6151; www.bestwestern.com
72 rooms. Pool. Fitness center. High-speed Internet access. **$**

★BOWEN MOTEL

169 N. Main St., Moab, 435-259-7132, 800-874-5439; www.bowenmotel.com
40 rooms. Complimentary continental breakfast. Pets accepted. Pool. Wireless Internet access. **$**

★★★SORREL RIVER RANCH RESORT

Highway 128, Moab, 435-259-4642, 877-359-2715; www.sorrelriver.com
Set in a dramatic landscape of red rock formations, this full-service resort is just 30 minutes from Arches National Park. Many of the Western-themed guest rooms, all of which have kitchenettes, overlook the Colorado River. Family loft suites are also available. Fireplaces and jetted hydrotherapy tubs are found in the deluxe suites. The resort offers horseback tours, tennis and a spa. After an activity-filled day, enjoy an upscale meal at the River Grill. 59 rooms. High-speed Internet access. Restaurant. Children's activity center. Spa. Tennis. **$$**

SPECIALTY LODGINGS

PACK CREEK RANCH

Pack Creek Ranch Road, Moab, 435-259-5505; www.packcreekranch.com
This complex of widely spaced, rustic cabins is 15 miles from downtown in a spectacular setting. The ranch is set in a valley with the La Sal Mountains on one side and the red rocks of Moab on the other. All the cabins have a full kitchen and a large sitting area with a rock fireplace. With no TVs or phones, you might actually relax. 11 rooms. Pets accepted. Pool. **$$**

SUNFLOWER HILL BED AND BREAKFAST

185 N. 300 E. Moab, 435-259-2974, 800-662-2786; www.sunflowerhill.com
12 rooms. Children over 10 years only. Whirlpool. **$**

RESTAURANTS

★★CENTER CAFÉ

60 N. 100 W., Moab, 435-259-4295; www.centercafemoab.com
International menu. Dinner. Business casual attire. Outdoor seating. **$$**

★MOAB BREWERY

686 S. Main St., Moab, 435-259-6333; www.themoabbrewery.com
American menu. Lunch, dinner. **$$**

★★SLICKROCK CAFÉ

5 N. Main St., Moab, 435-259-8004; www.slickrockcafe.com
American menu. Breakfast, lunch, dinner. **$**

MOAB AND BEYOND

This three- to four-day tour out of Moab includes magnificent vistas, unique rock formations and the upper reaches of Lake Powell. From Moab, head south on Highway 191 to Highway 211; follow 211 west to Newspaper Rock, a huge sandstone panel with petroglyphs that are up to 1,500 years old. Prehistoric peoples such as the Fremonts and ancestral Puebloans, as well as the Utes, Navajo and European-American settlers, left images etched into this wall of stone. From Newspaper Rock, it is an easy drive west on Highway 211 to the Needles District of Canyonlands National Park. You probably visited the Island in the Sky District of Canyonlands during your stay in Moab, but this section of the park offers a different perspective. Although best explored by mountain bike or in a high-clearance four-wheel-drive vehicle, there are several roadside viewpoints from which you can see the district's namesake red-and-white-striped rock pinnacles and other formations. Several easy hikes offer additional views.

Retrace your route back to Highway 191 and continue south to Highway 95, where you will head west to Natural Bridges National Monument. This easy-to-explore monument has a scenic drive with overlooks that offer views of three awe-inspiring natural stone bridges and some 700-year-old ancestral Puebloan cliff dwellings. There is also prehistoric rock art and a demonstration of how solar energy is used to produce the monument's electricity. The viewpoints are short walks from parking areas. You can also hike to all three of the natural bridges, which were created over millions of years as water cut through solid rock.

Returning to Highway 95, head northwest to the Hite Crossing section of Glen Canyon National Recreation Area. Encompassing the northern end of Lake Powell, this is one of the least developed (and least crowded) sections of the recreation area. Hite Crossing has scenic views, boat rentals and plenty of available lodging (including houseboats).

From Hite, continue northwest on Highway 95 across rock-studded terrain to Hanksville; head north on Highway 24 to the turnoff to Goblin Valley State Park. This delightful little park is a fantasyland where whimsical stone goblins seem to be frozen in mid-dance. From Goblin Valley, return to Highway 24 and continue north to Interstate 70 (I-70). Head east to the community of Green River, where you'll find several motels. Here you'll discover Green River State Park, a good spot for a picnic under the Russian olive and cottonwood trees along the river, or perhaps a round of golf at the park's nine-hole championship course. Nearby, the John Wesley Powell River History Museum tells the incredible story of explorer Powell, a one-armed Civil War veteran who did what was considered impossible when he charted the Green and Colorado rivers in the late 1800s. From Green River continue east on I-70 to Highway 191, which leads south back to Moab. Approximately 448 miles.

CANYONLANDS NATIONAL PARK

Set aside by Congress in 1964 as a national park, this 337,570-acre area is largely undeveloped and includes spectacular rock formations, canyons, arches, ancestral Puebloan ruins and more. Road conditions vary; primary access roads are paved and maintained while others are safe only for high-clearance four-wheel-drive vehicles.

Island in the Sky, North District, south and west of Dead Horse Point State Park, has Grand View Point, Upheaval Dome and Green River Overlook. This section is accessible by passenger car via Highway 313 and by four-wheel-drive vehicles and mountain bikes on dirt roads.

Needles, South District, has hiking trails and four-wheel-drive roads to Angel Arch, Chesler Park and the confluence of the Green and Colorado rivers. You'll also see prehistoric ruins and rock art here. This section is accessible by passenger car via Highway 211, by four-wheel-drive vehicle on dirt roads and by mountain bike.

Maze, West District, is accessible by hiking or by four-wheel-drive vehicles using unimproved roads. The most remote and least-visited section of the park, this area received its name from the many maze-like canyons. Horseshoe Canyon, a separate unit of the park nearby, is accessible via Highway 24 and 30 miles of two-wheel-drive dirt road. Roads are usually passable only in mid-March-mid-November.

Canyonlands is excellent for calm-water and white-water trips down the Green and Colorado rivers. Permits are required for private and commercial trips.

Campgrounds, with tent sites, are located at Island in the Sky and at Needles; water is available only at Needles. Visitor centers are in each district and are open daily.

Information: Canyonlands National Park, 2282 S. West Resource Blvd., Moab, 435-719-2313; www.nps.gov/cany

MONTICELLO

The highest county seat in Utah (San Juan County), Monticello was named for Thomas Jefferson's Virginia home. On the east slope of the Abajo Mountains, the elevation makes for delightful weather.

Information: San Juan County Visitor Center, 232 S. Main St., 435-587-3235, 800-574-4386; www.monticelloutah.org

WHAT TO SEE AND DO
CANYON RIMS RECREATION AREA

82 E. Dogwood St., Monticello, 435-259-2100; www.blm.gov/utah/moab/canyon_rims.html

Two overlooks (Anticline and Needles) into Canyonlands National Park are located here, as are well as two campgrounds (Wind Whistle and Hatch).

MANTI-LA SAL NATIONAL FOREST, LA SAL DIVISION
599 W. Price River Drive, Price, 435-637-2817; www.fs.fed.us/r4/mantilasal
The forest land of this division ranges from red rock canyons to high alpine terrain. Ancient ruins and rock art contrast with pine and spruce forests and aspen-dotted meadows. Fishing; hiking, snowmobiling, cross-country skiing, hunting, camping.

SPECIAL EVENTS
MONTICELLO PIONEER DAYS
Monticello; www.sanjuancounty.info
Parade, booths, food, games, sports. Weekend nearest July 24.

SAN JUAN COUNTY FAIR & RODEO
Monticello, 360-378-4310; www.sanjuancountyfair.org
Second weekend in August.

HOTEL
★BEST WESTERN WAYSIDE MOTOR INN
197 E. Central Ave., Monticello, 435-587-2261; www.bestwestern.com
37 rooms. Complimentary continental breakfast. Pets accepted. Pool. High-speed Internet access. $

NEPHI
Named for Mormon prophets who share the same name, Nephi is about 85 miles south of Salt Lake City.

Information: Juab Travel Council, 4 S. Main St., 435-623-5203, 800-748-4361; www.juabtravel.com

WHAT TO SEE AND DO
YUBA STATE PARK
Nephi, 435-758-2611; www.stateparks.utah.gov/stateparks/parks/yuba
Waterskiing and walleyed pike fishing, and the sandy beaches, are the big attractions of this lake. Daily.

SPECIAL EVENT
UTE STAMPEDE RODEO
795 S. Main St., Nephi, 435-623-5608; www.utestampederodeo.com
Three-day festival featuring Western and Mammoth parades, carnival, PRCA rodeo, contests, arts and crafts, concessions. Second weekend in July.

HOTEL
★BEST WESTERN PARADISE INN OF NEPHI
1025 S. Main St., Nephi, 435-623-0624; www.bestwestern.com
40 rooms. High-speed Internet access. Complimentary continental breakfast. Pets accepted. Pool. Fitness center. $

OGDEN

Brigham Young laid out the streets of Ogden, the fourth-largest city in Utah, in traditional Mormon geometrical style: broad, straight and bordered by poplar, box elder, elm and cottonwood trees. In 1846, Miles Goodyear, the first white settler, had built a cabin and trading post here, which he sold to the Mormons a year later. During the last 30 years of the 19th century, Ogden was an outfitting center for trappers and hunters heading north. Its saloons and gambling halls were typical of a frontier town, and there was considerable friction between the Mormons and the "gentiles." With the coming of the railroad, Ogden became one of the few cities in Utah whose inhabitants were not primarily Mormons.

Today, Ogden is a commercial and industrial center. Hill Air Force Base is nearby. Mount Ben Lomond, north of the city in the Wasatch Range, was the inspiration for the logo of Paramount Pictures.

Information: Convention & Visitors Bureau, 2501 Wall Ave., 866-867-8824; www.ogdencvb.org

WHAT TO SEE AND DO
DAUGHTERS OF UTAH PIONEERS MUSEUM AND RELIC HALL
4046 South 895 E., Ogden, 801-621-4891; www.dupinternational.org
See old handicrafts, household items and portraits of those who came to Utah prior to the railroad of 1869. This is also the site of Miles Goodyear's cabin, the first permanent house built in Utah. Mid-May-mid—September, Monday-Saturday.

ECCLES COMMUNITY ART CENTER
2580 Jefferson Ave., Ogden, 801-392-6935; www.ogden4arts.org
This 19th-century castle-like mansion hosts changing art exhibits. It also has a dance studio and outdoor sculpture and floral garden. Monday-Saturday.

FORT BUENAVENTURA STATE PARK
2450 A. Ave., Ogden, 801-399-8099; www.utah.com/stateparks/buenaventura.htm
The exciting era of mountain men is brought to life on this 32-acre site, where Miles Goodyear built Ogden's first settlement in 1846. The fort has been reconstructed according to archaeological and historical research. No nails were used in building the stockade; wooden pegs and mortise and tenon joints hold the structure together. April-November.

GEORGE S. ECCLES DINOSAUR PARK
1544 E. Park Blvd., Ogden, 801-393-3466; www.dinosaurpark.org
This outdoor display contains more than 100 life-size reproductions of dinosaurs and other prehistoric creatures. There's also an educational building with a working paleontological lab, as well as fossil and reptile displays. Daily; closed November-March.

HILL AEROSPACE MUSEUM
7961 Wardleigh Road, Hill Air Force Base, 801-777-6868; www.hill.af.mil
More than 55 aircraft on display here, including the SR-71 "Blackbird" reconnaissance plane and the B-52 bomber. Helicopters, jet engines, missiles, uniforms and other memorabilia are also featured. Daily.

UTAH

★
★
★
★
★

PINE VIEW RESERVOIR

Ogden, nine miles east on Highway 39 in Ogden Canyon in Wasatch-Cache National Forest, 801-625-5306; www.fs.fed.us/r4/wcnf/recreation/pineview.shtml

UNION STATION

2501 Wall Ave., Ogden, 801-393-9886; www.theunionstation.org

See some of the world's largest locomotives. The Browning-Kimball Car Museum and Browning Firearms Museum are also here (John Browning was the inventor of the automatic rifle), plus a 500-seat theater for musical and dramatic productions, art gallery and restaurant. Visitors Bureau for Northern Utah is located here. Monday-Saturday. 10 a.m.-5 p.m.

WEBER STATE UNIVERSITY

3848 Harrison Blvd., Ogden, 801-626-6000; www.weber.edu

Established in 1889; 17,000 students. On campus is the Layton P. Ott Planetarium with Foucault pendulum; shows Wednesday; no shows summer. The Stewart Bell Tower, with 183-bell electronic carillon, also offers performances. Daily. Campus tours.

WILLARD BAY STATE PARK

900 West 650 N., Ogden, 435-734-9494;
www.stateparks.utah.gov/stateparks/parks/willard-bay

This park features a 9,900-acre lake. Swimming, fishing, boating (ramps), sailing; picnicking, tent and trailer sites. Daily.

WOLF MOUNTAIN FAMILY SKI RESORT

3567 Nordic Valley Way, Eden, 801-745-3511; www.wolfmountaineden.com

Two chairlifts; patrol, school, rentals. Longest run 1½ miles, vertical drop 1,000 feet. December-April, daily.

SPECIAL EVENTS

PIONEER DAYS

Ogden Pioneer Stadium, 1875 Monroe Blvd., Ogden; www.ogdenpioneerdays.com

Rodeo, concerts, vintage car shows, fireworks, chili cook-off. Monday-Saturday evenings. Mid-late July.

UTAH SYMPHONY POPS CONCERT

Lindquist Fountain/Plaza, 1875 Monroe Blvd., Ogden

Music enhanced by a fireworks display. Late July.

HOTELS

★BEST WESTERN HIGH COUNTRY INN

1335 W. 12th St., Ogden, 801-394-9474, 800-594-8979; www.bestwestern.com

109 rooms. Pets accepted. Pool. Fitness center. High-speed Internet access. **$**

★COMFORT SUITES OGDEN

2250 S. 1200 W. Ogden, Ogden, 801-621-2545; www.ogdencomfortsuites.com

40 rooms. High-speed Internet access. Pool. Fitness center. Pets accepted. **$**

★HAMPTON INN & SUITES

2401 Washington Blvd., Ogden, 801-394-9400; www.hamptoninn.com

135 rooms. Fitness center. Wireless Internet access. Whirlpool. Business center. $

★★MARRIOTT

247 24th St., Ogden, 801-627-1190, 888-825-3163; www.marriott.com

292 rooms. High-speed Internet access. Restaurant, bar. Pool. Business center. $

SPECIALTY LODGING
ALASKAN INN

435 Ogden Canyon Road, Ogden, 801-621-8600; www.alaskaninn.com

12 rooms. Whirlpool. Complimentary continental breakfast. $$

PARK CITY

Soldiers struck silver here in 1868, starting one of the nation's largest silver mining camps, which reached a population of 10,000 before declining to a near ghost town when the silver market collapsed. Since then, however, Park City has been revived as a four-season resort with skiing, snowboarding, golf, tennis, water sports and mountain biking.

Information: Park City Chamber/Visitors Bureau, 1826 Olympic Parkway, Park City, 435-658-9616, 800-453-1360; www.parkcityinfo.com

WHAT TO SEE AND DO
BRIGHTON SKI RESORT

12601 E. Big Cottonwood Canyon Road, Brighton, 801-532-4731, 800-873-5512; www.skibrighton.com

THE CANYONS

4000 The Canyons Resort Drive, Park City, 435-649-5400; www.thecanyons.com

16 high-speed quad, triple, double chairlifts; gondola; patrol, school, rentals; restaurant, cafeteria, bar, lodge. 155 trails. Winter lift daily 9 a.m.-4 p.m. Thanksgiving-April, daily.

DEER VALLEY RESORT

2250 Deer Valley Drive S., Park City, 435-649-1000, 800-424-3337; www.deervalley.com

Eight high-speed quad, eight triple, two double chairlifts; rental, patrol, school, snowmaking; restaurants, lounge, lodge, nursery. Approximately 1,750 skiable acres. Vertical drop 3,000 feet. No snowboarding. December-mid-April, daily. Summer activities include mountain biking, hiking, horseback riding and scenic chairlift rides.

EGYPTIAN THEATRE

328 Main St., Park City, 435-649-9371; www.egyptiantheatrecompany.org

Originally built in 1926 as a silent movie and vaudeville house, this is now a year-round performing arts center with a full semiprofessional theater season. Wednesday-Saturday; some performances other days.

KIMBALL ART CENTER

638 Park Ave., Park City, 435-649-8882; www.kimball-art.org

Exhibits in various media by local and regional artists. Admission: free. Gallery, Monday, Wednesday-Friday 10 a.m.-5 p.m., Saturday-Sunday noon-5 p.m.

PARK CITY MOUNTAIN RESORT

1310 Lowell Ave., Park City, 435-649-8111, 800-222-7275; www.pcski.com

Gondola; two quad, four double, five triple, four six-passenger chairlifts; patrol, school, rentals, snowmaking; restaurants, cafeteria, bar. Approximately 3,300 acres; 104 trails; 750 acres of open-bowl skiing. Lighted snowboarding. Mid-November-mid-April, daily. Alpine slide, children's park, miniature golf in summer.

ROCKPORT STATE PARK

9040 N. Highway 302, Peoa, 435-336-2241;
www.stateparks.utah.gov/stateparks/parks/rockport

This 1,000-acre park along east side of Rockport Lake offers great opportunities for viewing wildlife, including bald eagles (winter) and golden eagles. Swimming, water-skiing, sailboarding, fishing, boating; cross-country ski trail (six miles), camping, tent and trailer sites. Daily.

SOLITUDE MOUNTAIN RESORT

12000 Big Cottonwood Canyon, Solitude, 801-534-1400; www.skisolitude.com

Dining, lodging, solitude community, mountain biking are available daily.

TANGER FACTORY OUTLET

6699 N. Landmark Drive, Park City, 435-645-7078, 866-665-8681;
www.tangeroutlet.com

The more than 45 outlet stores here include Gap, Nike and Eddie Bauer. Daily.

UTAH WINTER SPORTS PARK

3419 Olympic Parkway, Park City, 435-658-4200; www.olyparks.com

Recreational ski jumping is available at this $25-million park built for the 2002 Olympic Winter Games. Lessons are offered, followed by two-hour jumping session. Olympic bobsled and luge track (high-speed rides available). Wednesday-Sunday.

WHITE PINE TOURING CENTER

1790 Bonanza Drive, Park City, 435-649-8710; www.whitepinetouring.com

Groomed cross-country trails (12 miles), school, rentals; guided tours. November-April, daily. Summer mountain biking; rentals.

SPECIAL EVENTS
ART FESTIVAL

Main St., Park City

Open-air market featuring work of more than 200 visual artists. Also street entertainment. First weekend in August.

SUNDANCE FILM FESTIVAL

Park City, 435-776-7878; www.sundance.org/festival

This 10-day festival for independent filmmakers attracts lots of celebrities. Workshops, screenings and special events. Mid-January. Events held throughout city.

HOTELS

★★★THE CANYONS GRAND SUMMIT RESORT HOTEL

4000 The Canyons Resort Drive, Park City, 435-649-5400, 866-604-4171;
www.thecanyons.com

This lovely mountain lodge, one of three at the Canyons Resort, is set at the foot of Park City's ski slopes. Guest rooms, most of which have balconies and fireplaces, have excellent views of the mountains and the valley below. If you need a break from skiing, check out the resort's Village Shops, where regularly scheduled concerts and other events are held. Summer brings warm-weather activities like horseback riding, hiking and fly-fishing and the gondola remains open for scenic rides. 358 rooms. Wireless Internet access. Two restaurants, two bars. Children's activity center. Spa. Ski-in/ski-out. Pool. $$$$

★★★CHATEAUX AT SILVER LAKE

7815 E. Royal St., Park City, 435-658-9500, 888-976-2732;
www.chateaux-deervalley.com

Situated in the heart of Deer Valley Resort's Silver Lake Village, the Chateaux at Silver Lake offers guests a comfortable stay in an elegant and picturesque setting. Rooms are decorated with custom-designed furniture and feature pillow-top mattresses and feather beds, gas fireplaces and wet bars. Onsite amenities include a full-service spa, heated covered parking, free local shuttle service and winter sports equipment rentals. 95 rooms. Wireless Internet access. Restaurant, bar. Spa. Airport transportation available. Pool. Business center. $$$$

★★★CLUB LESPRI BOUTIQUE INN & SPA

1765 Sidewinder Drive, Park City, 435-645-9696; www.clublespri.com

This is one of the area's most intimate spa destinations, with only 10 suites, all of which feature fireplaces, hand-carved furniture, custom beds, oversize tubs and full kitchens. 10 rooms, all suites. Restaurant, bar. Spa. Whirlpool. Airport transportation available. $$$

★★★GOLDENER HIRSCH INN

7570 Royal St. E. Park City, 435-649-7770, 800-252-3373; www.goldenerhirschinn.com

Warm and inviting, this exceptional ski resort blends the services of a large hotel with the charm of a bed and breakfast. The romantic guest rooms and suites have warm colors and hand-painted furniture. All-day dining and après-ski service are available at the hotel's Austrian-themed restaurant. 20 rooms. Closed mid-April-early June, early October-early December. Complimentary full breakfast. Wireless Internet access. Restaurant, bar. Whirlpool. Ski-in/ski-out. Airport transportation available. $$$$

★HOLIDAY INN EXPRESS
1501 W. Ute Blvd., Park City, 435-658-1600, 888-465-4329; www.hieparkcity.com
76 rooms. Wireless Internet access. Airport transportation available. Pool. Pets accepted. Complimentary continental breakfast. **$**

★★★HOTEL PARK CITY
2001 Park Ave., Park City, 435-200-2000, 888-999-0098; www.hotelparkcity.com
This all-suite resort pampers its guests. The amenities are top notch, from triple-head showers and jetted tubs to Bose audio systems and Bulgari bath products. The suites have a residential air about them with cozy fireplaces, spacious sitting areas and traditional alpine-style furnishings. Set at the base of the Wasatch Mountains, this hotel has a scenic location that is ideal for skiers. Those who prefer a less rigorous route can visit the comprehensive spa. The charming Western-style restaurant wins raves for its mountain views and its delicious cuisine. 100 rooms, all suites. Wireless Internet access. Two restaurants, bar. Spa. Ski-in/ski-out. Airport transportation available. Golf. Skiing. **$$**

★★★MARRIOTT
1895 Sidewinder Drive, Park City, 435-649-2900, 800-234-9003; www.marriott.com
This newly renovated hotel is located a mile from downtown Park City and the historic Main Street. Take the complimentary shuttle to Utah Olympic Park, outlet stores and old Main Street. Starbucks fans will find a coffee kiosk in the lobby, and the hotel also rents ski equipment in winter and bicycles in summer. This hotel is non-smoking. 198 rooms. High-speed Internet access. Restaurant, bar. Pets accepted. Pool. Business center. **$$**

★★★★★STEIN ERIKSEN LODGE
7700 Stein Way, Park City, 435-649-3700, 800-453-1302; www.steinlodge.com
Nestled mid-mountain at Utah's Deer Valley ski resort, this Scandinavian masterpiece calls a magnificent alpine setting home. The resort offers visitors unparalleled levels of service. Heated sidewalks and walkways keep you toasty, while the ski valet service takes care of all your needs on the slopes. The dining is outstanding, and the Sunday Jazz Brunch and Skiers Lunch Buffet are local sensations. The blazing fireplace and inviting ambience of the Troll Hallen Lounge make it a cozy spot for après-ski or light fare. Guests rest weary muscles at the spa or unwind in the year-round outdoor heated pool. Rooms are all distinctive but all feature jetted tubs; suites have gourmet kitchens, stone fireplaces and master bedrooms. 180 rooms. Wireless Internet access. Restaurant, bar. Children's activity center. Spa. Outdoor pool, whirlpool. Ski-in/ski-out. Airport transportation available. Fitness center. Business center. **$$$$**

SPECIALTY LODGINGS
SILVER KING HOTEL
1485 Empire Ave., Park City, 435-649-5500, 800-331-8652; www.silverkinghotel.com
66 rooms, all suites. Wireless Internet access. Ski-in/ski-out. Pool. **$$$**

WASHINGTON SCHOOL INN
543 Park Ave., Park City, 435-649-3800, 800-824-1672;
www.washingtonschoolinn.com
Built in 1889, this historic stone schoolhouse is charming and well appointed with turn-of-the-century country décor and modern amenities. 15 rooms. Children over

8 years only. Complimentary full breakfast. Wireless Internet access. Whirlpool. Airport transportation available. $$

WOODSIDE INN BED AND BREAKFAST

1469 Woodside Ave., Park City, 435-649-3494, 888-241-5890; www.woodsideinn.com
Six rooms. Complimentary full breakfast. Wireless Internet access. Airport transportation available. $$

RESTAURANTS
★★★THE CABIN

4000 The Canyons Resort Drive, Park City, 435-649-8060; www.thecanyons.com
This upscale restaurant at the Canyons Grand Summit Hotel has rustic décor and a friendly staff and serves an eclectic Western menu, including buffalo tenderloin, lamb osso bucco and the signature crispy trout. American menu. Breakfast, lunch, dinner. Bar. Children's menu. Casual attire. Reservations recommended. Valet parking. $$$

★★CHEZ BETTY

1637 Short Line Drive, Park City, 435-649-8181; www.chezbetty.com
American menu. Dinner. Closed Tuesday-Wednesday (open all week December-March). Casual attire. Outdoor seating. $$$

★★★CHIMAYO

368 Main St., Park City, 435-649-6222; www.chimayorestaurant.com
Park City's most stylish come to this restaurant to sample Southwestern cuisine. Dishes include scallops wrapped in wild boar bacon and served with a tortilla tomato casserole with salsa verde and trout fajitas. A fireplace at one end of the dining room enhances the warm colorful atmosphere. Southwestern menu. Dinner. Children's menu. Casual attire. Reservations recommended. $$$

★★★★THE GLITRETIND

7700 Stein Way, Park City, 435-649-3700; www.steinlodge.com
The celebrated Stein Eriksen Lodge claims not only the most impressive of views of the Wasatch Mountains but one of the most lauded restaurants in Utah as well. Executive chef Zane Holmquist prepares delicious New American cuisine. Try the scallop and lobster burger or the loin of organic Utah lamb. The wine selection is also impressive. Managed by Sommelier Cara Schwindt, the selection houses more than 350 types of wine that total more than 8,000 bottles. The restaurant also provides a wide selection of dessert and after dinner drinks, including a wide range of single malt scotch, bourbon, Cognac and brandy. American menu. Breakfast, lunch, dinner, late-night, Sunday brunch. Bar. Children's menu. Business casual attire. Reservations recommended. Valet parking. Outdoor seating. $$$

★★★GRAPPA

151 Main St., Park City, 435-645-0636; www.grapparestaurant.com
Located in a former boarding house on Park City's historic Main Street, this upscale restaurant offers dining on three levels. Many of the dishes feature just-picked herbs and flowers from the adjacent gardens, such as the polenta and herb-crusted rainbow trout served over mushroom risotto. Italian menu. Dinner. Closed one month in spring and fall. Children's menu. Casual attire. Reservations recommended. Outdoor seating. $$$

★★KAMPAI
586 Main St., Park City, 435-649-0655; www.latituderg.com
Sushi menu. Lunch, dinner. Casual attire. Reservations recommended. $$

★★★★RIVERHORSE ON MAIN
540 Main St., Park City, 435-649-3536; www.riverhorsegroup.com
Even ski bunnies (and bums) must eat, and when they do, they come to Riverhorse on Main, a bustling, happening scene. Located in the renovated historic Masonic Hall on Main Street, this modern restaurant, with dark woods, soft candlelight and fresh flowers offers lots of fun, Asian-inspired eats such as chicken satay, shrimp potstickers, crispy duck salad, macadamia-crusted halibut, grilled lobster tail and charred rack of lamb. While the dress code is informal, reservations are a must. American menu. Dinner. Children's menu. Business casual attire. Reservations recommended. Outdoor seating. $$$

SPA
★★★★THE SPA AT STEIN ERIKSON LODGE
7700 Stein Way, Park City, 435-649-3700; www.steinlodge.com
The Spa at Stein Eriksen Lodge was designed to appeal to guests needing remedies for sore and tired muscles after skiing or those affected by the resort's high altitude. All spa services grant complimentary use of the fitness center, steam room, sauna, whirlpool, and relaxation room. Aromatic and exhilarating treatments refresh and renew at this European-style spa, where Vichy showers and kurs are de rigueur. The extensive massage menu includes Swedish, deep tissue, aromatic, stone, reflexology, and a special massage for mothers-to-be. In-room massages are available for additional privacy. $$

PAYSON
Payson sits at the foot of the Wasatch Mountains, near Utah Lake. Mormons first settled the area after spending a night on the banks of Peteneet Creek.
Information: Chamber of Commerce, 439 W. Utah Ave., 801-465-5200;
www.payson.org

WHAT TO SEE AND DO
MOUNT NEBO SCENIC LOOP DRIVE
Payson
This 45-mile drive around the eastern shoulder of towering Mount Nebo (elevation 11,877 feet) is one of the most thrilling in Utah. Mount Nebo's three peaks are the highest in the Wasatch Range. The road travels south through Payson and Santaquin canyons and then climbs 9,000 feet up Mount Nebo, offering a view of Devil's Kitchen, a brilliantly colored canyon. (This section of the drive is not recommended for those who dislike heights.) The forest road continues south to Highway 132; take Highway 132 east to Nephi, and then drive north on I-15 back to Payson.

PETEETNEET CULTURAL MUSEUM AND ARTS CENTER
10 N. 600 East, Payson, 801-465-5265; www.peteetneetacademy.org
Named after Ute leader Chief Peteetneet, the center and museum (also called the Peteetneet Academy) is housed in a historic Victorian-style building, which includes an art gallery, photography exhibit, blacksmith shop and visitor's center. Open Monday-Friday 10 a.m.-4 p.m.

SPECIAL EVENT
GOLDEN ONION DAYS
Payson; www.payson.org
Includes community theater presentations, 5K and 10K runs, horse races, demolition derby, parade, fireworks and picnic. Labor Day weekend.

HOTELS
★CHERRY LANE MOTEL
240 E. 100 N. Payson, 801-465-2582
10 rooms. $

★COMFORT INN
830 N. Main St., Payson, 801-465-4861; www.comfortinn.com
62 rooms. Complimentary continental breakfast. Pets accepted; fee. Pool.

RESTAURANT
★DALTON'S FINE DINING
20 S. 100 W. Payson, 801-465-9182;
www.daltonsrestaurant.com
American menu. Lunch, dinner. Closed Sunday. $

PRICE
Price, the seat of Carbon County, bases its prosperity on coal. More than 30 mine properties are within 30 miles. Several parks are located here.
Information: Carbon County Chamber of Commerce, 81 N. 200 E.,
435-637-2788; www.pricecityutah.com

WHAT TO SEE AND DO
CLEVELAND-LLOYD DINOSAUR QUARRY
125 S. 600 W. Price, 435-636-3600;
www.blm.gov/ut/st/en/fo/price/recreation/quarry.html
Since 1928, more than 12,000 dinosaur bones representing at least 70 different animals have been excavated on this site. Visitor center, nature trail, picnic area. Memorial Day-Labor Day, daily; Easter-Memorial Day, weekends only.

COLLEGE OF EASTERN UTAH PREHISTORIC MUSEUM
155 E. Main St., Price, 435-613-5060, 800-817-9949; www.museum.ceu.edu
This museum includes dinosaur displays and archaeology exhibits. Memorial Day-Labor Day, daily; rest of year, Monday-Saturday.

GEOLOGY TOURS
90 N. 100 E., Price
Self-guided tours of Nine Mile Canyon, San Rafael Desert, Cleveland-Lloyd Dinosaur Quarry, Little Grand Canyon and more. Maps available at Castle Country Travel Region or Castle Country Regional Information Center, 155 E. Main, 800-842-0784.

UTAH

★
★
★
★
☆

MANTI-LA SAL NATIONAL FOREST, MANTI DIVISION

599 W. Price River Drive, Price, 435-637-2817; www.fs.fed.us/r4/mantilasal

This 1,413,111-acre area offers scenic mountain drives, riding trails, campsites, winter sports and deer and elk hunting. Joe's Valley Reservoir on Highway 29 and Electric Lake on Highway 31 have fishing and boating. Areas of geologic interest, developed as a result of massive landslides, are near Ephraim.

PRICE CANYON RECREATION AREA

Price, 15 miles north on Highway 6, then three miles west on unnumbered road, 435-636-3600; www.blm.gov/utah/price/pricerec.htm

Scenic overlooks, hiking, picnicking, camping. Roads have steep grades. May-mid-October, daily.

SCOFIELD STATE PARK

Highways 6 and 96, Price, 435-448-9449 (summer), 435-687-2491 (winter); www.stateparks.utah.gov

Utah's highest state park has a 2,800-acre lake that lies at an altitude of 7,616 feet. Fishing, boating (docks, ramps), ice fishing; camping; snowmobiling; cross-country skiing in winter. May-October.

HOTELS
★BEST WESTERN CARRIAGE HOUSE INN

590 E. Main St., Price, 435-637-5660, 800-937-8376; www.bestwestern.com

40 rooms. Complimentary continental breakfast. Pool. High-speed Internet access. **$**

★★HOLIDAY INN

838 Westwood Blvd., Price, 435-637-8880, 888-465-4329; www.holiday-inn.com

151 rooms. High-speed Internet access. Restaurant, bar. Pool. **$**

PROVIDENCE

Very close to Logan (about a mile away), Providence is located where Spring Creek meets the Logan River. The small town was named by leaders of the LDS Church, who found its location providential.

Information: www.providence-city.com

SPECIALTY LODGING
PROVIDENCE INN

10 S. Main, Providence, 435-752-3432, 800-480-4943; www.providenceinn.com

This historic bed and breakfast has rooms decorated in various periods: Early American, Victorian and Georgian. Built in 1869, the structure has been accurately restored. A hearty breakfast is provided. 17 rooms. **$$**

PROVO

Provo received its name from French-Canadian trapper Etienne Provost, who arrived in the area in 1825. But it wasn't until 1849 that the first permanent settlement, begun by a party of Mormons, was established. The Mormon settlers erected Fort Utah as their first building, and despite famine, drought, hard winters and the constant danger of attack, they persisted and the settlement grew. Today, Provo is the seat of Utah

County and the state's third-largest city. An important educational and commercial center, Provo's largest employer is Brigham Young University.

Provo lies in the middle of a lush, green valley: to the north stands 12,008-foot Mount Timpanogos; to the south is the perpendicular face of the Wasatch Range; to the east Provo Peak rises 11,054 feet; and to the west lies Utah Lake, backed by more mountains. Provo is the headquarters of the Uinta National Forest, and many good fishing, boating, camping and hiking spots are nearby.

Information: Utah County Visitors Center, 111 S. University Ave., Provo, 801-851-2100, 800-222-8824; www.utahvalley.org

WHAT TO SEE AND DO
BRIGHAM YOUNG UNIVERSITY
Provo, 801-422-4636; www.byu.edu
Established 1875; 27,000 students. Founded by Brigham Young and operated by the Church of Jesus Christ of Latter-day Saints. This is one of the world's largest church-related institutions of higher learning, with students from every state and more than 90 foreign countries. One-hour, free guided tours arranged at Hosting Center Monday-Friday; also by appointment.

EARTH SCIENCE MUSEUM
1683 North Canyon Road, Provo, 801-422-3680; cpms.byu.edu
Geological collection, extensive series of minerals and fossils. Closed on university holidays.

HARRIS FINE ARTS CENTER
HFAC Campus Drive, Provo, 801-422-4322; www.cfac.byu.edu
Includes periodic displays of rare instruments and music collection. Concert, theater performances.

MONTE L. BEAN LIFE SCIENCE MUSEUM
645 E. 1430 N., Provo, 801-442-5051; www.mlbean.byu.edu
Exhibits and collections of insects, fish, amphibians, reptiles, birds, animals and plants. Closed Sunday.

MUSEUM OF ART
North Campus Drive, Provo, 801-422-8287; www.moa.byu.edu
Exhibits from the BYU Permanent Collection; traveling exhibits.

MUSEUM OF PEOPLES AND CULTURES
105 Allen Hall, Provo, 801-422-0020; mpc.byu.edu
Material from South America, the Near East and the Southwestern United States. Admission: free. Monday, Wednesday, Friday 9-5 a.m., Tuesday, Thursday 9-7 a.m.

PIONEER MUSEUM
500 W. 500 N. Provo, 801-852-6609; www.provo.org
This museum includes an outstanding collection of Utah pioneer relics and Western art. Pioneer Village. May-August, Wednesday, Friday and Saturday 1-4 p.m.

UINTA NATIONAL FOREST

88 W. and 100 N. Provo, 801-342-5100; www.fs.fed.us/r4/uwc

Scenic drives through the forest give an unsurpassed view of colorful landscapes, canyons and waterfalls. Stream and lake fishing; hunting for deer and elk, camping, picnicking. Reservations accepted.

UTAH LAKE STATE PARK

4400 W. Center St., Provo, 801-375-0731; www.stateparks.utah.gov/parks/utah-lake

The park is situated on the eastern shore of Utah Lake, a 150-square-mile, freshwater remnant of ancient Lake Bonneville that created the Great Salt Lake. Fishing, boating (ramp, dock); ice skating; roller skating; picnicking, play area, camping. Visitor center. Summer daily 6 a.m.-10 p.m.; winter 8 a.m.-5 p.m.; closed holidays.

SPECIAL EVENT
FREEDOM FESTIVAL

4626 N. 300 W., Provo, 801-818-1776; www.freedomfestival.org

Bazaar, carnival, parades. Early July.

HOTELS
★BEST WESTERN COTTONTREE INN

2230 N. University Parkway, Provo, 801-373-7044, 800-662-6886;
www.bestwestern.com

80 rooms. High-speed Internet access. Complimentary continental breakfast. Pool. Fitness center. Pool. **$**

★★COURTYARD PROVO

1600 N. Freedom Blvd., Provo, 801-373-2222; www.marriott.com

100 rooms. High-speed Internet access. Restaurant, bar. Pool. **$**

★FAIRFIELD INN

1515 S. University Ave., Provo, 801-377-9500; www.marriott.com

72 rooms. Complimentary continental breakfast. Pool. **$**

★★★MARRIOTT PROVO HOTEL AND CONFERENCE CENTER

101 W. 100 N. Provo, 801-377-4700, 800-777-7144; www.marriott.com

Nearby attractions include two shopping malls, as well as the Seven Peaks Water Park and Ice Rink, where the ice hockey competition and practices for the 2002 Winter Olympics were held. The comfortable rooms feature views of the Wasatch Mountains. This hotel is nonsmoking. 330 rooms. Wireless Internet access. Restaurant, bar. Airport transportation available. Pool. Business center. Fitness center. **$$**

RESTAURANT
★★BOMBAY HOUSE

463 N. University Ave., Provo, 801-373-6677; www.bombayhouse.com

Indian menu. Dinner. Closed Sunday. Casual attire. **$**

RICHFIELD

Located in the center of Sevier Valley in South Central Utah, Richfield has become the commercial hub of the region. Today, some of the world's best beef is raised in and shipped from this area.

Information: Chamber of Commerce, 435-896-6439; www.richfieldcity.com

WHAT TO SEE AND DO
BIG ROCK CANDY MOUNTAIN

Richfield, 25 miles south on Highway 89, in Marysvale Canyon, 435-896-4241
Burl Ives popularized this multicolored mountain in a song.

FISHLAKE NATIONAL FOREST

115 E. and 900 N. Richfield, 435-896-9233; www.fs.fed.us/r4/fishlake
This 1,424,000-acre forest offers fishing, hunting, hiking, picnicking and camping. It is named for the biggest lake in the forest area. Fish Lake (33 miles southeast, via Highways 119 and 24, then seven miles northeast on Highway 25) offers high-altitude angling on a six-mile-long lake covering 2,600 acres. Monday-Thursday 8 a.m.-noon, Monday-Thursday 1-5 p.m., Friday 8 a.m.-noon.

CAPITOL REEF NATIONAL PARK

Capitol Reef, at an elevation ranging from 3,900 to 8,800 feet, is composed of red sandstone cliffs capped with domes of white sandstone. It was named Capitol Reef because the rocks formed a natural barrier to pioneer travel and the white sandstone domes resemble that of the U.S. Capitol.

Located in the heart of Utah's slickrock country, the park is actually a 100-mile section of the Waterpocket Fold, an upthrust of sedimentary rock created during the formation of the Rocky Mountains. Pockets in the rocks collect thousands of gallons of water each time it rains. From A.D. 700-1350, this 378-square-mile area was the home of an ancient people who grew corn along the Fremont River. Petroglyphs can be seen on some of the sandstone walls. A schoolhouse, farmhouse and orchards, established by early Mormon settlers, are open to the public in season.

The park can be approached from either the east or the west via Highway 24, a paved road. There is a visitor center on this road about seven miles from the west boundary and eight miles from the east (Daily). A 25-mile round-trip scenic drive, some parts unpaved, starts from this point. There are evening programs and guided walks Memorial Day-Labor Day. Three campgrounds are available: Fruita, approximately one mile south off Highway 24, provides 70 tent and trailer sites year-round; Cedar Mesa, 23 miles south off Highway 24, and Cathedral, 28 miles north off Highway 24, offer five primitive sites with access depending on the weather. The Visitor Center is open daily (except for some major holidays) from 8 a.m.-4:30 p.m. with extended hours during the summer season. Ripple Rock Nature Center is open from Memorial Day-Labor Day from 10 a.m.-3 p.m. Tuesday-Saturday, closed Sundays and Mondays. Information: Torrey, 10 miles east of Richfield on Highway 119, then 65 miles southeast on Highway 24, 435-425-3791; www.nps.gov/care

UTAH

★
★
★
★
★

HOTELS

★DAYS INN

333 N. Main St., Richfield, 435-896-6476, 888-275-8513; www.daysinn.com
51 rooms. Restaurant. Pets accepted. Pool. $

★QUALITY INN

540 S. Main St., Richfield, 435-896-5465, 800-228-5151; www.qualityinn.com
79 rooms. Restaurant. Whirlpool. Pool. $

ROOSEVELT

Roosevelt, in the geographic center of Utah's "dinosaur land," was named after Theodore Roosevelt, who once camped on the banks of a nearby river. Nine Mile Canyon, with its American Indian petroglyphs, can be reached from here. A Ranger District office of the Ashley National Forest is located in the town.

Information: Chamber of Commerce, 50 E. 200 S., Roosevelt; 435-722-4598

HOTEL

★BEST WESTERN INN

2203 E. Highway 40, Roosevelt, 435-722-4644; www.bestwestern.com
40 rooms. High-speed Internet access. Pool. Airport transportation available. Fitness center. Complimentary continental breakfast. Pets accepted.

SALINA

Mormon settlers established this town in the mid-1800s and named their settlement after the abundant salt deposits nearby. Salina's biggest claim to fame is the annual pageant, performed by hundreds of members of the LDS Church.

SPECIAL EVENT

MORMON MIRACLE PAGEANT

4 N. 100 E., Manti, 435-835-3000, 800-255-8860; www.mormonmiracle.org
A cast of more than 600 portrays events from the Book of Mormon. Performances begin at dusk and ends about 11 p.m., and admission is free. Early-mid-June.

HOTEL

★BEST WESTERN SHAHEEN MOTEL

1225 S. State St., Salina, 435-529-7455; www.bestwestern.com
40 rooms. High-speed Internet access. Complimentary continental breakfast. Pool. $

SALT LAKE CITY

Salt Lake City, with its 10-acre blocks, 132-foot-wide, tree-lined streets and mountains rising to the east and west, is one of the most beautifully planned cities in the country.

On a hill at the north end of State Street stands Utah's classic Capitol building. Three blocks south is Temple Square, with the famed Mormon Temple and Tabernacle. The adjacent block houses the headquarters of the Church of Jesus Christ of Latter-Day Saints, whose members are commonly called Mormons.

Once a desert wilderness, Salt Lake City was built by Mormon settlers who sought refuge from religious persecution. Followers of Brigham Young arrived and named their new territory Deseret. In the early days, the Mormons began a variety of experiments in farming, industry and society, many of which were highly successful. Today, Salt Lake City is an industrious, businesslike city, a center for electronics, steel, missiles and a hundred other enterprises.

West of the city is the enormous Great Salt Lake, stretching 48 miles one way and 90 miles the other. It is less than 35 feet deep and between 15 and 20 percent salt—almost five times as salty as the ocean. You can't sink in the water—instead you'll just bob up and down. The lake is what remains of ancient Lake Bonneville, once 145 miles wide, 350 miles long and 1,000 feet deep. As Lake Bonneville's water evaporated over thousands of years, a large expanse of perfectly flat, solid salt was left. Today, the Bonneville Salt Flats stretch west almost to Nevada.

Salt Lake City was laid out in grid fashion, with Temple Square at the center. Most street names are coordinates on this grid: Fourth South Street is four blocks south of Temple Square, Seventh East is seven blocks east. These are written as 400 South and 700 East.

Information: Convention & Visitors Bureau, 90 S. West Temple, 801-534-4900; www.saltlake.org

WHAT TO SEE AND DO

ASSEMBLY HALL

500 W. North Temple, Salt Lake City, 801-240-3318; www.lds.org
(1880) Victorian gothic congregation hall. Tours daily 9 a.m.-9 p.m.

BRIGHAM YOUNG MONUMENT

Salt Lake City, Main and South Temple streets
This statue honoring the church leader was first seen at the Chicago World's Fair in 1893.

CLARK PLANETARIUM

110 S. 400 W., Salt Lake City, 801-456-7827; www.hansenplanetarium.net
The Hansen Dome Theatre and the IMAX Theatre are the two main attractions here. Daily. Free exhibits include images from the Hubble Space telescope and a fully functioning weather station.

COUNCIL HALL

300 N. State St., Salt Lake City, 801-538-1900; www.utah.com
Council Hall was once the meeting place of the territorial legislature and city hall for 30 years. It was dismantled and then reconstructed in 1963 at its present location. Visitor information center and office; memorabilia. Daily.

FAMILY HISTORY LIBRARY

35 N.W., Temple, Salt Lake City, 801-240-2584, 800-346-6044; www.familysearch.org/eng
This genealogical library is the largest such facility in the world. Monday 8 a.m.-5 p.m., Tuesday-Saturday 8 a.m.-9 p.m.

SALT LAKE CITY'S MORMON HERITAGE

The centerpiece of downtown Salt Lake City is Temple Square, the city block bordered by three streets named Temple West, North and South and Main Streets on the east side. Utah's top tourist attraction, Temple Square is the hub for the Church of Jesus Christ of the Latter-Day Saints, where guests are invited to join a free guided tour that offers a glimpse of several architectural and cultural landmarks, including the Mormon Tabernacle, the Museum of Church History and Art and the Joseph Smith Memorial Building. (Tours start at the flagpole every few minutes.) If your timing is right, you can also take in a film, choir rehearsal or organ recital here.

From Temple Square, head east on South Temple to a pair of historic homes, the **Lion House** *(63 E. South Temple)* and the **Beehive House** *(67 E. South Temple)*. No tours are available of the Lion House, which served as Brigham Young's home during the mid-19th century, but there is a restaurant on the lower level that is a good spot for a lunch break. Next door, the Beehive House, another former Young residence and a National Historic Landmark, offers free tours every day. Just east of these houses on South Temple is **Eagle Gate** *(at the intersection of State Street)*, an impressive arch capped by a 2-ton sculpture of an eagle with a 20-foot wingspan.

South of Eagle Gate on the east side of State Street are two of Salt Lake City's standout cultural facilities: the **Hansen Planetarium** *(15 South State St.)* and the **Social Hall Heritage Museum** *(39 South State St.)*. The former features daily star shows and a free space museum with hands-on exhibits. The latter includes remnants of Utah's first public building and the West's first theater. From the museum, it's best to reverse course and walk north on State Street, passing under Eagle Gate. Just beyond North Temple, hop on the paths that run through the lush City Creek Park and head north to the adjoining Memory Grove Park. From here, it's only a two-block walk west to the **Utah State Capitol** *(just north of the intersection of State Street and 300 North St.)*, an exemplary Renaissance Revival-style structure built from Utah granite in 1915. The building is open to the public daily and guided tours are offered on weekdays.

Two blocks west of the State Capitol is the **Pioneer Memorial Museum** *(300 North Main St.)*, a majestic replica of the original Salt Lake Theater (demolished in 1928) with 38 rooms of relics from the area's past, including photographs, vehicles, dolls and weapons. The museum is on the eastern edge of one of the city's oldest neighborhoods, the tree-lined **Marmalade District** *(between 300 and 500 North Streets to the north and south and Center and Quince Streets to the east and west)*, a good place to meander and gaze at historic homes.

UTAH

★
★ ★
★ ★
★

GOVERNOR'S MANSION

603 E. South Temple St., Salt Lake City, 801-538-1005; www.utah.gov/governor

Built by Thomas Kearns, a wealthy Utah senator in the early 1900s, this mansion is the official residence of Utah's governor. It was painstakingly restored after a fire in 1993. President Theodore Roosevelt, a personal friend of Senator Kerns, dined here often. Tours. June-September, Tuesday and Thursday 2-4 p.m.

INNSBROOK TOURS

Salt Lake City, 801-534-1001; www.saltlakecitytours.org

This is the best way to see all the famous sites in Salt Lake City. Pick-up begins at 9:15 a.m., and then you're off to see landmarks like the Mormon Tabernacle, the Salt Lake Temple and the Olympic Stadium and Village. Daily.

LAGOON AMUSEMENT PARK, PIONEER VILLAGE AND WATER PARK

Salt Lake City, 17 miles north on Interstate 15, 800-748-5246; www.lagoonpark.com

Besides fun rides and waterslides, the village includes a re-creation of a 19th-century Utah town with stagecoach and steam-engine train rides. Camping, picnicking. Memorial Day-August, daily; mid-April-late May and September, Saturday-Sunday only.

LIBERTY PARK

1300 South St., Salt Lake City, 801-972-7800;
www.slcgov.com/publicservices/Parks/default.htm

This 100-acre park is Salt Lake's largest. Go for a run, play tennis or enjoy a picnic. Paddleboats are available in summer, and there's a playground for kids. Park: daily 7 a.m.-10 p.m. Aviary: daily 9 a.m-6 p.m.; November-March: daily 9 a.m.-4:30 p.m.

393

LION HOUSE

63 E. South Temple, Salt Lake City, 801-363-5466;
www.diningattemplesquare.com/pantry.html

Lion House was home to Brigham Young's family. Today it houses a restaurant. Next door is another residence, Beehive House, which is open to the public for tours. Monday-Saturday 11 a.m.-8 p.m.

MAURICE ABRAVANEL CONCERT HALL

123 W. South Temple, Salt Lake City, 801-355-2787;
www.finearts.slco.org/facilities/abravanel/abravanel.html

Home to the Utah Symphony, this building is adorned with more than 12,000 square feet of 24-karat gold leaf and a mile of brass railing. It has been rated one of the best halls in the U.S. for acoustics. Free tours by appointment. The symphony has performances most weekends.

MOKI MAC RIVER EXPEDITIONS

6006 S. 1300 E. Salt Lake City, 801-268-6667, 800-284-7280; www.mokimac.com

Offers one to 14-day white-water rafting and canoeing trips on the Green and Colorado rivers.

MUSEUM OF CHURCH HISTORY AND ART

45 N. West Temple St., Salt Lake City, 801-240-4615;
www.lds.org/churchhistory/museum
Exhibits of Latter-Day Saints church history from 1820 to present. Admission: free.
Monday-Friday 9 a.m.-9 p.m., Saturday-Sunday 10 a.m.-7 p.m.

PARK CITY MOUNTAIN RESORT

1310 Lowell Ave., Park City, 435-649-8111, 800-331-3178; www.pcski.com
Ski and snowboard resort also open daily during the summer season. Monday-
Thursday noon-6 p.m., Friday-Sunday 11 a.m.-6 p.m.

PIONEER MEMORIAL MUSEUM

300 N. Main St., Salt Lake City, 801-532-6479; www.dupinternational.org
This extensive collection of pioneer relics includes a carriage house, with exhibits relating to transportation, including Brigham Young's wagon and Pony Express
items. One-hour guided tours by appointment. Monday-Saturday 9 a.m.-5 p.m.; June-
August, also Sunday 1-5 p.m.

PIONEER THEATRE COMPANY

300 S. 1400 E. Salt Lake City, 801-581-6961; www.pioneertheatre.org
Two auditoriums host dramas, musicals, comedies. Mid-September-mid-May.

RED BUTTE GARDEN AND ARBORETUM

300 Wakara Way, Salt Lake City, 801-581-4747; www.redbuttegarden.org
Includes more than 9,000 trees on 150 acres, representing 350 species; conservatory.
Self-guided tours. Special events in summer. Daily.

SALT LAKE ART CENTER

20 S. West Temple, Salt Lake City, 801-328-4201; www.slartcenter.org
Changing exhibits feature photographs, paintings, ceramics and sculptures. The
school hosts lectures and shows films. Tuesday-Thursday, Saturday 11 a.m.-6 p.m.,
Friday 11 a.m.-9 p.m.; closed Sunday, Monday and holidays.

SOLITUDE RESORT

12000 Big Cottonwood Canyon, Salt Lake City, 801-534-1400; www.skisolitude.com
Three quad, one triple, four double chairlifts; racecourse, patrol, school, rentals. Longest run 3½ miles, vertical drop 2,047 feet. November-April, daily. Cross-country
center.

TEMPLE SQUARE

50 W. North Temple Street, Salt Lake City, 801-240-1245, 800-537-9703;
www.mormon.org/mormonorg/eng
This 10-acre square is owned by the Church of Jesus Christ of Latter-Day Saints.
Two visitors' centers provide information, exhibits and guided tours; daily, every 10
minutes.

TABERNACLE

50 W. North Temple, Salt Lake City, 801-240-4150, 866-537-8457;
www.mormontabernaclechoir.org

The self-supporting roof, an elongated dome, is 250 feet long and 150 feet wide. The tabernacle organ has 11,623 pipes, ranging from ⅝ inch to 32 feet in length. The world-famous Tabernacle Choir may be heard at rehearsal (Thursday 8 p.m.) or at broadcast time (Sunday 9:30 a.m., be seated by 9:15 a.m.). Organ recitals Monday-Saturday noon, Sunday afternoon.

TEMPLE

50 W. North Temple, Salt Lake City, 801-240-4150, 866-537-8457;
www.mormontabernaclechoir.org

Used for sacred ordinances, such as baptisms and marriages. Closed to non-Mormons.

THIS IS THE PLACE HERITAGE PARK

2601 E. Sunnyside Ave., Salt Lake City, 801-582-1847; www.thisistheplace.org

This historic park is located at the mouth of Emigration Canyon, where Mormon pioneers first entered the valley, and includes Old Deseret Pioneer Village and This Is the Place Monument (1947), commemorating Brigham Young's words upon first seeing the Salt Lake City site. Hundreds of people depict pioneer life. Admission to the monument and visitors' center, which includes an audio presentation and murals of the Mormon migration, is free. Monument and grounds, daily, dawn-dusk. Visitor center Monday-Saturday 9 a.m.-6 p.m. Village late May-early September, Monday-Saturday 10 a.m.-6 p.m.

TROLLEY SQUARE

600 S. 700 East St., Salt Lake City, 801-521-9877; www.trolleysquare.com

This 10-acre complex of trolley barns has been converted into an entertainment/shopping/dining center. Monday-Saturday 10 a.m.-9 p.m., Sunday noon-5 p.m.

UNIVERSITY OF UTAH

201 S. Presidents Drive, Salt Lake City, 801-581-7200; www.utah.edu

Established in 1850. On campus is the J. Willard Marriott Library. Named for the hotel magnate, this library includes a vast Western Americana collection. Monday-Thursday 7 a.m.-midnight, Friday 7 a.m.-8 p.m., Saturday 9 a.m.-8 p.m., Sunday 10 a.m.-midnight; closed holidays, also July 24.

UTAH MUSEUM OF FINE ARTS

410 Campus Center Drive, Salt Lake City, 801-581-7332; www.umfa.utah.org

Representations of artistic styles from Egyptian antiquities to contemporary American paintings; 19th-century French and American paintings and furniture. Tuesday-Friday 10 a.m.-5 p.m., Saturday-Sunday 11 a.m.-5 p.m., Wednesday 10 a.m.-8 p.m.

UTAH MUSEUM OF NATURAL HISTORY

1390 E. Presidents Circle, Salt Lake City, 801-581-6927; www.umnh.utah.edu

Shows exhibits of the Earth's natural wonders and honors Utah's native cultures. Monday-Saturday 9:30 a.m.-5:30 p.m., Sunday noon-5 p.m.; closed July 24.

UTAH JAZZ (NBA)

301 W. South Temple, Salt Lake City, 801-325-2500; www.nba.com/jazz
Professional basketball team.

UTAH OPERA COMPANY

123 W. South Temple, Salt Lake City, 801-533-5626; www.utahopera.org
Grand opera. October-May.

UTAH STARZZ (WNBA)

301 W. South Temple, Salt Lake City, 801-355-3865; www.utah.com/sports/starzz.htm
Women's professional basketball team.

WASATCH-CACHE NATIONAL FOREST

125 S. State St., Salt Lake City, 801-236-3400; www.fs.fed.us/r4/uwc
This wilderness area has alpine lakes, rugged peaks and several canyons. Fishing, boating, deer and elk hunting, winter sports and camping.

WHEELER HISTORIC FARM

6351 S. 900 E. St., Salt Lake City, 801-264-2241; www.wheelerfarm.com
This living history farm on 75 acres depicts rural life from 1890 to1918 and includes a farmhouse, farm buildings, animals, crops and hay rides. Tour. Visitors can feed the animals, gather eggs and milk cows. There is a small fee for various activities and events. Monday-Saturday dawn-dusk.

ZCMI (ZION'S CO-OPERATIVE MERCANTILE INSTITUTION) CENTER

Main and South Temple, Salt Lake City
A department store established in 1868 by Brigham Young anchors this 85-store, enclosed downtown shopping mall. Monday-Saturday.

SPECIAL EVENT
UTAH ARTS FESTIVAL

230 S. 500 W., Salt Lake City, 801-322-2428; www.uaf.org
This four-day festival featuring visual, performing and culinary artists, draws more than 80,000 people every year. Last week in June.

HOTELS
★DAYS INN

1900 W. North Temple, Salt Lake City, 801-539-8538, 800-329-7466; www.daysinn.com
110 rooms. Complimentary continental breakfast. Airport transportation available. Pets accepted; fee. Pool. High-speed Internet access. **$**

★★EMBASSY SUITES

110 W. 600 S., Salt Lake City, 801-359-7800; www.embassysuites.com
241 rooms, all suites. Complimentary full breakfast. High-speed Internet access. Restaurant, bar. Pool. **$**

★★★★THE GRAND AMERICA HOTEL

555 S. Main St., Salt Lake City, 801-258-6000, 800-621-4505; www.grandamerica.com

Set against the beautiful backdrop of the Wasatch Mountains, the Grand America is a tribute to the glory of Old World Europe. This esteemed hotel is the pinnacle of refinement. The guest rooms are classically French, with plush carpets, luxurious fabrics, fine art and Richelieu furniture. The world-class spa is a sanctuary and includes a full-service salon. Both the indoor and outdoor pools are spectacular. 775 rooms. High-speed Internet access. Restaurant, two bars. Spa. Airport transportation available. Pool. **$$$**

★★HILTON SALT LAKE CITY AIRPORT

5151 Wiley Post Way, Salt Lake City, 801-539-1515, 800-999-3736; www.hilton.com

278 rooms. High-speed Internet access. Restaurant, bar. Airport transportation available. Pets accepted. Pool. Business center. **$**

★★★HILTON SALT LAKE CITY CENTER

255 S. West Temple, Salt Lake City, 801-328-2000; www.hilton.com

Located in the heart of downtown, this large hotel offers spacious and very nicely appointed rooms and friendly service.499 rooms. High-speed Internet access. Two restaurants, bar. Spa. Airport transportation available. Pets accepted. Pool. **$**

★★★HOTEL MONACO SALT LAKE CITY

15 W. 200 S., Salt Lake City, 801-595-0000, 877-294-9710; www.hotelmonaco.com

The Hotel Monaco stands out for its haute décor and personalized services. Located in the heart of downtown Salt Lake City, this refurbished 14-story landmark hotel makes an instant impression with its vibrant lobby featuring velvet furnishings. The rooms are equally delightful with beds swathed in Frette linens. Tall rooms are available with eight-foot beds and heightened showerheads. Amenities include coffeemakers with Starbucks coffee, Yoga programs (grab a mat from the basket and flip on the Yoga channel) and gourmet minibars. If all you're missing is a travel companion, you can adopt a goldfish during your stay. 225 rooms. Wireless Internet access. Restaurant, bar. Airport transportation available. Pets accepted. **$**

★★★LITTLE AMERICA HOTEL

500 S. Main St., Salt Lake City, 801-596-5700, 800-453-9450;
www.littleamerica.com/slc

This elegant hotel offers a variety of accommodations. Rooms in the tower are decorated in rich French brocade fabrics and English wool carpets, and offer large parlor areas with views of the city. There's also a separate dressing area and bathroom with an oval-shaped tub. Garden rooms are also spacious and have private entrances. There's a large indoor pool, salon and barber shop. 850 rooms. High-speed Internet access. Two restaurants, bar. Airport transportation available. Spa. Pool. **$**

★★★MARRIOTT SALT LAKE CITY DOWNTOWN

75 S. West Temple, Salt Lake City, 801-531-0800; www.marriott.com

Located across from the Salt Palace Convention Center, this hotel caters to business travelers and is close to the airport and major ski resorts. Everything is on hand here, including a heated pool, fitness center and a Starbucks. 515 rooms. High-speed Internet access. Restaurant, bar. Business center. **$$**

★★★MARRIOTT SALT LAKE CITY-CITY CENTER

220 S. State St., Salt Lake City, 801-961-8700, 866-961-8700; www.marriott.com

Situated adjacent to the Gallivan Center, which hosts concerts in summer and skating in winter, this hotel is within walking distance to numerous restaurants and shops. The contemporary and comfortable guest rooms are decorated in a relaxing palette and feature down comforters, large marble baths and views of either the city or the mountains. The hotel's restaurant, Piastra, serves up continental cuisine in a sophisticated setting. 359 rooms. High-speed Internet access. Restaurant, bar. **$**

★★PEERY HOTEL

110 W. Broadway, Salt Lake City, 801-521-4300, 800-331-0073; www.peeryhotel.com

73 rooms. Wireless Internet access. Restaurant, bar. **$**

★★★RADISSON HOTEL SALT LAKE CITY DOWNTOWN

215 W. S. Temple, Salt Lake City, 801-531-7500, 800-333-3333; www.radisson.com

Located downtown next to the Salt Palace Convention Center, all rooms in this hotel have spacious work areas with Herman Miller-designed ergonomic chairs and complimentary high-speed Internet access. There's also an indoor pool, fitness center, sauna and whirlpool. 381 rooms. High-speed Internet access. Restaurant, bar. Airport transportation available. Fitness center. Pool. **$**

SPECIALTY LODGING
ARMSTRONG MANSION

667 E. 100 S., Salt Lake City, 801-531-1333, 800-708-1333;
www.armstrongmansion.com

This bed and breakfast built in 1893 is tastefully decorated with antiques and carved wood. 16 rooms. Complimentary full breakfast. Spa. **$$**

RESTAURANTS
★★★BAMBARA

202 S. Main St., Salt Lake City, 801-363-5454; www.bambara-slc.com

This chic New American bistro housed in a former bank serves up creations such as seared halibut with basil mashed potatoes and tomato pine nut truffle vinaigrette, and house made tagliattelle and organic English peas, shaved truffle and wild mushroom-thyme cream sauce. American menu. Breakfast, lunch, dinner. Children's menu. Business casual attire. Reservations recommended. Valet parking. **$$$**

★★CREEKSIDE AT SOLITUDE

12000 Big Cottonwood Canyon, Solitude, 801-536-5787; www.skisolitude.com
American menu. Dinner, Saturday-Sunday brunch. Closed May, late September-mid-November. Bar. Casual attire. Outdoor seating. **$$**

★★★FRESCO ITALIAN CAFE

1513 S. 1500 E., Salt Lake City, 801-486-1300; www.frescoitaliancafe.com
A winding brick walkway lined with flowers leads the way to this charming neighborhood bistro, where you'll find a fireplace in winter and alfresco dining during the summer. Guests will enjoy the fresh and authentic flavors of Italy in dishes such as the chef's nightly risotto and delicious herb gnocchi. Italian menu. Dinner. Casual attire. Reservations recommended. Outdoor seating. **$$**

★★★LA CAILLE

9565 S. Wasatch Blvd., Little Cottonwood Canyon, 801-942-1751; www.lacaille.com
This impressive country French chateau is surrounded by beautiful gardens populated by peacocks, llamas, ducks and a host of other exotic creatures. Inside, the friendly staff is dressed in 18th-century costumes, and the menu features innovative fare such as champagne ravioli. French menu. Dinner, brunch. Bar. Children's menu. Casual attire. Reservations recommended. Valet parking. Outdoor seating. **$$$**

★★★LOG HAVEN

6451 E. Millcreek Canyon Road, Salt Lake City, 801-272-8255; www.log-haven.com
This rustic log mansion is one of Utah's most innovative and elegant restaurants. The fresh specialties change daily, but you might see fire-grilled corn soup or jumbo lump crab cakes. The restaurant also has an extensive wine list. International menu. Dinner. Bar. Business casual attire. Reservations recommended. Outdoor seating. **$$$**

★★MARKET STREET BROILER

260 S. 1300 E., Salt Lake City, 801-583-8808; www.gastronomyinc.com
Seafood menu. Lunch, dinner. Children's menu. Casual attire. Outdoor seating. **$$**

★★MARKET STREET GRILL

48 W. Market St., Salt Lake City, 801-322-4668; www.gastronomyinc.com
Seafood menu. Breakfast, lunch, dinner, Sunday brunch. Closed Labor Day. Children's menu. Casual attire. Valet parking. **$$**

★★★METROPOLITAN

173 W. Broadway, Salt Lake City, 801-364-3472; www.themetropolitan.com
This contemporary and whimsical restaurant specializes in "handcrafted New American cuisine." Indulge your inner kid with the TV dinner: a choice between fish and chips or wild boar ribs with peas and carrots and peach crisp. End with a sno-cone in a variety of flavors including spicy chocolate and cherry limeade. American menu. Dinner, late-night. Closed Sunday. Bar. Business casual attire. Reservations recommended. Valet parking. **$$$**

★★MIKADO AT COTTONWOOD

6572 S. Big Cottonwood Canyon Road, Salt Lake City, 801-947-9800;
www.latituderg.com

Sushi menu. Lunch, dinner. Children's menu. Casual attire. Reservations recommended. Outdoor seating. **$$**

★★★THE NEW YORKER

60 W. Market St., Salt Lake City, 801-363-0166; www.gastronomyinc.com

Recognized as one of Salt Lake's best dining spots since 1978, this elegant restaurant serves excellent traditional fare. Appetizers (including fruit, cheese and seafood) are offered as guests arrive. Steak menu. Lunch, dinner. Closed Sunday. Bar. Reservations recommended. Valet parking. **$$$**

★★RINO'S

2302 Parleys Way, Salt Lake City, 801-484-0901; www.rinositalianrestaurant.com

Italian menu. Dinner. Casual attire. Reservations recommended. Outdoor seating. **$$**

★RIO GRANDE CAFE

270 S. Rio Grande St., Salt Lake City, 801-364-3302

Southwestern menu. Lunch, dinner. Bar. Children's menu. Casual attire. Outdoor seating. **$**

★SQUATTERS PUB BREWERY

147 W. Broadway, Salt Lake City, 801-363-2739; www.squatters.com

American menu. Lunch, dinner, late-night, brunch. Bar. Children's menu. Casual attire. Outdoor seating. **$$**

★★TUCCI'S CUCINA ITALIA

515 S. 700 E., Salt Lake City, 801-533-9111; www.tuccis.qwestoffice.net

Italian menu. Lunch, dinner, brunch. Children's menu. Casual attire. Reservations recommended. Outdoor seating. **$$**

★★★TUSCANY

2832 E. 6200 S., Salt Lake City, 801-277-9919; www.tuscanyslc.com

This tremendously popular place maintains a high quality of service and offers authentic Tuscan fare while incorporating modern American culinary trends. One of the most popular items on the menu is the hardwood-grilled double cut pork chop with scallion mashed potatoes. Italian menu. Lunch, dinner, Sunday brunch. Bar. Casual attire. Reservations recommended. Valet parking. Outdoor seating. **$$$**

SNOWBIRD

In 1971, a Texas oilman recognized the potential of Little Cottonwood Canyon in the Wasatch National Forest and developed the area as a ski resort. Once home to thriving mining communities, the resort village of Snowbird, 29 miles east of Salt Lake City, now offers year-round recreational activities. With an average of 500 inches of snowfall annually, Snowbird claims to have the world's best powder.

Information: www.snowbird.com

WHAT TO SEE AND DO
SNOWBIRD SKI AND SUMMER RESORT
Highway 210, Snowbird, 801-933-2222, 800-232-9542; www.snowbird.com
Includes 89 runs on 2,500 acres; 27 percent beginner, 38 percent intermediate, 35 percent advanced/expert. Elevations of 7,800 to11,000 feet. Six double chairlifts, four high-speed quads, 125-passenger aerial tram. Patrol, school, rentals. Four lodges. Night skiing, Wednesday, Friday. Heli-skiing, half-pipe. Snowboarding, snowshoeing, ice skating. Mid-November-early May, daily. Summer activities include rock climbing, hiking, mountain biking, tennis, tram rides and concerts.

SPECIAL EVENT
UTAH SYMPHONY
Snowbird Ski and Summer Resort, Highway 210, Snowbird,
801-533-5626, 888-355-2787; www.utahsymphony.org
Snowbird Ski and Summer Resort is the summer home of the orchestra. Several Sunday afternoon concerts. July-August.

HOTELS
★★CLIFF LODGE & SPA
Little Cotton Canyon, Snowbird, 801-933-2222, 800-232-9542; www.snowbird.com
511 rooms. 12 restaurants, bar. Ski-in/ski-out. **$$$**

★★LODGE AT SNOWBIRD
Little Cottonwood Canyon, Snowbird, 801-933-2222, 800-232-9542;
www.snowbird.com
125 rooms. Restaurant, bar. Children's activity center. Airport transportation available. **$$**

RESTAURANT
★★STEAK PIT
Snowbird Center, Snowbird, 801-933-2260; www.snowbird.com
Steak menu. Dinner. Children's menu. Casual attire. Valet parking. **$$**

SPRINGDALE
This small village is right outside Zion National Park.
Information: www.zionpark.com

HOTELS
★CLIFFROSE LODGE AND GARDENS
281 Zion Park Blvd., Springdale, 435-772-3234, 800-243-8824;
www.cliffroselodge.com
40 rooms. Pool. High-speed Internet access. **$**

★★FLANIGAN'S INN AND DEEP CANYON SPA
450 Zion Park Blvd., Springdale, 435-772-3244, 800-765-7787; www.flanigans.com
36 rooms. Restaurant, bar. Spa. Pool. **$**

SPECIALTY LODGING
NOVEL HOUSE INN
73 Paradise Road, Springdale, 435-772-3650, 800-711-8400; www.novelhouse.com
This literary-themed bed and breakfast is set among the towering sandstone cliffs of Zion National Park. It is secluded but within walking distance of shops and restaurants. Complimentary breakfast and afternoon tea are served in the dining room with a view of West Temple Mountain. 10 rooms. Children not allowed. Complimentary full breakfast. Whirlpool. **$**

ST. GEORGE
Extending themselves to this hot, arid corner of southwest Utah, members of the LDS Church built their first temple here and struggled to survive by growing cotton. With determination and persistence, members of the church constructed the temple. Hundreds of tons of rocks were pounded into the mud until a stable foundation could be laid. Mormons from the north worked 40-day missions, and southern church members gave one day's labor out of every 10 until the temple was complete. The workers quarried 17,000 tons of rock by hand. A team of ox hauled the stones to the construction site, and for seven straight days, timber was hauled more than 80 miles from Mount Trumbull to build the structure. Made of red sandstone plastered to a gleaming white, the Mormon temple is not only the town's landmark but also a beacon for passing aircraft.

In St. George, warm summers are balanced by mild winters, and the village is fast becoming a retirement destination. The seat of Washington County, St. George is the closest town of its size to Zion National Park.

Information: St. George Area Chamber of Commerce, 97 E. St. George Blvd., 435-628-1658; www.stgeorgechamber.com

WHAT TO SEE AND DO
BRIGHAM YOUNG WINTER HOME
67 W. 200 N., St. George, 435-673-5181; www.lds.org
Brigham Young spent the last four winters of his life in this two-story adobe house, which still includes period furnishings. Winter, daily 9 a.m.-5 p.m.; summer, daily 9 a.m.-6 p.m.

PINE VALLEY CHAPEL
St. George, 30 miles north via Highway 18, 435-634-5747
Shipbuilder, Ebenezer Bryce built this white-framed chapel, which is still in use, in 1868 as an upside-down ship. The walls were completed on the ground, then raised and joined with wooden pegs and rawhide. Memorial Day-Labor Day, daily.

ST. GEORGE TEMPLE
250 E. 400 S., St. George, 435-673-3533
This red sandstone structure was built between 1863-1876 with local materials and resembles a colonial New England church. Daily.

TEMPLE VISITOR CENTER
490 S. 300 E., St. George, 435-673-5181; www.lds.org
A guided tour of the center explains local history and beliefs of the Latter-Day Saints; audiovisual program. Daily.

HOTELS

★BEST WESTERN CORAL HILLS

125 E. St. George Blvd., St. George, 435-673-4844, 800-542-7733; www.coralhills.com
98 rooms. Complimentary continental breakfast. Wireless Internet access. Airport transportation available. **$**

★COMFORT INN

1239 S. Main St., St. George, 435-673-7000, 800-428-0754; www.comfortsuites.net
122 rooms. Complimentary continental breakfast. Wireless Internet access. Airport transportation available. Pets accepted. **$**

★★HOLIDAY INN

850 S. Bluff St., St. George, 435-628-4235, 800-457-9800; www.histgeorgeutah.com
164 rooms. High-speed Internet access. Restaurant. Airport transportation available. Pets accepted. Business center. **$**

SPECIALTY LODGING

GREEN GATE VILLAGE

76 W. Tabernacle St., St. George, 435-628-6999, 800-350-6999; www.greengatevillage.com
Situated in the historic district of St. George, these elegantly restored pioneer houses are perfect for those who want nostalgic charm with modern conveniences. 14 rooms. Complimentary full breakfast. Pool. **$**

SUNDANCE

This popular ski resort was purchased by Robert Redford in 1968 and is named after the role Redford played in the film *Butch Cassidy and the Sundance Kid*. The popular Sundance Film Festival, held 30 miles north in Park City, is one of the largest independent film festivals in the world.

WHAT TO SEE AND DO

SUNDANCE SKI AREA

8841 N. Alpine Loop Road, Sundance, 801-225-4107, 800-892-1600; www.sundanceresort.com
Three chairlifts, rope tow; patrol, school, rentals; warming hut, restaurants. Longest run two miles, vertical drop 2,150 feet. Cross-country trails. Late November-April, daily.

HOTEL

★★★SUNDANCE RESORT

8841 N. Alpine Loop Road, Sundance, 801-225-4107, 800-892-1600; www.sundanceresort.com
This resort offers standard rooms, studios and cottages, all of which, like the resort itself, are intended to blend with the surrounding landscape. All of the rooms feature natural wood and Native American accents; most have fireplaces and private decks. The resort also offers fine dining and endless recreation, from artist workshops to nature programs. The general store is so popular that a mail-order catalog has been designed. A fabulous spa completes the well-rounded experience available at this unique resort. 110 rooms. Two restaurants, bar. Children's activity center. Fitness room. Spa. Ski. **$$$**

UTAH

★
★
★
★
★

RESTAURANTS

★★FOUNDRY GRILL

8841 N. Alpine Loop Road, Sundance, 801-223-4220, 800-892-1600;
www.sundanceresort.com

American menu. Breakfast, lunch, dinner, Sunday brunch. Bar. Outdoor seating. **$$**

★★★THE TREE ROOM

8841 N. Alpine Loop Road, Sundance, 801-223-4200, 800-892-1600;
www.sundanceresort.com

Located at the base of the Sundance ski lift, this restaurant's two-story windows offer stunning views of the rugged mountains and surrounding wilderness. The upscale-yet-casual room is filled with beautiful displays of Native American dolls and pottery. The sophisticated new American cuisine includes wild game, steaks and seafood, prepared with herbs and vegetables from the resort's own organic gardens. American menu. Dinner. Bar. Reservations recommended. **$$$**

VERNAL

This is the county seat of Uintah County in Northeastern Utah, which boasts oil, natural gas and many mineral deposits. Vernal is in an area of ancient geologic interest. Nearby are beautiful canyons, striking rock formations and majestic peaks.

Information: Dinosaurland Travel Board, 55 E. Main St., 435-789-1352, 800-477-5558;
www.dinoland.com

WHAT TO SEE AND DO

ASHLEY NATIONAL FOREST

355 N. Vernal Ave., Vernal, 435-789-1181; www.fs.fed.us/r4/ashley

The Uinta Mountains run through the heart of this nearly 1½ million-acre forest. Red Canyon, Kings Peak and Sheep Creek Geological Area are also here. Swimming, fishing, boating (ramps, marinas), white-water rafting, canoeing; hiking and nature trails, cross-country skiing, snowmobiling, improved or backcountry campgrounds. Visitor centers.

DAUGHTERS OF UTAH PIONEERS MUSEUM

500 W. 186 S. Vernal, 435-789-0352; www.dupinternational.org

This museum contains relics and artifacts dating from before 1847, when pioneers first settled in Utah. Includes period furniture, quilts, clothing, dolls, early medical instruments and more. June-weekend before Labor Day, Monday-Saturday.

FLAMING GORGE DAM AND NATIONAL RECREATION AREA

Vernal, 42 miles north on Highway 191 in Ashley National Forest, 435-784-3445;
www.utah.com/nationalsites

This area surrounds the 91-mile-long Flaming Gorge Reservoir and 502-foot-high Flaming Gorge Dam. Fishing on reservoir and river (all year), marinas, boat ramps, waterskiing; lodges, campgrounds. River rafting below dam. Visitor centers at dam and Red Canyon (on secondary paved road three miles off Highway 44).

OURAY NATIONAL WILDLIFE REFUGE

Vernal, 30 miles southwest on Highway 88, 435-545-2522; www.fws.gov/ouray

The desert scenery here includes waterfowl nesting marshes. Daily.

RED FLEET STATE PARK

8750 N. Highway 191, Vernal, 435-789-4432;
www.stateparks.utah.gov

This scenic lake is highlighted by red rock formations, and you can see several hundred well-preserved dinosaur tracks. Boating, swimming, fishing; camping. Summer, daily 6 a.m.-10 p.m.; winter, daily 8 a.m.-5 p.m.

HATCH RIVER EXPEDITIONS

55 E. Main St., Vernal, 800-856-8966; www.hatchriverexpeditions.com
Guided white-water trips on the Green and Yampa rivers.

STEINAKER STATE PARK

4335 N. Highway 191, Vernal, 435-789-4432;
www.stateparks.utah.gov

This state park encompasses approximately 2,200 acres on the west shore of Steinaker Reservoir. Swimming, waterskiing, fishing, boating; picnicking, tent and trailer sites. April-November; fishing all year. Summer 6 a.m.-10 p.m. Winter 8 a.m.-5 p.m.

UTAH FIELD HOUSE OF NATURAL HISTORY AND DINOSAUR GARDENS

496 E. Main St., Vernal, 435-789-3799;
www.stateparks.utah.gov

Guarded outside by three life-size cement dinosaurs, this museum has exhibits of fossils, archaeology, life zones, geology and fluorescent minerals of the region. The adjacent Dinosaur Gardens contain 18 life-size model dinosaurs in natural surroundings. Daily 9 a.m.-5 p.m.; Memorial Day-Labor Day 8 a.m.-7 p.m.

WESTERN HERITAGE MUSEUM

28 E. 200 S., Vernal, 435-789-7399; www.co.uintah.ut.us/museum/whMuseum.php
Relive the town's outlaw past at this museum that houses lots of local memorabilia and artifacts of the ancient people of Utah. Memorial Day-Labor Day, Monday-Friday 9 a.m.-6 p.m., Saturday 10 a.m.-4 p.m.; Labor Day-Memorial Day, Monday-Friday 9 a.m.-5 p.m., Saturday 10 a.m.-2 p.m.

HOTELS

★★BEST WESTERN DINOSAUR INN

251 E. Main St., Vernal, 435-789-2660; www.bestwestern.com
60 rooms. Restaurant, bar. Hot tub. Pool. Spa. High-speed Internet access. **$**

★THE SAGE MOTEL

54 W. Main St., Vernal, 800-760-1442; www.vernalmotels.com
26 rooms. Restaurant. Complimentary continental breakfast. Pets accepted. **$**

SPECIALTY LODGINGS

HILLS HOUSE

675 W. 3300 N., Vernal, 435-789-0700
Four rooms. **$**

LANDMARK INN BED AND BREAKFAST

288 E. 100 S., Vernal, 435-781-1800, 888-738-1800; www.landmark-inn.com

10 rooms. Complimentary full breakfast. **$**

RESTAURANT
★7-11 RANCH

77 E. Main St., Vernal, 435-789-1170

American menu. Breakfast, lunch, dinner. Closed Sunday. Children's menu. **$**

WHAT TO SEE AND DO
RIVER RAFTING

Dinosaur National Monument, 435-781-7700; www.nps.gov/dino

Go rafting down the Green and Yampa rivers. Get an advanced permit from National Park Service or with concession-operated guided float trips.

DINOSAUR NATIONAL MONUMENT/UTAH ENTRANCE

On August 17, 1909, paleontologist Earl Douglass discovered dinosaur bones in this area, including several nearly complete skeletons. Since then, this location has revealed more skeletons, skulls and bones of Jurassic-period dinosaurs than any other dig in the world. Utah's Dinosaur Quarry section can be entered from the junction of Highways 40 and 149, north of Jensen, 13 miles east of Vernal. Approximately seven miles north on Highway 149 is the fossil exhibit. Another five miles north is Green River Campground, with 90 tent and trailer sites available mid-May-mid-September. A smaller campground, Rainbow Park, provides a small number of tent sites from May to November. Lodore, Deerlodge and Echo Park campgrounds are available in Colorado.

The dinosaur site comprises only 80 acres of this 325-square-mile park, which lies at the border of Utah and Colorado. The backcountry section, most of which is in Colorado, is a land of fantastic and deeply eroded canyons of the Green and Yampa rivers. Access to this back-country section is via the Harpers Corner Road, starting at monument headquarters on Highway 40, two miles east of Dinosaur, Colorado. At Harpers Corner, the end of this 32-mile surfaced road, a one-mile foot trail leads to a promontory overlooking the Green and Yampa rivers, more than 2,500 feet below. The entire area was named a national monument in 1915.

Some areas of the monument are closed from approximately mid-November-mid-April because of snow.

Information: 4545 E. U.S. 40, Vernal, 435-374-3000; www.nps.gov/dino

ZION NATIONAL PARK

The spectacular canyons and enormous rock formations in this 147,551-acre national park are the result of powerful upheavals of the earth and erosion by flowing water and frost. Considered the grandfather of Utah's national parks, Zion is one of the nation's oldest national parks and one of the state's wildest, with large sections virtually inaccessible. The Virgin River runs through the interior of the park, and Zion Canyon, with its deep, narrow chasm and multicolored vertical walls, cuts through the middle, with smaller canyons branching from it like fingers. A paved roadway following the bottom of Zion Canyon is surrounded by massive rock formations in awe-inspiring colors that change with the light. The formations, described as temples, cathedrals and thrones, rise to great heights, the loftiest reaching 8,726 feet. The canyon road runs seven miles to the Temple of Sinawava, a natural amphitheater surrounded by cliffs. Another route, an extension of Highway 9, cuts through the park in an east-west direction, taking visitors through the mile-long Zion-Mount Carmel Tunnel and then descends through a series of switchbacks with viewpoints above Pine Creek Canyon.

Zion's main visitor center, open daily, is near the south entrance. Check here for maps, information about the park and schedules of naturalist activities and evening programs. Each evening in spring through the fall, park naturalists give illustrated talks on the natural and human history of the area. Pets must be kept on leash and are not permitted on trails. The park is open year-round.

Information: Zion National Park, Springdale, 435-772-3256; www.nps.gov/zion

WHAT TO SEE AND DO
BICYCLING
Zion
Biking is permitted on roads in park, except through Zion-Mt. Carmel Tunnel.

ESCORTED HORSEBACK TRIPS
Zion, 435-772-3967
Special guide service may be obtained for other trips not regularly scheduled. Contact Bryce/Zion Trail Rides at Zion Lodge. March-October, daily.

PARK TRAILS
Zion, 435-772-3256; www.nps.gov/zion
Trails lead to otherwise inaccessible areas: the Narrows (walls of this canyon are 2,000 feet high and as little as 50 feet apart at the stream), the Hanging Gardens of Zion, Weeping Rock, the Emerald Pools. Trails range from half-mile trips to day-long treks, some requiring great stamina. Trails in less-traveled areas should not be undertaken without first obtaining information from a park ranger. Backcountry permits

required for travel through the Virgin River Narrows and other canyons, and on all overnight trips.

ZION NATURE CENTER

Zion, adjacent to South Campground, 435-772-2356; www.nps.gov/zion
Kids between the ages 6-12 can sign up for the junior ranger program. Memorial Day-Labor Day, Monday-Friday.

INDEX

413

Colorado River Indian Tribes Reservation (Parker, AZ), *41*

Colorado River Runs (Avon, CO), *116*

Colorado Rockies (MLB) (Denver, CO), *147*

Colorado School of Mines (Golden, CO), *177*

Colorado Shakespeare Festival (Boulder, CO), *122*

Colorado Ski Museum & Ski Hall of Fame (Vail, CO), *215*

Colorado Springs Balloon Classic (Colorado Springs, CO), *136*

Colorado Springs Fine Arts Center (Colorado Springs, CO), *132*

Colorado Springs Pioneers Museum (Colorado Springs, CO), *132*

Colorado Stampede (Grand Junction, CO), *181*

Colorado State Fair (Pueblo, CO), *202*

Colorado State University (Fort Collins, CO), *172*

Colorado Trails Ranch (Durango, CO), *164*

Colorado's Ocean Journey (Denver, CO), *147*

Comanche Crossing Museum (Denver, CO), *147*

Comfort Inn (Estes Park, CO), *170*

Comfort Inn (Fallon, NV), *228*

Comfort Inn (Farmington, NM), *310*

Comfort Inn (Las Vegas, NM), *315*

Comfort Inn (Logan, UT), *368*

Comfort Inn (Ouray, CO), *199*

Comfort Inn (Payson, UT), *385*

Comfort Inn (Safford, AZ), *59*

Comfort Inn (Silver City, NM), *344*

Comfort Inn (St. George, UT), *403*

Comfort Inn (Taos, NM), *349*

Comfort Inn (Tucumcari, NM), *354*

Comfort Inn Downtown (Denver, CO), *152*

Comfort Inn Santa Fe (Santa Fe, NM), *333*

Comfort Suites Ogden (Ogden, UT), *378*

The Compound Restaurant (Santa Fe, NM), *338*

Coney Island Emporium (Las Vegas, NV), *233*

Connie Mack World Series Baseball Tournament (Farmington, NM), *309*

Cooperage (Albuquerque, NM), *295*

Coors Brewery Tour (Golden, CO), *177*

Copper Manor Motel (Silver City, NM), *344*

The Copper Mill (Logan, UT), *369*

Copper Mountain Resort Ski Area (Dillon, CO), *160*

Copper Queen Hotel (Bisbee, AZ), *12*

CopperWynd Resort and Club (Fountain Hills, AZ), *23*

Coral Pink Sand Dunes State Park (Kanab, UT), *366*

Coronado Café (Phoenix, AZ), *53*

Coronado National Forest (Sierra Vista, AZ), *80*

Coronado National Forest (Tucson, AZ), *90*

Coronado National Memorial (Hereford, AZ), *80*

Coronado State Monument (Bernalillo, NM), *290*

Cosanti Foundation (Paradise Valley, AZ), *60*

Cosmopolitan (Telluride, CO), *215*

Cottonwood Valley (Las Vegas), *233*

Council Hall (Salt Lake City, UT), *391*

Country Bounty (Salida, CO), *205*

The Country Club (Las Vegas, NV), *259*

Country Fair and Livestock Show (Elko, NV), *225*

Country Inn & Suites (Tempe, AZ), *83*

Country Inn & Suites by Carlson (Scottsdale, AZ), *64*

Country Inn & Suites By Carlson (Tucson, AZ), *93*

Country Sunshine Bed & Breakfast (Durango, CO), *164*

Coup des Tartes (Phoenix, AZ), *53*

Courtyard Albuquerque Airport (Albuquerque, NM), *293*

Courtyard Boulder (Boulder, CO), *122*

Courtyard Las Vegas Convention Center (Las Vegas, NV), *247*

Courtyard Provo (Provo, UT), *388*

Courtyard Tucson Airport (Tucson, AZ), *93*

419

★
★
★
★
★

421

★
★
★
☆
☆

429

INDEX

★
★
★
★
☆

Monarch Stables and Wagon Rides (Fraser, CO), *219*

Mondrian Hotel (Scottsdale, AZ), *66*

Montagna (Aspen, CO), *113*

Montauk Seafood Grill (Vail, CO), *218*

Monte Carlo Resort and Casino (Las Vegas, NV), *251*

Monte L. Bean Life Science Museum (Provo, UT), *387*

Monte Vista Crane Festival (Monte Vista, CO), *196*

Monte Vista National Wildlife Refuge (Alamosa, CO), *196*

MonteLago Village (Henderson, NV), *228*

Montezuma County Fair (Cortez, CO), *141*

Monticello Pioneer Days (Monticello, UT), *376*

Montrose County Historical Museum (Montrose, CO), *197*

Monument Course at Troon North Golf Club (Scottsdale, AZ), *61*

Mormon Lake Ski Center (Flagstaff, AZ), *20*

Mormon Miracle Pageant (Manti, UT), *390*

Mormon Tabernacle (Logan, UT), *367*

Mormon Temple (Logan, UT), *367*

Morton's, The Steakhouse (Denver, CO), *158*

Mosaic (Scottsdale, AZ), *72*

Mount Lemmon Ski Valley (Mount Lemmon, AZ), *90*

Mount Nebo Scenic Loop Drive (Payson, UT), *384*

Mount Rose Ski Area (Reno, NV), *275*

Mountain Film Festival (Telluride, CO), *213*

Mountain Man Rendezvous and Festival (Santa Fe, NM), *331*

Mountain Spirit Winery (Salida, CO), *204*

Mule Trips into the Canyon (Grand Canyon, AZ), *27*

Murphy's (Prescott, AZ), *58*

Museum of Archaeology and Material Culture (Cedar Crest, NM), *301*

Museum of Art (Provo, UT), *387*

Museum of Church History and Art (Salt Lake City, UT), *394*

Museum of Fine Arts (Santa Fe, NM), *325*

Museum of Geology and Institute of Meteoritics Meteorite Museum (Albuquerque, NM), *291*

Museum of Indian Arts and Culture (Santa Fe, NM), *326*

Museum of International Folk Art (Santa Fe, NM), *326*

Museum of Northern Arizona (Flagstaff, AZ), *20*

Museum of Northwest Colorado (Craig, CO), *142*

The Museum of Outdoor Arts (Englewood, CO), *167*

Museum of Peoples and Cultures (Provo, UT), *387*

Museum of Spanish Colonial Art (Santa Fe, NM), *326*

Museum of the American Numismatic Association (Colorado Springs, CO), *134*

Museum of Western Colorado (Grand Junction, CO), *180*

Musical Theater Southwest (Albuquerque, NM), *292*

Mystere by Cirque du Soleil (Las Vegas, NV), *240*

Mystery Castle (Phoenix, AZ), *46*

N

National Atomic Museum (Albuquerque, NM), *291*

National Automobile Museum (The Harrah Collection) (Reno, NV), *275*

National Basque Festival (Elko, NV), *226*

National Center for Atmospheric Research (Boulder, CO), *121*

National Championship Air Races (Reno, NV), *277*

National Finals Rodeo (Las Vegas, NV), *246*

National Mining Hall of Fame and Museum (Leadville, CO), *189*

National Radio Astronomy Observatory (Socorro, NM), *344*

National Western Stock Show, Rodeo & Horse Show (Denver, CO), *152*

The Native American Influence (Alamogordo, NM), *288*

433

★ ★ ★ ★ ★

438

INDEX

★
★
★
★
★

439

INDEX

★
★
★
★
★

The Swift Trail (Safford, AZ), *58*

Swiss Chalet Inn (Ruidoso, NM), *322*

Swiss Days (Midway, UT), *369*

Sylvan Dale Guest Ranch (Loveland, CO), *191*

Syzygy (Aspen, CO), *114*

T

T. Cook's (Phoenix, AZ), *54*

T. J. Bummer's (Sterling, CO), *212*

Tabernacle (Brigham City, UT), *359*

Tabernacle (Salt Lake City, UT), *395*

Table Mountain Inn (Golden, CO), *178, 179*

Tableau (Las Vegas, NV), *268*

Tabor Opera House (Leadville, CO), *189*

Tag-A-Long Expeditions (Moab, UT), *372*

Tahoe Biltmore Lodge and Casino (Crystal Bay, NV), *225*

Takah Sushi (Aspen, CO), *114*

Talavera (Scottsdale, AZ), *74*

Taliesin West (Scottsdale, AZ), *62*

Talking Stick Golf Club-South Course (Scottsdale, AZ), *62*

Tall Timber Resort (Durango, CO), *165*

Tamarisk (Green River, UT), *364*

Tamarron Resort (Durango, CO), *165*

Tanger Factory Outlet (Park City, UT), *380*

Tanque Verde Guest Ranch (Tucson, AZ), *95*

Tao (Las Vegas, NV), *268*

Taos Arts Festival (Taos, NM), *349*

Taos Pueblo (Taos, NM), *348*

Taos Pueblo Dances (Albuquerque, NM), *293, 349*

Taos Pueblo Deer or Matachines Dance (Taos, NM), *349*

Taos Rodeo (Taos, NM), *349*

Taos Ski Valley (Taos Ski Valley, NM), *348*

Tarbell's (Phoenix, AZ), *54*

Taste of Vail (Vail, CO), *216*

The Tavern (Aspen, CO), *115*

Taylor Park Reservoir (Gunnison, CO), *185*

Telephone Pioneer Museum (Albuquerque, NM), *292*

Telluride Bluegrass Festival (Telluride, CO), *213*

Telluride Gondola (Telluride), *212*

Telluride Historical Museum (Telluride, CO), *213*

Telluride Ski Resort (Telluride, CO), *213*

Tempe Bicycle Program (Tempe, AZ), *82*

Tempe Festival of the Arts (Tempe, AZ), *83*

Tempe Historical Museum (Tempe, AZ), *82*

Tempe Improvisation Comedy Theatre (Tempe, AZ), *82*

Tempe Mission Palms Hotel (Tempe, AZ), *84*

Tempe Town Lake (Tempe, AZ), *82*

Temple (Salt Lake City, UT), *395*

Temple Hoyne Buell Theater (Denver, CO), *151*

Temple Square (Salt Lake City, UT), *394*

Temple Visitor Center (St. George, UT), *402*

Ten Thousand Waves (Santa Fe, NM), *329*

Tenderfoot Drive (Salida, CO), *204*

Tennessee Pass Cookhouse (Leadville, CO), *190*

Tequila's (Pagosa Springs, CO), *201*

Terrace Dining Room (Scottsdale, AZ), *74*

Territorial Days (Tombstone, AZ), *87*

Territorial House Bed and Breakfast (Sedona, AZ), *78*

Territorial Prescott Days (Prescott, AZ), *57*

Territorial Statehouse State Park (Fillmore, UT), *363*

Tesuque Pueblo Flea Market (Santa Fe, NM), *333*

Tex's Riverways (Moab, UT), *372*

This Is The Place Heritage Park (Salt Lake City, UT), *395*

Thomas & Mack Center (Las Vegas, NV), *244*

Three Rivers Petroglyph Site (Three Rivers, NM), *287*

Thunderbird Lodge (Chinle, AZ), *14*

Thunderbird Lodge (Grand Canyon, AZ), *28*

Titan Missile Museum (Sahuarita, AZ), *91*

Tlaquepaque (Sedona, AZ), *76*

Tohono Chul Park (Tucson, AZ), *91*

445

INDEX

★★★★★

NOTES

NOTES

447

NOTES

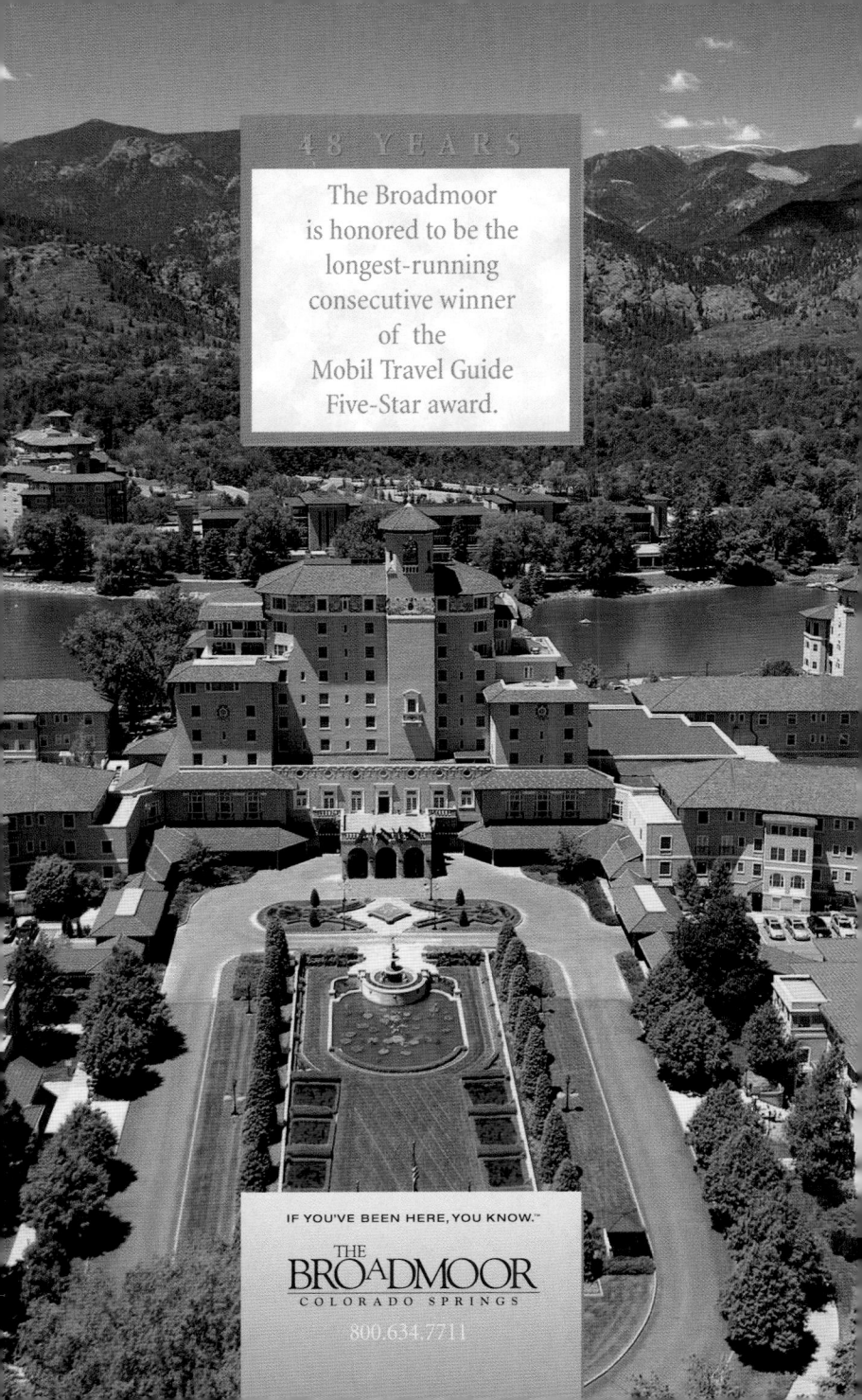

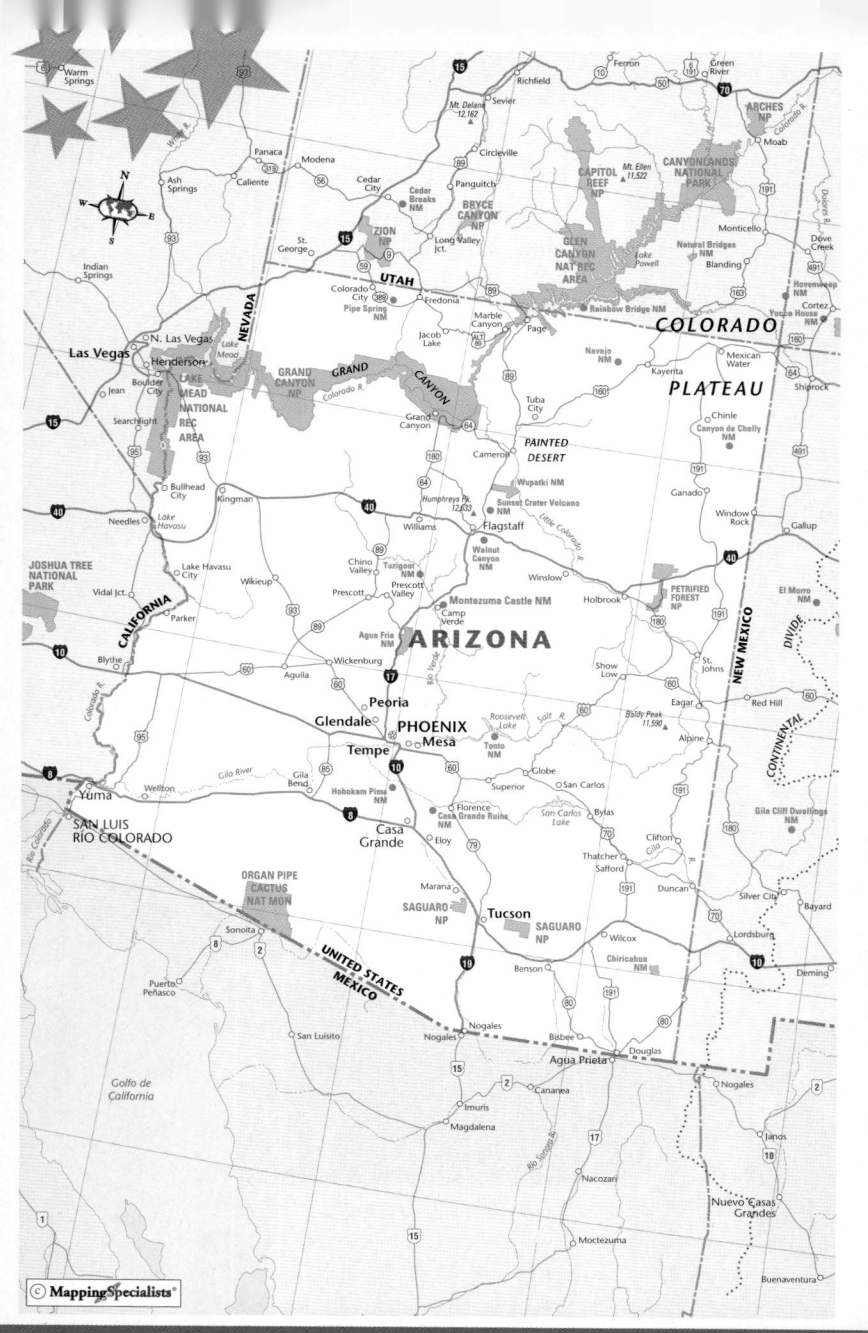

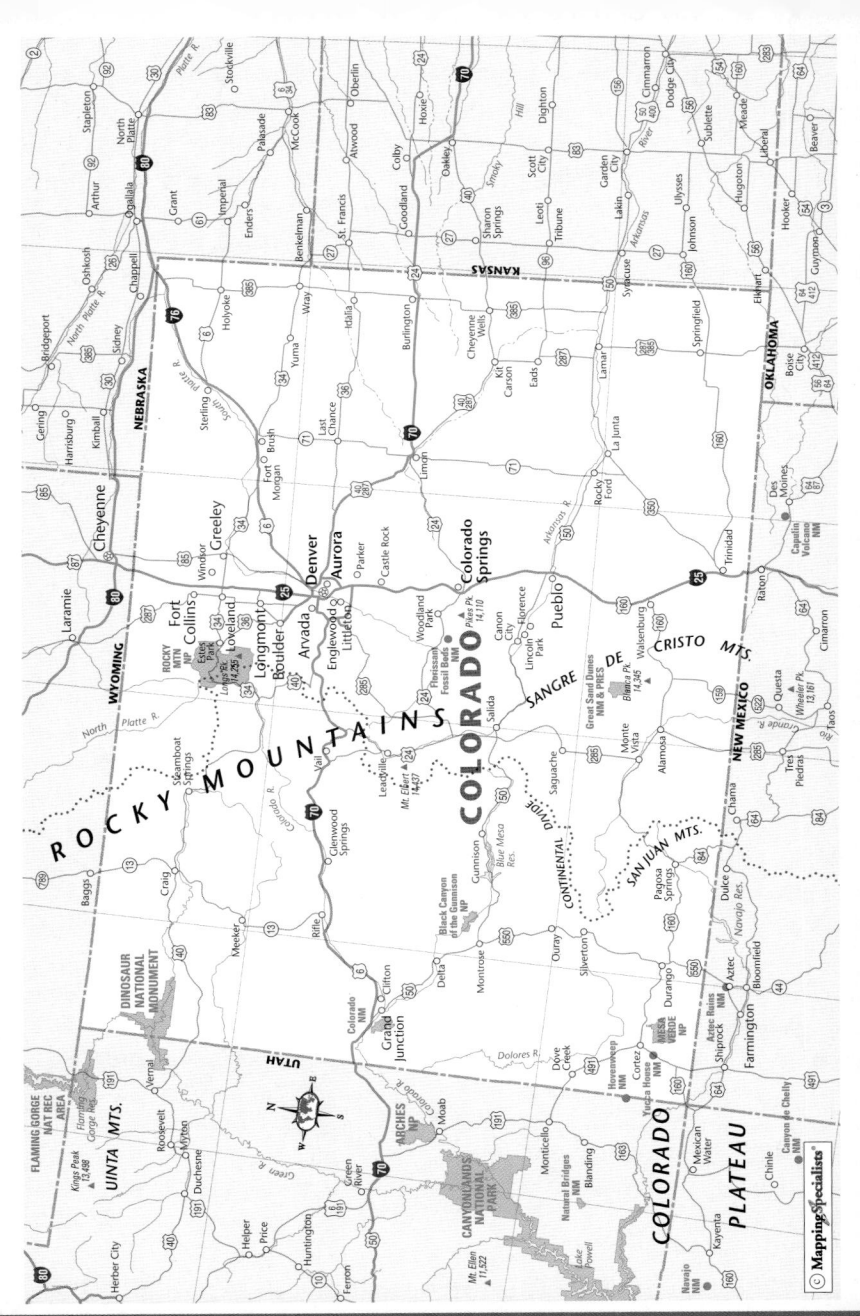

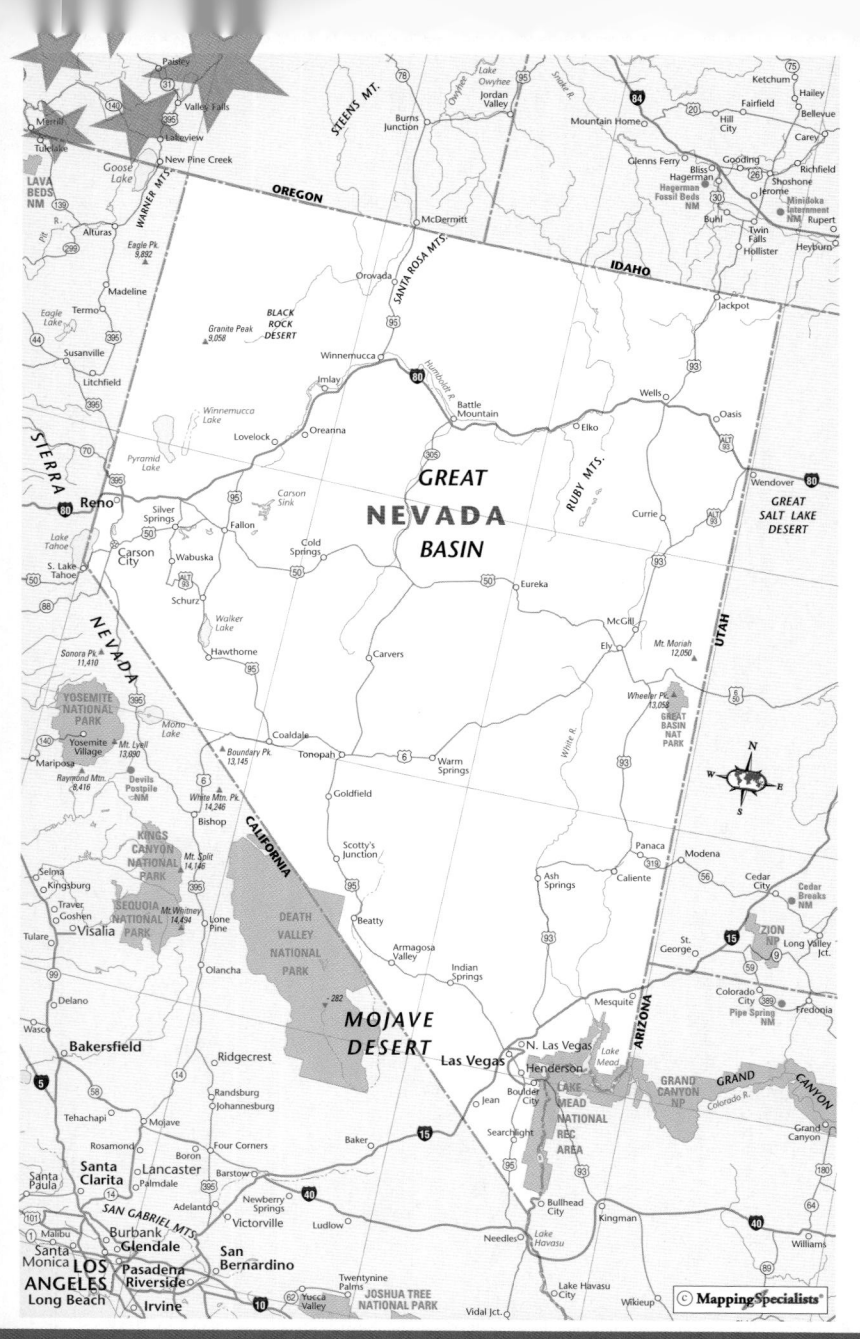

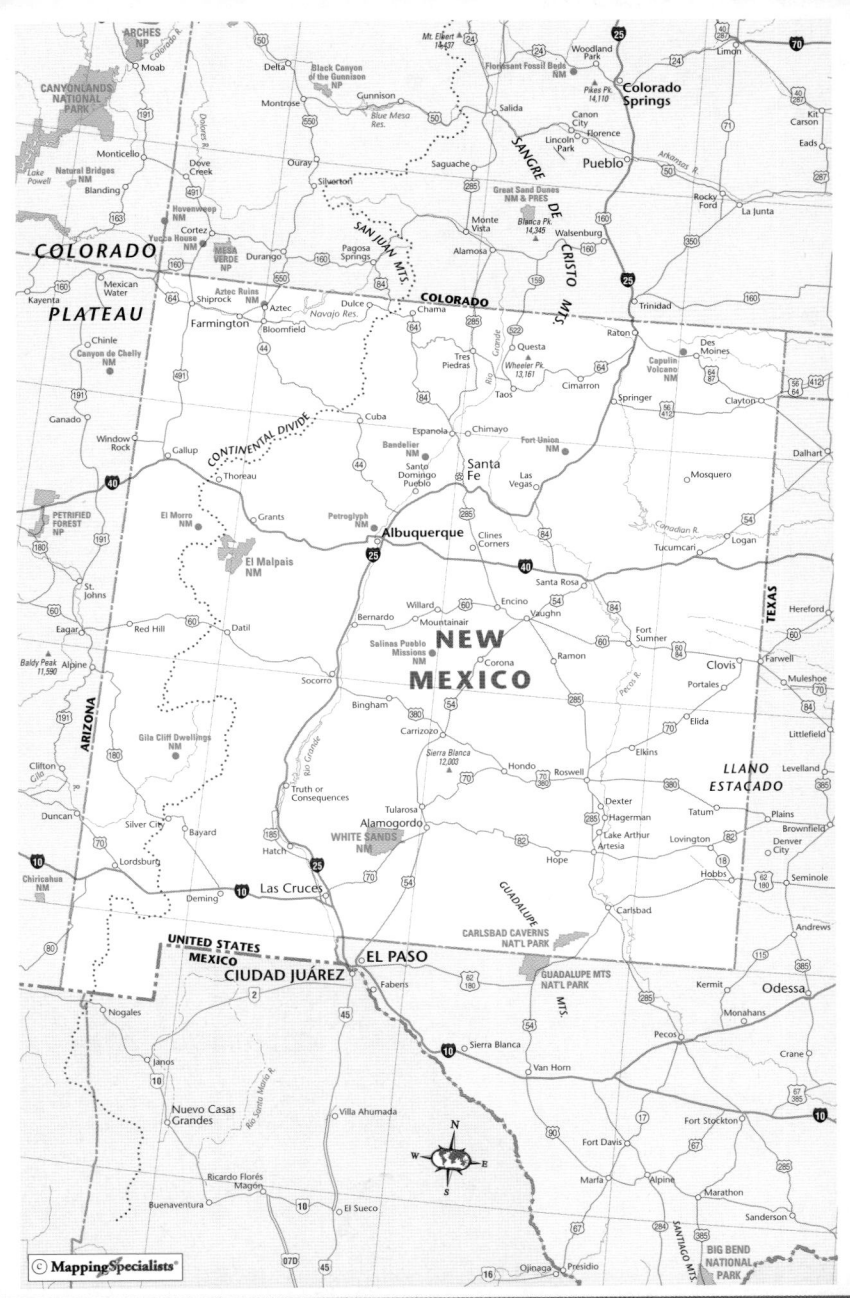

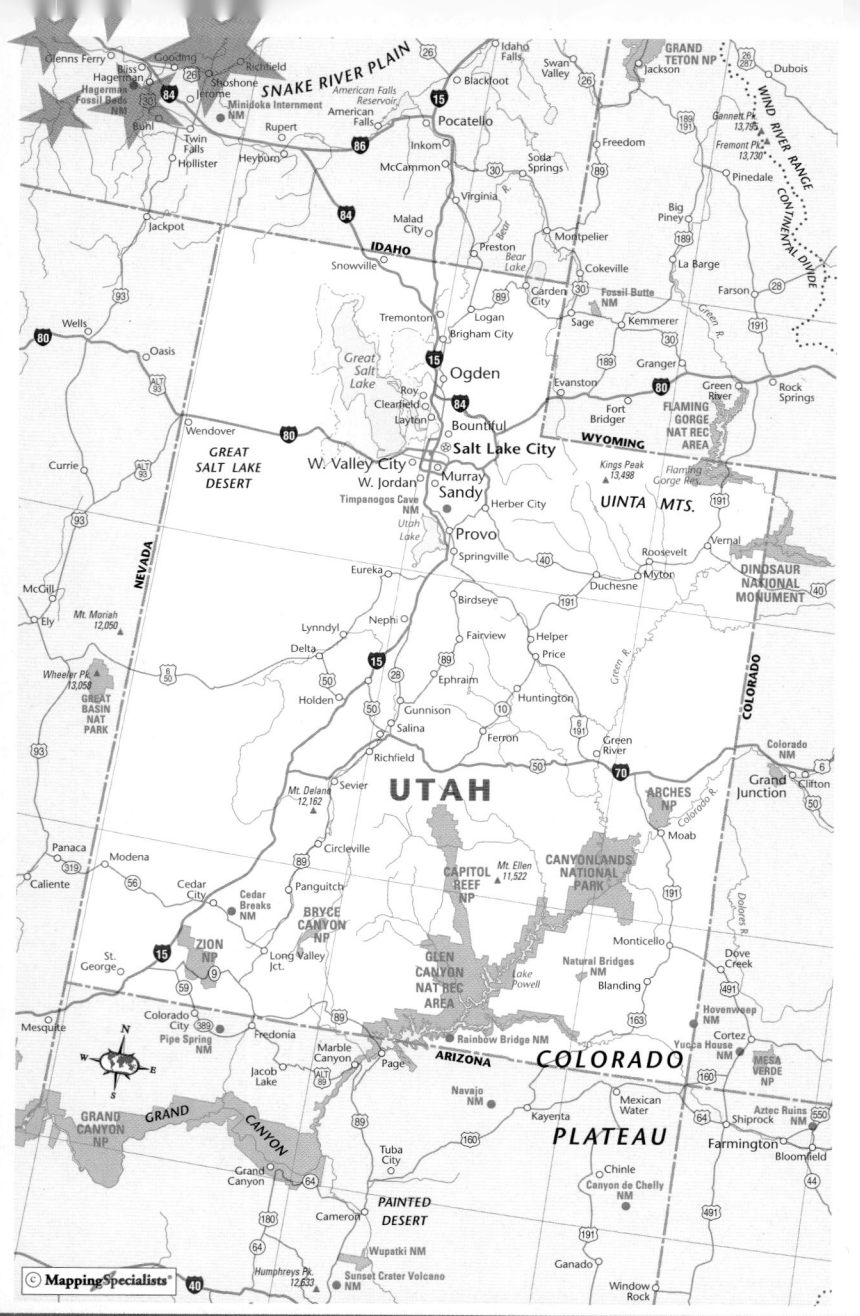

Les Éditions du Boréal
4447, rue Saint-Denis
Montréal (Québec) H2J 2L2
www.editionsboreal.qc.ca

LES DIMANCHES
SONT MORTELS

Francine D'Amour

LES DIMANCHES
SONT MORTELS

roman

Boréal

Les Éditions du Boréal remercient le Conseil des Arts du Canada ainsi que
le ministère du Patrimoine canadien et la SODEC pour leur soutien financier.

Les Éditions du Boréal bénéficient également du Programme de crédit d'impôt
pour l'édition de livres du gouvernement du Québec.

Diffusion au Canada : Dimedia
Diffusion et distribution en Europe : Les Éditions du Seuil

Données de catalogage avant publication (Canada)

D'Amour, Francine

Les dimanches sont mortels

 3e éd.

 (Boréal compact ; 164)

 Éd. originale : [Montréal : Guérin], 1987.

 Publ. à l'origine dans la coll. : Guérin littérature.

 ISBN 2-7646-1338-X

 I. Titre.

PS8557.A496D55	2004	C843'.54	C2004-940856-9
PS9557.A496D55	2004		

À Jean(s)

[…] *je lui versai donc une nouvelle rasade de vin aux reflets de feu. Je lui en apportai et donnai trois fois, et trois fois il but, l'imprudent !*

HOMÈRE, *Ulysse*

MIDI

Elle colle son front contre la vitre embuée. Le froid lui fait du bien. Elle a mal à la tête : la migraine rituelle des dimanches. Le givre dessine des entrelacs, une fine géométrie derrière laquelle le fleuve, paralysé sous une épaisse couche de glace, se devine à peine. Le mois de décembre s'achève.

Elle sera en retard. Elle devrait prévenir. Ou regagner son lit. Si elle sort, le froid risque de lui monter à la tête. Oui, se mettre au lit et dormir jusqu'à minuit. Débrancher le téléphone et laisser s'enfoncer au creux de l'oreiller la tempe endolorie. Abolir ce dimanche et, du coup, effacer tous ceux qui l'ont précédé. Dormir jusqu'au Premier de l'An : un peu moins de deux jours. Une année nouvelle. Mais non, un mirage ! Au-delà, il y a l'hiver qui continue, le culte des dimanches qui se perpétue. Celui-là sera le dernier. D'ailleurs, tout ira bien. Elle a tout prévu.

La tasse de café est posée en équilibre sur le rebord de la fenêtre. Elle avale la dernière gorgée. S'approche du téléphone, décroche le récepteur, allume une cigarette, compose le numéro et, finalement, raccroche.

Elle va à la cuisine se préparer un autre café. La migraine s'installe, localisée sur la droite. Le café fort la soulagera peut-être.

Elle frissonne. Un bain chaud, voilà ce qu'il lui faut avant de partir. Pendant que la baignoire se remplit, elle parcourt rapidement toutes les pièces de la maison, secoue les coussins, remet un disque dans sa pochette, vide un cendrier, ramasse un verre sale, range les livres et les papiers épars en les empilant minutieusement selon un ordre apparemment décroissant quant à la taille et au volume.

Elle allume une cigarette. Regarde attentivement le téléphone. Elle tremble un peu.

L'eau est bouillante. Elle coule. Prendre le temps de se détendre. Rouler un joint ? L'herbe et le papier sont dans la chambre, il faudrait sortir de la baignoire. Si elle mettait à l'essai la technique de Marie-Paule ? Un brin de naïveté, et le tour est joué. Elle rit.

calme de plus en plus calme détendue lourde de plus en plus lourde vous êtes calme   les épaules   laissez tomber les épaules   relâchez la nuque   détendue complètement détendue   vous coulez vous êtes très lourde très lourde   le jour est venu   tu m'attends je ne tarderai plus maintenant   souviens-toi une robe bleu de Chine la mer est calme et je flotte jusque chez toi.

Le café répandu forme une tache brune que le tapis absorbe peu à peu. Étourdie, les pieds rougis, elle s'appuie contre le lavabo. Elle allume une cigarette. Enroulée dans une serviette, elle s'observe avec soin dans le miroir de la pharmacie. L'effet Halcion, ces petites pilules bleues qui font tomber dru le sommeil et décapitent les rêves, se voit à peine : légère buée sous laquelle perce une lueur verte et résolue. Le jour est venu. Elle sort ses griffes, enlève le vernis écaillé. Pas de maquillage aujourd'hui. Pas le temps. Pas envie. Satisfaite, elle sourit. Ses yeux brillent maintenant. Feux verts. Plus qu'à s'habiller, donner un coup de fil, partir.

Sur le lit, Jasmine et Jérômine enlacées forment une sorte de magma félin compact. L'une contre l'autre, l'une sur l'autre, follement éméchées, elles se livrent à des débordements amoureux, tendres morsures, caresses délicates, langues tièdes, qui, peu à peu, se transforment en une lutte acharnée dont Jasmine, la mère, sort une fois de plus victorieuse : souveraine, elle quitte le champ de bataille en se secouant les pattes dédaigneusement. Les vêtements soigneusement disposés sur le lit sont couverts de poils. Elle enfile sa vieille robe bleue à col chinois, cherche la brosse pour la nettoyer, parcourt à nouveau toutes les pièces de la maison, secoue les coussins, vide un cendrier, range les livres et les papiers, découvre la brosse sous une pile de journaux, secoue les coussins, vide… Elle s'arrête.

vous vous sentez calme de plus en plus calme détendue très très calme

Elle allume une cigarette. Tend la main vers le téléphone, hésite, recule. Elle fouille dans son sac : argent, papiers d'identité, clefs de la maison et de la voiture. Surtout ne rien oublier.

Elle revient dans la chambre, attrape son walkman qui traîne sur la commode, ouvre le premier tiroir, en sort une bouteille de rhum Clément, un rhum vieux de la Martinique, l'emballe dans un sac de plastique, met ses bottes, son manteau, ses gants fourrés — il y a la voiture à déneiger —, embrasse les chattes qui, roulées en boule aux deux extrémités du lit, observent une trêve en léchant leurs blessures.

Elle décroche le récepteur, fait le numéro.

— Maman. C'est Mathilde. Oui. Oui. J'arrive. T'inquiète pas. Oui. Un seul apéritif. J'ai compris. Trois onces de scotch, pas plus. Oui. Tu peux partir tranquille. Mais oui j'ai la clef. Un steak oui. De toute façon, il a si peu d'appétit. T'inquiète pas, tout ira bien.

Mais, oui, voyons ! Non, on ne se disputera pas. Je serai patiente. Tu n'as rien à craindre. Amuse-toi, repose-toi, oublie-le. Et fais attention toi aussi. Tu sais très bien ce que je veux dire ! Qu'est-ce que tu dis ? Mais non, je n'ai pas besoin d'argent. J'en ai assez. Oui.

Quoi ? Ça non, pas question ! Même si ça tourne mal, je n'appellerai pas le docteur Patenaude. Je ne peux pas le supporter. Non. Je ne l'ai pas revu depuis ce dimanche, tu sais bien, oui, il y a presque un an, oui, oui, c'était en janvier. Je sais, je sais, c'est son médecin et le tien aussi, mais moi je refuse de parler à ce vieil imbécile.

Écoute, maman, laisse Marie-Paule tranquille ! Je n'ai pas besoin d'elle. Je peux très bien rester seule avec lui. T'inquiète pas, je te dis.   C'est ça, oui, j'arrive bientôt. Évidemment. Toute la soirée s'il le faut. Je ne le laisserai pas seul.

Il dormait. Une sorte de coma prolongé duquel il émergeait périodiquement tel un gros bébé maussade et hargneux. Ce serait bientôt l'heure de la tétée. Elles le savaient, et c'est à voix basse que, réunies toutes trois au salon en ce dimanche de janvier, elles discutaient. Le docteur Patenaude se faisait attendre.

Il y avait longtemps qu'elles avaient perdu le sommeil et qu'elles s'agitaient ainsi, fébriles, à bout de force et d'arguments, pendant que lui dormait. Des années et des années vouées à la survie de ce petit enfer familial : les mêmes gestes cent fois répétés (cacher la clef de la sainte armoire aux liqueurs à laquelle les trois prêtresses, seules, ont accès), la stérile litanie psalmodiée en chœur (« ça ne peut pas continuer comme ça fait attention tu ne penses qu'à ça boire toujours boire tu es malade maman est épuisée »), les larmes vaines, la colère et le désespoir, les supplications et le silence, l'impuissance.

Elles s'observaient mutuellement et s'efforçaient de faire taire la panique qui s'emparait de chacune quand elle reconnaissait sur le visage las des deux autres le masque têtu de la folie raisonnable.

Marie-Paule et Mathilde sont venues en catastrophe, bien décidées à prendre les choses en main. Ça ne peut plus continuer comme ça ! Elles en ont assez de ce nourrisson vorace jamais rassasié. Il est temps de le sevrer avant qu'il ne soit trop tard et qu'il ne les ait toutes trois avalées. Père goule, sangsue obstinée, vampire boulimique (anémique selon le diagnostic médical le plus récent) : il ne se lave plus, ne se rase plus, ne s'habille plus, ne marche plus sans tomber, ne mange presque plus, entend mal, souffre de confusion mentale. Mais il boit encore.

Voilà près de deux heures qu'elles essaient de convaincre leur mère. Explorant les solutions possibles, les éliminant une à une, tournant indéfiniment autour du pot, elles en arrivent au seul aboutissement logique de leur argumentation, à la solution finale qu'elles exposent avec précaution : il faut le placer (les mots ont du mal à passer et forment une boule dure qui étrangle la gorge) dans une maison spécialisée (Marie-Paule en a visité une, très confortable) où on en prendra soin et où on lui rendra visite très souvent (tous les dimanches).

Estelle disparaît dans son fauteuil. Elle a froid. Maudit soit le sort qui la condamne à passer encore un hiver dans la neige ! Partir. Loin d'ici. Hawaii, la Floride. Prendre le soleil. Marcher sur la plage. Elle l'a bien mérité.

Laisser la mer bercer ses pauvres oreilles dont le bourdonnement tenace la fait tellement souffrir. L'acupuncture et les massages, vivement recommandés par Marie-Paule, n'en viennent pas à bout.

C'est lui qui la retient ici, prisonnière et geôlière. Fatiguée. Elle est fatiguée. Remettre son sort entre les mains de ses filles. S'abandonner. L'abandonner. Fuir. Oh! bien sûr, elle se permet, ici et là, quelques petites escapades : une fin de semaine à Québec, quatre jours à La Malbaie, une semaine à Boston, un mois dans le New Jersey avec Marie-Paule et Jean-Louis.

Et tous les après-midi, même quand il neige, elle sort. Elle court à travers la ville — il y a toujours des courses à faire, Dieu merci! Elle court, éperdue, à bout de souffle, à la recherche d'une oasis où s'allonger enfin, loin de l'alcool, de la merde et des vomissures.

La Floride! Estelle pense à son père, si élégant, se promenant à pas mesurés à l'ombre des palmiers royaux, le regard clair sous le panama, la fleur à la boutonnière, le dos bien droit, une main posée négligemment sur le pommeau d'ivoire de sa canne, saluant au passage de vieux amis.

Elle entend cracher : il vient sans doute de se réveiller. Se lever, aller voir s'il a besoin d'elle. Elle n'en a pas la force. De toute façon, il n'hésitera pas à le lui faire savoir impérieusement. Il dépend entièrement d'elle. Elle a fait de son mieux pourtant. Mais ils en sont là. Et voilà que Marie-Paule et Mathilde la pressent de s'en défaire. Le confier à d'autres? Seront-ils plus habiles? Et qu'est-ce que les gens vont dire ? Estelle Dalpé abandonne son mari, son vieux mari malade ! Aurait-elle oublié sa mère, impotente pendant plus de quinze ans, capricieuse, prompte à s'emporter, mais dorlotée jusqu'à sa mort par un mari attentionné ? Évidemment, à l'époque, tout était plus facile. Une bonne et une infirmière se partageaient les soins à donner. Des années fastes. La main-d'œuvre à bon marché. Et c'est ainsi que ses parents avaient vieilli ensemble tous les deux, heureux, encore amoureux. Ils le paraissaient du moins.

Charles n'aime rien tant que s'attaquer à eux. Il les accable de défauts imaginaires. On dirait qu'il prend plaisir à déformer ses plus chers souvenirs et à la faire pleurer. Par exemple, il prétend que son beau-père, qui l'a bien aidé pourtant (un prêt considérable, et sans intérêt), cachait mal son mépris pour ses origines campagnardes. Il dit n'importe quoi. Elle n'aurait jamais dû l'épouser. Papa le lui avait bien dit.

Il crache encore. Il va bientôt vouloir se lever. Qu'est-ce qu'elles vont lui dire ? Il n'acceptera jamais. Il lui en voudra, la soupçonnera d'avoir dressé ses filles contre lui, et ce sera pire encore. Il fera semblant de ne pas entendre, de ne pas comprendre, ou il ne comprendra pas réellement. Depuis quelques jours, il ne tient que des propos confus.

Elle est fatiguée, tellement fatiguée qu'elle ne va pas tarder à mourir. C'est elle qui mourra la première. Elle mourra ici, dans cette maison qui sent le scotch et la vieillesse et qui lui fait les jambes molles dès qu'elle y pénètre, au retour de ses courses folles à travers Montréal et ses magasins. Elle regarde ses mains ridées desquelles le sang semble s'être retiré. Elle a envie de pleurer.

Mal à l'aise, Marie-Paule dévisage sa mère. Cette mère qui l'exaspère et à qui elle ressemble tant. Elle voit sa lèvre inférieure trembler. Non, elle ne va pas encore se mettre à pleurer ! Elle est malade. Ou plutôt elle se croit malade. Mais elle n'est que fatiguée. Incapable de se contrôler. Toujours à se lamenter sur son sort. Comme si elle avait le monopole du troisième âge et du malheur conjugal ! Les autres ont souvent à peine de quoi se nourrir convenablement et, elle, elle réclame la Floride comme son dû. Pauvre maman ! Comment lui venir en aide ? En convainquant le docteur Patenaude de placer son patient dans une institution spécialisée ? Mais réussira-t-elle à se débrouiller sans son mari ? Sera-t-elle capable de meubler sa solitude ? À son âge, il n'est pas si facile de changer ses habitudes.

Marie-Paule n'a que vingt-huit ans, mais elle en sait déjà quelque chose. Depuis qu'il a fait la connaissance d'une certaine Annie, Jean-Louis la néglige. Elle passe des soirées entières à se morfondre en l'attendant. À l'en croire, cette fille ne serait rien de plus qu'une copine — une copine « géniale », qui fait du cinéma. Derrière la caméra évidemment. Jean-Louis n'a que faire des aspirantes starlettes ! La géniale Annie tourne un film de politique-fiction. Quelque chose qui tient à la fois du documentaire, du récit traditionnel et du journal intime.

« Tout à fait actuel ! » s'émerveille Jean-Louis, chaque fois qu'il relit le scénario.

En entendant son père tousser, Marie-Paule se ressaisit. Elle regarde sa mère qui se mouche et sa sœur qui allume une cigarette. Elle a les larmes aux yeux, mais elle prend une profonde respiration (abdominale) et se lève en disant qu'elle va voir si son père est réveillé. Jean-Louis et le docteur Patenaude ne devraient plus tarder.

Mathilde se ronge les ongles. Elle observe sa mère à la dérobée. Depuis que Marie-Paule s'est éloignée, elle n'a plus qu'une envie : se lever d'un bond, prendre sa mère dans ses bras, la bercer indéfiniment, lécher ses blessures, lui raconter une histoire, lui chanter une chanson douce jusqu'à ce qu'elle s'endorme. S'enfuir avec elle. Partir au bout du monde. Qu'ils se débrouillent seuls ! Jusqu'à la fin, jusqu'à ce que son père consente enfin à mourir. Quand elle a évoqué sa mort tout à l'heure, dans le style pourtant indirect des relations familiales, Marie-Paule l'a fait taire d'un regard impérieux. Ça va, elle a compris, elle n'en parlera plus. Plus rien à dire. Tout a déjà été dit.

Elle allume une cigarette et ferme les yeux. Rêver. Échapper au cauchemar dominical. Fuir. L'enlever de gré ou de force. De force. Un rapt. Lui bander les yeux jusqu'à ce qu'elle oublie. La coucher sur un lit de sable, s'y enfouir avec elle et attendre, sans mot dire, que les vagues viennent mourir à leurs pieds enlacés.

Elle se rappelle son grand-père maternel, un jour

d'automne il y a bien longtemps, jouant à l'enterrer sous une mer de feuilles mortes, et elle, muette, immobile, respirant à peine, fiévreuse et ravie comme une amoureuse, pendant que ses parents et sa sœur font mine de la chercher partout, inquiets de sa disparition, sous l'œil complice du vieil homme qui multiplie les fausses pistes.

Elle sursaute. Elle ne supporte plus cette toux, cette façon qu'il a de se racler la gorge, ce corps qui fermente dans son lit et qu'elle n'approche plus qu'avec répugnance.

Elle se lève, regarde par la fenêtre le jardin qui étouffe sous la neige. Se taire. Attendre. Elle se tient immobile, une main sur la tempe. C'est dimanche, elle a mal à la tête. La démarche qu'elle entendait mener à bien, cet après-midi, avec l'aide de Marie-Paule, est vouée à l'échec. C'est sûr. Seule la mort viendra les délivrer de cet homme qui pèse sur leur vie de tout son poids et les presse comme des citrons amers.

Cesser de s'exalter ainsi. Voilà ce que dirait Marie-Paule. La décision finale appartient à sa mère. Elle se tourne vers elle. La berce des yeux. Suffit ! Apprendre à se contrôler, agir avec calme et efficacité, ranger au magasin des accessoires ce destin tragique qu'elle s'attribue volontiers et revenir tranquillement sur terre prendre rendez-vous avec le docteur Patenaude. C'est ce que Marie-Paule a fait dès son arrivée. Tout de suite, sans perdre de temps à se répandre en jérémiades et colères inutiles, elle a pris le téléphone, a réussi à parler au médecin, à lui exposer rapidement l'état des choses, le gâchis, jusqu'à ce qu'il accepte de venir faire une visite à domicile ce dimanche après-midi, à l'heure de la télédiffusion du match de hockey Canada-U.R.S.S. Un exploit de plus qui s'ajoute à l'interminable liste de ses actes de bravoure et d'abnégation filiale. Alors qu'elle, Mathilde, se démène en vain, frénétique, montée sur ses grands chevaux du dimanche, clamant sa fureur, mêlant les prières aux imprécations. Quelle sottise ! Sans recommandation médicale, le projet n'aboutira certainement pas. Les établissements qui accueillent les personnes âgées, ces mouroirs pudiquement baptisés « manoirs », sont très sélectifs. Les alcooliques irrécupérables comme son père, même suffisamment fortunés pour payer la pension fabuleuse qu'on exige, sont facilement rejetés. On leur préfère ces bons vieillards qui savent attendre la mort avec élégance en jouant au bridge. Bien que ce soit elle qui ait la première prononcé les mots fatidiques — « le placer », oui, une bonne fois pour toutes —, la réalisation matérielle du projet, son exécution plutôt dépend entièrement des initiatives de sa sœur aînée.

Elle attend ce médecin qui n'arrive pas. La vitre est glacée. Le froid engourdit son front douloureux. Le jardin a cessé de respirer. Les peupliers de Lombardie, ces vieux arbres malades qu'elle déteste, reposent immobiles. Le ciel est pétrifié. Elle regarde le cabanon dont le toit défoncé disparaît sous la neige. On y rangeait autrefois les pelles et les outils de jardinage. Il ne sert plus à rien, des ouvriers italiens se chargent maintenant de l'entretien. Son père ne s'intéresse plus au jardin, pas même aux peupliers qu'il prétendait pourtant avoir plantés lui-même. Il ne s'intéresse plus à rien. Il boit.

Elle a treize ans. Lui, son œil valide courroucé (l'autre bandé depuis son opération), un verre de scotch à la main, profère solennellement sa menace favorite : « Je vais te placer, moi, ma petite, une bonne fois pour toutes ! » La « placer », la dompter, lui interdire formellement l'accès à ce cabanon où, le dimanche, elle s'enferme à clef avec les garçons du voisinage. Ils s'allongent sur elle. C'est chaud. Une pelisse. Quand il n'y a personne à la maison, elle emprunte la pelisse de maman. Nue sous le poil soyeux. Il a caché, bien sûr, la clef du cabanon mais jamais il n'est parvenu à la « placer ». Elle sourit : l'ironie du sort — et du lexique — est décidément impitoyable. Elle a grandi depuis, rebelle et se mesurant à lui avec une égale férocité. Maintenant, il est vieux et malade. Sa main tremble autour de ses verres de scotch. Elle allume une autre cigarette.

Marie-Paule revient s'asseoir au salon. Elle dit que son père ne veut pas se lever, qu'il n'en a pas la force, qu'il se plaint de douleurs au ventre.

On sonne à la porte. Le docteur Patenaude sans doute. Ce n'est que Jean-Louis. Il apporte la tradition-nelle bouteille de vin rouge qui accompagne obligatoire-ment l'inévitable gigot, et les embrasse toutes les trois. Estelle se lève, rajuste sa robe et ses cheveux, s'efforce de faire bonne figure devant ce gendre qui l'intimide depuis qu'il est devenu impossible de lui cacher son déshonneur conjugal. Elle constate avec effroi qu'il est plus de cinq heures et court à la cuisine.

Mathilde voudrait parler à Jean-Louis. S'il allait s'opposer à la solution envisagée ? Sans doute n'interviendra-t-il pas : il se retranchera dans une indifférence simulée. Pour l'instant, c'est Marie-Paule qui l'accapare en l'interrogeant, mine de rien, sur les raisons de son arrivée tardive.

On entend un fracas de vaisselle cassée. Estelle sort de la cuisine et fond en larmes. Mathilde se précipite vers elle, l'aide à s'asseoir, décrète qu'il est complètement ridicule de manger en de telles circonstances, que d'ailleurs personne n'a faim et que sa mère est épuisée. Marie-Paule répond qu'il faut garder son calme, qu'elles sont toutes épuisées, que ça n'est pas le moment de jeûner et que Jean-Louis va s'occuper du repas. Elles se regardent, hargneuses, n'osant s'affronter davantage devant leur mère qui, effondrée, se reproche amèrement son indignité : Estelle Dalpé ne sait plus recevoir !

Jean-Louis se réfugie dans la cuisine. Réparer les pots cassés, il en a l'habitude. Il met le gigot au four. Le gigot ! Chez lui, le dimanche soir, on a toujours mangé du bœuf, parfois de la dinde, de l'agneau jamais : « Ça goûte la laine », soutient son père. Sa « belle »-famille est tout entière névrosée, Marie-Paule la première.

Mathilde pousse la porte, se plante devant lui et le dévisage de ses yeux railleurs. Elle lui demande de préparer des apéritifs pendant qu'elle terminera de vider le lave-vaisselle : comme ça, Marie-Paule ne pourra pas l'accuser de se croiser les bras. Il la gratifie d'un petit sourire complice et la quitte en faisant remarquer que ce repas du dimanche promet d'être comme les autres. Elle hausse les épaules.

Le docteur Patenaude est enfin arrivé. C'est un vieil ami de la famille qui ne pratique presque plus. Jean-Louis lui offre un apéritif.

Abandonnant aussitôt ses activités ménagères, Mathilde s'empresse de tracer un portrait détaillé de la situation. Son père est vraiment très malade, sénile, incurable. Récemment, il ne l'a même pas reconnue, il la confond de plus en plus souvent avec Marie-Paule. Il harcèle sa mère, il la menace : l'autre jour, il a tenté de la frapper avec sa canne. Son caractère, déjà peu accommodant, s'aigrit de plus en plus. Il exige maintenant des soins constants que sa mère n'est plus en mesure de lui donner. Hier encore, elle a fait une mauvaise chute en s'efforçant de le hisser hors d'un fauteuil. Il faut le placer dans une institution. C'est la seule solution possible.

Mathilde exagère un peu, dit Marie-Paule. Estelle ne dit rien. Le docteur Patenaude la terrifie. Elle n'ose affronter son regard qui stigmatise son incompétence. Non, elle n'est pas une bonne épouse, tendre, dévouée. Elle est au contraire maladroite et peu patiente.

Marie-Paule croit que son père vient de s'éveiller. Elle va voir. Le docteur s'intéresse maintenant à Jean-Louis qu'il n'avait jamais rencontré. Il l'interroge sur son métier. Jean-Louis répond poliment, puis se lève en expliquant qu'il doit aller arroser le gigot. Le docteur affirme que les temps ont bien changé et que les jeunes gens d'aujourd'hui ne dédaignent point de mettre la main à la pâte. Lui-même, l'été, il aime bien cuisiner, faire cuire des steaks sur le gril, cela le détend. Tiens donc! il allait oublier de raconter à Estelle les péripéties de son récent voyage au Japon. Mathilde allume une cigarette. Elle est exaspérée, elle aurait envie de bâillonner ce vieux bavard qu'elle imagine sortant du bain, ses chairs flasques pendant hors de son kimono.

Marie-Paule appelle Jean-Louis. Elle a besoin de lui.

Charles Dalpé fait une entrée remarquée. Dès qu'il apparaît aux portes du salon, soutenu par sa fille et son gendre, le docteur Patenaude se tait. Estelle lui cède son fauteuil, le plus confortable. On l'y installe. Mathilde évite de le regarder. Ses yeux vitreux, ses joues où pousse une barbe malingre, son cou où saillent les os, son corps décharné malgré le ventre proéminent qui pointe avec indécence, tout en lui la révulse. Le docteur lui demande comment il va. « Bien sûr, on ne rajeunit pas », répond-il en se raclant la gorge. Estelle est un peu fatiguée ces temps-ci mais lui, somme toute, se porte assez bien en dépit de cette douleur lancinante à l'estomac. Une quinte de toux met fin à ce laborieux discours. Épuisé, il se tait. Les trois femmes sont stupéfaites. Il y a des semaines qu'elles ne l'ont pas entendu parler ainsi, avec une élocution un peu difficile certes, mais sans qu'on puisse y déceler le moindre signe de confusion mentale. Jean-Louis ne peut se défendre de lui jeter, à l'insu de Marie-Paule, un bref regard admiratif. Le docteur enchaîne en évoquant de vieux souvenirs de collège. Historien, Charles Dalpé possède depuis toujours une mémoire prodigieuse. Il est devenu incapable de se souvenir de ce qu'il a fait la veille, il oublie tout ce qu'on lui dit, il oblige tout le monde à se répéter, mais c'est sans hésiter qu'il retrouve maintenant le nom de camarades qu'il n'a pas revus depuis presque cinquante ans.

Mathilde se mord les lèvres pour ne pas crier. Elle en a assez de cette réunion mondaine qui n'en finit plus. Son père participe du mieux qu'il peut à la conversation. Elle a remarqué qu'il ne quitte pas des yeux les verres que Jean-Louis vient de remplir à nouveau. Exceptionnelle-ment, il ne demande pas à boire. Mathilde est sidérée devant l'audace de la ruse paternelle.

Le docteur, sans même l'examiner, prescrit un lave-ment qui, dit-il, soulagera un peu son patient. Estelle le lui donnera, lui, il a perdu la main et d'ailleurs rien ne presse, demain matin il enverra une petite infirmière. Il félicite son ami Charles qui, malgré les innombrables interventions chirurgicales qu'il a subies sous anesthésie générale chaque fois, demeure solide comme un chêne et vivra au moins jusqu'à cent ans. Mathilde avale d'un coup le bloody mary qu'elle sirotait distraitement entre deux cigarettes. Elle s'étouffe, Jean-Louis a encore mis trop de Tabasco.

Charles déclare qu'il est fatigué et qu'il a décidé de retourner au lit. Il se lève en vacillant, manque de tomber. Jean-Louis se précipite et le raccompagne à sa chambre.

Le docteur tient à rassurer Estelle et ses filles. Charles n'est pas du tout sénile. Bien entendu, un bref séjour à l'hôpital ne lui ferait pas de mal. Il termine son verre et ouvre sa mallette. Il en sort une poignée de sédatifs, légers précise-t-il, qu'il distribue généreusement à la ronde : elles ont toutes besoin de repos. Marie-Paule déclare que sa mère et sa sœur sont déjà suffisamment intoxiquées comme ça ; quant à elle, elle ne se soigne plus que par homéopathie. Mathilde a reconnu les pilules bleues qui enterrent les dimanches dans l'oubli et tend une main avide. Estelle fouille dans son sac, elle cherche la carte qui permettra au bon docteur de toucher ses honoraires.

Promettant de faire les démarches nécessaires pour l'entrée de Charles à l'hôpital, le docteur Patenaude s'en va. Mathilde tente de le retenir, elle insiste, répète qu'il faut faire vite : sa mère est à bout. Elle crie presque, met en doute la compétence professionnelle du médecin, réprime difficilement son désir de l'injurier encore plus grossièrement. Sans paraître s'en formaliser, il répond, sur ce ton pontifiant qu'elle exècre, que ce n'est pas facile pour Estelle, il le reconnaît, mais qu'après tout elle n'est pas seule, elle a la chance d'avoir deux filles dont le devoir est de lui venir en aide. Mathilde, médusée devant cette manifestation sereine de l'outrecuidance masculine, lui tend son manteau. Elle est tout simplement folle de rage. Elle étranglerait ce vieil ours gâteux, engoncé dans sa fourrure, et qui s'en va maintenant, pressé de retrouver sa confortable tanière où l'attendent sa télévision, sa tarte au sucre du dimanche, sa femme et ses grands enfants, un garçon et une fille, qui étudient tous les deux la médecine comme papa.

Jean-Louis, qui s'affaire dans la cuisine où il s'est tenu discrètement à l'écart de l'affrontement final, annonce que le repas est servi. Évidemment, le gigot est beaucoup trop cuit. Peu importe, personne ne mange avec appétit. N'osant pas vraiment s'avouer qu'elle est soulagée par le verdict médical, Marie-Paule s'accorde ce soir un verre de vin qui s'ajoute à ses deux précédents apéritifs — une fois n'est pas coutume. Mathilde partage le reste de la bouteille avec Jean-Louis. Elle sait que son projet vient d'avorter définitivement. Sans la caution du médecin, sa mère ne bougera pas. Après l'hôpital, tout redeviendra du pareil au même et, progressivement, la situation se détériorera. Elle regarde sa mère qui mange du bout des lèvres cette viande qui a perdu tout son sang. Estelle fait ses excuses à Jean-Louis : dimanche prochain, quand elle reviendra de sa visite à l'hôpital, elle préparera elle-même un repas convenable. Charles, qui a trop dormi aujourd'hui, lui fera sans doute passer une nuit blanche, mais, si le docteur Patenaude est efficace, son mari entrera demain à l'hôpital et elle pourra enfin se reposer.

Marie-Paule propose de rester à coucher. Jean-Louis dit qu'il doit partir : il a une réunion ce soir. Mathilde quitte la table. Estelle la suit au salon, pendant que Marie-Paule, pendue au cou de Jean-Louis, l'embrasse comme si elle n'allait plus jamais le revoir.

La mère et sa fille n'ont rien à se dire. Mathilde met son manteau. Elle presse sa joue contre le col de renard blanc et adresse à sa mère un dernier regard où se lisent, confondues, la déception, la rancœur et la pitié. Estelle lui demande timidement si elle aime son manteau, un cadeau de Noël, s'il est assez chaud, si elle a besoin d'argent pour payer le notaire. Mathilde répond qu'elle n'a pas encore reçu le compte. Sa mère les aide, elle et son amie Josée, à financer une boutique de vêtements. Elle n'ose pas avouer, pas plus à l'une qu'à l'autre, que le projet a déjà cessé de l'intéresser. Elle enlève son manteau. Elle partira un peu plus tard. Estelle sort son carnet de chèques et, soudainement enthousiaste, elle se met à l'interroger sur l'état des travaux en cours.

Marie-Paule, que cette conversation irrite, feuillette une revue. De toute façon, cette entreprise est vouée à une faillite certaine, si jamais elle voit le jour.

Estelle et Mathilde ont vite fait le tour du sujet. Le silence se rétablit. On entend tousser. Marie-Paule sursaute. Sa mère se lève. Elles vont voir s'il est éveillé, disent-elles en même temps. Elles se sourient.

Il dort encore. Les trois femmes veillent au salon. Les verres sont sales et les cendriers pleins. Demain, la femme de ménage viendra et tout rentrera dans l'ordre.

Marie-Paule écrit dans le petit carnet fleuri qu'elle traîne partout avec elle. C'est une habitude qu'elle a prise et qui agace sa sœur. Estelle range son carnet de chèques. Mathilde fume, les yeux rivés sur sa mère. Elle rêve.

Les trois femmes veillent, pareilles à des survivantes qui, tard dans la nuit, s'endormiront enfin, vaincues par les pilules bleues du docteur Patenaude.

maman t'endormir maman en te me berçant   ton nom
comme une longue plainte une berceuse   te prendre en
moi t'emporter te cacher loin au bout du monde là où il ne
viendra pas   une cave nue et nous nous tenons serrées
l'une contre l'autre enlacées l'une sur l'autre soudées follement éméchées   nous sommes malades   tu es malade
maman tu es vieille épuisée défaite sous ton maquillage
de scène   tu joues les héroïnes les martyres et de toutes tes
forces tu attends que le rideau tombe tu prends sur toi je
prends sur moi nous prenons sur nous nous savons émerger
de la torpeur bleu Halcion   et vite nous fuyons vite nous
faisons des affaires nous téléphonons à des notaires nous
oublions l'inoubliable nous nous sentons déjà mieux nous
ne savons plus où donner de la tête   tu as peur la peur de
faillir mais tu tiens bon oh ! de plus en plus mal tu le sais
mais tu mourras à la tâche s'il le faut   jusqu'à la fin tu dis-
penseras sans compter ton temps ton amour et ta haine
tu régneras tu exerceras sur lui un contrôle continuel   ce
pouvoir dérisoire tu as peur maman tu as peur qu'on te
l'enlève   c'est ta raison de vivre qui te retient fidèle à ses

côtés jusqu'à en perdre la raison   je ne veux plus   crois-
moi je ne veux plus encenser ton courage te plaindre joindre
ma voix au chœur des lamentations   crois-moi je ne veux
plus ça me tue   je ne supporte plus de te voir le supporter
        oh ! t'offrir sa mort tant rêvée car c'est tout ce que je peux
encore t'offrir   sa mort que victime tour à tour consen-
tante et récalcitrante il t'arrive d'implorer dans le secret de
tes nuits de veille   t'offrir sa mort comme tu me donnes ton
argent   quelle pitié maman

TREIZE HEURES

Elle tape du pied et secoue désespérément les mains. Bien entendu, la voiture refuse de démarrer. Il fait moins vingt-cinq. Pas un nuage. Le ciel est bleu cru, un bleu ironiquement méditerranéen, et la neige si blanche qu'elle fait mal aux yeux. L'air sec pince les narines et brûle les poumons. Elle tousse, cherche une cigarette dans son sac.

Jasmine et Jérômine, assises sur le rebord de la fenêtre qui surplombe le radiateur, l'observent, narquoises. La fille se tient prudemment à l'écart de la mère. Elles s'étirent avec volupté, bâillent, agitent leurs oreilles, font des mines et des sourires de « pachattes » confortables et bien nourries. Puis, brusquement, elles mettent fin à ce duo de pantomime réglé avec une remarquable précision et, d'un double bond, elles quittent la fenêtre. Le labrador noir, cette bête énorme et maudite qui hélas ! habite le voisinage, vient de jaillir comme un diable hors de sa cour.

Un vrai temps de chien ! Ses doigts paralysés n'arrivent même pas à tenir la cigarette, encore moins à l'allumer. Rageuse, elle la jette par terre et la piétine. Le labrador s'approche. Elle se précipite dans la voiture, le cœur battant et les mains moites. Du coup, elle parvient enfin à allumer une cigarette. Et, miraculeusement, la voiture consent à démarrer. Le chien la poursuit en aboyant. Elle déteste cet animal sinistre qui répand la terreur dans le monde félin.

Elle conduit à l'aveuglette. Les vitres sont gelées et le dégivreur automatique met du temps à agir. Heureusement, les routes sont désertes : les promeneurs du dimanche ont préféré rester au chaud devant leurs jeux vidéo. Le volant est glacé ; cette voiture est un vrai tombeau, ses doigts sont déjà morts. Le chauffage ne fonctionne pas, du moins pas encore.

Elle tremble, elle a mal à la tête. Un grand frisson la secoue tout entière. Elle boirait bien une gorgée de ce rhum Clément qui attend sur la banquette arrière que son heure soit venue, rien qu'une petite gorgée, un petit coup de soleil de la Martinique qui ferait se déplier les doigts, se dilater la poitrine et fondre le corps entier.

Pas question ! Cette bouteille de rhum est le cadeau de Noël qu'elle apporte, avec quelques jours de retard, à son père malade.

Elle frissonne de nouveau. Allume maladroitement une cigarette. Ses gants, pourtant fourrés de laine d'agneau, ne valent rien. Elle tourne le bouton de la radio. Tombe aussitôt sur Keith Jarrett. La musique coule comme une petite pluie d'été, bienfaisante. Elle sourit. Autant en profiter. Elle fume. Le chauffage fonctionne maintenant : depuis quelques minutes, une chaleur diffuse se répand dans la voiture.

Elle freine brusquement. La chaussée est défoncée. La voiture qui la suit dérape et évite de justesse un tête-à-queue fatal. Le chauffeur l'invective et lui montre le poing. Elle n'entend pas ce qu'il dit. Elle hausse les épaules. Appuie sur l'accélérateur.

C'est Marie-Paule qui lui a enseigné cette dangereuse technique de relaxation. Mais au fond elle n'y arrive pas. Elle ne réussit jamais à se concentrer, aussitôt les images se mettent à défiler et elle s'oublie, quelque part entre la cuisse et le mollet, jusqu'à ce qu'elle se retrouve, étonnée, à l'autre bout du monde. Marie-Paule, elle, s'endort très facilement depuis que, comme elle dit, elle « inspire l'énergie » et « expire les tensions ». D'autant plus qu'elle a cessé de fumer, ne boit jamais de café, évite le vin et la viande rouge. Pauvre Marie-Paule ! Cela l'aide à mieux « assumer » sa rupture avec Jean-Louis.

vous vous sentez calme de plus en plus calme calme calme calme merde

La détente aggrave son mal de tête. Elle sent une veine saillir le long de sa tempe droite. Elle n'a pas assez dormi. Ce soir, quand tout sera fini et que la bouteille de rhum, complètement vide, roulera par terre, elle croquera deux petites pilules et elle dormira au moins douze heures. Elle préfère la torpeur bleue, qui engourdit le corps pendant que les images défilent et l'emmènent au bout du monde, aux bienveillants conseils de sa sœur aînée.

La migraine s'amplifie. Elle promène un doigt sur la veine gonflée. C'est vrai qu'elle n'a rien mangé depuis hier soir, elle n'a bu que du café noir. Elle fouille dans son sac. Rien. Elle a oublié de prendre du chocolat. Marie-Paule lui reproche souvent de manger mal et se risque même à faire d'inquiétants diagnostics. Ces temps-ci, sa sœur s'intéresse à l'hypoglycémie et elle l'a mise en garde plusieurs fois contre les méfaits du sucre.

Elle retire ses gants, ses doigts endoloris commencent à virer du blanc au rouge. La maison familiale n'est plus très loin, il n'y a que le pont Mercier à traverser. Elle aperçoit un restaurant qui ne paie pas de mine mais paraît ouvert. Elle va descendre un moment. Se calmer. Vaincre ce mal de tête avant qu'il ne la paralyse complètement et ne compromette ses projets.

Le restaurant est désert. Elle commande un sandwich et un café. Elle devrait téléphoner. S'il ne dort pas, il doit l'attendre avec impatience — l'heure de l'apéritif est proche — et chercher déjà la clef de l'armoire. Elle boit une gorgée de café, avale deux aspirines, allume une cigarette. Elle se dirige vers le téléphone. Sa gorge est nouée. Sa nuque se raidit. C'est toujours comme ça. Elle déteste lui parler au téléphone. Entendre sa voix baveuse, ses déglutitions laborieuses.

À la neuvième sonnerie (il devait dormir), il répond enfin.

— Papa. C'est moi. Non. Pas Marie-Paule. MATHILDE. Maman est partie? Oui. J'arrive. Mais non, ça me fait plaisir. J'ai dit ÇA ME FAIT PLAISIR. Oui. J'arrive. Je suis dans un garage près du pont.

Dans un GARAGE. Non. Un petit ennui mécanique, rien de grave. Je repars dans quelques minutes.

Mais non. Non. Une simple vérification, j'ai eu du mal à démarrer tout à l'heure. Mais oui j'arrive, tu peux bien attendre un peu. C'est ridicule, non, je ne viendrai pas en taxi. À cette heure-ci, un dimanche, tu sais bien qu'il n'y a personne sur le pont. Bon, le garagiste me fait signe. À tantôt. J'arrive. Oui, papa.

Elle raccroche. Même pas deux heures, et il quémande déjà sa ration d'alcool. Elle tremble et jette un coup d'œil au miroir qui lui fait face. Elle est pâle, sa veine bleuie se détache avec précision sur la peau tendue. Elle constate que ce restaurant, bien que minable, n'en possède pas moins un bar étonnamment bien garni. Et si elle s'emparait d'une bouteille de scotch, en déversait méthodiquement le contenu, goutte à goutte, dans le bassin de fausses pierres rempli de pièces de monnaie?

Elle n'a plus faim. Chipote dans son assiette. Mange le cornichon mariné. Commande un autre café et un cognac. Avale le tout. Paie et quitte le restaurant.

Le froid la surprend. Elle se tasse à l'intérieur de son manteau. Jamais elle ne s'habituera aux hivers de son pays natal. Elle a toujours froid. Même l'alcool ne parvient pas à la réchauffer.

Elle reprend la route. Allume une cigarette. Il fait vraiment trop froid. Elle a beaucoup trop mal à la tête. Elle téléphonera à Marie-Paule, lui demandera de la remplacer auprès de son père. Même Jean-Louis, à la rigueur, pourrait prendre sa place. L'un ou l'autre. Ils seraient tellement plus efficaces. À moins qu'elle ne le conduise à l'hôpital? Mais oui, il n'y aurait qu'à le déposer à l'urgence, on l'y garderait peut-être plus d'un mois, comme en février dernier, et sa mère pourrait prendre un peu de repos. Le dimanche, les chances sont bien minces : on le renverra à la maison. Non, elle va tout simplement rebrousser chemin. Se blottir sous l'édredon entre Jasmine et Jérômine. Et, bien au chaud, partir avec elles au bout du monde.

Impossible. Elle est coincée. Bêtement. Impossible de changer de voie. Pas moyen de revenir en arrière. Il faudrait faire une manœuvre illégale et dangereuse. Elle aperçoit une voiture de police. Rien à faire. Elle n'a pas le choix.

Le fleuve est mort sous l'épaisse couche de glace. Elle traverse le pont Mercier, les yeux à demi fermés, une main sur la tempe.

Il rêvait. Sur la petite table à côté du lit s'entassaient pêle-mêle les médicaments, les vieux journaux, un livre sur la Louisiane, des pommes vertes et du chocolat. Il préférait qu'on ne lui apporte pas de fleurs. Sa femme et ses filles viendraient bientôt lui rendre visite.

Du fond de son sommeil, il les aperçut montant la garde, hostiles, autour du lit. Estelle et Marie-Paule parlaient. Il n'entendait pas ce que disaient ces voix tour à tour geignardes et emportées. On aurait dit une musique ancienne, ou encore un concerto baroque, un air familier mais dont le titre pourtant lui échappait. Elles se mirent soudain à vociférer en mesure, chacune se dépouilla de son sautoir de perles, et elles lui ligotèrent les bras aux montants du lit. Mathilde se haussa sur la pointe des pieds et lui tendit un verre. Il sourit. Il remarqua qu'elle portait la robe bleue à col chinois qu'il lui avait lui-même achetée dans la plus élégante boutique de San Francisco. Il regardait le verre avec convoitise mais ses mains entravées n'arrivaient pas à s'en saisir. Il n'avait pas la force de se défaire de ses liens de perles.

Il avait soif. Maintenant qu'il était presque guéri, rien ne s'opposait à ce qu'il boive une petite goutte de temps à autre, le médecin le lui avait même conseillé. Il avait tellement soif que ce verre tendu allait le rendre fou. Mathilde mit un genou sur le lit, ses tresses blondes lui balayèrent la poitrine. Elle le fit boire comme un nourrisson. Il aimait ce feu qui lui brûlait la gorge. La petite fille remplit le verre à nouveau et il but avec volupté. Il avait reconnu le goût du rhum et des beaux jours. Il était si ému qu'il voulut embrasser sa fille, sa tendre complice qui le dévisageait gravement, mais elle se déroba, sauta en bas du lit et annonça froidement qu'elle n'avait pas encore fini ses devoirs et n'avait plus de temps à perdre. Elle s'arrêta devant un miroir, défit ses tresses, fit mousser ses cheveux, se mit du rouge à lèvres et, devenue grande, partit sans se retourner. Estelle et Marie-Paule resserrèrent doucement ses liens en lui chantant une berceuse.

Une infirmière ouvrit délicatement la porte. Son rêve s'évanouit et il sombra dans un sommeil profond.

La chambre était spacieuse. Charles Dalpé, renonçant aux convictions nationalistes et populistes qu'il avait défendues dans sa jeunesse malgré la désapprobation d'Estelle issue d'une famille traditionnellement libérale, acceptait maintenant de remettre son sort (et son corps) entre des mains anglophones et particulièrement compétentes. L'hôpital se dressait, solennel et victorien, au flanc du mont Royal et le malade séjournait dans son pavillon le plus luxueux réservé à une clientèle fortunée.

La nourriture y était soignée, le personnel affable et nombreux, la vue sur les érables et les conifères magnifique.

L'infirmière remit un peu d'ordre dans la chambre et s'approcha de la fenêtre panoramique. Il neigeait faiblement. Elle attendrait qu'il se réveille pour lui faire sa piqûre. Son patient se montrait toujours aimable avec elle, il l'interrogeait sur le pays qu'elle avait fui, vitupérait les crimes des Duvalier, père et fils, évoquait la révolte des esclaves dirigée par Toussaint-Louverture, enchaînait en lui racontant, inlassable, toute l'histoire de Dessalines, premier empereur d'Haïti. Elle l'écoutait, silencieuse, et pensait à son père qui ne devait plus se nourrir que d'ignames depuis que les macoutes lui avaient confisqué la barque avec laquelle il allait pêcher au large de l'île de la Gonave. C'est ce que Jérémie, son fiancé, lui avait écrit.

Immobile, les mains dans les poches de son uniforme immaculé, elle regardait la neige tomber en imaginant son père à demi mort de faim ou de peur. Quant à elle, elle finirait bien par mourir de froid, comme Toussaint-Louverture dans son cachot de fort de Joux par une nuit humide de germinal, si cet hiver ne consentait pas bientôt à s'adoucir. Elle se sentait faner de jour en jour, tel un hibiscus maladroitement transplanté ; sa peau, privée de soleil, fade et anémiée, ne contrastait plus qu'à peine avec tout ce blanc qui sévissait inexorablement autour d'elle, au dehors comme au dedans.

Monsieur Charles dormait, pelotonné dans ses rêves. Son sommeil était très agité. Quand il se réveillerait, il l'entretiendrait sans doute de son sujet favori : le divin

Barbancourt, les irrésistibles petits punchs faits de rhum pur coupé par un trait de sirop de canne et quelques gouttes de citron vert. Il évoquerait sa visite à la distillerie, le bar au toit de bambou, à Cap-Haïtien, où il venait boire l'après-midi avec les pêcheurs pendant que sa femme se baignait à la piscine ou faisait du lèche-vitrines devant les boutiques de l'hôtel. Monsieur Charles allait parfois jusqu'à prétendre qu'après trois ou quatre verres de rhum vieux sa langue se réchauffait suffisamment pour qu'il ait le créole bien en bouche. Il lui demandait alors de dire quelques mots dans sa langue, mais, gênée, elle faisait mine de ne pas entendre.

Il n'y avait que dans cette chambre qu'elle s'accordait, depuis bientôt un mois, le loisir d'avoir le mal du pays en contemplant sans les voir les épinettes du mont Royal. Dès qu'elle poussait la porte, il lui semblait sentir flotter dans l'air une tiède odeur de mélasse. Elle se sentait un peu seule dans cet hôpital étranger où ses quelques collègues antillais, tous originaires de la Barbade ou de la Jamaïque, ne savaient parler d'autre chose que de Bob Marley et du reggae.

Monsieur Charles se retourna dans son sommeil. Elle s'approcha du lit et remit de l'ordre dans ses couvertures.

Estelle est en retard. Elle est à bout de souffle. Le parking est toujours plein le dimanche après-midi et elle n'a trouvé de place où se garer qu'à l'extrémité opposée à l'entrée du pavillon : elle doit escalader la pente raide qui y conduit. Marie-Paule lui a conseillé de venir en taxi, mais elle n'aime pas dilapider son argent. Elle préfère le conserver pour ses voyages (Hawaii… la Floride… l'hiver prochain), le distribuer à ses filles.

La neige qui tombe de plus en plus fort la prend à la gorge. On est en février, dans le creux de l'hiver. Elle étouffe, vérifie si son vaporisateur est bien dans son sac : la crise d'asthme n'est pas loin. Est-ce qu'elle va finir comme sa mère, assise dans un fauteuil à économiser son souffle des années durant ? C'est nerveux, prétend Marie-Paule, asthmatique elle aussi à ses heures. Peut-être bien. Mais si elle ne se dépêche pas un peu, il sera de très mauvaise humeur. Surtout qu'elle n'est pas venue hier, elle a pris un congé. Il faut bien qu'elle refasse ses forces : dans quelques jours, il sera de retour à la maison. Après un mois de soins constants, de traitements divers et surtout de régime sec, il va beaucoup mieux. Mais ça n'a pas été facile, pas du tout. À chaque visite, il quémande de l'alcool, il la supplie, l'implore, finit par l'insulter et menace de s'enfuir. Elle a du mal à résister à ce chantage permanent. Elle sait de quoi il est capable. Comment oublier son arrivée inopinée, en pleine nuit, alors qu'il venait de s'enfuir de l'hôpital sous le nez du gardien ? Il y a déjà plusieurs années de cela. Aujourd'hui, il n'en aurait plus la force. C'est ce que lui répète Marie-Paule pour la rassurer, mais elle se méfie.

Appuyée contre le mur, Estelle reprend son souffle. L'ascenseur est long à venir. Dès qu'il reprend du mieux, Charles se remet à ses petites combines. Il y a deux ans, il avait réussi à soudoyer par téléphone un chauffeur de taxi et à se faire apporter une bouteille de scotch à l'hôpital.

La maudite engeance des chauffeurs de taxi ! Combien de fois n'y a-t-il pas fait appel dans ses moments de disette ?

C'est dimanche, aujourd'hui. Il aura encore plus de mal à s'en passer. L'an dernier, de peur qu'il ne mette sa menace à exécution et ne reste pas jusqu'au jour de l'opération, elle avait fini par céder : elle avait apporté du scotch à l'hôpital, pas beaucoup, quelques onces seulement. La honte ! Surprise par le chirurgien lui-même, un intimidant spécialiste de renom, elle avait été forcée de vider le contenu de la bouteille dans le lavabo. Le médecin lui avait ensuite reproché vertement son geste qui, disait-il, allait contrarier les efforts qu'il ne ménageait pas pour rendre la santé à son mari. D'ailleurs si l'opération était un succès, comme il l'escomptait, il publierait un article dans une revue médicale américaine. Estelle avait baissé les yeux comme une petite fille désobéissante sans oser s'expliquer. Elle avait pourtant consulté le docteur Patenaude qui avait donné son accord : un peu de scotch n'avait jamais fait de mal à personne !

Elle entre dans la chambre. Il ne dort pas. Elle a apporté des fruits : des poires et des kiwis. Il l'accueille en lui demandant si elle a vu le médecin et si sa date de sortie est enfin fixée. Elle n'en sait rien, elle tâchera de le rencontrer demain. Il dit qu'il n'est pas malade, qu'il n'a plus rien à faire ici. Est-ce qu'elle a un petit quelque chose pour lui ? Elle ne répond pas. Il insiste. Elle le prie de se montrer raisonnable. Il se met à crier : elle ne se soucie pas de lui, ne lui veut que du mal, elle l'enterrera, elle les enterrera tous, elle a déjà laissé mourir ce fils qu'il désirait tant et qui aurait su, lui, prendre sa défense contre toutes ces femmes qui l'entourent.

Estelle pense à cet enfant qu'elle a perdu quelques jours après sa naissance, alors que Marie-Paule avait à peine deux ans. Elle sent une douleur ancienne sourdre dans les replis de son ventre.

Une infirmière les interrompt. Elle vient voir si tout va bien. Charles tend la carte jaune sur laquelle il a inscrit ses choix pour les repas du lendemain. L'infirmière, s'adressant à Estelle, fait remarquer que le malade a bien meilleur appétit qu'à son arrivée. C'est qu'il n'est pas difficile, répond Charles sur un ton moqueur. Il ajoute qu'il aime les taquineries, cela fait sourire les jolies infirmières des Philippines. « De Bornéo », corrige-t-elle. Voilà qui est très intéressant. Alors qu'il s'apprête à faire le récit de l'invasion japonaise de l'île, Marie-Paule et Jean-Louis frappent à la porte entrouverte. L'infirmière, dont on ne saura jamais si elle est indonésienne ou malaise, s'éclipse discrètement.

Marie-Paule met fin à la conférence paternelle sur le Sud-Est asiatique. Ces manies de vieux professeur d'histoire l'ont toujours agacée. Il y a longtemps qu'il n'enseigne plus, ne publie plus; l'alcoolisme l'a forcé à prendre une retraite prématurée, mais il aime bien faire montre de son érudition, surtout devant Jean-Louis. C'est néanmoins le signe manifeste de ce qu'il est convenu d'appeler sa guérison; toutes ces drogues dont on le bourre semblent avoir eu raison, très provisoirement comme d'habitude, des méfaits causés par l'alcool.

Le voilà justement qui demande à Jean-Louis où il cache le petit quelque chose indispensable à qui veut fêter ça dignement. Avec lui, il y a toujours quelque chose à fêter. L'anniversaire de Jean-Louis par exemple : il a eu trente et un ans jeudi dernier. Le jeune homme en profite pour annoncer la grande nouvelle : le journal l'envoie en reportage à Cuba, trois semaines en mai, toutes dépenses payées.

Marie-Paule, qui pense sans arrêt à ce voyage depuis que Jean-Louis lui en a parlé, constate qu'il ne paraît toujours pas disposé à lui proposer de l'accompagner. Son père insiste : il faut arroser ce double événement. Elle aurait envie de le gifler, mais s'efforce tout de même de lui faire entendre raison : il exagère, tout ça n'est pas sérieux, il ne doit pas recommencer à boire autant qu'avant à moins qu'il ne veuille mourir ou faire mourir sa femme et ses filles. Estelle et Jean-Louis approuvent. Charles soutient qu'il n'a jamais bu que modérément, qu'il n'est pas un ivrogne comme ce collègue, aujourd'hui décédé, qui commençait à boire au petit matin. Il ne se lève jamais avant midi et réclame au bout d'une heure à peine son premier verre, réplique Marie-Paule, excédée devant autant de cynisme et de mauvaise foi. Le ton monte. Charles menace sa fille : il va la déshériter. Marie-Paule éclate de rire. Il la déshérite deux ou trois fois par année, alors qu'il n'a pas le sou, enfin presque ; c'est sa mère qui a de l'argent, et puis, de toute façon, elle et Jean-Louis se débrouillent très bien tout seuls, merci !

Estelle fond en larmes. Jean-Louis, mal à l'aise

comme chaque fois que Marie-Paule se met en colère, propose de les emmener au restaurant. Il vient de décider d'annuler son rendez-vous avec Annie, son amie cinéaste. Il avait oublié d'en parler à Marie-Paule; le moment serait mal choisi maintenant. Les deux femmes acceptent. Charles se laisse embrasser en bougonnant. Il leur recommande de boire à sa santé.

Mathilde croise le trio au moment où elle sort de l'ascenseur. Ils la préviennent : son père n'est pas d'humeur facile aujourd'hui. Elle voit que sa mère a pleuré. Non, elle ne croit pas qu'elle ira les rejoindre au restaurant. Elle les regarde partir et, tout à coup, la ressemblance entre sa mère et sa sœur, s'éloignant toutes deux d'un même pas un peu trop assuré, solides et en même temps si vulnérables, lui serre le cœur. Elles entrent dans l'ascenseur et font un petit signe de la main en agitant leurs boucles blondes.

Mathilde reste là comme une étrangère, ou une orpheline, pense-t-elle avec un sourire, les bras ballants, ses bras trop longs comme sa mère dit souvent. Elle est terrifiée à l'idée de se retrouver seule avec son père et se reproche de n'être pas venue plus tôt.

Elle se dirige lentement vers la chambre et se résigne à frapper à la porte. Il est seul bien entendu. Il paraît étonné, avoue qu'il ne s'attendait pas à sa visite. Elle est pourtant venue tous les dimanches.

Ils se taisent l'un et l'autre. Charles évite ces yeux verts qui virent si facilement au gris acier, ce regard aigu qui se pose sur lui comme s'il allait le décapiter. Elle ne semble pas d'humeur à plaisanter. Va-t-il se risquer à lui demander si par hasard elle n'aurait pas un petit quelque chose, une goutte, une larme de scotch?…

Il se souvient de la petite Mathilde, obstinée déjà, intransigeante, peu encline à pardonner, mais ne dédaignant point, le soir venu, ses invitations à partager sa promenade. Il était jeune encore, le scotch et le vin mêlés au café secouaient la léthargie qui l'envahissait de plus en plus souvent dès qu'il rentrait dans la grande maison de Notre-Dame-de-Grâce. Ils marchaient lentement sans mot dire et parfois, l'hiver, elle se jetait tout à coup sur lui sans prévenir, elle le bousculait, le houspillait, lui lançait ses tresses à la figure jusqu'à ce qu'il consente à lutter avec elle et alors, heureuse, elle le bourrait de coups de poing. Elle devait avoir huit ou dix ans et les poignets si menus qu'on aurait dit une princesse. La victoire était accordée à qui parvenait à faire tomber l'autre dans la neige. Elle gagnait toujours et, emportée par son élan, s'abattait sur lui comme une avalanche. Ils riaient aux éclats. Ensuite, ils jouaient à l'ange : couchés sur le dos, immobiles, les bras seuls battant de haut en bas, ils imprimaient dans la neige molle des silhouettes aux ailes déployées que le vent demain balaierait. Une fois relevés, ils admiraient leurs anges et rentraient à la maison, mouillés et ravis. Elle prenait un bain chaud, lui un cognac. Elle rouspétait un peu, puis allait se coucher. Il ne tardait pas non plus à se mettre au lit. Seuls les anges veillaient dans l'immensité blanche.

Il attend. Mais elle se tait obstinément. A-t-elle trouvé

un nom pour sa boutique, qu'est-ce qu'elle y vendra au juste, des vêtements féminins ? Elle répond évasivement que le projet est au point mort ; toutes sortes de difficultés imprévues sont survenues et elle n'a pas envie d'en parler aujourd'hui.

Charles n'ose pas l'interroger davantage. Mais qu'est-ce qui a bien pu lui arriver ? Sa fille n'est plus la même, elle était si enthousiaste autrefois, multipliant les projets d'avenir et de voyages, déclarant qu'elle serait ambassadeur, puis anthropologue ou reporter à l'étranger. Elle ne se gênait pas pour affirmer qu'elle ne deviendrait pas, elle, une momie enfouie sous les livres d'histoire, non, pas elle, elle ne moisirait pas longtemps dans ce pays abêtissant, une province à vrai dire, où l'on étouffe parce que tout le monde se connaît, se tutoie et s'appelle par son prénom. Il la revoit discourant, entrant en transe presque, maudissant ce pays où elle avait eu le malheur de naître, un désert surgelé dans lequel il ne se passait jamais rien, mis à part quelques soubresauts provoqués par de velléitaires aspirations à l'indépendance. Marie-Paule se moquait de ces enfantillages et engageait sa sœur à militer avec elle au sein du mouvement indépendantiste, plutôt que d'attendre passivement quelque hypothétique appel du bout du monde. Les deux sœurs devaient avoir quinze et dix-huit ans environ et elles se prenaient fréquemment aux cheveux. Maintenant, Mathilde ne s'enflamme plus que rarement pour le sort du monde et elle semble même se désintéresser du sien. Elle se tient droite, figée devant la fenêtre. Charles ne sait pas quoi dire.

Mathilde n'aime pas cette neige qui tombe, languissante. Elle préfère les tempêtes qui bouleversent le quotidien et montrent la vraie mesure de son pays. Mais, la plupart du temps, l'hiver traîne comme une tumeur qui se développe lentement. Pourtant, elle ne déteste pas la neige. Hier encore, elle a fait une longue promenade avec Hugo, un garçon qu'elle a rencontré dans un magasin de disques, il y a deux semaines ; c'est elle qui lui a proposé de venir à la maison écouter tout de suite le nouvel album de *Tears for Fears*. Ils se voient souvent depuis. Hugo est drôle : il n'a pas vingt ans, des cheveux soyeux comme un ange et des mines de bande dessinée. Ils se roulent dans la neige, puis ils font l'amour toute la nuit jusqu'à ce que le plaisir les rejette à l'aube comme des noyés parmi les disques épars. Alors il la quitte pour aller à ses cours. Il est si jeune, et elle si légère dans ses bras.

Mais le lendemain, c'est dimanche, l'hôpital et le silence. Et son père qui dort encore. Elle s'attendait au pire. Or, ils ne se sont pas encore disputés. Il n'a rien demandé, n'a pas dit un mot de sa querelle avec Marie-Paule. En fait, ils ne se sont rien dit.

Elle se tourne vers lui. Il a les yeux fermés. On dirait un gisant sculpté dans une pierre friable. Il se décompose sous son regard. Elle souhaiterait qu'il disparaisse, emporté par ses rêves.

Quand elle était petite, elle lui racontait ses rêves. Elle rêvait souvent qu'elle était une héroïne vagabondant de par le monde comme dans ces romans d'aventures qu'il lui achetait. À cette époque, il la comblait de cadeaux. Une fois, il lui avait rapporté de San Francisco une robe bleue à col chinois ; sa mère avait dit que la couleur ne lui allait pas, trop sombre pour une petite fille, surtout en été. Il s'était fâché. Cette robe avait été l'enjeu d'une dispute qui avait duré presque tout l'été. Sa mère prenait un malin plaisir à critiquer le mauvais goût de son mari devant tout le monde et lui, vaincu, avait fini par l'admettre. Elle n'avait plus jamais porté la robe, la fille de la femme de ménage en avait hérité, mais quelques années plus tard Mathilde avait acheté une autre robe, presque pareille, une robe bleue avec un col chinois.

Elle hésite à partir pendant qu'il dort. Elle fume des cigarettes à la chaîne. Il ouvre les yeux, se redresse, demande l'urinoir. Elle a horreur de ça. Elle n'est pas une infirmière et, de toute façon, il serait capable de se lever. Il lui apparaît soudain dans toute son indignité. Un vieil ivrogne maintenu artificiellement en vie. On le soigne pour qu'il puisse continuer à boire. Elle examine avec dégoût ce visage marqué par la couperose. Elle veut partir. Elle dit qu'elle est en retard, qu'on l'attend, qu'elle va appeler une infirmière.

Elle sort presque en courant, ses bottes et son manteau à la main. Elle voudrait qu'on l'attaque pour qu'elle puisse se défendre et battre à mort son agresseur. Elle ne comprend pas cette violence qui la secoue comme un vent mauvais. Mais elle la reconnaît.

Elle ne devrait plus le voir. Jamais. C'est dangereux. Il est temps de couper les ponts.

j'ai fait un rêve papa   un inconnu se jetait du haut du pont police sirènes ambulances pompiers photographes   un suicide mais moi je passais tout droit papa sans m'arrêter la nuque raide j'étais en retard tu comprends   je n'avais plus de temps à perdre et d'ailleurs cela ne me concernait pas   je n'avais vraiment pas le temps de m'arrêter j'étais en retard je te dis très en retard j'avais commis une erreur en prenant le pont Mercier   une erreur bête tu vois coincée tout à coup forcée de suivre la file des voitures impossible de changer de voie pas moyen de revenir en arrière   alors je voulais en finir papa en finir au plus vite avec ce pont interminable cette maudite traversée   et je passais tout droit sans m'arrêter éblouie par la pluie les phares les projecteurs toutes ces taches criardes dans la nuit   je ne faisais que passer   aveugle et sourde   je passais tout droit sans m'arrêter entre les feux les signaux les appels de code les secours la détresse   cela ne m'intéressait pas alors je filais droit devant   une fuite délibérée   je fendais la foule la haie des bras tendus poings levés doigts accusateurs   on aurait dit un téléroman un feuilleton une série

*noire   pas de temps à perdre en retard tout droit sans
m'arrêter imperturbable   c'était un cauchemar papa
cet individu anonyme qui se jetait du haut du pont c'était
toi papa   tu avais deviné n'est-ce pas   c'était bien toi
qui n'en finis plus de te laisser mourir pendant que moi
je rêve la nuit je m'endors et je fais de beaux rêves   je vois
le revolver s'enfoncer dans ton ventre ballonné   la bile le
sang l'alcool giclent   et tu n'as plus mal tu n'as plus envie
de boire tu meurs enfin papa   la délivrance   tu gis le
ventre ouvert une balle blanche en plein cœur tu te sou-
viens   un jeu que tu m'avais appris autrefois   couchés
tous les deux dans la neige   alors papa je me couche par
terre allongée sur le dos bras et jambes écartés   je bats des
ailes et je dessine un ange rouge   c'est avec ton sang papa*

QUATORZE HEURES

La maison de la rue Oxford se dresse, immuable, derrière la rangée de peupliers. Elle est désespérément solide. Des glaçons effilés comme des piques pendent au-dessus de la galerie de bois blanc que les écureuils bruns adoptent en été, en dépit de la réprobation maternelle.

Elle se gèle les pieds devant la double porte en chêne massif, malveillante, et promène ses doigts sur les rainures de plomb qui enceignent les vitraux. Il est encore temps de faire demi-tour. Elle fixe le verre rouge sombre où son visage anxieux se mire comme une grenade. La veine bat, affolée, sous la tempe, de plus en plus fort comme si elle allait exploser.

Elle lève la tête vers la chambre d'où, quand elle était petite, les jours de colère, elle jetait par la fenêtre les ballons et les poupées. Il l'attend. Il est inquiet peut-être.

Au moment où elle se décide à entrer, elle se rend compte qu'elle a oublié le rhum dans la voiture. Elle redescend en courant les trois marches et manque de s'étaler sur le trottoir glacé. Ses nouvelles bottes italiennes ne sont pas antidérapantes, mais pas du tout.

Elle enlève son manteau. Comme d'habitude, l'air est irrespirable dans cette maison surchauffée. Pas un son ne vient troubler le silence qui sévit. Sa mère a mis des fleurs partout, les bouquets qu'elle a reçus à Noël ; on se croirait dans un sépulcre.

Elle renifle l'odeur familière de l'alcool et des médicaments. La chambre paternelle est au bout du couloir, là où couchait la bonne quand il y en avait une. Il ne peut plus utiliser l'escalier et sa mère préfère dormir seule dans le lit conjugal. De toute façon, ils avaient fait chambre à part dès que Marie-Paule avait quitté la maison et libéré la pièce qu'elle occupait à côté de la salle de bains. Même avant, il arrivait fréquemment que la mère se glisse dans le lit de sa fille aînée au milieu de la nuit. Elle disait qu'il ronflait trop fort. Mais jamais elle ne venait la trouver, elle, Mathilde, frémissante sous les couvertures ; l'oreille tendue, les yeux grands ouverts, elle épiait les chuchotements et les pleurs étouffés, se jurait qu'elle ne dormirait qu'à l'aube pour, le lendemain, exhiber triomphalement des cernes vengeurs.

Il a renoncé à l'attendre. Il dort. Il a débranché le téléphone. Immobile sur le pas de la porte, elle retient son souffle. Qu'il ne se réveille surtout pas !

Elle passe au salon. Il y a encore des cadeaux sous le sapin artificiel ininflammable. Mardi dernier, on fêtait Noël et elle buvait du champagne en rêvant au radeau qui l'emmènerait au bout du monde. Si elle n'y prend garde, tout recommencera dans deux jours : la grande bouffe, les vins fins, les oncles et les tantes, les cadeaux, les souvenirs du bon vieux temps. Son père évoquera son enfance à la campagne, les oranges que sa pauvre mère, veuve, distribuait le matin des étrennes après la messe, les vœux du Nouvel An échangés sur le perron de l'église. Il est temps de mettre fin à tout cela, à cette comédie cent fois répétée, ce vaudeville sinistre, cette évocation obscène du passé. Chaque année, son père, qui a pourtant délaissé depuis longtemps la religion de son enfance et les curés qui lui ont jadis payé ses études, se permet une allusion timide à l'antique rituel de la bénédiction paternelle. Elle ne supporte plus la nostalgie qui perce alors sous les rires de la parenté réunie, l'attendrissement qu'elle lit dans les yeux de sa mère, et même dans ceux de Marie-Paule. Elle chasse le souvenir de cette bouffonnerie : son père, debout, irrémédiablement grotesque, et elles, agenouillées toutes trois devant lui, recevant sa bénédiction. Heureusement, elle avait à peine sept ou huit ans quand on a mis fin à ce cérémonial impie, l'évolution des mœurs et les progrès de l'alcoolisme ayant eu raison des prétentions de son père à la dignité patriarcale.

Ce salon est morbide. Elle le quitte sans regret et passe dans la bibliothèque voisine. Les livres d'histoire et les atlas s'entassent jusqu'au plafond. Un rayon spécial est réservé aux publications paternelles toutes consacrées à la vie de la colonie sous le Régime français. Elle les a lues distraitement, autrefois. Elle fouille parmi les livres entassés sur le bureau : des biographies surtout, les Mémoires de ses grands hommes favoris, Napoléon, de Gaulle, Georges-Émile Lapalme le malheureux, et même une vie de Staline offerte par Marie-Paule et Jean-Louis, à l'époque où ils étaient membres d'un groupuscule maoïste. Elle les feuillette. Ils sont poussiéreux, son père ne lit presque plus maintenant.

Elle s'assoit dans le fauteuil en acajou derrière le bureau et se frotte la tempe. Elle allume une cigarette ; son paquet est presque vide. Devant elle, Charles Dalpé, immortalisé, prononce un discours dans un cadre doré : il vient d'être nommé vice-doyen de la faculté d'Histoire à l'Université de Montréal. Il a cinquante ans environ et il boit trop depuis déjà longtemps. Cinq ans plus tard, on le forcera à remettre sa démission et il le fera sans amertume, heureux d'abandonner un travail qu'il n'aime plus et des collègues qui l'ennuient. À côté, il y a une grande photo de son grand-père maternel serrant la main du premier ministre fédéral Louis Saint-Laurent ; c'était peu de temps avant sa mort et sa mère l'époussette amoureusement tous les jours. Elle prend aussi un soin jaloux du portrait de Sir Georges-Étienne Cartier, qui figurait en bonne place au panthéon du grand-père.

Elle soupire jette un coup d'œil à sa montre. À peine deux heures quarante. On s'ennuie le dimanche comme chacun le sait. Elle a encore mal à la tête. Rien à faire. Elle ne va tout de même pas entonner à nouveau le refrain : *calme vous vous sentez calme de plus en plus calme parfaitement détendue…* Voilà qu'elle se met à radoter maintenant. Elle ferait mieux d'allumer une autre cigarette et d'invoquer le ciel pour qu'il continue à dormir.

Elle n'a plus de feu. Elle ouvre le tiroir, son père a toujours des allumettes. Elle tombe sur une enveloppe bleue, décachetée. Qui peut bien encore lui écrire? Elle succombe tout de suite à l'envie d'y jeter un coup d'œil. Inouï! Elle reconnaît la grande écriture penchée de Marie-Paule. La lettre est datée du lundi 12 mars. Elle serre la petite main de Fatima qu'elle porte à son cou depuis que Marie-Paule la lui a offerte en cadeau d'anniversaire. En mars dernier, justement.

Il sommeillait en attendant son apéritif. Sa fille avait avancé le meilleur fauteuil près du radiateur et ses pieds reposaient sur un gros pouf en cuir marocain. L'appartement de Marie-Paule et Jean-Louis était sombre et mal chauffé. Il avait froid et se recroquevillait dans son sommeil.

Une faible lueur filtrait encore à travers les rideaux de dentelle écrue. Il préférait fuir dans les rêves le crépuscule précoce des après-midi d'hiver. De la cuisine lui parvenaient l'écho indistinct des voix féminines, le fracas assourdi des chaudrons. Il lui sembla entendre le bruit d'un verre qui tintait comme un appel. Il avait la gorge sèche et irritée.

Sa tête bascula contre son épaule et il agita faiblement les bras. Il n'arrivait pas à s'envoler, ses ailes atrophiées lui collaient à la peau, et il trottinait gauchement sur le sable, le bec tendu vers la mer lointaine. Il devrait attendre la marée haute pour soulager son gosier douloureux.

Des pas résonnèrent sur le plancher de bois dur, des talons hauts qui s'avançaient résolument vers le salon, et il s'éveilla sans pourtant ouvrir les yeux. Il songea que l'heure de l'apéritif était enfin venue. Sous ses paupières flétries, des nuées d'oiseaux de malheur passaient à tire-d'aile, pendant que, solitaire, un vieux cormoran aptère à demi mort de soif errait sur la plage.

Les pas s'éloignèrent et, déçu, il se rendormit. Une araignée géante, que Marie-Paule devait certainement arroser tous les jours, pendait au-dessus de sa tête qui s'enfonçait maintenant dans le velours bordeaux du fauteuil.

Marie-Paule badigeonne les cailles de moutarde ; ensuite, il faudra mettre sur chacune (il y en a dix !) une barde de lard fumé, puis attacher les petites pattes maigrelettes avec de la ficelle. Elle aime bien cuisiner mais, aujourd'hui, ces chairs mortes qu'elle manipule délicatement lui lèvent le cœur. Il y a de ces dimanches comme ça. Tout va mal depuis que, les yeux encore gonflés de sommeil, elle a vu sur l'oreiller la note laissée par Jean-Louis : il rentrera vers quatre heures, qu'elle ne s'inquiète surtout pas, Annie lui a demandé de l'aider à repérer les extérieurs pour son film. Et voilà qu'il est maintenant plus de cinq heures, Jean-Louis n'est pas encore de retour, toute la famille est là, et il n'y a rien de prêt.

Elle jette un regard impatient à Mathilde qui essore négligemment la salade depuis plus de dix minutes. Enfin, puisque c'est aujourd'hui l'anniversaire de sa petite sœur chérie, autant ne pas intervenir, cela risquerait de tourner au vinaigre un fois de plus. Elle soupire sans mot dire ; Mathilde excelle depuis toujours à feindre l'inexpérience et c'est leur mère qui a jadis encouragé cette indolence naturelle. Marie-Paule entend Estelle crier depuis la salle à manger que les verres en cristal de Bohême, un acompte sur son héritage, ne sont pas tout à fait impeccables. Elle ne répond pas, mais ses doigts véloces se mettent à peler frénétiquement les pommes de terre qui accompagneront les petits pois.

Estelle a les traits tirés. Elle étouffe dans sa robe de lainage qui lui comprime la taille. Elle, qui était mince comme ses filles, comme Marie-Paule plutôt, pas comme Mathilde dont la silhouette efflanquée de chatte mal nourrie dépasse la mesure, se voit maintenant affublée d'un petit ventre qui s'attire les plaisanteries de Charles quand il est en verve.

Depuis son retour de l'hôpital, son mari se montre plus docile. Il sait qu'à la moindre incartade, à la prochaine « crise », le cercle familial se réunira de nouveau. Estelle s'est donc remise à la tâche, le cœur vaillant et le souffle court. Et quand, dans ses oreilles, le bourdonnement se fait entendre, strident comme un signal d'alarme que lui enverrait son corps fatigué, elle avale rapidement un cachet avec une gorgée de gin.

La table est bien mise, la nappe brodée qu'elle a donnée à Marie-Paule, ravissante. Il ne manque plus que les couteaux à fromage qu'elle n'arrive pas à trouver. Brandissant le tire-bouchon, Marie-Paule la rejoint et dit que, de toute façon, on ne mangera pas de fromage, pas même de pain puisque c'est Jean-Louis qui devait passer en prendre à la boulangerie, mais maintenant c'est fermé il est plus de cinq heures, on ne peut jamais compter sur lui, alors tant pis, on n'en fera pas un drame et on s'en passera. Mathilde, qui en a enfin terminé avec la salade, signale qu'il y a dans la cuisine une casserole qui menace de déborder. Marie-Paule se précipite et, au même moment, Jean-Louis apparaît, les bras chargés : il dépose, avec un grand sourire, deux baguettes de pain sur la table.

Charles, son verre vide à la main, se demande si Jean-Louis va lui en offrir un deuxième. Estelle, à qui rien n'échappe, termine rapidement son apéritif et, adressant à Marie-Paule un sourire entendu, déclare qu'elle meurt de faim. Le message est aussitôt reçu et, de connivence avec elles, Jean-Louis propose de passer à table tout de suite.

Mathilde repousse son assiette en soupirant bruyamment. Marie-Paule se dit que sa sœur, à force de vivre avec ses deux chattes, s'est mise à leur ressembler : on dirait Jasmine secouant une patte dégoûtée au-dessus de son plat, comme si elle voulait enterrer cette nourriture merdeuse qu'elle vient pourtant d'engloutir goulûment. Elle, elle n'a pas de chat, Jean-Louis n'en veut pas et elle connaît par cœur ses arguments : il soutient qu'il faut se méfier de ces animaux-là, ils sont hypocrites, fourbes, en plus ils ne sont pas très intelligents et on ne peut rien leur apprendre, enfin toutes les inepties habituelles que récitent sans se lasser les ennemis des chats. Cette mésentente existe entre eux depuis qu'ils se connaissent, bientôt six ans, et elle va s'accentuant. Marie-Paule se rappelle tous ces chatons de son enfance qui faisaient des galipettes dans les escaliers et s'endormaient nichés dans ses cheveux en lui pétrissant le cou, comme s'ils tétaient encore. Et elle sourit à cette Mathilde impossible, dont les petites mines et les grands airs l'agacent, mais qui fête ses vingt-quatre ans aujourd'hui et qu'elle a une envie soudaine d'embrasser, avant qu'il ne soit trop tard et que ces dimanches pervers ne les aient séparées. Prendrait-elle un petit morceau de ce savarin qu'elle a commandé exprès pour elle à La Gascogne, là où on trouve les meilleurs gâteaux en ville? Elle a trop mangé à midi chez Julien, mais elle veut bien y goûter, répond Mathilde.

Estelle félicite Marie-Paule : vraiment, elle a bien fait les choses, cette crème froide à l'avocat qui précédait les cailles, délicieuses elles aussi, était particulièrement originale et réussie. Marie-Paule la remercie et ajoute que, ces temps-ci, elle et Jean-Louis mangent surtout des légumes peu cuits et vite faits. Les légumes sont chers au mois de mars, s'étonne Estelle. Jean-Louis précise qu'ils consomment aussi de plus en plus de riz complet et boivent de moins en moins de vin. Charles, absorbé par la lecture minutieuse qu'il fait depuis plusieurs minutes de l'étiquette de la bouteille de beaujolais, lève un sourcil perplexe. Mathilde déclare qu'elle ne connaît rien de plus triste qu'un chou-fleur cuit à la vapeur un soir d'hiver.

Estelle, en l'entendant, se rappelle tous les efforts autrefois déployés pour lui faire manger ses carottes, toutes ces ruses utilisées en vain pour qu'elle consente au moins à avaler quelques bouchées de viande, ces visites répétées chez le pédiatre qui, chaque fois, prescrivait un nouveau médicament destiné à transformer en fringale ce manque chronique d'appétit ; parfois l'été, quand elle déguisait les repas en pique-niques improvisés, la petite fille, seule dans le jardin, acceptait enfin de s'alimenter sans faire de scène.

Mathilde délaisse son gâteau. Elle pense à Julien, à ces nourritures délicates qu'il avait préparées pour elle, des hors-d'œuvre, des bouchées, une infinité de petites choses fines et fondantes qu'ils ont mangées comme des oiseaux en buvant du champagne rose. De temps à autre, Claire et Camille, les filles jumelles de Julien, venaient picorer dans les assiettes puis retournaient à leurs jeux. Ensuite, elle a fermé les yeux et, quand elle les a rouverts, Julien avait disparu, caché derrière un paravent de soie où elle a tout de suite reconnu Jasmine et Jérômine parmi un foisonnement de fleurs des tropiques. Éblouie, elle avait pensé que son nouveau voisin l'étonnerait long-temps, ce Julien qui avait la patience de peindre sur la soie vierge ces paysages troubles et luxuriants où les bêtes s'ac-couplaient avec les plantes, cet appel du bout du monde que, comme elle, il devait entendre jusque dans ses rêves. Elle lui avait sauté au cou et l'avait embrassé pendant plus d'une heure. Puis, elle les avait quittés à regret, lui et ses filles, pressée malgré tout par la hâte de montrer son cadeau à Jasmine et Jérômine à qui elle conseillerait fer-mement de faire patte de velours sur la soie peinte. Elle allume une cigarette en se disant que Julien sera toujours là maintenant, quoi qu'elle fasse, précieux comme une rose des sables qu'elle aurait ramassée en plein désert. Même si elle s'en va, car elle s'en ira, elle s'en va toujours, sans savoir pourquoi, elle le quittera, elle filera comme une comète aspirée par sa trajectoire fatale.

Charles demande à Mathilde ce qu'elle compte faire de l'argent qu'ils lui ont donné en cadeau, sa mère et lui. Elle répond qu'elle va s'inscrire à des cours de pilotage et s'enfuir au Népal à bord d'un avion volé. Estelle la regarde, navrée. Un long silence s'établit. Mathilde se tourne vers son père et lui verse à boire : « un ange passe », murmure-t-elle. Interloqué, il ne dit mot et vide son verre d'un trait.

Jean-Louis, décidé à rompre le silence qui précède souvent les tempêtes dominicales, annonce qu'il va commencer la semaine prochaine à suivre des cours de danse africaine. Marie-Paule, persuadée que c'est Annie qui est à l'origine de ce revirement subit puisqu'il a toujours refusé de l'accompagner à son cours de tai-chi de même qu'à ses séances de gymnastique douce, lui coupe aussitôt la parole en demandant à Mathilde pourquoi elle n'a pas invité Julien, son adorable voisin. Sa sœur répond que Julien déteste les dimanches en famille. Ce Julien réagit comme un adolescent attardé, conclut Marie-Paule.

Estelle gigote sur sa chaise droite en pin décapé et se retient de commenter à nouveau (la dernière fois, cela avait entraîné une dispute) l'inconfort de ces meubles anciens que sa fille aînée affectionne tant. Charles, assis dans le confortable fauteuil victorien que Jean-Louis a transporté du salon à la salle à manger, pérore sur les origines du mobilier, louant les mérites de ces premiers colons inexpérimentés qui taillaient grossièrement dans le pin blanc, le plus facile à travailler, des meubles de fabrication rudimentaire. De telles simplifications exaspèrent Jean-Louis dont l'arrière-grand-père était un habile artisan ébéniste.

Estelle a un malaise : ses oreilles se sont mises à bourdonner, elle est étourdie, elle a peut-être bu trop de vin. Elle a envie de s'effondrer sur la belle nappe maintenant tachée. Elle entend Charles raconter ses souvenirs des Galapagos, le dernier long voyage qu'il a fait alors qu'il avait réussi à s'introduire dans un groupe de chercheurs en biologie, délégués par l'Université. Les cormorans aptères et les fous à pattes bleues atterrissent comme un cheveu sur la soupe dans l'indifférence générale. Mathilde note pourtant les noms colorés de ces oiseaux rares pour les répéter à Julien. Mais sa mère se lève brusquement en bredouillant qu'elle va s'étendre quelques minutes sur le lit de Marie-Paule. Elle repousse sa chaise, puis s'écroule, sa tête évitant de justesse la baratte à beurre que Marie-Paule a transformée en panier à couture.

Tout le monde se précipite, sauf Charles, muet dans son fauteuil. Jean-Louis l'aide à se relever, tout va bien, un petit étourdissement passager, et la conduit jusqu'à la chambre. Elle s'étend et éclate en sanglots.

Mathilde voit sa mère trembler. Elle pense au saule pleureur, un arbre centenaire, magnifique, que ses voisins d'en face, propriétaires aussi de la maison de Julien et de la sienne, ont abattu l'été dernier parce qu'il était atteint d'une maladie imaginaire. Et c'est à cette race de bûcherons incultes qu'elle appartient !

Estelle pleure encore. Elle est malade, son corps usé se révolte contre le contrôle qu'il a subi pendant tant d'années. Elle digère mal, il lui arrive même de vomir devant Charles qui la harcèle avec impudeur jusque dans ces moments de misère intime ; l'autre jour, il quémandait la clef de l'armoire aux liqueurs pendant qu'elle vomissait sa vie dans les toilettes. Mais c'est à son tour maintenant de tomber et d'exiger des soins, de l'attention. Estelle Dalpé peut tomber elle aussi ! Comme Charles quand il s'écrase parce qu'il a trop bu.

Mathilde lui caresse le front. C'est la mort qu'elle a vue passer dans ses yeux, peu avant sa chute. Sa mère est condamnée désormais. Il y longtemps que la mort est là, attentive, élégante même dans ses habits du dimanche, une convive discrète invitée à la table familiale.

Mathilde déballe le cadeau que Marie-Paule vient de lui offrir. Jean-Louis a proposé de ramener les parents fatigués à Notre-Dame-de-Grâce : il reviendra en taxi. Marie-Paule est soulagée, elle n'aime pas voir sa mère conduire dans cet état et, quand à son père, il y a longtemps qu'il a renoncé à tenir le volant.

Émue, Mathilde découvre la petite main de Fatima en argent ciselé que Marie-Paule avait ramenée d'Afghanistan, quand elle avait suivi à dix-neuf ans la grande migration de la jeunesse nord-américaine vers l'Asie ; à son retour, Mathilde, dévorée par la jalousie, trop jeune encore pour faire la route, lui dérobait à la moindre occasion le bijou qui la fascinait, et d'interminables querelles s'ensuivaient. Marie-Paule a ajouté de longues boucles d'oreilles en vieil argent qu'elle a trouvées chez un antiquaire de la rue Sherbrooke. Les deux sœurs s'embrassent et Marie-Paule court chercher la bouteille de mirabelle qu'elle avait soustraite à la vue de son père.

Elle remplit les verres et se met à confier à Mathilde les doutes qui l'assaillent depuis quelques mois : Jean-Louis est obnubilé par Annie, cette idée de s'inscrire à des cours de danse alors qu'il consacre déjà tellement de temps à toutes sortes d'activités sportives, mais voilà maintenant qu'il s'enfonce dans les lieux communs et répète à qui veut l'entendre qu'il en a assez de la compétition, qu'il ressent le besoin de laisser son corps s'exprimer plus librement. Serait-elle jalouse ? Quand ils font l'amour, elle imagine Annie qui les filme derrière sa caméra. Le moment est venu de faire une mise au point sur leur relation, si Jean-Louis accepte enfin de s'y prêter au lieu de toujours s'esquiver.

Mathilde écoute en silence, à mille lieues de ces fastidieuses histoires de couple. Sa sœur raconte maintenant son dernier stage : passionnant mais très dur, un vrai laboratoire de relations humaines, un groupe stimulant, une approche mêlant la pratique théâtrale à l'abandon corporel ; cela l'aidera sûrement à développer des rapports plus authentiques avec les autres, peut-être même avec Jean-Louis; elle y arrivera bien un jour au terme de toutes ses expériences. Mathilde, que la croissance personnelle en conserve n'attire guère et qui ne se plaît d'ailleurs que dans les situations équivoques, étouffe un bâillement. Comme la vie serait terne, si tout le monde se soumettait à cet impératif édifiant, la nouvelle morale de l'authenticité! Au moment où Jean-Louis ouvre la porte, Marie-Paule, inquiète devant le regard fermé de sa sœur, lui conseille de suivre une thérapie: cela vaudrait mieux que les somnifères. Mathilde, agacée, allume une cigarette.

Jean-Louis affirme que tout ira bien dans la grande maison de la rue Oxford. Il propose à Mathilde de venir jeter un coup d'œil sur la peinture qu'il fait à temps perdu. Résignée, elle le suit jusqu'à son bureau récemment converti en atelier. Elle regarde distraitement ces taches criardes, le dessin maladroit et se dit que, décidément, le ridicule ne tue pas les amateurs. Jean-Louis, volubile, explique que ce sont là ses premiers essais, que bien sûr il n'a aucun souci technique pour le moment, mais que l'important pour lui c'est de s'exprimer. Gênée, Mathilde sourit. Irait-elle jusqu'à lui faire remarquer que sa façon de s'habiller, malgré ses efforts depuis qu'il a abandonné l'uniforme du militant, témoigne à elle seule d'un mauvais goût irrémédiable?

La visite de l'exposition est interrompue par l'arrivée inopinée d'une amie de Marie-Paule qui est venue, malgré l'heure tardive, emprunter le livre dont elle a absolument besoin pour son séminaire demain. Elle aussi habite le plateau Mont-Royal mais c'est la première fois qu'elle vient, et elle s'exclame devant le puits de lumière, les boiseries, la baratte à beurre, le mur de briques naturelles et les violettes africaines en pleine floraison. Jean-Louis, modeste, avoue que c'est Marie-Paule qui prend soin des plantes, mais qu'il a lui-même fabriqué les coussins de cretonne, il adore la couture.

Mathilde en profite pour s'esquiver. Marie-Paule et elle téléphoneront pour fixer l'heure, et surtout le lieu, du prochain dimanche.

Immobile dans sa baignoire, Marie-Paule essaie de se détendre comme on le lui a appris dans une infinité de stages qui ont occupé une multitude de soirées et de fins de semaine. Elle est triste soudain, immensément triste. Jean-Louis s'est enfermé dans son atelier. La soirée n'était pas très réussie. Sa mère est malade et, comme d'habitude, c'est à elle, la fille aînée, qu'elle fera appel quand, épouvantée par sa propre détresse, elle perdra tout contrôle. C'est elle qui accourra comme une « bonne » sœur dévouée, pendant que Mathilde promènera ses grands airs Dieu sait où.

Elle pense à son père, si sage, ce soir, un enfant puni résolu à se racheter. Quand arrivera-t-elle à lui parler ? Elle en a un tel désir. Il serait important qu'elle clarifie ses rapports avec lui. Si Mathilde l'entendait, elle dirait encore qu'elle parle une langue de bois, mais Mathilde n'est qu'une enfant qui se cache derrière ses airs supérieurs. Bon, de toute façon, ça ne peut plus durer. Elle ne va pas continuer à transférer sur Jean-Louis son conflit œdipien mal résolu.

Elle masse ses points de tension en se disant qu'il faut qu'elle réfléchisse encore, mais qu'elle devrait peut-être essayer d'écrire à son père.

Elle a tellement de choses à lui dire.

tu ne dis jamais rien   bêtises et fadaises   chimériques
paroles d'ivrogne   pourquoi   dis-moi papa   plus de
vingt-huit ans que j'interroge en vain aruspices et devins
aveugles   et personne ne dit rien jamais   tu es seul tu
règnes souverain sur le silence et la déraison   tes machines
de guerre prêtes à l'assaut final   autrefois pourtant tu
racontais inlassable les victoires et les défaites le récit fabuleux de l'Europe mutilée le débarquement sur les plages
de la Normandie que j'imaginais grises et caillouteuses
comme les plates étendues du Maine où nous creusions
des abris dans le sable mouillé   j'écoutais sage et en boule
sur tes genoux je suivais des yeux comme une espionne
les retraites et les avances des Alliés que tu pointais
magistral sur les cartes géographiques déployées telles des
invitations au voyage   la guerre était finie depuis longtemps   mais ses cicatrices bourgeonnaient vivaces dans la
terre   fertile   de   ta   mémoire   certains   soirs   tu
chantais maladroit les vieilles chansons du folklore de la
Nouvelle-France et je m'endormais en battant la mesure
        puis Elle est venue au monde par un petit matin

neigeux   aux ides de mars tel un poison funeste   un
vrai poison qui hurlait nuit et jour et le monde d'un
seul coup a basculé vers son centre nouveau-né
    Mathilde soudain dans tes bras infidèles   minuscule
courtisane tapageuse piaillant jacassant sautillant   pendant que moi j'émigrais chez les bonnes sœurs parmi les
pensionnaires   col amidonné et bottines lacées   première
communiante en bas de fil hideux   et Mathilde sa menotte
vindicative dans ta main indulgente   une arracheuse de
cheveux   je vous observais cachée derrière les peupliers
    et déjà je demandais pourquoi mais pourquoi   comme
aujourd'hui je demande pourquoi mais pourquoi boire ainsi
    je n'ai pas su n'est-ce pas pas su m'y prendre pas su y faire
pas eu le tour la main le doigté   Estelle non plus ta femme
du monde cassante un quartz névrotique une reine déchue
    tu n'étais pas à la hauteur une demoiselle de Lotbinière
a ses exigences   tu bois séduit puis abandonné tour à tour
par Estelle et Mathilde les impitoyables   tu bois et nous
sommes coupables   je suis coupable   tu bois et tu ne veux
rien entendre cures thérapies désintoxication pas question
tu as choisi l'alcool le silence la mort   mais pourquoi   je
n'ai pas su pas pu pas voulu   une incapable   tu vas
mourir   un interminable suicide   kamikaze de l'eau-de-
vie et je resterai seule jusqu'au jour du pardon   mais en
attendant nous continuerons à jouer le jeu la petite guerre
des nerfs   puisque je proclame l'amnistie mais que tu
n'entends rien ne dis rien jamais rien   permets au moins
qu'un jour demain ce soir même je prenne ma plume et
mon courage à deux mains et te l'écrive noir sur blanc

QUINZE HEURES

Elle allume une cigarette, la dernière du paquet. Cette lettre n'est qu'un fatras de naïvetés, un appel à la grande réconciliation truffé d'explications laborieuses auxquelles son père n'a certainement rien compris. C'est bien là l'écriture de Marie-Paule, atteinte de logorrhée chronique ; son journal, fréquemment lu à son insu quand elles habitaient encore sous le même toit, était déjà symptomatique. Ce lyrisme de pacotille qui affleure sous le parti pris de l'authenticité ne saurait en rien ébranler son destinataire. Marie-Paule se sera humiliée en vain. Elle remet soigneusement la lettre à sa place parmi les comptes à régler et les polices d'assurance.

Charles apparaît soudain dans l'embrasure de la porte tel un revenant tout juste sorti des décombres. Elle ne l'a pas entendu venir. Elle le regarde, impassible, bien que de son ventre lui parvienne aussitôt un tiraillement familier. Il vacille légèrement, sa robe de chambre bâille, ses chevilles sont enflées. Il a la peau bleuâtre, repoussante, des extraterrestres.

Il se racle la gorge et la salue selon l'usage : « Tiens, ma

Mathilde, tu es déjà là. » Il paraît avoir complètement oublié ses précédentes récriminations téléphoniques. « Tu es bien gentille d'être venue », ajoute-t-il comme s'il ignorait qu'il est impensable de le laisser seul. Elle le regarde d'un œil froid et répond brièvement à ses manifestations captieuses de bienvenue. Affolée, elle pense que cet après-midi s'écoulera, interminable, jusqu'à la minute de vérité qu'elle ne cessera de différer.

« On s'installe au salon, il y a peut-être quelque chose d'intéressant à la télévision ? » propose-t-elle, se raccrochant comme à une bouée au monde merveilleux du petit écran. Il accepte et, poussif, se met en branle. Elle implore le ciel que dans les arcanes de la programmation soit prévue une quelconque rétrospective historique, quelque récit de guerre si possible, raconté comme si l'on y était par un vieux général revenu hanter les lieux de son passé.

« Je crois bien que je vais faire un petit détour par les toilettes », annonce-t-il. C'était prévisible : gavé de diurétiques, il est le champion incontesté des allers et retours éliminatoires. Comme il a la détestable habitude de ne jamais fermer la porte, simple négligence ou précaution élémentaire en cas de chute accidentelle, elle attend, plaquée contre le mur adjacent.

Ils atteignent enfin le but de leur périple, lui échouant dans son fauteuil, et elle allumant le poste de télévision en même temps que deux de ces infectes cigarettes américaines qu'il affectionne. Dieu soit loué et la France bénie ! la voix profonde d'Henri de Turennes se fait aussitôt entendre comme par enchantement.

Ils fument tous les deux pendant que les images apocalyptiques de la guerre du Viêt-nam, amoncellement de ruines et de chairs souffrantes, défilent sous leurs yeux. Il n'a rien demandé encore. Elle a caché le rhum Clément derrière les dictionnaires, peu avant son apparition dans la bibliothèque.

Elle invoque toutes les puissances occultes, sa cabale intime : surtout qu'il n'ait pas de malaise, lui donner à boire d'accord, mais le toucher, pas question !

Après quelques hésitations, elle décide de recourir à un piètre subterfuge pour gagner du temps. D'ailleurs, elle ne supporte pas le goût mielleux des Camels. « Si ça ne t'ennuie pas, je vais sortir quelques minutes acheter des cigarettes », dit-elle très rapidement. Il marmonne une réponse indistincte. Elle se lève et s'enfuit.

La rue Sherbrooke flotte dans l'air glacé comme un iceberg. Le temps n'est pas à la promenade et les magasins sont tous fermés. Elle songe un instant à courir jusqu'à sa voiture, s'y réfugier, partir au bout du monde dans la chaleur et la musique.

Pas possible ! Non, elle se refuse à y croire, impossible de fuir, elle a encore perdu ses clefs. Et du coup la clef de la maison paternelle aussi. Elle entreprend une fouille minutieuse de son sac, puis de ses poches. Bon, il n'y a plus qu'à se rendre à l'évidence et souhaiter les avoir oubliées dans la bibliothèque ou le salon, dans la serrure de la porte d'entrée peut-être, ou, mais là ça se complique, dans la voiture verrouillée de l'intérieur. Avait-elle ou non en main ces satanées clefs quand elle est entrée dans la maison ? Estelle, encline à la paranoïa du troisième âge, ferme toujours à clef la porte de sa prison quand elle s'en évade. Le trousseau devrait donc traîner quelque part sur une table ou une chaise.

Elle s'en remet à sa bonne étoile qui, plusieurs fois par semaine, accomplit le prodige de préserver des voleurs les clefs, l'argent et tous les menus objets, foulards, gants, sacs, qu'elle égare ici et là. Marie-Paule interprèterait sans doute son oubli comme la manifestation de son désir inconscient (!) de ne plus retourner chez son père.

Elle aperçoit enfin une pharmacie ouverte et presse le pas tout en évitant de glisser. Inutile de multiplier les actes manqués. D'ailleurs, n'en déplaise à Marie-Paule et à ses interprétations ingénues, elle n'ignore pas que, si elle s'oublie ainsi, puis se retrouve et repart à la dérive comme un continent emballé, elle ne s'en va pas moins sûrement vers l'échéance promise.

Elle s'engouffre dans la pharmacie, se laisse tenter par un analgésique qu'elle ne connaît pas, des pastilles effervescentes, et achète toute une cartouche de cigarettes. La veine se débat encore tel un petit animal en cage et fou de rage. Si les théories de Marie-Paule sur les origines psychosomatiques des maladies étaient fondées, elle aurait pour le moins déjà succombé à la mononucléose, au choléra ou à la fièvre jaune plutôt qu'à la migraine ordinaire du dimanche. Mais non, elle se porte bien, beaucoup trop bien, et il lui faudra survivre à ce dimanche dont la saveur acide lui remonte dans la gorge, semblable à un relent nauséeux de quinine.

Elle sort, réconfortée tout de même par la certitude intime de sa totale immunité ; le virus paternel ne se développe qu'en milieu favorable, là où, comme chez Marie-Paule, se cultivent le remords et les bons sentiments.

Il fait froid, le ciel s'obscurcit déjà. Le bleu méditerranéen observé à midi s'estompe rapidement et la nuit polaire s'abat prématurément sur les trottoirs déserts. Elle marche au hasard des rues de ce quartier où elle est née, différant son retour vers la maladie et la mort en sursis.

Une douce torpeur l'envahit peu à peu : c'est le froid qui fait son chemin jusque dans ses nerfs, et elle avance telle une somnambule. Elle porte une main à son cou et presse entre ses doigts le talisman qu'elle ne quitte plus depuis que Marie-Paule le lui a offert, la petite main de Fatima cachée sous les poils de renard blanc.

Elle marche sans penser à rien. Si elle continue ainsi, le froid l'emportera peut-être à son insu vers un nouveau monde. Elle revoit tout à coup une scène du passé maintes fois racontée par sa mère, un fait divers tiré de la légende familiale, plus exactement de la geste de son héros favori, le grand-père de Lotbinière : dans sa jeunesse, alors que dans des circonstances obscures il travaillait comme bûcheron sur un chantier éloigné, il s'était subitement endormi dans la neige, à la tombée du jour, vaincu par la fatigue et le froid de l'un de ces hivers fabuleux d'autrefois et, à son réveil dans la nuit noire où gisaient les squelettes des arbres abattus, il avait constaté que sa jambe droite, gelée, ne lui obéissait plus. Et, de fait, elle l'avait toujours connu ainsi, la patte folle mais le corps droit malgré sa canne. Un jour, à la belle époque des miracles du frère André, on avait fait appel au thaumaturge qui, pour ce fidèle de bonne famille, avait accepté de déplacer sa sainte personne jusque dans le salon de la rue Oxford alors qu'il officiait d'ordinaire dans la chambrette de son couvent. Les entreprises du bon frère avaient lamentablement échoué, se heurtant à l'agnosticisme du grand-père secrètement mécréant qui, en ces années très catholiques, avait d'abord refusé de s'agenouiller pour finalement se plier aux ordres du guérisseur offusqué devant pareille insoumission, et là, tout bonnement, il s'était évanoui sous l'effet de la violence faite à sa jambe infirme. Le frère André s'en était allé en concluant que la grâce de Dieu n'échoit qu'à ses serviteurs sincères.

Sans doute, mais elle, pendant ce temps, incrédule elle marche, elle poursuit son pèlerinage vers les lieux neigeux de son enfance en quête d'une révélation. Elle ne sait plus quelle sera l'issue de ce dimanche dont elle a pourtant prévu minutieusement le déroulement. La voilà justement qui traverse le parc des anges où son père et elle déployaient leurs ailes dans la neige et elle essuie la larme qui lui monte aux yeux tellement le froid se fait soudain déchirant.

Elle doit rentrer maintenant, s'arracher à cet état second qui engourdit sa détermination. Son père et la bouteille de rhum l'attendent.

Mais, en remontant la rue Melrose, elle souhaite tout

à coup qu'une rencontre fortuite, Gisèle peut-être surgie de l'ancien monde des amours et querelles enfantines, la contraigne à faire marche arrière sur ce chemin trop difficile. Gisèle ne se montre pas : elle habite en banlieue maintenant et berce son bébé ou bien elle parcourt le monde, belle comme une aventurière, elle est devenue une jeune avocate active qui partage habilement son temps entre son étude, ses amants et son enfant qu'elle élève seule, à moins qu'elle ne soit déjà morte et que son ombre plane au-dessus de la rue Melrose.

La maison n'est plus très loin et elle va s'interrogeant sur ses amitiés perdues. Et si une vieille amie oubliée se présentait à la barre des témoins, prenait sa défense, siégeait sur le banc du juge, qui sait ? Pourvu qu'elle n'en reconnaisse aucune parmi les psychologues préposés à son évaluation future et qui s'attacheront à elle pareils à une horde de sangsues avides de questions, d'explications et d'analyses. Elle tourne le coin de la rue Oxford, fuyant à l'avance les bonnes paroles et les mouchoirs tendus.

Les clefs sont sur la porte comme prévu. Quant à lui, il s'est endormi devant la télévision. On le dirait plongé dans un sommeil catatonique.

Elle manipule distraitement la commande à distance qui donne accès à une dizaine de chaînes dont la plupart présentent différents aspects, tous plus affligeants les uns que les autres, de l'*American way of life* : du jeu-questionnaire où le candidat futé qui a su deviner le prix exact de la marchandise convoitée emporte le congélateur ou le four à micro-ondes indispensable à son bonheur, à la sempiternelle petite maison dans la prairie où l'on ne batifole pas, tout occupé que l'on est à conquérir les grands espaces en famille, dans la joie et le labeur récompensé.

Elle allume une cigarette et réprime une envie de tousser qui risquerait de le réveiller. Il lui proposerait peut-être un cognac comme au temps où, victime de la coqueluche, elle devait avaler un grand verre de ce liquide qui lui raidissait la bouche et l'endormait aussitôt. Elle n'a pas oublié les heureux effets de ce premier somnifère qui tuait dans l'œuf les mauvais rêves et, si elle n'apprécie guère aujourd'hui la saveur médicamenteuse du cognac, elle s'en remet désormais aux petites pilules bleues.

La cigarette se consume lentement. Le temps ne passe pas. Il stagne, et sa migraine aussi. La longue promenade, le sandwich et le café-cognac n'ont pas produit les effets escomptés. Lui aussi, il faudra bien qu'il mange dans quelque temps. Elle n'a pas l'habitude de le nourrir. La dernière fois, quand sa mère était partie à Windsor, il avait dû se contenter de crème glacée.

Elle se lève, décidée à essayer le nouvel analgésique qui viendra peut-être à bout de la douleur à la tempe. Une ritournelle à la mode scande ses pas qui la conduisent vers la salle de bains, loin du vieillard endormi : *vous vous sentez calme de plus en plus calme complètement détendue vous vous posez déposez enfin…*

Il somnolait tapi sous les draps, guettant son retour avec l'indolence des vieux matous. Elle avait osé partir sans lui. Une fois de plus, Estelle parcourait le monde pendant que lui, abandonné, végétait dans son lit. Elle avait d'abord proposé qu'il l'accompagne là-bas, chez de vagues cousins établis à Windsor en Ontario, mais, agacée par ses hésitations, elle n'avait pas insisté. Elle était ravie de lui échapper : cela se voyait bien. Un peu inquiète tout de même, mais quinze jours sont vite passés. Elle téléphonerait souvent.

Il comptait profiter de sa solitude, jouir de sa liberté provisoire, délivré enfin de cette surveillance perpétuelle, de ce contrôle policier exercé sur ses appétits. La femme de ménage viendrait tous les jours, elle préparerait les repas, l'aiderait à se laver, mais il lui ferait vite comprendre qu'en fait il n'avait pas besoin d'elle : parfaitement, il se débrouillerait seul et fort bien. Marie-Paule et Mathilde téléphoneraient, Marie-Paule surtout, et elles lui rendraient visite à l'occasion. Il se montrerait alors très prudent.

Lui aussi autrefois avait aimé voyager, sillonner

religieusement les routes de France en quête de ses origines, se gorger de vins fins, liqueurs merveilleuses, philtres et élixirs du monde entier, et dans sa mémoire affluaient les souvenirs de mille nuits capiteuses, d'infinies ivresses, quand, hôte singulier de ses frères les fainéants de la terre, il trinquait dans toutes les langues. Il ne voyageait plus maintenant que dans ses rêves et jongleries confuses, reclus dans sa chambre et emporté vers de lointaines nébuleuses par les vapeurs de ses alcools familiers.

Puis, cet accident stupide était survenu, il avait fait une chute en se relevant de ce fauteuil que sa femme s'obstinait à conserver en mémoire de son père qui le lui avait légué en même temps que la maison, et il s'était cassé le bras droit.

La femme de ménage avait aussitôt donné l'alarme et Marie-Paule, les bras battant l'air et la langue vipérine, n'avait pas tardé à se rendre maître de la place. Un rigoureux service de gardiennage avait été mis sur pied et les sentinelles, ses filles, Jean-Louis, une horrible infirmière moustachue se relayaient ponctuellement. À tout prendre, il aurait préféré l'hôpital, Rose-Marie, l'adorable petite Haïtienne, les jolis minois des Philippines. Ici, on ne lui épargnait pas les remontrances, et même Mathilde s'employait à lui faire la morale.

Sa liberté n'aurait duré que le temps d'un aller et retour vers le paradis retrouvé, là où l'eau-de-vie coule en abondance, une courte permission d'à peine vingt-quatre heures. Il avait trop vite dépassé la mesure et le payait chèrement de ses déboires actuels. Estelle n'en avait rien su, en accord avec la consigne du silence que ses filles avaient établie.

Et depuis, il somnolait dans la cellule qu'il avait docilement réintégrée, se remémorant les audaces des nègres marrons terrés au fond de la forêt impénétrable, entre les fougères arborescentes et les palétuviers géants, là où le versant abrupt du piton s'ouvre sur l'abîme. Le parfum du rhum vieux se répandait dans l'air et il croyait entendre Rose-Marie chantonner une berceuse créole.

Marie-Paule secoue ses cheveux semés de flocons. Le mois d'avril s'achève mais, depuis la veille, il tombe une désespérante petite neige. Jean-Louis a bien de la chance, lui qui s'envolera bientôt pour Cuba où son journal l'envoie en reportage.

Quant au malade, il dort ou fait semblant, le bras inerte dans son plâtre ; au moins, pendant ce temps, il ne boit que ce qu'on lui sert. Il semble que le plan de campagne qu'elle a élaboré, à la suite de l'incident fâcheux survenu dès le lendemain du départ de sa mère, fonctionne à merveille et que le rationnement en vigueur commence déjà à porter ses fruits. Tout indique que depuis qu'il se contente d'une quantité raisonnable d'alcool, son père ait peu à peu retrouvé ses esprits et qu'il ressente même quelque tardif mais légitime remords.

Elle ne fait que passer aujourd'hui, c'est au tour de Mathilde de prendre en charge le repas du soir et la nuit qui vient. Estelle s'accorde de petites vacances bien méritées, mais ses filles en font les frais.

Or, c'est à la fin du mois précisément que Marie-Paule doit présenter son mémoire à l'université, « Le parricide dans la tradition romanesque », et de sa réussite dépend la permanence de son emploi au centre de recherches en études littéraires. Entre les longues heures consacrées à des lectures souvent arides — on n'entre pas en psychanalyse comme dans un moulin — et la fréquentation quotidienne, depuis deux ans, des Œdipe, Iphigénie, Karamazov et autres victimes ou bourreaux de la scène familiale, voilà qu'elle trouve à peine le temps de prendre soin de ses propres parents. Enfin, elle est un peu nerveuse, mais presque certaine de s'en tirer honorablement. Le sujet la passionne. Son analyse est fondée sur le caractère récurrent des fonctions attribuées aux actants tant dans la constellation familiale que dans l'acte criminel lui-même et, des résultats de ses modestes observations, elle tire quelques conclusions : les infanticides sont nettement plus fréquents que les parricides et par ailleurs, plus souvent qu'autrement, c'est le père qui tue sa fille et le fils son père, mis à part Médée, le cas douteux d'Abraham qui n'appartient pas tout à fait à la tradition littéraire, et quelques autres exceptions qui ouvrent le champ de ses spéculations à de nouvelles perspectives.

La voix paternelle, plutôt impérative aujourd'hui, interrompt la répétition intérieure à laquelle elle s'adonne constamment depuis que la date de son examen est fixée. Elle accourt à son chevet pendant que Jean-Louis s'affaire à déballer les provisions dans la cuisine ; il ne faut pas compter sur Mathilde pour ces préoccupations bassement domestiques et, à son arrivée, elle trouvera son repas servi sur un plateau d'argent sans même s'en étonner.

Charles paraît s'intéresser aux propos cubains de Jean-Louis, et Marie-Paule lui est reconnaissante d'alimenter ainsi la conversation. Incorrigible toutefois, son père se lance dans un éloge circonstancié du Habana Club, ce rhum peu parfumé mais qui ne s'en laisse pas moins boire fort agréablement. Jean-Louis acquiesce sans entendre Marie-Paule qui grommelle quelque perfidie entre ses dents.

Cuba exaspère Marie-Paule. Elle en a assez de la voix suave de Silvio Rodriguez qui chante la révolution, assez du spectacle de Jean-Louis se déhanchant maladroitement sur des rythmes de salsa, assez des analyses et commentaires nuancés des événements de Mariel. Jean-Louis sera parti dans moins d'un mois et Annie, par un bienheureux concours de circonstances, l'accompagnera sans doute. Justement, le voilà qui enchaîne en avouant la hâte qu'il a de partir : ce reportage promet d'être tellement intéressant !

Marie-Paule se réfugie dans la cuisine, loin de ces confidences odieuses. Et dire qu'il y a six ans, sept peut-être, c'est ensemble qu'elle et Jean-Louis partaient à Cuba. De vraies vacances : une sorte de lune de miel, l'année de leur rencontre. Elle avait eu le coup de foudre pour les cocotiers qui inclinaient leur tête gracile devant la mer et le soir, quand le soleil plongeait à l'horizon, elle sentait monter du plus profond d'elle-même de vagues moiteurs qui la laissaient frémissante. Son désir se nourrissait à même le sable, le sel et la bouche odorante de Jean-Louis. Oh! bien sûr, ils savaient respecter la limite au-delà de laquelle leur amour risquait de sombrer dans la mièvrerie, et ils entendaient tous les deux mettre leurs vacances à profit pour mieux connaître le peuple cubain. Pour cela, il fallait fuir les « tabarnacos », ces compatriotes mal embouchés qui proféraient ineptie sur ineptie, allant jusqu'à s'attendrir sur le sort des enfants cubains privés de chewing-gum. En fait, cette île semblait relativement prospère, en regard surtout de sa misérable voisine haïtienne, et ses habitants plutôt heureux ; voilà qui était contraire à l'orthodoxie maoïste et n'allait pas sans les amener à s'interroger, mais ils ne doutaient pas qu'à leur retour les éléments les plus avancés du groupe accepteraient de débattre la question en de fort démocratiques assemblées jusqu'à ce que l'un et l'autre se rangent à l'avis clairvoyant de l'avant-garde.

Le sauté de veau sera bientôt prêt. Haussant les épaules, Marie-Paule avale d'un trait un petit verre du rosé qu'elle a mis dans la sauce. Pourquoi n'arrive-t-elle pas à digérer tout ça ? Oublier, tout effacer, jusqu'au souvenir du Cambodge, ce Kampuchéa dont le parti proclamait bien haut le nom tout en niant sa fulgurante agonie. Comme ils avaient été naïfs à l'époque, elle, Jean-Louis et plusieurs autres ! Lors de ces vacances à Cuba, ils avaient même voulu aller entendre Fidel qui faisait son grand discours annuel à La Havane ; le guide, qui paradoxalement ne se souciait que du bien-être des « tabarnacos », n'avait rien fait pour leur faciliter les choses et, à son sourire narquois, ils avaient compris que leur condition petite-bourgeoise sautait indéniablement aux yeux. Ils s'étaient tout de même fait quelques amis cubains, et, le matin du départ, ils avaient quitté l'île au son des guitares, bouleversés par cette soudaine flambée de la chaleur latino-américaine qu'ils partageaient pour la première fois ; Pilar, la chanteuse qui apprenait l'anglais et s'extasiait devant les vêtements des touristes, pleurait, toute menue dans le jean de Marie-Paule. Puis Jean-Louis avait appris, tout à fait par hasard, que Pilar avait été du nombre des fuyards à Mariel, bien que leurs amis n'en aient jamais glissé un mot dans les lettres qui arrivaient à Montréal avec plusieurs semaines de retard.

Marie-Paule continue, songeuse, à éplucher les pommes de terre. Elle s'ennuie déjà de Jean-Louis et il n'est pas encore parti ! Il lui vient une brusque envie de danser au milieu des épluchures et elle ferme les yeux à l'écoute du désir qui se balance dans ses hanches. Mais voilà qu'aux cheveux clairs de Jean-Louis se mêlent maintenant les boucles sombres de Juan frôlant sa joue alors qu'il murmure tendrement : « Vamos a bailar ? » Juan dansait bien, mais les choses en étaient restées là et Jean-Louis n'avait rien su de cet émoi qu'elle-même ne comprenait pas, l'attribuant aux effets combinés du rhum cubain, du soleil et de la sensualité particulière de la langue espagnole.

Il y a six mois environ, Marie-Paule s'est appliquée à faire le récit, plus ou moins transposé certes, de ces vacances à Cuba, mais, à la lecture de sa courte nouvelle, Jean-Louis n'a fait que quelques remarques laconiques. Pourtant, elle avait rédigé son texte après un stage en création littéraire, un atelier passionnant où on lui avait inculqué ce que Mathilde, peu loquace elle aussi mais combien démoralisante, appelle les nouveaux poncifs de l'écriture : la perméabilité aux émotions, l'éclatement du langage, la multiplication des blancs qui assurent au lecteur comme à l'auteur des échappées hors-texte, le corps qui s'écrit sous la poussée du désir textuel et, un peu passée de mode maintenant, la narration de l'aventure narrative elle-même. Mathilde n'hésite jamais à tout balayer ainsi du revers de la main à coups de réflexions cyniques et d'approximations lapidaires ; un aveu de sa propre impuissance, voilà tout !

Tout en faisant cuire les pommes de terre, Marie-Paule se dit qu'elle devrait s'y remettre et qu'un jour Jean-Louis saura peut-être lire entre les lignes. En attendant, elle va le retrouver au salon où son tête-à-tête avec son père se prolonge. D'ailleurs, l'heure de l'apéritif approche. Elle doit voir à ce que tout se passe bien.

Mathilde apparaît soudain, traînant ses souliers boueux sur les fleurs du tapis chinois. Personne ne l'a entendue venir ; Estelle lui a remis une clef afin de faciliter ses visites au père veuf que l'alcool console trop facilement. Elle affirme mourir de froid. Évidemment, commente Marie-Paule, elle n'a rien sur le dos, même pas de bottes alors qu'il neige depuis le matin.

Souriante, Mathilde s'affale sur un divan et déclare qu'elle est épuisée, mais qu'elle en a enfin terminé de Radio-Canada et de son rôle de charmante hôtesse guidant son troupeau de visiteurs à travers les couloirs, studios et arcanes de la « maison ». Finies les questions insipides et les remarques admiratives ! La télévision d'État lui a signifié son congé vendredi dernier : on a décrété que sa conduite laissait à désirer, elle aurait été à quelques reprises impolie, grossière même, avec le public. Cette nouvelle l'a aussitôt mise en joie. Elle aura quand même tenu le coup plus de cinq mois. Mais il y a longtemps qu'elle en avait assez. Et elle s'est même offert le luxe de partir en beauté, claquant la porte au nez du directeur du personnel. On ne la reprendra plus à se payer deux fois par jour la traversée du pont Mercier, à l'heure de pointe la plupart du temps, pour un salaire dérisoire.

Marie-Paule contemple bouche bée cette petite sœur qui décidément ne grandira jamais et se joue de ses emplois, parfaitement inconsciente de la crise économique qui sévit. Insupportable Mathilde ! C'est bien elle, oui, l'enfant capricieuse qui s'amusait autrefois à décapiter les poupées, à précipiter par la fenêtre les jouets dédaignés, pendant que sa grande sœur s'ingéniait déjà à recoller tant bien que mal les morceaux. Qu'elle se débrouille maintenant ! Qu'elle moisisse toute seule dans sa cabane humide de l'autre côté du pont ! Les prestations de l'assurance-chômage suffiront amplement à en payer le loyer. Et maman sera toujours là pour offrir à son parasite chéri le luxe indispensable à sa survie. Une voiture, par exemple, pour éviter à la délicate enfant les longues courses en autobus quand elle condescend à quitter sa tanière.

Alors que Marie-Paule s'apprête à gratifier Mathilde d'une leçon d'économie élémentaire, Jean-Louis l'entraîne. C'est à lui pourtant que Mathilde doit cette occasion, pour tout autre qu'elle inespérée, de s'introduire à Radio-Canada. Mais Jean-Louis n'a qu'une envie : quitter au plus vite cette maison qui suinte la tension, l'abandonner à son mauvais génie qui sommeille, maintenant que la bouteille de Habana Club est à moitié vide. Pourvu que Marie-Paule n'en sache rien ! Pendant qu'elle s'affairait à la cuisine, le beau-père et le gendre ont en effet célébré le départ à Cuba grâce à une bouteille de rhum tirée de l'une de ces innombrables cachettes que compte la maison depuis que l'alcool en est devenu le dieu tutélaire.

Charles voit partir Marie-Paule et Jean-Louis à regret. Ému par la complicité inhabituelle de son gendre, il est à peine conscient de la présence de Mathilde auprès de lui.

Mathilde contient difficilement son exaspération. Elle fume cigarette sur cigarette. Voilà déjà trois fois qu'elle propose de passer à table et qu'il trouve tout juste l'énergie de marmonner que non, il n'a pas faim mais « mange, toi, ma Mathilde, mange si tu as faim… » Il est odieux, absolument odieux. Elle devrait le gaver comme une oie. Elle examine ce corps qui se faisande dans son fauteuil, ces chairs déjà mortes, cet œil éteint derrière le verre épais. Il vaut mieux lui servir à boire, devancer son désir.

Qu'il boive s'il ne veut pas manger ! Elle l'accompagnera d'ailleurs. Elle non plus n'a pas faim. Toute une nuit à tuer, seule avec lui… Elle le secoue : il grogne, puis ébauche un vague sourire quand elle lui tend un grand verre de rhum, son « p'tit apéro ».

Charles n'a fait de son verre qu'une gorgée. Toute une soirée en tête à tête avec sa fille… Il voit bien qu'elle n'en a pas envie, elle demeurera butée et silencieuse, lui jetant parfois un regard abrupt. Si au moins il savait encore comment provoquer sa colère, se mériter un accès de rage brutale, mais elle ne lui consent plus qu'une feinte indiffé-rence à peine teintée parfois d'une impatience vite maîtrisée. Se méfier de l'eau qui dort, songe-t-il, pendant que dans son rêve une petite fille en robe bleue de Chine le guide vers un étang qui exhale une terrible odeur de mélasse.

Le sauté de veau préparé par Marie-Paule disparaît, emporté par la chasse d'eau : Mathilde vient de le jeter dans les toilettes. Elle se roule un joint. Se calmer. Elle doit se calmer. Elle prend de longues bouffées, aspire profon-dément et avale une dernière gorgée de rhum avant de regagner courageusement le salon.

Elle repasse par la cuisine, dispose deux bols pleins de crème glacée sur un plateau et s'exhorte de nouveau au calme. Il y a en elle une bombe qui menace d'exploser si elle ne la désamorce pas tout de suite. Si ça tourne mal et que le barrage qui s'élève désormais entre eux cède sous la pression, elle téléphonera à Julien. Il n'y comprendra rien, mais accourra s'il le faut, flanqué de ses jumelles qu'il emmène partout. Julien qui élève seul ses filles dans la maison voisine face au fleuve mais trouve encore le temps de la câliner, de lui faire l'amour, de la nourrir, elle, Mathilde, qui pourtant se dérobe aussitôt rassasiée; Julien, oui, c'est lui qui doit venir tout de suite, au plus vite, avant qu'elle ne meure de faim.

Mathilde passe sa langue sur la boule de crème glacée. Elle oublie toujours d'en acheter, bien que Jasmine et Jérômine en raffolent. Sans doute parce que sa mère, elle, n'y a jamais manqué : c'est le dessert favori de son mari. Charles avale sans mot dire. C'est mou et sucré, donc facile à manger. Mathilde le regarde. Elle ne touche plus à son bol, allume une cigarette. Elle n'a plus faim ; elle reste là, assise, la nuque raide et le ventre creux, devant un mort dont le menton dégoutte de crème fondue.

Elle se détourne et ouvre la télé. Un vieux film avec Elvis Presley. Hawaii. Les filles ont des fleurs piquées dans les cheveux. C'est idiot, mais il lui vient une brutale envie de fuir. Les îles ! Voilà ce qui les réunit tous, elle, lui, sa mère, Marie-Paule et même Jean-Louis. Une passion, une maladie contagieuse : tous en sont atteints aussi sûrement que si elle était inscrite dans le code génétique familial.

Charles Dalpé se tourne et se retourne dans son lit. Il a mal au ventre. Son œil malade brûle. Il sait qu'il a trop bu. Il ne dort pas. Il a le foie douloureux mais ne prendra pas ses pilules, cette panoplie de pilules qui encombre sa table de chevet. Bien fait pour Estelle si à son retour elle découvre un moribond.

Il s'entend parler à voix haute, sursaute : c'est à peine s'il reconnaît sa propre voix.

Mathilde ma Mathilde viens   oui viens là   étends-toi là
près de moi   laisse ta tête reposer sur l'oreiller tout contre
la mienne   tu entends Mathilde c'est la sirène le jour du
départ est enfin venu   sous le lit il y a la mer   nous dérivons Mathilde   immobiles tous les deux les nerfs brûlés
pansant nos blessures   le vent se lève le lit tangue maintenant   mais nous reposons inertes car nous sommes les
énervés du dimanche   le lit d'apparat nous emporte
nous ne dormirons pas Mathilde   nous veillerons les yeux
tournés vers le large   ne me touche pas Mathilde pas encore
    défais plutôt tes tresses laisse mousser tes cheveux   tu
es belle dans ta robe bleue comme la mer de Chine
regarde Mathilde toutes ces îles entre lesquelles nous dérivons   vois ces fleurs de paradis ces pétales étoilés sur l'eau
    l'air est parfumé   seuls les grands oiseaux de mer nous
accompagnent et nous allons au fil de l'eau frayant entre les
îles   nous ne ferons pas escale Mathilde   ne bougeons pas
nous arriverons au bout du monde

dis-moi Mathilde tu ne reconnais pas cette odeur particu-

lière un parfum lourd et sucré l'odeur de la mélasse
Mathilde   vite donne-moi à boire   j'ai soif   mais pourquoi souris-tu   nos réserves sont à sec nous n'avons plus
rien à boire   j'ai soif   aide-moi Mathilde   vite   je
meurs de soif   ce parfum me rend malade   je t'en prie
Mathilde rien qu'une goutte une petite goutte   mais qu'y
a-t-il ne bouge pas ainsi nous allons chavirer   non
Mathilde non l'eau est lourde comme du sirop   c'est un
océan de rhum et je me noie Mathilde je ne peux plus respirer   arrête Mathilde aide-moi plutôt   cette eau lourde
me colle à la peau   vois cet îlot là-bas c'est La Désirade je
vais mourir au large de La Désirade   non Mathilde ma
Ma ma ma

mais qu'est-ce que cette masse informe   une méduse qui
étire ses tentacules gélatineux   qu'est-ce qui m'arrive bon
dieu   je suis à bout   les poumons gorgés de mélasse   on
dirait un fœtus   c'est un garçon avorté   Jean-Louis c'est
toi Jean-Louis aide-moi Jean-Louis   merci Jean-Louis
    mon fils   nous sommes deux survivants nous avons
survécu à la colère des femmes   nous irons là où tu voudras Jean-Louis ne me laisse pas seul   vois le Nil est une
mer étale et l'appel du muezzin une blessure dans l'air
évitons les côtes Jean-Louis et buvons ensemble pendant que
la mer est belle   fuyons la terre   non Jean-Louis ne me
laisse pas pas maintenant

quelle est cette silhouette que j'aperçois sous un nuage de
tulle blanc   Estelle mais c'est toi Estelle nue derrière le flot

des rubans satinés   Estelle alanguie dans un transatlan-
tique un verre à la main   elle m'attend sur le quai elle me
tend les bras elle m'offre à boire   bonjour Estelle   mais
non plus jamais je te le promets   oui tu as raison Estelle je
suis à toi   oui je ferai tout ce que tu voudras   merci il y a
si longtemps que j'avais soif   j'ai encore soif   non pas ça
Estelle non   va-t'en Estelle va-t'en   je suis épuisé tu me
tues Estelle tu cries et ton cri est guttural c'est le cri étince-
lant de l'oiseau-guêpier   va-t'en vieille bête volatile caque-
tant sous tes rubans de satin que le vent effiloche et rejette à
la mer   cela fait autant de petits éclats colorés qui fusent
au travers de l'eau   je suis un chasseur Estelle un chasseur
de proie jacassante

chasseur chassé mais immortel je vivrai au moins jusqu'à
cent ans

DIX-SEPT HEURES

Elle a dormi près de deux heures, en plein après-midi et sur un divan. Voilà qui est tout à fait inhabituel : les effets de l'analgésique sans doute. Elle se masse le front. La douleur se réveille aussitôt. Elle ferme les yeux, prête à se rendormir, à récupérer toutes ces nuits blanches peuplées de rêveries sonores, tintamarre de paroles éclatées, fracas et débris de verre charriés jusqu'à l'aube, lorsque enfin le sommeil la prend. Si elle pouvait dormir encore un peu… Les heures dormies sont autant de cases vides qu'elle parcourt avec insouciance, avant de réintégrer son casse-tête inachevé et de se remettre au jeu de patience infinie du dimanche. Elle est fatiguée, si fatiguée qu'il lui semble que ses membres vont se détacher d'elle, qu'elle pourrait perdre un bras, une jambe, la tête, n'importe lesquels de ces morceaux épars accidentellement réunis. Plus tard. Elle dormira plus tard.

Elle sait qu'elle ne dormira qu'après.

Parfaitement éveillée maintenant, elle le regarde. Il dort encore, lui. Il ne sait peut-être pas qu'elle est rentrée, munie de cigarettes et de médicaments, bardée de souvenirs et plus déterminée que jamais, prête à tenir un siège.

Elle tousse. Il remue dans son fauteuil. Elle allume une cigarette. Elle devrait le réveiller ; c'est ce que sa mère ferait si elle était là, sinon il n'aura pas faim, refusera de manger quelque chose de chaud avant de se mettre au lit pour la nuit. Dormir, boire, dormir, boire, manger, dormir et boire encore, pisser plus souvent qu'à son tour : à quelques cabrioles près, c'est la vie quotidienne de Jasmine et Jérômine. Elle va le laisser dormir. Estelle et Marie-Paule absente, la nuit leur appartient.

La première fois, elle avait seize ans. Quinze jours seule avec lui. Ils se parlaient à peine. Rapidement, ils en étaient venus à ne plus reconnaître le jour de la nuit. Ils lisaient, lui buvant sans retenue, elle fumant. Les effluves mêlés de l'alcool et de l'herbe, Chivas sélect et pur « mexican gold », se répandaient dans toute la maison. Ils ne s'habillaient plus qu'exceptionnellement, ne sortaient plus, se rencontraient parfois dans la cuisine, en robe de chambre et pantoufles, le cheveu hirsute, pris d'une fringale subite à cinq heures du matin. Alors ils mangeaient n'importe quoi. Sans se concerter, ils avaient opté pour un mode de vie identique : horaire anarchique, boulimie de lectures et réclusion volontaire. Dehors, l'été était chaud et ensoleillé, mais une commune inertie les retenait à l'intérieur. Pareils à des fantômes, ils erraient rue Oxford déjà complices et définitivement taciturnes. Cela avait continué ainsi, jusqu'à ce qu'il se mette à boire vraiment trop, à s'endormir le nez dans sa soupe en marmonnant des paroles dénuées de sens, à ne plus manger du tout, à tomber par terre, et qu'elle prévienne sa mère, la suppliant d'écourter ses vacances.

Il ouvre enfin les yeux. Il ne sait plus où il en est, ce qu'elle fait là, où est Estelle, quand arrivent Marie-Paule et Jean-Louis. Son œil malade paraît prêt à sortir de son orbite. Elle répond à toutes ses questions.

Calmé, il annonce qu'il est déjà cinq heures largement passées et qu'il est plus que temps de s'offrir mutuellement un petit apéritif. « Mais bien sûr, papa. J'ai amené quelque chose de bon, tu vas voir. Un cadeau de Noël pour toi. C'est Julien qui me l'a offert, mais j'ai pensé que tu apprécierais plus que moi. Je cours le chercher. Attends ! » Elle se dérobe aux interrogations paternelles (qu'est-ce que c'est, qui est ce Julien ?) et file à la bibliothèque.

Elle respire mieux. Le salon embaume la fleur mourante, mais dans la bibliothèque l'air sent bon le tabac refroidi et le vieux papier. Le rhum Clément est là, caché derrière les dictionnaires. Il fait frais, la pièce est peu chauffée puisque son père n'y vient presque plus. La bouteille à la main, il lui vient l'envie de l'ouvrir tout de suite. Une bonne rasade, et elle s'endormirait aussitôt, succombant à la chaleur et remettant à un autre dimanche la recherche de la pièce manquante du puzzle. Elle secoue les mains. Grimace. Suit du doigt le tracé de la veine saillante qui menace de percer la tempe. Et machinalement elle s'exhorte au calme. *Vous êtes calme de plus en plus calme détendue…* Suffit ! L'image repoussante de

Marie-Paule surgit, zélatrice de la médecine douce et des tisanes de tout acabit.

Un livre. Cela seul dispensera le calme et la distance nécessaires. Elle feuillette au hasard l'album illustré qui vient de lui tomber sous la main. C'est une étude de Roger Caillois sur l'art fantastique. *Les énervés de Jumièges* : deux jeunes suppliciés de sang royal sont étendus côte à côte sur un radeau à la dérive, une sorte de lit d'apparat qui flotte, somptueux entre les rives désertes d'un fleuve aux eaux jaunes. Elle s'aperçoit que son père a marqué la page, mais sans hésiter elle l'arrache. Cela devrait plaire à Julien. Elle lit le texte d'accompagnement. Les jeunes princes ont subi l'énervation : on leur a extirpé les nerfs des genoux et ils gisent paralysés.

Un calme effrayant. Voilà exactement ce qu'elle ressent. Elle aussi se sent flotter, énervée, sereine et tourmentée. Elle empoigne la bouteille de rhum. Il attend.

Il n'en croit pas ses yeux, celui de gauche surtout qui depuis des années lui a joué plus d'un mauvais tour. Sa fille brandit fièrement la bouteille. « Regarde, papa : c'est un rhum agricole de la Martinique. On ne l'exporte plus depuis longtemps, tu sais, il faut aller le chercher sur place. Du rhum Clément : rappelle-toi, tu en as déjà parlé. Goûte ! Ça se boit pur comme un bon cognac. Je me fais un verre moi aussi. Je n'y ai pas touché, j'attendais le moment de trinquer avec toi. Vas-y, goûte ! »

Elle remplit les verres. Ils boivent cérémonieusement. Elle remplit les verres de nouveau. Ils se taisent vaguement émus.

Elle se masse la tempe. L'alcool est une menace, elle ne doit pas succomber, boire trop vite et s'endormir. Il faut qu'elle soit alerte et vigilante jusqu'à la fin.

Charles regarde sa fille qui bâille à plusieurs reprises. Et rompant le silence, il murmure en un bredouillis à peine distinct : « Tu as l'air fatiguée, ma Mathilde. » Oui, elle dort mal depuis quelques jours. Mais comment lui confier l'obsession qui la retient éveillée, seule et obstinée au milieu de la nuit ?

Alors, il se met une fois de plus à évoquer le souvenir du bébé insomniaque qu'il devait bercer, quand Estelle à bout de nerfs enfouissait rageusement la tête sous l'oreiller. Elle connaît par cœur l'histoire de ce bébé qui, de rage, se heurtait la tête contre les barreaux de la bassinnette, de la mère enragée à son tour, du bébé veillant seul dans le salon obscur, les yeux grands ouverts dans la nuit, toutes larmes taries, seul et vigilant pendant que les parents feignaient de dormir là-haut, l'histoire de bébé Mathilde, seule et souveraine parmi les ombres de la nuit.

Elle ne l'écoute plus, remplit les verres. Ils boivent en silence. Au bout de quelques minutes, il se remet à radoter : « Où est Estelle, qu'est-ce qu'elle fait ? Elle exagère ! Et Marie-Paule, Jean-Louis, comment se fait-il qu'ils ne soient pas encore là, il est presque six heures et demie ? » Oui, sa mère devrait rentrer, Marie-Paule et Jean-Louis arriver bientôt main dans la main comme avant, la pièce de bœuf saigner dans les assiettes, et elle, Mathilde, ranger la bouteille de rhum et se mettre sagement à table.

Son verre est vide. Tout en pensant à sa mère partie se refaire une vie chez des amis qui vieillissent paisiblement (un couple modèle qui se consacre à « gérer » sa vieillesse avec intelligence), elle pose la bouteille de rhum à portée de la main de son père. « Joyeux Noël, papa ! » Charles, réjoui, contemple l'étiquette, puis déclare : « Mais qu'est-ce que tu attends, ma fille, pour nous inviter chez toi et nous présenter ton Julien ? Il y a des mois que je n'ai pas vu le bord de l'eau. »

Ils sont tous venus passer un dimanche devant le fleuve. C'était au début de l'été et seul Jean-Louis manquait à la fête. Elle pense que ce dimanche aura été le dernier, que son tour ne reviendra plus désormais, et elle ne répond pas.

Il feignait de dormir. Jérômine, roulée en boule sur ses genoux, ronronnait dès qu'il la flattait. Il n'osait plus bouger de peur de l'incommoder. Jasmine les observait, la mine sévère, outrée devant cette familiarité tapageuse que sa fille se permettait de témoigner à l'envahisseur ; Mathilde les avait toutes deux chassées de la causeuse pour l'offrir à ce vieux monsieur qui sentait la mélasse et grimaçait dans son sommeil en se racontant à lui-même d'inaudibles histoires.

Il soupira. Quand se décideraient-elles enfin à rentrer ? L'avaient-elles oublié là, sur la véranda, pour mieux se livrer à leur passe-temps favori : parler de lui, sinon contre lui ?

Ainsi Mathilde avait déposé les armes. Marie-Paule avait su la convaincre. Oh ! il était sans illusion. Ça n'était pas pour lui qu'elle était revenue à de meilleurs sentiments. Estelle, privée depuis bientôt deux mois de son rituel dominical, en était tombée malade. Un cocktail indigeste de somnifères, calmants divers, alcool avait eu raison de sa santé déjà affaiblie. Car Estelle buvait, raisonnablement bien sûr, mais enfin elle buvait ; tous les jours, l'heure de l'apéritif venue, elle l'accompagnait. Il l'encourageait parfois à forcer un peu la mesure. Rien de tel pour se détendre et prédisposer au sommeil, il en savait quelque chose. Et avantage non négligeable, elle oubliait alors de faire le compte de ce qu'il buvait, lui.

Hélas ! les choses avaient mal tourné. Elle s'était mise tout à coup à pleurer des après-midi entiers, à vomir indéfiniment un flot continu de paroles hargneuses, récriminations, appels au secours, réclamant Mathilde et encore du gin, prophétisant entre deux haut-le-cœur sa mort imminente, jusqu'à ce que Marie-Paule intervienne, la console et la sermonne, téléphone à Mathilde, l'enjoignant de cesser immédiatement ses enfantillages, empoche flacons et bouteilles dissimulés jusque sous le lit, et lui confie à lui (le monde à l'envers !) la surveillance de son épouse repentante.

Tout était finalement rentré dans l'ordre. Mathilde réapparue (mais qu'est-ce qui lui avait pris de disparaître ainsi sans prévenir ?), ce dimanche se déroulerait sans heurt, tels tous ceux qui l'avaient précédé selon la tradition imposée par Estelle.

Retenant Jérômine de la main, il se redressa légèrement et tenta de les apercevoir. Elles devaient se promener sous les trembles. Le sol était encore boueux ; il avait manqué de s'étaler tantôt mais Marie-Paule lui avait prestement tendu le bas. L'été tardait à venir.

Il aimait bien cette maison, un vieux chalet mal rafistolé (comment s'en arrangeait-elle en hiver ?), un abri précaire exposé au vent du nord. On y arrivait par le rang de l'Équerre tracé entre de vastes étendues plates, la masse liquide du Saint-Laurent refoulée derrière la barrière des trembles, une longue route droite qui se terminait par un tournant abrupt, cul-de-sac inattendu que clôturait la maison. N'eût été la silhouette du pont Mercier qu'on devinait au loin, on se serait cru à mille lieues de Montréal, égaré aux confins de l'un de ces déserts américains qui surgissent au beau milieu des banlieues.

Le jour déclinait. Le coucher de soleil serait magnifique. Jérômine ponctuait ses ronrons de roucoulements béats pendant que Jasmine posait sur lui un regard implacablement vert. Il pensa que cette chatte avait les mêmes yeux que Mathilde quand elle était seule avec lui.

Elles viendraient le rejoindre sur la véranda dans quelques minutes. Mathilde servirait à boire. Elle trouvait toujours le moyen de dénicher quelque part l'une de ces bonnes bouteilles de rhum des Antilles. Estelle commencerait par ne s'accorder qu'un doigt de Cinzano. Pauvre Estelle ! si délicate, elle n'était pas de taille à rivaliser avec lui. Mais elle n'en était pas moins devenue, peu à peu, son inavouable complice.

Marie-Paule se demande comment sa sœur, si démunie devant les exigences de la vie quotidienne, arrive à se débrouiller seule dans cette cabane déglinguée qui pue la moisissure. C'est vrai qu'il y a ce Julien dont Mathilde parle parfois, mais qu'elle cache à la famille comme si elle craignait qu'on ne l'abîme ; il habite à côté, une sorte de grange plus ou moins retapée, et il ne serait pas étonnant, pour peu qu'il ait la tête de l'emploi, qu'elle vive totalement à ses dépens. C'est Julien qui doit veiller à l'entretien général, réparer, déboucher, pelleter, nettoyer, cuisiner même, balayer, recoudre ses boutons, et elle, la petite princesse, le sonner dès qu'il y a quelque chose qui cloche. Sans compter que cet homme idéal est aussi un artiste accompli : il a offert à Mathilde une peinture sur soie magnifique, mais cet univers équivoque inquiète plus qu'il ne séduit. Une douceur un peu perverse qui laisse mal à l'aise, mais une réussite tout de même à côté de laquelle les essais de Jean-Louis font figure de croûtes baveuses.

Marie-Paule se reproche aussitôt cette comparaison odieuse que sa rancœur envers Jean-Louis vient de susciter. Elle lui en veut, c'est entendu, mais elle doit vivre maintenant avec ces émotions contraires qui l'envahissent, exprimer sa colère tout comme sa tristesse, faire de cette rupture une étape enrichissante sur le chemin de sa croissance personnelle, et pour cela se garder précisément de semblables accès de puérilité. Elle tend la main vers le paquet de cigarettes qui traîne sur la table voisine. Et puis, non, elle ne va pas se remettre à fumer, elle qui tient le coup depuis plus de cinq ans !

Mathilde propose un apéritif. Estelle approuve, elle a bien besoin de se réchauffer ; on est déjà en juin, mais les nuits sont encore fraîches et cette maison, terriblement humide. Mathilde rétorque que justement on est en juin, donc il ne fera pas nuit avant au moins trois heures, alors pourquoi ne pas réfléchir avant de parler, et que sous-entend ce « déjà », pourquoi revenir sur la parenthèse close du mois de mai ? Sa mère, qui n'a pas compris, ne répond pas. Marie-Paule cherche en vain à détendre l'atmosphère ; quand Mathilde fait la raisonneuse, il vaut mieux ne pas insister. Tant de sujets de conversation sont tabous : sa rupture avec Jean-Louis, les récents excès maternels, la disparition de Mathilde rentrée au bercail sans une explication. Pas un mot, pas un signe, pendant tout le mois de mai. Et la voilà aujourd'hui qui comble de ses largesses la famille à nouveau réunie (en oubliant Jean-Louis, bien sûr…) : le meilleur rhum, du saumon fumé, des pâtes fraîches qu'elle prétend avoir faites elle-même, un menu alléchant qu'elle a énuméré tout à l'heure du bout des lèvres comme si tout à coup, exténuée par tant d'efforts, elle n'avait plus la force de cacher le déplaisir qu'elle a à les recevoir.

Marie-Paule propose son aide à Mathilde ; sa sœur a si peu l'habitude, elle est certainement paniquée. D'ailleurs, cette histoire de pâtes paraît douteuse. A-t-elle au moins prévu une sauce, une salade, un dessert ? Et puis, peut-être pourront-elles en profiter pour échanger quelques confidences ?

Tout est sous contrôle. L'eau bout. La sauce mijote. Mathilde demande à Marie-Paule si elle veut bien préparer la vinaigrette. Julien n'a pas eu le temps de la faire. Car c'est lui bien entendu qui a tout fait : les pâtes, la sauce, et même le baba au rhum. Elle a presque envie de l'avouer à sa sœur.

Mais elle n'aime pas parler de Julien. D'ailleurs, elle ne l'a finalement pas invité, à la dernière minute elle l'a chassé ; elle ne veut pas de lui parmi les convives désenchantés des dimanches qui se mettent à saliver dès qu'elle prononce son nom. Et parler de Julien risque d'amener Marie-Paule à aborder le sujet de sa récente rupture avec Jean-Louis. Elle préfère ne pas entendre l'inévitable succession des lieux communs, ce discours raisonnable, déjà mâché, vite digéré, dans lequel il sera certainement question de « parcours », de « conflit des émotions », de « couple à penser, repenser, assumer », de « désir », « autonomie », « pouvoir », de « rapport à », de « notion de », de…, il n'y a pas de quoi rire, l'eau des pâtes est en train de déborder !

Le repas est servi. Charles et Estelle mangent avec peu d'appétit, les apéritifs leur ont coupé la faim. Marie-Paule et Mathilde évitent de se regarder. Les deux sœurs mesurent avec effroi le fossé qui les sépare. Elles n'ont plus rien à attendre l'une de l'autre.

Marie-Paule rumine l'échec de sa tentative de dialogue avec Mathilde. Sa sœur n'y est pas allée par quatre chemins. Ainsi, Jean-Louis serait un imbécile infatué de son image, un gars correct, progressiste, féministe, internationaliste, terriblement ennuyeux en fait, incapable de la moindre idée personnelle, englué jusqu'au cou dans les stéréotypes actuels ; petit cinéaste qui réfléchit les clichés ambiants dans ses productions raisonneuses, maladroites, et d'une fadeur telle que seul un grand bol de tisane paraîtrait aussi insipide. L'incompréhensible rancœur, la hargne qui habitent Mathilde depuis quelques temps expliquent ce portrait sommaire exécuté à gros traits. Elle en veut au monde entier. Marie-Paule sait bien que Jean-Louis, au fond, ne demande qu'à l'aider à assumer cette rupture dont elle sortira grandie. Quant à Estelle, elle serait, selon Mathilde, une mère indigne, condamnée à marcher sur les traces de leur père dont elle aurait par ailleurs favorisé la déchéance. Il suffirait pourtant d'un minimum de compassion et d'autorité pour contenir cette tendance au mimétisme. Mathilde seule, à l'en croire, parviendrait à survivre, intacte, imperméable aux tempêtes familiales que l'alcool distille régulièrement. Mais qu'est-ce que cette pharmacie où s'entassent les somnifères et les tranquillisants, et ces joints roulés finement qui traînent un peu partout, comme si la petite sœur n'allait jamais sortir de son adolescence prolongée ? Mathilde a prononcé un verdict sans appel. Dommage ! Marie-Paule enroule une pâte autour de sa fourchette et l'avale, étonnée : sa sœur aura tout de même appris à cuisiner.

La bouteille de vin est déjà vide. Charles et Mathilde fument. Le silence est total. Même Marie-Paule s'est tue. Mathilde dévisage sa mère, elle tousse, sa gorge est douloureuse, une séquelle d'un rhume mal soigné de l'hiver dernier. Quand elle était encore une écolière, elle avait souvent le rhume, et cela lui valait par la suite de brèves mais merveilleuses périodes de convalescence. Par de brumeux après-midi d'hiver, pelotonnée dans la voiture, seule avec sa mère, elle feignait de tousser gravement afin de prolonger ces moments ravis. La longue Lincoln noire, héritée du grand-père récemment décédé, ronronnait doucement et mère et fille se lovaient dans ses flancs. Elles s'offraient un jour de congé, en plein hiver, s'imaginant en fuite vers la Floride et le soleil qui empêcherait le virus de dégénérer en bronchite. Sages cependant, elles se contentaient de rouler au hasard des rues de la ville, s'arrêtant çà et là pour acheter des vitamines et du foie de veau, s'enfermant pour quelques heures dans un cinéma. En retard pour l'apéro, elles se pressaient vers la rue Oxford, prêtes à subir les récriminations paternelles. L'image de monsieur Hulot se débattant avec son jet d'eau resterait gravée dans la mémoire de ces escapades rieuses faites à l'insu du médecin de famille, ce bon docteur Patenaude toujours enclin à prescrire les antibiotiques et le lit. Mais aujourd'hui Estelle a encore bu trop de vin, elle mange à peine, divague, rend compte des démarches erratiques qu'elle a entreprises : il faut que cette boutique de vêtements voie le jour avant qu'elle ne soit trop vieille pour assister à l'ouverture, « Qu'est-ce que tu attends Mathilde pour te secouer un peu, et toi, Marie-Paule pourquoi ne pas t'associer avec ta sœur, non Charles tu seras malade demain si tu bois encore, tu te tiendras le ventre à deux mains tant pis pour toi ».

Mathilde regarde sa mère avec dégoût : une vieille femme geignarde et acariâtre que la haine défigure. Victime de son impuissance, incapable d'abandonner un alcoolique que ce seul geste aurait peut-être suffi à sauver, lâche et résignée, elle n'a trouvé que l'alcool à portée de la main pour s'enfoncer davantage dans son malheur quotidien. Elle sait pourtant, depuis quelques semaines, que sa fille n'en veut plus de cette boutique, mais elle en parle encore comme on rêve à voix haute.

Non, Mathilde ne deviendra pas vendeuse. De toute façon, depuis Radio-Canada, elle n'a nulle envie de travailler, non plus que de s'exprimer d'une manière ou d'une autre. Elle ne va certainement pas se mettre à peindre, à danser, à écrire, à chanter, à jouer du tam-tam, à faire des films, ainsi que Marie-Paule l'y incite. Il y a déjà bien assez d'amateurs et d'exhibitionnistes autour d'elle, l'atmosphère culturelle qui sévit ici est suffisamment polluée comme ça. Non, elle n'a plus envie de rien, même pas de sortir, voyager, manger au restaurant avec des amis en racontant ses états d'âme, rencontrer des gens « intéressants » ; elle ne souhaite plus que leur départ à tous, qu'ils s'en aillent et ne reviennent jamais. Avec une infinie délicatesse, elle découpe le baba au rhum et sert à chacun la part qui lui revient.

Si Charles réclame encore à boire, si Estelle lui répond en simulant l'exaspération et en adressant à ses filles l'un de ses regards complices si terriblement ambigus, si Marie-Paule s'empresse de desservir et en profite pour se livrer de nouveau à quelque confidence sur Jean-Louis, sa propre renaissance, le jeu complexe de ses énergies mutantes (!), Mathilde sait qu'elle éclatera, pour de vrai et non métaphoriquement comme l'entend Marie-Paule quand elle se gargarise avec ses modèles thérapeutiques, elle éclatera, frappera, griffera, rugira, tuera s'il le faut, mais elle arrivera à s'en défaire, à les chasser définitivement. Elle a commencé à faire ses griffes ; la semaine dernière encore elle s'est battue avec un inconnu qui voulait l'empêcher de fumer à la sortie du cinéma. Elle allume une cigarette. Maintenant, il faut faire du café, ils en ont tous besoin.

Estelle termine son café. La cafetière est vide et elle n'ose pas en redemander. La machine infernale s'est remise en marche. Ce maudit bourdonnement d'oreilles ! Sa fille aînée paraît triste ; ce Jean-Louis ne mérite pourtant pas qu'on le regrette à ce point. Mathilde s'est enfermée dans un silence impénétrable. Qu'est-ce qui lui prend encore ? Son repas était réussi, tout le monde lui en a fait compliment. Charles somnole comme d'habitude. Marie-Paule et Mathilde lui en veulent ; il n'y a pas de doute, elles lui reprochent son laisser-aller. Il y a des jours, c'est vrai, où elle n'arrive plus à donner le change. La vie est difficile rue Oxford. Ses filles la négligent depuis ce dimanche de janvier où elle a capitulé devant le docteur Patenaude. Comment se défaire de Charles après tant d'années ? N'importe qui comprendrait ça. Oui, la vie est difficile rue Oxford ; elle est longue, si longue. Que va-t-elle devenir si même Marie-Paule, sa grande fille, son meilleur soutien, l'abandonne ?

Les larmes ne sont pas loin. Estelle a un malaise. Si elle pouvait faire taire ces démons qui bourdonnent dans ses oreilles malades et finiront par la rendre folle !

mais qu'est-ce que j'ai fait au Bon Dieu pour qu'Il m'inflige ce châtiment quotidien   ma pauvre tête colonisée qu'il me faut partager avec cette horde malfaisante   grincements sifflements mugissements bourdonnements grognements   allez-vous vous taire à la fin cesser de me crier dans les oreilles   une petite goutte une larme de gin encore une et qu'ils s'endorment enfin repus   ils sont pressants ils réclament exigent vocifèrent à boire à boire   je les connais bien j'ai l'habitude de les servir   quand je les oublie ils se vengent pire encore que Charles et moi qui déteste l'alcool j'avale je leur donne des pilules aussi ils aiment bien alors j'avale j'avale valiums équanils halcions plus je leur en donne plus ils en veulent   ça je connais c'est du Charles tout craché   et Marie-Paule qui s'obstine à ne rien comprendre   je ferme les yeux et j'avale je les nourris comme une mère Marie-Paule une bonne mère quand ils sont à jeun ils crient mais le gin les calme et les endort   je fais la grimace le cœur me lève devant toutes ces bouteilles mais ensuite ils se taisent ils dorment engourdis   tu vois maintenant ils se sont tus   je me tue c'est ce que tu crois Marie-

*Paule mais tu ne sais pas ce que c'est que de vieillir   dites-
moi chère madame mais ce ne sont pas vos filles ces grandes
filles déjà on dirait plutôt trois sœurs   rappelle-toi ce monsieur sobre et élégant sur la plage de Wells nous étions toutes
trois allongées sous le parasol dans nos jolis maillots neufs
achetés la veille à Boston et Mathilde feignait de lire pendant qu'il nous complimentait   il mentait dis-tu tais-toi
je suis vieille Marie-Paule je sais j'ai les mains tachées et tu
ne te prives pas de me le rappeler   « la Floride c'est beaucoup trop loin il faut te reposer maintenant rester à la maison tranquillement »   oui je suis une vieille femme fatiguée mais ils ont encore besoin de moi   tous   Charles
Mathilde Marie-Paule et cette horde qui m'appelle légère
stridulation dans l'oreille gauche la rumeur allant se gon-
flant ils ne sont jamais rassasiés   je proteste mais je cède
toujours à mes parasites intimes ils le savent et ils en profitent   je leur sacrifie jusqu'à ma dignité jusqu'à mon sang
qui draine l'alcool   ils sont avides ils pompent si bien que
parfois les forces me manquent je fléchis perds l'équilibre
tombe   oh ! retiens-moi Marie-Paule   ils me font mal je
les hais ils sont voraces   je crois qu'ils sont téléguidés c'est
Charles qui me les envoie je les hais je les tuerai   mais ils
sont habiles ils me prennent par les sentiments c'est Charles
qui leur a appris   alors moi tu me connais Marie-Paule je
succombe je me dévoue je leur donne tout ce qu'ils veulent
    j'ai une longue expérience je soigne mon mari le fais
boire le ramasse remets les morceaux en place je cours à l'hôpital panse les blessures faites en tombant sillonne la ville
achète l'alcool les médicaments   et la viande le beau bœuf*

saignant la santé j'en extrais le jus les vitamines et je cours à l'hôpital vive et menue il va mourir c'est le cancer papa va mourir les médecins l'ont confirmé alors je cours vers lui avec le sang de bœuf frais et il le boit il ne boit que ça car il déteste l'alcool le cancer est généralisé mais je viens tous les jours j'ai la bouteille de sang dans mon sac   Mathilde m'accompagne parfois elle ne va pas à l'école elle tousse elle vient à l'hôpital avec moi elle aime les promenades courir à travers la ville dans la longue Lincoln noire sa dernière voiture il ne peut plus la conduire   alors c'est moi qui conduis j'aime conduire tu entends Marie-Paule je ne suis pas si vieille je sais encore conduire et j'irai au bout du monde j'emmènerai Mathilde je lui ferai manger du foie de veau   et puisqu'ils ne veulent pas me quitter je les emmènerai eux aussi   ils me donnent la nausée mais il ne sera pas dit qu'ils me garderont couchée dans mon salon à attendre la mort à côté de lui qui dort dans son fauteuil

la mort en robe de chambre à quatre heures de l'aprèsmidi un verre à la main   je suis vieille je sais ils n'arrêtent pas de me le crier dans les oreilles   j'aurais besoin d'un petit gin pour les faire taire   il faut les comprendre ce sont des enfants   tu as peut-être raison Marie-Paule je sais tu veux m'aider   je sais Mathilde tu les détestes toi aussi tu me détestes parce que je les héberge mais vous ne les connaissez pas ils ne lâchent pas prise si facilement   n'ayez crainte pourtant je tombe mais je sais me relever toute seule   et c'est toute seule que je mourrai un jour bientôt quand je n'aurai plus personne à nourrir

DIX-NEUF HEURES

Elle fume. À moitié vide déjà, la bouteille de rhum est posée entre eux. Elle n'y touche plus. Lui n'ose pas. Les deux verres qu'elle a bus, trois onces à peine, ont aggravé sa migraine. Chaque heure qui passe vient battre contre sa tempe. Le temps est lancinant.

Qu'est-elle venue faire ici ? Mais oui ! du gardiennage, du daddy sitting, de la suppléance en somme. On dit que les enfants délaissés sont agités, qu'ils en profitent, les petits monstres, et qu'aussitôt que papa, maman et la maîtresse ont le dos tourné ils font les fous. Lui pourtant se contente de hoqueter bien tranquille dans son fauteuil.

Elle le fait boire. Comme il est docile ! Il ne reste plus qu'à le faire manger maintenant. Le réfrigérateur est plein : les restes du repas de Noël, de quoi nourrir un village entier du Sahel, puisque seul ce pauvre Jean-Louis, tout à la joie de réintégrer sa famille d'accueil, a mangé avec appétit. Sa mère lui a recommandé de ne pas s'en faire, un petit steak vite fait et le tour est joué, ou encore une pointe de la tourtière de tante Adèle. Elle imagine la déglutition laborieuse, la fourchette qui pique à côté, le pantalon souillé, la bave au menton, et prend la résolution d'ignorer délibérément l'heure du souper. Ce dimanche ne sera pas comme les autres. Estelle et Marie-Paule ont pris congé, aussi bien en profiter pour lui faire plaisir et réaliser son rêve en prolongeant indéfiniment l'heure de l'apéritif jusqu'à ce que la bouteille soit complètement vide.

Un dimanche en trop, pense-t-elle, une parenthèse inutile entre Noël et le Jour de l'An, mais puisqu'elle a cédé et qu'elle est venue, il ne sera pas dit que cette année s'achèvera comme elle a commencé. Elle a tout prévu. Seule la retient encore cette insidieuse tentation de lâcher contre laquelle elle doit sans cesse lutter. Ne pas rater l'occasion, le faire ce soir : elle en est capable. Elle ne continuera pas plus longtemps à tourner en rond dans le manège familial. Rien n'est plus simple : il suffit d'accélérer le mouvement pour que le mécanisme s'enraye. Pris de peur, les chevaux de bois montés par les enfants sages s'emballent et, délivrés, ils foncent droit devant.

En finir une fois pour toutes. Voilà ce qu'elle est venue faire ici. Se le répéter encore et encore pour mieux s'en convaincre. Elle doit réussir à lui faire boire tout le rhum qui reste. Sinon, si elle s'en va maintenant, si elle court se blottir sous l'édredon, bien serrée entre Jasmine et Jérômine, si elle s'arrête dans le tournant du rang de l'Équerre et reste accrochée à Julien, son père se paiera encore un verre ou deux, puis il s'endormira, par terre puisque sans doute il sera tombé sur le chemin semé d'embûches qui va de son fauteuil à son lit, et il se réveillera le lendemain en maudissant son âge, le climat et cette mauvaise « grippe » qu'il couve depuis des années.

Pour le moment, il se racle la gorge, crache dans son mouchoir, éternue. Cet éternuement est le premier d'une interminable et retentissante série. Ainsi qu'il en a l'habitude, il ouvre grand la bouche, laisse monter, évite tout particulièrement de se moucher et, triomphant, explose. Puis, il remet ça. D'ordinaire, c'est à table qu'il lâche ainsi ses petites bombes, ce feu roulant qui s'éteint de lui-même une fois que les convives, abasourdis et le cœur soulevé, ont tous abdiqué devant leur assiette.

Elle attend calmement que la pantomime prenne fin. Grâce à ses écouteurs et à la cassette providentiellement oubliée dans le minuscule appareil que Julien lui a offert à Noël, elle voit son père qui s'agite, pendant qu'emportée sur les routes minérales de *Paris-Texas* elle n'entend rien que la voix rauque et nasillarde qui avoue : « *That was all she dreamed about, escape.* »

Le verre paternel est vide. Elle le remplit. Il ne s'en apercevra même pas, croira qu'il n'en avait pas encore fini, tout occupé qu'il est maintenant à se curer le nez.

Elle rajuste son walkman ; une guitare sèche griffe ses oreilles, traverse le désert granuleux qui s'étend derrière son front douloureux. La migraine ne l'effraie plus maintenant. Dès qu'elle en aura fini, le malaise disparaîtra à jamais. Sitôt couchée, à peine aura-t-elle fermé les yeux qu'elle s'endormira ; ses nuits seront longues, fécondes, à la mesure de ses jours qui, enfin, lui seront rendus.

La guitare se fait déchirante. Elle allume une cigarette et s'absorbe dans la contemplation des ombres qui se pressent dans le salon. Il somnole et, bien que la nuit soit tombée depuis longtemps, seul l'écran de la télévision allumée éclaire le crâne à demi chauve qui ballotte sur le cuir du fauteuil.

Solitaire sous ses écouteurs dans le salon obscur, elle erre parmi les roses de sable qui fleurissent dans ses oreilles. Elle ne sent plus la fatigue. Demain, elle aussi arpentera le désert qui l'attend au bout de la nuit. Elle ira dormir dans la lumière blanche, le corps tourné vers le soleil, apaisée, rayonnante, pareille à Jérômine quand elle s'étend sur son lit de gravier devant le fleuve par un bel après-midi d'été. Quand elle s'éveillera, elle retournera peut-être à New York se promener dans les rues de Soho jusqu'à ce qu'elle tombe sur Dean et qu'il l'invite à boire du champagne californien dans son loft. Et quand elle en aura assez de faire la belle devant les beaux esprits newyorkais, elle s'embarquera pour le bout du monde, là où la mer et transparente et l'air lourd des vapeurs de la canne à sucre.

Elle chipe une gorgée de rhum dans le verre de son père, qui semble maintenant profondément endormi. De temps à autre, il émet quelques grognements malaisés. Les années qui viennent le vouent à une dégradation certaine. Il continuera à boire et à tourmenter son entourage. Économe de ses mouvements, dépensant une énergie minimale, il peut vivre encore longtemps. D'un verre à l'autre, son sang éclairci et son cœur pompé par l'alcool maintiendront la machine en état, les inévitables embardées vite maîtrisées par Estelle et Marie-Paule. Et quand elles ne suffiront pas à la tâche, Estelle ponctuellement frappée par l'un de ses accès de mimétisme conjugal et Marie-Paule à bout de nerfs, elles l'inciteront à faire sa part — « c'est ton père, Mathilde, ne l'oublie pas ! »

Les dimanches succéderont aux dimanches comme autant de barrières contre lesquelles les semaines, les mois, les années viendront inéluctablement buter. Elle commencera à vivre à quarante ans quand il sera mort, si tant est qu'il ne se révèle pas immortel comme elle en a le soupçon, elle ira rejoindre la cohorte des morts-vivants qui se félicitent de leur maturité et chérissent les rides qui les défigurent. Voilà ce qui l'attend, si elle n'agit pas tout de suite.

Impossible de chercher à fuir, toutes ses précédentes tentatives ont échoué. Marie-Paule la ramènera encore comme elle l'a fait en juin, elle devra interrompre ses vacances comme en août dernier quand elle a été forcée de venir rejoindre à Wells la famille réunie, où qu'elle aille on la retrouvera, et du bout du monde elle accourra au chevet de l'éternel moribond qu'elle devra veiller ainsi qu'elle le fait ce soir alors que quatre jours à peine se sont écoulés depuis Noël.

Elle se secoue, allume les lampes, monte le volume de la télévision — on entend la musique funèbre des *Beaux dimanches*—, tapote l'épaule paternelle. Il se réveille, termine son verre, se lève en chancelant et, d'un pas mal assuré, se dirige vers la salle de bains.

Quand il revient quelques minutes plus tard, sa fille, souriante, *vous vous sentez calme de plus en plus calme*, lui tend un verre plein.

Bientôt, elle retournera à l'air libre et, débarrassée enfin de cette migraine qui lui scie la tempe, elle ira baigner dans la mer son front poissé d'alcool. Ne s'est-elle pas promis, l'été dernier, de revenir un jour occuper seule la vieille maison verte ?

Affalé dans la vaste berceuse en rotin garnie de coussins fleuris, il cognait des clous. « *You need a rest* » : la vieille maison de bois, ainsi baptisée par l'avocat bostonien qui la leur avait louée pendant des années, était toujours peinte en vert, flanquée de sa tourelle victorienne dominant la mer.

On l'avait traîné jusqu'ici, à Wells Beach dans le Maine, et il était fermement résolu à n'en plus bouger. Non qu'il appréciât particulièrement ce salon dédié au culte animalier, une invraisemblable ménagerie de porcelaine encombrant les tables, les rayonnages de la bibliothèque, et jusqu'aux marches de l'escalier menant aux chambres, mais il était prêt à fermer les yeux sur cet aimable fatras pourvu qu'on le laissât tranquille et qu'il n'ait plus à se déplacer.

Le voyage avait été une épreuve dont il commençait à peine à se remettre. Huit heures de voiture par une chaleur torride qui l'avaient laissé complètement déshydraté malgré les haltes. Un double scotch, deux peut-être, avalés en vitesse pendant que Marie-Paule, d'un *lady's room* à l'autre, s'évertuait à réconforter sa mère affligée de ce malaise désormais chronique : nausées, maux de tête, état dépressif perpétuel. Huit interminables heures sous la conduite nerveuse de Marie-Paule assistée d'un Jean-Louis soucieux de se faire pardonner son absence prolongée. C'était lui, ce cher Jean-Louis, qui, s'il fallait en croire Marie-Paule, avait suggéré ce retour aux sources sur les lieux de vacances estivales tant de fois évoqués par chacun des membres de la famille Dalpé. Cela ferait du bien à Estelle dont nul n'ignorait plus maintenant qu'à son tour elle s'était mise à boire un peu trop. En fait, elle lui tenait tout simplement compagnie ; il n'y avait pas là de quoi s'alarmer ; d'ailleurs elle n'en continuait pas moins à lui faire quotidiennement la morale et à exercer sur lui son habituelle surveillance. Malheureusement sa femme avait toujours eu le gin triste, mais, longtemps, ses accès de découragement (« comment le supporter davantage il ne pense qu'à ça me harcèle jour et nuit refuse de s'habiller j'en ai assez de le voir dormir ») avaient été interprétés comme la rançon de son dévouement à un mari indigne. Ce double jeu ayant été récemment percé à jour par ses filles, le séjour au bord de la mer était donc destiné à entretenir les illusions thérapeutiques de Marie-Paule. Lui, il n'avait jamais accepté de se soumettre à une cure de désintoxication ; ces artificieuses bouffonneries n'étaient pas faites pour lui, Charles Dalpé, alcoolique peut-être (tout de suite les grands mots), mais anonyme certainement pas. Il avait toujours fui le prosélytisme des buveurs repentis, goûtant peu la confession, l'absolution et moins encore le ferme propos subséquent. Tous ces thérapeutes, professionnels ou non, n'étaient somme toute que des curés en mal de brebis égarées et de droit chemin.

Il entendait le vent lutter contre la mer. Les vagues devaient être belles aujourd'hui. Demain, il ferait l'effort de s'habiller et de descendre sur la plage.

Au terme de cette équipée insensée, il retrouvait non sans plaisir le décor familier des vacances d'autrefois : cretonne fleurie aux teintes un peu passées, bimbeloterie de *Christmas shop,* meubles rustiques glanés sur les routes de la Nouvelle-Angleterre par la femme de l'avocat entichée de ces antiquailles du début du siècle. Il y avait sans doute été heureux, bien que ce passé fût si lointain qu'il lui était même impossible de le dater.

Il pourrait tout aussi bien mourir ici, pensait-il, à quelques pas de la mer que ses yeux affaiblis, éblouis par la luminosité du sable trop blanc, devinaient à peine. Plus rien ne le retenait, sinon la perspective de noyer son amertume dans le scotch que Jean-Louis ne tarderait pas à lui servir.

Derrière ses lunettes noires, les images défilaient, portées par la rumeur grandissante de la marée montante. Un montage enchevêtré accompagné d'une trame sonore faite de cris mêlés d'éclats de rire enfantins : une poupée projetée du haut de l'escalier, des poneys trottant sur la plage, le faisceau des lampes de poche qui fouillent les hautes dunes, une battue en pleine nuit, l'océan qui crache ses secrets enfouis, la peur charriée par les vagues.

Puis, au matin, quelques *clams* et du vin doux sur la jetée pendant que la maisonnée endormie récupère. Des cerfs-volants qui trouent le ciel gris d'éclairs colorés, les ongles pointus d'Estelle qui lui déchirent la poitrine, les mouettes frénétiques qui aboient toutes ensemble. Le paisible alignement des maisons de bois devant la mer. La petite fille terrée dans sa forteresse de sable. L'air marin qui monte à la tête et, du coup, dessoûle. Un film désuet qu'Estelle, quand elle reviendrait de son simulacre de bain de mer, allait bientôt interrompre.

Ce premier dimanche du mois d'août rassemblerait toute la famille puisque Mathilde avait promis de venir les rejoindre. Elle arriverait aujourd'hui, il en était sûr. Elle aimait tant la plage de Wells. Elle quitterait ce Julien (mais qu'est-ce qu'elle attendait pour le leur amener?) avec qui elle voyageait quelque part dans Charlevoix et accourrait vers la maison verte de son enfance. Il l'attendait. Mathilde, même si elle ne travaillait plus, avait besoin de vacances; la mer seule parviendrait à émousser le caractère de sa fille dont il avait hâte de revoir le regard vert et fatal.

Marie-Paule et Jean-Louis ont dressé la table sur la terrasse; le vent souffle un peu fort, c'est vrai, mais il est si agréable de manger dehors. Charles a commencé par rouspéter comme d'habitude: il craint un orage subit, son œil malade ne supporte pas l'éclat du soleil sur la mer. Un deuxième scotch, inespéré en ce début d'après-midi, a eu raison toutefois de sa mauvaise humeur.

Le repas s'achève. Les homards, des *chicken lobsters* de

moins d'une livre, étaient délicieux. Le mois d'août est le meilleur moment de la saison, par ailleurs plus tardive que sur les côtes québécoises, explique Marie-Paule à Jean-Louis.

Mathilde observe sa sœur qui n'en finit pas de parfaire l'initiation de Jean-Louis aux us et coutumes de la région. Les voilà donc de nouveau ensemble. Marie-Paule doit certainement mourir d'envie de raconter l'évolution qui a abouti à cet heureux état de fait. Les poches qu'ils ont tous les deux sous les yeux témoignent de la ténacité avec laquelle ils ont travaillé à édifier les bases nouvelles d'une relation méthodiquement disséquée. Quel récit ennuyeux en perspective ! se dit Mathilde qui, rassasiée, ne songe plus maintenant qu'à quitter la table et à se précipiter dans l'eau avant qu'il ne soit trop tard pour profiter de la marée haute.

Il fait déjà frais. Charles et Estelle ont trop bu et le spectacle de leurs visages bouffis fait frissonner. Il faut vite prendre le large, pense Mathilde. Cette fois encore elle a cédé, succombant davantage au charme suspect de la nostalgie qu'à l'appel insistant de Marie-Paule toujours prompte à la culpabiliser. Incapable de dormir, elle s'est levée à l'aube, brusquement résolue à prendre la route de l'océan et du marasme familial. Julien n'a pas cherché à la retenir. Sensible au désarroi dans lequel elle plonge inévitablement à la veille de chacun de ses rendez-vous manqués avec ses parents, il a plutôt proposé de l'accompagner. Elle a eu vite fait de refuser : Julien ne figurera jamais au générique des beaux dimanches.

Charles réclame du café. Pendant qu'elle le prépare, Mathilde a le temps de se tremper, déclare gentiment Marie-Paule.

L'eau est atrocement froide. Certains baigneurs arrivent tout de même à s'y maintenir quelques minutes. Mathilde, qui n'est pas d'un naturel héroïque, se contente de sautiller sur place en battant des mains. On dirait un grand échassier retombé en enfance, pense Marie-Paule qui sert le café. La petite sœur continue à trépigner. Les vagues viennent lui mordre les mollets qui virent du rouge au bleu. Jean-Louis l'appelle : le dessert est servi. Elle feint de ne pas entendre. Avec une lenteur étudiée, elle avance de quelques pas jusqu'à ce qu'une vague l'asperge presque totalement. Elle recule en bondissant et se remet à gesticuler. Marie-Paule, que ce premier bain de mer prolongé commence à inquiéter, se décide à faire le récit d'un morceau choisi de l'anthologie familiale. Jean-Louis, résigné, prend une cigarette dans le paquet de Mathilde.

Ce jour-là, Marie-Paule avait accompagné ses parents à Boston. Mathilde, elle, avait été confiée à la garde d'une voisine ; comme ça, elle ne risquait pas de s'ennuyer non plus que d'embêter les autres dans les musées, les magasins et les restaurants. On avait pris soin d'acheter la plus jolie poupée de la ville à la petite fille présumée sage. La nuit était tombée depuis longtemps lorsqu'on regagna enfin Wells. Persuadée que Mathilde était profondément endormie, Estelle s'apprêtait à déposer la poupée au pied du lit quand elle constata qu'il était vide. La voisine, absorbée par son *patchwork,* n'avait rien remarqué sinon que la petite fille, malgré ses efforts pour se remémorer les quelques rudiments de français appris à l'école et la dérider un peu, avait boudé obstinément toute la journée, refusant même de goûter à ses muffins tout juste sortis du four et acceptant enfin, à dix heures passées, de monter se coucher.

On avait fouillé les dunes, arpenté la plage et, vers quatre heures du matin, Charles avait retrouvé l'enfant cachée dans le grand trou qu'elle avait elle-même creusé dans le sable à plusieurs kilomètres de la maison. On l'avait ramenée, grelottante mais butée, et la poupée découverte sur le lit avait été rageusement piétinée avant d'être lancée à la tête des parents consternés.

« Elle n'en fera jamais d'autres », conclut Jean-Louis agacé par la manière enfantine qu'a Marie-Paule de raconter. D'ailleurs, qu'on se rassure, elle n'est pas perdue, la petite sœur, l'enfant précoce appliquée à ne pas grandir, pas encore : la voilà qui sort de l'eau et revient en gambadant, certaine qu'on la regarde et prête à poser devant la complaisante caméra familiale. C'est une comédienne avertie maintenant et bien aise d'être de retour sur les lieux de ses débuts. Les sarcasmes de Jean-Louis font sourire Marie-Paule, qui pourtant le fait taire avant que Mathilde ne l'entende.

Charles propose de fêter ces joyeuses retrouvailles avec le passé en faisant un sort à la bouteille de cognac que Jean-Louis a eu la bonne idée d'apporter. Estelle ne proteste pas.

Mathilde, montée passer des vêtements secs, revient avec deux paquets enrubannés. Le mois dernier, sa mère et sa sœur, nées presque le même jour à une trentaine d'années d'intervalle, ont fêté leur anniversaire. Bien que satisfaite sur le moment de rompre avec les traditionnelles festivités du dimanche, c'est avec une sorte de plaisir rancunier que Mathilde a manqué une fois de plus à sa promesse d'ivrogne et, chemin faisant, elle s'est arrêtée dans les boutiques de Perkin's Cove, paradis du *gift shop*. Une vendeuse au sourire terriblement angélique s'est précipitée vers elle, sa première cliente de la matinée. Expéditive, Mathilde n'a pas hésité longtemps : un carnet à la couverture fleurie que Marie-Paule déballe maintenant en lui décochant une œillade complice (le futur journal, roman qui sait, de ses démêlés avec Jean-Louis) et une robe de nuit avec garnitures de dentelles à l'ancienne pour sa mère.

C'est en l'essayant que, s'y prenant les pieds, Estelle est tombée. Elle ne s'est pas fait mal mais depuis, elle n'arrête pas de pleurer. Elle est étourdie. Les bébés homards s'agitent dans son ventre. Elle a trop mangé et ferait mieux de se mettre au lit. Mathilde ne croyait pas si bien faire en lui offrant ce cadeau empoisonné, pense-t-elle : une défroque de vieille femme malade et empotée.

Avec une impatience apitoyée, Marie-Paule aide sa mère à s'étendre. Charles, laissé seul sur la terrasse, surgit, le cheveu et la canne en bataille. Ses chevilles démesurément enflées le portent difficilement, il bute contre la porte entrouverte, vomit une bouillie d'injures, s'indigne de l'ignorance dans laquelle on le tient, gratifie Estelle de quelques paroles de réconfort assorties d'une petite remarque fielleuse sur l'âge qui n'épargne personne, la modération et le juste retour des choses puis il termine en déclarant qu'il couve une grippe et que le meilleur moyen de la prévenir est encore de se coucher jusqu'à ce que les forces lui reviennent. Jusqu'à l'heure du prochain verre, murmure Mathilde. Les deux sœurs quittent la chambre d'Estelle pendant que Charles s'ébranle lourdement vers la sienne.

Jean-Louis a débarrassé la table. Tel est son rôle et il le joue avec autant d'élégance que de naturel dès que pareil incident vient à se produire, inévitable raté dans le déroulement des repas du dimanche.

Pâle sous le hâle qui creuse ses traits fatigués et accuse les rides naissantes où se lisent les épisodes successifs de la décadence parentale, Marie-Paule s'avoue vaincue. Ce voyage maudit n'amène que des désillusions. Autrefois, l'eau de mer cicatrisait les blessures de l'hiver et le vent du large dissipait bien vite les émanations éthyliques de l'année entière. Wells était encore cette parenthèse ouverte permettant à chacun de reprendre son souffle. Mais il semble qu'il soit maintenant beaucoup trop tard. Charles et Estelle transportent partout le malheur qui les retient ensemble, leur petite misère mise en bouteilles. Les jeter toutes à la mer, songe Marie-Paule en empilant dans l'évier les assiettes et les verres sales. Sans Jean-Louis, comment aurait-elle supporté les désagréments de ces huit heures de route, son père particulièrement odieux et chicanier, responsable d'un départ par deux fois différé le lendemain de veilles trop arrosées, exigeant qu'on le dépose à l'aéroport de Burlington parce que la chaleur l'incommode et qu'un avion l'emmènerait tellement plus rapidement et confortablement à Boston où il suffirait que Jean-Louis vienne le chercher, menaçant de rentrer à Montréal en taxi, maugréant et ronchonnant pendant toute la durée du trajet ? Sans parler de sa mère, malade, revenant sur le passé et confessant son peu de goût pour l'eau glacée et le ciel gris de la côte du Maine où son mari l'a traînée pendant des années, et de l'altercation qui suivit cette cynique confidence maternelle ! Un voyage infernal au terme duquel Wells, l'étape finale, ne tient pas non plus ses promesses, conclut Marie-Paule, qui songe elle aussi à passer le reste de l'après-midi au lit. Elle aurait tant voulu rendre ses parents heureux, leur faire don du passé recelé dans la vieille maison verte au bord de la mer.

Un peu déconcerté par la sortie désabusée de Marie-Paule, Jean-Louis lui conseille de se reposer. Il ira rejoindre Mathilde déjà descendue sur la plage ; une bonne marche devrait l'aider à se remettre les idées en place. Bien que rares maintenant, ses contacts avec la famille Dalpé ne manquent jamais de l'insécuriser. Une famille à la dérive que Marie-Paule s'épuise à maintenir à flot. Elle en fait trop, elle risque de sombrer à son tour dans le scotch et la déraison s'il ne lui tend pas une ultime bouée de sauvetage. À moins qu'il ne soit lui-même la victime ignorée de ces naufragés insouciants qui, gorgés d'alcool et d'argent, réussissent toujours à surnager, redressant tant bien que mal le gouvernail et repartant de plus belle vers de nouvelles aventures dont d'incorrigibles naïfs comme lui font obligeamment les frais.

Qu'est-il venu faire dans cette galère, pense Jean-Louis, rejetant à la mer les galets qui lui tombent sous la main en même temps que la colère soudaine qui l'habite? D'où peut bien venir cette fascination équivoque qui le ramène régulièrement dans les bras de Marie-Paule et de sa famille? De ses origines sociales plutôt modestes, de la compassion qu'il ressent devant la vieillesse malheureuse, de la peur de vieillir ainsi conjurée, de l'éducation qu'il a reçue (il faut prendre soin de ses vieux parents), de Marie-Paule elle-même dont la dépendance amoureuse l'irrite moins qu'elle ne le flatte?

Il faudra qu'il en discute avec Annie, ou encore avec Christiane dès son retour. Pourquoi pas avec Mathilde qu'il aperçoit là-bas assise sur le sable? Bien sûr, il faudra d'abord faire tomber le masque protecteur, trouver la parade à ses attaques, l'empêcher de se retrancher derrière le persiflage et les railleries habituelles. Contournant une énorme méduse qui étale sa chair gélatineuse à quelques centimètres de ses pieds nus, Jean-Louis, dégoûté mais revigoré autant par l'air salin que par ses propres performances analytiques, se dirige d'un bon pas vers Mathilde qui, regardant la mer, ne le voit pas venir.

Cela fait plus de dix minutes que Jean-Louis monologue, encouragé par les sourires et les onomatopées bien placées de Mathilde. Il aura bientôt l'âge des premiers bilans, poursuit-il. Il commence déjà à s'y préparer. Heureusement, il a peu à peu appris à faire face à ses désirs, à se mettre à l'écoute de ses émotions. Bien entendu, cela n'a pas été facile : les hommes sont si peu entraînés à ces sortes de choses. Mais ses amitiés féminines l'ont aidé. Il voit plus clair maintenant, il comprend mieux le jeune homme superficiel qu'il s'est longtemps contenté d'être. Avec Marie-Paule, il se sent parfois coincé, presque contraint de régresser, forcé d'interrompre sa croissance personnelle. En fait, il étouffe au sein de la famille Dalpé.

Mathilde réagit peu ; elle semble absorbée par la fabrication du cataplasme de sable qu'elle applique sur ses jambes étendues. Jean-Louis aborde maintenant le prévisible sujet de l'homosexualité. Il dit qu'il se prépare à en faire l'expérience et que Marie-Paule s'avoue elle aussi intéressée. Et elle, Mathilde, où en est-elle, où en sont ses désirs, ses découvertes ?

La réponse tardant à venir, Jean-Louis n'ose pas insister davantage. Il s'apprête à emprunter une cigarette à son aimable mais peu loquace interlocutrice quand il découvre tout à coup que, sous le capuchon de son gilet en coton ouaté, Mathilde a son walkman sur les oreilles. Ulcéré, il se redresse d'un bond, secouant le sable qui colle à ses vêtements. Croyant qu'il se décide enfin à la quitter, Mathilde éteint l'appareil et s'informe de l'heure. La plage est presque déserte, il doit être tard. Jean-Louis la renseigne. Puis, n'y tenant plus, il explose : ces petits engins de malheur tuent la communication, la société de consommation multiplie les gadgets destinés à endormir les masses obéissantes et chacun de se promener, pareil à un zombi, retranché derrière ses écouteurs.

« Le walkman a précisément été inventé pour permettre à son utilisateur d'échapper aux ratiocinations, lieux communs et confidences malvenues de son entourage », rétorque Mathilde. D'ailleurs, elle rêve depuis longtemps d'un dimanche où chaque convive, muni de son appareil, jouirait en silence de sa petite musique personnelle. Quand Jean-Louis cessera-t-il de se griser de fadaises ? Entre deux chansons, elle a tout de même saisi quelques bribes de ces assommantes paraphrases de la sous-culture psychothérapeutique des dernières années.

L'arrivée d'un inconnu dispense Jean-Louis de répondre. Incroyable ! Mathilde reconnaît Dean qu'elle n'a pas vu depuis au moins quinze ans. Lui aussi venait autrefois passer ses vacances à Wells, puis il rentrait à New York et on l'oubliait jusqu'à l'année suivante.

Dean raconte sa vie. Il possède une boutique de posters dans Soho, fait lui-même des encadrements *new wave* très recherchés, des objets immenses qui couvrent des murs entiers des lofts new-yorkais et se vendent beaucoup plus cher que le bout de papier préalablement acheté chez lui ou ailleurs.

Mathilde, son walkman autour du cou, est tout oreilles ; elle n'entend pas rater cette occasion de mieux connaître New York et, qui sait, de refaire sa vie loin de l'interminable agonie paternelle.

Cet Américain aux dents blanches et cheveux gominés exaspère Jean-Louis. Dean s'inquiète maintenant de Marie-Paule : qu'est-elle devenue ? Oh ! elle est à Wells elle aussi, Marie-Paule *so charming* sur son poney trottant au bord de l'eau, comme il sera plaisant de la revoir !

Le soir descend. Invité à se joindre à eux pour l'apéritif, Dean passe chaleureusement son bras autour des épaules de Jean-Louis qui, mal à l'aise, n'ose cependant pas protester. Ravie, Mathilde court devant tant elle a hâte de prévenir Marie-Paule.

Charles et Estelle sont étendus côte à côte sur la terrasse. Un plaid sur les genoux, commodément installés dans les rocking-chairs que Marie-Paule a dénichés à la cave, ils contemplent, muets, le jour qui meurt sur la mer apaisée. Le vent est tombé, Marie-Paule prépare un repas léger. Mathilde et Jean-Louis ne devraient pas tarder. Tout ira bien maintenant.

Le soleil a disparu derrière les dunes roussâtres et la lune se lève déjà. Demain, à l'heure où il est si difficile de se rendormir, ils se pencheront tous les deux à la fenêtre et regarderont la mer accoucher du soleil. Et l'espace d'un matin, eux aussi se croiront immortels.

Perdus dans leurs pensées jumelles, ils rêvassent côte à côte, tels deux ennemis qui s'accordent une trêve bien méritée.

ma chère Estelle tes joues pendent fripées et les perles disparaissent dans les plis de ton cou   mais rassure-toi tu as toujours la jambe fine la démarche guillerette   ça n'est qu'un
accident tu es tombée voilà tout tu me survivras va   au
fond de ton regard mouillé se cache une impitoyable ténacité   tu demeureras la gardienne de ma vie posthume car
je ne vais pas tarder à te laisser seule avec tes filles tes
malaises et tes flacons   bientôt Estelle bientôt je partirai
comme une algue desséchée que la mer emporte   j'irai
flotter lâche et violacé membre coopté du peuple des
méduses   tu n'en crois rien n'est-ce pas j'entends tes railleries   oui j'ai peur de l'eau c'est vrai j'ai terriblement peur
de l'eau   mais ce bonheur pourtant cet apaisement de
l'être devant la mer et sa tranquille insolence   je veux
mourir comme on meurt au bord de la mer Estelle   un
bon mari un père respecté diront-ils   une contrefaçon
maladroite penseras-tu   ma chère Estelle mon épouse
pour le meilleur et pour le pire partagée entre la sollicitude
et le ressentiment   j'attends patiemment la mort qui se
mire au fond des bouteilles que tu caches mais que nous

buvons ensemble maintenant qu'enfin résignée tu consens à t'asseoir à mon côté   faisons la noce consommons Estelle dans le balancement de nos rocking-chairs   il n'est jamais trop tard pour bien faire   je te déteste Estelle oh! combien je hais la fille de son père foulant de sa canne à pommeau d'ivoire les tapis chinois de la rue Oxford la jeune femme se prêtant dédaigneusement à l'amour plus raide que l'eau-de-vie   oh! Estelle tu ressembles à la mer au mois d'août quand elle est grise et que toutes choses abdiquent devant son incommensurable passivité

quelle fatigue Charles dormir dormir enfin toute une nuit sans le secours de ces petites pilules qui broient le malheur quotidien et laissent au matin la bouche râpeuse   sommeil extorqué   et le lendemain le corps qui trahit   je tombe Charles et c'est ici au bord de cette mer du nord que tu me conduis   vaine transhumance jusqu'à la maison verte   You need a rest   dans mes oreilles le cri des mouettes se répercute à l'infini   on dirait la mort qui bour-donne   je vais bientôt mourir Charles le sais-tu et qui veillera à te mesurer chaque jour ton dû   tu me survivras les médecins ébahis continueront à te palper le foie   tu seras encore le plus fort le vainqueur de ce combat que nous ajournons depuis que l'ivresse le seul bien qui nous ait été donné en partage a fait de nous des alliés de la dernière heure
    quand je bois du gin Charles j'oublie le silence se fait dans mes oreilles j'oublie les plaisirs étriqués les nuits écra-sées sous le poids de tes soupirs avinés ton ignorance massive et satisfaite   c'est en Floride qu'il fallait me conduire

Charles là où la mer est tiède quand papa les pieds nus pro-
mène sa canne sur le sable blanc   je voudrais mourir en
Floride au beau milieu de l'hiver mais pas tout de suite
Charles pas maintenant dans ce rocking-chair défraîchi
alors que le gin me monte à la tête et que je m'enfonce dans
un brouillard nauséeux   tu te berces à mon côté et je crois
bien que je te hais Charles mon bébé plus vorace que les
requins qui croisent en haute mer

nous allons bientôt mourir   l'alcool brûlera nos organes
dévastés   Marie-Paule et Mathilde rangeront les rocking-
chairs à la cave   et la rumeur de la mer bercera les rêves
des morts comme des vivants

VINGT-DEUX HEURES

Elle fume. Lui, affaissé dans son fauteuil depuis plus d'une heure, ne bouge plus. La bouteille est vide ; il a tout bu, jusqu'à la dernière goutte. Sans mot dire, il s'est laissé sombrer au plus profond, dans le secret de son sang pollué. De temps à autre, il fait entendre une sorte de feulement, un grognement étouffé qui chaque fois la surprend juste au moment où elle croit l'oublier. Elle ne le regarde plus, elle fume, occupée à nier la réalité alarmante que ses rêves ont préméditée.

Le quitter tout de suite pendant qu'il en est encore temps, téléphoner à Julien, lui demander de prévenir le docteur Patenaude et s'enfuir avant son arrivée ? Car, autant se l'avouer, elle n'y connaît rien. Son sommeil paraît si lourd. Est-il entré dans un coma définitif, ou fait-il simplement une de ces longues siestes dont il a l'habitude ? Il a dormi presque toute la journée. Une infirmière vérifierait les signes vitaux, Marie-Paule saurait elle aussi faire un rapide diagnostic. Et pendant ce temps, elle, elle fume et lui tourne prudemment le dos.

Elle empoigne le téléphone. Une petite voix ensommeillée répond que Julien est sorti, qu'il n'a pas dit à quelle heure il rentrerait, que le message sera fait et que Jasmine et Jérômine ont passé l'après-midi à la fenêtre. Elle a réveillé Camille ; Julien s'est enfin résolu, depuis quelques semaines, à laisser les jumelles toutes seules quand il s'absente inopinément.

Où peut-il bien être allé, lui si casanier d'ordinaire ? De toute façon, elle ne saurait pas lui expliquer. Il accepterait sans doute de prévenir le docteur, lui conseillerait de l'attendre. Elle n'osera jamais lui avouer ses chimères puériles. Il n'y comprendrait rien d'ailleurs, lui qui habite un autre monde peuplé de soieries délicates et de jumelles malicieuses. Aussi bien continuer de le tenir à l'écart de tout ça, le plus loin possible du merdier familial. D'autant plus qu'elle le voit beaucoup moins souvent depuis qu'elle est revenue de New York ; il n'a pas encore digéré les quelques mots griffonnés à la hâte sur la carte postale qu'elle lui a envoyée, un baiser amusé et puis « bye bye » on se reverra dans deux ou trois mois ».

La respiration paternelle est difficile, un souffle inégal entrecoupé de râles étouffés. On croirait entendre le grondement lointain qui monte des entrailles d'une voiture récalcitrante, l'un de ces matins où le mercure indique moins trente. Avertissement de froid intense, préviennent les météorologues. De fait, la nuit qui vient s'annonce mortellement froide. Il faut boire. Il n'y a que ça pour se réchauffer, boire le bon rhum qui avale la peine des vieillards alcooliques et de leurs filles légitimes.

Elle termine son verre de rhum et allume une cigarette. À combien évaluer ce qu'il a bu aujourd'hui ? Une vingtaine d'onces, peut-être plus s'il avait commencé à « célébrer » avant qu'elle n'arrive. Quand, exceptionnellement, il admet avoir forcé un peu la mesure, il dit qu'il célèbre. Aujourd'hui c'est l'absence d'Estelle et de Marie-Paule qu'il célèbre, un dimanche entier avec sa fille cadette, sa préférée bien qu'elle le néglige. Vingt onces vont-elles suffire à en venir à bout ? Elle tire sur sa cigarette, troublée par la crudité de l'expression.

Sa dose quotidienne a longtemps dépassé la quantité absorbée aujourd'hui, mais c'était avant qu'il ne tombe sous le joug des médecins. Ces dernières années, on a plusieurs fois annoncé sa mort imminente, mais lui se réveillait frais comme une rose après chacune de ces anesthésies dont les spécialistes redoutaient les effets cumulés. Elles se retrouvaient toutes trois à son chevet et il ouvrait des yeux étonnés, tandis que le soluté s'écoulait comme l'eau-de-vie dans ses rêves de malade. Ce soir, pourtant, il semble qu'il accuse nettement le coup.

Elle triture le fil du téléphone qui court à portée de sa main. Marie-Paule viendrait tout de suite. Bien sûr, il ne serait pas facile de lui faire avaler l'histoire de la bouteille de rhum. Il faudrait détourner ses soupçons. Marie-Paule irait-elle jusqu'à imaginer la vérité ? Elle ne croirait jamais sa sœur capable d'une telle machination. Tout rentrerait rapidement dans l'ordre. À moins qu'il ne soit déjà trop tard ? Mais non, son père reviendrait vite à lui, et cet incident irait grossir les pages du journal intime où Marie-Paule consigne scrupuleusement ses émotions quotidiennes.

De Charles à Estelle, d'Estelle à Marie-Paule, la boucle est bouclée, en attendant que sa sœur accouche à son tour de son propre bâton de vieillesse. Alors elle pourra elle aussi s'adonner aux plaisirs de l'alcool en toute quiétude. Qui sait ? Marie-Paule joue peut-être le même jeu que leur mère. Et, sous ses dehors de jeune femme saine et soucieuse de son alimentation, se cache la tare familiale qui accomplit sa croissance souterraine. Comment pourrait-elle résister à la contagion quand elle s'y expose avec une telle bonne volonté, une disponibilité totale ? La tâche est trop lourde. Marie-Paule y laissera sa peau. Il faut lui venir en aide. Et tenter l'impossible, sauver la mère en même temps que la fille aînée.

Le téléphone sonne au moment précis où elle prend la décision de n'y plus toucher. C'est Estelle, la voix pâteuse et le propos brouillon, qui prévient de son retard. La mère Estelle a manifestement beaucoup trop bu ! Il vaut mieux en effet qu'elle accepte l'invitation de ses amis et se repose un peu, pourquoi pas jusqu'à demain, avant de rentrer. Oui, cela ne pose aucun problème ; Charles a bien mangé, il dort déjà, et elle peut compter sur sa fille qui se fera un plaisir de passer la nuit rue Oxford.

Elle raccroche. *Vous êtes calme de plus en plus calme vous êtes affreusement calme tellement calme que pour un peu vous fondriez en larmes.* Encore un couple de vieillards fortunés qui se soignent au gin entre deux voyages en Floride ! Mais ils ont sans doute plus de santé que la pauvre Estelle. Il n'est pas impossible que celle-ci se décide à rentrer ce soir, elle aura peur de gêner ses hôtes, et elle conduira sa voiture à travers les rues, la main lourde sur le volant et la tête dans les nuages de Miami, guidée par sa longue expérience de la fuite automobile.

En attendant, son père semble revenir à la vie. Il tousse, crache, se passe la main sur le crâne, caressant les stigmates laissés par ses récentes chutes. Il bredouille quelque chose. Il a soif, croit-elle entendre. Il prendrait bien un verre d'eau. Elle se lève, soulagée et pourtant déçue.

Elle a mal à la tête, mais elle n'essaie plus de combattre la douleur. C'est comme ça, elle n'a pas la forme, mais son calme est absolu — *vous êtes calme de plus en plus calme* — et elle revient, tenant d'une main le verre d'eau demandé et de l'autre la bouteille de gin qu'elle a trouvée, cachée dans l'armoire sous l'évier. Estelle devait se la garder pour elle, celle-là.

Les pieds dans ses nouvelles pantoufles, un cadeau d'anniversaire, il cherchait le sommeil. Depuis quelque temps, il avait parfois du mal à s'endormir. Il en était réduit à prendre lui aussi ces somnifères dont Estelle faisait si grand usage. L'alcool ne suffisait plus à diluer la misère de ce monde qu'il allait bientôt quitter. Il avait eu soixante-quatorze ans mercredi dernier. Franchir le cap des soixante-quinze ans serait bien au-dessus de ses forces. Il en avait assez de la rue Oxford et de son salon déjà funéraire où ses filles venaient le voir, en feignant de croire qu'il était encore en vie.

Son anniversaire tombait en novembre, en même temps que la première neige qui marquait l'ouverture de l'hiver. De fait, il avait neigé toute la nuit et, aujourd'hui, on le fêterait en déplorant une fois de plus la coïncidence. Il avait le sentiment que cette année il ne passerait pas l'hiver. Il ne quitterait plus cette maison, ça il le savait. Finies les escapades dans le Maine ou ailleurs, il en avait terminé avec les voyages. À son retour de Wells, il avait compris que son fauteuil serait le dernier rivage où il viendrait échouer.

Il était infiniment las. Une dépouille, un arbre dénudé. On n'était qu'en novembre, pourrait-il seulement tenir jusqu'à Noël, se rendre au bout de cette année qui égrenait platement ses jours? On le croyait immortel et lui-même en était venu à s'en convaincre. Il continuerait à boire et à narguer les médecins, faisant le désespoir de sa femme et de ses filles. Et, pourtant, il souhaitait mourir puisqu'il était devenu incapable même de dormir.

Marie-Paule viendrait bientôt changer son pansement. Il s'était blessé au front en tombant sur le plancher du garage. Ça n'était pas la première fois que pareille mésaventure lui arrivait mais cette fois la blessure était vilaine, il avait perdu beaucoup de sang, sa tête avait heurté violemment le béton et il avait même cru sa dernière heure venue quand Estelle, prise de nausées et courant d'abord s'occuper d'elle-même, avait été forcée de le laisser seul, à demi inconscient. Ils revenaient tous les deux d'une visite au cabinet du docteur Patenaude, qui leur avait offert un petit remontant avant de les reconduire jusqu'à la voiture. Ce cher Fernand avait bu à la santé de ses clients et amis qui n'en étaient pas à leur premier verre de la journée, autant le reconnaître. Fernand était vraiment le meilleur des médecins, bien plus compétent au fond que tous ces spécialistes qui n'avaient réussi qu'à lui faire perdre un œil, puis le sommeil en lui prescrivant ces maudits diurétiques qui l'obligeaient à se lever plusieurs fois durant la nuit. Il s'arrangeait d'ailleurs pour en prendre le moins souvent possible.

Il jeta un coup d'œil à sa montre. Estelle était encore couchée. Marie-Paule devait s'occuper du repas. La semaine dernière sa femme et lui avaient eu une petite dispute qui avait mal tourné. Oh ! rien de bien grave, les bêtises habituelles, des remarques sur l'âge, les étourderies et les maladresses d'Estelle qui, depuis quelque temps, ne goûtait plus du tout les plaisanteries. À la moindre allusion à ses parents décédés, à son père en particulier, ce vieux renard irréprochable jusque dans la mort, elle éclatait en sanglots ou se mettait à crier. Cela pouvait aller jusqu'à la crise de nerfs. Ce soir-là, elle s'était jetée sur lui, enfonçant ses ongles dans l'encolure de sa chemise jusqu'à ce que le sang perle entre les poils. Il l'avait calmée, et elle avait regagné sa chambre en maudissant sa vie vouée à l'entretien d'un monstre dont l'ingratitude n'échappait à personne. Elle buvait trop et devenait mauvaise. Bien que par le passé, si sa mémoire ne le trompait pas, elle n'eût pas toujours été non plus un modèle de douceur. Non, il n'avait pas oublié Wells, oui, c'était à Wells, une nuit d'été, ils étaient encore jeunes en ce temps-là et les voisins, un pasteur anglican et sa femme, les avaient invités — pas une goutte de scotch, rien que du sherry et du porto ; puis, au retour, Estelle s'était déclarée humiliée parce que, soi-disant, il avait trop bu et le ton avait monté jusqu'à ce qu'elle se mette à lui écorcher la poitrine. Toujours les mêmes histoires !

Il savait bien qu'Estelle irait se plaindre à Marie-Paule et qu'il passerait encore une fois pour un goujat, un mari dégénéré qui bat sa femme. Sa monstrueuse ingratitude n'échapperait à personne, ainsi que l'en menaçait Estelle. D'accord, il lui était arrivé en de très rares occasions de la rudoyer un peu, mais il se savait maintenant bien incapable de lui faire mal. Il était beaucoup trop faible, vieux et fatigué. Toute sa vie d'ailleurs, il n'avait été qu'un faible grossièrement manipulé. Il s'était laissé mener par le bout du nez et ne s'en était pas plus mal porté.

Tout ce malheur de leur vie commune venait de ce qu'en fait ils s'ennuyaient terriblement ensemble. Ils effilochaient les souvenirs comme des guenilles délavées que le temps avait trouées et, quand ils en avaient fait le tour, ils se retrempaient dans les vapeurs amnésiques de l'alcool. Ils s'ennuyaient à mourir dans cette maison qui refermait sur eux ses murs et son passé. Heureusement que Marie-Paule téléphonait souvent et leur rendait de fréquentes visites. Quant à Mathilde, elle était à New York et il ne l'avait pas revue depuis le dimanche de Wells. Elle viendrait aujourd'hui, elle allait bientôt l'embrasser, plutôt deux fois qu'une puisque c'était son anniversaire. Il lui ferait comprendre qu'elle ne pouvait plus se permettre de l'abandonner aussi longtemps, il était trop vieux, soixante-quatorze ans déjà, et il avait besoin d'elle pour mourir.

Mathilde n'a presque rien mangé. Saturée de tacos épicés et de légumes cuits à l'orientale, le gigot maternel lui avait manqué pourtant. Ce retour au bercail ne s'effectuait pas sans difficulté ; ses parents avaient encore vieilli et on pouvait lire le tracé de la courbe alcoolique sur leurs visages gonflés. Sa cabane au bord de l'eau lui était apparue peu avenante et mal chauffée. Il faisait ici beaucoup plus froid qu'à New York. Jasmine et Jérômine l'avaient à peine reconnue, doucettement abandonnées aux petits soins de Julien et de ses filles.

Répondant à l'appel intérieur de ses dimanches, elle avait quitté Dean et ses amis sans le moindre regret. Personne cette fois ne lui avait intimé l'ordre de revenir ; elle était d'ailleurs partie sans laisser d'adresse, une vague allusion à Dean mais aucunes coordonnées précises, et elle avait cru s'en être enfin tirée. Elle en avait peut-être eu assez de traîner dans cette ville supposée fascinante, assez de Dean obnubilé par sa prochaine installation dans une galerie alternative, assez des expositions, du théâtre d'avant-garde et des boîtes de jazz, assez du tango, des épaulettes rembourrées et de la post-performance. Dean prenait de la coke et, ensuite, il faisait l'amour avec le doigté méticuleux d'un ordinateur de la troisième génération. Elle préférait Chiquito, le grand Chiquito mince comme un bambou, avec qui elle parcourait la ville, étendue sur la banquette arrière de son taxi en fumant l'un de ses énormes joints.

Elle allume une cigarette et termine à voix haute le récit expurgé de ses aventures new-yorkaises en annonçant qu'elle compte repartir bientôt. Charles avale de travers sa gorgée de vin. Pendant qu'il se livre à l'une de ses coutumières séances de toux et de raclements de gorge ponctués de sonores éternuements, Marie-Paule prie sa sœur de débarrasser la table. Elle-même se rend à la cuisine pour préparer le café. Estelle essaie de se lever, après tout c'est elle aujourd'hui qui reçoit ses filles, mais elle a la tête qui tourne, toujours ce maudit bourdonnement, et elle se rassoit en faisant la moue.

Marie-Paule est particulièrement volubile ce soir. Elle a plein de choses à raconter à Mathilde. D'abord, ça y est, elle s'est mise sérieusement à écrire : une autobiographie romancée, un récit quoi, un peu à la manière de…, bon, évitons les comparaisons trop osées, mais enfin elle va tenter de retracer son itinéraire sentimental, sa rupture avec Jean-Louis en sera bien sûr l'élément central, ce sera l'occasion d'une mise au point intime, elle a un tel désir d'y voir plus clair là-dedans et surtout d'arriver à se mettre là où il le faut, c'est-à-dire au plus près de ses émotions. Voilà, tout cela prend forme peu à peu, laborieusement mais sûrement, et les stages, les ateliers, les cours qu'elle a suivis trouvent enfin leur aboutissement.

Mathilde l'écoute sans broncher et, mine de rien, lui demande quand elle se décidera à écrire sur la famille et sur toute cette merde qui se brasse ici puisqu'elle aime tant les analyses psychologiques. Marie-Paule feint d'ignorer le ton sarcastique que dissimule mal le regard intéressé de sa sœur. Elle enchaîne au contraire en faisant un rapport circonstancié de ses plus récentes conquêtes. C'est qu'il faut bien trouver un remplaçant à Jean-Louis. Marie-Paule le revoit souvent, il demeurera toujours son meilleur ami. Avant-hier encore, ils se sont rencontrés à la première du film d'Annie, oui, la cinéaste qui partage maintenant la vie de Jean-Louis. Et le film promet d'être le succès de la production cinématographique de l'année, québécoise s'entend.

Non, Jean-Louis n'est pas facile à remplacer et il serait présomptueux de déclarer que l'affaire est dans le sac. Elle a rencontré un adepte du tarot, l'instrument idéal du dragueur occasionnel. À l'entendre, elle n'aurait que des raisons de se réjouir, sa rupture annonce le début d'une ère nouvelle et les cartes l'encouragent à se mettre en mouvement et à travailler à son propre accouchement, une épreuve certes mais dont elle sortira grandie et prête à tomber dans les bras de son gourou. Mathilde sourit. Sa sœur avoue que le crâne rasé et la barbe du prophète la laissent froide mais qu'il ne faut pas croire pour autant qu'il n'y a rien de vrai dans ce qu'il raconte. Il lui semble en effet que, peu à peu, ses énergies se libèrent; elle devient plus créative, de moins en moins inhibée.

Mathilde l'interrompt en demandant qui sont les autres énergumènes qu'elle a rencontrés. Eh bien, après le prophète, pendant un stage en créativité, oh! elle ne pensait pas du tout à ça mais quand l'un des participants a lu son texte devant le groupe, une sorte de réflexion sur les enjeux de l'écriture, quelque chose de très émouvant, à la manière de... « Bon, comment s'appelle celui-là et de quoi a-t-il l'air ? » coupe Mathilde qui en a assez des mystères de la création. « Il s'appelle Roland », répond Marie-Paule en précisant que sous ce prénom vieillot se cache un jeune homme féru de modernité. Roland lui raconte tous ses rêves qu'il consigne dans un petit agenda spécialement conçu à cet effet ; il lui en a d'ailleurs acheté un et depuis ils échangent régulièrement leurs productions oniriques. Mathilde dit qu'elle ne rêve plus depuis qu'elle prend des somnifères, les petites pilules bleues de maman qui assèchent la bouche et les lendemains. Hélas ! continue Marie-Paule, qui jette à sa petite sœur un regard inquiet, Roland ne va jamais plus loin que le rêve ; il ne drague pas, ne s'intéresse aux femmes que si elles se contentent de confidences et d'émotions partagées, mais, conclut Marie-Paule, Roland est un gars correct, soucieux de se démarquer des stéréotypes masculins. Marie-Paule n'a qu'à lui sauter dessus, commente Mathilde qui imagine un Roland aussi lourd et ennuyeux que son prénom.

La vie tumultueuse de Marie-Paule, ses histoires de machos et de maos repentis ont cessé de l'intéresser. Mathilde songe à revenir auprès de ses parents, à s'asseoir devant eux, à les regarder boire jusqu'à ce que le scotch les emporte dans le rêve de leur commune origine. Elle a envie de boire elle aussi, elle aime l'alcool, elle lui voue une passion haineuse qu'elle fait taire en s'évadant parfois loin de ces dimanches stériles auxquels elle revient toujours, assoiffée comme une pierre du désert.

Elle écoute distraitement Marie-Paule qui raconte maintenant le film d'Annie. Non, elle n'ira pas le voir, répond-elle à Marie-Paule qui insiste, elle ne veut pas voir ces héroïnes errer à la dérive sur les traces de Wim Wenders, pas ça, pas encore. Marie-Paule, un peu choquée mais secrètement ravie, dit que peut-être…, en effet Annie n'innove pas tellement, l'errance toujours, mais enfin… Jean-Louis était là, au premier rang bien entendu, et il a promis de venir fêter Noël rue Oxford. Voilà tout compte fait ce qui fut l'événement de la soirée. Il a gardé pour Charles et Estelle, et pour Mathilde aussi, ajoute Marie-Paule avec un sourire, un certain attachement et il a envie de les revoir.

Mathilde jette un coup d'œil rapide au calendrier pendu derrière la porte de l'armoire où elle range la vaisselle propre et constate avec frayeur que Noël tombe cette année un mardi. Le temps des Fêtes risque d'être un moment difficile à passer. Il faudra multiplier les visites aux parents, ne pas les laisser seuls « célébrer » en tête à tête la fin de cette année impossible. Les dimanches perturbent déjà tellement ses semaines et son moral qu'elle voit mal comment elle pourrait en supporter davantage, avoue-t-elle à sa sœur.

Elle n'a sans doute pas remarqué que les parents se portent de plus en plus mal et que c'est elle, l'aînée, qui en fait les frais, réplique Marie-Paule outrée. Oui, c'est elle qui accourt quand l'alcool les transforme en bêtes malades et furieuses, privées de raison comme d'appétit.

Mathilde promène un doigt sur les cernes qui lui mangent le visage et se tait. Exaspérée, Marie-Paule lui remet le gâteau planté de ses bougies d'anniversaire. Avec la tête qu'elle fait, leur père croira qu'elle lui apporte un cadeau empoisonné. Portant le plateau de liqueurs, Marie-Paule ouvre la marche vers le salon.

sonner l'alarme   un ultime appel au secours et que reten-
tisse enfin dans toute la rue Oxford à travers la ville entière
et par-delà les frontières jusqu'aux confins de la terre là où
une vieille maison verte baigne dans l'air salé le fracas de
toutes les bouteilles renversées   ce plateau je le sens va me
glisser entre les mains   il est si lourd beaucoup trop lourd
pour moi   alcool répandu cours lent des chagrins jetés à la
mer   scotch cognac mirabelle eau-de-vie un petit verre
puis un autre   j'en meurs d'envie   laisser l'alcool se promener dans la bouche caresser la langue jusqu'au moment
différé de la déglutition   ils m'auront eue moi aussi
comme les autres   derrière moi la grande Mathilde la
petite sœur aux yeux cernés fait claquer ses talons sur le
plancher de bois franc telle une marionnette tirée de son
sommeil artificiel et qui se met en branle petit soldat persi-
fleur terré dans son armure   Mathilde cuirassée contre la
désillusion toujours prête à vous clouer le bec à vous poi-
gnarder dans le dos l'air indifférent comme si elle était
ailleurs à vous tomber dessus au moment où vous vous y
attendiez le moins et à vous abandonner ensuite bouche bée

devant pareille intolérance   mais cette envie qui me prend parfois de tout laisser tomber tout ce fatras glané au hasard des stages régimes cours exploration des émotions créativité

le scepticisme est contagieux lui aussi et ça y est voilà où j'en suis on croirait l'entendre elle la railleuse   si seulement Jean-Louis était là avec ses yeux confiants enthousiastes ses mains tendres le creux de son épaule   Mathilde me dirait d'acheter un chat et d'arracher des murs ces horribles dessins qu'il y a laissés   c'est Annie maintenant qui accroche aux murs les essais de Jean-Louis la belle Annie si douée tellement efficace une femme productive vraiment indépendante tout ce qu'il faut pour plaire à un homme nouveau

qu'est-ce qu'elle a bien pu faire Annie de ses trois chats Jean-Louis ne supporte pas   et si je les prenais en pension

c'est Mathilde dans mon dos qui me souffle ces méchancetés   tu te laisses aller Marie-Paule attention tu vas tomber dans la facilité et la dérision encore plus facilement que dans la mirabelle   trop facile   demain j'ai besoin de toute ma tête la gueule de bois surtout pas   toute mon énergie tendue vers demain un bon massage ne me ferait pas de tort car c'est demain le grand jour   ma thèse est terminée et je donne mon premier cours je vais enfin partager avec d'autres les petites découvertes que j'ai faites   le parricide dans la tradition romanesque tel est le titre de mon plan de cours   demain j'ai peine à y croire je ne me sens pas prête encore mais de toute façon je ne dois pas entrer trop vite dans le vif du sujet ce qui prime demain c'est le contact le premier contact avec les étudiants être proche d'eux tout de suite   si ce dimanche se terminait bien une

fois n'est pas coutume je passerais ensuite une bonne une
vraie bonne nuit mais j'en ai peur les larmes viendront puis
les cris les chutes la folie ordinaire   le mutisme cruel de
Mathilde la grossièreté paternelle les plaisanteries la sénilité
et ma mère qui pue le dentifrice voilà où elle en est mon
Dieu ! comment tout cela va-t-il se terminer entre le men-
songe et la pitié je finirai par y laisser ma peau   oh ! bien
sûr il y a Mathilde derrière moi qui avance lentement et
recule ensuite incapable de nous aider Mathilde dans mon
dos inutile et rêche ses yeux de comédienne verts et cernés
cette fébrilité contenue elle me fait peur elle marche dans
mon dos et on la dirait prête à tout pendant que moi seule
fais tourner la roue d'un dimanche à l'autre

deux pleureuses voilà ce que nous sommes devenues nous
formons cortège une lente procession vers le salon   je ferme
la marche   il y a des courants d'air et les bougies s'étei-
gnent une à une   Marie-Paule la voyante saura-t-elle lire
le mauvais présage   chère Marie-Paule ma bonne sœur
confite en générosité soumise à son destin familial comme à
ses enthousiasmes puérils devant les idées qui courent et plus
vite elles courent plus vite elles tombent et l'entraînent
chaque fois dans la chute mais toujours elle se relève et en
attrape une autre par le bout de sa grosse ficelle   c'est cela
qui l'aide à supporter le regard paternel quand il devient
mauvais déformé par l'alcool   affronter le courroux de
Charles le déchu   chaque nouvelle chute le laisse un peu
plus défait   papa pourquoi es-tu tombé si bas comme on
dit dans les mélodrames   combien de temps peut-il tenir

nous tenir telle est la question combien de temps est-ce que je pourrai tenir sans me laisser aller   du fond de sa peur il m'adresse une prière muette   et du mélodrame on passe à la série noire de la condamnation à vie à la mort douce

Marie-Paule avance tel un forçat son boulet au pied et elle ne se doute de rien chère Marie-Paule j'en ai assez de te suivre   il ne reste plus qu'une seule bougie et la petite flamme vacille   bon anniversaire papa

nous allons chanter pour toi papa tes filles vont entonner la chanson rituelle la ritournelle des années soixante-dix la chanson de la fraternité l'espoir d'un peuple gelé que seul l'alcool peut réchauffer   mon cher papa c'est à ton tour de te laisser parler d'amour

VINGT-TROIS HEURES

Elle se masse les pieds. Ils sont gelés. La maison est surchauffée et pourtant elle grelotte. Les nuits de décembre sont mortellement froides. Sans doute n'a-t-elle pas assez mangé aujourd'hui. Le banquet du dimanche n'aura pas lieu. Estelle et Marie-Paule ne viendront plus reprendre leur place à table, il est trop tard maintenant, et ce tête-à-tête lugubre avec son père se poursuivra jusqu'au lendemain dans la peur, la fatigue et l'alcool partagés.

Le temps... Elle avait tout prévu sauf le temps, l'écoulement parcimonieux du temps, les heures qui tombent goutte à goutte, l'échéance sans cesse différée. Et cette maudite migraine qui depuis le début la tient paralysée.

Son père, lui, remplit parfaitement son rôle; à le voir ainsi, dévasté, répandu dans son fauteuil, la tête pendante et le pantalon défait, on dirait un moribond qui n'attend plus que la piqûre qui endormira sa souffrance. Elle seule peut encore la lui donner. Pauvre papa, il a du mal à digérer le champagne du réveillon, le cognac des lendemains de veille, le scotch de toute une vie. Les chevilles enflées, le teint gris, il fait bien plus que ses soixante-quatorze ans.

Sa cigarette lui brûle le bout des doigts. Elle en allume une autre. Quand elle ose le regarder, elle le surprend qui grimace, ses lèvres roulent mollement et, de temps à autre, il grommelle entre ses dents.

Mathilde ma Mathilde tu le sais tu comprends toi seule sais ce qui est bon pour moi   tu aimes ton vieux père Mathilde ne le laisse pas sur sa soif comme on dit   aide-moi la nuit sera longue   désert infini sécheresse crevasses partout   j'avance et plus j'avance plus je tombe sous le sable il y a le vide le vide Mathilde   prends-moi et fais de moi ce que tu voudras   Estelle n'en saura rien ma colombe prison- nière envolée qui bientôt regagnera son nid ma belle Estelle ma pigeonne ventrue que j'ai un jour baguée   toutes serres déployées elles reviendront mes femmes en colère elles reviendront se disputer mes restes   il faudra fuir Mathilde fuir Estelle et Marie-Paule échapper à leur vengeance   dépossédées de leur trésor honni elles essaieront de te pla- cer toi aussi sous surveillance   oh ! Mathilde cette fureur ravie qui éclate dans tes yeux quand tu me regardes telle une princesse rétive muette nue sous ta robe bleu de Chine comme un aveu   rappelle-toi Mathilde je te l'avais offerte alors que tu gambadais dans ma vie crédule encore et que nous dessinions des anges de neige   tu me poussais à peine et aussitôt je tombais prêt à tout tout pour te plaire à toi Mathilde qui ne me jugeais pas encore   je t'aime Mathilde le sais-tu   aide-moi à me rendre jusqu'à la fin de la nuit

*Mathilde chérie emmène-moi par-delà les déserts jusqu'à
cette oasis où le scotch et le cognac coulent en abondance et
que parvenu en ces terres fertiles je meure enfin dans la
démesure et le pardon   mon scotch mes amours   étourdi
étouffé l'odeur acétique me prend à la gorge   la vague
m'emporte   Mathilde mon amour viens viens toi aussi
vois nous dérivons parés stagnants tels ces* Énervés *de*
Jumièges *cloués sur leur lit-bateau   donne-moi à boire
Mathilde je meurs de soif.*

Elle éteint sa cigarette et se précipite. Le voilà qui sans
prévenir tente de se lever. Elle qui croyait ne plus jamais
avoir à lui parler, encore moins à le toucher, s'approche,
le cœur soulevé. Il veut uriner, croit-elle entendre. Encore
heureux qu'il ne demande pas l'urinoir caché sous son lit.
Depuis l'hôpital, il en a pris la détestable habitude. Elle le
suit, le bras tendu mais se refusant à le soutenir. Et, tel l'un
de ces oiseaux des îles, survivants d'une espèce menacée,
il pique du nez et atterrit sur le plancher de bois verni.
Une fois de plus, ses chevilles ont cédé. Elle se penche sur
lui, essaie de le soulever, il respire encore, mais il est lourd
comme une momie, et il s'enfonce irrémédiablement.
L'urine forme une petite mare au-dessus de laquelle ils
surnagent tous les deux.

Elle le chevauche, ne sait plus très bien si elle tente de
le ranimer ou de l'achever et pense en souriant à Marie-
Paule et à tous les ratiocineurs de la terre, les ratiocineuses
surtout, qui feraient de sa posture et de ses dimanches des
preuves à l'appui de leurs théories simplettes. Elle fouille

les poches du pantalon paternel, y trouve la cigarette qu'elle cherchait, aspire profondément et lui souffle la fumée au visage. Il ouvre un œil ahuri. Il est immortel, pense-t-elle en se redressant.

Il reste du gin dans la bouteille, ça n'est pas ce qu'il préfère mais il s'en contentera. Estelle trouvera la maison vide à son retour, plus une goutte, tout aura été consommé.

Elle revient, écarte les jambes, s'assoit sur son ventre ballonné et lui verse à boire. Il ouvre le bec et avale en grimaçant un sourire. Elle lui tient la tête soulevée et il boit sans même prendre le temps de respirer.

L'alcool se mêle à l'urine répandue. Ils sont mouillés, euphoriques presque. Au moment où il s'étouffe, crachant la dernière gorgée de gin et souillant la robe bleue, elle s'abat sur sa poitrine, glisse une main sous sa chemise, promène un doigt étonné sur le poil blanchi, la peau rêche, déshydratée. Elle observe, interdite, l'alcool que vomit la bouche rassasiée, la salive mêlée aux larmes et à la sueur qui s'échappent de tous les orifices béants, le sang qui suinte de sa blessure à la tête rouverte. Il se liquéfie sous ses yeux.

Elle se redresse, s'éloigne un peu et contemple la *liquidation* progressive du corps paternel, l'écoulement de toutes ses liqueurs organiques et mauvaises humeurs. L'euphorie fait place à la stupeur devant ce spectacle qu'elle a elle-même mis en scène.

Elle empoigne la bouteille de gin qui a roulé par terre et la lui fourre dans la bouche. Il en recrache la moitié. Elle termine ce qui reste.

Il a les yeux fermés maintenant. Il se roule sur le dos, étire ses membres, se prélasse sur le plancher de bois, puis, tout à coup, il se met à tousser et à vomir. Elle nettoie les filaments bilieux qui s'agglutinent en poches sur sa poitrine et éponge sa robe maculée. Il semble bien qu'il soit méchamment étouffé. Elle envoie rouler la bouteille de gin qui s'immobilise au milieu des immondices.

Elle le regarde, fou des Galapagos abattu, battant des ailes, le souffle court. C'est le rêve qui se réalise, une mort déjà vécue, tant de fois anticipée. Elle ramène ses jambes l'une contre l'autre et, le couvrant de son corps entièrement déployé, elle colle sa bouche à son oreille.

ne t'inquiète pas papa tu vas mourir mais je suis là à tes côtés mon grand fou gavé   on dira le malheureux il avait trop bu et sa fille n'a pas su l'en empêcher elle devait dormir quand il s'est trouvé mal   on découvrira des bouteilles encore pleines cachées un peu partout sous les lits derrière les meubles dans la bibliothèque et entre les draps partout on butera contre des bouteilles vides   elle aura voulu lui faire plaisir diront-ils regardez il a vidé la bouteille de rhum de la Martinique   ils te ramasseront ils auront la nausée et ils t'emporteront   Marie-Paule fera le grand ménage le tri dans tes papiers et dans ses sentiments elle versera tant de larmes que le jour sera enfin venu où elle séchera sur son journal intime   Estelle étourdie confuse s'en remettra à sa fille aînée   elles tourneront autour de toi comme des toupies oscillant de la culpabilité au soulagement de la colère à la pitié cachant le dégoût la honte   je dirai ça n'est pas ma faute je dirai je dirai mais qu'est-ce que je dirai papa non je ne l'ai pas battu n'ai même pas eu à le frapper il est mort de sa belle mort pas de trace de poison de doigts sur son cou de balle dans la peau il a bu et il en est mort voilà tout je lui ai offert du rhum seulement du rhum un cadeau de Noël je ne croyais pas si bien faire pardon je ne sais plus ce que je dis

tu me souffleras les mots papa toi qui les connais si bien les juges les avocats les médecins tu plaideras ma cause s'il le faut oui c'était un tyran un impitoyable bourreau il nous tenait toutes les trois nous allions en mourir Estelle ma mère en avait déjà pris le chemin et personne pour nous venir en aide l'incompréhension générale nous étions seules avec lui le corps médical unanime nous renvoyait toutes à notre rôle qu'il tombe qu'il tombe et que ses femmes le ramassent j'en ai eu assez il ne fallait pas compter sur moi mesdames et messieurs les psychologues de tout acabit vous ne le saviez pas quelle naïveté vous croyiez que j'allais me satisfaire de paroles en l'air gestes symboliques et songes creux coups donnés dans le vide serviettes tordues en lieu et place cris poussés entre quatre murs insonorisés et alors et après où aviez-vous la tête non je n'allais pas faire de mon papa chéri maudit une petite chanson un long métrage un beau roman une toile à mettre au mur alors je l'ai tué et il est mort ivre de nos amours un dimanche comme les autres le dernier dimanche de force finis les repas en famille le dimanche l'ennui le dialogue impossible la folie qui mijote en même temps que la sauce du rôti je t'apporte la mort papa je te l'offre sur un plateau prends c'est pour toi une bouteille parmi les autres pour toi seul Estelle ne sera pas assez maligne pour en

profiter   prends laisse-toi aller mon ange voilà que tu t'en-
fonces dans la neige de décembre

Il halète et fait entendre une sorte de râle sibilant. Secoué de spasmes, il tremble. Elle se relève et étend sur lui une couverture qui traîne sur un fauteuil. Elle allume une cigarette, la lui glisse entre les lèvres. Lui aussi aime fumer. Il bave, n'a plus la force d'aspirer. L'air passe difficilement dans sa gorge obstruée par les déjections. Il s'accroche à son bras. Des paroles indistinctes s'emmêlent aux plaintes et aux gémissements, formant une monodie qui emplit la maison et bourdonne douloureusement dans ses oreilles. Elle se tient la tête à deux mains comme Estelle quand elle endort ses parasites intimes.

longue vie inutile stérilité et désirs mort-nés   n'ai enfanté que livres démodés filles manquées un plein panier de fruits secs rancœur accumulée humiliations répétées   Estelle éternelle insatisfaite veuve inconsolée de son père le vieux renard cancéreux mort décemment entre les draps propres d'un lit d'hôpital qu'il repose en paix   viens plus près Mathilde ça n'est pas facile pas si facile il y a le froid le cœur qui serre l'air qui déchire et dans la tête ce mouvement de va-et-vient pensées débandées qui montent s'accrochent et puis éclatent s'effacent disparaissent envolées délayées quelque chose se passe casse   je fonds   ton ange fond Mathilde j'ai chaud trop chaud décembre la neige on se croirait en été soleil torride Haïti si tu le voulais Mathilde tu

prendrais des branches de corossol et tu frotterais longue-
ment mon corps comme on le fait là-bas dans les veillées
funèbres   mourir en décembre le mois des morts en Haïti
    on m'emporte   mon corps se fraie un chemin entre les
îles terres d'ivresse et de misère   mon dernier voyage
Mathilde alcools inconnus cafés bars l'après-midi pêcheurs
flâneurs chômeurs du monde entier on m'attend tout ce que
j'aime Mathilde tout ce que j'ai su faire voyages et beuveries
    le dernier voyage paroles banales tout ce que tu hais
rien à attendre plus rien pas même envie   je ne t'entends
plus Mathilde alors tais-toi plus rien à nous dire laisse-moi
seul avec les voix venues d'ailleurs portées par l'odeur de la
mélasse et plus douces que la musique des anges

tu t'en vas je reste là muette plantée comme une vigie
bientôt minuit envie de dormir fatiguée dormir un sommeil
bien mérité petites pilules bleues inutiles à conserver toutefois on ne sait jamais   bon voyage papa   un jour quand
j'aurai retrouvé la voix je raconterai ton histoire l'histoire
d'un historien raté je serai dépositaire de ta mémoire
rappelle-toi tu disais autrefois que tu écrirais tes mémoires
le moment venu dans ta retraite dorée et puis tout s'est
embrouillé tes souvenirs se sont dilués dans le scotch

père et fille suivent le cours fluvial étendus côte à côte mais
voilà que les eaux se séparent et que chavire le lit-bateau
    l'un prend le large file vers la mer pendant que l'autre
part à la dérive solitaire et hardie

Il ne tremble plus, ne peine plus à courir après son souffle. Il est mort, la bouche entrouverte sur une parole demeurée imprononcée.

Elle allume une cigarette, installe commodément ses écouteurs. Le bourdonnement fait place à la musique. Elle entend la voix nasillarde sur fond râpeux de guitare : « *That was all she dreamed about, escape* ».

Il est temps de partir. Elle n'a plus mal à la tête, son front est lisse. Elle ne sent plus rien. Plus qu'à le quitter maintenant. Rien à dire, rien à expliquer, pas plus à Estelle qu'à Marie-Paule ou Jean-Louis. Rien à personne. Et le désert de l'autre côté de la porte.

Elle s'en va. Ses pas résonnent sur le trottoir de la rue Oxford. La neige fond. Le temps s'est radouci. Elle se sent calme, de plus en plus calme, complètement détendue. Tellement calme que ses genoux fléchissent sous le poids de la fatigue et de la faim. Elle tangue en marchant vers sa voiture telle une énervée qui s'en va à vau-l'eau.

Des sapins décorés illuminent la rue. Le dernier dimanche de l'année s'achève. On ne fêtera pas le Nouvel An chez les Dalpé mardi prochain. On ne sablera pas le champagne en famille autour d'une table bien garnie. La mort aura fait son trou entre les convives.

Elle met la clef dans la serrure, elle se sent calme, très calme. Un peu faible. C'est la faim. Elle ouvre la portière, un gros chat tapi sous la voiture détale en miaulant. Jasmine et Jérômine doivent mourir de faim elles aussi. Elles seront là à guetter derrière la fenêtre.

La voiture démarre doucement et s'éloigne en direction du pont Mercier. On l'attend. Elle allume une cigarette et franchit les eaux blanches du fleuve emprisonné entre ses rives gelées.

Novembre 1985-août 1986

MISE EN PAGES ET TYPOGRAPHIE :
LES ÉDITIONS DU BORÉAL

ACHEVÉ D'IMPRIMER EN SEPTEMBRE 2004
SUR LES PRESSES DE L'IMPRIMERIE AGMV MARQUIS
À CAP-SAINT-IGNACE (QUÉBEC).

THE WORDS OF
DESMOND TUTU

THE WORDS OF

DESMOND TUTU

SELECTED BY

NAOMI TUTU

Newmarket Press
New York

10 9 8 7 6 5 4 3

Library of Congress Cataloging-in-Publication Data

Tutu, Desmond.
   The words of Desmond Tutu.

   Bibliography: p.
   1. Tutu, Desmond—Quotations. I. Tutu, Naomi.
II. Title.
BX5700.6.Z8T875   1989   283'.68   88-34567

Quantity Purchases
Professional groups, firms, and other organizations may qualify for
special terms when ordering quantities of this title. For information
call or write the Special Sales Department, Newmarket Press,
18 East 48th Street, New York, N.Y. 10017 (212) 832-3575.
Manufactured in the United States

First edition

To the next generation, especially Talesa and Xabiso—
may your struggle be one of building
and not tearing down.

CONTENTS

INTRODUCTION

How does one go about introducing the thoughts and words of one's father? Initially it appeared to me that this introduction would be the easiest part of compiling this book. After all, I have known him for nearly thirty years and have heard him speak and preach more than most. However, as I prepared to write the introduction and thought about the selections, it became obvious that the task was going to be much more complicated. This is mainly because, though I have intellectually accepted him as Archbishop Tutu, Nobel Peace Prize recipient, emotionally he is and always will be my *Tata*, first and foremost. While a handful of people might be reading this because they want to know Naomi's *Tata*, that is not who I am asked to introduce. Rather, I am introducing a man who has come to symbolize for many around the world the nonviolent struggle against apartheid.

What is it that takes the son of a schoolteacher and washerwoman from the townships of South Africa and a life as a parish priest, and makes him a world figure? I think the key is the priesthood, and that is where it is best for me to begin. It is easiest for me to start there because that is a role he has had all my life and it is also the most honest because, as you will see in this book, he considers himself a Christian and a priest above all. That is what guides his words and actions.

Almost all the sayings collected in this book refer in some way to Desmond Tutu's faith. This is through no conscious effort on my part; in fact, I struggled to find more that did not. But almost all the addresses and speeches I selected from, to diverse audiences and in a wide range of situations, made some reference to faith, God, and the response they require of those who believe. In the same way his actions and statements in opposition to apartheid are based on this faith and the teachings of Christianity. If you attempt to understand the man, his words, or his actions divorced from this faith, they have no meaning. Even the ambiguities about him, such as the abhorrence of violence but the belief that it might, in some circumstances, be the lesser of the two evils, are the result of his beliefs. He himself says over and over again he is forced by his faith to speak out against injustice and oppression. As he says in *Why We Must Oppose Apartheid,* "My passionate opposition to the evil and pernicious policy of apartheid has nothing to do with a political or any other ideology. It has everything to do with my faith as a Christian and my understanding of the imperatives of the gospel of Jesus Christ." And again in his reply to the State President P.W. Botha's question published in periodicals in South Africa and the world on who he is guided by in his opposition to the South African government, "My theological position derives from the Bible and from the teachings of the Church, both of which predate Marxism and the African National Congress by several centuries."

The role that my father plays in South Africa is, I believe, the role he thinks the Church must play throughout the world. In South Africa the role of the Church as critic of social and economic systems is made simpler because the injustice is so blatant. (In fact he has said on numerous occasions that it is almost easier to be a Christian in a situation of oppression.) However, this should be the Church's role in all societies, for nowhere is there a place where all people are living in peace and security. Christian peace is not simply the absence of conflict, but rather the presence of justice, reconciliation, fullness of life, health and well-being for all people. No country has achieved this, no country can achieve it in isolation, and it is the Church's role to encourage all people to strive for this, the true peace. The Church must be a constant critic of all forms of government until this is achieved.

Having listened to my father speak fairly often, my mother, sisters, and I now murmur to each other, "Speech number 14," or 21, or whatever number once he has started a presentation or sermon. He himself has stated on numerous occasions that he is very repetitive, because, he insists, he has only one fundamental message—the importance of community and respect for others. In his eyes, once we have all recognized this and have chosen to live by it, the world will be a better place.

It is interesting that these themes are of the utmost importance in the two systems that are his foundation, Christianity and African culture. A solitary Christian is a contradiction in terms as is, in African culture, a solitary human being. We are only Christians in our caring for and sharing with others, and we are human through our relationships with other human beings. So in Xhosa we say *U muntu ngu muntu ngabantu,* meaning a person is a person through other people. It is a call to respect others as part of ourselves, others on whom we rely in some way or another. Likewise, in Christianity we are one body and no part of the body can be unaffected by the pain or loss of another. But as we share each other's pain, so do we share each other's joy.

Thus, for my father, the Nobel was not *his* prize, but the prize of so many in South Africa and around the world who are part of the fight for a better society. In practical terms this led to some headaches for the organizers of the Nobel prize-giving ceremony in 1984, because my father insisted that representatives of all those who had assisted him in some way be present in Oslo. In the end his party consisted of people from around the world, from Terry Waite, the Archbishop of Canterbury's special envoy, to the Dean of General Seminary in New York where he had been when he was notified of his selection, to a contingent from the South African Council of Churches. The full party must have numbered at least forty, which was a blessing when, after a bomb scare during the presentation, the orchestra did not return and we were called upon to supply the music! The real importance of this crowd, however, was the statement it made of our need for one another in all situations, and that no one person no matter how gifted can achieve anything alone.

Rather than gifted, I think my father would consider himself blessed. Blessed in the people he has met throughout his life, from Bishop Trevor Huddleston, who showed him that respect is something due to others no matter the color of their skin or their situation in life, to my mother who taught him that a certain irreverence in life is necessary if you are to remain sane and enjoy life to its fullest.

All the above seems to paint a picture of a humorless, all-suffering human being, but the one thing most everyone who has heard my father speak comments on is his sense of humor. Even when talking about the insanity of apartheid to those who suffer it daily, he is able to draw laughter by comparing the basing of rights on skin color to basing them on the size of one's nose, as he has a fairly large one. There is some truth to the theory that he laughs and tries to get others to do so to stop himself from crying. However, I think there is also the realization that no situation is completely devoid of any joy or hope, for once that becomes true, then there is no reason to struggle or live. In addition, he believes that humor is liberating because once you begin to take yourself or your situation in life too seriously, you become a prisoner of your self-perception. That is one of the things that he believes the majority of white South Africans are guilty of. They have taken to heart the belief that they are innately superior to blacks and are therefore afraid of what would happen once they gave an inch and accepted our humanity. They are afraid that this would result in us doing to them what they have done to us but with vengeance. So he asks black South Africans to understand this fear while urging white South Africans to release themselves from it by taking those first steps towards a free South Africa. Not an easy role to play by any stretch of the imagination, because whites continue to vilify him as a trouble-maker, and many young blacks see people like him as standing in the way of liberation, so that I wonder if he would ever be able again to stop a crowd from killing a suspected informer as he did a few years ago. It seems more likely that the anger would be turned on him instead.

It is strange to hear the South African government and its supporters speak of my father as one who encourages violence and hate. If there is anybody I know who finds it impossible to hate another human being it is he. On many occasions I have felt frustrated by his attempts to teach us that hating someone else is hating ourselves and God. I finally decided it was impossible to change his view in 1982. I was to be married on July 3rd and on June 16th my fiancé, my sisters, and I went with my father to a service to commemorate those young people killed in the Soweto uprising of 1976. After the service, he left the churchyard, which was surrounded by police, to try to ensure that people were able to leave peacefully. A contingent of police stormed into the churchyard chasing some young people. My fiancé Corbin tried to intervene when three police then began to attack the parish priest—so they turned on us. When they were through, Corbin's glasses were broken and he had *sjambok* marks on his head and face while my arm was bleeding and my back was throbbing. When we got home, I asked my father, "Can you still ask us to forgive? Can you still believe they are our brothers, that we have some responsibility to them?" He had no profound statement that will be remembered for generations, but simply said, "I cannot ask you to do anything since you were the one beaten, but I can hope that if I am ever the one, I will still be able to forgive and pray for them. That is the strength I ask for."

Throughout this introduction, I have spoken of the importance of his faith to my father: Perhaps what is strangest about it is that he came by most of it after he decided to become a priest. Growing up, I knew my parents had been married in the Catholic church, so how did we end up as Anglicans? I decided, rather romantically, that married and with two children, my father had been dramatically called by God to the priesthood and therefore became an Anglican. I later found out that upon leaving teaching after the introduction of Bantu Education, he chose the priesthood rather as another form of service close in many ways to that of a teacher. But however he considers the decision at the time, I still believe that he was "called" because it is unlikely that he would have the strength to continue the struggle, or even to be able to survive, without his faith. He is too easily hurt and too needing of love to thrive in the position he now holds within South Africa without this anchor. A Desmond Tutu without his belief in an all loving, all forgiving God who created us for his purposes could not play the role he plays today. He *is* his faith, and it is his faith that sustains him and has made him what he is.

I hope these words will give to some a better understanding of my father's faith, and more importantly, of the part that the struggle against apartheid is playing in the greater struggle for a world governed by true peace.

—Naomi Tutu
London
December, 1988

FAITH
AND
RESPONSIBILITY

"The word of God calls his people to work for justice, for only thus can there be peace."

"The church must be ready to speak the truth in love. It has a responsibility for all, the rich and the poor, the ruler and the ruled, the oppressed and the oppressor, but it needs to point out that God *does* take sides. Incredibly, he sides with those whom the world would marginalize, whom the world considers of little account. That was what he did in the founding of Israel. He took their side when they did not deserve it against the powerful, against pharoah. That was a paradigmatic act that gave an important clue about the sort of God he is."

"One day at a party in England for some reason we were expected to pay for our tea. I offered to buy a cup for an acquaintance. Now he could have said, "No, thank you." You could have knocked me down with a feather when he replied, "No, I won't be subsidized!" Well, I never! I suppose it was an understandable attitude. You want to pay your own way and not sponge on others. But it is an attitude that may have seemed to carry over into our relationship with God—our refusal to be subsidized by Him. It all stems very much from the prevailing achievement ethic which permeates our very existence. It is drummed into our heads, from our most impressionable days, that you must grind the opposition into the dust. We get so worked up that our children can become nervous wrecks as they are egged on to greater efforts by competitive parents. It has got to the stage where the worst sin in our society is to have failed.

"What a tremendous relief it should be, and has been to many, to discover that we don't need to prove ourselves to God. We don't have to do anything at all, to be acceptable to Him. That is what Jesus came to say, and for that He got killed. He came to say, 'Hey, you don't have to earn God's love. It is not a matter for human achievement. You exist because God loves you already. You are a child of divine love.' The Pharisees, the reli-

gious leaders of His day, they couldn't bu
thought Jesus was proclaiming a thoroug
ble God with very low standards—any T
Harry, Mary and Jane would soon be jos
with the prim and proper ones. Stupendously this was true;
no, just part of the truth. Jesus was saying that the unlikely ones, those despised ones, the sinners, the prosti-
tutes, the tax collectors, would in fact precede the prim
and proper ones into the Kingdom of God. That really
set the cat among some ecclesiastical pigeons, I can tell
you.

"When a chap is in love, he will go out in all kinds of
weather to keep an appointment with his beloved. Love
can be demanding, in fact more demanding than law. It
has its own imperatives—think of a mother sitting by
the bedside of a sick child through the night, impelled
only by love. Nothing is too much trouble for love."

"To ignore people of other faiths and ideologies in an
increasingly plural society is to be willfully blind to what
the scriptures say about Christian witness. We are severely impoverished if we do not encounter people of
other faiths with reverence and respect for their belief and
integrity."

"The heart of the Christian Gospel is precisely that God the all holy One, the all powerful One is also the One full of mercy and compassion. He is not a neutral God inhabiting some inaccessible Mount Olympus. He is a God who cares about his children and cares enormously for the weak, the poor, the naked, the downtrodden, the despised. He takes their side not because they are good, since many of them are demonstrably not so. He takes their side because He is that kind of God, and they have no one else to champion them."

"An authentic Christian spirituality is utterly subversive to any system that would treat a man or woman as anything less than a child of God. It has nothing to do with ideology or politics. Every praying Christian, every person who has an encounter with God, must have a passionate concern for his or her brother and sister, his or her neighbor. To treat anyone of these as if he were less than the child of God is to deny the validity of one's spiritual experience."

"If we are to say that religion cannot be concerned with politics then we are really saying that there is a substantial part of human life in which God's writ does not run. If it is not God's then whose is it? Who is in charge if not the God and Father of our Lord Jesus Christ?

"Is it not interesting just how often people and churches are accused of mixing religion with politics?—almost always whenever they condemn a particular social political dispensation as being unjust. If the South African Council of Churches were to say now that it thought apartheid was not so bad, I am as certain as anything that we would not find ourselves where we are today. Why is it not being political for a religious body or a religious leader to *praise* a social political dispensation?"

"My passionate opposition to apartheid stems from my understanding of the Bible and the Christian faith. If anyone can prove that apartheid is consistent with the teachings of the Bible and Jesus Christ then I will burn my Bible and cease forthwith to be a Christian. Praise to God that no one can do that."

"It is interesting to note that many who have been Christian activists, such as St. Francis of Assisi, who went on a crusade and was deeply concerned with the poor and downtrodden, and St. Teresa of Avila, the Spanish nun who reorganized her Carmelite religious community, were people who put first things first. St. Francis is known to have spent a whole night in prayer enraptured as he repeated over and over again the phrase 'My God and my all,' and you recall that after a lengthy Lenten period of fasting and meditation he emerged from his cave bearing the marks of the nails of Christ in his hands and the wound in his side—the stigmata.

"All I am saying is that the Bible and our faith and its tradition declare unequivocally that for an authentic Christian existence the absolute priority must be spirituality. A church that does not pray is quite useless. Christians who do not pray are of no earthly worth. We must be marked by a heightened God consciousness. Then all kinds of things will happen."

"If you take your Christianity seriously you can't support apartheid, for Christianity and apartheid are totally incompatible. That is what our church and others are saying when they declare apartheid a heresy."

"Let me warn the government again: You are not God. You may be powerful, but you are mortal. Beware when you take on the church of God. Emperor Nero, Hitler, Amin, and many others have tried it and ended ignominiously. Get rid of apartheid, and we will have a new South Africa that is just, nonracial, and democratic, where black and white can exist amicably side by side in their home country as members of one family, the human family, God's family."

"True Christian worship includes the love of God and the love of neighbour. The two must go together or your Christianity is false. St. John asks in his first epistle how you can say you love God, whom you have not seen, if you hate your brother, whom you have. Our love for God is tested and proved by our love for our neighbour. This is what the churches, and perhaps especially the South African Council of Churches, attempt to do in that beautiful but sadly unhappy land which is South Africa."

"Jesus was quite categorical in expressing solidarity with those he called the least of his brethren: the naked, the hungry, the thirsty, the sick, the imprisoned. To act with compassion toward these is to act with compassion toward Jesus himself. In Isaiah 61 Jesus summed up the nature of his ministry:

> The spirit of the Lord is upon me, because he has anointed me to preach good news to the poor. He has sent me to proclaim release to the captives and recovering of sight to the blind, to set at liberty those who are oppressed.

"If we are the representatives of God, we must take sides. We have no choice really. To be neutral in a situation of injustice is to have chosen sides already. It is to support the status quo. We must look to our Lord and Master who is our peace.

"I would hope we could show our solidarity with those who are uprooted, that we would walk through the squalor of the slums, which are the result of deliberate government policy, that we would attend those horrific funerals, that we would be at the treason trials with the families of the detained. I know we do many of these things already. That is where we must be."

"We who have the privilege of working in situations of injustice and oppression, where God's children have their noses rubbed in the dust daily and their God-given human dignity is trodden callously underfoot with a cynical disregard for their human rights, are filled with an anamolous exhilaration. We are filled with an indomitable hope and exhilaration because we know that ultimately injustice and oppression and evil and exploitation cannot prevail and that the kingdoms of this world are becoming the kingdom of our God and his Christ.

"In a setting that claims we are made for alienation, separation, dividedness, hostility, and war, we must, as the church of God, proclaim that we are made for togetherness, for fellowship, for community, for oneness, for friendship, and peace. In a situation of injustice, oppression, and exploitation, we must proclaim that the justice and righteousness and equity of God will prevail. In a place where truth is a constant casualty, with many in high places taking loosely the demands of verity and truthfulness, we must declare that truth matters and that a people who have become immoral are in grave danger of collapse. In a situation where human life seems dirt cheap, with people being killed as easily as one swats a fly, we must proclaim that people matter and matter enormously, because they are created in the image of God. We must proclaim that apartheid must go and that a new dispensation will take its place, a dispensation where black and white will live together as members of one family, the human family, God's family."

"Christians from all over the world form a tremendous variety and rich diversity. How I have longed for my compatriots to experience a World Christian Conference— sponsored ecumenical event just to glory in the wonderful variety of people God has united in the *koinonia* of His Son's body—people from bewilderingly different ethnic, cultural, geographical, social, economic, and ecclesiastical backgrounds and yet remarkably able to confess Jesus Christ as Lord to the glory of the Father.

"You really cannot describe the texture of these gatherings at which you catch a glimpse of the true *oikumene*. There are tall people, short people, clever people (most seem so) and others not so clever, fat people, lean people, black, yellow, Caucasian people in a splendidly variegated array of national costumes and speaking a veritable Babel of languages, all (or nearly all) able to worship together, to receive the body and blood of our Lord and Savior together and all able to understand one another because of the marvel of simultaneous translation. You realized what God intended the church to be, a first fruit of the redeemed, a sign of hope that God intends us to be a family."

"My passionate opposition to the evil and pernicious policy of apartheid has nothing to do with a political or any other ideology. It has everything to do with my faith as a Christian and my understanding of the imperatives of the gospel of Jesus Christ. My opposition is based firmly and squarely on the Bible and on the injunctions of the Christian gospel. I have yet to hear the oppressed say, 'Archbishop Tutu, you are too political.' If anything, they will probably declare that we are not political enough. If I were to stand up here and say that I don't think apartheid to be too bad, then none of my erstwhile critics would accuse me of that heinous crime of mixing religion with politics."

APARTHEID

"I come from a beautiful land, richly endowed by God with wonderful resources, wide expanses, rolling mountains, singing birds, bright shining stars out of blue skies, with radiant sunshine, golden sunshine. There is enough of the good things that come from God's bounty; there is enough for everyone, but apartheid has confirmed some in their selfishness, causing them to grasp greedily a disproportionate share, the lion's share, because of their power."

"Humans are of infinite worth intrinsically because they are created in God's image. Apartheid, injustice, oppression, exploitation are not only wrong; they are positively blasphemous because they treat the children of God as if they are less than His."

"Ours is a deeply polarized society. It is a house divided against itself, hagridden by fear, suspicion, division, hostility, alienation, characterized by violence, injustice, oppression, unrest, and yet also by compassion, caring, concern, courageous witness for the truth, refusal to compromise on principle by people of all races."

"You remember the story of the Zambian boasting to a South African about their minister of the navy. The South African scoffed: 'You are landlocked. How can you have a minister of the navy?' The Zambian retorted: 'Ah, but you claim to have a minister of justice.' "

"I visited one of the banned people, Winnie Mandela. Her husband, Nelson Mandela, is serving a life sentence on Robben Island, our maximum security prison. I wanted to take her Holy Communion. The police told me I couldn't enter her house. So we celebrated Holy Communion in my car in the street in Christian South Africa. On a second occasion I went to see her on a weekend. Her restriction order is more strict on weekends.

She can't leave her yard. So we celebrated Holy Communion again in the street. This time Winnie was on one side of the fence and I was on the other. This in Christian South Africa in 1978."

"The consequence of sin is to divide, to break up, to cause to disintegrate, to separate, to alienate, to split apart. Apartheid partakes of this centrifugal nature of sin for it is in fact the essence of sin to separate. That is why we have said that apartheid is fundamentally, in its very nature, evil, immoral, and un-Christian."

"Let us all identify the problem. It is not Soviet expansionism, even if the Russians may have their eyes on our lucrative natural resources. The enemy is not the agitator. Let him try telling denizens of the affluent suburbs that they are suffering and oppressed and see how far he can get with that. The enemy is not 'out there.' It is not on the border. It is not an interfering hostile world. The enemy is right here. The enemy is apartheid, which has turned this country into the pariah of the world."

"For us blacks, the victims of apartheid, the declaration of a state of emergency is merely making *de jure* what has been *de facto*, because we have, in the black community, been living in a virtual state of emergency. We have been accustomed over the years to having meetings banned and community leaders detained. We have been used over the years to our leaders being tried for high treason or muzzled in some way or another, with quite extraordinary bail conditions imposed."

"A person banned for three or five years becomes a non-person, who cannot be quoted during the period of her banning order. She cannot attend a gathering, which means more than one person. Two persons together talking to a banned person are a gathering! She cannot attend the wedding or funeral of even her own child without special permission. She must be at home from 6:00 P.M. of one day to 6:00 A.M. of the next and on all public holidays, and from 6:00 P.M. on Fridays until 6:00 A.M. on Mondays for three years. She cannot go on holiday outside the magisterial area to which she has been confined. She cannot go to the cinema, nor to a picnic. That is severe punishment, inflicted without the evidence allegedly justifying it being made available to the banned person, not having it scrutinized in a court of law. It is a serious erosion and violation of basic human rights, of which blacks have precious few in the land of their birth."

"It won't do to tinker with this system. It cannot be reformed. It must be dismantled. It must be destroyed so that a new South Africa can rise."

"Apartheid has decreed the politics of exclusion. Seventy-three percent of the population is excluded from any meaningful participation in the political decision-making process of the land of their birth. . . . Blacks are expected to exercise their political ambitions in unviable, poverty-stricken, arid, Bantustan homelands, ghettoes of misery, inexhaustible reservoirs of cheap black labor, Bantustans into which South Africa is being balkanized. Blacks are systematically being stripped of their South African citizenship and being turned into aliens in the land of their birth. This is apartheid's Final Solution, just as Nazism had its Final Solution for the Jews in Hitler's Aryan madness."

"Detention without trial is an abrogation of the rule of law; it is a subverting of justice. It is to punish someone and to punish him severely without the inconvenience of having to prove his guilt in an open court. It is a very handy device greatly beloved of totalitarian, repressive governments."

"When a priest goes missing and is subsequently found dead, the media in the West carry his story in very extensive coverage. I am glad that the death of one person can cause so much concern. But in the same week that this priest is found dead, the South African police kill 24 blacks who had been participating in a protest, and 6,000 blacks are sacked for being similarly involved, and you are lucky to get that much coverage. Are we being told something I do not want to believe, that we blacks are expendable and that blood is thicker than water, that when it comes to the crunch you cannot trust whites, that they will club together? I don't want to believe that is the message being conveyed to us."

"It won't help the antisanctions lobby to vilify me. Even if they were to liquidate me, what I say is true: apartheid is filthy, it is vile, it is immoral, it is violent, it is vicious, it is evil, it is un-Christian. Even if I am not there, even if I can be shown to be a scoundrel of the first water, it won't help to change the nature of apartheid. Apartheid is the problem and the world agrees with us."

"Apartheid cannot survive without an enemy and so apartheid has to create enemies. If they are not external enemies, then they must be internal enemies."

"Apartheid says our value resides in a biological attribute, in this instance, skin color. A particular skin color is by definition not a universal phenomenon possessed by all human beings. The Bible, on the other hand, declares that what makes each and every person of infinite, incalculable worth is not this or that biological attribute. It is the fact that we are each created in the image of God."

"Only those who have been victims of oppression and injustice and discrimination know what I am talking about when I say that the ultimate evil is not the suffering, excruciating as that may be, which is meted out to those who are God's children. The ultimate evil of oppression, and certainly of that policy of South Africa called apartheid, is when it succeeds in making a child of God begin to doubt that he or she is a child of God."

VIOLENCE
AND
NONVIOLENCE

"Stability and peace in our land will not come from the barrel of a gun, because peace without justice is an impossibility."

"There is no peace in South Africa. There is no peace because there is no justice. There can be no real peace and security until there is first justice enjoyed by all inhabitants of that beautiful land. The Bible knows nothing about peace without justice, for that would be crying 'peace, peace,' where there is no peace. God's Shalom, peace, involves inevitable righteousness, justice, wholesomeness, fullness of life, participation in decision making, goodness, laughter, joy, compassion, sharing, and reconciliation."

"There will be more and more political harassment, bannings and detention, but these will not deter those who are determined to become free. The international community must make up its mind whether it wants to see a peaceful resolution of the South African Crisis or not. If it does, then let it apply pressure (diplomatic, political, but above all economic) on the South African Government to persuade them to go to the negotiating table with the authentic leaders of all sections of the South African population before it is too late."

"We are preparing for a society that is going to be able to discriminate between good and bad, and we must not allow ourselves to become like the system we oppose. We cannot afford to use methods of which we will be ashamed when we look back, when we say, *'Ja, magtag,* we shouldn't have done that.'

"We must remember, my friends, that we have been given a wonderful cause, the cause of freedom! And you and I must be those who will walk with heads held high. We will say, 'We used methods that can stand the harsh scrutiny of history.' "

"The paradigms that we've got to follow are biblical paradigms. Moses went to see the Pharoah not once but several times. Who are we to prejudge the grace of God. It's very difficult for me as a church leader to say, 'Go to hell,' to say God's grace cannot operate on P. W. Botha."

"Many are beginning to think the only way forward is the way of armed struggle. But I am certain that if we were to say today the government is serious about dismantling apartheid most people would be glad. None of our people is really bloodthirsty. They just want their place under the sun, a place where they are acknowledged for what they are—human beings made in the image of God."

"We must recognize that apartheid is the primary violence in South Africa. It's the violence of the migratory labor system, the violence of detention without trial, the violence that forces children to starve, the violence that stunts intellectual and spiritual growth. Apartheid is an evil and immoral system that must be destroyed."

"I am opposed to both the violence of those who maintain an unjust system and the violence of those who seek to overthrow it. The important point to make is that many people think violence is something that is going to be introduced from the outside by the so-called terrorists, the people of the liberation movements. The situation in South Africa is already a violent one. It is the institutional violence, the structural violence of apartheid, that has caused the answering violence of the liberation movements."

"When blacks—after many years during which their cautious protest was consistently ignored—in desperation opted for armed struggle, whites dubbed them 'terrorists,' which meant they could be ruthlessly imprisoned, hanged, or shot. The will to be free is not, however, defeated by even the worst kind of violence. Such repressive violence has only succeeded in throwing South Africa into a low-intensity civil war. Already South Africans are staring at fellow South Africans through gunsights."

"I will never tell someone to pick up a gun. But I will pray for the man who picks up the gun, pray that he will be less cruel than he might otherwise have been, because he is a member of the community. We are going to have to decide: if this civil war escalates, what is our ministry going to be?"

"I am a lover of peace and I try to work for justice because only thus do I believe we can ever hope to establish durable peace. It is self-defeating to justify a truce based on unstable foundations of oppression. Such a truce can only be inherently unstable, requiring that it be maintained by institutional violence."

"International action and international pressure are among the few nonviolent options left. Yet how strident is the opposition to economic sanctions. Blacks cannot vote. We are driven therefore to invoke a nonviolent method that we believe is likely to produce the desired result. If this option is denied us, what then is left? If sanctions should fail, there is no other way but to fight."

"The problem is not sanctions. The problem is apartheid. I want apartheid destroyed, not reformed. If it can be done away without sanctions I will sing Alleluia. The onus is still on those who oppose sanctions to provide us with a viable nonviolent alternative."

"When a clash occurs between the laws of man and the laws of God, then for the Christian there can be no debate or argument about which he must obey. Our Lord told those who questioned Him: "Render unto Caesar the things that belong to Caesar and render unto God the things that belong to God." Caesar is God's servant to ensure that good and just order prevail. He cannot claim absolute authority without becoming blasphemous.

"We are a normally law-abiding people, but when the honor of God is at stake, we will disobey iniquitous and unjust laws. Please let us be mindful of the important distinction between what is legal and what is morally right."

"My father used to say 'Don't raise your voice. Improve your argument.' Good sense does not always lie with the loudest shouters, nor can we say that a large unruly crowd is always the best arbiter of what is right."

"All violence is evil, but a time may come when you have to decide between two evils—oppression or a violent overthrow of the oppressive regime. This happened in World War II. Did you allow Hitler to put children into gas ovens unhindered or did you go to war to stop him? Which was the lesser evil? Did you accept the tyranny of taxation without representation or did you fight the American War of Independence? Which was the lesser evil? I am sick and tired of those who would say that I support violence. I support the African National Congress in its aims to found a just, democratic, and nonracial South Africa, but I do not support its methods."

"Some of us, at great cost to our credibility, still talk about peaceful change in the face of escalating government intransigence and violence and growing impatience and frustration in the black community. We are seen especially by young blacks as standing in the way of revolution, and it is possible that whites may one day realize what we actually did and how much they owe to those whom they have most loved to hate, those whom they have delighted in seeing vilified and discredited."

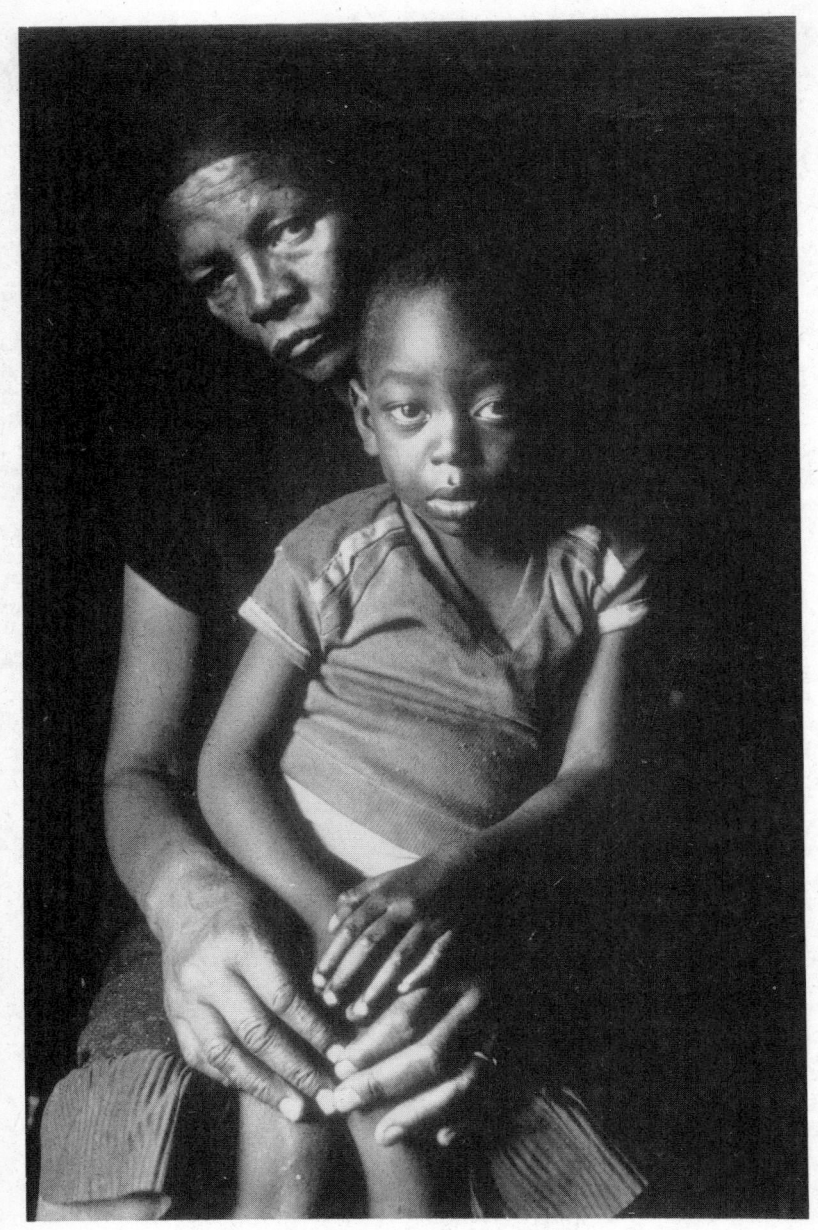

FAMILY

"A person is entitled to a stable community life, and the first of these communities is the family."

"Children are a wonderful gift. They are young and small persons, with minds and ideas, hating to be talked down to. They have an extraordinary capacity to see into the heart of things, and to expose sham and humbug for what they are. We must not idealize them too much, but I know that most of those I have had any dealings with respond wonderfully to being treated with respect, as persons who are responsible."

"Every day in a squatter camp near Cape Town, called K.T.C., the authorities have been demolishing flimsy plastic shelters that black mothers have erected because they were taking their marriage vows seriously. They have been reduced to sitting on soaking mattresses, with their household effects strewn round their feet, and whimpering babies on their laps, in the cold Cape winter rain. Every day the authorities have carried out these callous demolitions. What heinous crime have these women committed, to be hounded like criminals in this manner? All they have wanted is to be with their husbands, the fathers of their children. Everywhere else in the world they would be highly commended, but in South Africa, a land that claims to be Christian, and that boasts a public holiday called Family Day, these gallant women are treated so inhumanely, and yet all they want is to have a decent and stable family life. Unfortunately, in the land of their birth, it is a criminal offense for them to live happily with their husbands and fathers of their children. Black family life is thus being undermined, not accidentally, but by deliberate government policy. It is part of the price human beings, God's children, are called to pay for apartheid. An unacceptable price."

"The fulfillment of God's dream for human beings happens in the new dispensation when we are incorporated in Christ where 'there is neither Jew nor Gentile, slave nor free, male nor female, but we are all one in Christ.' Thus, it is not trying to be in vogue—to be climbing the latest bandwagon—to be concerned about the place of women in society and in the church. There can be no true liberation that ignores the question raised by the movement for the liberation of women."

"I believe that males and females have distinctive gifts, and both sets of gifts are indispensable for truly human existence. I am sure that the church has lost something valuable in denying ordination to women for so long. There is something uniquely valuable that women and men bring to the ordained ministry, and it has been distorted and defective as long as women have been debarred. Somehow men have been less human for this loss."

"There is something in the nature of God that corresponds to our maleness and our femaleness. We have tended to speak much more of the maleness, so we refer to the Fatherhood of God, which is as it should be. But we have missed out on the fullness that is God when we have ignored that which corresponds to our femaleness. We have hardly spoken about the Motherhood of God, and consequently we have been the poorer for this."

"I would like to refer to one aspect—a tremendous quality that women have—which relates to a like quality in God. It is the faith women have in people. Take a child who is a cause of much frustration and disillusion in others. The mother of that child can see the beauty and goodness hidden deep down, and women are much more patient than men in trying to bring that goodness to the surface. They have the capacity, more than men, to cherish that good and bring it to fruition. Women, we need you to give us back our faith in humanity."

"The father leaves his family in the Bantustan homeland, there eking out a miserable existence, whilst he,
if he is lucky, goes to the so-called white man's town as
a migrant, to live an unnatural life in a single-sex hostel for eleven months there, being prey to drunkenness,
prostitution, and worse. . . . This cancer, eating away
at the vitals of black family life, is deliberate government
policy. It is part of the cost of apartheid, exorbitant in
terms of human suffering."

"In pursuance of apartheid's ideological racist dream, over
3,000,000 of God's children have been uprooted from
their homes, which have been demolished, whilst they have
been dumped in the Bantustan homeland resettlement
camps. . . . These dumping grounds are far from where
work and food can be procured easily. Children starve,
suffer from the often irreversible consequences of mal-
nutrition. . . . They starve in a land that could be the
breadbasket of Africa, a land that normally is an exporter
of food."

"We should be appalled that the world has a refugee population of over ten million people—not just statistics, but people who are mothers, fathers, children, husbands, wives to somebody. They are not just faceless digits but human persons for whom our Lord and Savior died. He identified fully with them as one who had himself been a refugee."

"Apartheid has spawned discriminatory education, such as Bantu education, education for serfdom, ensuring that the government spends only about one-tenth on one black child per annum for education what it spends on a white child. It is education that is decidedly separate and unequal. It is to be wantonly wasteful of human resources, because so many of God's children are prevented, by deliberate government policy, from attaining their fullest potential. South Africa is paying a heavy price already for this iniquitous policy because there is a desperate shortage of skilled manpower, a direct result of the short-sighted schemes of the racist regime. It is a moral universe that we inhabit, and good and right and equity matter in the universe of the God we worship. And so, in this matter, the South African government and its supporters are being hoisted with their own petard."

"Apartheid is upheld by a phalanx of iniquitous laws, such as the Population Registration Act, which decrees that all South Africans must be classified ethnically, and duly registered according to these race categories. Many times in the same family one child has been classified white whilst another with a slightly darker hue has been classified colored, with all the horrible consequences for the latter of being shut out from membership of a greatly privileged caste. There have, as a result, been several child suicides. This is too high a price to pay for racial purity."

"In one area of Soweto the youth erected barricades to stop the security forces from evicting those who refused to pay rent. The police went indiscriminately into homes in the area, ordered the children into the streets, and beat them. When the children ran away, they shot them. I went to one such home, where a thirteen-year-old boy had been shot dead. His younger brother, who had been shot in the stomach, was in critical condition in the hospital. The stunned mother sat silently in her chair. She kept wiping her eyes but there were no tears. I tried to talk to her about the love of God and silently asked, 'How long, oh Lord.' "

"Because there is global insecurity, nations are engaged in a mad arms race, spending billions of dollars wastefully on instruments of destruction, when millions are starving. Just a fraction of what is expended so obscenely on defense budgets would make the difference in enabling God's children to fill their stomachs, be educated, and given the chance to lead fulfilled and happy lives. We have the capacity to feed ourselves several times over, but we are daily haunted by the spectacle of the gaunt dregs of humanity shuffling along in endless queues, with bowls to collect what the charity of the world has provided, too little too late. God created us for fellowship. God created us so that we should form the human family, existing together because we were made for one another. We are not made for an exclusive self-sufficiency but for interdependence, and we break the law of being at our peril."

"Our children are being used as hostages in the power game of the government of South Africa. By controlling our children, the government hopes to control the parents. I am not just talking about black children, though they are by far the group that suffers the most. I speak also of white children, poor white youngsters who learn to hate at a very young age, who learn to salute, to march, to fear children with black skin, who are being trained in their bodies and their minds and their spirits to prepare for war."

"We of an older generation are on the whole still scared of arrest, of police dogs, of tear gas, of prison, and of death. But these young people are quite something else. They have experienced it all—yes, they have seen friends, brothers, and sisters die, and they are no longer scared. They are just determined. They are determined that they are going to be free, they and their reluctant, cowed parents. They have, they believe, sat for too long, listening night after night to the stories of their parents' daily humiliations just because they were black. They have decided that enough is enough. They are people with iron in their souls."

"My wife and I decided early on in our marriage that we were going to try to let our children do a lot of things that we had been denied in our childhood. We had been brought up to know that children are meant to be seen and not heard. So as children we used to feel so terribly frustrated when those gods of our household—our parents and their grown-up friends—were discussing something really interesting. We were burning to ask 'who' or 'what' in order to clarify some obscure point, but we never dared to interrupt.

"So we did not want our children to go through all those traumas. But it was not easy. I remember for instance saying to our youngest, who was then a very chirpy three-year-old, and quite sure that there were very few things that she did not know in the world: 'Mpho, darling, please keep quiet, you talk too much.' Do you think she was at all deflated by this rebuke? Not at all—quick as a shot she retorted: 'Daddy, you talk a lot too.'

"We stuck it out very painfully. We let them join in discussions with our adult friends—they interrupted, they argued, they contributed. We discovered there was much fun in the home, and we parents developed as we pitted our strengths against those of our children. They were persons in their own right, and we had to think out many things that previously we had taken for granted. I did not mean letting go of discipline, because a rebellious child is really testing out the parameters of acceptable conduct, and that is part of the painful process of growing up."

THE COMMUNITY—
BLACK AND WHITE

"One of the ways of helping to destroy a people is to tell them that they don't have a history, that they have no roots."

"Africans believe in something that is difficult to render in English. We call it *ubuntu, botho*. It means the essence of being human. You know when it is there and when it is absent. It speaks about humaneness, gentleness, hospitality, putting yourself out on behalf of others, being vulnerable. It embraces compassion and toughness. It recognizes that my humanity is bound up in yours, for we can only be human together."

"There is an old film called *The Defiant Ones*. In one scene, two convicts manacled together escape. They fall into a ditch with slippery sides. One of them claws his way to near the top and just about makes it. But he cannot. His mate to whom he is manacled is still at the bottom and drags him down. The only way they can escape to freedom is together. The one convict was black and the other white: a dramatic parable of our situation in South Africa. The only way we can survive is together, black and white; the only way we can be truly human is together, black and white."

"Large crowds are scurrying home past the cathedral on their way to the main Johannesburg railway station; they seem like so many ants. In the morning it is the same story, only the traffic is in the opposite direction. Blacks live more than twelve miles away, mainly in the twin city of Soweto (abbreviation for South Western Township), with nearly a million black inhabitants. They start from home in the dark and return when the street lights (where they have them) are on. They hardly see their children except over the weekend, and their transport is woefully inadequate, with dangerously overcrowded trams and buses."

"The black community can be dealt with effectively only through its recognized leaders. Anything else the government attempts will be like fiddling while the fires of revolution burn in our country."

"In our African language we say 'a person is a person through other persons.' I would not know how to be a human being at all except I learned this from other human beings. We are made for a delicate network of relationships, of interdependence. We are meant to complement each other. All kinds of things go horribly wrong when we break that fundamental law of our being. Not even the most powerful nation can be completely self-sufficient."

"We were meant to be as caring as a good farmer who tends the soil, not being unwantonly wasteful of irreplaceable natural resources and not behaving irresponsibly toward nature, polluting the air and water so recklessly."

"The African, on his side, regards the universe as one composite whole; an organic entity, progressively driving toward greater harmony and unity, whose individual parts exist merely as interdependent aspects of one whole realizing their fullest life in the corporate life where communal contentment is the absolute measure of values. His philosophy of life strives toward unity and aggregation, toward greater social responsibility."

"I understand why white people have the kind of perceptions that they have, which are totally different from the perceptions of blacks. If my wife and I had lived in the northern suburbs of Johannesburg always, what would we know about the state of emergency. I mean, you say to white people, 'We are in a state of emergency.' 'State of emergency? What state of emergency are you talking about?' What do they know about rubber bullets that shoot through their own children? What do they know about tear gas? What do they know about Caspirs, which rumble through our townships? State of emergency? We wake up on a Sunday in our northern suburban home. The salubrious, clean air, the breeze floating through the trees. . . . And I drive out of there with my wife, as we are going to Soweto. At nine o'clock we come to Soweto, and we have to put on our headlights because of the smog."

"People have been turned into aliens in the land of their birth, because aliens cannot claim any rights, least of all political rights. Millions have been deprived of their birthright, their South African citizenship; stable black communities have been destroyed, and those who have been uprooted have been dumped as you dump not people but things, in arid poverty-striken Bantustan homeland resettlement camps. Three and a half million people are treated in such a callous and heartless fashion in a land whose newest constitution invokes the name of God to sanctify a vicious, evil, and totally immoral and utterly un-Christian system, a system as evil, as immoral, as un-Christian as communism and Nazism."

"The university is dedicated to the pursuit of truth and imbued with a passion to follow the evidence wherever it might lead. Sadly, far too many of the institutions claiming to be universities in South Africa actually base themselves on a lie, which, if not consciously espoused, is acquiesced to by what those institutions do. The lie is that people should be separated because of fundamentally irreconcilable ethnic differences. How can you say that people are dedicated to the pursuit of truth when they have tried to provide intellectual respectability to this horrendous lie, which has caused so much unnecessary suffering to millions. A university must have a social conscience."

"We shall be free, all of us, black and white. Let us sit down together, black and white. I have said before and say again the minimum conditions for starting negotiations: lift the state of emergency; release detainees and political prisoners and allow exiles to return freely; unban political organizations; and then talk to those whom the people identify as their representatives and leaders. We shall be free only together, black and white. We shall survive only together, black and white. We can be human only together, black and white."

"I am black and there are many times when I have asked whether God really cared for us when I have looked at some of the things that our people have suffered. When the South African Defense Forces raided Maputo and Maseru a few years ago, we were told we could not hold memorial services. I held such services because I did not think then, nor do I think now, that I can be told by a secular authority what services I may or may not hold. They kill our children and then prescribe how we may bury them and they think we do not hurt. What do they think happens to us? For them we are really less than human, spoken of as 'those people.' Our pain, our anguish one day will burst forth in an unstoppable flood."

"White South Africans are not demons. White South Africans are ordinary human beings. Most of them are very scared human beings, and I ask the audience, 'Wouldn't you be scared if you were outnumbered five to one?'

"Now my brothers and sisters, let me tell you something. I am the bishop of the Diocese of Johannesburg. My flock is black, my flock is white. One has got to say to our people, 'I love you, I care for you, enormously.' And when I care about black liberation, it is because I care about white liberation."

"To the white community in general I say express your commitment to change by agreeing to accept a redistribution of wealth and a more equitable sharing of the resources of our land. Be willing to accept voluntarily a declension of your very high standard of living. Isn't it better to lose something voluntarily, and to assist in bringing about change—political power sharing—in an orderly fashion, rather than seeing this come about through bloodshed and chaos, when you stand to lose everything?"

"All of us [blacks worldwide] are bound to Mother Africa by invisible but tenacious bonds. She has nurtured the deepest things in us blacks. All of us have roots that go deep into the warm soil of Africa, so that no matter how long and traumatic our separation from our ancestral home has been, there are things we are often unable to articulate but which we feel in our very bones, things which make us different from others who have not suckled the breasts of our mother, Africa. Don't most of us, for instance, find the classical arguments for the existence of God just an interesting cerebral game, because Africa taught us long ago that life without belief in a supreme being was just too absurd to contemplate? And don't most of us thrill as we approach the awesomeness of the transcendent when many of our contemporaries find even the word God an embarrassment? How do you explain our shared sense of the corporateness of life, our rejection of Hellenistic dichotomies in our insistence that life, material and spiritual, secular and sacred, is all of a piece?"

"Unless we work assiduously so that all of God's children, our brothers and sisters, members of one human family, all will enjoy basic human rights, the right to a fulfilled life, the right of movement, the freedom to be fully human, within a humanity measured by nothing less than the humanity of Jesus Christ Himself, then we are on the road inexorably to self-destruction, we are not far from global suicide—and yet it could be so different."

TOWARD A NEW
SOUTH AFRICA

"I long and work for a South Africa that is more open and more just; where people count and where they will have equal access to the good things of life, with equal opportunity to live, work, and learn. I long for a South Africa where there will be equal and untrammeled access to the courts of the land, where detention without trial will be a thing of the hoary past, where bannings and other such arbitrary acts will no longer be even so much as mentioned, and where the rule of law will hold sway in the fullest sense. In addition, all adults will participate fully in political decision making, and in other decisions that affect their lives. Consequently, they will have the vote and be eligible for election to all public offices. This South Africa will have integrity of territory with a common citizenship, and all the rights and privileges that go with such a citizenship, belonging to all its inhabitants."

"If it weren't for faith, I would have given up long ago. I am certain lots of us would have been hate-filled and bitter. For me, the scriptures have become more and more thoroughly relevant to our situation. They speak of a God who, when you worship him, turns you around to be concerned for your neighbor. He does not tolerate a relationship with himself that excludes your neighbor."

"There is no such thing as separate freedom—freedom is indivisible. At the present time we see our white fellow South Africans investing much of their resources to protect their so-called separate freedoms and privileges. They have little time left to enjoy them as they check the burglar proofing, the alarm system, the gun under the pillow, and the viciousness of the watchdog. These resources could be employed in more creative ways to improve the quality of life of the entire community. Our white fellow South Africans think that their security lies in possessing a formidable and sophisticated arsenal of weapons. But they must know in their hearts that the security of all of us consists in a population whose members, black and white, are reasonably contented because they share equitably in the good things, which all, black and white, have cooperated to produce."

"We shall be free because our cause is a just cause. We do not want to dominate others, we just want to have our humanity acknowledged. Our freedom is not the gift of white people. They cannot decide to give or to withhold it. Our freedom is an inalienable right bestowed on us by God."

"The award [the Nobel Prize] is a tremendous political statement. It says that despite all distortion of truth, the world recognizes that we are striving for peace. It is a tremendous affirmation that our cause is just and our methods are praiseworthy."

"The world is on our side—on the side of justice, of liberation, of South Africa, of South Africans, black and white who want a new South Africa. The world is not anti–South African, nor antiwhite (it would be odd for a white English person or American to be antiwhite). It is firmly and decidedly anti-apartheid, anti-oppression, anti-injustice, and the world knows that we are on the winning side."

"There are two things we need to say to our people: that the liberation is certain and it is going to be costly. I use this extraordinary vision in the Revelation of St. John the Divine. It's a vision of souls who have been killed during some persecution or other. And they are lying under the altar, and they are crying to the Lord. 'How long, Lord. How long is this thing going to go on?' And the extraordinary answer is not 'Don't worry, it will be all right.' The extraordinary answer is 'Wait a bit, because more of your brothers and sisters are going to die before the consummation.' "

"We believe that there can be no real peace in our beloved land until there is fundamental change. Please believe us when we say there is much goodwill left, although we have to add that time and patience are running out. We recognize that fundamental change cannot happen overnight, so we suggest that only four things need to be done to give real hope that this change is going to happen:

"1. Let the Government commit themselves to a common citizenship in an undivided South Africa. If this does not happen we will have to kiss a peaceful change good-bye.

"2. Please abolish the Pass Laws. Nothing is more hateful in a hateful system for blacks than these laws. I wish God could give me the words that could describe the dramatic change that would occur in relationships in this country if the real abolition of the Pass Laws were to happen.

"3. Please stop immediately all population removals and the uprooting of people. It is in my view totally evil and has caused untold misery.

"4. Set up a uniform educational system. We want to suggest that all universities be declared open and that the black universities be free to appoint blacks who have credibility in the black community. Otherwise we fear that unrest in these institutions will remain endemic.

"If these four things were done as a beginning, then we would be the first to declare out loud: please give the government a chance; they seem, in our view, to have embarked on the course of real change."

"Fundamentally, I believe history teaches us a categorical lesson: that once a people are determined to become free, then nothing can stop them from reaching their goal."

"God called Steve Biko to be his servant in South Africa—to speak up on behalf of God, declaring what the will of this God must be in a situation such as ours, a situation of evil, injustice, oppression, and exploitation. God called him to be the founding father of the Black Consciousness movement, against which we have had tirades and fulminations. Steve knew and believed fervently that being problack was not the same thing as being antiwhite. The Black Consciousness movement is not a 'hate white movement,' despite all you have heard to the contrary. He had a far too profound respect for persons as persons to want to deal with them under ready-made, shop-soiled categories.

"Steve has started something that is quite unstoppable. The powers of evil, of injustice, of oppression, of exploitation have done their worst and they have lost. They have lost because they are immoral and wrong, and our God, the God of Exodus, the liberator God, is a God of justice and righteousness, and he is on the side of justice and liberation and goodness. We thank and praise God for giving us such a magnificent gift in Steve Biko, and for his sake, and the sake of ourselves and our children, let us dedicate ourselves anew to the struggle for the liberation of our beloved land, South Africa."

"We need Nelson Mandela, because he is almost certainly going to be our first black prime minister. He represents all our genuine leaders, in prison and in exile. So to call for his release is really to say, please let us sit down, black and white together, each with our acknowledged leaders, and work out our common future so that we can move into this new South Africa, which will be filled with justice, peace, love, righteousness, compassion, and caring."

"We must demonstrate to the people of South Africa, both black and white, that the people of the world are not only watching, they are singing a new song, they are raising the trumpets of a new day. And their song will resonate around the world. And their song will break down the walls that isolate my people in their townships and in their hearts. I call for the reverberation of their song to free the hearts of my people, and to shift the tone of conversation and action forever."

"Nothing could have been deader than Jesus on the cross on that first Good Friday. And the hopes of his disciples had appeared to die with the crucifixion. Nothing could have been deeper than the despair of his followers when they saw their Master hanging on the cross like a common criminal. The darkness that covered the earth for three hours during that Friday symbolized the blackness of their despair.

"And then Easter happened. Jesus rose from the dead. The incredible, the unexpected, happened. Life triumphed over death, light over darkness, love over hatred, good over evil. That is what Easter means—hope prevails over despair. Jesus reigns as Lord of Lords and King of Kings. Oppression and injustice and suffering can't be the end of the human story. Freedom and justice, peace and reconciliation are His will for all of us, black and white, in this land and throughout the world. Easter says to us that despite everything to the contrary, His will for us will prevail, love will prevail over hate, justice over injustice and oppression, peace over exploitation and bitterness.

"The Lord is risen. Alleluia."

"If God be for us who could be against us?"

Acceptance of the Nobel Peace Prize
The Right Reverend Desmond Mpilo Tutu
Bishop of Johannesburg
Oslo, Norway, December 10, 1984

Many thousands of people round the world have been thrilled with the award of the Nobel Peace Prize for 1984 to Desmond Mpilo Tutu. I was told of a delegation of American churchpeople who were visiting Russia. On hearing the news they and their Russian hosts celebrated the Nobel Peace Prize Winner.

There has been a tremendous volume of greetings from heads of state, world leaders of the Christian church and other faiths as well as from so-called ordinary people— notable exceptions being the Soviet and South African governments.

The prize has given fresh hope to many in the world that has sometimes had a pall of despondency cast over it by the experience of suffering, disease, poverty, famine, hunger, oppression, injustice, evil and war—a pall that has made many wonder whether God cared, whether He was omnipotent, whether He was loving and compassionate. The world is in such desperate straits, in such a horrible mess that it all provides almost conclusive proof that a good and powerful and loving God such as Christians and people of other faiths say they believe in could not exist, or if He did He really could not be a God who cared much about the fate of His creatures or the world they happened to inhabit which seemed to be so hostile to their aspirations to be fully human.

I once went to a friend's house in England.

There I found a charming book of cartoons entitled *My God*. One showed God with appeals and supplications bombarding Him from people below and He saying, "I wish I could say, 'Don't call me, I'll call you.' " And another declared "Create in 6 days and have eternity to regret it."

My favourite shows God somewhat disconsolate and saying, "Oh dear, I think I have lost my copy of the divine plan." Looking at the state of the world you would be forgiven for wondering if He ever had one and whether He had not really botched things up.

New hope has sprung in the breast of many as a result of this prize—the mother watching her child starve in a Bantustan homeland resettlement camp, or one whose flimsy plastic covering was demolished by the authorities in the K.T.C. squatter camp in Cape Town; the man emasculated by the Pass Laws as he lived for 11 months in a single sex hostel; the student receiving an inferior education; the activist languishing in a consulate or a solitary confinement cell, being tortured because he thought he was human and wanted that God-given right recognised; the exile longing to kiss the soil of her much loved motherland, the political prisoner watching the days of a life sentence go by like the drip of a faulty tap, imprisoned because he knew he was created by God not to have his human dignity or pride trodden underfoot.

A new hope has been kindled in the breast of the millions who are voiceless, oppressed, dispossessed, tortured by the powerful tyrants; lacking elementary human rights in Latin America, in South East Asia, the Far East, in many parts of Africa and behind the Iron Curtain, who have their noses rubbed in the dust. How wonderful, how appropriate that this award is made today—December 10, Human Rights Day. It says more eloquently than anything else that this is God's world and He is in charge. That our cause is a just cause; that we will attain human rights in South Africa and everywhere in the world. We shall be free in South Africa and everywhere in the world.

I want to thank the Nobel Committee, I want to thank the Churches in Norway and everywhere for their support, their love and their prayers.

On behalf of all these for whom you have given new hope, a new cause for joy, I want to accept this award in a wholly representative capacity.

I accept this prestigious award on behalf of my family, on behalf of the South African Council of Churches, on behalf of all in my motherland, on behalf of those committed to the cause of justice, peace, and reconciliation everywhere.

If God be for us who can be against us?

CHRONOLOGY

1931
  October   Tutu is born to Zachariah (a schoolteacher)
                         and Aletha Malthare (a housewife) Tutu in
                         Klerksdorp in the Western Transvaal.

1945–1950   Tutu attends the Johannesburg Bantu High
                         School (Madibane) in Western Native
                         Township.

1948   South Africa's National Party wins the
                         national election on an apartheid platform,
                         vowing to broaden and further institutional-
                         ize state racism.

1950   The National Party enacts some of the cor-
                         nerstones of apartheid, including: the Pop-
                         ulation Registration Act, classifying all South
                         Africans by race; and the Group Areas Act,
                         enforcing racial segregation, uprooting
                         blacks, "coloureds," and Indians from their
                         communities and stripping them of their
                         property.

1951–1953	Tutu attends the Pretoria Bantu Normal College, receiving a teacher's diploma.
1951	The Bantu Authorities Act, creating the "homelands" system, is enacted.
1952	The African National Congress wages the Defiance Campaign against the new apartheid laws.
1954	Tutu receives a BA from the University of South Africa, then teaches for a year at his old high school, Madibane.
1955 March	The government passes the Bantu Education Act, depriving all non-whites of an academic education. Tutu will eventually quit teaching as a result.
June	The Freedom Charter—the South African resistance's statement of principles—is drafted by 3,000 delegates assembled by the national Action Council of the Congress of the People.
July	Tutu marries Leah Nomalizo.
1955–1958	Tutu teaches at the Munsieville High School in Krugersdorp.
1958–1960	Tutu receives ordination training at St. Peter's Theological College in Johannesburg.
1960	South Africa's first black bishop, Alpheus Zulu, is consecrated.

March	The Sharpeville Massacre. Police kill 69 and wound 180 at a peaceful demonstration against pass laws. The government subsequently bans the ANC and the Pan-Africanist Congress.
December	Tutu is ordained as deacon.
1962	Nelson Mandela, leader of the ANC, is imprisoned on Robben Island.
1962–1966	The Tutu family lives in London, where Desmond Tutu is part-time curate at St. Alban's and receives BA honours and a Masters in Theology from King's College.
1966–1970	Tutu serves on the teaching staff of the Federal Theological Seminary, Alice.
1967	The Terrorism Act is passed, allowing police to detain suspects indefinitely.
1968	Steve Biko and others form the South African Student's Organization and spearhead the growing Black Consciousness Movement.
1970–1972	Tutu is lecturer in theology at the University of Botswana, Lesotho, and Swaziland.
1973	Steve Biko is banned.
1975	Tutu is named Dean of Johannesburg, thereby becoming the Anglican church's first black Dean. The family moves to Soweto rather than into the posh deanery in Johannesburg's "white's only" section.

1976
May   In his first public political initiative, Tutu
                           sends an open letter to Prime Minister John
                           Vorster appealing for an end to the home-
                           lands system and other reforms.

June   The Soweto Uprising. On June 16, 15,000
                           schoolchildren march in protest of Bantu
                           education; over the next three weeks,
                           600 people—most of them students and
                           schoolchildren—are killed.

July   Tutu is consecrated Bishop of Lesotho in St.
                           Mary's Cathedral, Johannesburg.

1977
September   Steve Biko is killed by security police while
                           in custody and buried in Kingwilliamstown.
                           Tutu gives the funeral oration.

1978
March   Tutu becomes General Secretary of the South
                           African Council of Churches.

September   P.W. Botha becomes Prime Minister after
                           John Vorster resigns in scandal.

1979   Tutu is awarded an Honorary Doctorate of
                           Law by Harvard University.

1980   The government confiscates Tutu's passport
                           in reprisal for his call for an international
                           boycott of South African coal.

May	Tutu becomes Rector of St. Augustine's, Orlando West in Soweto.
1982	Tutu is awarded the Honorary Doctorate of Sacred Theology by Columbia University.
1984 **October**	Tutu is awarded the Nobel Peace Prize. He had been nominated twice before.
November	Tutu is elected Bishop of Johannesburg, the Anglican Church of Southern Africa's second most important title after Archbishop of Cape Town.
1985 **March**	Police massacre 19 black demonstrators in Uitenhage during an increasingly turbulent year. 700 die in township unrest by September.
Spring	The divestment movement, begun at Columbia University, spreads throughout campuses and businesses in the United States.
July	The government declares a State of Emergency, subjecting citizens to arrest, imprisonment and torture without warrant.
1986	Tutu is awarded the Martin Luther King, Jr., Peace Award in Atlanta.
January	Tutu visits the U.S. and issues outspoken attacks on South Africa's State of Emergency.

April	Tutu calls for international economic sanctions against the apartheid regime, exposing himself to potential charges of treason.
June	After a brief respite, the State of Emergency is reimposed with even tighter restrictions on the public and the press.
September	Tutu is enthroned as Archbishop of Capetown.

1987

| June | Tutu warns in Mozambique that black South Africans could be justified in taking up arms against an unjust government. |
| August | Tutu is elected President of the All African Conference of Churches. |

1988

February	Tutu and other church leaders are arrested as they march on the South African Parliament to protest the banning of anti-apartheid organizations.
May	Tutu is awarded his 25th honorary doctorate by Northeastern University, Boston.
September	Tutu illegally urges South Africans to boycott apartheid municipal elections to be held in October. The government seizes a recording of his sermon, but backs down on threats to prosecute.
November	South African Angelican bishops give Tutu his strongest backing yet on his call for sanctions against apartheid.

SOURCES

Address given at a Home and Family Life Conference, Hammanskraal, 1979. (Home)

Address given at Natal University, 1980. (Natal I)

Address given at Natal University, 1981. (Natal II)

Address given at the University of the Western Cape, 1987. (UWC I)

Address given at the University of the Western Cape, 1988. (UWC II)

Address given in New York City, 1988. (New York)

Address on acceptance of the Nobel Peace Prize, 1984. (Nobel)

Address to the World Council of Churches Central Committee, Kingston, Jamaica, 1979. (Kingston)

Article dated November 8, 1978. (Article)

Article written for the African-America Institute, 1981. (AAI Article)

"Blessed are the meek for they shall inherit the earth," BBC Lent Series, 1988. (Lent)

"The Challenges of God's Mission," address to the United Methodists, Louisville, Kentucky, 1987. (Louisville)

"Change or Illusion," address to a Black Sash Conference, 1980. (Black Sash)

Charge delivered to the Episcopal Synod, 1987. (Charge)

Charge delivered to the Special Synod of the Archdiocese of Cape Town, 1987. (Special Synod)

"A Christian Vision of the Future of South Africa." (Christian Vision)

Christianity and Crisis, "Voices of South Africa." (Christianity and Crisis)

Crying in the Wilderness, by Desmond Tutu, Grand Rapids, Michigan: William B. Eerdmans Publishing Company, 1982. (Crying)

"Freedom Fighters or Terrorists." (Fighters)

Funeral Oration for Steve Biko, 1977. (Biko)

Hope and Suffering, by Desmond Tutu, Grand Rapids, Michigan, William B. Eerdmans Publishing Company, 1983. (Hope)

SOURCES

"Major contributions of the World Council of Churches over 40 Years—A Personal View." (WCC Article)

New York Times Magazine, 1988 (Times)

Presentation to the Eloff Commission of inquiry, 1982. (Eloff)

"Scape-Goatism," address given to the Cape Press Club, 1987. (Cape Press Club)

Sermon delivered on the feast of Epiphany, Kingston, Jamaica, 1979. (Epiphany)

Sermon delivered at St. George's Cathedral, 1987. (St. George)

Sermon delivered at St. George's Cathedral, Pentecost, 1987. (Pentecost)

"Speaking within the South African Context." (Context)

Tutu: Voice of the Voiceless, by Shirley de Boulay, Grand Rapids, Michigan: William B. Eerdmans Publishing Company, 1988. (Tutu)

Welcome to Gustav Gutierrez, 1988. (Welcome)

"Whither South Africa," address given at Woodstock Town Hall, 1985. (Woodstock)

"Why We Must Oppose Apartheid." (Oppose)

Following is a list of the above sources in order of their appearance within each section of the book. Sources are identified by the key words which appear in parentheses at the end of each citation.

FAITH AND RESPONSIBILITY: Context, Context, Natal II, WCC Article, Lent, Pentecost, Eloff, Oppose, Pentecost, UWC II, St. George, Kingston, Charge, Welcome, Special Synod, WCC Article, Oppose.

APARTHEID: Nobel, Oppose, Special Synod, UWC I, Epiphany, Christian Vision, Cape Press Club, Woodstock, Nobel, Special Synod, Nobel, UWC I, Nobel, UWC II, Woodstock, Oppose, Christianity and Crisis.

VIOLENCE AND NONVIOLENCE: Woodstock, Nobel, AAI Article, Woodstock, Times, Hope, Christianity and Crisis, Hope, Fighters, Fighters, Fighters, Fighters, UWC II, St. George, Cape Press Club, Cape Press Club.

FAMILY: Hope, Home, Nobel, Louisville, Crying, Crying, Crying, Nobel, Nobel, Hope, Nobel, Nobel, Fighters, Christianity and Crisis, New York, Crying, Home.

THE COMMUNITY—BLACK AND WHITE: Christianity and Crisis, Christian Vision, Christian Vision, Tutu, Hope, Oppose, Louisville, Tutu, Woodstock, UWC I, UWC II, Oppose, St. George, Woodstock, Black Sash, Tutu, Nobel.

TOWARD A NEW SOUTH AFRICA: Crying, Christianity and Crisis, Article, Hope, Times, UWC II, Crying, Crying, Crying, Biko, Natal I, New York, Crying, Nobel.

PHOTO CREDITS

p. 2 Portrait of Desmond Tutu in New York, 1984. (Jerry Soloway, UPI/Bettmann Newsphotos)

p. 20 Young African boy praying before a statue of a dark-skinned child Jesus in the Church of Christ the King, Johannesburg, 1955. (UPI/Bettmann)

p. 34 Black South African risks a fine of $20 or 20 days in prison for sitting on a "Europeans Only" bench, 1970. (UPI photo)

p. 44 Black student demonstrators in Leandra throw smoking teargas canisters back at police during a clash following the detention of 40 black youths by South African officials, 1985. (Reuters/Bettmann Newsphotos)

p. 54 Mother and son in Muthare Valley, a slum outside of Nairobi in Kenya, 1988. (Rex Miller)

p. 60 Two girls from Nairobi are fed through funds from a Western relief agency, 1988. (Rex Miller)

p. 68 A young black man, in an act of resistance, rides a bus restricted to whites in Durban, 1986. (Reuters/Bettmann Newsphotos)

p. 80 Striking black mineworkers as they are bussed out of Vaal Reefs gold mine west of Johannesburg, 1987. (Wendy Schwegmann, Reuters/Bettmann Newsphotos)

p. 90 Relief worker in Muthare valley, Kenya, 1988. (Rex Miller)

p. 92 Tutu leads funeral march for four victims killed in clash with police in Dacluza, 1985. (Reuters/Bettmann Newsphotos)

THE ACCLAIMED NEWMARKET *WORDS OF* SERIES

The Words of Peace
Selections from the Speeches of the Winners of the Nobel Peace Prize
Edited by Professor Irwin Abrams. Foreword by President Jimmy Carter.
A new compendium of excerpts from the award winners' acceptance speeches from 1901 to 1990, including the Dalai Lama, Mother Teresa, Lech Walesa, Martin Luther King, Jr., and Elie Wiesel. Themes are: Peace, Human Rights, Violence and Nonviolence, the Bonds of Humanity, Faith and Hope, plus much more. 144 pages. 4" x 6". ISBN 1-55704-250-0, $6.95 pocket paperback.
5 1/4" x 8". ISBN 1-55704-060-5, $14.95 hardcover.

The Words of Desmond Tutu
Selected and Introduced by Naomi Tutu
Nearly 100 memorable quotations from the addresses, sermons, and writings of South Africa's Nobel Prize-winning archbishop. Topics include: Faith and Responsibility, Apartheid, Family, Violence and Nonviolence, The Community—Black and White, and Toward a New South Africa.
10 photos; chronology; text of acceptance speech for the Nobel Peace Prize, 1984; 112 pages.
5 1/4" x 8". ISBN 1-55704-038-9, $12.95 hardcover. ISBN 1-55704-282-9, $10.00 paperback.

The Words of Gandhi
Selected and Introduced by Richard Attenborough
Over 150 selections from the letters, speeches, and writings collected in five sections—Daily Life, Cooperation, Nonviolence, Faith, and Peace.
21 photos, glossary. 112 pages. 5 1/4" x 8". ISBN 0-937858-14-5, $12.95 hardcover.
ISBN 0-55704-290-X, $10.00 paperback.

The Words of Harry S Truman
Selected and Introduced by Robert J. Donovan
This entirely new volume of quotations from Truman's speeches and writings gives the essence of his views on politics, leadership, civil rights, war and peace, and on "giving 'em hell."
15 photos, chronology. 112 pages. 5 1/4" x 8". ISBN 1-55704-283-7, $10.00 paperback.

The Words of Martin Luther King, Jr.
Selected and Introduced by Coretta Scott King
Over 120 quotations and excerpts from the great civil rights leader's speeches, sermons, and writings on: The Community of Man, Racism, Civil Rights, Justice and Freedom, Faith and Religion, Nonviolence, and Peace. 16 photos, chronology, text of presidential proclamation of King holiday. 128 pages. 5 1/4" x 8". ISBN 0-937858-28-5, $14.95 hardcover.
ISBN 0-937858-79-X, $10.00 paperback. 4" x 6". ISBN 1-55704-151-2, $5.95 pocket paperback.

The Words of Albert Schweitzer
Selected and Introduced by Norman Cousins
An inspiring collection focusing on: Knowledge and Discovery, Reverence for Life, Faith, The Life of the Soul, The Musician as Artist, and Civilization and Peace.
22 photos, chronology. 112 pages. 5 1/4" x 8". ISBN 0-937858-41-2, $14.95 hardcover.
ISBN 0-55704-291-8, $10.00 paperback.

More Inspirational Biography
Gandhi: A Pictorial Biography
Text by Gerald Gold, Photo Selection and Afterword by Richard Attenborough
The important personal, political, and spiritual periods of Gandhi's life. "First Rate."—*LA Times*.
150 photos, bibliography, map, index. 192 pages. 7 1/4" x 9". ISBN 0-937858-20-X, $9.95 paperback

Newmarket Press books are available from your local bookseller or from Newmarket Press, 18 East 48th Street, New York, NY 10017. (212) 832-3575. Catalogs are available on request. Please add $3.00 per book for postage and handling, plus $1.00 for each additional item ordered. (New York residents, please add applicable state and local sales tax.) Please allow 4-6 weeks for delivery. Prices and availability are subject to change. For information on quantity order discounts, please contact the Newmarket Special Sales Department.